A HISTORY OF WESTERN ARCHITECTURE

,F T

A HISTORY OF WESTERN ARCHITECTURE

THIRD EDITION

David Watkin

 LAURENCE KING

First published in Great Britain in 1986

Third edition published in 2000 by Laurence King Publishing
an imprint of Calmann & King Ltd
71 Great Russell Street
London WCIB 3BN
Tel: + 44 20 7831 6351
Fax: + 44 20 7831 8356
e-mail: enquiries@calmann-king.co.uk
www.laurence-king.com

A catalogue record for this book is available
from the British Library.

ISBN (h/back) 1 85669 227 2
ISBN (p/back) 1 85669 223 X

Picture research:
    First edition: Susan Bolsom
    Second edition: Mary-Jane Gibson
    Third edition: Peter Kent

Book design: Barbara Mercer
Cover design: Pentagram

Printed in Italy

Frontispiece
Guggenheim Museum, Bilbao by Frank Gehry

Front cover
The Musée du Louvre, with I. M. Pei's Pyramid
© Roy Rainford/Robert Harding
Back cover
The Ishtar Gate from Babylon (Berlin, Pergamon Museum)

Contents

Preface

The new edition of this book has been expanded in both text and illustration. As well as containing new material on ancient Egyptian and Mesopotamian architecture, where the roots of western architecture can be seen, it has been reshaped so that each chapter now contains a full account of urbanism. The opportunity has also been taken of expanding the account of twentieth-century architecture from the 1930s to the present day. The book is thus brought right up to date by its survey of the extraordinary flowering of architecture around the world at the start of the millennium. From Berlin to Ohio, from Bilbao to London, a series of spectacular public buildings have captured the popular attention to an unexpected degree. And, though this book remains a history of western architecture, it is also now appropriate to take a fuller look at the remarkable contribution of modern Japanese architects from Arata Isozaki to Tadeo Ando.

The preface of the first edition presented this book as the first history of western architecture from the ancient world to the present day to have appeared since the demise of the certainties of the Modern Movement. According to modernist doctrines, the birth of something called 'modern man' in the twentieth century called for a new architecture devoid of historical resonances. However, contemplating the whole history of architecture from ancient times onwards, it seemed improbable to me that traditional forms would never recur. Indeed, in the last decades traditional architecture has re-established itself inescapably as a solution to the many problems presented by new needs and new materials.

The years since the appearance of the first edition also saw other events which few anticipated: the demise of the totalitarian Communist systems in Eastern Europe and even in Soviet Russia itself. The architect Robert Adam, who has designed extensive classical additions at the Ashmolean Museum, Oxford, makes a bold claim for a comparison between Marxism and Modernism:

Above all it was Karl Marx who drew together these strands into a single philosophical system that laid the foundations both of Communism and Modernism. He combined a wholly technological view of society with a belief that history was rolling relentlessly towards a predestined end, and considered that only a revolutionary destruction of the old order could create a truly modern world unencumbered with its past . . . this vision of a technological future lies at the centre of the Modern Movement.

Adam describes his realization that revivals, so far from being the product of what Corbusier described as 'contemptible enslavement to the past', were the vital moving spring for many of the great phases of architecture.

Certainly, it had always seemed to me that this was the only way in which one could make sense of the history of western architecture. Looking at the successive rebirths of classicism of which that history chiefly consists, it is clear that each generation has had to rediscover the classical language for itself, finding in it what it wanted to find. Alberti in the fifteenth century, Palladio in the sixteenth, Perrault in the seventeenth, Adam in the eighteenth, Schinkel in the nineteenth, Lutyens in the twentieth: all made a personal rediscovery of the language of the orders; all brought expectations of their own to their search for the secrets of ancient design, expectations that coloured their response to what they found or thought they found.

Architectural and archaeological scholarship has also kept pace in the 1980s and 1990s with this new receptivity to our continuing historical legacy. Learned books that are beacons of enlightenment in this essentially creative attitude to the past include *Hadrian's Villa and its Legacy* (1995) by William MacDonald and John Pinto; *Pliny's Villa: from Antiquity to Posterity* (1994) by Pierre de la Ruffinière du Prey and *The Lost Meaning of Classical Architecture: Speculations on Ornament from Vetruvius to Venturi* (1988) by George Hersey. Charles Jencks, the influential writer on architectural Post-Modernism, has also sought to restore meaning to architecture in books such as *Towards a Symbolic Architecture: The Thematic House* (1985). He proposes working out iconographic programmes for 'an architecture which contains coherent meanings, from the private and everyday to the public and philosophical.' The modernists, by contrast, had assumed that an architecture of resonance was no longer feasible because the past was dead. They thus gave its various phases names and dates like those on tombstones. But it will be more helpful if we remember that the architects of buildings we describe as 'Mannerist', 'Baroque', 'Neo-Classical', and so on, did not themselves use these terms. This will help us to see a living continuity rather than a museum of styles, a garden rather than a cemetery.

For example, it may be stimulating to consider architects as different as Alberti and Soane, not as examples of 'Quattrocento' or 'Neo-Classical' styles, but as students of Vitruvius. The same form can be revived with quite different intentions and can evoke different sets of meaning and resonances in different periods. Thus, a Grecian-inspired classicism was used by Thomas Jefferson to symbolize democratic ideas in eighteenth-century America, though similar forms were to have very different implications in Germany in the 1930s. But architecture in itself is neither totalitarian nor democratic, so that we can admire Greek temples while being repelled by the animal sacrifice for which they were designed. 'Architecture', as Léon Krier has said, 'can express nothing else but its own constructive logic, meaning its origin in the laws of nature and human labour and intelligence. Architecture and Building are only concerned with creating a built environment which is beautiful and solid, agreeable, habitable and elegant.'

Moreover, we no longer believe in the historical inevitability of particular stylistic or cultural developments. Ernst Gombrich, in essays such as 'The Logic of Vanity Fair: Alternatives to Historicism in the Study of Fashion, Style and Taste' (1974), undermined the assumptions of Hegelian determinism in art-historical studies. We thus accept that, but for the accident of human personalities, the story could have been quite different and its future unfolding cannot be predicted. Nor can the functional explanation of architecture always be taken at face value, for the will to build can be an end in itself: the expression of power or of an aesthetic urge, justified in terms of functional necessity.

In the recovery of reverence which is now a cultural desideratum, we might reflect on the following lines:

> While stands the Coliseum, Rome shall stand;
> When falls the Coliseum, Rome shall fall;
> When Rome falls – the World.

Thus the 19th-century poet Lord Byron, in *Childe Harold's Pilgrimage* translated the words of the Venerable Bede, the 8th-century saint who has been called 'the father of English history'. Who are we to break that chain, to assume that we have nothing to learn from the past?

Allan Greenberg, the leading traditional architect in America, has recently written that,

> The classical language of architecture is always modern because it is rooted in the physiology and psychology of the individual human being . . . . Classical architecture . . . is the most comprehensive architectural language that human beings have yet developed. Three millennia of western architecture – which is largely a history of classical architecture – demonstrate how successfully this classical language has responded to building needs in diverse political realms, cultures, climates, and geographies.

It will be a principal aim of the present book to tell the exciting story of that success.

However, this language acquires some of its significance by alternating with explosive bursts of a kind of near anarchical architecture which seems to be produced in response to a recurring human demand for excitement, even danger. This is demonstrated in the recent Deconstructivist movement associated with Peter Eisenman which has flowered internationally in the work of architects such as Coop Himmelbau, Frank Gehry, Daniel Libeskind, Rem Koolhaas and Zaha Hadid. It is probably too soon to judge their buildings, or to guess how soon they will fall out of fashion, for, according to one opinion, they merely express the ageold 'will to shock', and thus seem to have no other function than to attract attention. However, it is not for this book to predict the future, other than to confirm the truth of the claim in the *Apocalypse* that, 'Behold, I make all things new.'

DAVID WATKIN
Cambridge, November 1999

1 Mesopotamia and Egypt

WESTERN CULTURE AND ARCHITECTURE DERIVE MUCH OF their richness and resonances from the fact that their origins lie outside of Europe. It is in the Near East and Egypt, in the valleys of the rivers Tigris and Euphrates in Mesopotamia, and, further west, of the Nile in Egypt, that the earliest buildings are to be found. Our story must thus begin outside Europe, though little was known of the Sumerian civilization of Mesopotamia until excavations began in the mid-nineteenth century. Yet it was here that growing mastery of irrigation led to surpluses of grain, which enabled the cultivation of a variety of life styles so that some might cultivate the soil, while others moved to cities.

Mesopotamia

We can trace the origins of monumental architecture and of urban consciousness to the fourth millennium BC in the 'land between rivers' which is what Mesopotamia means. The origins of Sumerian culture in southern Iraq and the marsh country at the northern tip of the Persian Gulf can be found after 5000BC in the prehistoric sacred city of Eridu. Here mud-brick temples, including elevations with alternating buttresses and recesses, retain echoes of earlier reed construction, a building type which continues today. Here began the long story of Mesopotamian temple architecture which reached a climax in the giant ziggurats and palatial temples of Sumer, Babylon and Assyria. Gods were believed to own the city so that it was essential to protect and house them with the utmost strength and security.

South of Babylon in the large Sumerian city of Uruk (the Biblical Erech; today Warka) during the fourth millennium BC one third of the area was eventually given over to temples and public buildings. In the precinct dedicated to Inanna (later Ishtar), the goddess of love and war, groups of temples were connected by a remarkable portico of two rows of massive circular columns of mud brick, the first free-standing columns known. The walls and pilasters were decorated with an early form of architectural ornament in the form of terracotta cones, about 4 inches (10cm) long, coloured red, buff and black, and placed in geometrical patterns.

1 Eridu: perspective reconstruction of Temple 1 (c.5000BC)

2 Uruk: detail of mosaic courtyard (4th millennium BC)

Here, too, were discovered fragments of the world's earliest written documents.

In the adjacent precinct dedicated to Anu, the sky god, is a building known as the White Temple. It stands on top of a high platform with sloping sides which is perhaps the origin of the ziggurat or temple-tower. We thus find that here in the Euphrates delta there was already a sophisticated brick architecture, including walls with projecting decorative buttresses, which influenced subsequent developments until the Hellenistic age. Even the buttresses remained a distinguishing feature of sacred buildings throughout this period. Painted and relief decorations were now not merely ornament but emphasized the structure, as at the temple at Al 'Ubaid near Ur built by King A-annipadda in the mid-third millennium BC.

Built in flat terrains, Mesopotamian cities contained temple-ziggurats perhaps recalling mountains. The most remarkable of these staged towers, consisting of diminishing square platforms, is the huge ziggurat at Ur of c. 2125BC. Here the core of mud brick has a facing of burnt brickwork and dramatic ramped staircases. Since one stage of it survives to a height of roughly 59 feet (18m), it is the best preserved of the staged towers that arose in most Sumerian cities during this and succeeding periods. Ur was a walled city built by masters of engineering with two enclosed harbours to accommodate shipping from the Euphrates. The principal public buildings, temples and palaces were enclosed in

3 Khorsabad: perspective reconstruction (c.700BC)

an inner fortification where stood the great ziggurat. All this was part of a wealthy urban culture based on trade as well as agriculture. It saw key inventions in our civilization such as writing on clay tablets in c. 3200BC, monumental architecture, sculpture and the origin of the city state.

The principles of Sumerian architecture were continued by the warlike Assyrian kings from northern Mesopotamia from around the end of the second millennium BC to 612BC. Little evidence survives of the great cities of Nineveh and Nimrud, which were expanded with one-storeyed mud brick houses, formed round a central court, with no outside windows. Larger houses were two-storeyed and whitewashed. Though vaulting and even domed construction were known to them, they did not make technical advances, their buildings simply becoming grander and more lavish,

4 Ur: ziggurat (c.2000BC)

ornamented with glazed bricks and sculptured decorations both free-standing and in relief.

A characteristic Assyrian achievement is the royal city of Khorsabad in northern Iraq, built by Sargon II (reigned 721–705BC), a square-planned city with towered walls, covering nearly a square mile (2.6km²). It was here, incidentally, that the first Assyrian excavations began in 1843. The site contained a palace for the king's brother, the grand vizier; a temple to Nabu, god of writing and wisdom, most important of the Assyrian gods; official buildings; and the vast palace of Sargon himself. Covering 10 hectares (23 acres) and arranged round three courtyards, this was a terraced building with ramps and stairs, raised on a platform with a heavy facing of dressed stone and incorporating a complicated system of terracotta drains. Notable for its multiplication of detail rather than for its coherence of overall composition, it featured rich woods such as cedar and cypress, few columns, but painted plaster walls, polychrome glazed bricks, arches, winged lions, bulls with humanoid heads, reeded ornament and crenellations.

The palace was not only the official residence but the administrative headquarters of a monarch who, as well as fulfilling his sacred and practical role as defender of the nation from external enemies, oversaw the distribution of grain and the maintenance of the vital dykes and canals. In one corner of the palace there was a temple-ziggurat, an arrangement that was an early example of the increasing Assyrian stress on the rule by autocratic sovereigns over church and state.

Following the fall of Nineveh in 612BC and of the Assyrian Empire, the centre of power moved from the upper Tigris to the lower Euphrates where the kings of a neo-Babylonian dynasty rebuilt the city of Babylon with such splendour that Herodotus observed in the mid-fifth century BC, 'It surpasses in splendour any city of the known world'. Indeed, its very name comes from *Bab-ili*, 'gate of the Gods'.

No notable buildings survive from Babylon's first period of predominance under Hammurabi (reigned

5 Khorsabad: winged bull from throne-room entrance (Paris, Louvre)

1792–1750BC), but there is evidence from its second, so-called neo-Babylonian period when it was rebuilt by Nebuchadnezzar II who reigned from 604–562BC. Excavations in Iraq have revealed the city's grid plan with its double walls, towers and canal connecting it to the river, as well as the foundations of brick-built temples, palaces, fortifications and the famous ziggurat which was the origin of the legend of the Tower of Babel in the Old Testament.

The main approach to the city was from a wide paved road now known as the Processional Way, its façades faced with polychrome glazed bricks. The entrance to the inner city was through the Ishtar Gate, also faced with glazed bricks of a vivid blue, with yellow and white bulls and dragons in relief. Surviving elements of the Ishtar Gate have been reconstructed in the Pergamon Museum in Berlin. To the west of the gate was Nebuchadnezzar's palace, planned round five courtyards, with façades ornamented with glazed brick. It is possible that in one corner of the palace were the Hanging Gardens about which little is known, though,

6 Babylon: perspective reconstruction, as rebuilt by Nebuchadnezzar (reigned 604–562BC)

7 Persepolis (founded c.515BC): staircase

like the walls of Babylon they were one of the Seven Wonders of the ancient world.

Modern scholars have written little on the town planning of this period. It used to be supposed that palaces and temples in the cities of the ancient Near East such as Khorsabad, Nimrud and Ur, were haphazardly placed and that the coherent relation of buildings to each other in a civic context only developed with the Greek influence which followed the conquest of Mesopotamian lands by the Persians. However, the credit for this is increasingly given to the ancient cities of the Near East, as in the Processional Way at Babylon, and at Egypt.

Mesopotamian civilization and, with it, the architecture were brought to an end in 539BC with the conquest of Babylon by Cyrus the Great, who founded the Achamenid dynasty in Persia, the country we now know as Iran. Removed until then from the kind of political developments at which we have been looking, Persia suddenly became a great imperial power. Like others who have found themselves in such a position, the Persians eagerly adopted the style of those they had vanquished. Persepolis, begun as a ceremonial centre for Darius in c.518BC and completed in 460BC by Artaxerxes I, was a glorious conclusion to Mesopotamian architecture, with its magnificent double stairways and superb relief sculpture. The whole

8 Babylon: Ishtar Gate (Berlin, Pergamon Museum)

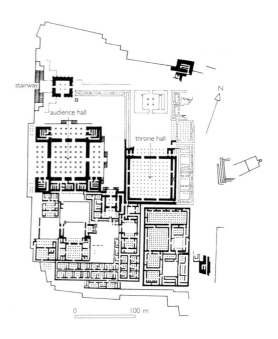

9 Plan of Persepolis

deliberately incorporated echoes of Babylonian, Assyrian, Egyptian and Greek architecture, bearing the marks of the Greek craftsmen whom Darius brought back from his wars in the Aegean. Though Persepolis was largely destroyed by Alexander the Great, its ruins, unlike those of the other buildings we have seen in this chapter, were long known to western traveller from the seventeenth century onwards, though systematic excavation did not begin until 1931. To make sense of our story it is more than time that we turned our attention to the monumental achievement of the ancient Egyptians.

Egypt

The investigation of Egyptian architecture is challenging because we have to erase our modern expectations about the artistic need for change and innovation, and the architectural need for an appropriate relation between material and form. The combined monarchy and religion of ancient Egypt, as well as the forms that defined them, retained common elements for 3000 years despite successive innovations. In its narrow river valley, insulated from the outer world by the hostile barriers of the Arabian and Libyan deserts, Egypt was a closed society, largely untouched by foreign influence. Architects and artists attached no value to originality: indeed, some of the finest examples of Egyptian architecture were put up by Roman emperors, including Augustus, Trajan and Hadrian, who would today be condemned for creating 'pastiche'. The ancient Egyptians had no belief in expressing the nature of materials, for theirs was an architecture of symbolical rather than practical function. In the early period it incorporated elements derived from mud-brick buildings and from trees and plants, forms not ideally suited to stone. The significance lies not in the form but in the iconography, for the forms are bearers of meaning, so that art is the same as writing.

Pharaoh is the ancient Egyptian word for king, deriving from the word *pr-o* meaning 'great house'. The king, or pharaoh, is always referred to as god, for only a divine king was able to carry out the rituals that preserved Egypt and hence the universe. The official cults were dedicated to the perpetuation of the cosmic order in which the king and god were mutually interdependent, the god granting favours to the king in return for the performance of ritual functions. The king was also, via the gods, the source of architectural inspiration, so he is sometimes depicted as preparing the foundations of monumental buildings. No plan for a major building has survived, and it is clear that it was customary to rely on standardized plans. However, the names of three architects are known, of whom two, Imhotep (*fl.* 2600BC) and Amenhotep (c.1440–c.1340BC), were held in such high regard that they were deified for their achievements.

Herodotus, the first visitor to leave an account of Egypt, recorded in c.460BC that the Egyptians regarded their dwelling house as a temporary lodging and the tomb as a permanent abode until the resurrection. Though Egyptian tombs and temples were monumental in character, their origins were in the modest secular buildings of an agricultural people. Most buildings by the Nile were of degradable materials, mud-brick, wood and reed mats, still used today and most notably by the architect Hassan Fathy (1900–89) who continued a tradition dating to the 4th millennium BC. Though little of the vernacular architecture of the ancient Egyptians survives, this mud-brick architecture ultimately accounts for much in mature Egyptian buildings of stone. Thus the massive pylons, which normally form the entrance gateways to temples, have the canted sides required in mud-brick buildings. Also, it was customary to strengthen the corners of those mud buildings with plant stems which were echoed in stone architecture in the form of three-quarter roll mouldings.

From Saqqara to the Great Pyramid

The first colossal stone-built structure in Egypt, and perhaps the world, is the funeral complex at Saqqara, south of Cairo, built in 2650BC by King Djoser (reigned c.2630–2611BC), founder of Dynasty III. This early example of axial planning, combining architecture, painting and sculpture, is dominated by a vast stepped pyramid almost 200 feet (60m) high, surrounded by a columned processional hall and other buildings. Providing a habitation for the dead king as well as a realistic stage setting for ritual, it includes a throne and a statue of the king.

The precinct is enclosed by a limestone wall incorporating imposing façades, which echo in masonry the shape of temporary, tent-like shrines constructed of timber and matting. This might be seen as a parallel to the way in which the forms of Doric were, according to Vitruvius, imitations in stone of carpentry. These dummy façades conceal cores of solid rubble, containing no interior spaces. As often, Egyptian architecture challenges all modern expectations of architectural 'truth' and propriety which are ultimately of eighteenth-century rationalist origin. The entrance hall is flanked

10 Saqqara: stepped pyramid and reconstruction of enclosure wall (c.2650BC)

by semi-columns, ornamented with reed bundles that echo the trunks of palm trees. These are still not free-standing columns but the rounded ends of short spur walls, a form unexpectedly echoed in the Greek world in the celebrated temple of Apollo Epicurius at Bassae, designed by Ictinus in c.429BC.

The remarkable achievement at Saqqara initiated a period of powerful architectural expansion. The use of stone represented a technological revolution that enabled the erection of pyramids, reaching to heaven as a symbol of the sun's rays, their sides sometimes inscribed with solar discs. A rapid development from the step pyramid group of King Djoser culminated a century later in the Great Pyramid of Cheops at Giza.

The Great Pyramid, built in 2500BC for the kings of Dynasty IV, was regarded by the ancients as one of the Seven Wonders of the world. Indeed, covering 123 acres (49.2 hectares) and 480 feet (146m) high with sides 755 feet (230m) long, it is still one of the largest structures ever raised by man, its plan twice the size of St Peter's in Rome. How it was constructed is still mysterious. Without the wheel, there were no carts, cranes or pulleys to assist in moving the giant stones, but we know that wedges, cradles, levers and rockers were used.

Rubble ramps, serving as roadways for the transport of materials on hand-drawn sledges, were built round the outside of the stone casing of the pyramid. These ramps were removed once the pyramid was completed. The construction workers included prisoners of war, captive peoples and agricultural labourers employed during the annual period when the Nile inundated the land.

The interior of the Great Pyramid has three tomb-chambers of which the central room and the granite burial chamber, containing the stone sarcophagus, are connected by an enormous grand gallery with a corbelled roof of limestone slabs, ascending diagonally through the heart of the pyramid. The exterior was originally covered with fine polished limestone emphasizing the mathematical precision of a monument which strives dynamically upwards towards the heavens. By this 'ramp to heaven', the dead monarch was to rise after death.

Within a few decades the Great Pyramid was followed by the adjacent pyramids of Cheops' son, King Chephren, and of his successor, King Mycerinus, forming, together with the Sphinx, an impressive royal necropolis. Each pyramid had an associated temple linked to the pyramid complex by a causeway, while there were also smaller pyramids for the pharaohs' wives. The Sphinx, seemingly an enigmatic portrait of Chephren, lies by the side of the causeway leading to his pyramid. Hewn from a rocky outcrop of limestone in c.2500BC, the Sphinx is 241 feet (73.5m) long, the largest monumental sculpture of Ancient Egypt. Showing the king in divine form as the son of Re, direct offspring of the sun god, it has the body of a recumbent lion and the head of the king, framed by a royal headdress, looking east to the rising sun.

Thebes

The tradition represented by the royal pyramid temples came to an end with the collapse of the Old Kingdom and the replacement of Memphis as a power centre by the city of Thebes in Upper Egypt. The nation was reunified by King Mentuhotep II (2040–2010BC) who,

11 Sphinx of Chephren and Pyramid of Cheops, Giza (c.2500BC)

12 Deir el-Bahri: mortuary temple of Queen Hatshepsut

together with his military and political associates, created rock-cut tombs for themselves at Deir el-Bahri (Arabic for 'northern monastery'), near the bank of the Nile in western Thebes. King Mentuhotep's tomb, buried deep in the mountains, was approached by a terrace resembling a formalized primeval hill, planted with a grove of trees. Orientated to the east where the sun rises, this seems to be an image of the creation of the world and the daily rebirth of the sun. The whole complex can be seen as a kind of landscape architecture placed at the foot of the vertical rock-face of the towering cliffs which bound the valley on three sides, leaving it open only to the east. The three courts rising above each other are approached up ramped causeways and lined with double colonnades of an austere, proto-Doric character, which are the origin of the Greek Doric order some thousand years later.

Five or six hundred years later, in c.1470BC, Queen Hatshepsut commissioned her architect, Senmut, Overseer of Royal Works, to build her a mortuary temple at Deir el-Bahri as a deliberate, if grander, echo of the adjacent ramped temple of Mentuhotep.

In Beni Hasan in Middle Egypt, large underground tomb halls were an important new development in religious architecture, yet still echoing the forms of secular buildings. In the Tomb of Khnumhotep (Middle Kingdom, Dynasty XII, c.1900BC), wood and mud-brick forms are translated into stone. Some of the columns are 16-sided like those at Deir el-Bahri, while the vaulted roof is painted in imitation of textiles and timber beams. This recalls tent-like buildings in which wooden poles were hung with mats or carpets.

Karnak and Luxor

At the north end of Thebes, which remained the religious centre of Egypt for 2000 years, was the temple-city of Karnak, dedicated to Amon-Re, soon to become known as the 'king of the Gods'. The origins of Karnak lay at beginning of the Middle Kingdom around 2000BC with the creation of a modest shrine to Amon-Re. Successive additions made this the most important religious centre in the country, for the god Amon-Re was believed to emit from Karnak a vital energy which sustained the whole rhythm of the seasons, including the annual flooding of the Nile. This guaranteed successful crops of grain and the stability of the Egyptian state which was upheld by the king or pharaoh, the living son of Amon-Re.

The temple complex of Karnak was balanced by that of Luxor at the south end of Thebes to which it was eventually connected with a straight processional way, over a mile (3km) long, lined with statues of sphinxes. Some of the numerous sacred festivals and lavish feasts took place in the city rather than the temple, and the proximity of the temple complexes of Karnak and Luxor to the urban life of Thebes suggests a parallel to the relation of the cities of medieval Europe to their great cathedrals. Also, though they did not exactly serve a community function, the temples played religious, artistic and educational roles a little like medieval monasteries. They were power centres with great wealth derived from their ownership of land, the temple authorities sometimes exercising tax-collecting functions.

13 Temple of Amenhotep III, Luxor (c.1370BC)

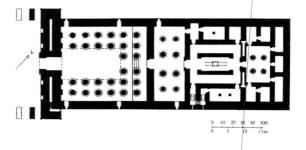

14 Plan of the Temple of Khonsu, Karnak (c.1180–1160BC)

Their importance meant that successive pharaohs felt obliged to add to them so that, unlike Greek temples which were to be planned as a homogeneous whole, Egyptian temples became a succession of buildings including great hippostyle halls. The extended temples diminished in height behind a chain of towering pylons. The temple of Amon-Re at Karnak, for example, was constantly extended over a period of 2000 years until it became one of the most inspiring and spatially enthralling buildings in the history of world architecture.

In front of the entrance pylon is a harbour basin, connected with a canal to the Nile, enabling the divine image of Amon-Re to sail ceremonially in a barque to the temple at Luxor. An avenue of sphinxes, each with the body of a lion and the ram's head of Amon, leads to the entrance pylon, the first of a set of six added by successive rulers. With slits for the fastening of flag poles, the pylon represents the horizon from which the sun rises and features incised images, originally gilded and painted, of the king vanquishing the enemies of Egypt.

Next comes a great court, representing a link between earth and heaven, open to the sky and flanked by columns sprouting with plant capitals like the trees in the fertile Nile valley. This leads to the heart of the complex, the amazing Hypostyle Hall, 238 by 170 feet (104×84m), begun by Seti I and completed by Rameses II as the largest enclosed space in Egyptian architecture. Its 134 columns in 16 rows have papyrus capitals creating the impression of a plantation. In the central aisles, the columns are 69 feet (21m) high, while those in the outer aisles are lower, 42½ feet (13m) high, allowing the central area to be lit by stone window grilles in a raised clerestory which anticipated the lighting of medieval cathedrals. The interiors were covered with incised coloured reliefs and inscriptions in honour of the kings and gods.

Another pylon leads to the sanctuary which housed the barque, beyond which lies another vast court. The axial line is now abandoned and replaced by a mysterious path which includes the tent-like festival hall of King

Tuthmosis III (c.1450BC). This features 'tent pole' columns which echo the wooden poles supporting the canopy over the throne. Approached circuitously from here is the actual inner sanctuary of Amon-Re, where his golden statue stood on a block of red granite which survives today. Reserved for the king or high priest, this was the climax of the whole sequence of spaces where man and god met in the daily cult rituals surrounded by representations of the cosmos on the walls and ceilings. These rituals extended to the holy lake, a regular feature of temples, which was an image of the primeval ocean where the sun-god Re first appeared. South of the temple of Amon is that of the god Konsu, the 'advice giver', a well-preserved monument begun by Rameses III in c.1180BC.

The temple at Luxor, the centre of the mystic relationship between the king and the god Amon, where the king celebrated his divine marriage annually, was laid out on similarly grandiose lines to that at Karnak. The entrance pylon was erected in c.1250BC by one of the greatest builders in Egyptian history, Rameses II, whose long reign dominated much of the XIX Dynasty in the New Kingdom (1307–1196BC). One of the two red granite obelisks from before this pylon is still *in situ*, the other has been in the Place de la Concorde, Paris, since 1836.

While Karnak and Luxor on the east bank of the Nile house temples to the gods, the west bank is the kingdom of the dead. Here Rameses II built his immense mortuary temple, the Ramesseum, in 1250BC, featuring giant pillar statues of himself in mummy-form. Further colossal statues of him recur in his celebrated rock-cut tomb at Abu Simbel.

The Ptolemaic period

As we mentioned at the outset, one of the most extraordinary examples of continuity in the history of architecture is the temples, such as those at Edfu, Dendera and Philae, erected following the defeat of the Egyptian empire. These were commissioned by the Macedonian Ptolemaic dynasty (304–30BC), the Greek-speaking inheritors of Alexander the Great's Egyptian province, and then by the Roman emperors (30BC–AD395), alien rulers who adopted the title of pharaoh. The outstanding quality of these buildings is a fitting termination to one of the greatest architectural traditions the world has known.

15 Abu Simbel: rock-cut tomb of Rameses II (c.1250BC)

16 Temple of Hathor at Dendera (110BC–AD68)

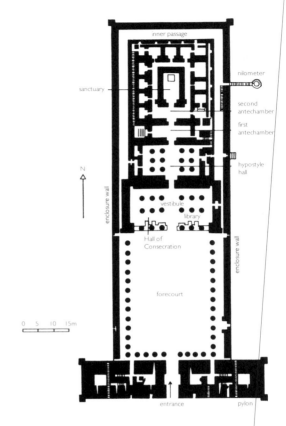

17 *Above* Plan of the Temple of Horus, Edfu (237–57BC)

18 *Below* Temple of Horus, Edfu

2

The Classical Foundation: Greek, Hellenistic, Roman

The Bronze Age heritage

To begin at the beginning means that we must look far beyond the serene composure and shining intellectual coherence of the Parthenon to a mistier world of primeval romance which the ancient Greeks could not forget, though its details were even to them mysterious. This was the Helladic civilization of the mid- and later second millennium BC, during which period there was opposition between Greece, represented by Mycenae and the plain of Argos, and north-west Asia (the modern Turkey), dominated by the city of Troy. The legendary heroes of this civilization were subsequently celebrated by the Homeric poets, while modern excavations on the island of Crete have revealed the importance, as the earliest examples of European architecture, of the palaces at Knossos (begun c. 1600BC), Phaistos, Mallia and Hagia Triada. Contact through trade with advanced eastern cultures in Egypt and Syria during the Middle Bronze Age from shortly after 2000BC enabled the

Cretans, by 1600BC, to develop an indigenous architecture enlivened with Asiatic and, increasingly, Egyptian touches such as pillars, central courtyards and frescoed interiors.

This Cretan culture, often known as Minoan after the mythical King Minos of Knossos, developed from the Neolithic period, c.5000BC, and was not immediately brought to an end by the Mycenean invasion from mainland Greece from about 1450BC. The palaces built towards the end of this period were constructed of stone rubble or sun-dried mud brick coated with plaster. They were large dense accumulations of informally or asymmetrically arranged rooms and halls grouped round a courtyard and enlivened with loggias, terraces, porticoes, verandahs and light-wells. The 'Palace of Minos' at Knossos, a four-storeyed building covering three to four acres (1.2 to 1.6 hectares), contains a grand columnar staircase, the first of its kind in recorded history.

Little is known of the exterior of Cretan palaces and it seems unlikely that their façades were architecturally impressive. Their interiors were sometimes frescoed, though the famous examples at Knossos with their gaudy nautical air are largely inventions by the archaeologist Sir Arthur Evans (1851–1941). The fact that the palaces were unfortified suggests that their richly furnished rooms, approached through cloister courts or peristyles of gaily painted wooden columns, were designed for a relaxed and civilized way of life. A proper drainage system allowed for bathrooms and lavatories; some rooms were provided with charcoal braziers for cooking and heating in winter; while the ground floor contained

19 The throne-room of the palace at Knossos

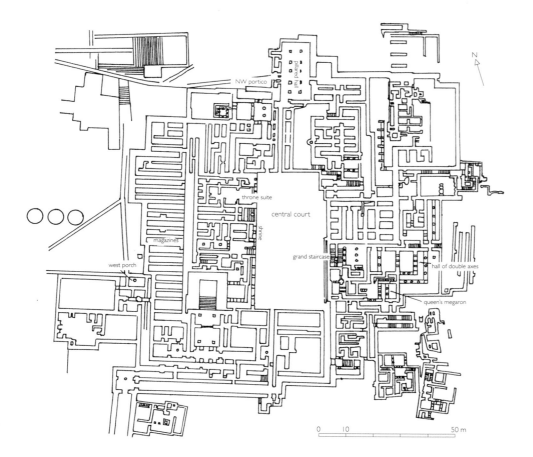

20 Restored plan of the palace of Minos, Knossos (c.15th century BC)

enormous storage areas for the main products of an island more fertile then than today: grain, wine, olive oil and wool. The complexity of the storage area at Knossos may partly account for the legend amongst the early Greeks that King Minos fed annually seven Athenian youths and maidens to the monstrous Minotaur housed in a specially designed labyrinth. The size of the storage area suggests too that the palace was the central point of distribution for a large part of the island. Certainly this was not a culture based on the tomb, like that of the Egyptians, or on the temple, like that of the Sumerians in Mesopotamia. Nor was it a warrior culture, for Cretan towns, like Cretan palaces, were not capable of being defended. This was an island or naval power for which the barrier of the sea formed the most effective defence.

Mycenae

Meanwhile a parallel culture had been developing in mainland Greece, known today as Mycenean or Late Helladic. These Mycenean Greeks ruled the Aegean world during the last centuries of the Bronze Age from 1400–1200BC. One of the centres of their world was doubtless Mycenae, in the plain of Argos, where the principal surviving remains of the city and citadel date from c.1300BC. The grim fortresses of Mycenae and nearby Tiryns are in marked contrast to the gracious indefensible palaces of Crete. Indeed it may have been the warrior kings of Mycenae who brought Minoan civilization to an end by invading Crete and taking over Minoan trade between 1450 and 1400BC, though they subsequently incorporated Minoan building forms and even employed Minoan artists.

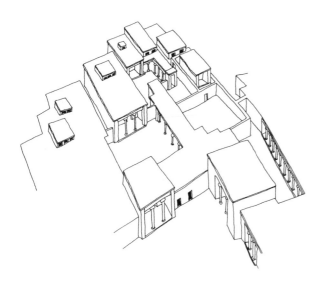

The name Mycenae is recorded in the Homeric epics as the seat of King Agamemnon. Agamemnon's exploits are vividly recorded in Aeschylus's great dramatic trilogy, the *Oresteia*, where his home is given as Argos. Though lacking the romantic associations of Mycenae, Tiryns is better preserved. At the citadel of Tiryns the earliest work, dating from shortly before 1400BC, is a wall 20 feet (6m) thick and at least as high. Formed from immense rough-hewn blocks of stone weighing several tons, this display of strength seemed so superhuman to the later Greeks that they called this technique Cyclopean, since it seemed that the stones must have been set in place by the Cyclops, mythical gigantic creatures with a single eye in the centre of the forehead. In fact the method seems to have been an importation of a practice current in Asia Minor. Inside these extravagant fortifications the palace, dating from the final extension of Tiryns in the late thirteenth century, was a comparatively limited affair. It reflected Minoan influence in its construction of sun-dried bricks and wooden columns, its asymmetrical planning and its lively frescoes.

21 *Above* Reconstruction of the palace at Tiryns as in the late 13th century BC

22 *Below* Plan of the palace at Mycenae (late 13th century BC)

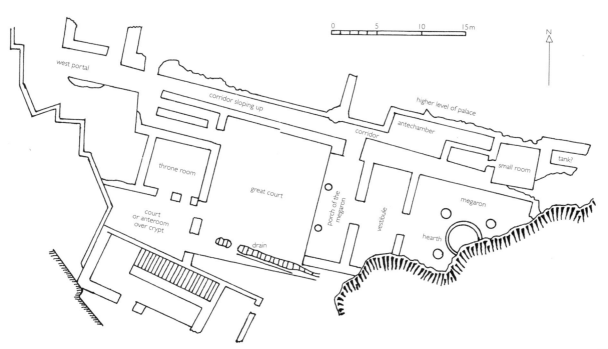

23 The Lion Gate at Mycenae (c.1250BC)

The citadel and palace at Mycenae were rebuilt at about the same time as Tiryns, probably with the same labour. The Lion Gate which forms the imposing entrance to Mycenae reveals a clear taste for the monumental. It consists of three giant stones surmounted by a triangular stone sculpture in which a central column of Minoan type is flanked heraldically by a pair of attendant (now headless) lions. This forceful composition with its somewhat Hittite flavour mingles Minoan and Mycenean themes in an image of kingly rule. Passing through the Lion Gate, the present-day visitor finds on his right a circular grave-yard containing shaft tombs preserved from an earlier dynasty by the builder of the Lion Gate. Beyond these a chariot ramp leads up to the palace, while for those arriving on foot a two-flight staircase of possibly Minoan inspiration was added in c.1200BC. The rather modest palace contained a small guard or guest room and an open courtyard leading to the megaron, a kind of baronial hall

corresponding with Homer's description of the house of Odysseus. Inside the megaron, which may have contained the throne, there were four columns supporting the roof, a central hearth, and frescoes of warriors, horses and chariots on the walls. It was approached through a small vestibule of which the entrance was marked by a pair of columns.

It has been argued that the design of this megaron, the inner sanctum of the king or chieftain, contains the seeds of the temples of the classical Greeks. There are two problems about deriving the Greek temple from the palace megaron: the survival of knowledge over a dark period of at least two centuries, and the greater complexity of the palace megaron in comparison with the earliest temples. Perhaps both should be seen as independent elaborations of a simple and long-lasting house type. Certainly parallels can be drawn between the prostyle temples and houses of the Greeks and the 'House of the Columns', which lies east of the palace at Mycenae. The most striking feature of this house was the central open courtyard flanked by free-standing columns on three sides, an arrangement recalling the even more imposing colonnaded courtyard in front of the principal megaron at Tiryns.

Outside the citadel of Mycenae lies the so-called Treasury of Atreus or Tomb of Agamemnon of c.1300BC, presumably built as the resting place of the king responsible for the last remodelling of the citadel and palace. The grandest of the tholos tombs, of which there were a dozen in and around Mycenae, it is also the noblest surviving architectural monument of prehistoric Greece. The tholos tomb, an Eastern Mediterranean type of great antiquity, consists of a subterranean circular chamber with a corbelled stone roof resembling a beehive. It is approached by a sloping pathway or 'dromos' cut into the mound so as to form a suitably chilling and imposing approach, especially in the 'Treasury of Atreus' where the walls of the 120-foot (36m) long dromos are lined with stone.

The entrance doorway to the 'Treasury of Atreus' has tapering sides as well as an inward batter or slant,

24 Tomb of Agamemnon, Mycenae (c.1300BC)

25 Plan and three cross-sections of the 'Treasury of Atreus', Mycenae (c.1300BC)

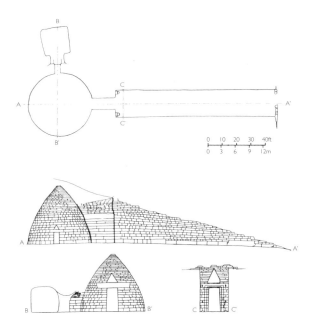

features which may be derived from Egypt. Above is a triangular opening intended to relieve pressure on the lintel from the surmounting stonework. This triangle, and the flanking areas adorned with a pair of half-columns, were originally veneered with decorative slabs of stone ornamented with friezes of running spirals, a Minoan motif. The door itself was flanked by half-columns of green limestone, parts of which survive and are now in the British Museum. The shafts are ornamented with zig-zags and running spirals and are crowned with a cavetto moulding which resembles the water-lily capitals of Egypt. The refined and luxurious decoration of this frontispiece with its ornament in green alabaster and red porphyry is one of the most unexpected products of the whole Bronze Age. The tholos chamber, 43 feet (13m) high and 47½ feet (14.5m) in diameter, has a span unequalled in masonry construction till the erection of the Pantheon in Rome over 1400 years later, though Hellenistic meeting-halls such as the Arsinoeion at Samothrace vaulted larger spans in timber. Considerable engineering skill was required at the 'Treasury of Atreus' in the positioning of the immense stones so as to resist pressure and provide a smooth interior surface for the decoration in gold, silver and bronze with which it was covered.

Hellenic culture

The prosperity on which such buildings depended had begun to decline by about 1300BC for reasons which are not entirely clear. It is sometimes supposed that invaders from the northern edge of the Helladic world, subsequently known as Dorians, destroyed the bases of Mycenean civilization in the twelfth century. By about 1100BC the Bronze Age culture was in ruins, its palaces burnt, its treasuries looted and its craftsmen disbanded; a wholesale movement of population had taken place and an illiterate Dark Age of poverty and barbarism ensued for four centuries. The ninth century saw an emphasis on the use of iron, a technology which had been known since the eleventh century. A sterner metal than bronze, it was especially suitable for a way of life based on the sword and the plough. Probably in the eighth century Homer sang the glories of the lost Bronze Age civilization and we can date the beginning of Hellenic culture to shortly after 800BC when the Greek script, incorporating certain letters from the Phoenician alphabet, was evolved from the script known as Linear B which was used in Mycenaean Greece. Linear B owed nothing to the as yet undeciphered Linear A, which the Minoans used in recording their business transactions. Other departures from Bronze Age precedent included the new emphasis on temples, a building type unknown to the Minoans.

Unlike the civilizations of Egypt and the ancient Near East, Hellenic culture had no clearly defined boundaries but was diffused from Greece itself to the Aegean islands, the coasts of modern Turkey and the Black Sea, to Sicily and southern Italy, southern France and even the Mediterranean coast of Spain. The population of Greece and the Aegean shores was largely divided between the Ionians and the Dorians who had arrived more recently from the north. The principal Ionian cities were Athens, which had also been a Mycenean town, Chalcis, Eretria, the twelve cities of Ionia on the west coast of Asia Minor (Turkey), and Massalia (Marseilles). The chief cities of the Dorians were Sparta, Argos, Aegina, Corinth and Thebes, while they were also established on the islands of Sicily, Corfu, Rhodes and Crete. Classical Greeks subsequently regarded the characteristic quality of their art as due to the mingling of a supposed Dorian masculinity and strength with an Ionian femininity and grace.

It was not until 179BC that these groups of peoples finally suppressed opposition from their principal rivals, the Persians and the Phoenicians. This new Hellenic order contained no common system of government. It was characterized by small self-governing states ruled variously by individual kings, by small groups, or by a majority of free male citizens (the Greek terms for these three systems being tyranny, oligarchy and democracy). Though these city-states were often at war with each other, they were proud of their common cultural identity. Their belief in their own unchallengeable cultural superiority was so strong that it has been accepted not only by their immediate successors, the Romans, but by subsequent generations down to and including our own.

The Bronze Age world of the second millennium recorded by Homer contained citadels dominated by the palaces of princes, but the Hellenic world after 800BC included cities containing the statues of gods in temples. Approached through a two-columned porch leading into the inner room or cella, these early shrines echoed the megaron of Mycenean palaces. Built of sun-dried brick with additional timber supports, the first of them were probably thatched so that they would have had pitched roofs rather than the flat mud roofs of the Minoans and Myceneans. The decision to extend the front columns all round the building in the form of an external colonnade (or pteron) was of particular importance for the future of temple architecture. The earliest example of this seems to have been at a rich grave discovered in 1981 at Lefkandi on the island of Evvoia (ancient Euboea) in northern Greece. Perhaps dating from as early as 1050BC, this long apsed building, which is a cross between a tomb and a temple, has a stone socle, mud-brick walls faced internally with plaster, a reed roof supported on posts, and is surrounded by a peristyle of rectangular posts. A rather later instance is the colonnade of wooden columns or posts which in c.750BC was wrapped round the long temple of Hera on the island of Samos (fig. 34), built about fifty years before. Hera, mother of the earth, was the sister and wife of Zeus, greatest of the Olympian gods. Her temple at Samos was replaced by another, perhaps early in the seventh century.

Terracotta roofing tiles, which were invented in the seventh century, probably at Corinth, played a vital part in the trend towards greater monumentality and durability, since their weight encouraged the adoption of stone rather than wooden columns, as well as leading to improvement in wall construction. They also popularized ridge-roof construction of shallower pitch than that needed for thatch, and buildings of a firmly rectangular plan. The temple of Apollo of c.630BC at Thermon in north-western Greece, a sanctuary since Mycenean times, was one of the earliest of the great tiled buildings. It was also important for the proto-Doric features of its entablature, that is, the superstructure between the capitals and the gutter. Its tiled roof was carried by fifteen wooden columns on each flank and five at each end, as well as by the mud-brick walls themselves. In the Hellenistic period these columns were replaced by stone ones but the entablature they supported seems always to have remained wooden, though enlivened with remarkable terracotta enrichments.

What survives of the entablature are the great terracotta metopes, each nearly three feet square, which filled the space between the triglyphs. These terracotta or wooden triglyphs were perhaps covers, at once decorative and protective, for the exposed grained ends of the heavy wooden ceiling beams. The metopes, which were fastened to a mud-brick backing, are brightly painted with red frames and rosette borders enclosing pictures of gorgons and other mythological scenes, characteristic examples of the Archaic painting style. The gutter above was ornamented with a row of painted terracotta masks, an early instance of the antefixes that were to crown the cornices of all subsequent classical buildings. The temple still retained the row of columns running down the centre of the cella, an ancient practice shortly to be abandoned, but it did introduce a rear porch or opisthodomus which was to be widely adopted in later temples.

Archaic temples c.600–480BC

The disposition of the Greek temple and, as we have seen at Thermon, the origins of the Doric order, were settled during the seventh century. Within the east front the vestibule (pronaos) led directly to the body or cella of the temple which housed the idol of the deity to whom it was dedicated. This statue was placed at the far end facing east. Behind it there was sometimes an inner room (adytum), used as a treasury, sanctuary or oracle chamber, as well as the rear porch (opisthodomus). Since the pronaos and opisthodomus often contained rich offerings to the gods, they were enclosed with metal railings and gates. It is important to realize that the altar on which animals were sacrificed in the hope of propitiating the gods was generally placed not inside the temple but in front of the main entrance façade. Most temples faced east so that the priest, who himself faced

east during the sacrifice, would have his back to the temple. Though this may seem odd to us, it is precisely the position which has been adopted by recent popes in celebrating open-air Mass in front of St Peter's in Rome. However, the Greek temple, unlike St Peter's, was specifically designed for such a form of worship so that it, in contrast to the Gothic cathedral, was more an object for the faithful to admire in repose than to enter and move around in. It is possible that part of the awe and mystery with which Greek temples were invested was due to the fact that except at festivals their interiors were closed to the general public, whose only view of the idol would be from outside the eastern door. In a hot climate life can be lived more outdoors than indoors, and the ancient Greeks may have demanded less from their buildings than we do, though they would doubtless have required cool thick-walled interiors. Certainly they were deeply sensitive to nature and possessed an imaginative spirituality which led them to see trees, water, mountains and skies as animated with the presence of the gods.

The transformation of these early experiments into what we recognize as the fully developed Greek temple came only after the Greeks began to carve stone both for architecture and for sculpture from the mid-seventh century. The various parts of what became established as the Doric order are clearly set out in fig. 28. In the first stone temples the Greeks tended to echo the construction and decoration of those they had earlier built in timber and sun-dried mud brick with terracotta enrichments: the result has sometimes been called petrified carpentry. This phrase well describes such details as the guttae resembling wooden pegs carved on to the mutules. According to this theory these slab-shaped mutules represent the ends of rafters protruding below the eaves along the flanks of a temple. On the other hand, it is unclear what function so many guttae would have performed, even in an all-wooden construction: it should also be remembered that features like the mutules habitually adorned not only the flanks of ridge-roofed buildings but also, illogically, the rafterless ends. But the theory that the features of the Doric order have timber origins goes back to Vitruvius, writing in the first century BC, so that it cannot entirely be rejected. Modern scholars prefer to stress the various Doric elements as a deliberately aesthetic or poetic commentary on the theme of function. Assembled in an abstract geometrical way, the elements are unnecessarily massive and not in themselves functional, but are eloquent of patterns of construction and support. Thus the Doric order may be less the result of a slow evolution from timber prototypes than a deliberate aesthetic invention in the mid-seventh century by builders of genius in the north-east Peloponnese who were anxious to create a new monumental effect in stone architecture.

Another open question concerns the possibility that the emergent Doric style was influenced by the massive architecture of masonry and columns developed by the Egyptians, for example in the temple of Amon at Karnak (c.1750–1085BC) or in the mortuary temple of Queen Hatshepsut at Deir el-Bahri (c.1470BC), where the shrine of Anubis has a distinctly proto-Doric order. We know that during the seventh century BC there was contact between Greece and the Nile delta but until the dates of some of the temples at Corinth and nearby Isthmia are calculated more accurately we cannot be certain that their designers owed much to Egyptian precedent. If they date from after c.660BC then Egyptian influence is more likely, since contact was especially close during the reign of the pharaoh Psamtik I, himself a great builder. The Greek tradition of monumental stone sculpture also began towards the mid-seventh century with stiff frontal figures of markedly Egyptian character. Egyptian influence in architecture seems to have been the greatest in the late seventh and early sixth centuries, especially in the technique of assembling and dressing massive stones. By the end of the sixth century the Greeks had replaced many of these techniques with some of their own invention, although as late as the fifth century BC the great historian and traveller Herodotus was impressed by Egyptian architecture.

26 Portico of the shrine of Anubis at the Temple of Hatshepsut, Deir el-Bahri (c.1470BC)

The large temple of Artemis at Garitsa on the island of Corfu was built in about 590 or 580BC as one of the earliest stone peripteral Greek temples. It is also important as an early instance of the incorporation of sculptured groups in the pediments. A fierce Gorgon is flanked by a pair of no less fierce panthers to frighten away all evil visitors and spirits from the sacred mysteries within. The temple itself has disappeared but fragments of its painted limestone sculpture and its architecture survive, though not *in situ*. This is unfortunate since it was probably the first in which the full Doric order was established: the tapered fluted columns, standing without bases on a stone stylobate, are crowned with shallow cushion capitals which support an entablature adorned with a triglyph and metope frieze, and punctuated with mutules and guttae. Many further refinements of detail and proportion were introduced during the succeeding centuries but nothing of substance was added to the Doric order.

Of similar date is the temple of Hera at Olympia, built in a combination of limestone masonry, sun-dried brick and timber columns which were gradually

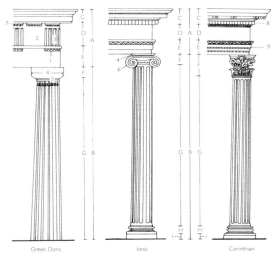

| Greek Doric | Ionic | Corinthian | Tuscan | Roman Doric | Composite |

27 *Top* Temple of Apollo at Corinth (c.540BC)

28 *Above* The orders of classical architecture (*A* entablature, *B* column, *C* cornice, *D* frieze, *E* architrave, *F* capital, *G* shaft, *H* base, *I* plinth; 1 guttae, 2 metope, 3 triglyph, 4 abacus, 5 echinus, 6 volute, 7 mutule, 8 dentils, 9 fascia)

replaced in stone from the mid-sixth century onwards. The oldest surviving colonnade of a sixth-century temple is the seven columns of the temple of Apollo at Corinth, dating from about 540BC. Nearly 21 feet (6.3m) high, the limestone columns, originally covered with white stucco, have a powerful elemental appeal which is partly due to their completely perpendicular profile. If the columns lack subtlety of line, the stone floors on which they stand rise towards the centre in a slight convex curve on all four sides of the temple, the earliest example of a refinement to which we shall

return when discussing the Parthenon. Another refinement at Corinth which obsessed all designers of Doric temples was the problem of the corner triglyphs. The Greeks insisted on placing a triglyph above each column in order to symbolize the load carried by the

27

column. To preserve the illusion of strength they also insisted on ending the frieze with a triglyph and not with the visually weaker metope. This meant that the corner triglyphs could not be placed centrally over the corner columns. To minimize the consequent irregularity in the spacing of triglyph and metopes the end columns were placed slightly closer together than the others; also, in the temple of Apollo at Corinth, the metopes next to the end triglyphs were made two inches (5cm) wider than their counterparts. Corinth was a rich commercial centre near the coast at the base of the isthmus connecting the Peloponnese with mainland Greece. It was thus ideally placed for trade by land between north and south, and by sea between east and west. Rising above the town is the mountainous Acrocorinth, which still impresses the visitor today as one of the finest natural citadels in the world. Occupied from before 4000BC, Corinth was perhaps at its most influential under the rule of the autocrat Kypselos and his son Periander in the seventh century when it colonized Syracuse and Corfu and was the leading manufacturer and distributor of pottery in the ancient world. Sacked and destroyed by the Romans in 146BC, it was refounded when it was adopted as a Roman colony in the first century BC under Julius Caesar. It then became the luxurious capital of Roman Greece and was chosen by St Paul as the centre of his mission to the pagan world.

The much visited temple of Apollo at Corinth should be related stylistically to a further two temples at Athens and one at Delphi. The temple of Athena Polias on the Acropolis at Athens was erected around the mid-sixth century BC during the rule of the 'tyrant' Pisistratus, who respectively founded and enhanced the Dionysiac and Panathenaic festivals as well as establishing an official text of Homer. The links which the Pisistratids maintained with their fellow rulers in the islands may explain the incorporation into their temple of marble brought from the Aegean islands as well as the use of the Ionic order, of which more later. The temple was thus the first in which the pedimental sculptures were carved

in marble, and also in the round, since they were created independently of their limestone background. The enormous temple of Olympian Zeus at Athens was begun under the Pisistratids in c.520BC but not completed until c.130AD under Hadrian. The prominent use of marble for the decorative upper parts and roof tiles of the Pisistratid temple of Athena Polias may have encouraged an exiled Athenian family, the Alcmaeonids, to face a whole temple front with marble for the first time: the temple of Apollo at Delphi of 513BC.

There are few more striking memorials of the Doric style between the mid-sixth and mid-fifth centuries than the ruins of the great temples erected in Magna Graecia, the Greek colonies of Sicily and the coast of Italy south of Naples. They have a stern and earthy virility which to some minds encapsulates the Doric 'spirit' more perfectly than the later and more sophisticated Doric of fifth-century Athens. Syracuse on Sicily was the greatest of the Dorian colonies and the largest city in the Greek world. The early-sixth century Temple of Apollo at Syracuse is a ponderously imposing example of early Doric with its close-set, massively tapered columns. Substantial portions remain at Selinus of a remarkable series of Doric temples of which there were four on the Acropolis and three on the plateau nearby. Another famous group of Doric temples survives fifty miles south of Naples in the city of Poseidonia, a colony of the Sybarites renamed Paestum by the Romans. The earliest of the three temples is the mid-sixth-century 'basilica' or first temple of Hera. Adjacent to it, and dating from about a century later, is the second temple of Hera (also called that of Neptune or Poseidon) which is similar to the temple of Zeus at Olympia of c.470–457BC. With its impressive two-storeyed interior, this second Hera temple at Paestum is the best-preserved of all ancient temples. On an eminence a little further to the north is the much smaller late-sixth-century temple of Athena (Ceres or Demeter).

The swelling profiles of the columns of the first temple of Hera and of the temple of Athena at Paestum,

they carry their well-nigh unendurable load. This earthiness, this sense of being close to nature, is accidentally emphasized by the rough porous surfaces of the local limestone (travertine) which was originally concealed beneath a smooth coating of brightly painted stucco. It has been claimed that entasis, which was echoed almost imperceptibly at the Parthenon shortly after the middle of the fifth century, was adopted in order to correct the impression of sinking in the middle which might be given by totally straight-sided columns. However, the fact that it is so pronounced at Paestum suggests that whatever the motive for its subsequent use, it was not originally a corrective optical expedient but rather an artistic device to be enjoyed in its own right as a symbol of the huge effect of load on support.

There are numerous other peculiarities in the design of the Paestum temples which suggest that their builders were men of fertile genius: capitals are carved ornamentally; Ionic elements are blended with Doric; and features such as cornices, mutules, regulae and guttae are from time to time omitted. Most remarkable is the treatment of the upper parts of the Temple of Athena. The horizontal cornice is omitted from the ends of the temple and, instead, the cornice on the sides of the building is continued up on either side of the pediment to form deeply projecting eaves, the undersides of which are decoratively coffered. The columns all tilt slightly inwards, heightening the tense vertical thrust of this home of the great goddess, Athena. Through its height and its site this is a building which would have challenged the eye and the mind of every visitor to Paestum by land or sea.

The largest and in some ways most remarkable of all Doric temples was that of Olympian Zeus at the then luxurious city of Acragas (Latin Agrigentum; now Agrigento) on Sicily. It was probably begun in c.500BC but left unfinished in 406BC following the sack of Acragas by the Carthaginians, which brought to an end the most flourishing century in the history of the city. Designed to overwhelm the visitor, this enormous monument, 173 by 361 feet (52 × 108m), was raised up

29 The second Temple of Hera, also called that of Poseidon or Neptune, at Paestum (mid-5th century BC)

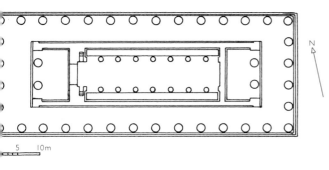

5   10m

30 Plan of the second Temple of Hera at Paestum

producing the effect known as entasis, are the most exaggerated of any antique temples (though they can be matched in some columns of the temple of Hera at Olympia). The profiles are echoed at Paestum in the spreading outlines of the squat capitals they support, so that we can almost hear the massive stones groaning as

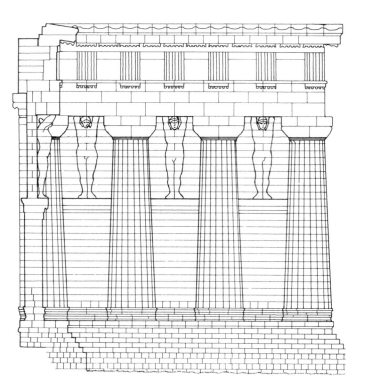

31 Reconstruction of the Temple of Olympian Zeus at Acragas (5th century BC)

helped carry the entablature, itself seemingly further strengthened with iron bars. This temple of Olympian Zeus is thus a more literal expression of a building groaning in labour which we have already observed at Paestum. The note of brutality introduced by these figures has been linked, perhaps fancifully, to the defeat of the Carthaginians at Himera in 480BC, after which bands of Carthaginian prisoners are supposed to have been put to forced labour on the building of the temple.

We have described the splendours and the subtleties of Doric temples but hardly their setting. Few Greek sites are more impressive than Acragas. The acropolis, set on a high ridge to the north, contains the remains of the temple of Athena but to the south runs another ridge, parallel to the coast, crowned poetically with no less than six temples within half a mile of each other. Since we can be sure of so little about the intentions of the ancient Greeks, it has been open to modern scholars to propose contrasting theories as to the relation of Greek buildings to each other and to the landscape. These range from the argument that it was arbitrary to the notion that the siting of a temple in relation to, say, a nearby mountain influenced the whole treatment of the order: aspiring as in the temple of Athena at Paestum, or restrained as in the temple of Apollo which crouches below the Acrocorinth at Corinth. Certainly the image of temples against mountains, of orderly columns against the rough rock from which they were hewn, is a compelling symbol of human control and dignity achieved in a hard battle against nature. Referring to the temple at Bassae, the neo-classical architect C. R. Cockerell wrote in the early nineteenth century that 'A work of order is like an oasis in the desert'. Moreover, we can perhaps see the combination of equilibrium and tensile strength in Doric temples as an echo of the spiritual process of aspiration confronted with opposition while the dedication of the temples to the gods reminds man that alone he is powerless against the forces of the natural world which surrounds him.

Another magnificently sited and well preserved late Archaic Doric temple is that of Aphaia, built in

on five steps on a platform 15 feet (4.5m) above ground level. In order to help carry the weight of the entablature, the outer columns were not free-standing but were half-columns engaged against a continuous solid wall. Despite the appearance of massiveness, the entablature was in fact built with comparatively small blocks of stone. The strangest and most mysterious features of the building are the surviving fragments of stone figures which have given it its popular name, 'The Temple of the Giants'. We know from these and from late medieval descriptions that the temple incorporated immense male figures (telamones or atlantes), some 25 feet (7.5m) high, holding their arms above their heads so as to support the upper stages of the building. Their precise location in the temple has been a matter of debate, but modern archaeologists assume that these somewhat barbaric figures stood on a ledge in the curtain wall between the engaged columns where they

c.510–490BC on the island of Aegina near Athens. Aphaia was the old goddess of the whole earth, protectress of sailors and hunters. Her temple, placed above her cave, commands superb views of the sea in both directions from its rocky hill-top site in the midst of verdant pine woods. It was built of local limestone faced with cream-painted marble stucco, while its many ornamental features – pedimental sculpture, acroteria, lion masks, griffins – were richly painted in bright colours. The pedimental sculpture of Homeric battle scenes at Troy forms the earliest substantial group of its kind to survive. The earlier and more archaic is on the west pediment of c.490BC, where the warriors have a calm detachment and smiling elegance suited to the mood of the temple, though they contrast strikingly with the far more aggressively muscular movement which characterizes the figures on the slightly later eastern pediment.

The temple displays numerous refinements of proportion: for example, apart from the temple of Athena at Paestum it is the first in which all the columns tilt inwards and those on the corners are slightly thickened; the columns also have entasis, while the stylobate has an upwards curve and the interior affords an early example of a two-storeyed colonnade. In features such as these it anticipates the Parthenon, but before we turn to fifth-century Athens to investigate the culmination of the Doric order we should glance at the origin and rise of the Ionic, the style of Greek Asia.

The rise of Ionic

We have already noted the establishment of the Ionian colonies on the seaboard of Asia Minor by Mycenean Greeks who, fleeing from the collapse of their civilization after 1100BC, founded coastal cities like Miletus, Priene, Ephesus and Smyrna by the eighth century BC. Here and in numerous Aegean islands such as Samos, Chios, Naxos, Paros and Delos they created a refined and luxurious civilization symbolized for us by the Ionic style with its curvaceous grace and its hint of sensuousness. The origin of the Ionic, like so much in the ancient world, is still uncertain. Some see its origin in the so-called Aeolic capitals ofthe late seventh or first half of the sixth century BC, discovered at Aeolis in north-west Asia Minor. Though very graceful, the Aeolic capital has a long rectangular spread which is in fact more functional as a support for longitudinally placed beams than the square slab of the Doric order. There are architectural antecedents for Aeolic capitals in Palestine and Cyprus, but it may be that the similarity with later work is an accident and that the Ionic style was invented around 550BC in two now destroyed buildings which were the first Greek temples of vast scale: the third temple of Hera at Samos and the temple of Artemis (Diana) at Ephesus, paid for by King Croesus of Lydia.

Theodorus, an architect and engineer of genius from Samos, worked on both of these immense temples and wrote a now lost book on that at Samos, the earliest architectural treatise of which we have the name. They were the first dipteral temples, that is they boasted a double peristyle (or pteron) of columns on all four sides, a feature which was to be characteristic of temples in Asia Minor and was probably derived from the imposing columned halls of Egyptian temples. The spacing of the columns on the west entrance front was gradually widened towards the centre, another feature inspired by Egypt. The sumptuous temple of Artemis was constructed almost entirely of marble, unlike the archaic Doric temples. Its columns established types for later Ionic buildings in their slenderness as compared with Doric columns; in the design of their capitals; and in the rich mouldings of their bases which are characterized by a horizontally fluted torus. The lower parts of some of the columns were carved with figure sculpture, and though this exotic feature did not set a fashion, prominent display of sculpture was characteristic of Ionic temples as part of an emphasis on ornament, rather than on construction as in Doric temples. Thus the Ionic style entirely omits the Doric frieze in which triglyphs and metopes act as a poetic interpretation of structural

33 The Treasury at Delphi (c.525BC)

34 Plan of the Third Temple of Hera at Samos (c.550BC)

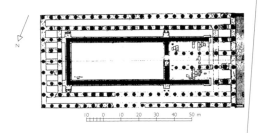

reality. This is replaced in Asiatic Ionic with a row of dentils or small square blocks immediately below the cornice, and in Ionic of the western Aegean with a band of stone which is often richly carved with figure sculpture.

A building of singular richness and charm which demonstrates early western Ionic at its most vivacious is the marble treasury built at Delphi in c.525BC by the island state of Siphnos. Its porch is flanked by two large caryatids (free-standing female statues) of a type later echoed by the architect of the Erechtheion at Athens. They carry on their heads bizarre capitals elaborately carved with figures of men and lions. The frieze and even the pediment are filled with sculptured figures carved in high relief and gaily painted in red, blue and green, while the architectural ornament carved round the cella doorway is scarcely less elaborate.

The classic phase: 480–400BC

The Parthenon, Propylaea and Erechtheion, grouped on the Acropolis or citadel of Athens, are traditionally seen as representing the high point in the development of the Doric and Ionic orders. The view that fifth-century Athens marks the climax of antique architecture is in part due to nineteenth-century scholars, who were accustomed to interpret historical periods and styles in terms of biological and sometimes even of moral development presupposing an inevitable process of rise, maturity and decline. However, the classical language in architecture has continued to produce buildings of magnificence and variety down to the present day and there is no reason to regard this tradition as only a pale imitation of something better done in the fifth century.

Nonetheless, these years saw the establishment of the first humane culture of the ancient world with which modern man can identify emotionally and intellectually. It was the work of architects and sculptors like Callicrates, Ictinus, Mnesicles and Phidias; of mural painters like Polygnotus, Micon and Panaenus; of the philosopher Socrates, who laid the foundations of logic; and of the poets and tragedians Aesehylus, Sophocles and Euripides, whose dramatic portrayal of human passions was unequalled until the time of Shakespeare. This cultural efflorescence took place in the fifty-year period of peace between the Persian and Peloponnesian Wars. Indeed, while it is untrue to claim that economic conditions create or determine the character of cultural achievements, it is clear that this kind of broad-ranging artistic flowering would have been impossible unless it had been rooted in a soil of economic prosperity and peace. In terms of public revenue Athens at this time was the richest of the Greek states. It is also widely supposed that she had developed a political system anticipating modern democratic procedure. However, the splendid architectural achievement of these years was due, as it always is, to powerful individuals, not to democratic committees.

The political destiny of Athens was in the hands of the military and political leader Pericles, from c.450 until his death in 429BC. A nobleman with inherited wealth, he had the vision and the power to create a new

35 Plan of the Acropolis at Athens

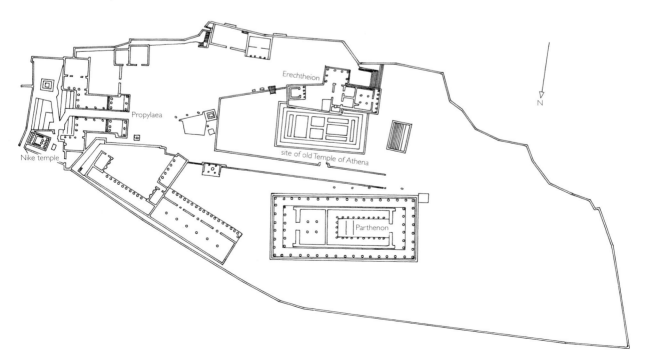

Erechtheion

Propylaea

site of old Temple of Athena

Nike temple

Parthenon

N

36 Interior of the Parthenon (completed 438BC)

37 Exterior of the Parthenon

Athens which would be the envy of the ancient world. The supremacy of Athens had been established as early as 490BC when it triumphantly defeated the Persians at Marathon, 26 miles (42km) from Athens. In 477BC the Delian League was established under Athenian direction in order to consolidate the victories of Marathon and of Salamis (480BC) and keep the invading Persians permanently out of Greek territory. Pericles was anxious to underline the political dominance of Athens by erecting a series of arresting public buildings and, in particular, by rebuilding the Parthenon, a temple dedicated to the city's guardian goddess, Athena. Religion and politics were here as difficult to disentangle as they were to be in medieval Europe. Indeed, so determined was Pericles to carry his vision into execution that he diverted to building purposes the

38 Detail of the Parthenon frieze (completed 432BC) showing an equestrian group from the Panathenaic procession

funds which members of the Delian League and other states subject to Athens had raised in order to repel possible Persian invasion in the future.

One of the most famous buildings in the world, the Parthenon was the subject of at least one contemporary monograph, now lost, and is universally acknowledged as the masterpiece of the Doric order. However, we know next to nothing of its building history beyond the fact that it is unlikely to represent the ideal vision of a single designer but is rather the result of a process of compromise and adaptation. We have said that Pericles aimed to 'rebuild' the Parthenon, but it is not clear how much was standing of what is known as the 'Older Parthenon' in 447BC when he commissioned the architect Ictinus to provide a permanent and magnificent home for a new statue of Athena, to be commissioned from the sculptor Phidias.

The first temple to Athena on the Acropolis was probably built around the mid-sixth century, but a more ambitious temple was begun in c.490BC on a vast artificial platform of solid limestone on the south side of the Acropolis. In the celebrated phrase of Demosthenes, this was 'built from the spoils of Marathon', but, save for the platform and the bottom drums of some of the columns, little seems to have been completed by the time of the terrible reprisal of the Persians in 480–479BC when, under the leadership of Xerxes, they looted Athens and destroyed its buildings. According to one theory, the Athenian statesman Kimon commissioned the architect Callicrates about fifteen years after this defeat to continue work on the unfinished temple. This building was about half-complete on Kimon's death in 450BC. His rival Pericles now dismissed Callicrates and in 447BC commissioned Ictinus to build a new temple, larger (8 by 17 columns as opposed to 6 by 16), but on the same site and incorporating substantial portions of Callicrates' work, including the columns and even some of the carved metopes, which are certainly stylistically earlier than the frieze and pedimental sculpture. The temple begun by Ictinus in 447BC was structurally complete by 438BC, in which year it was dedicated at the Panathenaic festival, though the pedimental sculpture was not ready until six years later. Having served variously as a Catholic cathedral and a mosque, the building remained well preserved until 1687 when an explosion of gunpowder temporarily stored in the cella destroyed the whole of the centre. Thereafter the building decayed rapidly until the point when Lord Elgin removed most of the sculpture to London in 1799–1803.

The Parthenon is the perfect embodiment of the Greek combination of the monumental with the delicate, the abstract with the sensual as expressed here in the ravishing sculptures of Phidias. It was constructed throughout of locally quarried Pentelic marble which lent itself more readily than the customary limestone to what are known as 'optical refinements'. We have touched earlier on these mysterious refinements and on the suggestions which archaeologists have made for their presence. At the Parthenon they include the convex curvature of the stylobate and entablature; the entasis of the columns and the thickening of those at the corners; and the inward tilting of both the columns and the outer face of the walls of the sanctuary rooms. One of the puzzling features of these refinements is that most of them are too subtle to be noticed by the eye: for example, the tilt of the columns inwards is so slight that the axes of those on both flanks would, if continued upwards, not meet until a point a mile and a half above the pavement of the temple. Another puzzle concerns the irregular spacing of the columns which some have seen as deliberate, others as accidental.

What separates the Parthenon from earlier Doric temples is not its optical refinements but the quality and profusion of its sculptural enrichment. This depicts on the metopes the battles between the gods and giants, the Amazons and Athenians, and the centaurs and Lapiths; on the frieze the Panathenaic procession in Athens which took place every four years; and on the pediments the birth of Athena and her contest with Poseidon for the Attic land. The building represents an unusual blend of Doric and Ionic elements, since sculpture on such a scale, especially the continuous figured frieze which runs unusually round the entire inner building, is more characteristic of the Ionic manner.

The author of this animated naturalistic sculpture was Phidias who, perhaps surprisingly, was also the general overseer of all Pericles' public works, a fact which gives one some idea of the status a successful sculptor was able to achieve and, consequently, of the importance attached to his art. Indeed Greek architecture as represented by the Parthenon has a sculptural basis. We can interpret the whole temple as a carved object: both its architecture and its sculpture were shaped in a similar process, with the same tools and from the same material, marble. Much of the carving was done *in situ*, for example the friezes on the north and south sides and the fluting on the columns, while all the salient architectural and sculptural points above the level of the capitals were emphasized in bright colours by an application of tinted wax. There is a kind of freehand quality about the way in which its architects and sculptors breathed life into the building and its sculptures. The optical refinements were the result of visual rather than mathematical considerations and some of them must have been worked out not in advance but in the process of execution.

We have already observed how Greek temples were not generally remarkable for their interior spaces. The celebrated frieze at the Parthenon, though over 500 feet (150m) long and more elaborately carved than any previous relief, was awkwardly placed so that it was not only ill-lit but also in great part obscured by the outer columns and architrave of the temple. It is not clear how attractive modern taste would find Phidias' colossal chryselephantine statue of Athena, which would have overwhelmed visitors to the cella. Over 40 feet (12m) high and constructed round a wooden core, it was faced with ivory for the face, arms and feet, and gold for the clothes and other features. However, Ictinus provided the interior of the cella with a livelier architectural disposition than usual by returning the flanking columns along the short fourth side, thus providing a more interesting background for the cult statue than the customary blank wall. This two-storeyed colonnade which created an architectural frame for the statue was the first development in the interior design of the Doric temple for over 150 years. There were further innovations in the interior of the lesser chamber or treasury, which seems to have contained four Ionic columns, the first introduction of Ionic elements into a Doric building.

39 The Propylaea on the Acropolis (437–432BC)

The two other principal buildings on the Acropolis, the Propylaea and the Erechtheion, are monuments of even greater ingenuity than the Parthenon. The Propylaea, which was constructed in 437–432BC as the gateway to the sacred enclosure of the temple, was the second building commissioned by Pericles. Like the Parthenon, it was built of marble and was one of the most expensive buildings of its day. Surprisingly, Pericles turned not to Ictinus but to Mnesicles, who was presumably a prominent architect though we do not know any other buildings designed by him. Unfortunately, it was left uncompleted on the outbreak of the Peloponnesian War in 432BC.

A ceremonial gateway had occupied this site from Mycenean times. Indeed Mnesicles was hampered in his aim of placing an impressive symmetrical building here, not only because the site was steeply sloping but also because the existing retaining wall followed the irregular line of the Acropolis cliff. The building is entered through a hexastyle Doric portico leading to an imposing columnar passageway which heightens the drama of approach. The Ionic columns of this passageway support a rich marble ceiling which, with its coffers adorned with gold stars on a blue ground, was one of the wonders of its time. Incidentally, the iron bars with which the architect supported a section of the architrave are structurally unnecessary. At the end of the passageway the visitor is confronted with the purpose of the whole building, the great entrance wall with its central doorway for wheeled traffic, flanked by two doorways on each side for pedestrians. The ground rises sharply so that the Doric portico, through which one emerges into the holy ground of the Acropolis at the east end of the Ionic passageway, is the frontispiece to a separately-roofed building, higher than that containing the west entrance portico. The junction of the two roofs was an awkward feature of the exterior elevation.

The entrance front is flanked by two lower colonnaded side wings. Since their columns are shorter than those of the portico, though they stand on the same level, Mnesicles was confronted with the problem of

40 The Erechtheion on the Acropolis (421–405BC)

relating two entablatures of different heights. He solved the problem by allowing the entablatures of the colonnades to continue uninterruptedly beyond the corner columns of the portico, creating small passage-like areas at the junction between the side wings and the portico.

The room in the northern side wing may have been intended for ritual dining; following the hanging of its walls with pictures in the second century AD, it has always been known as the Pinakotheke (picture gallery), though in the context of a gateway both functions seem mildly improbable. The planning of the southern wing shows Mnesicles at his most ingenious, since it is partly a sham required visually to balance the façade of the Pinakotheke but impossible to construct in its entirety because of the need for access to the projected temple of Athena Nike which occupies the adjacent south-west bastion of the Acropolis. The western end of the building

has a false north front, since there is nothing behind the last pillar of the colonnade of three columns *in antis* (ranging with the wall).

There are numerous other oddities and delicacies in the design of the Propylaea, including the use of optical refinements and the incorporation of bands of dark Eleusinian stone contrasting with the white marble. However, its special importance is as an early example of the grouping of a building with a complex plan and on different levels so as to create harmonious spatial relationships between its various parts. The potentialities of this have been exploited down the centuries, beginning in the ancient world with the terraced Hellenistic sanctuaries of Athena at Lindos on the island of Rhodes, and of Asclepios on the nearby island of Cos. The unusual grouping of the Propylaea is also echoed in that of the Erechtheion which was erected on the north side of the Athenian Acropolis in 421–405BC. A costly all-marble temple built on two levels with four porticoes of contrasting design and no fewer than five entrances, this is the most eccentric of all surviving Greek buildings. Unfortunately, the name of its initial architect is not recorded.

In its exceptional variety and complexity, the Erechtheion was obviously intended as a foil to the massive undeviating rhythm of the adjacent Parthenon. However, its irregular grouping was also influenced by the fact that it contained several separate sanctuaries, including those of Athena Polias, Erechtheus and Pandrosus, as well as a den of snakes. It also incorporated an incongruous assortment of existing sacred features such as Athena's olive tree, King Cecrops' tomb, and two souvenirs associated with Poseidon's contest on this spot with Athena for the dominion of Athens: the mark of his trident on the rock and a cistern of sea-water. The architect's solution was to provide a main block echoing the form of a normal temple with two porches of contrasting size projecting at its western end. The smaller of these, on the south side pointing towards the Parthenon, is the celebrated caryatid porch, while the northernmost is so much larger as to seem part of a separate temple. The site slopes from north to south as well as from east to west so that not only do the two western porches rise from different levels, but the main east entrance front is ten feet higher than the west front. The design of the west front thus differs markedly from that of the east front and its portico is raised up on a plain massive wall containing the entrance door to the basement.

Perhaps partly to distract attention from the irregularity of the building as a whole, tremendous emphasis was put on the carved ornament of its parts. Indeed, the ornament was so elaborate that it found no imitators in Greece. The north, east and west porticoes were all provided with figured friezes, while the capitals and necking bands of their columns and antae were exquisitely carved with meticulous filigree ornament of lotus and palmette motifs; similar adornment enhanced the doorway in the north portico, which made it the richest of its kind to survive. Indeed, we know from the building accounts that the cost of the architectural ornament exceeded that of the figure sculpture. The minutely detailed accounts, carved in marble in 409–407BC, comprise payments to about 130 workmen of whom 54 per cent were foreign residents, 24 per cent free citizens and 21 per cent slaves.

We may appropriately end our survey of fifth-century Greece in this chapter on a high point both architecturally and geographically: the isolated temple of Apollo Epicurius (the aid-bringer), 3700 feet (130m) up in the mountainous ravines of Bassae (the Greek word for ravines). Pausanias, who visited this remote and beautiful corner of Arcadia in the second century AD, told us in his admiring account of the temple that it was designed by Ictinus and commissioned by the little town of Phigalia nearby in fulfilment of a vow for deliverance from the plague. However, the aid for which Apollo was being thanked may have been in connection with military success rather than health, for the Epikouri were a group of Arcadian mercenary troops. There has also been much speculation about the date of construction but it is now often supposed to have been designed in c.429–427BC and completed in c.400BC.

The temple of Apollo Epicurius is largely built of grey local limestone and its external Doric colonnade has a certain archaic or old-fashioned flavour; it also lacks the optical refinements of the Parthenon, save for entasis. The interior, by contrast, displays a number of striking innovations which justify the traditional attribution to Ictinus. The cella is flanked by impressive Ionic half-columns, taller than the Doric columns outside and connected to the cella walls by curious spurs which are perhaps a recollection of the similar forms in the early archaic temple of Hera at Olympia not far away. The half-columns have extravagantly flared bases, the curvaceous lines of which are echoed in the startling three-faced capitals with their two canted volutes and curved tops. These are a surprising development from

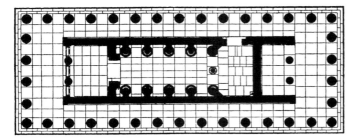

41 *Above* Plan of The Temple of Apollo at Bassae (c.429–400BC)

42 *Right* Reconstruction of the interior of the Temple of Apollo at Bassae

43 *Below* The Temple of Apollo at Bassae

the end capital of an Ionic colonnade which was carved with one diagonal volute at the corner. There was no precedent for the Bassae Ionic order or for the Corinthian capitals which crowned one, and probably all three, of the columns along the south end of the cella. The curling tendrils of the double row of acanthus leaves on these remarkable four-faced capitals are the earliest examples of a design which was to become a hallmark of Roman architecture.

Another novelty in the cella was the continuous figured frieze which ran round all four sides of its interior. Here one could appreciate the sculpture uninterruptedly, as one could not in the case of the Parthenon frieze. However, the interior must have been so dark that the frieze was presumably intended primarily for the enjoyment of the gods rather than of men. Stylistically this powerful representation in carved marble of the battles between the Greeks and Amazons, Lapiths and centaurs, which can be seen today in the British Museum, has greater force and vigour than the more gracious frieze of the Parthenon.

Most unusually the cella has no end wall but behind the central, free-standing Corinthian column (now destroyed) opens into an adytum or inner sanctuary which, again unusually, is open to the exterior colonnade through a door in its east wall. Since the temple untypically faces north, not east, this door would allow eastern light to flood into the adytum which may have housed the cult statue of Apollo against its west wall. This would have created a dramatic lighting effect within the dark cella where the freestanding Corinthian column at the south end would be intriguingly silhouetted, thus inviting the visitor to move towards the partially concealed statue. It is possible that the statue stood in the cella in front of the Corinthian column, in which case it would have been set against an architectural framework of the orders in a spatial relationship similar to that pioneered by Ictinus in the cella of the Parthenon.

The Hellenistic background

Though there must always be a set limit to the duration of earthly glory, the Athenians at the end of the fifth century BC seemed unluckier than most. Even as the stones of the Erechtheion rose the Athenian Empire was fighting for its life in the Peloponnesian War against Sparta, who was backed from 412BC by Athens' old enemy, Persia. The defeat of Athens in 406BC brought to an end not only her political supremacy but the stability of Greece as a whole. However, the power of Persia was hollower than it looked, for its empire was destroyed by Alexander the Great (356–323BC) who replaced it with a short-lived hellenizing empire of vast size in the Near East. This was effectively the old Persian Empire under Macedonian and Greek management. From c.306BC Alexander's generals and their successors carved it up into numerous kingdoms which we call Hellenistic because, though far from mainland Greece, they maintained a cultural allegiance to the memory of what Athens had been. Asiatic kings were thus proud to be counted honorary citizens of Athens, which they in turn enriched with temples, stoas and votive monuments.

The three principal Hellenistic kingdoms were the Antigonid in Macedon, the Seleucid in Syria, and the Ptolemaic in Egypt; other lesser groupings included the Attalid kingdom of Pergamum in northern Asia Minor, the Aetolian League in northern Greece, the Achaean League in the Peloponnese, and the prosperous trading centres on the islands of Rhodes and Delos. These form the historical background to Hellenistic architecture, but there has been much dispute as to the precise duration of a hellenizing style which, within the context of Greek architecture as a whole, we may usefully call Hellenistic. It is often agreed that it is too limiting stylistically to restrict it to the period of the Hellenistic kingdoms from 306BC, for the way was prepared during the course of the fourth century. For example, new life and prosperity were, perhaps ironically, brought to the old Ionic cities of Asia Minor with the ending of their subjugation by the mainland powers following a peace treaty with Persia in 387BC. Under their Persian rulers in the fourth century BC they developed a style that was monumental in scale and rich in ornamental detail.

Mainland Greece in the fourth century BC and the development of the Corinthian order

The tholos (a conically-roofed circular building of uncertain ceremonial purpose) at Delphi was built of marble in c.375BC by the architect Theodorus of Phocaea, who wrote a book (now lost) about it. The exterior of this fanciful, richly ornamented and original building was adorned with a colonnade or pteron of twenty Doric columns. Inside there was a ring of ten Corinthian columns which were inspired by those at Bassae, though they rose unexpectedly from a continuous bench of black limestone. Having arrived at Delphi we should linger there a moment for, although its buildings were architecturally less distinguished than those of the Athenian acropolis, it was and still is the most memorable Greek site after Athens. It impresses by the overwhelming poetry of its spectacular site, high up in a natural amphitheatre in the mountainous foothills of Parnassus, and by its awe-inspiring associations as the seat of the most celebrated oracle of the ancient world.

Larger than the tholos at Delphi was that at Epidaurus, designed by the architect-sculptor Polycleitus the Younger in c.360BC and built slowly during the next thirty years. The lively capitals of the fourteen Corinthian columns encircling its interior were delicately carved with naturalistic and richly detailed acanthus foliage, partly free of the bell-form behind. Several capitals survive, of which one seems to have been specially buried. If this is the architect's specimen rather than a later copy, then Polycleitus can be credited with inventing the form of the Corinthian capital which became standard in later Hellenistic and Roman architecture.

We have seen the tentative beginnings of the Corinthian capital in the cella of the temple at Bassae, where its decorative richness seemed to emphasize the holiness of the area round the cult statue. According to Vitruvius, the Corinthian capital was invented by Callimachus who is also known to have made a bronze chimney resembling a palm-tree for the Erechtheion. The sources for the Corinthian capital may lie in the world of metalwork and of interior furnishing and decoration. Certainly the Greeks were reluctant to use it on exteriors, but in the fourth century it appeared in the interiors of many buildings. Having been applied to the exteriors of a number of minor structures, the Corinthian order finally triumphed on the exterior of the greatest temple of mainland Greece, that of

44 The tholos at Delphi (c.375BC)

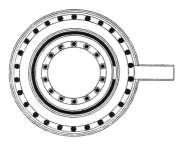

45 Plan of the tholos at Epidaurus (c.360BC)

46 The Temple of Olympian Zeus, Athens (begun 174 1BC): the Corinthian capitals

47 The Choragic Monument of Lysicrates, Athens (334BC)

Olympian Zeus in Athens. King Antiochus IV of Syria continued work on this sixth-century temple from 174BC as a gift to the Athenian people and as a statement of his belief in Greek ideals and of his devotion to Zeus. The architect, unusually, was a Roman citizen, Cossutius, who adopted the platform and the plan of the original sixth-century scheme for this temple though, significantly, he changed its order from Doric to Corinthian. Perhaps the earliest Corinthian temple on the grand scale, it was not completed till the time of the Emperor Hadrian in AD132. Cossutius' bold and fanciful capitals, close to those of the tholos at Epidaurus, exercised considerable influence on Roman architecture since, following his sack of Athens in 86BC, the dictator Sulla took some of them to Rome to adorn the temple on the Capitol.

The separation between structure and function which we have seen in the decorative use of the Corinthian order in fourth-century Greek architecture may have been encouraged by the ornamental or celebratory role of the tholos as a building type. It was given an elegantly fanciful expression in one of the most entertaining of the surviving small buildings of classical antiquity, the Choragic Monument of Lysicrates in Athens. This extravagant monument was built to display the bronze tripod won by Lysicrates in 334BC as a prize for providing a chorus in a contest in the theatre at Athens. This cylindrical monument is surrounded by six engaged columns with florid and elongated Corinthian capitals and is surmounted by an elaborate finial of acanthus ornament. Thanks to the measured drawings of it published by the pioneer English archaeologists Stuart and Revett in their *Antiquities of Athens* in 1762, it had considerable influence on neo-classical design in Britain and America.

Theatres

The theatre is an important building type of which the seeds had been sown by the end of the fifth century BC, but which achieved its finest flowering in the fourth century and later. The essence of the Greek theatre is the orchestra, i.e. dancing place, a circular piece of ground on which the actors and the chorus performed alternately. The spectators sat on a rocky slope overlooking this since Greek theatres, unlike Roman, were constructed on hillsides, not on man-made vaults or terraces. The prototypal Greek theatre was that dedicated to Dionysus on the slopes of the Acropolis in

48 The theatre at Epidaurus (c.300BC)

Athens. It had become the custom by about the later fifth century BC to erect wooden scenery against the back wall of a long thin stoa which stood between the orchestra and the adjacent temple of Dionysus, the god to whom the plays were offered. This stoa, which may date from the fourth century, became the origin of the foyer of all subsequent theatres down to our own age. Later, perhaps as early as the end of the fourth century BC, the wooden scenery was replaced by a permanent stone structure or scene-building, while a semi-circle of stone seating for as many as 17,000 spectators replaced earlier wooden benches.

The most beautiful as well as the best preserved surviving theatre in Greece is that at Epidaurus, perhaps dating from c.300BC. Its vast symmetrical auditorium, rather more than semi-circular in plan, is divided by radiating stairways and, unusually, has two distinct slopes, the upper being steeper. The seats in the lower two-thirds of the auditorium were evidently intended to be cushioned, while all command a clear view of the orchestra, as can be appreciated by anyone who attends a theatrical performance there today, one of the charms of the better preserved Greek theatres being that they still serve their original function after nearly 2,500 years. However, we are reminded that the theatre originally had a sacred function by the surviving base of the altar of Dionysus which formerly occupied the centre of the circular orchestra. Behind the orchestra rose the scene-building, which has now disappeared, together with the proscenium which was added in front of it in late Hellenistic times. At either end are elegant stone doorways which may also be additions later than the time of Polycleitus. The proscenium, a one-storeyed colonnade providing a flat top or stage on which the actors could perform, may be related to the popularity of the Hellenistic New Comedy which flourished ftom the later fourth century to around the mid-third century BC. The plays of authors such as Menander and Philemon now put emphasis on dialogue and on individual characters, rather than on the massive old choruses who were more suitably deployed in the orchestra below. The arrival of the stage raised above the level of the orchestra was obviously one of the most significant moments in the gradual development of the ancient Greek theatre into that of the present day. Most of the old theatres were provided with a proscenium-stage in the Hellenistic period. The well-preserved theatre at Priene, though less extensive than that at Epidaurus, gives one a clearer idea of the Hellenistic proscenium, while at Oropus the timber stage has been reconstructed in recent times.

Asia Minor in the fourth and third centuries BC

Elaborate tomb-houses were an Asiatic, not a mainland Greek tradition. The most impressive fourth-century tomb we know is that of a non-Grecian king, Mausolus of Caria in Asia Minor, who reigned from 377 to 353BC. He seems to have begun building this at Halicarnassus some time before his death in 353BC, but it was completed by his widow and sister, Queen Artemisia, in c.350BC as a monument to both private grief and dynastic self-regard. Its vast scale, rich ornament and extraordinary combination of pyramid and Ionic temple made it, according to ancient writers, one of the seven wonders of the world: indeed, such was its fame that it gave its name to a whole building type, the mausoleum. Its architects were Pythias, who was also the sculptor of the marble quadriga on the top, and Satyrus. They described their masterpiece in yet another of the now lost architectural treatises of the ancient world. This monument was a product of Athenian and Asiatic taste, for four of the leading sculptors of Greece – Bryaxis, Leochares, Scopas and Timotheus or Praxiteles – were shipped over the Aegean from the mainland to carve the three figured friezes and numerous other statues of men, lions and horses. The mausoleum was dismantled centuries ago to provide building materials, so that its precise form has long been a matter of intense speculation, though since the 1850s numerous carved details have been preserved in the British Museum.

Pythias, architect of the mausoleum at Halicarnassus, was also responsible for another great Ionic monument in Asia Minor, the marble temple of Athena Polias at Priene near Miletus, begun in about 340BC and dedicated in 334BC. It was begun in a period of prosperity under Persian rule but was one of those projects with which Alexander the Great, arriving as conqueror of the Persian Empire in 334BC, chose to identify himself by continuing. According to an inscription on one of the antae in the front porch it was thus dedicated by him in 334BC, though work on it was not completed until the middle of the second century BC. There is reason to suppose that Pythias regarded this costly, thoughtful, though not enormous building as a model of the Ionic order and he wrote a now lost book on it which seems to have concentrated on its proportions. Its plan was laid out in a grid of large and small squares with a proportion of length to breadth of about 2:1. The increasing emphasis on planned regularity of this kind is characteristic of Hellenistic as opposed to fifth-century architecture. Nonetheless, its Ionic capitals are models of Grecian elegance, with their volute cushions forming a gracefully sagging line which was to be straightened out in later Hellenistic and Roman architecture. These were the capitals which the leading Greek Revival architect in Britain, Sir Robert Smirke, chose to imitate in the 1820s for the external colonnade of his British Museum, though he could not resist 'correcting' Pythias by replacing his Asiatic bases with Attic ones (see Chapter 9).

We have admired at Halicarnassus one of the seven wonders of the ancient world. Elsewhere in Asia Minor we find another of these wonders in the form of the dipteral temple of Artemis at Ephesus, as rebuilt after a fire in 356BC. Ephesus was the principal of the twelve Ionian cities on the coast of Asia Minor and its temple, like that at Priene, was accordingly one with which Alexander chose to be culturally and politically identified. Indeed, we know from Arrian, Alexander's biographer in the second century AD, that at Ephesus he restored the democracy but 'gave orders to contribute to the temple of Artemis such taxes as they had paid to the Persians'. This colossal marble temple was an example of

49 Restoration drawing of the Mausoleum at Halicarnassus (completed c.350BC)

50 Columns of the Temple of Athena Polias at Priene (begun c.340BC)

the religious and architectural conservatism of the Greek world, since it reproduced the plan of the sixth-century Archaic temple which it replaced, though the details of its Ionic order are more sophisticated. Like its Archaic predecessor it was celebrated for the unusual drums of its columns, many of which were powerfully carved with figure sculpture. A similar temple, though lacking the carved drums, can be found north-east of Ephesus at the city of Sardis which, having been the capital of the Lydian monarchy, became the seat of the governor of Lydia under the Persian Empire. Dedicated to Artemis-Cybele, it was probably begun in c. 300BC but was left uncompleted in the second century AD. The Ionic columns of its peristyle, over 58 feet (17.5m) high, were the largest then erected in Asia Minor, while the 39-feet (11.5m) high doors of the pronaos and opisthodomus led to large spaces 60 by 45 feet (18 × 13.5m) in plan at each end of the temple. These impressive columnar interiors may have been hypaethral (open to the sky).

The second century BC: sacred and secular buildings

The almost overweening ambition responsible for these Asiatic temples found yet more grandiose expression in the gigantic oracular temple of Apollo at Didyma near Miletus. This was probably also begun in c. 300BC by architects from Ephesus and Miletus, but construction dragged on for over three centuries until it was finally abandoned uncompleted in the second century AD. Miletus was the southernmost of the twelve cities of the Ionian confederacy and had been a great maritime state which fought bravely but unsuccessfully against the Persians. After Alexander the Great had defeated the Persians at Miletus in 334BC the inhabitants began a new Ionic temple to replace that burnt by King Darius of Persia in 494BC.

One of the largest temples in the ancient world, the new building at Didyma boasted columns 64 feet 7½ inches (19.4m) high, the tallest and slenderest of any Greek temple. It borrowed from its Archaic predecessor its unusual plan with an open court, originally planted

with bay trees, containing a freestanding shrine in the form of a small Ionic temple. This shrine housed the Archaic bronze statue of Apollo which had been removed by Xerxes but was returned at the end of the third century BC. The exceptionally deep pronaos terminates at a higher level in an antechamber from which oracles may have been proclaimed. This supposed oracle chamber was flanked by two small stone staircases leading upwards while from its west front, adorned with Corinthian half-columns, an impressive flight of 24 steps, 50 feet (15m) wide, led down into the great

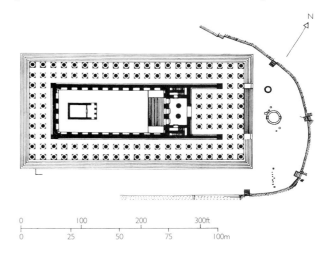

51, 52 *Above and below* The Temple of Apollo at Didyma (begun c. 300BC): plan and view

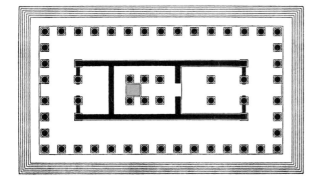

53 Plan of the Temple of Artemis Leukophryene at Magnesia-on-the-Meander, by Hermogenes (c.150BC)

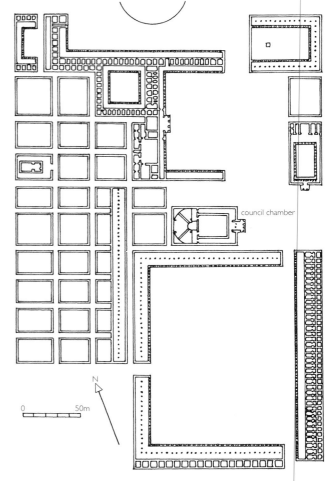

council chamber

N

0   50m

54 Plan of the city centre of Miletus as in 150BC

unroofed court of the cella. The walls of the court were unadorned up to a height of 17½ feet (5.25m), above which was a row of pilasters with rich foliage, griffins and lyres carved on their capitals and frieze. This festive ornament is likely to be late Hellenistic in date while the elaborate carved bases of the columns on the front of the temple, together with their bizarre angled capitals adorned with bulls' heads, busts of gods and winged monsters, must date from the Roman Empire.

From the second half of the second century BC we can recognize a number of works by a well-known architect from Priene called Hermogenes. These include the temple of Dionysus at Teos and that of Artemis Leukophryene at Magnesia-on-the-Meander, on both of which he wrote books since lost. He was much admired in Augustan Rome, especially by Vitruvius, and can thus be seen as influential on the whole tradition of Roman and Renaissance architecture. He rejected Doric as unsuitable for temples because of the endless problems with the corner triglyphs, and proposed a set of standard proportions for the Ionic order. He made the temple at Magnesia pseudo-dipteral, that is he omitted the inner colonnade of the two customary in dipteral temples. He thus created an impressive open space between the outer colonnade and the cella walls, an arrangement which had been attempted before but rarely with such a sense

of space and clarity. The three unusual openings resembling doors or windows which he introduced in the pediments also tend to minimize the classical Greek separation of part from part by dissolving the traditional role of the wall as barrier.

We do not think of the window as characteristic of Greek monumental architecture because the temple, as we have seen, was regarded as an isolated sculptural monument to be admired primarily from the exterior. However, there were already windows in the Propylaea and Erechtheion in Athens; the temple of the Athenians on Delos; the Philippeion at Olympia; and the Tholos at Epidaurus. From around the end of the third century BC windows began to play an important role in architectural design: for example, in the Council Chamber (Ecclesiasterion or Bouleuterion) at Priene of c.200BC, lit by a huge semi-circular window which is also an early instance of the architectural use of the arch; or in the Bouleuterion at Miletus, one of the most arresting of all Hellenistic buildings, erected partly at the cost of the Grecophile King Antiochus IV of Syria (175–164BC). Approached through a Corinthian propylon leading into a Doric colonnaded court, the Bouleuterion itself has upper walls pierced with numerous large windows and adorned with Doric half-columns, an early example of the extensive use of an engaged order.

Town planning

The adoption of features such as engaged columns and columns linked by walls or low screens clearly indicates the end of the classical Greek emphasis on the integrity of the free-standing column and the solid wall as separate load-bearing elements. This new approach, perhaps associated with the end of the temple as the dominant building type, encouraged architects to dispose buildings in a geometrical arrangement of lines rather than to concentrate on the 'correct' application of the order in a single monument. We can see this at Miletus where the second-century Bouleuterion is part of a noble complex of public buildings in the centre of the town.

The notion of the planned town is a product of the age of colonization, especially in the west. However, as early as c.466BC the architect Hippodamus had laid out his native city of Miletus in a large chessboard plan comprising about 400 blocks separated by streets which were at the most 14 feet (4.2m) wide. These were entirely residential, all public activities being conducted in a series of buildings and spaces forming a civic area at the centre of the city. But these public buildings were only added gradually, and it was not until the Hellenistic period that cities were commonly provided with

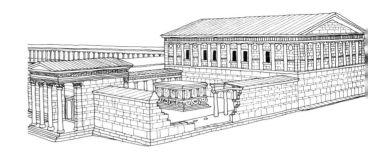

55 Restoration drawing of the Bouleuterion (Council Chamber) at Miletus, c.170BC

specialized buildings for the various functions of government. It was nonetheless Hippodamus of Miletus who can be credited with the concern to create the uniformity and rectangularity that was followed in most planned urban developments until the late nineteenth century.

The Greek agora

Until the arrival of these public and administrative buildings, the most important building in the agora (public square or market place) would be the stoa, which would provide shelter along one side.

This stoa or colonnaded porch was perhaps the most characteristic secular building type developed by the Greeks and became an essential feature of Hellenistic cities between the fourth and second centuries BC. The type was known in Archaic times and was adopted in the Athenian agora in the later fifth century BC. The employment of the freestanding portico as a monumental building was exclusive to the Greeks in the ancient world. A covered meeting-place for a wide range of activities, it was also of signal architectural importance as an aid to the organization of spaces and groups in Hellenistic city centres. Though it largely fell out of use under the Romans it undoubtedly influenced the long colonnaded streets which were characteristic of Roman town planning, especially in the Near East.

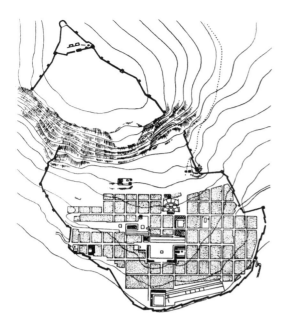

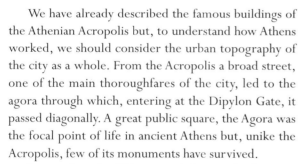

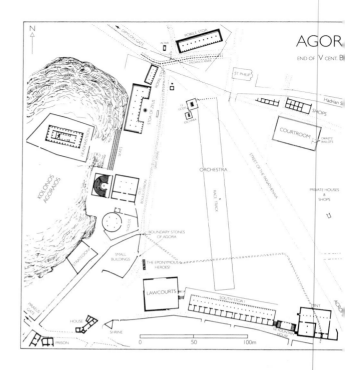

56 Plan of the city of Priene (4th–3rd century BC)

57 Plan of the Agora, Athens

We have already described the famous buildings of the Athenian Acropolis but, to understand how Athens worked, we should consider the urban topography of the city as a whole. From the Acropolis a broad street, one of the main thoroughfares of the city, led to the agora through which, entering at the Dipylon Gate, it passed diagonally. A great public square, the Agora was the focal point of life in ancient Athens but, unike the Acropolis, few of its monuments have survived.

From at least the fifth century BC onwards, the agora was the centre of civic affairs and political debate in Athens, as well as the setting for events such as religious processions and athletic displays. Near to its open space were the Senate House (Bouleuterion), where the 500 legislators of the Athenian senate met daily, the Headquarters of the General Staff (Strategeion), the Mint, the Law Courts and the Temple of Hephaestus (Hephaesteion), the most lavish building in the agora and the most complete surviving Greek temple. The agora was also dotted with shrines which were venerated on a regular basis, and were thus more visited than the major shrines on the Acropolis. The significance of the agora in the history of town planning was that it was the forerunner of the Roman fora and indeed of all subsequent piazzas and squares.

When work began on the agoras at Miletus and Priene in the later fourth century BC, U-shaped and L-shaped stoas were built to form impressive backgrounds to public buildings for the senate, gymnasia, market houses, as well as to temples and shrines. It is important to remember that Greek public and private life, like that of medieval Europe, was suffused with religion. Stoas, theatres and other public buildings were dedicated to the gods and contained altars and statues. The axial relationship to each other of these stoas at Miletus and Priene was partly determined by their subtle connection with the overall grid plan of the city itself. In this they were strikingly different from earlier agoras such as that at Athens which must have originally presented a rather fortuitous or scrappy appearance.

It could be claimed that the Greeks were among the first to conceive the role of the architect as involving the

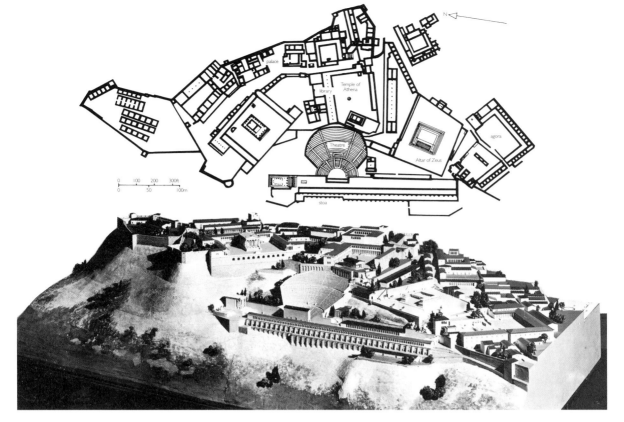

58, 59 Plan and model of the upper city of Pergamum (mid-3rd to mid-2nd centuries BC)

design of whole cities, not just of single buildings. The small city of Priene, consisting of about 4,000 inhabitants, was rebuilt in the late fourth and third centuries BC as a model of the Greek polis or city-state. The philosopher Aristotle (384–322BC), tutor to Alexander, had provided the intellectual model in his book, *Politics*, in which he celebrated the ideal city-state. Occupying a terraced and steeply sloping site south of an almost inaccessibly lofty acropolis, Priene was laid out on a grid plan with six principal streets running east-west on level ground crossed at right angles by fifteen streets ascending the hillside somewhat too sharply for comfort. Near the centre is the agora with its well-placed civic buildings forming a noble open space, while the stadium and palaestra (wrestling school) at the southern extremity of the town are balanced by the theatre cut into the rock of the acropolis at the north extremity. The precinct sacred to Athena Polias with its

superb Ionic temple forms a notable off-centre feature on a commanding terrace north-west of the agora. In the mid-second century BC the agora was remodelled to form a more enclosed interior space with an elegant semi-circular archway marking its entrance from the east. This is perhaps the first example of an ornamental Greek arch.

Massive masonry walls and towers enclosed not only the whole town but also the much steeper and unbuilt area of equal size which surrounded the acropolis. There was an eloquent contrast between the ordered but not obsessively symmetrical street plan of the town itself and the wholly irregular pattern outlined by these retaining fortifications which followed the natural lines of the acropolis and the ravines to its south. Though Priene housed a population which would be accounted today as of no more than village proportions, its great temple and public buildings, its fountains, gymnasia and spacious stoas, provided a setting for civilized urban living which can hardly fail to strike us as ideal.

Pergamum, further north in Asia Minor, represents a different example of the Hellenistic urban idea, since its plan is not constricted by the Hippodamian grid: indeed, where Priene ignores its sloping site, Pergamum exploits it. It was laid out as the imposing capital of the Attalid kingdom by Attalus I, second king of the Pergamene dynasty, and his son, Eumenes II, between the mid-third and mid-second centuries BC. We know virtually nothing about the principal cities of the Hellenistic world: Alexandria, as laid out under the Ptolemies, the Macedonian kings of Egypt, and Antioch, as laid out under the Seleucids, the Macedonian kings of Syria. However, the city of Pergamum, though politically less important, has been thoroughly excavated in modern times so that it has come to assume a special significance. But very little stands on the site, even the remains of the great Altar of Zeus having been taken to the Pergamon Museum in East Berlin where there is also a splendid model of the whole upper city.

The upper city, roughly crescent-shaped in plan, was dramatically situated on the crest of the hill, with its ceremonial buildings constructed on a series of irregular terraces following the lie of the land and thus placed at odd angles to each other. At the foot was the lower agora, a large completely enclosed court. Adjacent on the north was the upper agora which was dominated by the Altar of Zeus on a high terrace. North of this was the temple of Athena, built in the old-fashioned Doric style, perhaps in tribute to the Parthenon, though possibly simply an echo of the nearby temple at Assos. The temple of Athena stood in a large courtyard surrounded by colonnades behind one of which was the most celebrated library of its date, apart from that at Alexandria. This great library was adorned with a version of the statue of Athena in the Parthenon, which again underlines the extent to which these powerful Hellenistic kingdoms in Asia Minor acknowledged Greece as the mother of culture. An enormous theatre, partly Roman in date, was fitted into the hillside immediately west of the temple of Athena, while in front of the theatre ran a 700-feet (213m) long terrace or stoa projecting from the side of the acropolis on a retaining wall. At its north end was a small Ionic temple of Hellenistic origin rebuilt in the

60 Altar of Zeus, Pergamon (Berlin Museum)

early third century AD by the Emperor Caracalla, for Pergamum received many Roman embellishments after it had come under Roman rule in 133BC through the will of its last king, the Attalid dynasty having always favoured Rome. Indeed, one of the most dominant buildings of Pergamum was the Imperial Roman temple of Trajan which towered over the city from a colossal terrace added north of the theatre. The eastern edge of the acropolis was dominated by the modest Hellenistic palaces with their barracks and storehouses extending northwards.

Like every Greek city Pergamum was, of course, a man's world. While the women were confined to their modest mud-brick houses in the lower city, the men talked and strolled in the cool colonnades of the agora or admired the handsome youths being trained in the gymnasia. Architecturally the most distinguished building at Pergamum was the Altar of Zeus, built on the second terrace of the acropolis by Eumenes II in c.170BC. Although there was a tradition of monumental altars in Ionia from the sixth century, Greek altars were generally simple, consisting either of a long narrow pedestal in front of the temple or merely a mound of the ashes of former victims. But in Hellenistic times increasing emphasis was put on size and architectural adornment, so that the altar of Zeus the Liberator at Syracuse, built around 200BC for an annual sacrifice of 450 oxen, was nearly 650 feet (198m) long. Lest we deceive ourselves into thinking that we are in harmony

61 Reconstruction of the Stoa of Attalus in the agora of Athens (mid-2nd century BC)

with the Greek mentality we should consider for a moment the stench, squalor and noise of such an occasion as the flies settled on the blackening blood in the stifling heat.

There were other altars of great size at Lycosura and Samothrace but none more splendid than that at Pergamum. The largest sculptured monument in the ancient world, its scale and function were found so horrific by Christians that it is mentioned in the Bible as 'the seat of Satan' (Apocalypse 2:13). From the front the building appeared as a U-shaped Ionic colonnade set on a high podium, which was covered with an enormous sculptured relief. The whole area between the side wings of the podium was filled with a vast flight of steps leading up to the altar itself, which was a comparatively modest affair in the centre of a columnar court behind the

colonnade. Interest concentrates not on the interior but on the unparalleled dynamism of the carved figures on the 7½-foot (2.25m) high podium representing with frightening and emotional realism the battle between the Olympian gods and the giants. This symbolizes the victories of the king of Pergamum over the barbarian Gauls who invaded Asia Minor in 278BC. The Pergamene sculptural style exercised considerable influence over later Roman art through the close cultural and political links between Pergamum and Rome.

When in the mid-second century BC the haphazard planning of the agora in Athens was tidied up by the addition of new axially placed stoas, the most splendid of them, the Stoa of Attalus, was commissioned by the architecturally minded Attalus II of Pergamum, who must have been proud to introduce Hellenistic town-planning ideals into the heart of Athens. This unusually sumptuous stoa, which was entirely reconstructed as a museum in the 1950, was built of marble and boasted a

62 The Tower of the Winds, Athens (mid-1st century BC)

aligned on the four cardinal points and the four intermediate points from which the eight winds were supposed to blow. Each side was carved with a sculptural relief personifying a different wind. There were also sundials on the exterior, a water clock within and on the roof a bronze statue of a Triton holding a weather-vane. The capitals of the porch columns were elegantly carved with lotus and acanthus leaves which have been widely imitated in classical and neo-classical architecture. The building, paid for by Andronicus from far-away Cyrrhus on the Euphrates, is a perfect architectural and sculptural combination of Greek construction and Hellenistic science.

Domestic architecture

Very different from Priene, Pergamum or Athens as an example of a Hellenistic city is Delos with its informal unmonumental character. Though the smallest of the Cyclades islands, its claim to be the birthplace of Apollo and Artemis helped it become one of the leading sanctuaries in Greece. In honour of Apollo no one was allowed to be born or to die here, but despite this inconvenience it was a flourishing community which was the centre of the Athenian-led Confederacy after the Persian Wars. Having been made a free port by Rome in the second century BC, it took over from Rhodes as the leading trade centre in the Aegean and as such became the principal Roman slave market. Here on the irregular rocky surfaces of a small but beautiful island, the disposition of buildings could conform to no previously conceived plan so that, whether Greek or Hellenistic, they are scattered heterogeneously across its length and breadth.

From Mycenean times the cult centre on Delos had been by the Sacred Harbour near the north-western end of the island. Here, crowded together so as to form an extraordinary combination of the sacred and the commercial, are the three adjacent temples of Apollo, a number of third- and second-century stoas, the agora, houses, warehouses, a large merchants' club known as the Agora of the Italians, and the Hypostyle Hall or

two-storeyed colonnade with a row of shops at the back. Remarkably it combined as many as four different orders, one Doric, two Ionic, and one with rich leaf-capitals of consciously archaizing character. These seem to echo the capitals used near Pergamum around 600BC, so that we can perhaps see their introduction here as a subtle way of claiming historical authenticity for a modern Pergamene style.

Before leaving Athens we should glance at an unusual building which, though Roman in date, is essentially Hellenistic in character. The Tower of the Winds, probably dating from the mid-first century BC, is a handsome octagonal structure of marble with its sides

63 Plan of the city and sanctuaries of Delos

64 The Terrace of the Naxian Lions on Delos (c. late 7th century BC)

Exchange which was an elegant but functional building divided into five aisles by 44 Doric and Ionic columns. Immediately north of the Agora of the Italians is the Terrace of the Naxian Lions whose austere archaic forms in marble, smoothed by the sea-winds of centuries, are one of the principal memories carried away from the island by many modern visitors, as doubtless by many antique ones. These lithe creatures guard the approach to the Sacred Lake, now dry, west of which was a select residential area. Even finer houses were to be found in the neighbourhood of the theatre which lay to the south of the Sacred and Commercial Harbours. The substantial surviving or reconstructed fragments of late Hellenistic buildings of the second century BC, such as the House of Hermes and the House of the Masks, are well known for their lively mosaic floors, painted stuccoed walls, and two-storeyed colonnaded courtyards. The better type of house generally faced south and was a rectangular block built of sun-dried mud brick round an internal court which was occasionally ornamented with a colonnade on one or more sides. The planning was informal and asymmetrical with no attempt to create axial vistas, each house often differing in plan from the next even when they were regimented in urban blocks. With its flexibility and simplicity this type was adaptable to a range of functions including inn, factory, school, or hotel as in a block south of the theatre at Delos.

65 *Above* The House of the Vettii, Pompeii (early 1st century AD): the peristyle on to which all the principal rooms open

66 *Below* Plan of the House of the Vettii

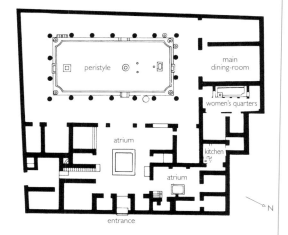

67 *Left* Wall painting at Pompeii

It is possible to distinguish three main types of Greek house, beginning with those of the later fifth century BC at Olynthos which are characterized by the pastas, a long room running east and west, generally for the whole width of the house. The south wall of the pastas opened through pillars into a courtyard. Later, when greater use was made of stone, we find at Priene the house centred on a prostas or loggia, which has been interpreted as a revival or survival of the ancient megaron. Finally there is the peristyle house which is originally associated especially with Delos.

From the third century BC the life and thought of the Romans was civilized by contact in countless ways with Greeks and the Greek way of life. The educated classes of Italy became gradually but completely hellenized. For an example of this we may turn to the small south Italian town of Pompeii which, though dating from the Roman Republic, is Hellenistic in architectural character. The oldest houses, dating from about 300BC, are dominated by a central open space, the atrium, which is related axially or symmetrically to the surrounding rooms. A good example is the House of the Surgeons where a small entrance hall, flanked by a pair of service rooms, leads to the atrium, from two sides of which open bedrooms. At the far end of the atrium lie the main living-rooms with windows looking on to the garden beyond. This type of house was gradually enriched with Hellenistic features such as columns in the atrium and, by the end of the second century BC, with a peristyle or colonnaded court at the back of the house, perhaps containing a garden. The House of the Vettii is a sumptuous late example of this type, with its atrium and handsome peristyle. In such houses private citizens created small-scale versions of the palaces of eastern kings in the Hellenistic world. At Delos in the late third and early second centuries BC interior decorators had simulated in paint architectural motifs and polychrome marble veneering. This technique was taken up in the so-called First Pompeian style (c.200–90BC) where, as in the House of the Centaur, the wall was divided into three horizontal layers and treated architecturally in stucco and paint.

The Pompeiian Second style (c.80–15BC), which accompanied the increasing use of columns in the atrium and peristyle, incorporated painted colonnades framing illusionistic views of countryside. A beautiful example of this type, perhaps inspired by Hellenistic stage paintings, is the painted cubiculum of c.40BC from a villa at Boscoreale near Pompeii. Now in the Metropolitan Museum, New York, the paintings are a product of a neo-Hellenistic Roman humanism in which the merits of philosophy are held up as a guide to the good ruler. Decorative mosaic floors, used at Delos in the House of the Masks, were another popular Hellenistic fashion which reached Italy in the first century BC. Famous Greek and Hellenistic paintings were imitated in mosaic, as can be seen in the depiction at the House of the Faun in Pompeii of Alexander the Great's victory over the Persians at Issus. This was evidently copied from a late classical painting and is now in the Museo Nazionale at Naples.

The rise of Rome

Before the end of the second century BC the great period of Hellenistic building activity was over. Indeed, the leading artists and thinkers had flourished before 200BC: the achievements of philosophers like Aristotle, Zeno and Epicurus, of scientists and mathematicians like Euclid and Archimedes, and of sculptors like Praxiteles and Lysippus, had helped determine the shape of the world we live in. They were the first to define the philosophies towards life which we know as stoicism, epicureanism and cynicism; the first to produce books of grammar, statics and hydrostatics, to measure the circumference of the earth, to come close to discovering the circulation of the blood; while it was the sculptors of this period who were imitated by the Romans and their successors down to the rediscovery of Archaic and fifth-century Greek art in the eighteenth century. The adventurous spirit which prevailed in science and mathematics was accompanied by a conservative outlook in cultural and artistic matters. The scattered Hellenistic kingdoms believed that what gave them identity was imitation of the public and representational arts as established in Greece. Thus, by the late fourth century artistic style could be said to have acquired a political significance by seeming to invest Hellenistic rulers with something of the authority of Alexander.

This self-conscious approach to the role of art encouraged the production in Alexandria around 300BC of the earliest written histories of art. Aristotle had come close to arguing for cultural relativism. Far from following Plato's belief that the works of man are pale imitations of divine reality or heavenly 'Ideas', he noted that temples, sculpture and paintings reflected the individual tastes of their creators and their patrons. This opened the way for their being considered as 'works of art' rather than as ritual or political images. Indeed, it was the Hellenistic period which saw the birth of art collecting.

The disintegration of the Hellenistic achievement in the second and first centuries BC must be seen in the light of the growing power of Rome. The prolonged but successful fight against Carthage by the highly militarized state of Rome in the Punic Wars of the third and second centuries BC had ensured by 201BC that it and not Carthage would control the western world. Rome dealt more swiftly with Greece and the Hellenistic kingdoms, conquering Macedonia in 168BC, Greece twenty years later, and Carthage with its north African territories in 151BC; Corinth was sacked in 146BC and Athens itself in 86BC, while the kingdom of Pergamum became a Roman province in 133BC, Syria in 64BC and Egypt in 30BC. Though the cultural impact of Rome throughout the Greek east was disastrous, especially in terms of the booty removed and the tribute money exacted, the cultural impact *on* Rome was wholly and permanently beneficial.

The Roman genius for organization and planning is demonstrated in the Roman Empire in the Lex Romana, the system of laws from which the subsequent legal codes of the western world derive; in the Pax Romana, the peace which reigned for a century and a half, thanks to wise administration; and, especially, in the architecture and planning of its great cities. With their public buildings, basilicas and temples formally set in monumental squares or fora, their wide streets lined with apartment blocks, shops and offices, and their warehouses and elaborate drainage systems, these cities marked a wholly new departure in urban architecture. The systematization of the construction industry and the introduction of new building techniques facilitated these great programmes of development and renewal which included bridges and aqueducts as well as new roads linking the cities.

This new range of building types called for an architecture of greater variety and flexibility than that which had existed in the Greek and Hellenistic cultures. Dependent on the column as a constructional element, Greek and Hellenistic architecture was essentially a trabeated system in which vertical lines contrasted with horizontal lines. The creation of interior space was not a guiding consideration. Roman architects, by contrast, reinstated the wall, developed the use of the arch, and were masters in interior design, especially when it involved domes, apses and vaults. The ultimate ancestry of the circular domed buildings of the Romans lay in the religious buildings and tombs of the ancient world, but it should be stressed that few of these had been designed to be entered by the general public. In exploiting the possibilities of public domed spaces in the design of baths, palaces, villas and especially in the Pantheon, the Romans developed the use of cast concrete for vaults.

Concrete grew between the third and first centuries BC out of the mortared rubble construction adopted by the Romans, who lacked the conveniently situated marble quarries of the Greeks. It was the increasing daring with which architects of the Empire used concrete, especially for vaults, that enabled them to create a new architecture of space in which the building became a kind of moulded shell. Roman concrete (*opus caementicium*) was a mortar strengthened with an aggregate of smallish stones (*caementa*) and was generally

68 The Maison Carrée at Nîmes (early 1st century AD)

laid in roughly horizontal courses. Though it could not be mixed and poured like modern concrete it did develop from a rubble infill between brick walls to a building material in its own right with which it was possible to construct walls, arches and vaults. It derived much of its strength from the composition of its mortar, which combined lime with the volcanic sand (pozzuolana) found near Rome.

It is important to remember that Roman architects of all periods never made the mistake of modern architects of exposing the actual surface of the concrete. Realizing that concrete adds to its initial visual crudity the subsequent disadvantage of staining disagreeably rather than weathering beautifully, the Romans always took care to conceal it internally by plaster, marble or mosaic, and externally by brick or stone facings, of which the three principal types are known chronologically as *opus incertum* (second and early first centuries BC), a random facing composed of small stones; *opus reticulatum* (first century BC and first century AD), small square stones set diagonally; and *opus testaceum* (mid-first century AD onwards), a facing of flat bricks or tiles. While concrete was used extensively for foundations, walls and vaults, a varied range of stones and marbles was adopted for other structural and decorative parts.

Travertine, quarried near Tivoli from the second century BC, is an attractive hard limestone of a creamy-grey colour and slightly pitted texture. The Carrara quarries in north Italy provided a dead white marble lacking the crumbly richness of Pentelic marble. Later in the Empire red and grey granite and red porphyry were imported from Egypt.

It should not be supposed that because of their use of a modern-sounding material like concrete the Romans made fundamental advances in technology, except in the field of vaulting. Like the Greeks they were not interested in pushing their knowledge very far beyond the techniques they knew so well, so that they habitually made their supporting walls far more massive than was structurally necessary. Indeed, one might even say that the Roman world was not greatly more advanced technologically than the Bronze Age cultures of two or three millennia earlier.

Roman life and architecture were permeated by politics. Rarely has architecture been put so completely to the service of politics as in the great temples and fora of imperial Rome. The direct political symbolism of these buildings is paralleled in their equally direct symmetrical layout. Unlike the Greeks, the Romans liked buildings to have an obvious front which would be approached axially. This different architectural approach meant that the characteristic Roman temple was itself also subtly different from the Greek. Let us take as an example one of the best preserved of all, the so-called Maison Carrée at Nîmes in southern France, built under Augustus in the opening years of the first century AD. It stands in un-Greek fashion on a high podium broken at the entrance front by a broad flight of steps flanked by low cheek-walls. It is thus actually impossible to approach the temple in any other way than axially up these steps. Moreover, though the columns make a splendid show in the entrance portico, they are not continued all round the temple in the form of a colonnade. Instead, at the back and sides of the building they are merged into the walls of the cella, so that the temple is an example of the type known as pseudo-dipteral. In other words, the columns are engaged and wholly decorative. The Roman wall, articulated with applied ornament, has invaded the temple and thus replaced the freestanding load-bearing columns of the Greeks.

Republican architecture

For the concept of a temple on a podium with a portico at only one end, as at Nîmes, the Romans were indebted to the Etruscans, while the relation of a temple to a colonnaded court was a Hellenistic idea. The Etruscan kings from Etruria in central Italy conquered Rome in the mid-seventh century BC and ruled it for about one hundred and fifty years. The civilization they introduced, of which tantalizingly few monuments survive, was influenced by contemporary Greece. They were the first to build monumentally in Rome, for example the late-sixth-century temple of Jupiter, Juno and Minerva on the Capitoline Hill, while their engineering achievements included the draining of the land subsequently occupied by the Forum. In 509BC the Etruscans were expelled and a republican city-state was established under the leadership of Roman patricians. A marked cultural decline ensued until about the middle of the second century BC. During this lengthy period the Romans were preoccupied with a succession of wars in which they established their dominance first over Italy and, by the end of the second Punic War against the Carthaginians in 202BC, over the whole Mediterranean. The sack of Corinth in 146BC brought Greece itself under Roman rule so that Italy, to her benefit, was flooded with Greek works of art as well as refugee craftsmen and architects.

A Greek architect, Hermodorus of Salamis, designed the first all-marble temple in Rome in the year that

69 The Forum Boarium in Rome: in the centre the Temple of Vesta or Hercules Victor, on the right the Temple of Fortuna Virilis (late 2nd century and early 1st century BC respectively)

Corinth fell. Dedicated to Jupiter Stator, it was commissioned by Q. Caecilius Metellus who had helped defeat the Macedonians. It no longer survives, but the Temple of Fortuna Virilis (Portunus) in the Forum Boarium (cattle-market) near the Tiber is a well-preserved example of an Ionic temple of the later Roman Republic. Dating from the second half of the second century BC, it is possibly the earliest pseudoperipteral temple and perhaps influenced the Maison Carrée at Nîmes. Though Greek in detail it was Italian in plan and Roman in construction, that is, the podium is concrete faced with travertine, the columns are travertine and the cella walls are tufa, a solidified volcanic dust or mud, faced with stucco.

A small number of attractive circular temples include the so-called Temple of Vesta (more probably Hercules Victor), also in the Forum Boarium. Perhaps of the first half of the first century BC, though restored under the Empire, it is built of Pentelic marble from Athens whence its architect may also have been brought. Its circular form echoes that of the Greek tholos; its Corinthian capitals resemble those of the Olympieion in Athens, while the steps surrounding it are also a Greek fashion. Subsequent Roman writers believed that the form of such temples was an echo of the round huts of the Early Iron Age in Italy, a resemblance which, in the case of the Temple of Vesta, has since been fortuitously heightened by the loss of the entablature.

Another well-known circular temple of similar date, variously described without authority as a Temple of Vesta or of the Sibyl, can be found picturesquely perched above the gorge at Tivoli. It has a concrete podium faced with travertine slabs, foundations of tufa, and travertine ashlar for the body of the temple itself, including columns, door and window frames. Its attractive Corinthian capitals are especially luxuriant with a large central flower prominently placed on the upper part of the bell. They support an Ionic entablature with oxheads linked by rich garlands carved in the frieze, a Hellenistic motif which became increasingly popular from the time of Augustus. Partly due to the beauty of its site, this

70 The Temple of Vesta at Tivoli (early 1st century BC)

charming temple has long been one of the most popular buildings of antiquity. Drawn and painted by numerous artists from the Renaissance onwards, it was restored in a celebrated drawing by Palladio in his *Quattro Libri* (1570) and was imitated by English architects such as William Kent (1685–1748) and John Soane (1753–1837) (see pp. 373, 387).

The Sanctuary of Fortuna Primigenia at Praeneste, some 30 miles (48km) east of Rome, is different from anything we have yet seen. One of the most imaginative buildings of antiquity, it was an extraordinary Republican foretaste of the scenic effects and the concrete vaulting of later Imperial architects. It may date from the late second century BC, though it has traditionally been associated with the dictator Sulla who settled his partisans here in c.80BC. It was sacred to the goddess of Fortune or Fate who had been delivering oracles on this spot from at least the third century BC. Higher up the hill from the earliest temple and forum is a series of seven terraces. These are connected by staircases and ramps which culminate in a theatre surmounted first by a semicircular double portico and finally by a small

circular temple. The great double-ramp staircase, surely of eastern origin since it seems to recall ancient ziggurats, is flanked by columns with eccentrically sloping capitals following the incline of the ramp. The fourth terrace is backed by a row of colonnaded shops and punctuated by two hemi-cycles with screens of Ionic columns and coffered barrel-vaults of concrete. Enough survives of this exhilarating assembly of classical symmetry, uniting concrete, tufa, travertine and stucco on an improbable site with superb views towards the sea across the Campagna, to convince us that rarely before or since have architecture and landscape been blended in so masterly a fashion.

Together with the Roman Baths the Roman Amphitheatre is a phrase which has passed into the language as immediately expressive of the Roman way of life. While the palaces of the Roman emperors have largely disappeared, the western parts of their empire are still scattered with the vast elliptical amphitheatres where their subjects enjoyed the frequently brutal spectacles which modern taste finds degrading. The amphitheatre is architecturally a development from the theatres of the Greeks as adapted by the Romans. One of the earliest stone theatres in Italy was that built at Pompeii in the second century BC, but the stern conservative sentiment in Republican Rome delayed the building of places of public entertainment as permanent structures. Thus the first theatre in Rome, of which little survives, was the Theatre of Pompey, built in 55BC. Pompey, who with Caesar and Crassus in 60BC formed the ruling Triumvirate in Rome, had recently returned from Greece and is supposed to have modelled his theatre on that at Mytilene on the island of Lesbos. Fortunately the Theatre of Marcellus, projected by Caesar but dedicated in 13 or 11BC by Augustus to the memory of his grandson Marcellus, survives as one of the principal monuments of late Republican Rome.

The Theatre of Marcellus typifies some of the differences between Greek and Roman theatres in being built not on a hillside but on an elaborated arcuated substructure with concrete barrel-vaults; and in having

71, 72 The Sanctuary of Fortuna Primigenia, Praeneste (possibly late 2nd century BC): axonometric reconstruction and view

a semicircular, not circular, orchestra, designed less for the chorus than as a reserved area of seats for senators. In Roman theatres, unlike Greek, the audience did not look out at the countryside across the orchestra because the *scaena frons* (stage building or back scene), though modest in the Theatre of Marcellus, became an object of increasing architectural size and consequence. Of especial importance for the future of theatre design was the semicircular façade of the Theatre of Marcellus with its tiers of arched openings framed with superimposed orders, Doric on the ground floor, the lighter Ionic on the next and, probably, Corinthian on the now lost top floor. This system of articulation, developed from key Republican buildings such as the sanctuaries of Praeneste and Tivoli and the Tabularium in Rome, is a perfect early statement of what was to become the characteristically Roman combination of a structural arch and a decorative column. It found its most monumental expression in a celebrated building which, because it was inspired by the Theatre of Marcellus, it is appropriate to discuss here: the Colosseum.

The earliest permanent stone amphitheatre surviving in Italy is that built on a comparatively modest scale at Pompeii in c.80BC. Augustus built one in Rome in the Campus Martius in 29BC but it was destroyed in the fire of AD64. The Colosseum, built by Vespasian in AD75–80, is thus the earliest as well as the finest surviving amphitheatre in Rome. Known originally as the Flavian Amphitheatre, after the family name of Vespasian, it has been known since the eighth century AD as the Colosseum, a name which may have been derived from the nearby Colossus of Nero. However, by building it on the site of the artificial lake in the private park of the Golden House of Nero, Vespasian was able to contrast his own magnanimity with Nero's self-indulgence. Certainly the Colosseum was built to gratify the tastes of the multitude, of whom it could accommodate as many as 50,000.

Built of travertine quarried at Tivoli, the exterior façade of the Colosseum is a visually compelling assembly of three tiers of 80 round-arched openings, each flanked

73 The Theatre of Marcellus, Rome (completed 13/11BC)

by engaged columns, surmounted by a taller but barer storey articulated with Corinthian pilasters. The serenity of this unbroken rhythm of superimposed orders, Doric, Ionic, Corinthian, was a powerful influence in the Renaissance on architects such as Alberti and Giuliano da Sangallo (see Chapter 6). Derived from the Theatre of Marcellus, the façades of the Colosseum may have been architecturally conservative, but as a feat of engineering construction and as an example of the Roman genius for organization, the building reached an unsurpassed level of achievement. The terraced seats, mostly of marble, were supported on the gradually rising vaults of an arcuated substructure of brick-faced concrete. The whole vast honeycomb was penetrated with radiating ramps, lateral passageways and ambulatories, and horizontal gangways, so as to enable safe and convenient circulation for the great crowds who entered by ticket through the 76 numbered entrances. Similar ingenuity was devoted to the design and construction of the maze-like subterranean chambers below the floor of the arena, where wild animals were confined in cages which could be hauled up to floor level.

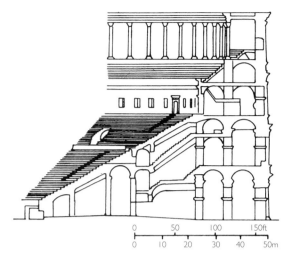

75, 76 *Left and above* The Colosseum, Rome (AD75–80): section and aerial view

The impact of the Colosseum was widespread, smaller but still impressive versions of it surviving at Verona and Pola in Italy, and at Nîmes and Arles in southern France. At Nîmes we also find an even more imposing arcuated monument, the Pont du Gard, built by Agrippa in the late first century BC to carry the aqueduct of Nîmes over the gorge of the river Gardon.

Constructed throughout of stone ashlar and 160 feet (49m) high, it spans the summer bed of the river in a single arch, like most Roman bridges and aqueducts, so as to avoid placing abutments in fast-running water. Even more striking is the aqueduct at Segovia in Spain, which towers dramatically nearly 100 feet (30m) above the rooftops near the middle of the modern town. Built some time in the first or early second century AD, the stonework of this gripping monument was left deliberately rough, perhaps so as to heighten the impression of strength. It still carries the water supply of the town on its two tiers of 128 arches.

Fora, basilicas and temples: the Roman synthesis

The plans of many Roman towns, echoing those of their forts, were often dominated by two straight streets crossing at the centre. Near the point of intersection was placed the forum, generally colonnaded, round which were grouped the principal public buildings, a disposition one finds in countless Roman cities from Pompeii to Damascus. The Roman forum replaced the Greek and Hellenistic agora as the principal focus of city life and planning. In Rome itself, the most famous as well

74 The aqueduct at Segovia (1st or early 2nd century AD)

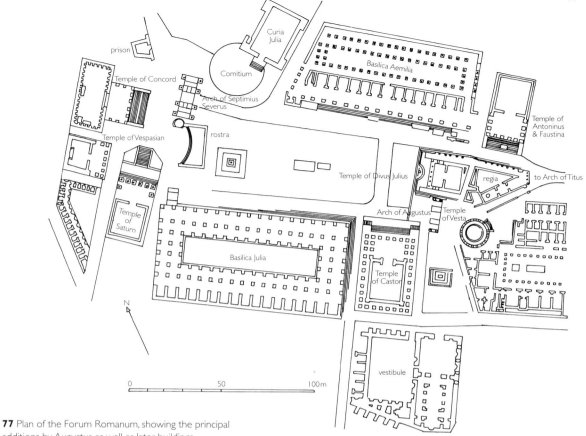

77 Plan of the Forum Romanum, showing the principal additions by Augustus as well as later buildings

as the oldest of the fora had a very different origin. This was the Forum Romanum which stood below the Capitol hill and served as a market-place, though near its north-west corner stood the Curia or senate-house for the ruling oligarchy. In the second century BC it was provided with basilicas, large covered halls serving as law courts, exchanges and markets.

By the beginning of the Empire the Forum Romanum had become very overcrowded, and during the next century and a half it was magnificently extended by successive emperors whose buildings were public demonstrations of their own political and military achievements. A precedent had been set by Julius Caesar who added the Forum of Caesar (or Forum Julium) immediately north-west of the Forum Romanum in c.54BC. It consisted of a colonnaded rectangle dominated by a temple dedicated to Venus Genetrix (Venus the Mother), mother of Aeneas whose son Iulus (Ascanius) founded the Julian clan. The plan of this

forum, which was to be so influential on later Roman fora, may have been inspired by such Hellenistic examples as the sanctuary of Asclepios on the island of Cos.

As part of his plan of bringing order to the haphazard if time-honoured Forum, Caesar completely rebuilt one of the old Republican basilicas, the Basilica Sempronia, which now became the Basilica Julia, and restored the Basilica Aemilia facing it on the north side of the Forum. The Basilica Aemilia, one of the earliest basilicas, dated from 179BC and seems to have had a two-storeyed colonnaded façade of sixteen bays like a Hellenistic stoa. Unlike a stoa it contained an enclosed hall, lit by a high clerestorey, in which a magistrate could conveniently conduct his business. Following its restoration by Julius Caesar it was entirely rebuilt by Augustus in 14BC. It emerged as a building richly articulated with an external order of engaged columns. The more extensive Basilica Julia, rebuilt by Augustus and again by Diocletian in the

... IX IMP·XI·COS·VI·P·COS·ET
... C·POTEST·VI·COS·PROCOS·E
... BVS·
... I·ROMANI·PROPAGATVM
... VES·P·Q·R

78 The Forum Romanum, showing (*left*) the Arch of Septimius Severus, in the distance the Arch of Titus and (*right*) the three columns of the Temple of Castor and Pollux

late third century AD, contained a central hall flanked by four aisles divided by arcades carried on rows of piers.

Caesar's vision of replanning Rome was achieved by Augustus and Agrippa. Augustus (63BC–AD14), great-nephew and adopted son of the last Republican dictator, Julius Caesar, became first emperor following his defeat of Antony and Cleopatra at the Battle of Actium in 31BC. The exploits of Sulla, Caesar and Augustus himself, too complicated and extensive even to summarize here, had made Rome master of a vast empire which, by the time of Trajan (AD98–117), incorporated most of Europe as far north as Scotland, as well as the whole Mediterranean world including the North African coast and much of the Near East. Bound together by Roman

law in a peace which lasted for 150 years, it was a phenomenon which has never been repeated.

One of Augustus's first ambitions had been the modernization of the road system in Italy, while in Rome he early entrusted to his friend and colleague Agrippa the task of building new aqueducts and improving the drainage system. According to Suetonius, Augustus boasted of the hub of his empire that he 'found Rome a city of brick and left it a city of marble'. The emphasis on marble was typical of his traditionalist taste for grandiose neo-classicism rather than for the experimental brick and concrete architecture of Praeneste. While he was dynamic as a military leader he was stylistically conservative as an architectural patron, for his buildings helped him in his task of emphasizing the political continuity between the old Republic and the new Empire. Thus he not only erected new public buildings but rebuilt or restored many of the existing temples: indeed, in his autobiographical testament, *Res Gestae Divi*

79 Restoration drawing of the Temple of Mars Ultor with part of the Forum Augustum, AD2

Augusti ('The achievements of the divine Augustus'), he claimed to have rebuilt as many as 82 temples in one year, 28BC.

As part of his remodelling and extension of the Roman Forum, a continuation of the work begun by Julius Caesar, Augustus completely rebuilt two temples in marble, the Temple of Castor and Pollux and the Temple of Concord. At the east end of the Forum he also added a third, the Temple of Divus Julius (the deified Julius), dedicated to his adopted father in 29BC as an uncompromising statement of his religious and political ideals. The Temples of Castor and Pollux and of Concord were carried out under the direction of Augustus's stepson and eventual successor as emperor, Tiberius (reigned AD14–37). The Temple of Castor and Pollux (dedicated in AD6) is a key building in the history of the Roman Corinthian order, since it established for the first time the standard Corinthian entablature with a richly moulded architrave, a plain frieze, prominent dentils supported on a border of egg-and-tongue, and a surmounting corona resting on elaborate scrolled modillions carved with acanthus leaves on their undersides. The three surviving columns, which have been a celebrated landmark in the Forum since the Middle Ages, are surmounted by succulently furled capitals, each carved from two blocks of Carrara marble. Together with the Temple of Concord, of which a restored marble cornice block survives, it is the perfect example of the late Augustan style which introduced a new opulence of detail executed with a Grecian crispness.

The architectural and iconographical climax of Augustus's contributions to Rome came in AD2 with the Forum Augustum and its grandiose temple of Mars Ultor. A colonnaded rectangular space north of and at right angles to Caesar's Forum Julium, it was similarly dominated by a temple placed at one end. Lying immediately north of the Forum Romanum, the Forum Augustum was built on land bought by Augustus and was his personal gift to the city. The temple was dedicated to Mars Ultor (Mars the Avenger) in accordance with a vow Augustus made before the battle of Philippi in 42BC in which Brutus and Cassius, who had murdered Caesar, were killed. This political iconography is celebrated in the sculpture which adorned the temple and the forum. In seeking to demonstrate the historical and political legitimacy of the Augustan Empire as the inevitable conclusion of the Republic, it recalled the dual founding of Rome by Aeneas and Romulus and their links with the god Mars and the goddess Venus, supposed foundress of the Julian family to which Augustus was heir. Thus in the apse which was the climax of the interior there were statues of Mars, Venus and the Deified Julius.

Both temple and forum incorporated a rich profusion of white and coloured marbles, many of them doubtless worked by imported Greek craftsmen, and it is unfortunate that little more survives of the temple than three Corinthian columns. The richly carved interior was flanked by two rows of freestanding columns which corresponded to pilasters on the outer walls. At the far end opposite the entrance was the apse. Raised on a high podium, the temple projected far into the colonnaded forum, creating that strong frontal emphasis which was part of the Italic tradition. The flanking colonnades of the forum carried an attic sumptuously adorned with caryatids copied from either the Erechtheion in Athens or the Inner Propylaea at Eleusis. Each colonnade opened out dramatically at the rear into a semicircular courtyard, introducing a cross-axis which was to be deployed more effectively in the Forum of Trajan.

This fusion of temple with forum, derived from Hellenistic precedent, is underlined by the fact that one of the two great building enterprises of the emperor Vespasian (reigned AD70–9) is known variously as the Temple of Peace, the Forum of Peace and the Forum of Vespasian. Built in AD71–9, this great dynastic monument commemorated Vespasian's conquest of the Jews and the capture of Jerusalem. It stood near the Forum of Augustus on the site of the former meat market, from which it probably derives its large square plan. The Forum was laid out as a formal garden, with trees leading up to the portico of the temple which was flush with the line of the colonnade surrounding the forum on three sides. The reticent front of the temple did not dominate the forum but was flanked to the right and left by a library and galleries which contained celebrated trophies from the Jewish Wars, such as the Ark of the Covenant and the Seven-branched Candlestick, as well as magnificent examples of Greek painting and sculpture. To Pliny the Temple of Peace, with the Forum of Augustus and the Basilica Aemilia, was one of the 'three most beautiful buildings the world ever saw'.

The emperor Domitian (reigned AD81–96) filled in the long narrow space between the Forum of Augustus and that of Vespasian with the Forum Transitorium (or Forum of Nerva), completed by the emperor Nerva who dedicated it in AD97. The two long sides of the Forum Transitorium were strikingly enlivened with freestanding columns, each with its own entablature breaking forward from the wall behind. A partially engaged order had already been adopted in interiors but the architect of this forum seems to have been the first to be bold enough to apply the technique to external architecture where its wholly decorative intent would be even more noticeable. The surviving section of this colonnade with its richly carved frieze and attic is one of the most attractive survivals of the imperial fora. The liveliness of its rippling order was echoed in subsequent buildings such as the library of Hadrian at Athens.

Adjacent to the Forum of Augustus on the northwest were the final extensions to the Roman fora, the Forum

80 The Forum of Nerva (completed AD97)

and Market of Trajan (c.AD100–112). The most extravagant of all, they were as large as all the others put together. Designed by Apollodorus of Damascus, the Forum of Trajan extended the area of the fora to the north-west so as to meet the Campus Martius. The east side of the Forum was a vast gently curved colonnade with a triumphal arch in the centre leading from the Forum Augustum. The balancing west side was taken up by the enormous Ulpian Basilica which formed a striking cross-axis within the Forum. Trajan built this in 113AD out of the spoils of the Dacian Wars as the largest basilica in Rome. It was a characteristically dynastic monument, called after his family name of Ulpius. Previous fora had been dominated by temples but here the dominating accent was the Basilica Ulpia, running the full 400 feet (122m) of one of the sides of the forum. Its central

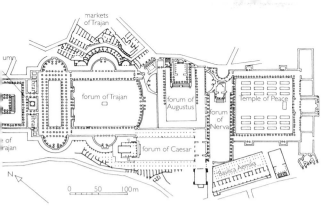

81 Plan of the Imperial Fora, Rome

rectangular nave was enclosed within two ambulatory colonnades which opened out at the two short ends into large semicircular spaces. The interiors were sumptuously decorated with variegated marbles and gilded bronze. The Roman basilica was of incalculable significance for its influence on builders in the Roman provinces and, more importantly, for the fact that the longitudinal type found at Trier or Lepcis Magna was selected by the emperor Constantine in the fourth century AD as the architectural model for Christian churches (see p. 89).

Built up against the west side of the Basilica Ulpia were two libraries, one Greek and one Roman, with between them a colonnaded enclosure containing Trajan's Column. This staggering object, 125 feet (38m) high, is composed from huge blocks of Carrara marble and forms a kind of illustrated stone book to match the books in the flanking libraries. Thus it is carved with a continuous figured spiral frieze about 600 feet (over 180m) long, which represents, with rapidly decreasing legibility as it mounts, the story of Trajan's Dacian Wars. The column is a monument of extreme originality in both conception and stylistic detail. Successive events are depicted against an uninterrupted background in vivid narrative carving which moved away from the formal classicizing traditions of relief sculpture commissioned by the state, and was influential on late antique sculpture. This colossal monument of self-veneration, containing Trajan's tomb in its podium, was complemented by the Temple to the Deified Trajan, which was built by Hadrian in c. AD119 about two years after Trajan's death. With the porticoed courtyard which

82 Trajan's Column, Rome (AD113)

surrounded it, this temple completed Trajan's Forum, and hence the whole complex of the Roman fora, on its north-west side.

Triumphal arches

A feature of the Forum Romanum we have not so far described is that its east and west ends are marked by freestanding commemorative arches. The triumphal arch, sometimes useless, often arrogant, yet rarely lacking in nobility, is perhaps the most characteristic of all Roman architectural inventions. Few empires can ever have devised a more instantly recognizable symbol, or one more widely used. The origin of the form remains obscure though, according to Livy, some commemorative arches were set up in Rome as early as the second century BC, while decorative archways, as we saw on p. 51, were occasionally found in Hellenistic cities such as Priene. It was Augustus who set the fashion for building triumphal arches throughout the Empire, and

83 The Arch of Tiberius at Orange (c.AD26)

the earliest to survive date from his reign, the plain but bold arch built in his honour at Susa in Italy in 9–8BC being a characteristic example. An especially rich early arch is the exuberantly carved Arch of Tiberius built at Orange in southern France in c.AD26 to commemorate the suppression of a rebellion. As the first triple arch it is an unusually early forerunner of the great arches of the later Empire.

The Arch of Titus in the via Sacra at the eastern approach to the Forum Romanum was built to honour Titus and celebrate his conquest of Jerusalem. It was completed by Domitian shortly after Titus's death in AD81. Built of concrete faced with Pentelic marble, it is one of the definitive monuments of the single-arch type as well as being one of the first significant public buildings to adopt a type of capital which had been known from the time of Augustus, the Composite. The distinguishing character of the Composite capital is the surmounting of the acanthus leaves of the Corinthian capital with the diagonal volutes of the Ionic. The Romans liked in general to follow the same rules for their designs of all their triumphal arches: the standard arch is flanked by Corinthian or Composite columns standing on pedestals and framing sculptured panels. In early arches these columns were engaged but from the second century AD they were usually detached; above them was an engaged entablature surmounted by a tall attic carved with a dedicatory inscription in large Roman capitals, always one of the most elegant features of the triumphal arch. This in turn was crowned by a sculptural group, normally including a quadriga, that is, a horse-drawn chariot.

A characteristically opulent late example of the triple-arch type is the Arch of Septimius Severus, built in AD203 on a crowded site at the west end of the Forum Romanum. The first arch with freestanding as opposed to engaged columns, its ornamental role is also emphasized by the steps which originally led up to it. The triumphal arch was adopted with special enthusiasm in the eastern and North African provinces of the Empire. In cities such as Lepcis Magna in modern Libya and Timgad in Algeria, towering above the flat sandy desert, it was an immediately comprehensible symbol of Roman rule and order.

Palaces, villas and the new architecture of concrete

We noted in describing the Hellenistic house in the last chapter that Roman Republican houses, for example, at Pompeii, were organized round a central atrium or hall. This generally had an opening in its roof and a water tank (*impluvium*) sunk into the floor beneath it. The atrium may have been a somewhat gloomy feature and by the second century BC it was common to add at the rear of the house a more cheerful peristyle, often containing a garden. One of the grandest of these peristyle houses is the Villa of the Mysteries on the outskirts of Pompeii, begun in the second century BC and extended by the mid-first century AD with a deeply projecting

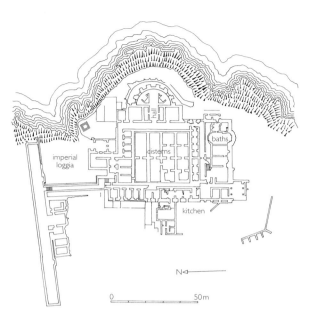

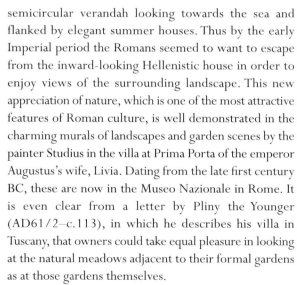

84 Plan of the Villa Jovis at Capri (AD14–37)

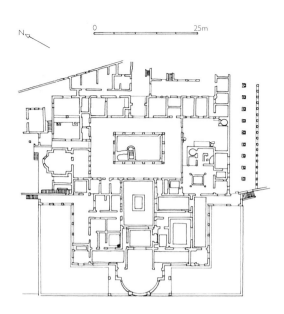

85 Plan of the Villa of the Mysteries, Pompeii (2nd century BC to mid-1st century AD)

semicircular verandah looking towards the sea and flanked by elegant summer houses. Thus by the early Imperial period the Romans seemed to want to escape from the inward-looking Hellenistic house in order to enjoy views of the surrounding landscape. This new appreciation of nature, which is one of the most attractive features of Roman culture, is well demonstrated in the charming murals of landscapes and garden scenes by the painter Studius in the villa at Prima Porta of the emperor Augustus's wife, Livia. Dating from the late first century BC, these are now in the Museo Nazionale in Rome. It is even clear from a letter by Pliny the Younger (AD61/2–c.113), in which he describes his villa in Tuscany, that owners could take equal pleasure in looking at the natural meadows adjacent to their formal gardens as at those gardens themselves.

One architectural consequence of the appreciation of nature by ancient Romans was strikingly shown at the Villa Jovis, which was built by the emperor Tiberius in AD14–37 on an improbable but picturesque site on top of the cliffs on the island of Capri. Little has survived of this exotic retreat with its breathtaking views towards the Bay of Naples, but its plan has been reconstructed

so that we can appreciate the scattered complexity of its terraces, ramps, belvederes, baths and numerous outbuildings. This represented an early and brilliant instance of the fusion of nature and architecture.

What was perhaps even more remarkable was that the spirit of the Villa Jovis was brought on more than one occasion into the heart of imperial Rome. The first and architecturally most striking instance of such an experiment was the Golden House of Nero, built by that emperor in AD64–68 after the fire of AD64 in which at least a third of Rome was destroyed. With the help of his engineer-architects, Severus and Celer, Nero created an astonishing area of parkland, over 300 acres in extent, which was approached from the Forum through a colonnaded vestibule containing a colossal bronze statue of himself, 120 feet (36m) high. In the centre of the park was an artificial lake with all the artful irregularity of outline now associated with Capability Brown in eighteenth-century England (see p. 383). Scattered through the park were temples, fountains, baths, porticoes and pavilions, of which the principal was Nero's long spreading palace, the Domus Aurea (Golden House).

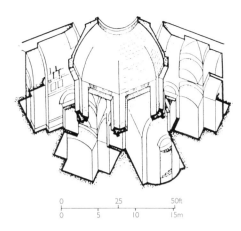

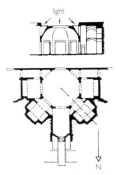

87 Nero's Golden House, Rome: plan and section of the octagonal room

86 Nero's Golden House, Rome (AD64-8): axonometric of the Octagonal room

88 Interior of the octagonal room of Nero's Golden House, Rome

The Golden House was memorable for its curious hexagonal entrance courtyard, perhaps designed as a sun-trap, its mechanical toys, and above all for its ingenious top-lit interiors. However unsatisfactory Nero may have been as an emperor, as a patron he was one of the most significant in the history of Roman architecture. Nonetheless, on his suicide in AD68 the ornamental buildings in his wonderland park were swept almost entirely away: indeed, on its site were erected the principal Roman monuments of the next half-century, including the Colosseum, on ground formerly occupied by the lake; the Temples of Venus and Rome, and of Peace; the Flavian Palace; and the Baths of Titus and of Trajan, the substructures of the latter incorporating parts of the residential wing of the Golden House. In the Renaissance these vaulted chambers, which had been decorated for Nero with plasterwork and paintings incorporating fanciful scrolls and arabesques, were discovered underground, that is in 'grottoes'. Imitated in the Renaissance by artists such as Raphael (see p. 227), Giovanni da Udine and Vasari, and in the eighteenth century by architects like Adam and Wyatt (see pp. 377ff and 386), this decorative style thus became known as 'grotesque'.

Less survives today than in the sixteenth century of this ornamental style of the mid-first century AD, but modern archaeologists have put us in a better position than Raphael to appreciate the astounding originality of the domed octagonal room in the centre of the eastern range of the Golden House. This room, which was conceivably of post-Neronian date, marked an important point in the development of brick-faced concrete, of which it was entirely constructed. The use of concrete which, unlike other building materials, holds firm as a monolithic unit, enables the eight-sided vault to modify imperceptibly into a normal dome as it rises. Like the Pantheon, the room is top-lit through a broad oculus in the dome and is otherwise windowless. However, it opens on five of its sides into rectangular vaulted rooms which are themselves lit from above by concealed lightwells around the outer edge of the dome. This dissolution of the wall in a rich and ambiguous play of light and shade which emphasizes voids rather than solids was a remarkable feat of spatial imagination. Moreover,

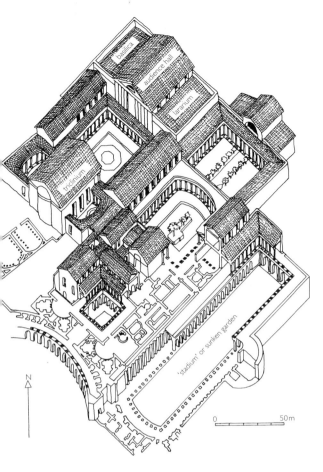

89 Restoration drawing of the Flavian Palace, Rome (inaugurated AD92)

the open dome may have been surmounted by a structure described by Suetonius as 'a rotunda, which rotated day and night like the heavens', while the walls here and elsewhere were adorned with marble pilasters and stucco-work or even 'inlaid with gold and highlighted with gems and mother-of-pearl'.

Showy and self-indulgent, the Golden House was run up very rapidly, for concrete is a material suited to fast construction. The most significant features of the Golden House were, however, soon taken up in a building of greater distinction, the Flavian Palace built for the emperor Domitian on the Palatine Hill and inaugurated in AD92. Known as the Domus Augustana or, more popularly, as the Palatium it remained the official residence of the emperors for three centuries and also gave us the word 'palace'. Domitian's architect,

Rabirius, designed a vast and complex building, a model of how to provide dignity and order on an irregular site which both contains and is surrounded by existing historic buildings. Rather than bulldoze the whole area in order to create a single symmetrical pile, Rabirius provided a palace which, though asymmetrical in its general grouping, is symmetrically disposed in all those subsidiary parts which are sufficiently small to be taken in by the eye. The lower parts also incorporated and preserved various earlier buildings of interest such as the late Republican House of the Griffins.

The official wing containing the state apartments occupied the north-west corner. A peristyle courtyard with a central fountain was flanked on one side by the throne room, basilica and 'chapel' (*Lararium*), and on the opposite side by an enormous triclinium (banqueting-hall). The sumptuous marble columns which lined the walls of the great rooms were entirely decorative, in accordance with the Roman custom of carrying the weight of the superstructure not on columns but on concrete piers and walls. The private apartments, in the south-west corner on ground sloping steeply down to the Circus Maximus, were approached from the north-east by two magnificent peristyle courtyards. From the ingenious honeycomb of small rooms of varying shapes and heights on the ground floor a staircase led down to the lower part of the palace. The great height of the whole building seems a natural consequence of the use of concrete, while its internal distribution, on two levels with suites of rooms on different floors for use at different seasons of the year, is extremely complex.

The lower part of the palace contained a remarkable group of top-lit rooms round a courtyard dominated by an elaborate fountain of curiously serpentine plan. On the north-east side of this court was a pair of domed polygonal chambers cutting into the rock of the hillside. Like much in the palace these were a sophisticated variant on features of the Golden House of Nero. From the opposite side of the courtyard access could be had to the unexpected curved south-west façade of the palace which Rabirius fronted with a segmental

73

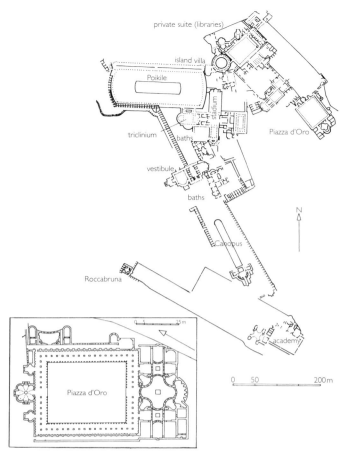

90 *Above* Plan of Hadrian's villa at Tivoli (AD118–34), and (inset) detail of the Piazza d'Oro, its peristyle court and pavilions

91 *Below* Hadrian's villa at Tivoli: the island villa

colonnade. Another surprise was the long walled garden, again approached from the courtyard, which lay along the south-east side of the palace. In an imaginative stroke the long narrow shape of this sunken colonnaded garden, with its segmentally shaped south end, imitated the form of a hippodrome or stadium. Indeed, the structure at the south end contained the box from which the imperial suite viewed events in the Circus Maximus below.

Though much of the palace survives, the great truncated blocks stripped of their ornamental architecture and decorative facings can seem gaunt and baffling to the modern visitor. For a similar building with an allure that is more readily comprehensible we have to turn to Hadrian's celebrated villa in the Campagna near Tivoli, about 15 miles (24km) from Rome.

Though the largest Roman villa ever built, it resembles no other in form or plan. Developed gradually between AD118 and 134 on a pre-existing Republican villa, it is a collection of largely unrelated structures of dazzling architectural virtuosity strung out haphazardly along a plateau for the length of half a mile or so. Buildings such as the Island Villa, the two pavilions flanking the Piazza d'Oro (Golden Square), the Academy and the Small Baths contain scarcely a straight line. They are the exaggeratedly fantastical statements of a designer determined to destroy at all costs the convention of the square room with four walls and a ceiling. The domed octagonal pavilion at the north-west end of the Piazza d'Oro goes even further along this path than anything we have yet seen in that its plan, in which rectangular and apsidal bays alternate, has entirely dictated the undulating shape of its exterior.

The uniquely curvilinear architecture of Tivoli with its spirited clash of concave and convex shapes, its circular colonnades, its concrete vaults and domes shimmering with glass mosaic, was everywhere enlivened with the sparkle of pools, fountains, cascades and canals, and further enhanced with Hadrian's collection of figure sculpture. For the villa was a kind of open-air museum of antiquities, in which Hadrian the connoisseur assembled his collection of Egyptian, neo-

92 The Canopus at Hadrian's villa, Tivoli

Egyptian, classical and modern works of art. Moreover, his keen historical appreciation and capacity for nostalgic reflection encouraged him to turn the very buildings into revivalist museum-pieces so that they were given names recalling celebrated monuments of antiquity which he had seen on his travels: for example, there was a Stoa Poikile, called after the one in Athens; an ornamental canal called the Canopus after the two-mile-long canal connecting Canopus with Alexandria, which was lined with copies of Greek sculpture including the caryatids of the Erechtheion, and which contained at one end a Serapaeum recalling the sanctuary of Serapis at Canopus; and a circular Greek Doric Temple of Venus, a copy of that at Cnidus in Asia Minor, overlooking a Vale of Tempe which recalled a celebrated valley in Thessaly.

Other buildings commissioned by Hadrian

Having seen his villa at Tivoli, we should turn to the most important building commissioned by Hadrian, the Pantheon in Rome. Hadrian, who reigned from AD117 to 138, was one of the greatest architectural patrons of all time, and the Pantheon, built in c.AD118–c.128, is a creative synthesis of the three major trends in the architecture of the day: the creation of interior space, the associated development of concrete construction, and the survival of traditional classical forms. The Pantheon vies with the Parthenon as the most celebrated architectural monument of the western world, and is certainly one of the most imitated. It is also fortunate in being the best preserved of all ancient buildings, though it has lost the colonnaded forecourt which, as in the Forum of Augustus, originally led the eye up to the portico at the end of the vista. The gradual raising of the ground level, with the subsequent loss of the steps leading up to the portico, has also slightly dimmed the impact of the exterior. However, the giant portico seems only to have been a conservative gesture to satisfy traditional expectations of what a temple ought to look like. The interest of Hadrian and his architect, whose identity is unknown, was evidently in the revolutionary rotunda behind. The disparity between the portico and the main body of the building is almost painfully emphasized by the brutality of their junction with one another. The traditional character of the portico is underlined by Hadrian's curiously misleading decision to adorn its frieze with a copy of the inscription on the very different earlier temple, built by Agrippa, which it replaced: M · AGRIPPA · L · F · COS · TERTIUM · FECIT (Marcus Agrippa the son of Lucius, three times consul, built this).

As we have seen, the Greeks and Romans had erected numerous circular buildings, the one closest to the Pantheon probably being the Arsinoeion, a tholos dedicated to the Great Gods built in c.270BC on the island of Samothrace in the northern Aegean. But none of these prepares one for the breathtaking scale, drama and majesty of the Pantheon. The span of its dome (142 feet; 43.2m) was unprecedented, that of St Peter's in Rome, over 1400 years later, being 139 feet (42.5m). The perfectly balanced proportions of the interior are

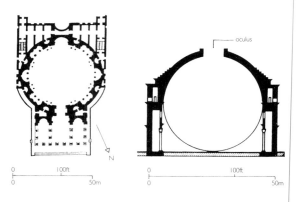

93 *Above* The exterior of the Pantheon, Rome (c.AD118–28)

94 *Above Right* Plan and section of the Pantheon

95 *Below* The interior of the Pantheon: painting by G.P. Pannini (National Gallery of Art, Washington DC)

due to the fact that the inner diameter of the dome is exactly equal to the height of its oculus from the floor. The Corinthian columns screening the exedrae which flank the walls of the rotunda are a brilliant device to give scale: knowing them to be tall like the columns of a temple, we can marvel that the building rises so far above them. The exedrae also emphasize the magic of the dome, since they dissolve the whole wall space so that the dome floats diaphanously above a mysterious shadowy curtain of solid and void.

The actual construction of the building is brilliant, complex and original, but it is not exposed internally, the whole of the drum and most of the dome being covered with ornamental architecture which is at variance with or structurally irrelevant to the building behind. Indeed, the coffering on the inner face of the dome is ingeniously modelled to create a false perspective. In the making of the concrete of which the building is largely constructed various filling materials were used: travertine, tufa, brick and a light volcanic pumice. In order gradually to lessen the weight of the building as it rises, these materials are employed in different combinations so as to create a series of six constructional layers, starting with the heaviest for the foundations and finishing with the lightest, pumice, for the upper portion of the dome. There is, in a sense, a seventh layer consisting simply of air, since the top of the dome is open to the sky through an oculus 28 feet (8.5m) in diameter.

This captivating eye of light at the apex of the dome is the irresistible climax towards which the gaze of every visitor is drawn. Wholly insulated from the noise and sight of the world, we have a seemingly miraculous contact through this luminous embrasure with the heavens above and with the gods who inhabit them. Indeed, we can sense the divine immanence by observing how the sun in its diurnal path illuminates now the floor, now the walls, and now the dome of this vast Pantheon, this temple dedicated to all the gods. Its form is circular, endless and without seam like the empire which conceived it, then in the meridian of its splendour. The near perfection of this circular domed interior, utterly unlike anything previously seen on the face of the earth, seemed the symbol and the consequence of an immutable union between the gods, nature, man and the state. It immediately became, and remained down the centuries, a symbol, more cogent even than the Parthenon, of man's highest religious and political ambitions, so that not only was its combination of rotunda and portico imitated from Palladio in Renaissance Italy to McKim, Mead and White in New York around 1900, but it could claim to be the father of

96 The Mausoleum of Caecilia Metella on the Via Appia, Rome (c.20BC)

every domed space up to and including the Durbar Hall in Lutyens's Viceroy's House at New Delhi (1912–31) (see pp. 247, 525, 636).

Of course our hints at the meaning which the Pantheon may have had for Hadrian and his unknown architect are largely speculative. We should beware of supposing either that a building we regard as noble must have been the work of men whom we would similarly call noble, or that an ugly building must have been produced by the depraved. It may, therefore, be sobering to recall that, according to the historian Dio Cassius in c.AD200, Hadrian summarily executed the distinguished architect, Apollodorus of Damascus, for no greater offence than having criticized, justly in modern judgement, Hadrian's own design for the Temple of Venus and Rome. What the architectural historian can say confidently, rather than speculatively, about the Pantheon is that it helped inaugurate a new phase of architecture in which, more than ever before, emphasis was concentrated on the creation of interior space.

By the time of the building of the Pantheon devotion to the old gods of the Mediterranean world was being supplanted by the attractions of new mystery cults from the East. The Pantheon, which seems designed to express the idea of the numinous rather than to function as the home of a particular cult, owes its preservation to its having been turned by Pope Boniface IV in c.AD609 into a place of worship for the most long-lasting of the new oriental religions. It remains to this day a Roman Catholic church and is known by Romans not as the Pantheon but as Sta Maria Rotonda.

His own Mausoleum (c.AD135), though now remodelled as the Castel Sant'Angelo, is another monumental circular building in Rome which we owe to Hadrian. It stands in a line which, deriving ultimately from Etruscan tumulus tombs or barrows, consists of a circular masonry drum covered with a conical mound of earth: a well-known early example is the Mausoleum of Caecilia Metella of c.20BC on the Via Appia in Rome. The Mausoleum of Augustus in the Campus Martius beside the Tiber in Rome is of about the same date.

97 The Temple of Venus and Rome, Rome (completed c.AD135)

Enough of it survives to enable us to know that it was a tall travertine-faced concrete drum, 290 feet (88m) in diameter, containing tomb-chambers separated by radiating walls of concrete. It was surmounted by an earthen tumulus planted with evergreen trees and dominated by a statue of Augustus. Hadrian's Mausoleum, a more elaborate version of the same theme, survives more completely though it lacks its crowning ring of trees.

The last of Hadrian's many contributions to Rome at which we should look is the Temple of Venus and Rome. Dedicated to the legendary ancestress of the Roman people and to a personification of Rome, this was built between the Temple of Peace and the Colosseum on land formerly occupied by part of the Golden House of Nero. Begun at an uncertain date and

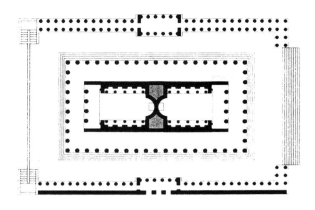

98 Plan of the Temple of Venus, Rome

99 Hadrian's Mausoleum (now the Castel Sant'Angelo), Rome (c.AD135)

consecrated in AD135, it was a striking memorial of Hadrian's admiration for Athens, since it might be interpreted as a version of the Olympieion built of blue-veined Greek marble, perhaps by workmen from Pergamum. However, it is not clear how successful visually was the experiment of placing a gigantic Corinthian temple on the low stepped plinth of the Greeks instead of on the imposing podium of the Romans. The surviving apse of the cella, with lozenge-shaped coffering in its semi-dome, may date from a remodelling by Maxentius in AD307–12.

Although Hadrian provided Rome with some of its most memorable buildings, he was happier living in Athens where, inspired by the example of Hellenistic kings, he became the most influential of the many non-Greeks to nurse a nostalgic enthusiasm for the memory of Athens at the height of her achievement in the fifth century BC. We have already noted how in AD131–2 Hadrian completed the gigantic temple of Olympian Zeus which had been begun in Athens in the sixth century and continued in the seventh century by Antiochus IV of Syria. At about the same time he built near this temple the Arch of Hadrian, a city gate like that in the agora at Priene but unexpectedly surmounted by a fanciful tripartite screen which originally contained statues of Hadrian and Theseus in its central columnar aedicule. Built as a mark of separation between the old city and the new, it was curiously inscribed 'This is

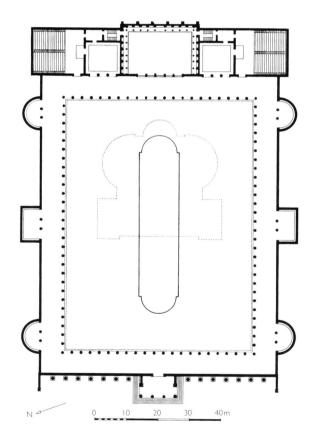

100 Plan of the Library of Hadrian, Athens (AD131)

Athens, the ancient city of Theseus' on its west front facing the temple, and 'This is the city of Hadrian not of Theseus' on the other side facing the Acropolis.

Its lively rhythm was echoed in the library which closes the rectangular stoa built by Hadrian in c.AD131, adjoining the Market of Caesar and Augustus near the Agora in Athens. The surviving entrance wall of the court which led up to the library proper is enlivened with freestanding Corinthian columns supporting a series of projecting entablatures, a decorative device inspired by the Forum Transitorium in Rome of AD97. The building is crisp but sumptuous, with its columns of green cipollino marble from Euboea standing out against a wall which is enlivened by the decorative drafting of its masonry, a form of rustication originating in Asia Minor. Further enhancements all now lost, were the statue-lined attic and the inner peristyle of 100 columns of Phrygian stone.

Baths

Much that was to be characteristic of the planning of the great imperial baths had been established in the early days of the Empire in the Baths of Titus (c.AD80). For the Romans the baths were a way of life. They contained not merely a succession of cold rooms, warm rooms and sweating rooms with their associated changing rooms, but also libraries, restaurants, museums and lounges, interspersed with courts and gardens, the whole forming a beguiling setting for physical, social, intellectual and sexual activity. The Baths of Titus popularized the double circulation plan in which a large, rectangular groin-vaulted frigidarium (cold room) with a cold plunge in each corner is the central point around which is symmetrically disposed a series of smaller rooms so as to duplicate facilities on each side of the building: e.g. caldarium (hot room), apodyteria (changing-rooms) and palaestra (exercise yards).

Little survives of either the Baths of Titus, now known principally from a plan drawn by Palladio, or of those of Trajan, designed about 25 years later by Apollodorus of Damascus whose Ulpian Basilica we have already admired. Inaugurated in AD109, the Baths of Trajan were not merely twice the size of those of Titus, but were disposed in an aesthetically more imaginative and imposing manner. The frigidarium was now placed near the centre of the whole complex where it could act as a visual pivot of the two axes running through the baths from the entrance on the north to the caldarium on the south, and from the palaestra on the west to the balancing palaestra on the east. The Baths of Trajan are of immense significance in the history of monumental interior planning for the way in which the architect

101 Plan of the Baths of Caracalla, Rome (AD212-16)

102 Interior of the Baths of Diocletian, Rome (AD298–306)

exploited the vistas through this great series of related and interlocking spaces. The construction of these interiors, like those of the Baths of Titus, was made possible by the use of concrete for the high, wide vaults.

The Baths of Caracalla (AD212–16) and of Diocletian (AD298–306) are among the most impressive surviving monuments of Roman antiquity, though their architects added little to what had been achieved at the Baths of Trajan. Occupying a site of nearly fifty acres and capable of accommodating 1600 bathers, the Baths of Caracalla were especially memorable for the vast circular caldarium which, projecting from the southwest front so as to derive the maximum heat from the sun, was spanned by a concrete dome, higher than that of the Pantheon and scarcely less in diameter. The subtle cross-vistas, the dramatic screens of columns, the contrast of light and shade and of high rooms and low rooms, the richly polychromatic marble veneers, the mosaic and stucco-work, all added up to a ravishing aesthetic experience which, it must be confessed, was hardly matched by the bleak and somewhat forbidding exterior architecture.

The Baths of Diocletian, though somewhat larger than those of Caracalla, had a more rigid plan and made far less play with the apsed and curved rooms which must have made the Baths of Caracalla so exciting.

However, the vista along the frigidarium was longer and more crowded with a variety of columns than that at the earlier baths. We can appreciate something of the drama and the scale of this conception, since the main three-bay block of the frigidarium survives as part of the church of Sta Maria degli Angeli which was carved out of the ruins of the baths by Michelangelo in the 1560s. However, the floor level has risen during the centuries so that the lower parts of the gigantic Roman columns of red granite are buried. Also, the cold plunge areas and other adjacent rooms were not incorporated into Michelangelo's church, while the vault has lost its mosaic covering of coloured glass. One of the most eloquent, though often forgotten, survivals of the Baths of Diocletian is the outlying circular chamber converted in 1598–1600 into a church which is known today as S. Bernardo alle Terme. The original coffered dome survives intact, like that of the Pantheon.

The popularity throughout the Empire of the institution of the Roman bath led to numerous imitations from Lepcis Magna and Timgad in North Africa to Trier in Germany. This ensured the spread not only of Roman habits but of the techniques of Roman monumental

103, 104 *Left and below* The Basilica of Maxentius, Rome: view and a restoration drawing of the interior (AD307–after 312)

architecture, though the lack of a sand comparable to pozzuolana prevented the full adoption of Roman practices in the provinces. The sumptuous interiors of the baths, providing a remarkably palatial setting for their function, must have made a special appeal to the masses of ordinary Roman subjects who were unlikely to see the interiors of actual palaces.

The impact of the baths is also felt in the greatest surviving, and also the last, basilica in Rome, the Basilica of Maxentius which occupies a large site near the Via Sacra between the Forum Romanum and the Colosseum. One of the major monuments of classical antiquity, this was begun by the emperor Maxentius in AD307–12 and completed by Constantine after 312. The columnar hall of the earlier basilicas nearby has here been abandoned in favour of the vast cross-vaulted spaces of the baths, such as the recently completed Baths of Diocletian. The high central nave, 260 by 80 feet (80 × 25m), rose in three bays to a concrete groin-vaulted roof, 115 feet (35m) above the floor. Supported by eight Corinthian columns, this was flanked on each of its long sides by three barrel-vaulted aisles, considerably lower in height and serving to carry the thrust of the high vaults. In completing the building Constantine shifted its axis by making a new entrance from the south on the Via Sacra in the middle of the long side, thus somewhat diminishing its internal spatial impact. He also added an apse in the centre of the north side in order to balance his new entrance. All that survives today is the north aisle, yet even this fragment of the whole has an overwhelming scale and grandeur.

Town planning

We have already seen Pompeii in the context of villa design, but in the last years before its destruction by the eruption of Vesuvius in AD79 the increased pace of commercialization had brought many changes to the city. Its spacious town houses with their fine paintings were divided into lodging-houses or shops, while even the Villa of Mysteries was turned over to industrial production. A corresponding change in Rome came with

the disastrous fire of AD64, which swept away much of the old city with its narrow winding streets and ramshackle tenements. It was replaced at the direction of Nero with new apartment blocks which were to be structurally independent of each other. Their street fronts were to be lined with porticoes with flat roofs from which fires could be fought; floors and ceilings were to be of concrete; and in each courtyard there was to be a water tank for help in repelling future fires. Built in fire-proof materials such as brick-faced concrete with barrel-vaulted rather than wooden-beamed ceilings, these imposing blocks lined the wide new streets of the post-fire city.

Little of this work survives but fortunately a related town-planning scheme in Rome exists in a remarkably good state of preservation. This is the new commercial quarter laid out under Trajan in c.AD98–117 on the north-east side of his monumental forum. Known as Trajan's Market, this was a commercial development of one hundred and fifty shops, offices and a great covered market-hall. Its principal feature was the great hemicycle of arcaded shops echoing the shape of the exedra in the Forum. The whole complex was laid out on three different levels round a street which followed a zig-zag line behind the hemicycle, these buildings both masking and being formed by the scarred face of the Quirinal Hill as cut away by Trajan for his Forum. The large, plain but subtly grouped commercial buildings of brick-faced concrete with travertine details and sensible window openings curiously resemble some aspects of Post-Modern architecture in the 1980s. They have greater flexibility than most modern work and, by the application in the hemicycle of classical motifs such as pediments and Tuscan pilasters, gradually accommodate themselves in a skilful way to the far greater architectural richness of the adjacent Forum of Trajan. As a revolutionary complex of vaulted spaces for commercial and social purposes, forming an architecture of solids and voids in which structural columns had been eliminated, Trajan's Market provided a totally new image for urban design.

107 Model of apartment housing at Ostia, near Rome (late 1st and 2nd centuries AD)

105, 106 *Above and below* Interior of Trajan's Market, Rome (c.AD100–112): view and an axonometric reconstruction

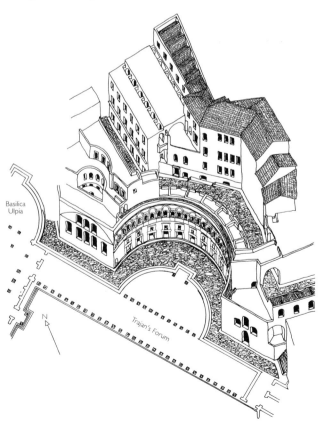

Basilica
Ulpia

N

Trajan's Forum

Trajan's Market is better preserved and rather earlier in date than most of the similar buildings at the town of Ostia, the imperial port about 15 miles (24km) from Rome. Essentially of the late first and second centuries AD, Ostia is nonetheless one of the best preserved Roman cities after Pompeii and Herculaneum. Whereas Pompeii is known for its sumptuous villas and private houses of Italic or Hellenistic inspiration, Ostia is characteristic of the type of Roman city which replaced that older and in many ways more gracious Italic culture. The growth in urban population spelt the end of the spacious one-storeyed villas and houses so that the streets of a town like Ostia are crowded with multistorey apartment blocks, often containing shops on the ground floor, offices, public warehouses and the inevitable baths. The apartment blocks (insulae), up to five storeys in height, were generally arranged round a central courtyard with stairs giving access to the individual apartments. Many of the street fronts incorporated the traditional one-roomed shop on the ground floor, each containing a wooden mezzanine for storage or sleeping purposes lit by its own small window. The form of these austere but dignified blocks in brick-faced concrete with the brick exposed, not covered with stucco, was echoed in other building types in Ostia such as the numerous warehouses and granaries, the Barracks of the Vigiles (headquarters of the fire brigade) and the seats of commercial guilds.

108 *Above* Timgad, Algeria (founded AD100): aerial view with the Arch of Trajan in the centre

109 *Right* Plan of Timgad, Algeria

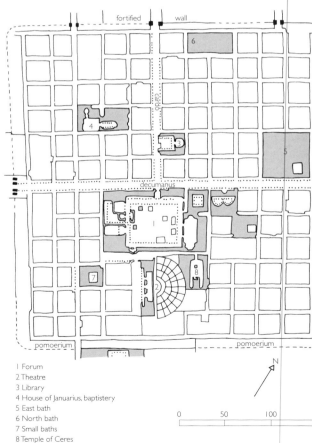

1 Forum
2 Theatre
3 Library
4 House of Januarius, baptistery
5 East bath
6 North bath
7 Small baths
8 Temple of Ceres

0 50 100

The street plan of the central part of Ostia sprang from that of the 'castrum' or fortified military colony set up by Rome in the late fourth century BC. This took the customary form of a walled square containing two streets crossing at right angles, and it was at the point of their intersection that the Forum was laid out. This was a long narrow rectangle with a temple at each end. Developed over a long period, Ostia contrasts with the city of Timgad, Algeria, as originally laid out under Trajan who founded it in AD100 as a colony of military veterans. Timgad is the classic example of the type of Roman city based on a chequer-board plan. Forming a perfect square, its neat grid of streets is approached through a monumental triple archway known as the Arch of Trajan, though it is probably of the later second century AD.

Lepcis Magna in Libya was a Carthaginian trading-centre with an Old Forum of the late first century BC and second century AD which contained several temples and was surrounded on three sides by a colonnade. By the end of the second century AD Lepcis Magna, birthplace of the emperor Septimius Severus (reigned AD193–211), was one of the richest cities in the entire Roman world. Septimius Severus now provided it with a new quarter containing a magnificent new forum and basilica. Adjacent to the forum was a handsome colonnaded street leading from a piazza at the Hadrianic Baths to the harbour which he also rebuilt. In gratitude the citizens of Lepcis Magna erected a four-way triumphal arch in honour of the emperor in c.AD205. Though standing at a crossroads near the centre of the city, it was a non-functional object of display not intended to accommodate traffic.

At Palmyra, a great merchant city in the heart of the Syrian desert, a colonnaded street about three-quarters of a mile (1km) long was built in the mid-second century AD in connection with a series of new public buildings. The street changes direction at two points, of which one is marked by an ornamental columnar pavilion (tetrakionion), and the other by a triple archway built in 220AD. In plan this arch is an elongated V in order to accommodate itself to the shift in axis between the main street and the proposed Sacred Way leading to the Sanctuary of Bel. The colonnaded streets and temples of Palmyra and Baalbek, lacking the concrete vaults which dominated Roman architecture in the west, are powerful echoes of the essentially columnar architecture of the Greek and Hellenistic world. While in the west Roman architectural genius was not deployed primarily in the temple, the tradition of the Greek and Hellenistic peripteral temple survived in the east, as can be seen at these two cities.

The extraordinary sanctuary of Jupiter Heliopolitanus at Baalbek, begun early in the first century AD and finished in the mid-third, is preceded by a monumental tower-flanked propylon leading dramatically into a hexagonal forecourt, which in turn leads to a yet larger colonnaded courtyard dominated by the vast temple of Jupiter at the far end. Parallel with the temple but just outside the sanctuary is the temple of Bacchus which, though considerably smaller than the Jupiter

110 The Temple of Jupiter at Baalbek (early 1st to mid-3rd century AD): one of the semicircular exedrae on the north side of the courtyard

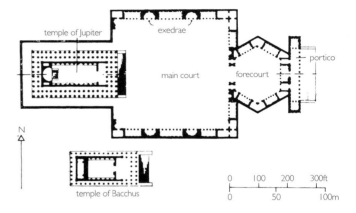

111 Plan of the sanctuary at the Temple of Jupiter, Baalbek

temple, is still larger than the Parthenon. Its well-preserved cella is memorable for its engaged Corinthian columns alternating with arched and pedimented niches in an eloquent combination of the Greek column and the Roman wall. While Roman architects were busy developing advanced engineering and vaulting techniques so as to create a new classical architecture of space and mass, eastern architects continued to elaborate the classical orders and were called to Rome to help design columnar architecture.

At Miletus in Asia Minor in the mid-second century AD the south agora was converted into a regular peristyle with a magnificent gateway in its north-east corner. The scenic grouping, play of light and shade, and central broken pediment of this monumental gate are derived from the elaborate *scaena frons* or stage building

112 The gateway to the market at Miletus, Asia Minor (mid-2nd century AD), reconstructed in the Pergamon Museum, Berlin

113 Diocletian's palace at Spalato (AD300–6): the great courtyard

of the Roman theatre. Now reconstructed in the Pergamon Museum in Berlin, it originally faced outwards so as to form an arrestingly theatrical feature of the square in front of the Bouleuterion (senate-house). The east side of this square was dominated by a Nymphaeum or monumental fountain, of which little survives, though it was one of the most extravagant examples of a type popular in Asia Minor. The Nymphaeum is stylistically close to the magnificent Library of Celsus at Ephesus (c.AD117–20), though the scenic groupings and complex contrapuntal rhythm of its three tiers of columnar aedicules made it an even more striking example than the adjacent gateway of what has been described as the proto-Baroque architecture of the Roman Near East.

The Roman castrum, which shaped the plan of many Roman cities, even influenced the design of an imperial palace at the start of the fourth century AD, in an unstable period when the distinction between military and public architecture was diminishing. In general spirit there could scarcely be a greater contrast between Hadrian's carefree and wholly unfortified villa at Tivoli, built at the height of the Empire, and Diocletian's imposing fortress-palace at Spalato in Dalmatia (now Split in Croatia), built in c.AD300–06 as the last of the great palaces of the pagan Empire. Diocletian's Baths in Rome had been surrounded by a great perimeter wall, but in the palace which he planned for his retirement on

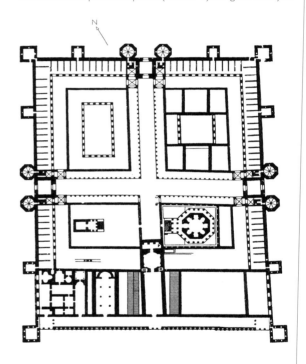

114 Plan of Diocletian's palace at Spalato (AD300–6)

the Dalmatian coast the massive outer walls and towers have a new and sombre purpose as part of the confrontation of the dying Empire against the threat of barbarian uprisings. Indeed, the whole plan of this vast palace, measuring roughly 595 by 710 feet (180 × 216m), echoes that of the traditional Roman fort crossed by two streets meeting at right-angles in front of the praetorium, the official residence of the legionary commander, in the centre of the camp. At Spalato the whole southern half of the enclosed area was devoted to the imperial palace, mausoleum and accompanying temple, while the northern half probably consisted largely of barracks.

Diocletian's octagonal mausoleum is surrounded both inside and outside by ornamental columns, those inside making no pretence of carrying the semicircular inner dome of brick since their entablatures break forwards from the wall. There is also a decorative outer dome of light concrete which rises into an octagonal pyramid. Between this towering mausoleum and the smaller temple to its west lies an unusual colonnaded street or peristyle which is the principal surviving feature of the palace. It forms a ceremonial forecourt with a flight of steps at one end leading up to the main entrance. The open colonnades on either side boast one of the earliest instances of the springing of arches directly from the column capitals. This lively disposition, which anticipates Byzantine and Romanesque procedure, had been foreshadowed in Asia Minor and North Africa in buildings such as the Severan Forum of AD216 at Lepcis Magna, and also in wall paintings, for example in the Villa of the Mysteries at Pompeii, as early as the first century BC. The presence of such features at Spalato is doubtless due to the employment of workmen from Asia Minor. Related features include the adornment of the sea front of the palace with engaged columns supported on corbels, and the cavalier bending up of an architrave so as to form an arch. This bold device had already been adopted at Baalbek in Syria, but its use in Diocletian's palace at Spalato to adorn both the main entrance and the sea front is perhaps its earliest appearance in the west.

Constantine and the adoption of Christianity

Christianity had risen from being one of the many eastern mystic sects which threatened the supremacy of the Roman gods, to the point at which it was legalized in the Empire in AD313. The emperor Constantine (b.272; reigned AD306–37), resented by the wealthy pagan aristocrats in Rome, transferred the imperial residence in 324 to the Greek city at the meeting-point of Europe and Asia which bears his name, Constantinople, the modern Istanbul. Six years later he took the momentous step of transferring the capital of the Empire to Constantinople which he now formally dedicated as 'the new Rome'. We shall investigate some of the consequences of this in the next chapter, but in the meantime let us look at two of his contributions to the old Rome.

The Arch of Constantine, the largest of all triumphal arches, was built by the Senate in AD313–15 on a handsome site near the Roman Colosseum to commemorate Constantine's victory over his rival as emperor, Maxentius, at the Battle of Pons Mulvius in AD312. It is extraordinary that this nostalgic attempt to recover the glories of pagan Rome should commemorate the campaign in which Constantine was supposed to have been converted to Christianity by the vision of a luminous cross in the sky, inscribed with the legend 'By this cross conquer'. The Arch is a curious essay in historical revivalism, for, feeling that modern sculptors could not rival earlier ones in quality, its builders

115 The Arch of Constantine, Rome (AD313–15)

116 *Above* Interior of S. Costanza, Rome (c.AD340)

friezes of Constantinian date which are superficially in a more primitive style. It is clear that Constantine's sculptors were not interested in the realistic presentation which had meant so much to Hellenistic artists, but in a kind of symbolical expression of historical and, shortly, of Christian truths.

We shall end with the mausoleum built in Rome for Constantine's daughter St Constantia, a building which takes us to the threshold of Early Christian architecture and beyond, though it will remind us that Constantinian Christian architecture can also be seen as the final stage of the architecture of Late Antiquity. Built in c.AD340 and now known as the church of S. Costanza, it is a circular domed structure with sixteen round-headed windows forming a clerestorey round the drum. It may be inspired by an important example of the Roman tradition of centrally-planned buildings, the early-fourth-century pavilion in Rome known as the 'Temple of Minerva Medica'. In place of the niches of this building, S. Costanza has on the ground floor a continuous circular arcade of twelve pairs of coupled Composite columns surrounded by a dark barrel-vaulted ambulatory which buttresses the central rotunda. This merging of a domed space with an arcade and circular passage in a building which straddles the pagan and the Christian worlds has finally brought us to the verge of Byzantine architecture.

incorporated sculptural panels of the first and second centuries AD. These came from monuments associated with the less depraved emperors, such as Trajan, Hadrian and Marcus Aurelius, with whom Constantine may have wished to identify. The crisply elegant naturalism of this early work contrasts strangely with the long narrative

117, 118 *Below, left and right* Section and plan of S. Costanza, Rome

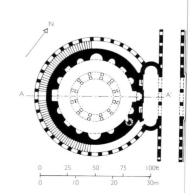

3 Early Christian and Byzantine

CONSTANTINE THE GREAT, THOUGH NOT BAPTIZED UNTIL HIS death-bed, had long seen himself as the thirteenth Apostle, the Viceroy of God divinely appointed to breathe new life into the decaying Empire by making it resemble the City of God on earth. He was able to give concrete expression to these seemingly extravagant beliefs because he was also a practical man and a soldier of genius. Remarkably, his successors shared his vision, so that by the end of the fourth century the emperor had become a Holy Emperor enshrined in the sacred Palace in the renamed Constantinople, encompassed with elaborate liturgical ceremony and ruling autocratically over his subjects, a majority of whom were Christian, even though scarcely more than one seventh had been at the time of Constantine's conversion in 313.

The establishment by Constantine of a new administrative and religious capital at Byzantium in 330 had the effect, not intended by him, of hastening the division of the Empire into its eastern and western components, the former speaking Greek, the latter Latin. This division was, incidentally, sealed in the eleventh century by the secession of the Christians in the Eastern Empire (the Orthodox Church) from the Catholic Church centred on the see of Rome. Less than thirty years after Constantine's death, the Emperor Valentinian, finding the problems of defending the Empire too much for one man, created his brother Valens co-emperor in the east in 364, a disposition which was to continue until the collapse of the Roman empire. This calamity, which happened during the fifth century as a result of Germanic invasions and of internal economic and social problems, drew attention to the greater political and cultural strength of the empire in the east.

Rome

The earliest Christians showed little interest in art, especially in times of persecution, but by the time of Constantine the walls of their meeting-houses and catacombs were frequently adorned with painted decoration. The new public image of Constantinian Christianity demanded a correspondingly public architectural expression. It sought inspiration not in Roman temple architecture with its obviously pagan associations, but in the aisled basilica which was the most prominent form of public building in Rome and in countless Romanized cities. From the early fourth century the Christian assembly halls consisted of various combinations of the following basilical features: the rectangular plan, the timber roof with trusses either exposed or concealed by a flat ceiling, the side aisles, sometimes colonnaded, the high clerestorey, and always the tribunal, often apsed, at the far end, formerly containing the magistrate's seat and now the bishop's seat with the altar in front of him. A splendid early example of this type was the Basilica Constantinia, the

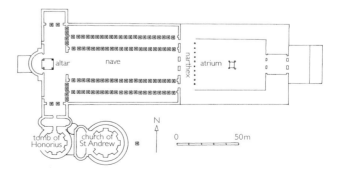

119 Plan of Old St Peter's, Rome (begun c.333)

89

120 Interior of S. Lorenzo, Milan

121 Plan of S. Lorenzo, Milan (probably 5th century)

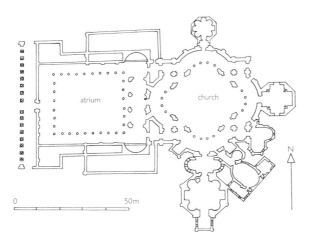

The largest Constantinian basilica, St Peter's in Rome, was entirely replaced in the sixteenth century by the present edifice. It was begun in c.333 as a pilgrimage shrine or martyrium over the tomb of the martyred apostle St Peter. This function meant that, unusually, the basilica was provided with a broad lateral transept between the apse and the nave. This was intended as circulation space for the thousands of pilgrims who came from the city and the empire to venerate the shrine situated on the chord of the apse beneath a baldacchino of spirally fluted columns. The colonnaded nave and aisles served as a covered cemetery and funeral banqueting-hall, while in front of the basilica was a large colonnaded atrium or courtyard with a central fountain for ritual washing in the form of a second-century bronze pine cone. This handsome object is today a celebrated feature of the upper courtyard of Bramante's Belvedere at the Vatican (see p. 225).

For half a century after Constantine's departure in 330 Rome became something of an architectural backwater and interest shifts to the imperial residences at Constantinople, Antioch and Jerusalem in the east, and Milan, Trier and Cologne in the west. S. Lorenzo in Milan (probably of the 5th century) is a church of startling originality. In plan it is a square with an apse projecting from each side, producing a quatrefoil shape which is echoed internally by the two-storeyed colonnades separating the central space from the surrounding ambulatory. It is an early adaptation for ecclesiastical purposes of centrally-planned Roman buildings such as the early-fourth-century pavilion in the Piazza d'Oro of Hadrian's villa at Tivoli (p. 73).

The twelfth-century church of S. Clemente in Rome incorporates in its basement parts of the original basilica begun in c.380. Indeed the later or upper church is so conservative in style that for centuries, until the excavations of 1857–61, it was assumed without question that it was the fourth-century church. Moreover, the upper twelfth-century church retained the existing choir of 872 surrounded by low marble walls ('cancelli') and containing an ambo (a stand for

cathedral of Rome now known as the Lateran Basilica or S. Giovanni in Laterano, which Constantine began in c.313. Built largely of brick-faced concrete, it has been much altered and extended, but we know that originally its interior was enriched with seven gold altars and mosaic decoration glittering in the light of over a hundred chandeliers and sixty gold or silver candlesticks.

reading the Epistle and Gospel) on each side. The whole of this elaborate enclosure, in which the monks or canons would sing their office antiphonally, invades the space of the nave, there being insufficient room for both it and the altar in the small apse. The history of church architecture in western Europe during the succeeding centuries is thus partly that of the gradual enlargement of the east or high altar end. S. Clemente is remarkable for preserving both architecturally and liturgically an arrangement evocative of Constantinian Christianity.

Preceded by a colonnaded atrium, the fourth-century lower church at S. Clemente, about 13 feet (4m) below the level of the upper church, incorporated substantial fragments of buildings dating from the preceding three centuries, including a temple of Mithras, one of the eastern cults which for a time rivalled Christianity in popularity. The modest nave was broad, short and very low. It was flanked on each side by eight broadly-spaced columns, differing from each other in size and material, supporting arches.

The church of S. Paolo fuori le mura (St Paul outside the walls) was begun in Rome in 385 to provide a setting for the shrine of the Apostle St Paul as splendid as that already provided for St Peter. The columns along the nave carry arches instead of the horizontal entablature of St Peter's, a theme further emphasized by the giant triumphal arch which separates the nave from the transept containing the shrine. In its present form the church is a partially accurate reconstruction of the original after a fire in 1823. The other leading basilica of

122 Interior of S. Clemente, Rome (mainly 12th century; choir 872)

123 Interior of S. Maria Maggiore, Rome (432–40)

124 Interior of S. Stefano Rotondo, Rome (468–83)

Early Christian Rome, S. Maria Maggiore (432–40), has been less rebuilt than St Paul's and it still gives one a convincing impression of the powerful classicizing style of the fifth century. It was built under Pope Sixtus III (432–40) at a time when Christianity had been flourishing more freely than ever since Emperor Theodosius's final overthrow of paganism in Rome in 392. The fact that Rome was sacked more than once during the fifth century by invaders from northern and central Europe did not prevent this period from being one of the greatest in its history of church building.

S. Sabina on the Aventine hill in Rome, built in 422–32, is a sophisticated and well-preserved example of the classical revival which is especially associated with the patronage of Sixtus III. Its nave, high, long and narrow, is far more elegant than that of the lower church of S. Clemente, and its reused antique columns selected with far greater care. To Sixtus III is also due the baptistery at the Lateran basilica, a centrally-planned domed structure with a lavish use of porphyry and other precious materials, as well as virtuoso decoration in mosaic and in marble *opus sectile*. The baptistery has been remodelled but more survives of a similar fifth-century Roman work, the church of S. Stefano Rotondo (468–83). Here two concentric rings of columns define the central area and the surrounding aisles or

ambulatories. The inner colonnade is Ionic and has a horizontal entablature, while the outer Corinthian colonnade carries arches, three of which, supported on two Corinthian columns, make a surprising leap across the central circular space. The centrally-planned mausoleum of pagan Rome was a building type especially suitable for adoption as a Christian martyrium. We may assume that this was such a martyrium, built to house a relic of the first martyr, Stephen.

Constantinople, Salonica and Ravenna

Virtually nothing survives of fifth-century ecclesiastical architecture in Constantinople except for the ruins of the monastic church of St John Studios (begun 463), with its typical semicircular apse and its colonnaded galleried nave. Salonica (modern Thessaloniki) in northern Greece, which eventually became the second city of the Empire after the loss of the eastern provinces – including Ephesus, Antioch, Jerusalem and Alexandria – is richer than Constantinople in fifth-century churches. Here is the elaborate and influential church of S. Demetrios, perhaps of the later fifth century, faithfully rebuilt after a fire in 1917. The nave arcades form a complex rhythm composed of groups of four, five and

125 Interior of the Mausoleum of Galla Placidia, Ravenna (c.425)

four columns separated by piers. The tomb of St Demetrios is in the crypt and does not dominate the striking architectural configuration of the church as a whole. An even richer fifth-century Greek church was that of St Leonidas in Lechaion, the harbour town of Corinth. Little of it survives, though it is clear that the total length of the forecourt, atrium and basilica was 610 feet (186m). The variety of floor levels, of the grouping of columns, of the deeply carved capitals and of the patterned marble pavements must have made it one of the most splendid Early Christian monuments of the Aegean coastlands.

Some of the finest examples of Early Christian architecture in the west are to be found in North Italy at Ravenna, the capital of the Western Emperors from 402 to 455, then of the Ostrogothic conquerors from the north, of whom the principal was the highly Romanized King Theodoric (490–526); finally it became the see of the Byzantine viceroys who were installed in 540 following Justinian's short-lived reconquest of Italy.

Here the empress Galla Placidia, daughter of the emperor Theodosius and mother of Valentinian III, built the church of S. Croce in c.425 and attached to one end of its narthex a cruciform building serving as a martyrium to St Lawrence and as an imperial mausoleum for herself, her husband and her half-brother Honorius. The mosaic decoration of the Mausoleum of Galla Placidia represents the art of the imperial court at its most naturalistic and Hellenistic, with Christ as a beardless young shepherd feeding his sheep beneath a cheerful blue sky. This relaxed and sunny mood had already disappeared by the sixth century when mosaics were remade for the church of S. Apollinare Nuovo, Ravenna, built in 490 by Theodoric. Above the arcades of its high broad nave solemn hieratic rows of male and female saints move in an undeviating and unearthly progress towards the altar. The whole interior is, unusually, swathed in mosaic so that it shimmers in a divine radiance enhanced by the light from the aisle windows which, unlike those in, say, S. Sabina, are by this time as large as those in the clerestorey.

The monuments of Ravenna have brought us to the style known as Byzantine, which might in some ways be regarded as the climax of Early Christian architecture. The origin of Byzantine architecture is intimately associated with the cultural and political ambitions of Justinian, the religious autocrat who ruled the Roman Empire of the East from 527 to 565. Like many another great ruler, Justinian promoted building on a vast scale as an expression of beneficent sovereignty and as a way of giving visual identity to his image of world order. It was presumably at Justinian's insistence that his own court historian, Procopius of Caesarea (c.500–560), devoted a whole volume, *Buildings*, to his architectural undertakings. From Procopius's descriptions of hundreds of Justinian's buildings, which strongly emphasize fortifications, it is clear that the emperor's principal tasks included the replacement of the two greatest churches in Constantinople and the extension of the Sacred Palace there; the development of Ravenna as a worthy capital of the reconquered province of Italy;

the repair of the shrines in Jerusalem and Mount Sinai; and the provision of fortifications and other public buildings throughout the Empire.

Whereas in the West churches were built during and after the Middle Ages according to a system which is ultimately inspired by the Roman basilica of the Early Christian period, in the East from the time of Justinian the characteristic church is a domed, vaulted and centrally-planned building which echoes the experimental architecture of the Romans such as the Golden House of Nero and the pavilions at Hadrian's Villa. The Justinianic domed church exercised, as we shall see, wide and unexpected influence in the East, not only in the later Byzantine churches of Russia and the Balkans but on the mosques of Islamic Persia, North India and Turkey.

Hagia Sophia

The greatest of Justinian's churches, Hagia Sophia (the church of the Holy Wisdom of God), in Constantinople, is architecturally somewhat outside the tradition outlined in the previous paragraph. The church which it replaced, founded by Constantine and Constantius, was burnt to the ground in the Nika Insurrection of 532. Justianian suppressed these riots and took the opportunity of marking his victory by erecting in 532–7 the new Hagia Sophia, one of the largest, most lavish and most expensive buildings of all time. His architects were two skilled scientists and mathematicians from Asia Minor, Anthemios of Tralles and Isidorus of Miletus. The fact that they were not trained primarily as architects or builders may partly account for the fresh approach which enabled them to design an unprecedented domed structure.

The plan consists of a huge rectangle measuring 230 by 250 feet (71 × 77m) enclosing a central square space defined by four piers carrying a dome so vast that it dominates the whole interior, though as originally constructed the dome was some 20 feet (6m) lower than the present one. Unlike the dome of the Pantheon (see p. 76) which, after the manner of an outsize igloo, was

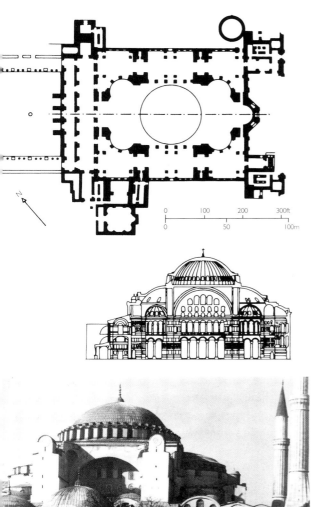

126 *Left above* Plan and section of Hagia Sophia, Constantinople (532–7)

127 *Left below* Exterior of Hagia Sophia, Constantinople. The minarets are a later addition

128 *Above* Interior of Hagia Sophia, Constantinople

supported in a structurally unimaginative way on the 20-foot thick walls of a hollow drum, the dome of Hagia Sophia (180 feet; 55m high) surmounted a square not a circular space, and was supported on pendentives (spherical triangles) rising from the piers. This method of constructing a dome, which may have originated in Persia though it had not been used on this scale before, meant that it was possible to dispense with the supporting walls beneath it. The square space below the dome could thus be opened out into further spaces surrounding it on all four sides, as at Hagia Sophia. Here

the central space is separated from galleried aisles on the north and south sides by dramatic two-storeyed screens of marble columns carrying arches, while on the east and west sides there are no subsidiary supports at all, so that the space flows uninterruptedly into the area beneath the two huge semi-domes which abut on to the east and west ends of the central dome. These semi-domes, of the same diameter (107 feet; 32.5m) as the principal dome, the thrust of which they help support, are themselves extended into lower semi-circular apses or conches.

The result is that though the whole structure is rationally and symmetrically organized it appears mysterious, for our eyes are continually led from one space to another whose precise extent and form we are unable to ascertain. The poetic ambiguity of this flickering contrast of light and shade is reflected in miniature in the characteristic capital which crowns the Byzantine column. Whereas in Roman Corinthian capitals the acanthus foliage sprang unequivocally from the solid bell, the bell of the Byzantine capital was masked by an intricately spiky overall foliage carving, undercut by drilling so that it resembled a kind of starched lacy veil.

It is tempting to try to relate the interior to the liturgy for which it was designed, and even to see the former as a necessary consequence or expression of the latter. However, the architectural historian is on difficult ground here because little is known with certainty about the services and the use of churches in sixth-century Constantinople. It has sometimes been claimed, on the basis of much later Byzantine usages, that mystery and concealment were essential to the early liturgy. According to this view, the nave or central space was reserved for the clergy while the ordinary congregation caught glimpses of the splendid ceremonies from the aisles and galleries. This would then be one reason why the centrally-planned church was adopted for the Eastern liturgy, since the attempt to provide adequate space for the clergy in the basilican plan produced a choir encroaching into a nave which, as at S. Clemente, would have looked better without this encumberment. It has also been suggested, and equally vigorously denied, that curtains in the aisles and sanctuary further concealed the Sacrifice of the Mass from the lay congregation. What we know with certainty is that at the beginning of Mass in Hagia Sophia the patriarch leading his clergy and, on state occasions, the emperor leading his court would go in procession into the nave. The patriarch would emerge from the sanctuary after the Consecration, the most solemn moment of the Mass, in order to exchange the Kiss of Peace with the emperor.

This sacred sealing of the divine pact between God, church and state took place in public view below the eastern rim of the great central dome which was itself a tangible symbol of the Dome of Heaven.

This earthly image of the celestial hierarchy was constructed throughout not with the heavy brick-faced concrete of Roman imperial architecture, but with thin bricks, except for the ashlar blocks which comprised the eight main piers. These light bricks were used to create a series of domes like diaphanous bubbles, an effect which led Procopius to describe the upper parts of the building as 'hanging in mid-air'. The experiment turned out to be too hazardous, for the shallow brick dome collapsed in 558 and was replaced by the ribbed dome of steeper pitch which, extensively repaired, survives today. The walls inside were covered with a shimmering skin of the coloured marbles, porphyry and basalt in which the Empire was so rich, while the vaults and domes were sheathed in mosaic composed of glass and semi-precious stones which glimmered in the light of the sun and especially of the numerous gold lamps, candlesticks and chandeliers.

The Parthenon (p. 34), the Pantheon (p. 76) and Hagia Sophia are amongst the three greatest buildings in the history of western architecture. The Pantheon stands mid-way both chronologically and stylistically between a building which is virtually all exterior, like the Parthenon, and one like Hagia Sophia where the exterior is merely the inside-out of the interior. The exterior of Hagia Sophia is composed of featureless cliff-like masses of plastered brick surmounted by domes of dull-grey lead. The gradual addition of massive buttresses and, following its adaptation as a mosque in 1453, of giant minarets, has not improved its architectural coherence. Since, as we lamented in the first chapter, we have lost all the monographs on classical Greek buildings written by contemporaries, it may be some compensation to quote here from the fascinating and beautiful account of Hagia Sophia written by Justinian's historian, Procopius. His poetic interpretation confirms that we are not too fanciful in seeing the interior as an exalted example of a specifically Byzantine spatial aesthetic:

It abounds exceedingly in sunlight and in the reflection of the sun's rays from the marble. Indeed one might say that its interior is not illuminated from without by the sun, but that the radiance comes into being within it, such an abundance of light bathes this shrine . . . [The dome is] marvellous in its grace, but by reason of the seeming insecurity of its composition altogether terrifying. For it seems somehow to float in the air on no firm basis, but to be poised aloft to the peril of those inside it . . . On either side of this are columns arranged on the pavement; these likewise do not stand in a straight line, but they retreat inward in the pattern of the semicircle as if they were yielding to one another in a choral dance . . . [The dome] seems not to rest upon solid masonry, but to cover the space with its golden dome suspended from Heaven. All these details, fitted together with incredible skill in mid-air and floating off from each other and resting only on the parts next to them, produce a single and most extraordinary harmony in the work, and yet do not permit the spectator to linger much over the study of any one of them, but each detail attracts the eye and draws it on irresistibly to itself. So the vision constantly shifts suddenly, for the beholder is unable to select which particular detail he should admire more than all the others. . . .

The whole ceiling is overlaid with pure gold, which adds glory to the beauty, yet the light reflected from the stones prevails, shining out in rivalry with the gold . . . who could recount the beauty of the columns and the stones with which the church is adorned? One might imagine that he had come upon a meadow with its flowers in full bloom. For he would surely marvel at the purple of some, the green tint of others, and at those on which the crimson glows and those from which the white flashes, and again at those which Nature, like some painter, varies with the most contrasting colours. And whenever anyone enters this church to pray, he understands at once that it is not by any human power of skill, but by the influence of God, that this work has been so finely turned.

Other sixth-century churches in Constantinople and Ravenna

Hagia Sophia has sometimes been interpreted as a merger of the longitudinal Basilica of Maxentius with the dome of the Pantheon. The theme of the domed basilica is echoed in the next largest church in Constantinople after Hagia Sophia, the church of Hagia Irene (Holy Peace), begun by Justinian in 532, rebuilt in 564 and again in 740. The eighth-century remodelling is significant for the additional dome which was provided over the first bay of the nave, thus creating a new longitudinal emphasis in a domed church. An intriguing sixth-century survival is the stepped synthronon (benches for clergy in Byzantine and East Christian churches), like a miniature stone amphitheatre following the curve of the apse.

In c.525 Justinian began the church of SS. Sergios and Bacchos in Constantinople. Like Hagia Sophia, which it slightly predates, it has a spatially complex interior in which a domed central area is surrounded by screens of columns, both straight and apsed, through which we can see the outer galleried aisles. Smaller and architecturally more concentrated than Hagia Sophia, the church is square in plan with a pumpkin-shaped octagonal dome, about 70 feet (21m) high, which is ribbed like an umbrella and thus able to dispense with pendentives. In proportions and ornament the church is less sophisticated than Hagia Sophia, save for its marvellously lacy capitals and entablature, ordered ready-made from the workshops of the government-run marble quarries on the nearby Proconnesian islands in the Sea of Marmara.

Outside Constantinople there is only one church which closely resembles the type of SS. Sergios and Bacchos. This is the lovely church of S. Vitale at Ravenna,

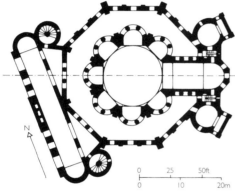

129 *Above* Capital in the gallery of SS. Sergios and Bacchos, Constantinople (begun c.525)

130 *Above left* Exterior of S. Vitale, Ravenna (c.532–48)

131, 132 *Left* Plan and section of S. Vitale, Ravenna

by the mosaics in the chancel depicting the haloed Justinian, accompanied by his empress Theodora, bringing gifts to the altar. Like SS. Sergios and Bacchos, the church consists of a central vaulted octagon opening into a continuous galleried ambulatory or outer aisle. However, the exterior form is here not a square but an octagon which produces a series of constantly shifting facets, creating a livelier and more compelling sense of movement both inside and outside the church. The spatial pulse and flow of the church is moreover heightened by the fact that each side of the inner octagon is apsed, except for that leading to the chancel, whereas at SS. Sergios and Bacchos there are only four such apses.

S. Vitale is built of long thin bricks imitating those used in Constantinople, while the marble columns and capitals were doubtless imported from the Proconnesian workshops. However, the dome, or rather the octagonal vault resting on squinches, is constructed according to a

begun in c.532 and completed in 546–8 as the finest building of its century in the West. Started under Ostrogothic rule by Ecclesius, Bishop of Ravenna, and paid for by a local banker, Julianus Argentarius, it was completed by Justinian after his reconquest of Italy. Its new role as an imperial court church was emphasized

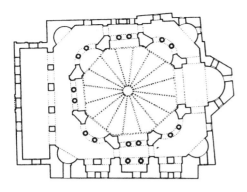

133 Plan of SS. Sergios and Bacchos, Constantinople

134 *Right* Exterior of S. Apollinare in Classe, Ravenna (c.532–49)

western technique of inserting hollow terracotta pots into each other. The weight of this was even less than that of the brick domes of Constantinople, so that the architect could dispense with buttresses. The contrastingly luminous and shadowy spaces of the lower half of the building are crowned by the glittering mosaics, mainly in green, white, blue and gold, which lead the eye past the figures of saints and bishops staring ethereally in front of them till it rests on the Lamb of God in the apex of the chancel vault.

Similar mosaic adorns the church of S. Apollinare at Classe, the harbour town of Ravenna, begun in c.532 under the Ostrogoths and completed under Byzantine rule in 549. The enchanting but non-illusionistic representation of St Apollinaris, first Bishop of Ravenna, surrounded by symbolic sheep in the Garden of Paradise, adorns the apse of a basilica which has preserved intact the Early Christian form, uninfluenced by the new architecture of Justinianic Constantinople. At S. Apollinare Nuovo, built in Ravenna by the Ostrogothic king Theodoric, there is another beautiful interior filled with mosaics (fig. 165).

Perhaps the most influential of Justinian's churches in Constantinople was the five-domed church of the Holy Apostles (c.536–550), destroyed by the Turks in 1469. In plan it was a Greek cross with a dome over each arm and a higher dome over the crossing. It was a disposition which influenced one of the most celebrated Byzantine churches of the West, S. Marco in Venice.

Later Byzantine architecture

A characteristic form for Byzantine churches of the eleventh century was the quincunx or cross-in-square plan. This consists of a rectangular or square building divided into nine bays of which the central one is a large domed square; this is flanked by four barrel-vaulted rectangular bays, while the four smaller bays, one in each corner, are square and generally also domed. The church of Panaghia Chalkeon (1028) at Salonica is a typical early example, with the lively grouping of its tall polygonal drums capped by small pantiled domes. The pure brick façades of Constantinople and Salonica, articulated with engaged columns, pilasters and niches, are not echoed in Greece from the eleventh century where the wall is ornamented by patterns of stone and brick known as cloisonné facing. Varied examples of this can be seen in two attractive churches of c.1020, the Katholikon at Hosios Lukas (Holy Luke) at Styris and the little Church of the Apostles in the agora at Athens. With its contrast of light and shade, solid and void, smooth marble sheathing and faceted mosaics, the interior of the Katholikon is the direct descendant of the luminous mystery of Justinianic architecture of the sixth century. Other fine examples of this style are the Theotokos, a smaller church added in c.1040 to the Katholikon at Hosios Lukas; the churches of H. Theodoroi and Kapnikarea in Athens, both of the 1060s; and the monastic church of the Dormition at Daphni, near Athens, of c.1080, which is a building of classic dignity, eschewing the Picturesque complexity of the Katholikon at Hosios Lukas. Daphni is well known

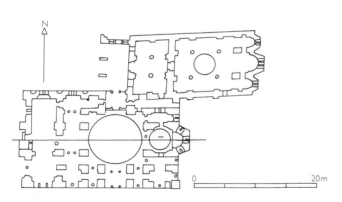

135 *Top* Exterior of the Katholikon, Hosios Lukas

136 *Above* Plan of the Katholikon, Hosios Lukas (c.1020) and the Church of the Theotokos (c.1040)

137 *Right* Mosaic of Christ Pantocrator in the dome of the Church of the Dormition, Daphni (c.1080)

138 *Above* Churches on the hillside at the Byzantine town of Mistra, Greece

139 *Right* Church of the Holy Apostles, Salonica

for its superb mosaics, probably the work of artists from Constantinople. Though the stern semitic face of Christ Pantocrator (ruler of all things) is typical of the grimmer side of Byzantine otherworldliness, a new spirit seems to inform some of the narrative scenes from the life of Christ which attempt to suggest movement and even human emotion.

Under the Paleologue Dynasty (1261–1453) in the Byzantine Empire the decorative treatment of exterior walls in the eleventh century was taken up with renewed emphasis in the herringbone, chequerboard and diamond-shaped patterns of the brickwork façades of churches such as St Kliment at Ohrid, Macedonia (1294), and in Greece at the Paregoritissa at Arta (1282–9), as well as at Hagia Theodoroi (c.1290) and the Brontocheion (c.1300), both at the enchanting Byzantine town of Mistra near Sparta. One of the most sophisticated examples of this very fetching late style is the church of the Holy Apostles at Salonica (1312–15). In the narthex façade the red bricks are contrasted with white stones, creating a colour scheme which was strikingly developed during the fourteenth century.

With its magnificent main façade composed of three storeys of arched openings with polychromatic voussoirs, the Tekfur Sarayi is the only surviving imperial palace building in Constantinople. By 1390, about sixty years after it was built, the remains of the Byzantine Empire were effectively in Turkish hands. The victory of Islam was finally sealed in 1453 with the triumphant entry into Constantinople of Sultan Mehmed, thus extinguishing the sacred empire which had preserved the literature of Greece and Rome for posterity as well as guarding European civilization for so long against invasions by the Turks.

Russia

The fall of the Empire does not mark the end of the story of Byzantine architecture, for it was developed in rich and sometimes surprising ways in Russia, Italy and France. Cultural and commercial links between Russia and Constantinople followed the conversion to Christianity of the Grand Duke Vladimir of Kiev in 988.

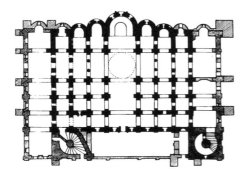

140 *Top* Plan of the cathedral of Hagia Sofia, Kiev, (c.1015–37)

141 *Above* Exterior of the cathedral of Hagia Sophia, Kiev

142 *Right, above* Exterior of the church of the Transfiguration, Kizhi (1714)

143 *Right* Plan of the cathedral of St Basil, Moscow (1555–60)

The architect and the master-mason who came from Constantinople to build the multi-domed Byzantine-style cathedral of Hagia Sophia at Kiev in c.1015–37 began a stylistic tradition which was to last for nearly 900 years. The cathedral of Hagia Sophia at Novgorod (1045–52) has only five main domes as opposed to the thirteen, representing Christ and the twelve apostles, of Kiev. However, in the twelfth century the central dome was remodelled externally with the bulging contour which was to become such a distinctive feature of Russian churches. The final onion-shaped form, which became universal in the fifteenth and sixteenth centuries, can be seen in the remodelled subsidiary domes of the cathedral at Novgorod and in the church of the Saviour at Nereditsa, near Novgorod (1199). Doubtless adopted in Russian as in Islamic architecture for its arresting aesthetic qualities, the onion dome had the additional advantage in northern climates of throwing off snow. It also resembled the shape of the helmets worn at that time by Russian soldiers.

We should not overlook the indigenous Russian tradition of building in wood which produced such striking buildings as the church of the Transfiguration at Kizhi in northern Russia (1714). This is an extremely late example of this kind of timber construction. The climax of this tradition had been reached with the cathedral of St Basil the Blessed (1555–60), built by Ivan IV (the Terrible) near the Saviour Gate of the Kremlin in Moscow (fig. 169). It draws elements from the domed Byzantine church and the wooden tent-shaped church of Russia into an unforgettable skyline. The bizarre plan consists of a small central church surrounded by eight independent chapels each commemorating a military victory and each separately domed. There is a legend that the Tsar was so delighted with the originality of the church that he ordered the architects' eyes to be put out so that they could never produce anything to rival it.

S Marco, Venice

Other outposts of Byzantine influence were to be found in Venice, Sicily and Aquitaine. Venice echoed on a smaller scale the ideal position of Constantinople at the meeting-point of the trade routes of the ancient world from east to west. Founded in the fifth century, she soon became a province of the Byzantine Empire but transformed herself into a virtually independent republic in the tenth century. This rich daughter of Byzantium soon grew greater than the mother, and it was Venetians who led the Crusaders in their shameful sack of Constantinople in 1204. Venice thereafter became for half a century the mistress of the Eastern Empire and adorned her shrines, treasuries and piazzas with loot from Constantinople.

The first church of S. Marco in Venice was built in 830 on the cruciform plan of Justinian's church of the Holy Apostles in Constantinople, though it is not known whether it reproduced the five domes of its model. It seems that in the late tenth century the four flanking domes of the Holy Apostles were replaced by those characteristic of later Byzantine architecture: high domes on tall drums encircled with windows. Certainly it was the higher windowed dome which was adopted for the present church of S. Marco, which was begun in c.1063 from the designs of a Greek architect. Following a fire in 976, the original church of 830 had been rebuilt, perhaps as a replica, so that the church of 1063 was the third on its

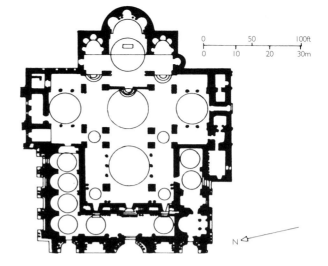

144 Plan of S. Marco, Venice (begun c.1063)

site, though it was approximately the same size as the first. Its cruciform plan is a version of the Byzantine quincunx with a dome over the centre of the nave and one in each of the four arms, providing interiors which were gradually encrusted with rich marble and mosaic sheathing. This even replaced some of the windows, thus creating that atmosphere of shadowy voluptuousness which has captivated visitors down the centuries as breathing the authentic spirit of oriental mystery (fig. 170).

The plain Byzantine brickwork of the five-arched west front, spreading amply like some triumphal arch, was encased from the thirteenth century beneath a riot of marble slabs, columns, capitals, sculpture and mosaic, some brought from earlier buildings, the most celebrated being the four Roman bronze horses above the centre portal which were brought from Constantinople in 1204. In the twelfth or thirteenth century the brick Byzantine domes were given fantastical outer shells with that bulbous profile we noted in Russian Byzantine architecture, while in the fifteenth century the upper parts of the west front were whipped into a great froth by the addition of ogee arches divided by tall canopied and crocketed niches.

S. Marco was built as a monumental chapel and martyrium attached to the adjacent palace of the Doges, the elected leaders of the Venetian republic, so that it filled something of the dynastic role of Hagia Sophia in Constantinople. Though it no longer retains this function, it has never ceased both to impress visitors with a sense of the power and mystery of historic Christian worship, and also to stimulate their imagination as an evocation of the gorgeous wealth of the east brought to the very doors of the west. No one has been more moved by the religious, historical and cultural resonances of this magical building than the influential nineteenth-century English critic, John Ruskin. In *The Stones of Venice* (London 1851–3), his highly romantic description of the west front of S. Marco is part of a rhetorical device to contrast the splendours of the Venetian church with the very different character of English medieval cathedrals. These he condemns on adjacent pages as 'melancholy' and 'grim'. At S. Marco:

> . . . there rises a vision out of the earth, and all the great square seems to have opened from it in a kind of awe, that we may see it far away; a multitude of pillars and white domes, clustered into a long low pyramid of coloured light; a treasure-heap, it seems, hollowed beneath into five great vaulted porches, ceiled with fair mosaic, and beset with sculpture of alabaster, clear as amber and delicate as ivory, sculpture fantastic and involved, of palm leaves and lilies, and grapes and pomegranates, and birds clinging and fluttering among the branches, all twined together into an endless network of buds and plumes . . . and above these, another range of glittering pinnacles, mixed with white arches edged with scarlet flowers, a confusion of delight, amidst which the breasts of the Greek horses are seen blazing in their breadth of golden strength, and the St Mark's lion, lifted on a blue field covered with stars,

145 West front of S. Marco, Venice (begun c.1063)

146 *Above* Interior of the Palatine Chapel, Palermo (1132–43)

147 *Right* Exterior of the east end of the cathedral, Monreale, (begun 1174)

until at last, as if in ecstasy, the crests of the arches break into a marble foam, and toss themselves far into the blue sky in flashes and wreaths of sculptured spray, as if the breakers on the Lido shore had been frost-bound before they fell, and the sea-nymphs had inlaid them with coral and amethyst.

Sicily and France

The architecture of Sicily represents another and rather different assimilation of oriental and western influences. From 535 it was a part of the Byzantine Empire, but it fell to the Arabs in 827. The Normans, who conquered it in 1061–91, renewed cultural ties with the Byzantine court but at the same time retained Muslim features such as pointed arches, rib work and honeycombed or stalactite ceilings. The enchantingly exotic result can be seen in interiors like that of the Palatine chapel at

Palermo, built by the Norman King Roger II in 1132–43 as a combination of a Latin basilica and a Greek domed nave. Byzantine columns and capitals in the nave support an arcade of pointed Muslim arches and a painted honeycomb ceiling. In the 1140s Greek artists were summoned from Constantinople to provide mosaics in the dome and drum according to the established Byzantine disposition of Christ Pantocrator with his court of archangels, angels, prophets and evangelists. Also dating from the 1140s is the small church of S. Maria dell' Ammiraglio, usually known as La Martorana, built for Roger II's admiral, George of Antioch. It has been much altered but it is still possible to interpret it as

148 Interior of the cathedral of S. Front, Périgueux (c.1125–50)

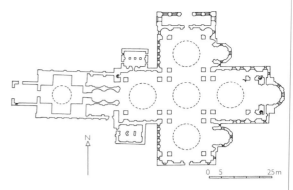

149 Plan of the cathedral of S. Front, Périgueux

a typical Byzantine square with a central dome supported on four columns, surrounded by an ambulatory with barrel-vaulted cross arms, and a triple apse at the east end. The pointed arches and squinches in the dome are of Muslim origin, while the chief glory of the church is its elaborate and lively mosaic decoration which has something of the human warmth we noted at Daphni.

The cathedrals at Cefalù, begun in 1131 by Roger II, at Palermo, begun 1172, and at Monreale, begun 1174, are architecturally not so much Byzantine as Sicilian Romanesque. However, the interiors of Cefalù, and more particularly of Monreale, are celebrated for their magnificent Byzantine mosaics, largely the work of craftsmen imported from Constantinople.

While the Sicilian cathedrals represent buildings erected in the Romanesque period in the Romanesque style but with Byzantine interior decoration, a puzzling group of domed churches in the heart of France was erected in the same period in a Byzantine style with no decoration. The earliest is perhaps Angoulême cathedral (1105–28), with its impressive line of four stone domes down the nave. The pendentives on which these rest, though Byzantine in inspiration, are carried on French pointed arches. The same is true of the two huge domes at the cathedral of Cahors (c.1100–19) which influenced Souillac (c.1130). The finest of this unexpected group, the cathedral of S. Front at Périgueux (c.1125–50), relates less easily to the French Romanesque tradition, since its form of a Greek cross with five domes is close to S. Marco in Venice and thus to the Holy Apostles at Constantinople. The unadorned stonework of this noble interior enables one to appreciate more easily than in Venice the massive articulation of its domes and piers. However, its ruthless modern appearance is in part due to a drastic restoration and rebuilding in the 1850s by the architect Paul Abadie (1812–1884), who thus acquired the necessary skill to design the church of the Sacré-Coeur (1874–1919), an outrageous but much-loved grandchild of Byzantium that screams across the rooftops of Paris from Montmartre.

4 Carolingian and Romanesque

The rise of monasticism

Western Europe was not architecturally barren between the death of Theodoric in 526 and the coronation of Charlemagne in 800. One of the chief civilizing forces was monasticism, which first reached Europe in the fourth and fifth centuries in the ascetical form practised by Christian hermits in their caves or huts in the deserts of Syria and Egypt. Without abandoning their individual huts, these hermits soon gathered themselves into groups which formed the first primitive monasteries. Out of these institutions grew the monastic system which enables men or women, by becoming monks or nuns, to devote their lives to the worship of God. Taking vows of poverty, chastity and obedience, they spend much of the day and night in common recitation of the divine office, the sequence of prayers largely consisting of the psalms. In addition, many monks were scholars and educators, in which capacity they helped to determine the whole pattern of medieval culture.

Spreading to Ireland from Britain and Gaul, the early monastic movement produced missionaries who in due course returned to work in north Britain and even on the continent. However, this Celto-Oriental version of Catholic monasticism came into unsuccessful conflict with the Roman version, promoted by missionaries such as St Augustine who reached the Anglo-Saxon south of England in 597. Roman monasticism was based on the Rule established by St Benedict in the monastery he founded at Monte Cassino in southern Italy in c.530. The idea of the monk as hermit or recluse had gradually given way to the Benedictine concept of the educated monk as the guardian of order at a time when the only order conceivable was that remembered from Roman antiquity. The Benedictine monk would chant the office with decorum and solemnity according to a rule that was uniform throughout all the houses of his order. In Britain the Synod of Whitby in 664 established the victory of Roman over Celtic ritual. In Gaul Pepin III replaced the Gallican liturgy with the Roman in 754–68, while Charlemagne imposed the Benedictine rule on all monks in 789.

The Carolingian Renaissance

Western civilization has been continuously coloured by attempts to emulate the achievements of the ancient Romans. The Roman empire of the west had fallen in the fifth century to barbarian Germanic tribes from the north who extended their sway across Europe: Lombards in Italy; Franks and Burgundians in Gaul; Anglo-Saxons in Britain; and Visigoths in Spain, replaced by Arabs in 711. However, at Poitiers in 732 the Frankish leader Charles Martel defeated an Arab army which had crossed the Pyrenees with the object of adding Gaul to the Islamic empire in the west that already included Sicily, part of southern Italy and most of Spain. Martel's son Pepin made himself king of the Franks in 751, establishing the Carolingian dynasty, which owes its name to Charles Martel. Pepin's son Charlemagne (c.742–814) was crowned first Holy Roman Emperor in St Peter's, Rome, on Christmas Day 800.

The boldness of this remarkable challenge to the Byzantine emperors, who were technically masters of what was left of the western Empire, was justified by the rapid expansion of Charlemagne's territories which included most of present-day Germany, the Netherlands, Belgium, Switzerland, France and Italy.

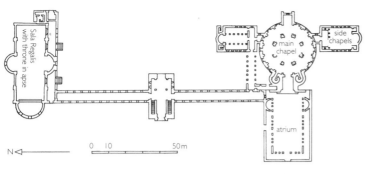

150 Plan of the palace and Palatine Chapel, Aachen (c.790–c.800)

151 Axonometric reconstruction of Palatine Chapel, Aachen

Although this empire had dissolved by the end of the ninth century, Charlemagne left behind him a vision of western Europe which has been of enduring significance in the creation of medieval and modern Europe. The Carolingian Empire had not time to develop the kind of stabilizing civil service, army and navy that the Byzantine Empire enjoyed. Instead, Charlemagne came to rely on Benedictine monasticism as a stabilizing force, thereby

setting an important precedent for the whole medieval period.

Charlemagne was primarily a military leader, yet he learned to speak Latin with fluency even though his native language was German. He also promoted Latin for official as well as for religious purposes throughout the empire. As part of this Roman renaissance he patronized the arts to a degree unprecedented in northern Europe and drew to his court European scholars who helped educate monks and priests to take their part in a new civil service. These learned men studied and thus helped to preserve Latin classical texts, and in transcribing them invented a new script which is known today as Carolingian minuscule. This was rediscovered by Early Renaissance scholars who, thinking it genuinely antique, caused it to be adopted for lower-case letters in printed books. In fact the ancient Roman alphabet lacked a lower case and consisted only of capital letters.

While lower-case lettering has been one of Charlemagne's principal legacies to the modern world, very little Carolingian architecture has survived. What was perhaps its single most important monument still exists intact: the celebrated Palatine chapel or Minster at Aachen, begun by Charlemagne around 790 to the designs of Odo of Metz and dedicated in honour of the Virgin probably in 800. The palace of which it formed a part has, however, almost entirely disappeared. Designed to recall imperial Rome, it was called the Lateran after the palace of the same name in Rome which was traditionally the gift to the Catholic church of Constantine, the first Christian emperor. The bronze equestrian statue, perhaps of Theodoric, in the colonnaded forecourt of Charlemagne's palace was an echo of the statue of Marcus Aurelius, now on the Capitol in Rome but displayed in the Middle Ages on the Lateran because it was believed to represent Constantine. Similarly, the vestibule of the chapel at Aachen contained a bronze statue of a she-wolf copied from the Capitoline wolf, then in the Lateran. The disposition of the palace, with a vast apsed throne-room

152 Interior of the oratory, Germigny-des-Prés (806)

153 Plan of St Riquier (790–99)

or *Sala Regalis* balancing the chapel at the other end of a long axis, recalled one of the most imposing Roman imperial monuments of northern Europe, the basilica or *Aula Palatina* at Trier of the early fourth century.

Like a temple commanding a Roman forum, Charlemagne's chapel stood at one end of a colonnaded forecourt capable of holding 7,000 people. The west-work of the chapel contained a tribune from which the emperor could address the crowd from his throne. The sixteen-sided chapel with its tall, vaulted, central octagon (fig. 164) surrounded by an ambulatory is obviously a reflection of S. Vitale at Ravenna (p. 98), though it has also been compared with the octagonal *Chrysotriclinion* or hall of state built in the Sacred Palace at Constantinople in c. 570. The delicate curves and spatial ambiguity of Ravenna have no place at Aachen, for the curved columnar niches surrounding the central octagon at S. Vitale have been eliminated and the ground-floor columns replaced with sturdy piers. Odo of Metz thus took a Byzantine type and rendered it with the bold no-nonsense manner which was to be typical of later Romanesque architecture. Nor did he adopt the light constructional methods of Byzantine buildings, such as light bricks and hollow terracotta pots for vaults. Instead, Roman ruins were demolished to obtain stone for the walls and for the heavy barrel and groin vaults, while sumptuous fittings like the marble columns and bronze parapets had to be brought from Italy, some from Ravenna itself.

More Byzantine and eastern in character was the Palatine group at Germigny-des-Prés near St-Benoît-

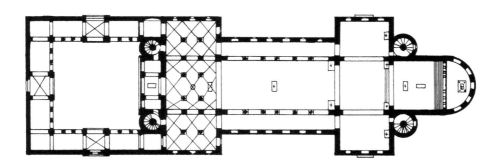

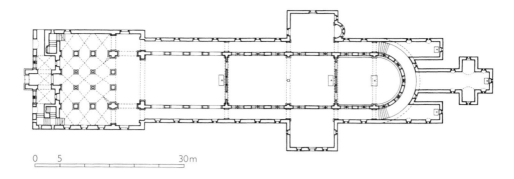

154 *Above* Plan of Corvey on the Weser (873–85)

155 *Left* Interior of the church at Corvey on the Weser, showing the westwork

sur-Loire in northern France, built in 806 for Theodulph, Bishop of Orléans and a member of Charlemagne's circle. This consisted of the surviving oratory, heavily restored in 1867–76, attached to a villa or palace which has almost entirely disappeared. The charming little oratory has the Byzantine quincunx plan with four columns in the centre and domes supported on squinches in the four corner compartments. This did not become popular in the Eastern Empire until the tenth and eleventh centuries so that its presence here, as well as that of the horseshoe-shaped arches and apses, may be explained by influence from the seventh- or eighth-century Christian architecture of Visigothic Spain. Theodulph, it should be pointed out, was a Goth from Septimania, the modern diocese of Narbonne near the Spanish border.

Apart from Aachen, the principal architectural contribution of the court of Charlemagne may have been the monastery of Centula, the modern St-Riquier, near Amiens in northern France. Completely rebuilt in the Gothic period, as built in 790–99 it incorporated details such as columns, bases and mouldings specially brought from Rome. If we can rely on an eleventh-century drawing of the building, it seems to have reflected something of the dynamism of its Abbot, Angilbert, one of the most colourful personalities of the Palatine court. According to this drawing, it was a complex and varied composition incorporating high towers over the crossing and over the elaborate westwork; an east end with a projecting apse flanked by two circular stair towers; and a screened and compartmented nave with superimposed gallery chapels. How much of this actually existed in the eighth century is uncertain so that we should turn, for a surviving example of a westwork, to the church at Corvey on the Weser, Germany.

First of all we should explain the term westwork, which we have already come across in connection with Aachen. It signifies the tower-like western end to a church containing an entrance vestibule with a chapel over. Perhaps originally it was seen as a symbol of the church militant, fortified against the hostile forces of the outer world. At Centula and Reims it formed a virtually independent parish church complete with a baptismal font. It had a long post-Carolingian afterlife, especially in Germany. It was adopted at Reims and Corbie in the

156 Gateway at the monastery of Lorsch (c.800)

east end of the axis. The island of Reichenau off the German shore of Lake Constance is an eloquent survival of Carolingian monasticism, beginning in the eighth century with its three churches: St Peter at Niederzell; the Minster at Mittelzell; and St George at Oberzell, with its nave walls enriched with narrative paintings in the tenth or eleventh centuries, the work of the Ottonian school of painting for which Reichenau became famous.

Perhaps the best known Carolingian monument is the gateway thought to have been built in c.800 at the eighth-century monastery of Lorsch in the Rhineland. Attributed to Abbot Richbod, a member of the Palatine school at Aachen, it is a freestanding three-arched gateway which occupies an isolated position in front of the entrance courtyard of the monastery. It thus recalls a Roman triumphal arch in a forum as well as the propylaeum in the forecourt of Old St Peter's in Rome (see p. 89). Its engaged columns and fluted pilasters with their imaginatively designed Composite capitals stand out against a polychromatic background of alternating slabs of browny-red and cream stone. This Gallo-Roman masoncraft is a provincial echo of classical Roman *opus reticulatum* (see p. 59).

The understandably powerful attraction for the Carolingian world of Old St Peter's, the central monument of Christian Rome, can be sensed elsewhere in the Rhineland, at the abbey church of Fulda. Having been rebuilt after 790 in imitation of St Riquier, the abbey was provided with a vast transept and apse west of the nave in 802–19 to receive the relics of St Boniface. This impressive addition was closely modelled on the western transept of Old St Peter's which contained the shrine of St Peter.

For the fullest expression of Carolingian monasticism as a kind of model town, with church, school, shops, mill, brew-house and farm buildings, we must turn not to any surviving buildings but to the celebrated plan for a monastery drawn in c.820 at St Gall, near Lake Constance in Switzerland. This astonishing triumph of organization served as a model for the great monasteries

ninth century, whence it passed to Germany at Corvey on the Weser, founded by monks from Corbie. The westwork at Corvey, built in 873–85, comprises a low vaulted entrance hall, divided by piers and circular columns, with above this the two-storeyed upper church. Here there is a lively emphasis on the play of light and shade created by the open arcades separating the nave from the aisles as well as from the outer wall of the west front.

Another novel Carolingian church is St-Germain, Auxerre, in eastern France, where a vaulted crypt, which has been variously dated to the sixth century and to the late eighth or early ninth centuries was remodelled in 841–59 so as to allow greater access to the relics of St-Germain. This involved the addition of canted aisles, which offer a precedent for the echelon apse of Romanesque and Gothic east ends (see p. 124). They lead to a rotunda unusually placed at the extreme

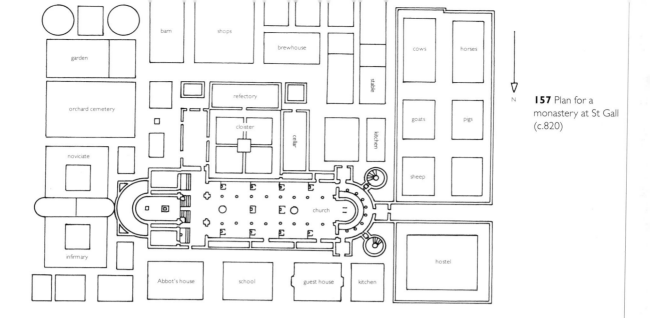

of the Middle Ages which acted not only as spiritual but also as administrative, cultural and agricultural centres for entire neighbourhoods.

Britain and Spain from the ninth to the early eleventh centuries

The cultural and intellectual light of the Carolingian Empire which burned so attractively and so unexpectedly against the background of the Dark Ages was extinguished in the late ninth and early tenth centuries. The heirs to the Carolingians were the Ottonians, but since their architecture is discussed more appropriately in an early Romanesque context we should now turn to the pre-Romanesque architecture of the two parts of Europe we have not investigated so far, Britain and Spain.

Britain

Despite the initial brutality of the pagan Angles and Saxons who invaded Britain in the fifth and sixth centuries from an area roughly corresponding to northwest Germany, an Anglo-Saxon culture was established by 700 which made Britain the most civilized country in Europe. Though Anglo-Saxon secular architecture was largely of timber, Roman missionaries introduced a new type of brick and stone building from the Mediterranean and Gaul. This was used in churches such as the austere little church of St John at Escomb, County Durham, probably of the late seventh century and apparently incorporating reused Roman stonework. It has a long narrow nave and a small chancel, both strictly rectangular in plan. More impressive is the parish church at Brixworth, Northamptonshire, a monastic foundation of the late seventh century founded by Benedictine monks from Peterborough. Probably dating from the eighth century, this is a four-bay aisled basilica, though the aisles are now lost, with a clerestorey and a polygonal apse at the east end. The arches of the arcade and clerestorey, constructed from two broad rings of Roman bricks, together with the imposing total length of 140 feet (42.5m), combine to give the church a certain Italianate flavour. The high level of contemporary achievement in sculpture can be seen in such moving monuments as the seventh-century Ruthwell Cross, with its figure reliefs probably copied from carved ivory panels and illuminated Gospel Books.

Little survives of the basilican churches and chapels of Gaul in these years, but the metalwork, stone sculpture and painting of the Anglo-Irish school in northern England and Ireland in the seventh and eighth centuries survive in sufficient quantity to enable us to see that it was one of the most brilliant achievements

anywhere in Europe. It produced monuments such as the Lindisfarne Gospels and the stone Cross of Nigg in a commanding abstract style which depends on the swirling vigour of indigenous barbarian art. Although this dazzling craftsmanship was not accompanied by architectural production of commensurate quality, an unusual and extensive example of the use of architectural sculpture, perhaps of the late eighth century, can be seen in the church of St Mary, Breedon-on-the-Hill, Leicestershire. The sculpture includes slabs carved with human figures, perhaps inspired by Carolingian ivories, and friezes, seven or nine inches (18 or 23cm) high and about 60 feet (18m) in total length. The carved decoration on these includes Greek key, vine or ivy scrolls, interlace and fantastic animals and birds.

The lower parts of the little church of St Lawrence at Bradford-on-Avon, Wiltshire, have sometimes been tentatively dated to c.700 and the upper to c.975, but it is now thought to be all of one date, possibly c.1000. It is a well proportioned and carefully built stone church attractively adorned with blind arcading on the exterior. It has projecting porches on the north and south sides, the latter now destroyed, and a narrow nave as high as it is long, 25 feet (7.5m). These steep and narrow proportions are further emphasized by the smallness of the chancel arch, which is only 3 feet 6 inches (107cm) wide.

Some Germanic Carolingian features were adopted, especially during the tenth-century monastic revival in England, in churches such as Canterbury, Durham, Ely, and Winchester where we ought to note the former existence of a true westwork. All this work has now disappeared and the church of Bradford-on-Avon, simple though it is, is perhaps architecturally more mature than any other surviving Saxon building, with the exception

158 *Above left* Exterior of St Lawrence, Bradford-on-Avon (c.1000)

159 *Below left* Exterior of the tower at All Saints, Earls Barton (late 10th or early 11th century)

of the Late Saxon church of St Mary-in-Castro, Dover, Kent, of c.1000. Though this is cruciform in plan, with a nave, chancel, transepts and low central tower, the fact that the chancel and transepts are narrower and lower than the nave diminishes the architectural impact. More zestful are the church towers at Barnack, Northamptonshire, of the early tenth century, and at Barton-upon-Humber, Humberside, and Earls Barton, Northamptonshire, both of the late tenth or early eleventh centuries. These are adorned not with the decorative arcading of Bradford-on-Avon but with vertical and horizontal pilaster strips forming patterns which, except at Barton-upon-Humber, seem somewhat childish. Inappropriate for stone construction, this decoration possibly recalls the timber buildings of Saxon England. As we have seen, the metalwork, sculpture and painting of the Anglo-Irish school in northern England and Ireland in the seventh and eighth centuries had been far more advanced artistically.

Spain

Architectural development in Spain in these years was complicated by the capture of most of the country by Muslim Arabs at the beginning of the eighth century. In the north-western corner of Spain, which had not fallen to this Moorish invasion, the Kingdom of the Asturias developed a sophisticated style between the eighth and tenth centuries. At his palace near Oviedo, King Alfonso II (reigned 791–842) built the church of S. Julián de los Prados in c.830 from designs by an architect called Tioda. Its exterior was grouped in the compartmental Germanic way, while inside there are remains of a scheme of classical decoration inspired by sources standing in the tradition of the Villa of the Mysteries at Pompeii (p. 71). In the early 840s Alfonso's successor, Ramiro I, built what is now the church of Sta María de Naranco adjacent to his palace and baths at Naranco, near Oviedo. This was built as a hall but was converted into a church and consecrated in 848. In general disposition it has some similarities with the Saxon church of St Lawrence at Bradford-on-Avon in England.

160 The east end exterior of Sta María de Naranco (c.840–8)

Sta María de Naranco is a remarkably well preserved if somewhat puzzling royal monument, part palace hall, part church, and part belvedere. Raised on a vaulted crypt, the body of the building is a rectangular hall approached up a stone staircase leading to a porch in the middle of one of the long sides. At each end of the building the hall or nave opens through an arcade on to unglazed exterior loggias, one of which is now blocked. The arches forming the open loggias are carried on rich Corinthian capitals but the coupled columns which line the interior walls of the chapel are crudely carved with spiral patterns and surmounted by no less crude block capitals. The chapel and crypt are roofed with stone tunnel vaults strengthened with transverse arches of ashlar. They are amongst the earliest of their kind in medieval church buildings in the west.

The conquest of most of Spain by Muslim Arabs in 710–11 led to an architecture which has no parallel in Europe. The Arabs, unlike other invaders in Europe in the Dark Ages, brought a high degree of civilization with them. Their religion, science and urban way of life were well expressed in the capital city of Islamic Spain, Córdoba, a former Roman city. Reaching a population of half a million under the Muslims, it became the largest and most prosperous city in western Europe. The

161 Interior (961–76) of the Great Mosque at Córdoba

162 Alhambra, Granada (1354–91)

dominant building was the Great Mosque (786–988), which was connected with the palace of the caliph by a bridge across a street. This arrangement recalls that of the principal court churches of Christendom, Hagia Sophia at Constantinople and the Palatine Chapel at Aachen. A vast building composed of eleven aisles, each twelve bays long, the Great Mosque is like an enlarged version of an ancient Roman basilica combined with a forest of columns. Its most significant architectural feature is its three small domes, each constructed of eight arches which intersect so as to form an eight-pointed star. The corners of the rectangular rooms beneath are cut across diagonally by the arches, which are technically called squinches. This is in contrast to the other main method of constructing masonry domes over rectangular bases at this time, the spherical triangle or pendentive as adopted at Hagia Sophia. In the Islamic domes of Córdoba the squinch is combined with the framework of ribs used by the ancient Romans to strengthen their concrete domes. With their love of geometry, the Muslims of Córdoba exposed and ornamented the structural system, unlike the Romans and Byzantines who had concealed theirs. However, Muslim architects did not develop the potentialities of the system which, as we shall see, was later exploited by

Gothic and Baroque architects.

Between the late ninth and the early eleventh centuries Christians in Spain developed a style known as Mozarabic, which combined Christian and Islamic themes. A bold example is the church of San Miguel de Escalada near León (913), with an arcade of arches of the horseshoe-profile so popular in Moorish Spain. Even the ground plan of the apses in this church follows the horseshoe-shape. The finest surviving monument of Moorish architecture in Spain dates from only a century before the final expulsion of the Moors from the country in 1492 by the Catholic sovereigns, Ferdinand and Isabella. This is the Alhambra at Granada (1354–91), a luxurious palace which contains, behind its fortified exterior, an enchanting network of cloistered courtyards enlivened with fountains, greenery and intricately carved ornament.

Ottonian architecture and its influence

The Carolingian achievement disintegrated into anarchy in the ninth century in the face of invasion from Vikings, Muslims, Arabs and Magyars. However, the imperial concept was at length revived by Otto I, the Great (936–73), who was crowned in Rome as first Saxon emperor in 962. The great Ottonian Empire, which survived until 1056, was less extensive than the Carolingian since it excluded the area of present-day France and consisted mainly of Germany and part of north Italy. France and Germany now went separate ways and began to develop their individual cultures. Against the background of the growing feudal system the princely bishops of the Ottonian Empire built castles as well as churches, raised armies as well as taught dogma, and so helped create the image of the Church Militant to which the architecture of Romanesque Europe was to give such forcible expression.

Many Ottonian churches have been destroyed or remodelled but the convent church of St Cyriakus at Gernrode, begun in 959, is a well-preserved example of a type which may look back to St-Riquier. It is also indebted to one type of Early Christian basilica in Rome, for example S. Lorenzo (579–90) and Sant' Agnese (625–38), whence it derives such details as its internal galleries. Its system of alternating supports – piers and columns – in the nave was equally to be of great

163 *Below* Exterior of St Michael, Hildesheim (1001–33)

164 *Opposite top* Aachen: the dome of the Palatine Chapel (c.790–c.800)

165 *Opposite bottom* The Basilica of S. Apollinare Nuovo, Ravenna (begun by Theodoric in 490 and consecrated in 549)

significance for the future. The Benedictine abbey church of St Pantaleon, Cologne, was rebuilt in c.966–80 by Otto I and II as a Germanic revival of a Roman type of unaisled church. The towered westwork survives, as does the nave though with the addition of later aisles. Characteristic features are the pilaster strips, arched corbel tables and blind arcading, all of which had been adopted in the early Romanesque style created around 800 in Lombardy in north central Italy.

The cathedrals at Mainz, begun in 978 and since rebuilt, and Paderborn, begun in 1009, combined Carolingian and Roman Early Christian forms in a massive way which we can begin to recognize as characteristically Germanic. The dynamically composed

166 Interior of the cathedral, Speyer (1030–1106)

church of St Michael at Hildesheim, recently reconstructed as originally built in 1001–33, has a semi-circular apse at both the west and east ends, like St Gall, as well as western and eastern transepts, each with a central tower and flanking circular stair towers like St-Riquier. The church goes beyond these sources in a number of important ways. Thus, the western apse is raised above a crypt or basement chapel approached by semi-subterranean staircases, while the whole church is, unusually, entered by doors in the south aisle which thereby becomes a kind of internal narthex. The crossings between the nave and transepts are emphasized by chancel arches on all four sides, resembling triumphal arches, and the nave is divided into a series of square bays by the alternating supports which consist of one pier followed by two columns. This kind of triple rhythm, probably of Carolingian origin in Saxony, became common in the Romanesque churches of central Europe. However, in western Europe, especially in England, the dual bay was adopted with the simpler rhythm of alternate thick and thin supports.

The notable shift towards greater spatial complexity at Hildesheim may be due to its patron St Bernward (c.960–1022; canonized 1193), bishop of Hildesheim, chaplain at the imperial court and tutor to Otto III, grandson of Otto I. In 1001 Bernward, who had made several visits to Rome, accompanied the twenty-year-old Otto III to Rome, where he lived for a time in the imperial palace on the Aventine hill. Here he would have seen the Early Christian basilicas, whose somewhat

167 *Below* Plan of St Michael, Hildesheim

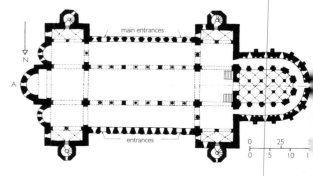

monotonous internal disposition he so decisively rejected at Hildesheim. From the 12-foot-high (3.6m) bronze Easter column, sculptured with scenes from the life of Christ, which he commissioned for the church in c.1020, it is clear that he was an admirer of Trajan's column of which it is a remarkable Christian echo. The bronze sculptured doors executed for him in 1015 are technically important as the first of their kind cast in one piece in the West since Roman times.

Strasbourg cathedral and the abbey church of Limburg an der Haardt, founded in 1025 by the emperor Conrad II, were both, in the first half of the eleventh century, provided with west fronts boasting the twin towers which became the norm for great churches instead of the more complex type supposed to have existed at St-Riquier. Strasbourg has been rebuilt and Limburg is a ruin so that we must look to Speyer, Maria Laach and Trier to gain an idea of the power of early German Romanesque. The vast cathedral of Speyer, with its 235-foot-long (72m) nave, was begun under Conrad II in 1030 as the dynastic pantheon of the ruling house of the empire. From this time dates the imposing groin-vaulted crypt but the original nave roof, perhaps executed in c.1060, was a flat timber construction. However, in 1082–1106 a new campaign involved strengthening alternate nave piers with additional shafts and dosserets to carry the present stone groin-vault, which was probably intended from the beginning. Drawing inspiration in scale as well as detail from Roman buildings such as the basilica at Trier and also from Lombard Romanesque architecture, Speyer is a classic example of what we mean by Romanesque with its surging rhythm uniting all the architectural parts into an overall system dominated by the endlessly repeated round arches of arcades, corbel tables, windows, apses and vaults.

At Trier the Roman cathedral begun by the age of Constantine was remodelled in the eleventh century with a west front containing a central apse. This and the four towers are a powerful restatement of a Carolingian theme, while the multi-towered cathedral of Worms, begun in the early eleventh century but greatly elaborated in the twelfth and thirteenth centuries, is the supreme example of the sober magnificence of Romanesque Germany. The grandiloquent spread of these weighty piles of stone seems the appropriate accompaniment to the achievement of the Hohenstaufen dynasty, under whose rule from 1138 to 1268 the territories and influence of the Holy Roman Empire were greater than ever before or since.

The church of St Maria im Kapitol, Cologne, begun in c.1040, has a trefoil-shaped east end which may echo the church of the Nativity at Bethlehem. The trefoil plan appears again at the church of the Apostles, begun in c.1190, also in Cologne. Despite its late date the apse is still richly adorned with Lombardic Romanesque details such as blind arcading and galleries in the thickness of the walls below the eaves. Another characteristically conservative building is the abbey church of Maria Laach (1093–1156). A late example of the influence of St

168 Exterior of the cathedral, Trier (mainly 11th and 12th centuries)

169 *Above* St Basil's cathedral, Moscow (1555–60), by the architects Barma and Posnik

170 *Opposite* S. Marco, Venice (begun 1063): the crossing and the central dome

171 Exterior of the abbey church of Maria Laach (1093–1156)

Michael, Hildesheim, it has a western apse approached through an atrium, and a vigorously composed exterior crowned with no less than six towers and adorned with Lombardic ornamentation. In its lovely pastoral setting near a lake it still functions today as the centre of a Benedictine monastery and a popular place of pilgrimage. Further afield we can admire other echoes of a similar form in the many-towered cathedral of Tournai in present-day Belgium, begun in 1110 and continued from c.1165 onwards, and in the mid-twelfth-century cathedral of Lund in Denmark.

France in the tenth and early eleventh centuries

France suffered more than Germany from the collapse of the Carolingian Empire and the accompanying invasions of Vikings, Hungarians and Muslims. During the tenth and eleventh centuries she found no unifying cultural and political influence such as that provided in Germany by the princes and bishops of the Ottonian Empire. Instead her history was characterized by feuds and fights between a series of small and hostile provinces owing reluctant allegiance to the Capet kings who ruled the Ile de France. The most successful of these warring duchies was that of the Dukes of Normandy. These Christianized heirs to the Viking invaders increased their power after their conquest of England in 1066. The dominating force in France was undoubtedly the church, and especially the two leading monastic orders of Benedictines and Cistercians, whose great houses of Cluny and Cîteaux, respectively, exercised powerful religious, architectural and artistic influence on the whole of western Christendom.

Though less architecturally productive than Germany in the post-Carolingian period, France did make important contributions to the development of Romanesque architecture, chiefly in the spatial organization and planning of the east or altar end of churches. These went hand in hand with developments such as the increasing popularity of pilgrimages and of the veneration of saints. Architectural historians are fond of attributing the apsed chapel to the growing custom of priests and monks saying mass daily, but the evidence for the establishment of this practice amongst the clergy in the eleventh and twelfth centuries is too patchy to be much stressed as a determinant on architectural development. An important early church is that of St Martin at Tours where the tomb of the saint, much visited by pilgrims, was near the apse east of the canons' choir. To allow pilgrims to visit it without disturbing the canons an ambulatory was carried round the outer edge of the apse, while subsidiary chapels with altars for the canons' masses radiated out from the ambulatory in the form of round-ended absidioles. This form of apsed east end with ambulatory and radiating chapels, generally known by its French name, chevet, became widespread in French Romanesque and Gothic architecture. The radiating plan of Tours can only be deduced from excavations, and its date is controversial though the archaeological evidence certainly indicates a late-eleventh-century ambulatory and possibly allows for one of c.1000 as well.

One of the earliest surviving examples of the radiating ambulatory is that of the Benedictine abbey-church of St-Philibert at Tournus in Burgundy, built from c.1008 to the mid-eleventh century with additions of c.1120. Here we find westwork, narthex and apsed east end boasting radiating chapels at both crypt and ground-floor level. Lacking in refined ornament or mouldings, St-Philibert movingly conveys the almost earthy austerity of the earliest French Romanesque. It is easy and it may even be right to interpret it as a symbol of permanence achieved slowly and with difficulty against a social background of instability and violence. At the same time, the various parts of the building are vaulted

172 The ambulatory of St-Philibert, Tournus (c.1008 to mid-11th century)

with stone in differing and novel ways. This reminds us that Burgundy, which had suffered in the first half of the tenth century from bands of invading Magyars burning and pillaging their towns and buildings, was a pioneer in the development of fireproof vaulted construction. At St-Philibert the nave and the chapel over the narthex were curiously vaulted during the first half of the eleventh century with parallel transverse tunnel vaults, while the aisles of both interiors are groin-vaulted.

The great Benedictine monastery of Cluny was not only the most important Romanesque building in Burgundy but was also one of the most influential institutions in medieval Europe. It was founded in 910 by William, Duke of Aquitaine, with a charter which exempted it from external interference, whether ecclesiastical or lay. During the next three centuries it more than realized the grandiose ambitions of the St Gall plan of c.820 for an ideal monastery. Breaking with Benedictine convention, by which each monastery was self-governing, the abbot of Cluny came to exercise direct control over as many as 1450 Cluniac monasteries. The successive abbey churches at Cluny are known today as Cluny I, II, and III. Cluny I, dedicated in 927, was replaced in c.955–81 by Cluny II, which was not tunnel-vaulted till c.1010. This in turn was replaced by Cluny III, built in c.1088–1130 as the largest church in Christendom. The stone tunnel vaults provided an ideal sounding-box for the solemn antiphonal chanting of the Latin office for which the Cluniac order became renowned. To visit Cluny today is a sad experience, for it was largely destroyed in 1810 by the so-called 'men of reason' who were one of the philistine consequences of the French Revolution.

Cluny II had the staggered east end or échelon apse in which small apses containing altars open off the eastern sides of the transepts. In addition, the aisles are continued eastwards beyond the transepts and are terminated with apses which flank the main apse at the east end of the church. Derived from ninth-century Carolingian churches such as St-Philibert-de-Grandlieu

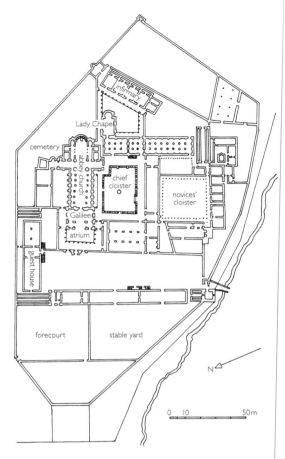

173 Plan of the abbey church at Cluny: Cluny II (c.955–81)

174 Plan of St-Bénigne, Dijon (1001–18)

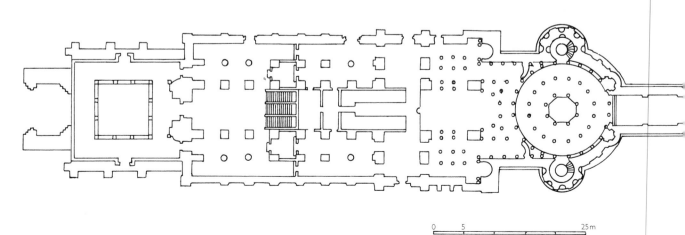

175 The west front of S. Miniato al Monte, Florence (11th to 12th century)

at Déas and St-Germain at Auxerre, this disposition was widely influential. So too was the external arrangement of Cluny II with twin bell-towers at the west end and a taller tower over the crossing.

The strikingly original church of St-Bénigne at Dijon is another Burgundian Cluniac monument which has now largely disappeared. It was built in 1001–18 by St

William of Volpiano, a civilized and widely travelled abbot who had numerous connections with the German imperial family, to whose empire the Duchy of Burgundy belonged in the eleventh century. He seems to have employed craftsmen from his native Italy as well as from Burgundy for a church which is an imaginative synthesis of revered architectural monuments of the past and of tenth-century architectural achievements.

Our image of this church owes much to Professor Conant's restorations on paper which, it must be confessed, are very speculative. He has proposed a church combining Carolingian and Germanic features, like the westwork and the picturesque nine-towered skyline, with a Burgundian tunnel vault of stone a double-aisled nave like the Early Christian basilicas of Rome, and architectural details in the Lombardic Romanesque style. The most interesting feature was the great circular rotunda at the east end of the church, which combined echoes of the Pantheon and of the centrally-planned Anastasis (Resurrection) Rotunda built in the mid-fourth century in the courtyard behind Constantine's martyrium-basilica of the Holy Sepulchre at Jerusalem. Rising from a vaulted crypt, the circular space at St-Bénigne contained no fewer than three concentric rings of two-storeyed columnar arcades. The innermost of these rose up to form a cupola-like third storey which was open to the sky through a central oculus. It has been suggested that this was inspired by Abbot Wulfric's Rotunda at St Augustine's Abbey, Canterbury, of c.1050. Though this is unlikely, the superimposed arches of the nave, resembling Roman aqueducts, produced an effect which can be appreciated today in an English Romanesque church such as Southwell Minster of c.1130. These connections across the channel prompt us to turn to eleventh-century England, for it is here, following the Norman conquest in 1066, that the finest Norman churches are to be found.

Normandy and England in the eleventh and twelfth centuries

We have already noted the dynamism of the Christianized Vikings known as Normans who developed a powerfully organized state on both sides of the channel, in France from 911. There seems no reason to dispute the customary view that the forceful cathedrals, abbeys and castles, forming a stone chain which bound the Norman provinces tightly together, are a direct visual reflection of the uncompromising statecraft of the Normans. In 1002 Duke Richard II of Normandy invited St William of Volpiano, Abbot of St-Bénigne, Dijon, to reform the Norman abbeys along Cluniac lines. One of

the architectural consequences of this mission was the abbey church of Bernay (1017–c.1055), the father of a long line of abbey and parish churches in Normandy and England. Especially influential innovations at Bernay were the engaged columns on the nave piers and the attempt at a three-storeyed elevation with a triforium and clerestorey. Bernay had what we may call the Burgundian staggered plan at the east end, but other Norman churches adopted the ambulatory plan with radiating chapels characteristic of the Loire country. An important example is the cathedral built at Rouen in c.1037–63.

The abbey church of Notre-Dame at Jumièges, begun in 1037 and dedicated thirty years later by William the Conqueror on his triumphant return from subduing England, established the standard type of Norman Romanesque. Its powerful west front adopted the twin towers of early-eleventh-century Germany but crowned them with octagonal upper stages of imposing originality. The high nave is characterized by the double bay system in which cylindrical piers alternate with compound piers articulated with wall shafts. Later Romanesque and Gothic churches were to be ceiled with stone vaults resting on wall shafts of this type, but the problem of high stone-vaulting had not yet been solved at this date. The roofing at Jumièges was thus largely wooden. In the transept we find the origin of the typical Norman thick- or double-shell wall technique. In this the wall is so massive that it becomes a building in itself with an arcaded ground floor supporting a deep internal gallery or tribune, while a further passageway sometimes runs in front of the clerestorey.

Jumièges is today a ruin, so that for a rare surviving example of a contemporary church retaining its original wooden roof we must visit the dramatically sited abbey of Mont-St-Michel (1024–84). Rather later and more highly articulated are the two abbey churches which William the Conqueror built at Caen as an act of penance for having married a close blood relation, Matilda, without papal dispensation: St-Trinité, the Abbaye-aux-Dames (begun 1062), and the more

176 West front of the abbey church of Notre-Dame, Jumièges (1037–67)

without an intermediate diaphragm arch, was constructionally more convenient than a tunnel vault since it distributed its weight more widely at four outer points. The walls needed to support it were thus less massive and continuous and could also be opened so as to admit more light.

At the end of the eleventh century the initiative in vaulting seems to have passed somewhat unexpectedly to England, where the Norman style had been imported by King Edward the Confessor at Westminster Abbey (c.1050–65) even before the Norman Conquest. Edward, who was in fact half Norman, had lived in Normandy between the ages of 13 and 40. The policy of construction rather than destruction adopted by the conquering Normans after 1066 is surely without precedent in scale and effectiveness. The two building types selected by the Normans to symbolize the new cultural and political unity were the church, especially the Benedictine abbey church, and the castle.

From Edward the Confessor's Westminster Abbey, with its triapsidal east end, twin western towers and crossing tower, it is clear that the Norman style would have been adopted in England even if the Conquest had never taken place. However, the process was immeasurably speeded up by the building expansion on an unprecedented scale in English architecture which followed the Conquest. The roll call of monumental new buildings in the 1070s alone includes the cathedrals of Canterbury, Lincoln, Old Sarum, Rochester and Winchester, and the abbeys of Bury St Edmunds, Canterbury and St Albans. The process continued unabated after the Conqueror's death in 1087 with the monastic cathedrals of Norwich, Ely and Durham; the secular cathedrals of Old St Paul's, Gloucester, Chester and Chichester; and the abbey churches of Tewkesbury, Blyth and St Mary's, York. These churches were in part rebuilt later in the Middle Ages but one can well appreciate the scale and power of this late-eleventh-century work from the surviving aisled transepts at Winchester and Ely with their great galleried tribunes and clerestoreys. These demonstrate the strength of the

magnificent St-Etienne, the Abbaye-aux-Hommes, probably also begun in the early 1060s. While the naves of both churches were originally covered with flat wooden ceilings, replaced with stone groin vaults in c.1105–15, the sanctuary of Matilda's Abbaye-aux-Dames was roofed, probably in the 1080s, with two large bays of groin vaulting. This is one of the earliest uses in Europe of the groin vault to cover so wide a span. It can be paralleled at Speyer cathedral where the timber nave ceiling was replaced in c.1082–1106 by a groin vault, though in order to carry the weight of this it was still found necessary to construct a transverse or diaphragm arch between each bay. The true groin vault, caused by the interpenetration of two tunnel vaults

177 The west front of Lincoln cathedral (c.1072–92)

178 The west side of the north transept, Winchester cathedral (1079–c.1090)

thick-wall technique derived from Jumièges and Caen in Normandy or from St Martin at Tours.

Simeon, appointed abbot of Ely in 1081, and his brother Walkelin, bishop of Winchester, were relatives of William the Conqueror. William was crowned at Winchester, England's second city, as well as in London, and the unadorned strength of his kinsmen's work at Winchester and Ely represents the political power and the architectural style of the early Normans at their most forthright. While the Ely and Winchester transepts typify the sober norm, the magnificent west front of Lincoln (c.1072–92) is unique in Norman architecture on either side of the channel. Its patron, Bishop Remigius, came from Fécamp in Normandy, an influence which may

account for the emphatic westwork though scarcely for its original form. The three great arched recesses of the Lincoln west front have sometimes romantically been interpreted as an echo of the triumphal arches of the Romans: an eloquent tribute from eleventh-century churchmen to what they regarded as a superior civilization. However, it found no immediate imitators except for the arresting early-thirteenth-century west front of Peterborough cathedral. The imperious arch which forms the west front of Tewkesbury, perhaps of the 1120s, may be an echo of the similar feature at Charlemagne's chapel at Aachen.

The monumentality of Lincoln and Tewkesbury is well matched in the field of eleventh-century secular architecture by such daunting fortresses as the White Tower (c.1077–97) at the Tower of London, and the even larger castle at Colchester, Essex, both probably the work of the same designer. The Normans were among the first in Europe to build such elaborate fortifications and castles, and the White Tower is the pioneer example of the type of huge stone keep which was to become increasingly familiar throughout their territories. William placed his great tower, a rectangle of 107 by 118 feet (32.5 × 36m), by the river Thames just inside the existing Roman wall of the city of London, where he could command the approaches to the city from the river and from the adjacent countryside. The Tower of London has been in continuous use almost to the present day as a prison, though the White Tower was not built primarily for this purpose but provided residential accommodation on a royal scale. The impact of this on Saxon England can be gauged by the fact that at the time of the Conquest there were probably few stone-built houses in the country. Indeed, this three-storeyed tower with walls c.12 feet (3.6m) thick at their base must have been the most impressive building erected in England since the Roman occupation. Like many other Norman buildings in England it was built of limestone imported from Caen in Normandy, as though to emphasize its character as an alien intruder on the English scene. Erected under the direction of Bishop Gundulf of Rochester, who had arrived in England from Caen in 1070, it contains an ambitious chapel on the second floor. This dominates the entire east front of the Tower, for its projecting semicircular apse is continued for the full height of the building. In the blunt and unornamented interior of the chapel the tunnel-vaulted nave is lined with massive circular piers, some of which are crowned with primitive scalloped capitals supporting two tiers of unmoulded arches. The White Tower was impregnable to all military engines of its day and was entered by a door at first-floor level approached by a wooden staircase which could be withdrawn in times of danger.

To guard Watling Street, the road which led from the continent via Dover to London, Bishop Gundulf also built a stone castle on the river Medway at Rochester, Kent, in the 1080s. William of Corbeuil, Archbishop of Canterbury, replaced this in 1127–39 with the superb keep of Caen stone which, like the twelfth-century keeps at Dover (Kent), Hedingham (Essex), Richmond (Yorkshire), and Newcastle-upon-Tyne

179 Exterior of the White Tower, Tower of London (c.1077–97)

180 Interior of St John's Chapel, White Tower, Tower of London

(Northumberland), is an eloquent tribute to the influence of the White Tower at London.

The combination at Durham of castle, monastery and cathedral, perched high on a precipitous rock above an encircling river, provides the most spectacular image in England or Normandy of Norman genius, both religious and military. The county of Durham was one of the last parts of England to fall, bloodily in this case, before William the Conqueror, and the magnitude of his achievement seems to be reflected in the heroic scale of the architecture. The cathedral at Durham was converted into a monastic chapter by the Normans, having previously been secular. This system, whereby monks lived under a bishop and chanted their office in a monastic church which was also a cathedral, was unknown on the continent. However, in England the other monastic cathedrals which existed up to the Reformation in the sixteenth century were Canterbury, Rochester, Winchester, Bath, Worcester, Coventry, Ely and Norwich. The Englishman's image of a cathedral was thus partly determined by the appearance of the typical Benedictine abbey church with its ancillary and residential buildings. This understanding of a cathedral operating within a social context has helped form the unique and beautiful character of the historic English cathedral cities. Similarly, the colleges of Oxford and Cambridge and the older public schools, though not monastic institutions, visually resemble the more gracious monasteries with their spreading lawns and cloisters so that in England, uniquely in Europe, education and scholarship acquired, and still retain, inescapably social overtones.

The new cathedral at Durham was begun in 1093 by its French bishop, William of St Calais, or St Carileph to give the name its anglicized form. Since it was one of the last of the majestic cycle of eleventh-century cathedrals, its designers were able to draw on what had already been achieved aesthetically and technically. Thus the relation between the height of the nave arcade and the gallery above is more harmonious than at Ely or Gloucester, and there is a subtle balance between the alternating circular and compound piers which, though totally different in form, are virtually equal to each other in visual importance. The massive circular piers are deeply cut with abstract patterns of zig-zag and lozenge form which produce an overpowering effect somehow suggestive of giants at play. The presence of overall linear patterning of this kind, which was to become a feature of English medieval architecture, has been linked to the school of manuscript illumination at Durham which preserved into the twelfth century the linear style characteristic of Anglo-Saxon illumination. But there is an even more striking example of this taut linearity at Durham in the form of the stone rib vault which, for the first time in any church in Europe, binds the whole

181 *Below* Durham cathedral (begun 1093): Interior of the nave

182 *Above* Durham cathedral from the north

183 *Below* Plan of Durham cathedral

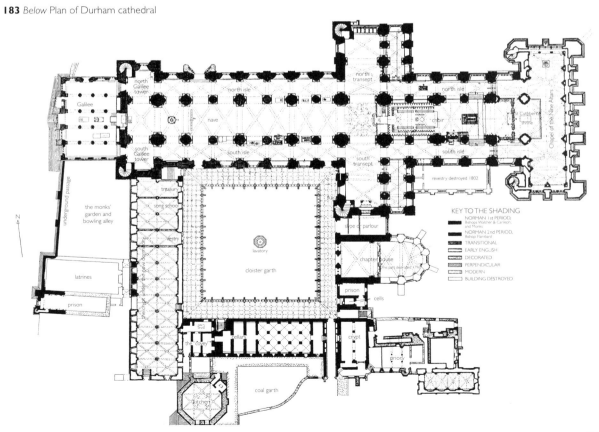

interior together in an enclosing network of stone lines and infilling panels. Whereas in earlier churches the nave walls were liable to be seen as separate and unrelated entities with a flat timber roof resting on top of them, the designer of the Durham high vaults made possible at a stroke the unified stone interior which we know, as he did not, would reach its climax in the stone and glass cages of Gothic Europe.

Durham was conceived from the start in 1093 as a church to be groin-vaulted throughout in stone and, as such, seems to have been the first in Europe. Work started at the east end, where the vaults over the aisles were complete by 1096, and those over the choir by 1107. The north transept vaults date from c.1110 to and those over the south transept and nave, used in conjunction with pointed arches, from c.1130. The transverse arches of the nave vaults are pointed so as to produce a steeper curve which carries the thrust more effectively than the flat curve of the semicircle. As a consequence of the way in which the vaults draw the church together in a single visual unity, the clerestorey is largely merged into the vault instead of existing as an independent horizontal layer. As we have noted, it is not only the presence of stone vaults throughout the church that is remarkable, but the fact that they are constructed with ribs and panels. In fact the panels were rather heavy, being formed from plastered rubble, and those in the chancel were so badly cracked by 1235 that they had to be replaced. The experiment was not continued in England until the second half of the twelfth century, and the next stage in the development of the rib vault was taken in Normandy at Caen and eventually in the Ile de France where the panels formed thin webs constructed of cut stone.

The early twelfth century also saw the adoption, again notably at Durham cathedral, of the chevron or zigzag ornament. Of ultimately prehistoric origin, this became one of the hallmarks of late Norman architecture. One of the loveliest examples is the Galilee or Lady Chapel, which was added at the west end of Durham in c.1170–5 by Bishop Hugh de Puiset (or Pudsey). Lady Chapels, dedicated to the Virgin Mary, are invariably situated near the east end of a church, but the unique western position of that at Durham has been attributed by long tradition to Bishop Pudsey's wish to prevent women from penetrating the body of the church further than was strictly necessary. It is clear, however, that the original site was near St Cuthbert's shrine at the east end where, according to another tradition, St Cuthbert's own hostility to women caused such grave structural failures that construction on that site had to be abandoned. Pudsey's spacious five-aisled Lady Chapel has lost the massiveness of early Romanesque and its light arcades seem to move inexorably forwards, for they are carved with aggressive zigzag work like the teeth of giant cogwheels. It should be noted that Pudsey's domestic interiors in the castle at Durham are similarly rich.

The Norman style, as Romanesque is often known in England, was developed with increasing decorative luxuriance until it began to give way in the 1170s to the Gothic style which, as we have seen, had been anticipated in the rib vaults at Durham as early as c.1100. This process is well appreciated at Ely cathedral where work, initiated in the 1080s, continued into the mid-thirteenth century. The striking west front of Ely, reached by the late twelfth century, boasts the great tower and transepts of German Romanesque, though it is difficult to find an exact German parallel. What is especially English as opposed to continental is the extraordinary way in which the walls, both exterior and interior are adorned with tier upon tier of blank arcading resembling an ornamental grid in front of the actual wall. This characteristic is emphasized in the two great polygonal turrets at the angles of the south-west transept, where the shafts are placed not at the corners but on the centre of each side so that where they meet an arch they run up playfully in front of it. This lively but illogical ornamentation, dating from c.1200, was echoed in the same years in the superimposed arcading in the south transept at Lincoln and in the triforium at Beverley of about thirty years later. The Ely theme of the freestanding shaft bisecting an arch recurs in the

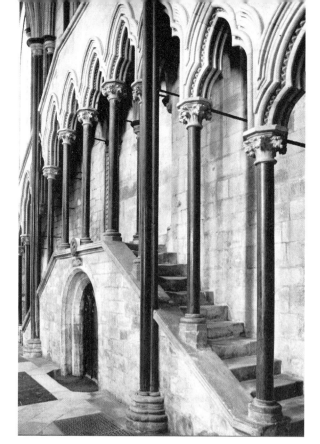

184 *Left* The west front of Ely cathedral (1080 to mid-13th century)

185 *Below left* Interior of the chapter-house, Bristol (c.1150)

186 *Above* Staircase of the chapter-house, Beverley (c.1230)

chapter-house stairs of c.1230 at Beverley. It is an important theme because the English love of an openwork pattern of shafts and mouldings let down like a grille in front of the wall behind eventually found its climax in a phase of Gothic which was unique to England: the Perpendicular Gothic of the late fourteenth to the early sixteenth centuries.

Endlessly repeated blind arcading as an ornamental pattern largely unrelated to the structure behind reappears in buildings such as the west front of Castle Acre Priory, Norfolk, c.1150, and the tower of Norwich cathedral, while the interior of the chapter-house at Bristol cathedral combines this with a rich diapering which is one of the earliest examples of the English obsession with surface patterning.

The pilgrimage churches of France and Spain

We have seen that the buildings produced in England under its Norman kings from c.1070 to c.1170 form one of the most impressive and consistent subdivisions of the Romanesque architecture of Europe. France, larger in area and less united politically, developed a number of regional schools of Romanesque of which the most important, apart from Normandy in the north, were in the central and southern parts of the country: Burgundy in the east, Aquitaine in the south-west, Auvergne in the centre, Poitou in the west, and Provence in the south-east. These were cut through by the architecture of the four pilgrimage routes which led from towns in different parts of France: St Denis or Chartres, Vézelay, Le Puy, and Arles. These joined on the Spanish side of the Pyrenees at Puente-la-Reina whence a single route led via Burgos and León to Santiago de Compostela in the north-west corner of Spain. On the strength of its rather tenuous claims to possess the body of the Apostle St James, this remote town became, somewhat surprisingly, the most popular place of pilgrimage in the Middle Ages after Rome and Jerusalem. These astonishing pilgrimages, which set serious religious activities such as prayer, penance and thanksgiving in a context akin to that of the modern package holiday tour, have been immortalized in Chaucer's *Canterbury Tales*. They were a vital part of the internationalism which was one of the happiest aspects of medieval culture: rich men and poor men, priests and laymen, though coming from widely different countries and backgrounds, were united not only by a common religious ideal but also by the physical ordeal of pilgrimage along hot and dusty roads punctuated with shrines and hospices.

This unity is expressed architecturally in a series of related churches begun in the late eleventh century on the Compostela pilgrimage route, including St-Martin at Tours and St-Martial at Limoges, both now destroyed,

Ste-Foy at Conques and the (originally) virtually identical St-Sernin at Toulouse, and Santiago de Compostela itself. In these dark atmospheric churches the tall clerestoreys and wooden ceilings of Norman churches were replaced with stone barrel-vaulting resting on single-storey galleries. Since they were designed to accommodate not only choirs of monks or canons but also large processions of pilgrims attending impressive ceremonies, the largest of these churches generally contained five aisles; a shrine at or below the high altar; and large transepts and an apse, all provided with an ambulatory and radiating chapels inspired by Tours and intended for relics and private masses. There can be little doubt, too, that their size and splendour were the consequence of a bid to rival the Constantinian basilica of St Peter in Rome which was the chief focus of the pilgrimage traffic in Europe.

Perhaps the most evocative of the surviving pilgrimage churches is Ste-Foy at Conques, one of the smallest yet with the high narrow proportions of the group as a whole. Picturesquely set on the edge of an unspoilt hillside village in Languedoc, both it and its setting have changed little in character since it was built in c.1050–1130, though the west towers are nineteenth-century. It is also remarkable for having preserved its Treasury so that the modern visitor can, for once, experience how the dark and austerely detailed interiors of the early twelfth century were offset on great feasts by the dazzling shrines and reliquaries of precious metals studded with jewels and enamels. The most stunning object in the Conques treasury is the gold reliquary – idol, one is tempted to say – of Ste-Foy. This enthroned hieratic doll, probably dating from the mid-tenth century, is a vivid expression of the cultural resonances and continuity of the Middle Ages, for the head is fashioned from a fifth-century Roman parade helmet and both it and the rest of the figure have been adorned with gems and ornaments down the centuries, culminating in a restoration in the sixteenth century.

Further south in the capital of Languedoc, Toulouse, is the largest barrel-vaulted church in France, St-Sernin

187 Reliquary from Ste-Foy, Conques (c.mid-10th century)

188 Exterior of Ste-Foy, Conques (c.1050–1130)

189 Exterior of St-Sernin, Toulouse (begun c.1080)

(c.1080 onwards), built of brick, the principal local building material. Its multi-apsed ambulatory is strikingly articulated on the exterior, though the outward appearance of the church is dominated by the immense octagonal tower, largely of Gothic date, which rises above the crossing like some Christianized pagoda. The exterior of Santiago de Compostela (c.1075–1150), the goal of the pilgrimage, has been even more completely transformed by a later period, in this case the Baroque. However, the Spanish architectural genius for accumulating the riches of the ages, rather than stripping in order to start from scratch, meant that the architects who remodelled the church in the 1730s lovingly preserved not only the Romanesque interior but even portions of the west front behind their magnificent new façade.

190 Portico de la Gloria, Santiago de Compostela (1168–88)

191 Plan of the cathedral of Santiago de Compostela (c.1075–1211)

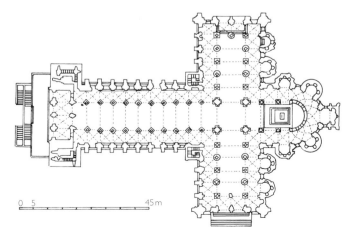

0 5   45m

The surviving sculptured portals of c.1111–16 on the south transept façade of Santiago de Compostela, though much of the carving is not *in situ*, remind us that the years around 1100 saw the revival of monumental stone sculpture after a gap of nearly six centuries. What is important for our purposes is that here and at the Porte Miègeville of c.1115–18 at St-Sernin, Toulouse, the designers began to use sculpture architecturally so as to integrate the architectural form with its sculptural adornment. Within the massive round-headed arch of the Porte Miègeville the tympanum depicts the Ascension of Christ above a lintel carved with the twelve Apostles and supported by two vivaciously carved corbels. In the spandrels on either side of the arch are carved figures of St Peter and St James. This animated style with its exaggerated drapery patterns reappears in the piers of the cloister at Moissac (c.1100), and in other churches on the pilgrimage route in Spain, notably Jaca, León and Santiago itself.

Cluny III and the provincial schools of French Romanesque

The construction in c.1088–1130 of the third abbey church at Cluny as the largest church in Christendom was contemporary with the unprecedented burst of building activity in Norman England. We have already commented on the exceptional status in Benedictine monasticism of the powerful and centralized Cluniac order, as well as on the importance of Cluny II (c.955–c.1000). This certainly helped popularize what is known as the staggered plan (see p. 124) but we should be cautious before accepting Professor Conant's exaggerated claims for its influence. Cluniac monks dedicated themselves to the pursuit of magnificence in the solemn worship of Almighty God. The stone tunnel vaults of their churches formed an appropriately imposing enclosure within which the characteristic Cluniac chant could echo and re-echo in an unceasing tide of rhythmical solemnity. Ruled by powerful abbots of whom the most celebrated was St Hugh (1049–1109), Cluny III was evidently intended as a counterbalance to the imperial splendour of Speyer. It

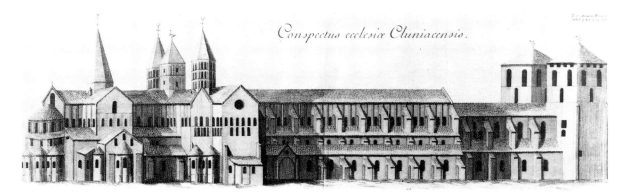

thus became a centre of papal as opposed to imperial power, though the conflict between popes and emperors was at its most acute in Italy.

Cluny III was designed by Gunzo who, in addition to being a monk of Cluny, was a musician with an interest in mathematics. The executant architect was called Hézelon and was also a mathematician. As a result, the dimensions of the various parts of the vast church, 600 feet long and 100 feet high (183 × 30.5m) to the apex of the nave vault, were related to each other by a complicated mathematical process which included a set of basic modules of 5, 8⅓, 25 and 31 feet (1.52, 2.6, 7.6 and 9.4m). This proportional system was not adopted on aesthetic grounds but rather as a practical convenience and as a reflection of the emphasis on aspects of number in the writings of philosophers from Plato to Augustine.

The overwhelming scale of Cluny III, its un-precedented length and height, its numerous towers and radiating chapels, its two sets of transepts and its choir housing three hundred monks, its frescoes and sculpture, all astonished visitors until its tragic destruction in the early nineteenth century. The eastern parts, with their complex massing ultimately derived from Speyer, were completed by 1100, and the church was dedicated by Pope Innocent II in 1130. Following the ambulatory plan of the pilgrimage churches and not the staggered plan of Cluny II, the eastern parts echoed the composition of a centrally-planned building, while the five-aisled nave followed the basilican type. Professor Conant, who spent a lifetime studying Cluny, regarded it as a learned combination of ancient Roman grandeur, Carolingian vivacity and proto-Gothic dynamism. Thus not only were

192 Engraving of the abbey church at Cluny: Cluny III (c.1088–1130)

193 The west portal of the abbey church of La Madeleine, Vézelay (c.1125)

the proportions of the nave already Gothic but the arches of the arcades were pointed.

The tympanum of c.1113 of the great west portal, 64 feet (19.5m) high, was carved with a tremendous allegorical representation of Christ enthroned in majesty in a hieratic Byzantine pose. Although this is almost entirely destroyed, it is clear from surviving fragments that, like much sculpture in the ancient world, it was painted. Indeed, probably the majority of early medieval, that is post-Roman and pre-Romanesque, sculpture was painted. The Cluny portal inaugurated the great series of Romanesque portals in the abbeys at Moissac (c.1125), Souillac (c.1125) and Conques (c.1130–35), all in Languedoc; and at Vézelay Abbey (c.1125), Autun cathedral (c.1130) and Charlieu Priory (c.1140–50), all in Burgundy. The drama of these depictions, originally coloured, of the Apocalypse, Last Judgement and Christ in Majesty, is heightened by their forceful compression within the varied shapes of their architectural surroundings. The tympanum of the Last Judgement at Autun is, most unusually for this period, signed by its sculptor, Gislebertus, while the most extravagant of all is the portal at Vézelay depicting the Commission of the Apostles. The dynamism of line creates a suggestion of supernatural forces at work in a way that is unparalleled in western sculpture.

A striking variant of the architectural use of sculpture at Moissac, Autun and Vézelay can be seen in the west front of Angoulême cathedral (c.1130), which is the first example of a sculptural programme occupying the whole façade of a church. The designer of this astonishing display treated the façade as a screen in a way which suggests that he may have been inspired by the *scaena frons* of the Roman theatre. This puzzling façade has been somewhat ignored by architectural historians, for whom the significance of the building is as an example of the regional school of Romanesque domed churches in Aquitaine (see p. 106).

The cathedral of Autun (c.1120-30) is one of the most attractive of the numerous architectural echoes of Cluny, with its pointed barrel vault and its neo-antique fluted Corinthian pilasters, possibly inspired by the Roman gate in the city, though they had also appeared

194 *Above* The west front of the cathedral, Angoulême (c.1130)

195 *Opposite left* The cathedral of Autun (c.1120–30): detail of the nave showing the pilasters

196 *Opposite right* The west front of Notre-Dame-la-Grande, Poitiers (c.1130–45)

197 *Opposite below* The west front of St-Gilles-du-Gard, Provence (c.1170)

at Cluny which lacks Roman remains. The Cluniac priory and pilgrimage church of St-Gilles-du-Gard in Provence takes us further from the model of the mother house. In c.1170 it was given a west front with richly carved arches which is a powerful restatement of the spirit of ancient Rome as evinced in the remains at the nearby Roman cities of Arles and Nîmes. Similar arched portals survive at the cathedrals at Arles and Avignon.

The abbey church of St-Benoît-sur-Loire (c.1080–1130) in central France, earlier than Cluny III in its

inception, is a noble surviving example of the Cluny type with radiating chapels and a boldly massed east end. It originally had a towered porch of which an impressive example survives at Evreuil. At Poitiers the church of Notre-Dame-la-Grande (c.1130–45) is chiefly memorable for its bizarre west façade which is completely encrusted with rich carving, creating an effect that has been likened to a Byzantine ivory casket. Its positively oriental profusion may owe something to the impact of the Crusades or to trade with the east. Its conically-capped towers are roofed with stone tiles of an ornamental fish-scale pattern. The rich carving of Notre-Dame-la-Grande is echoed in the noble pilgrimage church at Aulnay-de-Saintonge, Poitou, while the fish-scale motif is taken up with a vengeance at the remarkable pyramidal kitchen at the Benedictine abbey of Fontevrault near Angers in the Loire country, where the numerous apses containing fireplaces are capped by chimney turrets. The abbey church at Fontevrault was dedicated in 1119 as the pantheon of the Plantagenet dynasty, counts of Anjou and kings of England from the mid-twelfth century. Its aisleless four-bay nave was roofed with a series of domes which must be related to the unusual domed churches of Périgord in southern Aquitaine: St-Front at Périgueux, Cahors, Souillac and Angoulême cathedral. These have already been mentioned in the context of inspiration from the Byzantine church of S. Marco in Venice but, except for the markedly Venetian St-Front, they must be seen as an indigenous development in French Romanesque.

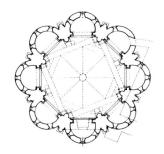

198 *Right* Plan of the kitchen of Fontevrault Abbey, near Angers (early 12th century)

199 *Opposite* Exterior of the kitchen at Fontevrault Abbey, Angers

In the meantime reaction against the sumptuous architecture and liturgy of the Cluniacs was growing in the Cistercian order, which had been founded in 1098 by Robert of Molesme. Cistercian monasteries such as Cîteaux (1125–50), Fontenay (1139–47) and Clairvaux (1153–74), though inspired in general form by the St Gall/Cluny model, eschewed luxurious objects like towers and stained glass. The monasteries in which Cistercian monks led their austerely contemplative lives were placed near running water in remote and beautiful valleys as at Tintern and Fountains in England.

Spain in the eleventh and twelfth centuries

The Christian kingdoms in the northern half of Spain more than doubled their territory in the eleventh and twelfth centuries during the course of their struggles against the Moors, whom they pushed further and further south. We have already noted the architectural impact of the pilgrimage routes from France, while the arrival of the Cluniac order around 1000 strengthened this French influence, of which an early instance can be seen at Jaca Cathedral (c.1060) onwards. A rather different example of Cluniac influence is found in the monastery of Sta María of Ripoll in Catalonia (c.1020–32), whose builder-abbot, Oliba, was a friend of St Hugh of Cluny. Like the later pilgrimage churches, it was evidently built in emulation of Old St Peter's in Rome, for it terminates in a huge seven-apsed eastern transept.

The fighting spirit of Spanish Catholicism – and it should be remembered that the Moors were not driven out of their last stronghold, Granada, until 1492 – is nowhere better expressed than in the superb fortified church and monastery of Loarre of the late eleventh century, and in the contemporary walled town of Ávila. The uncompromising genius of the Spaniards, their combination of grandeur and piety, is summed up in the splendid walls of Ávila which originally incorporated the fortified apse of the Romanesque cathedral. Though the cathedral has been replaced, the pilgrimage church

of S. Vincente, begun in c.1109, boasts a magnificent carved western portal of Burgundian inspiration.

The survival of influences from Mozarabic architecture and the use of Muslim craftsmen make Spanish Romanesque an especially intriguing subject for study, as can be seen in the church of the Holy Sepulchre in Torres del Río, in the north-eastern province of Navarra, with its octagonal dome of intersecting flying ribs clearly inspired by that in the mosque at Córdoba. Muslim influence flowed back along the pilgrimage routes from Spain into France, as can be seen in the remarkably Moorish-looking twelfth-century cathedral of Le Puy in the Auvergne, which even has Kufic inscriptions on its wooden doors. At the cloister of Sto Domingo de Silos (c.1085–1100), which contains some of the most famous architectural sculpture in Spain, the arabesque capitals are of Islamic inspiration while the corner piers are adorned with delicately carved figured panels which are based on Romanesque ivories and Mozarabic illuminated manuscripts.

The late-twelfth-century Old Cathedral of Salamanca, in Old Castile, could be regarded as the climax of Spanish Romanesque architecture although, in common with many other Spanish buildings, it is often omitted from standard histories of western architecture, presumably on the spurious ground that it does not lead anywhere stylistically. The first surprise is that it is immediately adjacent to the enormous New Cathedral, begun in 1512 in a retardataire Late Gothic style. This sympathetic preservation of an earlier monument would surely have happened in no country in Europe but Spain at that moment. As an example of dynamic conservatism it can perhaps be seen as a parallel to the design of the Old Cathedral itself, where the strange ribbed dome over the crossing is a deliberate echo of Moorish architecture. Raised on two tiers of arcaded lights, this

200 *Opposite top* The church and monastery of Loarre (late 11th century)

201 *Opposite below* The cloister at Sto Domingo de Silos (c.1085–1100)

202 The fortified walls of Ávila (late 11th century)

203 Exterior of the Old Cathedral, Salamanca (late 12th century)

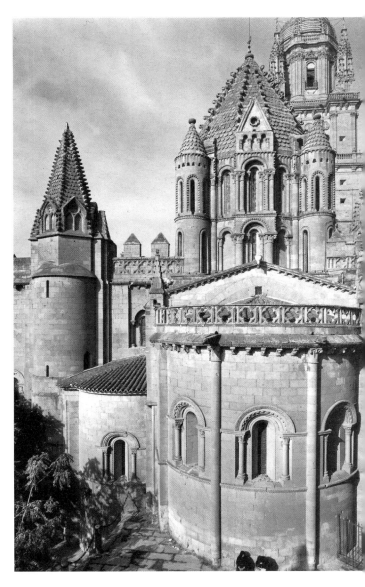

monumental dome is vigorously expressed externally where it is eight-sided, convex in profile, and covered with the fish-scale stone slates which we have already seen at Poitiers. Its subsidiary gables and conically-capped turrets add to the gaiety and the complex polyphony of the composition as a whole. Unusually for this date, the name of the architect of this masterpiece is recorded, Pedro Petriz. He was doubtless inspired by the cathedral at Zamora in the same province, which has a domed crossing tower of c.1174. This eclectic feature echoes that built in the 1140s over the Crusaders' transept at the church of the Holy Sepulchre at Jerusalem, though it is articulated with both French and Muslim features.

Italy

The different regions of Italy, like those of France, had widely differing architectural characters in the Romanesque period. The power struggle between the various states and between the pope and emperor meant that there could be no unified style, as there was in England under the Normans. The principal conflict was between the papacy with its spiritual supremacy and its temporal authority over the papal states in northern Italy, and the Holy Roman Empire with its historic claims to temporal power in both Italy and Germany. Elements of the style sometimes known as First Romanesque were developed in Lombardy as early as the ninth century. Little of this survives today, though the church of S. Vincenzo in Prato, Milan, apparently rebuilt in the eleventh century in its early-ninth-century form, has pilaster strips terminating in small arcaded galleries below the eaves. A revival of an ancient Roman decorative motif, this was a characteristic of the First Romanesque style. Subsequently developed in the Rhineland, this style was revived in northern Italy in the eleventh century where, as we shall see, it was elaborated with conspicuous success.

North of the Po the northern provinces of Lombardy, Piedmont, Emilia and parts of Venetia, centred on Milan and Pavia, developed a strenuously massive style in the late eleventh and early twelfth centuries, combining much use of brick with German Imperial and French Romanesque influences. In Tuscany the cities of Florence, Pisa and Lucca have recognizable vivacious styles of their own; while Rome and the south, each for different reasons, are less important as Romanesque centres. We have already noted in the previous chapter the marked conservatism of Rome, which continued the Early Christian manner so convincingly that the twelfth-century church of S. Clemente was believed, until the mid-nineteenth century, to date from the fourth century. Other well-known examples of this traditionalist approach in the Romanesque period include S. Maria in Cosmedin, S. Maria in Trastevere, SS. Giovanni e Paolo and the cloisters of S. Giovanni in Laterano and S. Paolo fuori le mura. The exceptional cases of S. Marco in Venice and of Sicily, with its astonishing blend of Byzantine, Romanesque and Muslim influences, have already been discussed as the conclusion of the same chapter.

Lombardy

The religious and political background to the Romanesque architecture of Lombardy, a prosperous agricultural province in northern Italy, is coloured by the expansion of Benedictine monasticism and by the growing resistance of its cities to the emperor. Milan, the capital of Lombardy, was for a time the capital of the Western Empire before the fear of barbarian invasions sent the last emperors in search of safety amid the marshes of Ravenna. Its nobles were conquered first in 744 by Charlemagne and then by the German emperor Otto I in 961, but in the ensuing centuries the indigenous princely families wished to give their power the sanction of legality by seeking investiture from the emperor, though they resisted his political authority. It was at the church of S. Ambrogio at Milan, served by both Benedictine monks and a chapter of canons, that the German emperors were crowned kings of Italy.

Lombard architects borrowed extensively from Saxon and Rhenish Romanesque, which they equalled

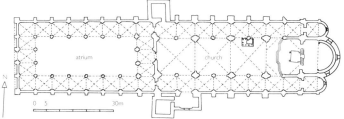

in quality during the twelfth century. S. Ambrogio at Milan was begun in c.1080 in the Imperial style, but was probably not vaulted until 1117 following an earthquake in that year. The dating of the vaulting is problematical but important, because the high rib vaults in the nave are amongst the earliest examples of their type in Europe. However, the plan is still basilican, because it is the rebuilding of a fourth-century church, and even incorporates the Early Christian feature of a spacious colonnaded atrium, dating from c.1098, before the west front. The church is flanked by two square belfry towers, one dating from the tenth century. Like the rib vault these towers became a feature of Lombard Romanesque.

S. Michele at Pavia (c.1100–1160), inspired by S. Ambrogio, and the cathedrals at Piacenza (1122–58), Parma (1117 onwards) and Modena (begun in 1099 by the architect Lanfranc), together with churches such as S. Zeno Maggiore at Verona (c.1123 onwards), are majestic examples of the north Italian type, often with huge screen façades crowned by a single broad gable, the little arched colonnades below the eaves which became a hallmark of the Lombardo-Rhenish style, and porches supported by detached columns resting on the backs of carved animals. Ruskin's *Stones of Venice* (1851–3) did much to popularize this kind of architecture amongst English-speaking peoples. Writing persuasively of 'this indraught of the Lombard energies upon the Byzantine rest, like a wild north wind descending into a space of rarefied atmosphere', he suggested:

The Lombard of early times seems to have been

exactly what a tiger would be, if you could give him love of a joke, vigorous imagination, strong sense of justice, fear of hell, knowledge of Northern mythology, a stone den, and a mallet and chisel; fancy him pacing up and down in the said den to digest his dinner, and striking on the wall, with a new fancy in his head, at every turn, and you have the Lombardic sculptor.

Parma cathedral has a huge crypt doubtless inspired by that at Speyer, and transepts with apses almost as large as that of the choir, a feature echoing St Maria im Kapitol, Cologne. Especially memorable at Parma is the towering octagonal baptistery begun in 1196 in a combination, like the cathedral itself, of stone and red brick. Its emphatic adornment with four tiers of open colonnaded galleries may have been inspired by Pisa cathedral to which, and to Tuscan Romanesque in general, we should now turn our attention.

Tuscany
The three principal monuments of Florentine Romanesque architecture are the Baptistery at Florence and the Benedictine abbey churches of S. Miniato al Monte, superbly placed on a hill overlooking Florence, and of the Badia at nearby Fiesole. They have a delicacy and a classical restraint which set them immediately apart from anything else of their date in Europe. The commercial cities of Tuscany, more peaceful and prosperous than those of Lombardy, flourished under the benign and civilized rule of Countess Matilda (1046–1115). The greater availability of stone and marble is immediately apparent in the monumental octagonal Baptistery at Florence. Dating originally from the fifth century, this was given its present form during the eleventh and twelfth centuries, though some exterior arcading as well as the mosaic and pavement inside are thirteenth-century. The patterning of the outside and the inside of the building with a veneer of polychrome marble is a typically Florentine reaction to the richly decorative aspect of ancient Roman and Byzantine architecture. It is in sharp distinction to the mass, weight and sculptural vigour of northern Romanesque. The celebrated bronze doors added by Ghiberti in the first half of the fifteenth century are amongst the earliest and finest monuments of the Renaissance in Europe. They thus add further resonance to an historic building which, together with the

207 *Left* Exterior of the Baptistery, Florence (mainly 11th and 12th centuries)

208 *Below* Interior of the Baptistery, Florence

209 *Above* Interior of S. Miniato al Monte, Florence (begun 1062)

210 *Above right* left Interior of the cathedral, Pisa

211, 212 *Below left and right* The Baptistery (1153–1265), cathedral (begun 1063) and Leaning Tower (1174–1271), Pisa, with section of the Baptistery

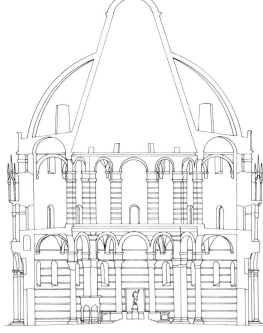

213 Exterior of the cathedral, Lucca (c.1204)

equally sumptuously ornamented basilica of S. Miniato al Monte (1062; exterior (fig. 175) completed in the twelfth century), is often regarded today as constituting a Tuscan 'Proto-Renaissance'. That is to say, they anticipate the revival of classicism in fifteenth-century Florence by architects like Alberti and Brunelleschi.

The same marble sheathing combined with tiers of open colonnades provides the dominant accent at the great cathedral of Pisa. Begun in 1063 after the victory of the Pisan fleet over the Saracens near Palermo, it was consecrated in 1118, though the nave was extended to the west in the same style in the 1260s. Unusually wide-ranging in its sources, the building is, in the end, triumphantly coherent from a visual point of view because of the dominance of its arcuated patterning. Its cruciform plan resembles the conjunction of three apsed and galleried basilicas, with uninterrupted arcades consisting of ancient Roman granite columns brought from the Isle of Elba. The capitals vary from imperial Roman to Byzantine, while the walls are encrusted in Byzantine fashion with Roman carvings and inscriptions. The mosaic in the apse is also Byzantine in style. It is interesting to note in this connection that, according to

Vasari, the sixteenth-century art historian, the architect was a Greek called Boschetto, although the architecture generally is of the imperial Lombard type. The oval dome over the crossing, on the other hand, with its squinches and shallow pendentives rising from high and narrow pointed arches, seems to be of Islamic inspiration.

The cathedral forms a group of magnetic visual impact with the twelfth-century baptistery, the celebrated belfry or Leaning Tower, and the thirteenth-century Campo Santo or cemetery. The astonishing circular domed baptistery (1153–1265) is the masterpiece of an architect called Diotisalvi, although only the lower parts with their Pisan arcading are Romanesque. The upper parts and outer dome are Gothic alterations by Nicola Pisano in 1260–65. The result is a building which, combining a bizarre profile with great strength of architectural character, has few equals before Leo von Klenze's Befreiungshalle at Kelheim of 1842–63 (see p. 485). Conant has pointed out the similarity of the building to the Rotunda of the Anastasis in Jerusalem. This may be related to the contact of Pisa, then a considerable seaport, with the East whither its navy transported both pilgrims and crusaders.

It is scarcely surprising that a style as dazzling as Pisan Romanesque should have spread widely and rapidly both in Tuscany and far beyond: to Apulia, Genoa, Sardinia, and Zadar in present-day Yugoslavia. Amongst the best-known products of its influence are the magnificent churches at Lucca, 13 miles (22km) from Pisa. At S. Michele, begun in 1143, the whole of the two upper tiers of the west façade is simply a false screen of ornamental arcading encrusted with marble decoration based on oriental textiles. As striking is the façade of c.1204 at the cathedral, which became a place of pilgrimage because of its possession of the 'Volto Santo' (Holy Face), a crucifix traditionally carved by Nicodemus. By this time in northern Europe, where the classical tradition was far less deeply embedded, Romanesque had been superseded by Gothic, a style with which it had, superficially, little in common, and which must be the subject of our next chapter.

5 The Gothic Experiment

FEW PHASES IN THE HISTORY OF WORLD ARCHITECTURE HAVE given rise to so many stylistic explanations as Gothic. This strange flowering of poetic and constructional genius, seemingly so at variance with the classicizing elements in the Romanesque tradition which it interrupted, has been variously explained as the inevitable expression of the Catholic religion, of national character, of structural honesty, of scholastic philosophy, and so on. However many useful insights these individual interpretations contain, taken together they necessarily cancel each other out. Some are current today: for example, a standard history of Gothic published in 1962 by Paul Frankl concludes with the argument that 'the common root' of the different aspects of medieval culture 'lay in the personality of Jesus'; others have been rejected, like the nationalistic claims made in England, France and Germany around 1800 that each country had given birth to the style as an expression of national genius.

It is now widely agreed that the Gothic style was born in the area round Paris – the Ile de France – in the 1130s, and that though characteristic features such as the rib vault and the pointed arch had appeared in both Islamic and Romanesque architecture, Gothic did represent a break with the past. The decisiveness of this break is characterized in aesthetic terms by the elimination of the massive wall structure and the frontality of Romanesque churches in favour of a lighter and more diaphanous structure with an emphasis on diagonal lines and views. This new sense of space is, however, combined with a division of interiors into a succession of ribbed cells, so that Gothic buildings, large or small, ecclesiastical or secular, are articulated in a way

that seems analogous to a skeleton. This method of articulation had not featured in antique or early medieval architecture. What is also new is the emphatic verticality in which horizontal lines are obscured and all lines soar upwards to heaven in seeming defiance of gravity. This sense of divine other-worldliness is heightened by the light which, suffused with rich colour from darkly glowing stained-glass windows, seems to derive from some non-natural source.

Though all Gothic buildings during the Middle Ages shared at least some of these characteristics, the Gothic style developed chronologically, from the early French style of the twelfth century to a more sophisticated version of this in the thirteenth century known as Rayonnant. This was succeeded in France by a richer variant, known as Flamboyant, which spread to many parts of Europe though not to England. There the progression from a simple lancet style in the twelfth century to a more elaborate style known as Decorated had ended in the Perpendicular style which, lasting into the sixteenth century, found no precise European parallel.

This new architecture grew as Europe itself entered a new phase of stability and prosperity after 1100: a confidence expressed, for example, in the numerous Crusades to win back the Holy Land from Islam. The isolated monasteries, castles and villages of the Romanesque world gradually gave way to cities and towns as centres of population and culture. Though still united by an international concept of Christendom, Europe saw in this period the birth of the idea of the nation state in England, France and Spain. The growth of intellectual life in the twelfth and thirteenth centuries, culminating in the scholastic philosophy of St Thomas Aquinas, was accompanied by numerous writings on religious mysticism and spirituality. This fruitful confrontation of spirit and matter was given overwhelming expression in the great cathedrals, built of stone yet aspiring heavenwards. With this new Christian architecture rose an art incorporating new narrative themes and devotional images. Through the medium of full-scale human figure sculpture, reappearing for the first time since the late-antique period, religious themes were expressed in human terms. This new humanity is encapsulated in the countless standing statues of the Virgin and Child in which the Mother of God is shown as a youthful figure, lovely and smiling.

France

'The new light': Abbot Suger and the origins of Gothic

The chevet and narthex of 1140–44 at the Benedictine abbey church of St-Denis near Paris are the earliest and most important stirrings of this new movement. The patron of the new work, Abbot Suger (1081–1151), was one of the most significant in the history of French civilization. He was first minister to Louis VI and VII and in some sense a founder of the centralized monarchy which was to culminate in the reign of Louis XIV. St-Denis was the burial place of the Capetian kings (the dynasty reigning from the late tenth to the early fourteenth century), so that in increasing its splendour Suger could not avoid making a gesture of national significance. His dynamic personality comes over powerfully in the two fascinating accounts which he left us of the abbey of St-Denis and all he had done to transform it. According to Suger, the Carolingian church was in a near-ruinous condition and was also too small to accommodate the crowds of pilgrims who came to venerate its relics, including those of the patron saint of France, St-Denis, and his companions. At the west end Suger built a twin-towered narthex with a rose window

in the centre of the façade. This combination of a twin-towered façade with a rose window was probably the first of its kind, but in general form the west end echoed the Norman Romanesque church of St-Etienne at Caen. It was in the ambulatory surrounding the choir that Suger and his architect, whose name we do not know, took their most decisive steps towards the new architecture.

The forms used in the ambulatory – pointed arches, ribbed vaults, chapels radiating round an apse – had been used before, as we have seen in the last chapter. What was new was the replacement of heavy dividing walls with slender columns so that space could flow freely in a pattern of light and shadow, creating a vertical tension which is at the heart of Gothic as opposed to Romanesque architecture. We know that this is not simply the reaction of the modern art historian, for Suger himself wrote in similar terms of his 'circular string of chapels, by virtue of which the whole church

214 The ambulatory of St-Denis (1140–44)

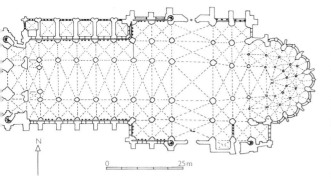

215 Plan of the abbey church of St-Denis, near Paris (west and east ends 1140–44; nave, transepts and choir 1231–81)

would shine with the wonderful and uninterrupted light of most luminous windows, pervading the interior beauty'. He also explains that the new chevet was 'ennobled by the beauty of length and width' and that 'the midst of the edifice was suddenly raised aloft by twelve columns . . . and secondarily, by as many columns in the side-aisles.'

The emphasis on light in Suger's writings is fundamental to the Gothic aesthetic. He wrote of the narthex and chevet with which he flanked the Carolingian nave:

> Once the new rear part is joined to the part in front,
>   The church shines with its middle part brightened.
>   For bright is that which is brightly coupled with the bright,
>   And bright is the noble edifice which is pervaded by the new light.

Suger derived his understanding of God as 'the superessential Light' from the writings of John the Scot (c.810–877) and from those attributed to 'Dionysius', later known as the pseudo-Areopagite, who had been (wrongly) identified with St-Denis himself, the apostle of the Gauls. Dionysius had united Christian teaching with the neo-Platonic philosophy of the third-century author Plotinus, who believed that all modes of being, including beauty, were emanations of 'the One' and 'the

Good'. Dionysius wrote that 'This stone or that piece of wood is a light to me' because all visible things are 'material lights' reflecting the infinite light of God himself. This enabled Suger to justify his love of richly ornamented and brightly shining objects such as reliquaries, shrines, metalwork, stained glass and mosaic, as a means of raising his thoughts from the material to the spiritual world by focusing in a trance-like concentration on their glitter.

The chevet of St-Denis was an important precedent for the emphasis on stained glass, especially figured glass, in Gothic interiors. Such glass had an obvious role to play in Suger's Gothic world, both as an object of contemplation in itself and as providing a glowing, mysterious and other-worldly light which would be a suitable background for religious reflection and aesthetic experience – for there is no doubt that Suger's reaction to the colour and splendour of Catholic worship was poetic and emotional.

For a patron of art and architecture of Suger's significance to have written a record of his aims and achievements is all but unique. We have therefore dwelt on him at some length, not only because of his importance in himself but because countless worshippers in and designers of churches during the course of the Middle Ages will have seen buildings and their contents in the same light. The medieval Catholic wanted to be reminded by everything he came across in his life of the truths of his religion. Thus, in the passage we have quoted from Suger about his new chevet, he goes on to emphasize that the twelve columns signify the twelve Apostles and, faced with the same number of columns in the side aisles, explains that these symbolize the number of minor prophets.

Other cathedrals in the Ile de France: Sens, Noyon, Laon and Paris

Suger's choir at St-Denis was replaced with a light and soaring structure in the Rayonnant Gothic style of the 1230s, but the choir at Sens cathedral of c.1140 survives as an example of the earliest Gothic style in the Ile de

France. Noyon cathedral, begun c.1150, still retains transept arms with rounded ends and the three-storeyed elevation of the imposing Romanesque churches of Normandy incorporating deep galleries, but the wall articulation was enlivened by the introduction of an additional fourth storey, a triforium or low wall-passage between the gallery and the clerestorey. This was combined with a system of alternating supports in the nave – massed compound piers and circular columns – supporting sexpartite vaults. Noyon represents the early Gothic balance between the verticality of the pointed arch and the horizontal effect of multiple storeys. The unifying spirit of the High Gothic of the thirteenth century, as we shall see at Chartres and elsewhere, was to eliminate the more compartmental character of churches like Noyon, Laon and Notre-Dame in Paris.

The cathedrals of Laon and Paris, built at the same time from c.1160 onwards, represent strikingly different interpretations of early Gothic: Laon has an ebullient and picturesque gaiety; Notre-Dame a serene gravity. The monumental nave of Laon echoed the four-storeyed elevation of Noyon but replaced the alternating supports in the arcade with a row of identical circular piers. This motif was widely adopted in High Gothic architecture, since alternating supports had been found to have the effect of slowing down the impression of movement along the nave. The round piers or columns of churches like Laon and Notre-Dame have an antique Roman grandeur which we know was appreciated by contemporaries. Suger claimed that his columns at St-Denis were an echo of those he had admired in Rome, at the Baths of Diocletian and elsewhere. It should thus not be thought that early Gothic patrons and designers supposed that their work was in any way hostile to the classical tradition.

Laon is especially memorable for its array of five towers, a pair at the west end, one at each transept, and one at the crossing. Their effect is heightened by the dramatic position of the cathedral on a hilltop, unusual for major churches in France. Inspired by the cathedral of Tournai, and therefore demonstrating the continuing

vigour of the Romanesque tradition, these towers were envisaged from the start, although they were not constructed until a later building campaign which began in c.1190. Their dynamism, openness and numerous diagonals create the kind of spatial complexity which has been defined by one scholar as a consequence of 'the Gothic desire for the "multiple image"'. Additional life is imparted to the towers by the unexpected presence of six enormous carved oxen near their summits, a charming tribute to the memory of the beasts who for years toiled up the hill with their burden of stone from the plain below. The towers were admired by the lively architect Villard de Honnecourt, author of the only

216 The nave of Noyon cathedral (begun c.1150)

surviving architect's sketchbook of the thirteenth century, though in his drawing of Laon he reduces their weightiness in favour of a High Gothic slenderness of line.

The mighty west façade of Laon, begun c.1190, has a plasticity and a depth which, though not typical of all High Gothic architecture, move decisively away from the flatter planes of Romanesque composition. Equally animated is the delightful south transept of c.1180 at Soissons cathedral, with its semi-circular apse consisting of four superimposed tiers of arches. As at Noyon and Laon this four-storeyed elevation dissolves the flesh of the Romanesque wall so as to leave a tense but luminous skeleton of straining arches. This picturesque and unexpected *tour de force* contrasts dramatically with the severer High Gothic forms of the nave at Soissons, built at the beginning of the thirteenth century. The transition to the unity and restraint characteristic of much High Gothic design can be immediately appreciated by a glance at the ground plan of the cathedral of Notre-Dame at Paris, begun in 1163. Notre-Dame is a single unified vessel with none of the compartmentalization in plan and grouping which characterized Romanesque architecture. When it was begun it was the tallest church in Christendom so that, as an insurance against its

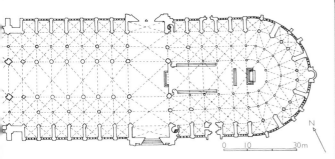

217 *Above* Plan of Notre-Dame cathedral, Paris (begun 1163)

218 *Top right* The west front of Laon cathedral (begun c.1190), showing the carved oxen on the tower

219 *Bottom right* Interior of the south transept at Soissons cathedral (c.1180)

collapse, flying buttresses were added in c.1180. Among the earliest of their kind, these helped the gallery over the nave arcade to carry the lateral thrust of the high vaults. The elevations were remodelled after 1230, when the four storeys were reduced to the more fashionable three introduced at Chartres.

Chartres

The cathedral of Chartres, as rebuilt after a fire in 1194, has long been seen as the key building in the development of the High Gothic style as well as one of the most compelling expressions of the strength and the poetry of medieval Catholicism. A lightening and clarification of the wall structure was effected at

Chartres by the dramatic abolition of the tribune galleries, thus reducing the internal elevation to three storeys only: a high arcade, low triforium passage, and clerestorey windows expanded so as to equal the arcade in height. The master of Chartres had evidently deduced that flying buttresses would be sufficient to stabilize the high vaults without any additional support from a tribune gallery. A spirit of unification and verticality is underlined by the presence on the nave piers of slender attached shafts which rise from the ground to the springing of the vaults, where they merge with the ribs. For the first time in a large Gothic church the architect of Chartres had made the single bay the basic unit of design in the nave, as opposed to the double bays of Romanesque churches. This immediately doubles the pace of the eastward drive.

The seat of a wealthy bishopric, the city of Chartres owed its prosperity to the bishop and chapter who had established four annual trade fairs held on the feasts of the Virgin Mary, to whom the cathedral was dedicated: her Nativity, Annunciation, Purification and Assumption. The choice of these was coloured by the cathedral's claim to possess the tunic, miraculously preserved in the great fire of 1194, which Mary wore when giving birth to Christ. The cathedral windows are filled with figured stained glass, many of them devoted to the cult of Mary, which bathe the building with that jewelled, other-worldly light which is an essential part of the full Gothic experience. Donations for this glass and for the sculptural ornamentation of the cathedral came from the nobility and gentry of the Ile de France as well as from the merchants, tradesmen and even the workmen of the city of Chartres.

A major pilgrimage church like Chartres cathedral reflected not only the realization on earth of the Celestial City as described in the Revelations of St John the Divine, but was also a symbol of the religious faith and commercial prosperity of the townspeople. It was at the

220 Chartres cathedral (from 1194): the interior of the nave showing the three storeys of the elevation

same time the background to many secular activities ranging from legal to commercial. Indeed, in the later Middle Ages when urban civilization assumed even greater importance, the architectural equivalents to cathedrals such as Chartres were great civic buildings such as the Cloth Halls of Ypres and Bruges.

Though a masterpiece which preserves almost all of its medieval glass as well as six thirteenth-century sculptural portals, Chartres is in fact a complex amalgam of many different periods. The lower parts of the west front of 1134–c.1150 survive from the pre-fire cathedral, while the north and south transept façades are early thirteenth-century. As many as nine towers were projected but only two were built, the northwestern tower of c.1140 being the earliest Gothic tower anywhere, though it was capped by a sumptuous

221 *Above left* The west front of Chartres cathedral (mainly after 1194; lower parts 1134–c.1150; left spire 1507)

222 *Above right* Chartres cathedral: the exterior of the south transept (early 13th century)

223 *Above* Cloth hall at Ypres (1200–1304)

Flamboyant spire in 1507. The contrast and irregularity of Chartres well express the changefulness and dynamic energy of the creators of the Gothic style. To see the logical aesthetic culmination of the ideals of the master of Chartres of around 1195 we must turn to early-thirteenth-century cathedrals such as Reims, Amiens, Beauvais and Bourges, all also in northern France.

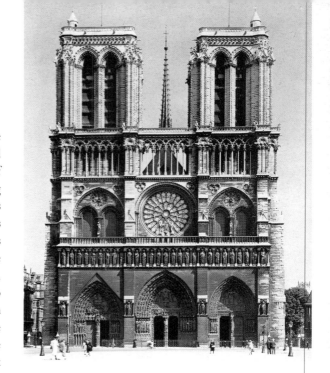

High Gothic: Reims, Amiens, Beauvais and Bourges

We have stressed the significance of Chartres as the symbolic heart of a prosperous urban and agricultural society. The even greater architectural splendour of Reims cathedral is similarly related to its unique standing as the solemn coronation place of the Capetian monarchs of the Ile de France. The slow process by which this dynasty, gradually assuming dominance over territories such as Normandy, Burgundy and Brittany, helped create and define something akin to the modern French nation, cannot be retold here. Nonetheless, it is important to realize that the Ile de France during the thirteenth century saw itself as the special representative of the cultural and material superiority of Catholic France. The costly splendour of Reims must be interpreted against that background. It was, moreover, from the Ile de France that the Gothic style radiated out to all the cultured capitals of Europe.

The designer of Reims, probably Jean d'Orbais, adopted in c.1210 the new three-tier elevation, quadripartite vaults, shafted piers and flying buttresses of Chartres. However, he animated these structural features with a new emphasis on sculptural enrichment, including angels in the external pinnacles; crockets; gargoyles; and carved vegetation on the portals, pier capitals and friezes. Reims also contains the earliest instances of bar tracery. In plate tracery, as at Chartres, openings are cut out of the solid stone so that the wall surface is still dominant. In the bar tracery of Reims the two-light windows form a single glazed opening surmounted by a circular oculus containing sexfoil tracery in which the linear patterns have almost entirely replaced solid mass. Tracery is a Gothic invention of the utmost importance, since it is no exaggeration to say

224 *Above right* The west front of Notre-Dame, Paris (c.1200–50)

225 *Right* Exterior of the Sainte-Chapelle, Paris, from the south-west (1243–8)

226 *Opposite* The west front of Reims cathedral (begun c.1235)

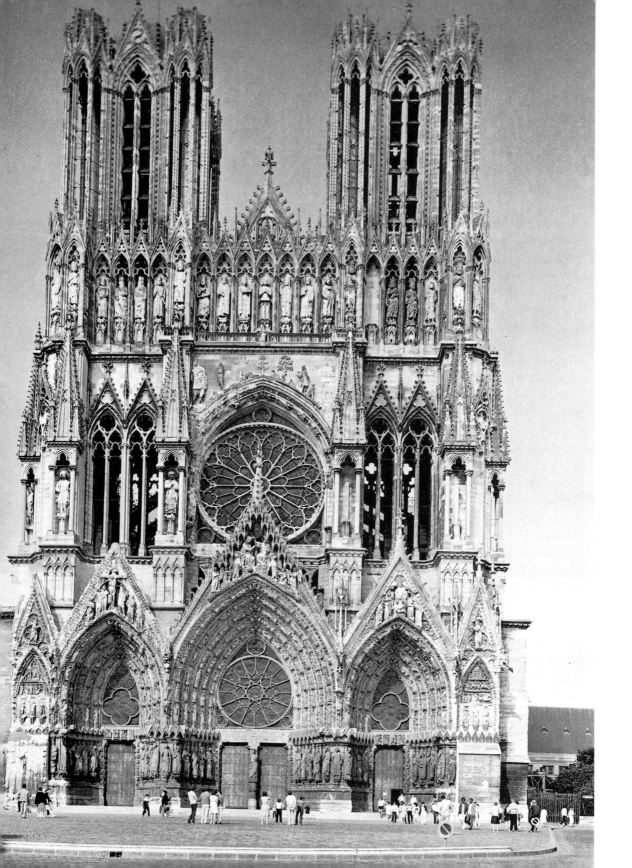

that eventually whole buildings, like the Sainte-Chapelle, were to be defined and composed of tracery and the glass it contained.

Reims was to have been crowned with six towers, or seven counting the *flèche* (spirelet) over the crossing, of which only the two on the west front were executed, both in the fifteenth century. It should not be forgotten that towers surmounted by spires were a Gothic invention and, though it may be a truism, that they have always been regarded as fingers pointing to heaven. The opulent west front of Reims was probably designed by Jean le Loup in the mid-1230s. Work proceeded slowly into the later thirteenth century while the upper gallery, with its figures of kings underlining the royal significance of the building – a common feature in Ile de France cathedrals – was not carried out until the fifteenth century. The trio of projecting gabled porticoes, logically marking the entrances to nave and aisles, forms an overwhelmingly impressive triumphal arch motif in a manner which had first been stated by the genius who designed the west front of Laon cathedral in the 1190s. But whereas Laon was still fundamentally a wall pierced with windows and ornamented with attached porches, the west front of Reims is one flickering sculptural composition into which the gabled porches, richly adorned with crockets and figure sculpture, are completely fused. Its qualities as a work of art, uniting monumentality with delicacy, and logic with fantasy, coupled with the high seriousness of its central role in the religious and political history of France, have made it for many a Gothic parallel to the Parthenon.

For some that comparison is suggested more forcefully by the west front of Notre-Dame in Paris (c.1200–50), with its wonderfully satisfying grid of horizontals and verticals. However, it is normally Amiens which is regarded as representing the classic moment of High Gothic. Designed in 1220 by Robert de Luzarches, following the destruction by fire two years earlier of the Romanesque church, the nave at Amiens is closely modelled on Reims. Its vaults soar even higher: nearly 140 feet (42.5m) as compared with 125 (38) at Reims

227 Interior of Amiens cathedral (1220–1250s)

228 Plan of Amiens cathedral

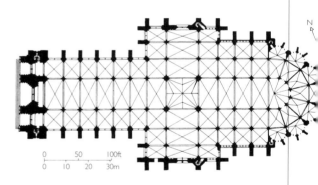

and 120 (36.5) at Chartres. The tracery, too, marks a development from Reims: here there are four-light windows surmounted by three traceried circles so that the wall dissolves into glass threaded with stone membranes like the veins on a leaf. This tracery pattern is now extended to the triforium, which thus resembles a row of unglazed windows echoing the clerestorey above. The eventual turning of the triforium into actual windows merging into the clerestorey is, as we shall see, one of the hallmarks of the unifying linear spirit of the so-called Rayonnant style which succeeded High Gothic.

The scintillatingly luminous effect of this disposition can be seen in the choir at Amiens, rising in the 1250s under the cathedral's third architect, Regnault de Cormont.

Another early instance of the same feature occurs strikingly at the cathedral of Beauvais, begun in 1225 as the last of the great Ile de France cathedrals. It was built with the deliberate ambition of achieving the highest vaults, over 150 feet (46m), of any known Gothic building. Ruskin wrote with awe in *The Seven Lamps of Architecture* that 'There are few rocks, even among the Alps, that have a clear vertical fall as high as the choir of Beauvais.' Soaring verticality on this scale suffered a setback with the collapse of the choir vaults in 1284, though this may have been less because of their height than because of inadequate foundations and supports.

Because of the expense the cathedral was never completed so that the three poignant fragments which survive today consist of the original polygonal apse, the choir as rebuilt in modified form after 1284, and the sumptuously Flamboyant transepts.

The emphatically vertical aspirations of Beauvais were not universally reflected in French architecture in the years following its design. Instead architects of the Rayonnant style were less concerned with height, monumentality and new spatial effects than with brittle, almost metallic elegance and a subtlety of linear pattern. Before investigating that tradition we should note that the cathedral of Bourges, begun c.1195, emphasizes multiplicity of vision in its interiors rather than the passion for unification which led from Chartres to Beauvais. The arcades, triforia and clerestorey of the nave are duplicated on a smaller scale in the tall inner aisles. This necessarily complicates the views across the church where, counting the inner and outer aisles, there are altogether five horizontal divisions or storeys. Echoes of this expansive system can be found in the thirteenth-century choirs of the cathedrals of Le Mans and Coutances in France, and in Toledo and Burgos cathedrals in Spain.

229 The choir of Beauvais cathedral (after 1284)

230 Bourges cathedral: the exterior from the east, showing the flying buttresses (begun c.1195)

The Court Style and Rayonnant Gothic

The earliest phase of the Rayonnant style of French Gothic which succeeded Amiens is sometimes known as the Court Style, from its close association with the reign of Louis IX (1227–70), canonized as St Louis in 1297. His prestige as Christian ruler and chivalrous soldier was higher than that of any European leader in his day. The veneration with which he was regarded, especially following his return from the Seventh Crusade in 1254, was given weight by the prosperity of his kingdom and the brilliance of its culture. The taut linearity of Court Style decoration is succinctly stated in the three masterpieces of the 1230s, all presumably by the same hand, in which Rayonnant Gothic was born: they are the cathedral of Troyes, the rebuilt abbey church of St-Denis, and Louis IX's chapel of St-Germain-en-Laye. In the choir of Troyes the clerestorey and triforium are tied together more completely than before, in the culmination of a process begun in 1220 in the apse of Reims where Jean le Loup had linked the two storeys with colonnettes.

St-Denis plays an important part in the development of the Court Style, as it had done in the origins of Gothic itself. Between 1231 and 1281 the upper parts of Suger's choir were rebuilt and connected to his western narthex with a handsome new nave and transepts. From the 1240s Pierre de Montreuil was a leading architect in this elaborate process. The close fusion at Amiens of the design of the triforium and the windows of the clerestorey led to the idea of turning the triforium itself into windows. This was done at St-Denis by glazing the outer wall of the triforium passage and retaining the unglazed tracery on the nave side as at Amiens. Triforia had previously looked into the dark roof space over the aisles or into blind passages in the thickness of the wall. However, the increasing height of churches meant that, as at St-Denis, the triforia could be above and independent of the aisle roofs. The dissolution of the entire wall area above the arcade into a luminous foil with little horizontal division between triforium and clerestorey was fraught with consequences for the future. The fully glazed wall is at its most astonishing in the transepts at St-Denis, where giant rose windows on the north and south walls entirely fill the space above the glazed triforia. Another important innovation was in the design of the piers, which abandoned the tradition of the column with attached shafts in favour of a lozenge-shaped mass of colonnettes which correspond to the ribs in the vault and to the orders of the arcade arches.

The jewel of the Court Style is the Sainte-Chapelle (fig. 225) at the royal palace in Paris, built for St Louis in 1243–8 as a national shrine to house a fragment of the True Cross, which he bought from the emperor of Byzantium, and another sacred relic believed to be the Crown of Thorns. The presence of this relic led Pope Innocent IV to proclaim that it meant that Christ had

231 The east end of the church of St-Urbain, Troyes (begun 1262)

crowned Louis with his own Crown. The chapel was thus a symbol of the French achievement at its most royal and most Catholic. It is a giant reliquary with a metallic quality which recalls, doubtless deliberately, the costly silverwork shrines, reliquaries and monstrances of the Middle Ages, many of which have now disappeared. The taut and brittle Court Style with its dissolution of wall in favour of glass and of wiry tracery patterns was ideally suited for a monument of this kind. The walls of this great glass cage, uninterrupted by transepts or any other projections, are filled with continuous stained-glass windows from the apex of the vault down to the floor, save for a low dado (figs 225, 236).

The style spreading from Paris produced the shrinelike collegiate church of St-Urbain at Troyes, begun in 1262 by the French pope, Urban IV, in honour of his patron saint and to commemorate his own birthplace. On the exterior the spiky gables and pinnacles create a nervous attenuation, while inside the triforium has at last been abolished and the church is two-storeyed with walls almost entirely of glass separated by fragile tracery. This is beautifully expressed in the mannered and capricious choir of c.1270 at Sées cathedral, Normandy, where the arches of the arcade are provided with prominent triangular gables, functionally inappropriate in an interior since they are properly the terminations of roofs. Borrowed from the choir triforium at Amiens of the 1250s, this device blurs the distinction between exterior and interior so that the arcade at Sées almost resembles an external portico.

In this new architecture of light we no longer find the dark stained glass of the early and High Gothic periods with its rich reds and blues, but more frequently white and grey glass creating a cooler, lighter effect. Architecture is seen as a giant reticulated web of brittle shafts and tracery. This had been anticipated in such High Gothic designs as the early-thirteenth-century south portal at Chartres, which is encased with tremendously slender and elongated shafts that seem to have strayed from some system of celestial scaffolding. If one adds to this the two layers of window tracery found at St-Urbain as well as vertical cusped panelling enlivening blank walls, one comes close to a linear architecture of autonomous tracery. This is what we find in the astonishing west front of Strasbourg cathedral, begun in 1275/77 perhaps from designs by a master Erwin. Erwin had evidently admired St-Urbain as well as the north and south transepts of Notre-Dame, the north begun by Jean de Chelles in the 1240s and the south begun by him in 1258 from designs by Pierre de Montreuil. However, these buildings are surpassed in capricious invention by Strasbourg, where slender shafts of stone rise up two feet in front of the traceried windows.

232 Interior of the choir of Sées cathedral (c.1270)

233 The Portail des Libraires or north transept of Rouen cathedral (begun 1281)

The façade of the north transept of Rouen cathedral, the Portail des Libraires, begun in 1281, belongs to the same family as Strasbourg and the Notre-Dame transepts. It introduces a new liveliness by extending blind architectural ornament on to the façades of the flanking houses. The cathedral thus appears as a living frame in constant aspiring motion, dominating the physical as well as the spiritual life of the city. The taut stylishness of late Rayonnant architecture, with its concern to create walls out of light defined by stone membranes, can be appreciated in the choirs of St-Thibault-en-Auxois, Burgundy, and of the abbey-church of La Trinité, Vendôme, and in the naves of Bayonne, Nevers and Auxerre cathedrals, all begun in the last decade of the thirteenth or the first decade of the fourteenth century. Perhaps the most exquisite example of this diaphanous linearity is the Benedictine abbey-church of St-Ouen at Rouen, begun in 1318.

Hall churches

From the later thirteenth century, cathedrals in the Rayonnant style were built in the south and west in the

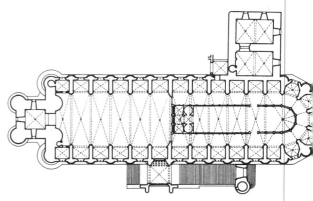

234 *Top* Albi cathedral (begun 1282), showing the Flamboyant south porch (1519)

235 *Above* Plan of Albi cathedral

236 *Opposite* The interior of the Sainte-Chapelle, Paris (1243–8)

wake of the growth of royal power, though areas such as the Plantagenet provinces of Poitou and Anjou in the west continued with their tradition of hall churches, that is with aisles the same height as the nave. An early example is Poitiers cathedral, contemporary with Laon and Notre-Dame. Hall churches were especially favoured by the Franciscan and Dominican orders founded in the early thirteenth century. The friars of these mendicant or begging orders, turning their backs on the monasteries of the Benedictines and Cistercians in secluded pastoral settings, set up their pulpits in town churches where they conducted crusading missions for the urban poor.

A related tradition, again deviating from the High Gothic norm, is the replacement of aisles with lateral chapels. Among the earliest examples of this in a Gothic church occurs in c.1270 in the nave of the Dominican church of Sta Catalina in Barcelona. The system became the norm for churches in Catalonia, whence it may have influenced the amazing fortified cathedral at Albi (1282–1390) in southern France. This was built by Bishop Bernard de Castanet, a Dominican and a vigorous persecutor of the followers of the Albigensian heresy, a negative and anti-social sect who believed that all matter was evil. The brick-built mass of Albi cathedral, rising sheer from the ground, has a twentieth-century bareness, unencumbered with transepts, eastern chapels or flying buttresses. The buttresses are to be found inside, projecting into the huge unbroken nave. Chapels were provided between them but these were later subdivided horizontally to provide an upper storey.

The Flamboyant style

After 1340 building activity on major churches considerably slowed down, partly as a result of the disastrous Hundred Years War against England (1337–1444). However, during this period the seeds were planted of the last phase of French Gothic, the style known as Flamboyant, characterized by double-curved tracery patterns resembling flames leaping upwards. The style flourished especially vigorously in northern France.

237 The west front (c.1500–14) of the church of St-Maclou, Rouen (1434–70)

The fantastic pentagonal west front of St-Maclou, Rouen, is the result of an ambition to dissolve solid mass into a diagonal polyphony of pinnacled ornament, disappearing imperceptibly in the air like a shimmering heat haze. Towers and spires lent themselves more readily than façades to this treatment, as can be seen in the lacy profusion of the Tour de Beurre (1485–1500) at Rouen Cathedral or of the north tower at Chartres of 1507. The Flamboyant aesthetic was difficult to apply to the creation of interior space, so that what lies behind the exotic porches and exterior walls of Flamboyant churches is often a repetition of the long-established Rayonnant style. The vocabulary of form deployed in the Flamboyant style had already been anticipated in the late Decorated or Curvilinear style in England. Indeed, English influence may well lie behind buildings such as the west front of Rouen which is essentially a screen hung with rows of statues. Though such a theme seems markedly un-French, it should be remembered that it had been adopted in the twelfth century at Angoulême cathedral (see p. 106).

Secular buildings in medieval France

In French secular architecture from the twelfth to the fourteenth centuries the outstanding monuments are the fortified castles and cities which were erected all over the country, particularly towards the end of this period during the Hundred Years War. Imposing walled towns survive, especially in the south of France at Carcassonne and Aigues-Mortes. Castles were centred on a keep, often circular as at Châteaudun, or polygonal as at Gisors and Provins, while the thirteenth-century castle of Villandraut is a rectangular walled enclosure flanked by circular towers placed with a fine regard for symmetry. The feudal splendour of these towered and pinnacled castles was poetically recorded in the illustrations to the *Très Riches Heures du Duc de Berry* (1413–16). This was the most celebrated of the popular books of devotion for the laity known as Books of Hours. One of the illustrations in the *Très Riches Heures* shows the walls of the royal palace in the Ile de la Cité in Paris, rebuilt by St Louis and his grandson Philip the Fair in the thirteenth and early fourteenth centuries. Little of this exists today except for the great room with its rib vaults on four rows of columns, and the neighbouring kitchen with its four hearths in the corners.

Many castles were destroyed in the seventeenth century as a result of the order of Cardinal Richelieu (see p. 319) that feudal fortresses should be dismantled. One of the finest survivals is the Palace of the Popes at Avignon, a vast fortified complex surrounded by towers and high walls. It consists of two palaces, one built by Pope Benedict XII in 1336–42 as a combined fortress

238 The Papal Palace, Avignon (1336–52)

239 *Above* The house of Jacques Coeur at Bourges (1445–53): the courtyard

240 *Left* Plan of the house of Jacques Coeur at Bourges

241 *Overleaf left* Lincoln cathedral: the nave (vaulted in 1233)

242 *Overleaf right* Bristol cathedral: the vaulting of the choir and south aisle (1298–c.1330)

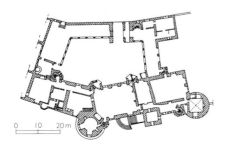

0   10   20m

165

243 The courtyard of the Palais de Justice at Rouen (1499)

and monastery, and the other by Pope Clement VI in 1342–52 from the designs of the architect Jean de Loubinère. This is a more luxurious building, graciously enlivened with wall-paintings and sculpture. Its increasing freedom reached a climax in the fifteenth century in sumptuous domestic buildings such as the Hôtel de Cluny, the Paris residence of the abbot of Cluny, and especially the house at Bourges of the wealthy Jacques Coeur, the king's treasurer. This was built in 1445–53 round a courtyard with an asymmetrical and functionally disposed plan which grouped banking offices on one side and domestic apartments on the other. Lit with generous windows, these are linked by open stone staircases, corridors and porches in a lively composition capped by a skyline of gables, turrets and chimneys. The Flamboyant style was equally successful in the context of civic architecture, as can be seen in one of the most magnificent public buildings of late medieval France, the Palais de Justice of 1499 at Rouen.

England

Canterbury and its impact

At Canterbury cathedral in 1174 a leading English ecclesiastical patron decided to follow the fashion in architecture newly set in the Ile de France: the resulting choir at Canterbury is one of the earliest major Gothic buildings in the country. Just as we have fascinating documents by Abbot Suger describing the construction of the first Gothic building in France in the 1140s, so, by a remarkable coincidence, we have a contemporary account by one of the monks of Canterbury, Gervase, of the ten-year building process following the great fire of September 1174 which had largely destroyed the Romanesque choir. After this disaster leading master-masons from England and France were invited to give their advice on how to rebuild this prestigious metropolitan cathedral, seat of the primate of England and of a flourishing Benedictine monastery, and the centre of a growing cult of devotion to St Thomas à Becket who was murdered in the cathedral in 1170. The choice fell on a Frenchman, William of Sens, who, unable to persuade the monks to replace the Norman choir entirely, was forced to raise his Gothic structure, inspired by Laon and Notre-Dame, Paris, on the old crypt and within the surviving outer aisle walls of the Norman choir. Nonetheless, his high three-storeyed Gothic elevation made a striking impact with its sexpartite stone rib-vaults, applied shafts, carved acanthus capitals, pointed arches and semi-circular ambulatory.

Gervase contrasted all this stylistically with the Romanesque work:

The pillars of the old and new work are alike in form and thickness but different in length. For the new pillars were elongated by almost twelve feet. In the old capitals the work was plain, in the new ones exquisite in sculpture. There the circuit of the choir had twenty-two pillars, here are twenty-eight. There the arches and everything else was plain, or sculpted with an axe and not with a chisel. But here almost throughout is appropriate sculpture. There used to be no marble shafts, but here are innumerable ones. There in the circuit round the choir, the vaults were plain, but here they are arch-ribbed and have keystones.

In stressing the applied shafting of polished black Purbeck marble contrasting in colour and texture with the paler background stone brought from Caen, Gervase drew attention to one of the principal and most influential features of the choir. Playful decorative patterning of this kind, largely unknown in France, was to become a persistent feature of native English Gothic, as it had been of much Anglo-Saxon and later manuscript illumination. Moreover, the constructional system at Canterbury, which has strong affinities with the Anglo-Norman thick-wall technique (see p. 126), was also out of step with developments in early French Gothic since it incorporates an internal wall-passage in front of the clerestorey window.

William of Sens was seriously injured by falling from the scaffolding in 1178, when his place was taken by a master-mason called William the Englishman who continued the work eastwards, providing the Trinity Chapel in the apse and the circular Corona at the east end, both designed as shrines for St Thomas. His work combines with that of his predecessor to provide the cathedral with an eastern end planned on typically English additive lines: that is, consisting of a leisurely series of linked but separate spaces which contrasts with the more cohesive and single-minded organization of French cathedrals. The monks' choir, with its alternating round and octagonal piers, is differently treated from the adjacent presbytery containing the High Altar where the piers have applied shafts. Different again is the Trinity Chapel with coupled columns inspired by those in northeastern France at Sens and at the lost cathedral of Arras. Finally, in the Corona at Canterbury the piers are replaced by Purbeck marble wall-shafts. This tendency to variety and dislocation is heightened by the picturesque

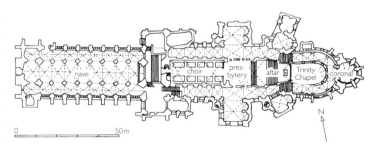

244 *Top* The choir and east end of Canterbury cathedral (1174–84)

245 *Above* Plan of Canterbury cathedral

raising of the floor of the Trinity Chapel sixteen steps above that of the choir, and by the spatial poetry of the unexpected circular Corona. Another departure from the French norm is the extreme length of the cathedral which had already been doubled in length in 1096–1130, while William of Sens's retention of the second pair of transepts, inspired by Cluny III, further emphasized that the composition was additive in character, in other words that it was Romanesque rather than Gothic.

It is a striking fact that these colourful and picturesque characteristics set a pattern which was to be widely followed in Gothic architecture in England: for example, double transepts as at Lincoln, Salisbury, Southwell and Worcester; exaggerated length from east to west; compartmental grouping; spatial play, as in the Decorated style; and especially the decorative use of features which in France would normally be handled with at least an appearance of logic. The length and complexity may be partly due to the unusual English

246 *Above* Interior of the nave of Wells cathedral (c.1185–c.1240), showing the strainer arch added in the 1330s

247 *Opposite* The Palacio del Infantado at Guadalajara (1480–3), by Juan Guas

combination in a single building of the different functions of a Benedictine abbey-church and a cathedral, a pattern which occurred at Bath, Canterbury, Coventry, Durham, Ely, Norwich, Rochester, Winchester and Worcester.

The immediate influence of Canterbury can be seen in the eastern parts of Chichester, Rochester and Winchester cathedrals with their liberal decorative use of Purbeck marble. In the north of England Gothic arrived at the same time as at Canterbury but through the influence of the Cistercians. We noted in the last chapter the founding of the Cistercian order in 1098 as a reaction against the growing opulence in architecture and liturgy of the Cluniac Benedictines. The architectural enthusiasm of the Cistercians for austerity and for functional innovation led them to adopt the early Gothic style at Kirkstall Abbey (c.1152) and Roche Abbey (c.1172), both in Yorkshire. South-west England also forms another school, centred on Wells cathedral as designed between c.1185 and 1200 and executed with

modifications up to c.1240. The original nave elevation of Wells is similar to that of Roche, but also assumes a spreading amplitude and elaboration in contrast to the leaner verticality to which France was aspiring at that moment. Thus the triforium is an emphatically horizontal element in the elevation with no wall shafts to link it with the arcade below. Moreover, the piers have as many as 24 attached shafts, which create a sumptuous rippling effect down the nave. This hint of a resurgence of an Anglo-Norman decorative richness recurs in the elaborate north porch of c.1210–15 and in the celebrated west front of c.1220–40, a picturesquely illogical screen on which are hung nearly four hundred carved and painted stone figures. Extended by flanking towers which stand outside the body of the church, it is the first of the decorative screen façades which are a feature of English cathedrals from Salisbury to Exeter.

Lincoln and its impact

Lincoln cathedral, rebuilt from 1192 by the master-mason Geoffrey de Noiers, is another masterpiece which is innovative in a way unparalleled in France. St Hugh's Choir, known after Geoffrey de Noiers's patron, the French-born Carthusian monk St Hugh of Lincoln, is roofed with what is known as the 'crazy vault' of Lincoln. It is perhaps the earliest instance in Gothic Europe of deliberate emphasis on the decorative as opposed to the functional role of ribs. The vault thus becomes a continuous linear net largely unrelated to the bay divisions and featuring for the first time tiercerons, that is to say decorative ribs which do not lead to the central point of the vault but to a place along a ridge rib which runs along the crown of the vault. The same spirit of almost wilful gaiety dictated the design of the blank arcading which adorns the walls in St Hugh's Choir. Here the Norman tradition of intersecting round-headed arcading has been developed in a three-dimensional way by superimposing one tier of pointed arches on top of another so as to produce a syncopated rhythm in two planes, which is emphasized by the contrasting material of the colonnettes: limestone for the lower layer and

polished black Purbeck marble, inspired by Canterbury, for the upper.

Lincoln is also notable for the continuing use of the Anglo-Norman thick or double-shell wall which first appeared in the mid-eleventh century in the transept at Jumièges and was adopted at Caen, St Albans, Durham and Winchester. In Gothic architecture this technique enabled the vaults to be supported less by flying buttresses than by the walls of the gallery over the aisles. The span of the arcades in the nave at Lincoln is so great that the eye can take in the aisles at the same time (fig. 241). Horizontal ornament is even more marked in the west front, which was reached by about 1230. Previously dominated by its three great Norman arches, this façade was now extended to both sides with repetitive tiers of blank arcading unrelated to the structure of the wall behind.

Not surprisingly, Lincoln exercised immediate and powerful impact, especially on Ely where the presbytery of 1234–52 is a lovely enrichment of Lincoln's nave. Salisbury cathedral (1220–c.1260) also bears the marks of influence from Lincoln and Wells, though its designer did not echo Geoffrey de Noiers's picturesque waywardness. There is a calmness and austerity about Salisbury which set it apart from the three other leading cathedrals in the Early English style, Canterbury, Wells and Lincoln. It is also unusual for an English cathedral in being built at one go on a virgin site with no subsequent additions save for the magnificent fourteenth-century crossing tower and spire. It is the tower and spire which, though not envisaged by the original designer, unite visually the numerous separately roofed parts of the cathedral. Indeed the two sets of transepts, projecting north porch and rectangular east end make Salisbury the classic example of

248 *Top* The vaults of St Hugh's choir in Lincoln cathedral (begun 1192), seen from the north-east transept

249 *Left* The blank arcading of the walls of St Hugh's Choir, Lincoln

250 The presbytery of Ely cathedral (1234–52)

French developments. It was intended to combine the functions of three buildings associated with Henry's brother-in-law, Louis IX: the coronation church of Reims, the royal mausoleum at St-Denis and the Sainte-Chapelle in Paris. French features at Westminster include the chevet and ambulatory; the tall narrow proportions of the nave, higher than any so far built in England; the thin upper wall technique with flying buttresses and no clerestorey passage; the springing of the vaults from single *tas-de-charges* (springing stones); the uninterrupted descent of shafts from the vaults to the pier bases; and especially the window tracery, including bar tracery from Reims, windows in spherical triangles from the

251 *Below* Salisbury cathedral from the north-east (1220–c.1260)

compartmentalism in English Gothic, in contrast to the unifying spirit of French Gothic as reflected in Amiens cathedral which, with its apsed east end and minimal transepts, was begun in the same year. The unadventurous repetition of simple Early English lancets, buttresses and pinnacles, and the low nave elevation, do not prepare the visitor for the spatial interest of the Lady Chapel at the east end, a miniature hall church with vaults which merge subtly with those of the rectangular ambulatory of the choir. Space flows freely here in a way which anticipates the Decorated style by creating a diaphanous quality, heightened by the extreme slenderness of the Purbeck marble pillars supporting the vaults.

Westminster Abbey

The small repertoire of Early English architectural motifs as constantly repeated at Salisbury perhaps just touches on sterility. Westminster Abbey, begun for Henry III in 1245, made that style immediately out of date by presenting in the most prestigious national context a blend of English traditions with the latest

252 Westminster Abbey (begun 1245): the interior of the choir and the vaults

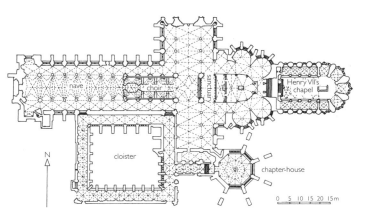

253 Plan of Westminster Abbey

Sainte-Chapelle, and rose windows from the north transept at Notre-Dame. It must be said that this French language is spoken with an English accent and that the master-mason from 1245 to 1253, Henry de Reynes, may have come from Reynes in Essex rather than Reims. Thus English tradition asserts itself in the considerable projection of the transepts; the dynamic effect caused by the recession of the clerestorey windows from the wall ribs; the deep triforium gallery; and the preoccupation with surface texture, as in the rich use of Purbeck marble and of blind arcading with diaper, foliage or figure sculpture.

The octagonal chapter-house, completed in 1253, is lit with great traceried windows of the most up-to-date Rayonnant type as established in the side chapels added to the nave at Notre-Dame in the 1240s. In a centrally-planned building of a kind virtually unknown in France they define an amazing space almost entirely surrounded by glass. The spatial impact of this interior and the passion of its designer for huge compound tracery windows were harbingers of the future style of English Gothic.

The impact of Westminster and the origins of the Decorated style

Lichfield, Hereford, Lincoln and Salisbury cathedrals all contain sparkling work influenced by the French Court Style as introduced to England at Westminster. The nave of Lichfield, begun in c.1258, shows the liberating and graceful impact of the new tracery patterns, while the west front, reached in c.1280, attempts to echo the French twin-towered type. The Lady Chapel of c.1320–35 is a stylish version of the Sainte-Chapelle. It has the same mannered, rather metallic quality of its model, which has itself been likened to a sumptuous metalwork shrine. These taut attenuated proportions had already featured in the north transept at Hereford cathedral, built in c.1260 by the courtier bishop Peter of Aigueblanche from Savoy, who had come to England with queen Eleanor of Provence, wife of Henry III. At Lincoln the sumptuous Angel Choir, added in 1256–80 as a splendid shrine for St Hugh, carries traceried windows to a new level of translucent opulence. The clerestorey windows are duplicated as an open screen on the inner side of the clerestorey passage looking into the choir. The climax of the Angel Choir is the vast traceried window which fills the east wall, the earliest eight-light window recorded and the parent of many, especially in the north of England. Less inventively, the chapter house and cloister at Salisbury, begun in c.1270, duplicate those at Westminster.

The mature Decorated style starts around 1290. It is particularly associated with the use of ogee, i.e. double, curves, which first appeared in the Eleanor Crosses, erected by Edward I in 1291–4 to mark the funeral procession of his queen from Lincolnshire to Westminster Abbey. The style is seen at its best in Exeter and York cathedrals; the choirs of Wells and Bristol; the tower, choir and Lady Chapel at Ely; and the porch of St Mary Redcliffe at Bristol. The nave of Exeter, begun about 1310, is memorable for the weighty richness

created by its massive vault, which appears to be a decorative end in itself rather than the logical roofing of the bay divisions. It spreads profusely like palm leaves because it is covered with extremely prominent ribs of which as many as eleven, more than in any previous building, spring from a single source.

The Decorated style at Wells, Bristol and Ely

The work begun at Wells cathedral in c.1285 and continued into the 1330s is both more subtle and more imaginative than Exeter. The octagonal chapter-house deploys the palm-leaf theme of Exeter with tremendous panache: 32 ribs spring out from the central pillar to meet the ribs radiating out from the eight engaged shafts round the edge of the room. Something of the same effect is captured in the Lady Chapel, an irregular octagon in shape with two western piers ambiguously interpenetrating the retrochoir which is considerably lower in height. This spatial play involving emphasis on cross vistas is echoed in two other important innovations

254 The nave of Exeter cathedral (begun c.1310)

255 The vault of the choir at Wells cathedral (c.1330)

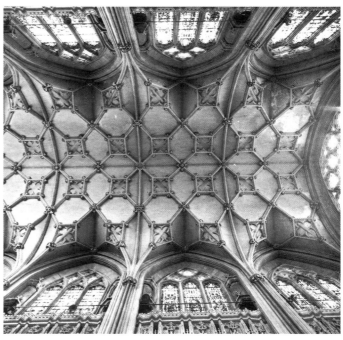

in the Lady Chapel: the nodding, i.e. three-dimensional, ogee arches of the sedilia, and the lierne vault, that is, a vault with ribs which do not spring from either the boss or the main springers but are introduced to create decorative patterns often, as at Wells, of star formation. This theme reached its climax at Wells in the breathtaking vault of the choir of c.1330, where the absence of diagonal ribs or ridge ribs blurs the distinction between the bays in favour of a continuous ornamental display of large cusped lozenges of varying sizes. The internal wall treatment was also of startling originality, for the substantial area between the arcade and the clerestorey windows was filled with an open stone grille of tall mullions standing directly on the arcade arches. This is an extreme development from the tracery we have observed on a more modest scale in the Court Style of thirteenth-century France, as in the choirs of St-Denis, Tours and Sées, the transepts at Notre-Dame and Amiens, and the apses at St-Urbain and Troyes. We shall return to this topic in discussing the origins of the Perpendicular.

The last novelty to be noted at Wells is the extraordinary strainer arches inserted in the crossing in the 1330s to help carry the weight of the tower. Resembling two intersecting ogee curves, or an upside-down arch standing on a normal arch, they reflect the diagonal emphasis of the Decorated style in an arresting manner. In fact they repeat on a larger scale what had already been tried in differing ways in the sedilia and flying arches at Bristol. To the Augustinian abbey-church, today cathedral of St Augustine, at Bristol, a new chancel and Lady Chapel were added in 1298–c.1330 (fig. 242). The chancel and its aisles form a hall church in which the weight of the choir vault is carried to buttresses in the outer aisle walls by means of curious arched stone bridges spanning the aisles, not dissimilar in effect to the strainer arches at Wells. There is no precedent for beams of precisely this kind, save perhaps in the aisles of the undercroft of the Sainte-Chapelle.

Pictorial and structural ingenuity is found in the hexagonal north porch added to the parish church of St

256 Exterior of the north porch of the church of St Mary Redcliffe, Bristol (c.1325)

257 The interior of the octagon at Ely cathedral (1322–42)

Mary Redcliffe, Bristol, in c.1325. The doorway has an oriental outline composed of a chain of six concave curves. Bristol was a major port with considerable trading contact with the East, a fact which may well explain the profuse carving of this exotic doorway, as well as the use of ogee arches and of vaults adorned with ribs in star formation.

The climax of the Decorated style, at any rate in spatial terms, is found at Ely cathedral, where the area of desolation caused by the collapse of the Norman crossing tower in 1322 seems to have suggested the creation of a centrally-planned space, over 65 feet (20m) in diameter, surmounted by an octagonal tower. As we have seen at Wells and Bristol, diagonal vistas were dear to Decorated designers. Nowhere was that spatial preoccupation given more poetic and dynamic expression than in the great octagon which so unexpectedly interrupts the steady repetitive rhythm of the long Norman nave at Ely. Light floods in from the four large windows placed across the diagonal sides of the octagon, and also from the lantern above, with its rib vaulting forming a lively star pattern. It is as though the chapter-house at Wells had miraculously lost its central pillar and had the crowning section of its vault cut away to allow views upwards into a lantern floating above it.

Ely was a monastic cathedral and it was beneath this tower that the monks set up their choir, a position of unique pictorial attraction. To assist them in the design of the great lantern the Ely masons called on the king's master-carpenter in London, William Hurley, since wood was the only possible material for such a construction. Doubtless they knew of the precedent recently set by the octagonal chapter-house of c.1300 at York, where the adoption of timber for the vault had dispensed with the need for a central supporting column. England is not specially rich in stone quarries, but the abundance of timber and the strength of the ship-building tradition encouraged the skills of the carpenters who produced a series of timber vaults in the thirteenth and fourteenth centuries in imitation of stone, above all at the octagon at Ely in the 1340s. These wooden ceilings, increasingly adorned with carved bosses, lent themselves more easily to applied ornamentation than the heavier stone vaults of France. Gothic architecture was believed in the nineteenth century by writers such as Pugin and Viollet-le-Duc to be a truthful way of building. However, nothing could be less truthful than the Ely octagon, where the lantern does not rest on the vault beneath, as it appears to, but on a cantilevered frame of timber brackets supporting eight mighty timber posts. Both the frame and the posts are deliberately concealed from the spectator; indeed, boarding and wooden ribs have been ingeniously applied to the underside of the brackets so as to give the illusion of a stone vault.

The three westernmost bays of the choir at Ely were rebuilt in c.1328–35 following the damage caused by the collapse of the tower. They develop the theme of the adjacent retrochoir with a new luxuriance, as in the starry lierne vault and the filigree tracery in the gallery openings. The Lady Chapel, begun in 1321 and completed in c.1335–49, is one of the loveliest Decorated rooms in England, with the huge spreading star patterns of its lierne vault, the flowing tracery of its windows and, above all, the rippling three-dimensional arcade of nodding ogee arches which runs round all four walls. This enchanting miniature architecture of niches, gables, vaults, crockets and pinnacles is enlivened with carved foliage and figure sculpture, wantonly damaged in the seventeenth century, and was originally brightly painted. The imposing west front of York Minster, dominated by the flame-like tracery of its great central window, shows that the Decorated style was equally capable of effects on the grandest scale.

St Stephen's Chapel and the origins of Perpendicular

The Rayonnant style introduced at Westminster Abbey in the mid-thirteenth century continued in some parts of the country well into the fourteenth century, for example in the north of England in the nave of York, begun 1292. However, the impact of Rayonnant also gave

258 A section of St Stephen's Chapel, Westminster (1292–1348), drawn for the Society of Antiquaries

birth to two contrasting but virtually contemporary developments: Decorated and Perpendicular, the latter so called because it is a rectilinear system of design and ornament based on the repetition of vertical panels with cusped heads. The story begins at St Stephen's Chapel, Westminster, built for Edward I in deliberate rivalry with the Sainte-Chapelle. The long building process consisted of three campaigns of 1292–7, 1320–6, and 1330–48 when the vault and clerestorey were added. Only the heavily restored crypt survives today.

Though it was primarily a monument in the Decorated style, sumptuously painted, and ornamented with ogee cusping and perhaps the earliest of lierne vaults in the crypt, it had something of the feel of a panelled cage: its wall surfaces were enlivened with blind tracery, including blank vertical panelling in the spandrels of the windows inside and mullions descending below the windows on the exterior. It is clear that its first architect, Michael of Canterbury, succeeded by his son Thomas in 1323, developed certain tendencies within the French Court Style in an early Perpendicular way. This was taken a stage further in 1332–49 in the now-destroyed chapter-house and cloister at Old St Paul's cathedral in London by the architect William Ramsey, who had already worked on St Stephen's Chapel. The work at St Paul's contained window mullions extended downwards on the wall face, the earliest rectilinear Perpendicular tracery, and virtually

the first use of the four-centred arch which became one of the hallmarks of the Perpendicular style. The flattened profile of the four-centred arch helps define the Perpendicular as a style of rigidity, as opposed to the mobility of the Decorated style. It was a form never adopted on the continent, except marginally in Flanders. Indeed, whereas English Decorated had a European impact and influenced a range of buildings from Bohemia to Portugal, the Perpendicular was never exported to the continent. Though the Decorated style did not cease in the mid-fourteenth century, the dominant style for two centuries from c.1330 was Perpendicular.

The Perpendicular at Gloucester

The Perpendicular features of Old St Paul's were applied for the first time to a major church when the south transept and choir of the Benedictine abbey-church, now cathedral, at Gloucester were remodelled in 1331–7 and c.1337–c.1350 respectively. The choir may have been conceived as a shrine for the remains of King Edward II, murdered in 1327, who it was hoped would become a royal saint like Edward the Confessor and would thus attract pilgrims. The work was probably supervised by royal architects from London, perhaps William Ramsey or Thomas of Canterbury. The latter was the king's chief architect when the south transept at Gloucester was begun, but the great window which it contains is close to those by Ramsey in the chapter-house at Old St Paul's.

The most amazing aspect of Gloucester is that the walls of the eleventh-century choir were left largely intact beneath a veneer or grid of descending mullions and cusped panels. It is a *tour de force* of joinery in stone, in other words it is the culmination of the imaginative recreation in stone of techniques originating in carpentry, a theme given early expression at St Stephen's Chapel. This marks an important shift from the Sainte-Chapelle, one of the models for St Stephen's Chapel, where forms derived from metalwork seem to have played a determining aesthetic role. The east end of the choir at Gloucester is a wall of glass, articulated with tracery composed of the same cusped panels which adorn the walls.

Late Perpendicular and the fan vault

The choir vault at Gloucester is of the complex lierne variety with countless small compartments emphasized by bosses. It was not long before a type of vaulting more in harmony with the panelling of the walls was invented. This is the fan vault, the essence of which is the application of decorative cusped panels to solid semi-cones. These panels are inspired by those in Perpendicular window tracery and are divided by

mouldings which resemble, but are not, ribs. The fan vault represents the last phase in the English preoccupation with decorative vaulting patterns. Weighty ornamental vaults of this kind had been facilitated structurally by the retention in England of the thick-wall technique which provided a supporting mass of adequate solidity. The first use of the fan vault is not known, though the east walk of the cloister at Gloucester, vaulted between 1331 and 1357, is frequently cited.

The style of Gloucester made an impact at York where, though the presbytery and choir were built from the 1360s to 1400 in a style similar to that of the Rayonnant nave, they were adorned with blind arcading and culminated in a vast east window obviously inspired by Gloucester. Screens of free-standing mullions descend in front of several windows, both inside and out, in the eastern limb of York as they do at Strasbourg and Ulm (p. 189). The naves of Canterbury, built in 1379–1405 perhaps by Henry Yevele, and of Winchester, built in 1394–1450 by William Wynford, both royal master-masons, are sweeping and confident statements of the new Perpendicular style, though both still have lierne vaults. A transitional stage is reached with the chancel vault of c.1430–59 at Sherborne Abbey, Dorset, which, though technically a lierne vault, is given the appearance of a fan vault. The largest of its kind so far erected, this may have fired the imagination of the designers of the high vaults at Bath Abbey, the brothers Robert and William Vertue, and of those of the royal chapels at King's College, Cambridge, and Westminster Abbey.

King's College and its chapel were founded by Henry VI in 1441 and St George's Chapel, Windsor, by Edward IV in 1475, but their completion was delayed by the Wars of the Roses and the accompanying dynastic shifts between Yorkists and Lancastrians. Reacting against the extremes of the Decorated style, Henry VI wrote in 1447 that he wanted his chapel to 'proceed in large form, clean and substantial, setting apart superfluity of too great curious works of entail [carving] and busy

259 The north wall of the choir interior at Gloucester cathedral (c.1337–c.1350)

260 The vaulting of Henry VII's chapel at Westminster Abbey (1503–12)

himself in which Mass would be said for the repose of his soul long after his death, and as a shrine for Henry VI who he hoped would be canonized. It was a religious and political monument in which Henry VII attempted to demonstrate with the utmost magnificence the power and legitimacy of the Tudor dynasty. Though its design is often attributed to the Vertue brothers, who were subsequently architects to Henry VIII, it is more probably by Robert Janyns the younger, one of the royal master-masons. The lavishly ornamented vault of Henry VII's Chapel is embellished with pendants, a form initiated at the Divinity School in Oxford designed by William Orchard in 1479. The enormous pendants take the form of fan cones carried by transverse arches whose crowns disappear behind the vault. The frilly cusped edges of these transverse arches, like the sumptuous ornament of the chapel as a whole, recall the Flamboyant Gothic of France and Spain. The weight is also carried by octagonal turrets, ornamented externally with horizontal panelling and merging with the trefoil-plan oriel windows in a continuous rippling flow of stone and glass. In the centre of the chapel stands the sumptuous tomb of Henry VII and his wife, Elizabeth of York, carved in 1512–18 by the Florentine sculptor Pietro Torrigiano as one of the earliest pieces of Renaissance design in England.

Parish churches and secular architecture

The buildings we have looked at so far were commissioned by kings, bishops and abbots. We should look finally at parish churches and secular buildings, many of which were commissioned by an increasingly prosperous merchant class and, especially in the case of town churches, by the religious guilds of laymen which grew in popularity during the fourteenth and fifteenth centuries. Stone vaulting was generally too expensive for modest parish churches, where a tradition of timber roofs came to a climax in the Perpendicular period with

moulding'. The chapel was originally planned with complex lierne vaults, but eventually a magnificent fan vault was constructed from designs by John Wastell in 1508–15. The great weight of delicately patterned stone seems to rest on nothing more substantial than walls of glass, for the chapel is in a line which goes back to the Sainte-Chapelle. In fact that weight is carried by enormous external buttresses whose projection is concealed by the side chapels inserted between them. 'Tax not the royal saint with vain expense', urged the poet Wordsworth in his celebrated sonnet on the chapel, in words which remind us that decorative fan vaults on such a scale were costly and extravagant toys which only royal wealth could support.

Even more sumptuous is Henry VII's Chapel, built in 1503–c.1512 on the site of the former Lady Chapel of 1220 at the east end of Westminster Abbey. Henry VII, the first Tudor king, intended it as a chantry chapel for

261 *Opposite* King's College chapel, Cambridge, showing the fan vaulting of 1508–15 and the organ screen of the 1530s

262 Westminster Hall in the Palace of Westminster (1390s), showing the hammer-beam roof

263 Harlech Castle, Gwynnedd (1283–90)

the hammer-beam roofs of churches such as Needham Market and Wymondham, in East Anglia. The earliest recorded hammer-beam roof, that is one in which the arches and braces are supported by horizontal brackets projecting from the walls, is in the mid-fourteenth-century Pilgrims' Hall at Winchester. The form was made respectable for ambitious structures in a royal building, Westminster Hall, where a hammer-beam roof was constructed in the 1390s by the king's master-carpenter, Hugh Herland, at a time when the hall was being rebuilt by Henry Yevele.

The great tower, often added at the crossing of a cathedral or abbey church, was especially influential on parish churches. An early example was that at Lincoln cathedral of 1307–11, followed in the fourteenth century by those at Hereford, Lichfield, Norwich and Salisbury cathedrals. This tradition reached a climax with the magnificent Perpendicular towers at Beverley, Canterbury, Durham, Worcester and York. The county of Somerset, made prosperous through wool like the Cotswolds and East Anglia, can boast an astonishing number of parish-church towers, of which that at St Cuthbert's, Wells, in the shadow of the cathedral, is amongst the most prominent.

We may begin the story of secular architecture in the Gothic period with the Welsh castles erected in the late thirteenth century by Edward I to seal his conquest of Wales. A strong aesthetic desire for symmetry shaped castles such as Harlech, where a concentric form inspired by French and Italian precedent (see pp. 165 and 199) is centred on the English feature of a keep-gatehouse. Symmetry is again the keynote of the never-completed grid-plan town of New Winchelsea, Sussex, laid out under Edward I in 1283 partly as a settlement for wine merchants trading with Gascony. In the same year Edward's chancellor, Bishop Burnell of Wells, began to build himself a large country house at Acton Burnell, Shropshire.

A dignified rectangular block with well-ordered fenestration and a square tower at each corner, Acton Burnell is one of the earliest surviving domestic buildings in the country, composed with the aesthetic intention of achieving visual harmony. It contrasts with the random agglomerative grouping of Stokesay Castle, Shropshire, begun only a few years before. The way in which the different functions of the various parts of a building like Stokesay are expressed in its asymmetrical exterior remained the norm for smaller manor-houses during the Middle Ages. A similar architectural disposition was adopted in France, as we have seen in the house of Jacques Coeur at Bourges. It was not until the impact of the Renaissance was felt that there was any major return to the symmetry of Harlech.

The principal apartment of houses such as Acton Burnell, as it was of all castles, palaces and colleges, was the hall, where meals were taken in common by the

264 Stokesay Castle, Shropshire: tower, solar with external staircase, and hall (c.1270–91)

265 The Great Hall of Penshurst Place, Kent (c.1341)

entire household. One of the best preserved is that at Penshurst, Kent, built in c.1341 by John Poultney, Lord Mayor of London, and one of the largest, 90 by 45 feet (27 × 14m) but now ruined, is that added to Kenilworth Castle in the 1390s by John of Gaunt, father of Henry IV. During the course of the fifteenth century the high table was often moved, in the interests of comfort and privacy, from the hall to a room known as the great chamber or solar, frequently situated on the first floor at the dais end of the hall.

The passion for towers, initially with a military function, coloured much fifteenth-century architecture when their justification was beginning to be largely aesthetic: for example, such brick-built and only partially defensive towers as Caister Castle, Norfolk, the first to be built of this material; Tattershall Castle, Lincolnshire, built for Henry VI's Lord Treasurer; and Buckden Palace, Huntingdonshire, a seat of the bishops of Lincoln. This tradition echoed the gigantic gatehouses erected by monasteries such as Thornton Abbey, Lincolnshire, in c.1382 and St Osyth's Priory, Essex, about a century later. It reached a climax in the lordly turreted gatehouses of the early sixteenth century which form the grandiose state entrances to Tudor palaces and colleges like Hampton Court and St John's and Christ's Colleges at Cambridge.

Oxford and Cambridge colleges

The colleges of Oxford and Cambridge are a unique treasury of English medieval architecture, housing to this day a corporate way of life with many echoes of the organization of medieval monasteries and manor-houses. The architectural pattern which had been growing in a haphazard way for a century was crystallized by William of Wykeham, Chancellor of England, who founded New College, Oxford, in 1379. Like Abbot Suger, another great architectural patron, he was a self-willed and largely self-made man. His architect William Wynford laid out a quadrangle in the 1380s which united in one handsome architectural composition hall, chapel, library, warden's lodgings and accommodation for Fellows and undergraduates. At Cambridge the concept of the college as a planned coherent entity was given sophisticated expression at Queens' College in the 1440s, probably designed by Reginald Ely, the first architect of King's College chapel. The planning of colleges is not monastic in inspiration, though several of them were founded by monks, but is closer to that of fourteenth- and fifteenth-century manor-houses. For example, Haddon Hall, Derbyshire, is built like Queens' College round two courtyards with a hall in the linking range, though its rambling picturesque grouping is far from the ordered restraint of the college. We might rather compare Queens' with the contemporary Herstmonceux Castle, Sussex, a largely symmetrical red brick building which originally contained a series of rectangular courtyards, one of them surrounded by a covered walk as in the second court of Queens'. Something of this formal grandeur would have been achieved at King's College, Cambridge, if any more of Reginal Ely's plan had been built than the chapel which forms the north side of the proposed main court. We have touched on that chapel in another context. Suffice to add here that its great carved wooden organ screen of the 1530s, and much of its Flemish-designed glass of 1515–17 and 1526–7, are already in the style of the Renaissance. Like Henry VII's tomb in his chapel at Westminster Abbey, these Renaissance masterpieces were carried out for Henry VIII who, in bringing about the Reformation in England, was to sever its art from the Roman Catholic church and from the European culture to which it had given birth. When we next look at England in this book it is a country which has been unhappily isolated from the sources of Renaissance design in Italy.

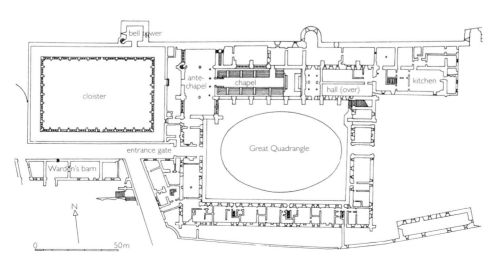

266 Plan of New College, Oxford (1380s), designed by William Wynford

bell tower

cloister

ante-chapel

chapel

hall (over)

kitchen

entrance gate

Great Quadrangle

Warden's barn

N

0   50m

Germany and Central Europe, Belgium, Italy, Spain, Portugal

The countries we shall now examine adopted Gothic later than France or England so that their most important monuments tend to be in a Late Gothic style. This has been much less studied than earlier Gothic because of the nineteenth-century belief that a late style must be more decadent than an early one, and because its profuse ornament has offended the twentieth-century aesthetic conscience. However, it is part of our present aim to establish it as one of the greatest moments in western architecture by investigating the work of leading architectural personalities such as Peter Parler, Benedikt Ried, Juan Guas, Simon de Colónia, Diogo Boytac and Diogo Arruda.

Cologne, Prague and the Parler dynasty

The territories of the Holy Roman Empire, especially its western regions along the Rhine basin, were initially resistant to the Gothic style which they rightly saw as a French invention. Buildings such as the choir of 1208 at Magdeburg cathedral in present-day East Germany, with its polygonal apse and ambulatory, and the collegiate church of St George at Limburg on the Lahn, Germany (1211–c.1235), which combines a rib-vaulted Gothic interior with an ambitious Late Romanesque exterior, are still Transitional in style. It was not until the 1230s that resistance to French forms was generally overcome. Thus in German-speaking territories the most interesting and, as we shall see, exciting churches are those in later rather than earlier Gothic styles, a rather different position from that prevailing in France. The key buildings in the earliest Gothic style, both begun in the 1230s, are the churches of St Elizabeth at Marburg on the Lahn, Hesse (begun 1236), and of the Virgin at Trier. The former is a hall church with bar tracery derived from Reims and an east end with a trefoiled plan, treated here in Gothic terms inspired by the east end of Noyon. The graceful church at Trier takes this centralized planning even further so as to produce a multi-apsed polygonal church of considerable originality.

If Reims lay behind many of the details of Marburg and Trier, Amiens was the principal source of inspiration for the architect Gerhard, who began designing Cologne cathedral in 1248, following the destruction by fire of the Carolingian cathedral earlier that year. Work proceeded slowly, so that the architects were able to incorporate the increasingly sophisticated streamlining effects introduced at Amiens by its third architect, Regnaut de Cormont, from the 1250s. The result was that by the time of the consecration of Cologne in 1322, the choir, with vaults soaring more than 141 feet (43m) high, rivalled Beauvais as the apotheosis of High Gothic aspirations. At Cologne, as at Beauvais, Gothic ambitions proved too great to be fully achieved, and only the choir was built in the Middle Ages. The successful completion of Cologne cathedral in the nineteenth century, according to the rediscovered original designs, was a remarkable product of the romantic nationalism of the day.

Less dependent on French sources was the Dominican church at Regensburg, Bavaria, built during the second half of the thirteenth century. While reflecting the High Gothic love of height and slenderness and of uniting nave and chancel in a single uninterrupted vessel, the church is also economical in spirit with a two-storeyed elevation in which the vast wall-space between the arcade and the clerestorey windows is left blank. This represented a type which became increasingly popular with the mendicant orders: a plain preaching hall with none of the diagonality inherent in fully-developed Gothic, but with a taut spirituality derived from the long high choirs lit with immensely tall lancets.

As in Italy and France the mendicant orders were also especially associated from the thirteenth century with this type, the hall church. In Germany this tradition was given early and sophisticated expression in the parish church of the Holy Cross at Schwäbisch-Gmünd,

267 *Above* The choir vaulting of the church of the Holy Cross, Schwäbisch-Gmünd (1351)

268 *Left* The interior of the choir of Cologne cathedral (1248–1322)

Swabia, begun in 1320. The simple round piers of the nave, expressive of mendicant simplicity as opposed to cathedral splendour, were continued in the choir which was begun in 1351 on the hall-church pattern, probably from designs by Heinrich Parler (born c.1290). Parler introduced new complexities in the decorative articulation of both the exterior and interior of the choir. These include the pronounced cornice above the arcade which bends forward in a triangular formation where it crosses over the wall shafts; and the rich tracery with its odd curves and semi-circles which brings what in England would be known as 'Geometrical' to the verge of Curvilinear.

At Soest in Westphalia are two hall churches, both in process of construction in c.1330, the Franciscan church and the Wiesenkirche, of which the latter is one of the most beautiful of its kind. Its virtually square plan with no distinction between nave and choir creates a remarkably balanced space. This sense of total unity is emphasized by the abolition of the clerestorey and triforium so that the arcade, which reaches colossal height in some churches, rises without interruption to the vaults. An accompanying refinement turns the slender piers of the arcade at the Wiesenkirche into bundles of delicately moulded shafts which themselves become the ribs of the vault, uninterrupted by capitals of any kind. This flowing linear device, more than hinted at in the chancel at Bristol of 1298, becomes a hallmark of Germanic late Gothic architecture.

This late style is especially associated with the Parler dynasty of master-masons, who worked in South Germany, mainly in Swabia, and in Bohemia, mainly in Prague, making professional marriages through several generations. We have already seen the inventive freedom

269 The east end of Prague cathedral, showing the pinnacled buttresses (designed 1344)

270 Prague cathedral: the interior of the sacristy with its hanging vaults by Peter Parler (1356–62)

and the interest in diagonality which Heinrich Parler or his son Peter demonstrated in the choir at Schwäbisch-Gmünd. In 1356 the Emperor Charles IV called Peter Parler (1333–1399) to Prague to continue work on the cathedral. Charles IV, an admirer of France, made Prague the capital of the empire and determined that it should be the greatest city in northern Europe. He established an archbishopric, a cathedral in 1344, began the New Town and founded the university at Prague in 1348, the first in German- or Slav-speaking lands. He commissioned designs for the new cathedral in 1344 from Matthias of Arras, a French architect who may have worked on Narbonne cathedral and on the Papal Palace at Avignon. Matthias was already using functional elements decoratively in, for example, the pinnacles attached to the buttresses at the east end of Prague cathedral. When Peter Parler took over in 1356, following Matthias's death four years earlier, he interrupted the smooth rhythm of the French-inspired ambulatory with its radiating chapels, by creating a two-bay sacristy on the north side in 1356–62. On the south side he added the large square chapel of St Wenceslas in 1366–7, adorned with semi-precious stones. This, unconventionally, takes in part of the south transept, which he provided with an elaborate projecting porch at the same time. In vaulting all these areas with tiercerons and liernes and in eliminating capitals on the shafts, Parler displayed an imaginative inventiveness which can only be paralleled in some English Decorated work of about half a century earlier. Indeed, the bizarre flying ribs of the sacristy and porch may be directly inspired by those in the Berkeley Chapel at Bristol and the Easter Sepulchre at Lincoln cathedral.

In the upper storeys of Parler's choir at Prague, built in 1374–85, curious emphasis on diagonality is contrived by bringing forward at a canted angle the ends of the glazed triforium in each bay. This undulating rhythm is echoed in the clerestorey windows, which also have obliquely set tabernacle niches with cusped ogee heads in each bay. Similarly placed niches had appeared in the choirs at Wells and at Selby in Yorkshire, while the flowing

271 *Above* Marienburg (Malbork) Castle, Danzig

272 *Top right* The interior of the choir at Aachen cathedral (1355–1414)

273 *Bottom right* The roof and tower of Vienna cathedral (tower c.1370–1433)

tracery in the clerestorey windows also recalls English sources. Moreover, the net-vaults, so-called because their ribs form net-like lozenges, are also an English speciality. They are reminiscent of the nave vault at Winchester, though Parler increased the flowing unity by dispensing with the ridge rib and, for the first time in a German-speaking country, by interrupting the transverse arches. It must be assumed that Parler was in touch with a number of English workshops, or that he had either visited England or seen drawings of English buildings.

The ornamental tierceron vaults of England were rarely used in Mediterranean countries but were taken up with enthusiasm in North Germany and along the Baltic coast. At the fortress-palace of Marienburg (now Malbork) near Danzig (Gdańsk), the seat of the Grand Master of the Teutonic Order of Knights which had subdued the pagan Slav population of West Prussia in the thirteenth century, the lower and upper chapels of 1335–44 have elaborate tierceron vaults, while the Grand Master's Refectory of c.1325–50 has a succession of billowing vaults echoing those of English chapter-houses but with Germanic triradial ribs. In 1370 Parler built the church of All Saints on the Hradčany, the great hill with its castle and cathedral which dominates the city of Prague. All Saints is a deliberate echo of the Sainte-Chapelle in Paris. Peter Parler may also have designed the Frauenkirche at Nuremberg, a noble hall church of 1355, and was certainly responsible for the Charles Bridge across the Vltava in Prague, approached through an impressive gate-tower.

The choir which was added between 1355 and 1414 to the cathedral at Aachen, coronation place of the German emperors, is another of the masterpieces commissioned by the Emperor Charles IV. The contrast between the low and solid octagon of the ninth-century Palatine Chapel, where Charles had been crowned in 1349, and the giant aspiring glass cage with which he confronted it is one of the most electric expressions in Europe of the fruitful combination of Gothic dynamism and medieval ideals of Christian kingship. Here pilgrims came to venerate the relics of Charlemagne in Charles IV's sumptuous Gothic shrine, which combined references to the Sainte-Chapelle, Cologne cathedral and to more Germanic churches such as the Wiesenkirche at Soest. Vienna cathedral, too, must be seen in this stylistic context. It has a hall-choir of 1304–40 and a nave and towers begun in 1359, though the net-vault of the nave was built in 1446. Each tower contains a chapel with a vault in which flying ribs terminate in hanging bosses, a lively device borrowed from Peter Parler at Prague. The first of these vaults is dated c.1370 and the splendid south tower can be dated from c.1370–1433. Its dissolution of separate storeys into a lacy interwoven thread of pinnacles, tabernacles, tracery, crockets and gables is a remarkable foretaste of the openwork towers of the Flamboyant Gothic style in France and of Late Gothic in Germany.

German late Gothic

The finest of the towers in the late style (sometimes called *Sondergotik*) are those at Strasbourg and Ulm, and are related to the circle of the four leading German architects working in the thirty-year period from 1390, all of whom were indebted to the school of the Parlers. They are Ulrich von Ensingen, Wentzel Roriczer, Hinrich von Brunsberg and Hans von Burghausen (sometimes wrongly called Stethaimer). All were South Germans except for Brunsberg, who worked in north-

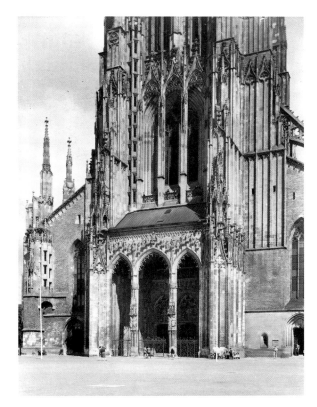

274 The west front of Ulm cathedral (begun in the late 14th century and completed in the 19th)

east Germany. In 1392 Ulrich von Ensingen took over as architect of Ulm, which had been begun by the Parlers. The west porch, completed in 1434, continues the Late Gothic decorative complexity. This high triple porch is at the base of the great tower, which is placed at the centre of the west front in contradiction of High Gothic ideals. The tower was continued after 1419 by Matthäus Ensingen, Ulrich's son, and increasingly smothered with decoration in 1478–92 by Matthäus Böblinger, the execution of whose design was not in fact completed until 1881–90 when the spire became the highest in Europe. The brilliantly designed eastern towers are also wholly nineteenth-century in date.

In 1399 Ulrich von Ensingen continued work on the west front of Strasbourg with its tower inspired, like those at Elm and Esslingen, by that built at Freiburg in 1275–c.1340. Ulrich's successor as architect, Johannes Hültz, heightened the fantasy of the Freiburg tower

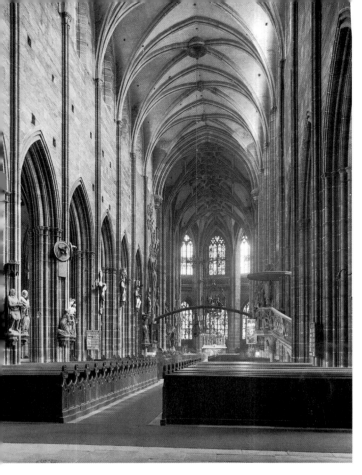

275 The interior of St Lorenz, Nuremberg (begun 1439), designed by Konrad Heinzelmann

276 The west front of Strasbourg cathedral (begun 1277; tower 1399–1419)

during the final building phase from 1419, so that its spire became a kind of transparent Gothic stepped pyramid or Tower of Babel threaded with open spiral staircases. It thus constitutes a prime example of that unifying Late Gothic style which blurs distinctions between exterior and interior. Just as walls now became stone frameworks filled with glass, so at Freiburg and Strasbourg tracery proper to windows has been applied to the construction of a spire which becomes an open web of filigree work in stone.

In the 1390s Heinrich von Brunsberg adapted the Parler style to brick architecture when he began the churches of St Mary at Stargard in Germanic Prussia and of St Catherine at Brandenburg. Hans von Burghausen built two major brick hall churches at

Landshut, Bavaria, the parish church of St Martin (1387–c.1432) and the Spitalkirche (1407–61), both of which create a unified, almost disembodied interior space with colossally high, slender and widely-spaced piers, uninterrupted by capitals, supporting a floating net-vault where all sense of bay division is abolished. The exaggerated restraint of this architecture of high tension is underlined by the use of brick and the minimal decoration. An especially poetic feature of the choir of the Spitalkirche is the way in which the central pier of the apse, merging into its palm-like vault, is silhouetted behind the high altar against the east window of the ambulatory. This device of blocking the central axis down the church with a pier recurs even more forcefully in Hans von Burghausen's choir at the

Franciscan church at Salzburg, begun in 1408, where again, by dissolving the finite east end, it has the effect of making the church fade away in a blur of light and shade, solid and void.

The grace and harmony of the Landshut churches influenced a generation of architects who produced a series of similar masterpieces, including Konrad Heinzelmann (c.1390–1454), Nicolaus Eseler (c.1400–92), and Jörg Ganghofer (d.1488). Among the finest are St George, Nördlingen (begun 1427), and the choir of St Lorenz, Nuremberg (begun 1439), both worked on by Heinzelmann; St George, Dinkelsbühl (1448–92), by Eseler; and the Frauenkirche at Munich (1468–88), by Ganghofer. St Lorenz is an unforgettable vision of late-medieval religiosity. The high stone spire of the sacrament house, carved by Adam Kraft in 1493, rises to the complex star vaults in a riot of nodding ogees, vegetal ornament and animated figure sculpture. The same joyous spirit is expressed in the figures of the Annunciation, carved by Veit Stoss (c.1450–1533) and suspended in their festively decorated oval frame in front of the high altar. The architectural tradition represented by these churches was continued on cathedral scale into the sixteenth century in, for example, the choir at Freiburg of 1510–13. Brick hall churches like those in Bavaria by Heinzelmann and Ganghofer were equally characteristic of north and north-eastern Germany, for example those, all now in Poland, at Danzig (Gdańsk), Breslau (Wrocław), Thorn (Toruń) and Stettin (Szczecin). These introduced the folded or diamond vault, which entirely dispenses with ribs so as to produce an effect like crinkled paper. A typical late example is the early-sixteenth-century vault of the Franciscan church at Bechin (Bechyně), Bohemia.

Ried and Bohemia

The tradition of the hall church was combined with a development of the spatial and decorative ingenuity associated with the Parler family, to produce a final flowering of fantasy between 1490 and 1520. This phase of German Gothic is still too little known. The key figure in Central Europe was Benedikt Ried (1454–1534), the German mason who became Master of the King's Works in Bohemia. This complex architecture of growth and interpenetration is characterized by double curved vaults, flying ribs and occasionally the organic device of ribs in the form of tree branches. Flying ribs or skeleton vaults, often silhouetted against a solid rib vault above them, are in a sense the logical climax of Gothic architecture, aesthetically expressing structural forces within the context of a poetic opening up of diagonal vistas. In 1493–1502 Ried created the Vladislav Hall in the upper parts of the old palace of Charles IV in the royal castle on the Hradčany in Prague. The largest secular hall of the late Middle Ages, this was intended to provide space for tournaments. Its amazing vault boasts intertwined double-curved or three-dimensional lierne ribs reaching almost to the floor. Similarly inventive is the vault over the Riders' Staircase with its twisting, asymmetrical, truncated ribs. Another novel aspect of the building is that, despite its Gothic form, it contains Quattrocento Renaissance details of astonishingly early date in the doors and windows.

At Annaberg, Saxony, the church of St Anne (1499–1522) is another startlingly beautiful variant of the net-vaulted hall church. The octagonal piers have

277 The Vladislav Hall, in the Hradčany Castle, Prague (1493–1502) designed by Ried

278 The church of St Barbara, Kuttenberg: the east end (begun 1388)

279 The interior of St Barbara, Kuttenberg, showing rib vaults; begun in 1512 by Ried

hollowed concave sides from which grow twisting intersecting ribs, forming a pattern which is echoed in the whole design of the vault. Annaberg eloquently expresses the desire to abolish separate elements such as wall, pier, shaft, rib and vault cell, in favour of intertwining fragments of all of them into a complex decorative and spatial unity of which the dominant impression is one of mobility in depth. This influenced a number of churches in Bohemia, particularly Benedikt Ried's vault begun in 1512 at St Barbara, Kuttenberg (Kutná Hora), Bohemia.

The church in the prosperous silver-mining town of Kuttenberg was begun in 1388 by Peter Parler, and continued by his son John. In the nave Ried provided twisting undulating ribs which rise uninterruptedly from the piers to form patterns of growth on the vault like the lithe tendrils of young plants in spring. This fresh naturalistic impression is poignantly heightened in the aisles, where descending tiercerons are abruptly terminated in mid-flight near the windows, leaving free-standing severed ends like those a gardener might leave in cutting back unwanted growth. The walls, almost entirely of glass divided by flowing tracery, are fringed externally with a continuous row of flying buttresses supporting the weight of the vault. This astonishing concentration of cusped arches and bristling pinnacles is crowned by the three tent-like roofs of the church which, like the similar ones at Louny, give the building a slightly Chinese flavour or a resemblance to a Turkish encampment.

Secular architecture in Germany and Bohemia

Castles and town halls are among the glories of medieval Germany, but their history has been far less studied than that of churches, for a range of reasons which include the fact that they have been more frequently altered, demolished or allowed to become ruinous. Their chronological relationship to the development of the Gothic style is not always clear, though we have noted the novel vaulting systems pioneered in the castles of Marienburg and Prague, to which we should add the Albrechtsburg at Meissen in Saxony, a castle designed in 1471 by Arnold of Westphalia with every conceivable version of tortured Late Gothic vaulting.

The builders of Marienburg created perhaps the greatest secular building of the Middle Ages, after the contemporary Palace of the Popes at Avignon. The Outer Castle leads to the quadrangular symmetrical Upper Castle of c.1270–c.1309, which is flanked by the three-sided fourteenth-century Middle Castle containing the Grand Master's apartments. The aggressive angularity of the brick exteriors contrasts stylistically with the spacious well-lit interiors with their lyrical rib vaults. The same is true of the combined cathedral and castle erected under the auspices of the Teutonic Order at Marienwerder (Kwidzyn) during the fourteenth century, about 25 miles inland along the Vistula. From the west end of the cloister a 200-foot-long (61m) passage leads to an immensely high gabled 'Dansker' tower, one of the immensely extravagant latrine towers with which the Order advertised its concern for hygiene.

Breslau (now Wrocław), nowadays in Poland but belonging to Bohemia from 1335, Austria from 1526 and Prussia from 1741, boasts an exceptionally ostentatious town hall exhibiting sophisticated Gothic work of all periods from the thirteenth to the sixteenth centuries. The local Silesian brick was here faced extravagantly with sandstone brought from the Bohemian border. Brick, sometimes glazed and coloured, was considered sufficient for the imposing

280 The cathedral and castle of the Teutonic Order at Marienwerder (Kwidzyn), Poland: the latrine tower (14th century)

town halls of flourishing trading towns on the Baltic such as Lübeck and Stralsund. Bremen and Brunswick are two other cities belonging to the Hanseatic League which was founded in the thirteenth century to protect foreign trading interests in north Germany. Both were severely damaged in the Second World War, but the great curved market place at Bremen, where the cathedral faces the sumptuous town hall begun in brick in 1405, has been sufficiently restored to serve as one of the most eloquent reminders in Europe of the cultural and commercial richness of the late Middle Ages. A similar pattern existed in the old market-place at Brunswick (Braunschweig), where St Martin's church was confronted by the equally magnificent town hall. This L-shaped building boasted two open arcades, filled with elaborate tracery, which were constructed in 1393 and 1447 respectively so as to form two sides of the market-place. Commodious urban life, providing security and prosperity far from the castle or the cloister, was here given early and convincing expression.

Belgium

Belgium, or the southern Netherlands, which was part of the diocese of Cologne in the Middle Ages, was certainly rich in ecclesiastical architecture from the

281 The Town Hall at Louvain (1448)

thirteenth century – for example the east end of Tournai cathedral, St Gudule, Brussels, and Hertogenbosch – to the great Flamboyant churches of the fifteenth century such as Notre-Dame at Antwerp, St Rombaut at Malines, St Jacques at Liège, and St Peter at Louvain. However, it is the secular architecture, the guild-halls and town halls of her prosperous commercial cities, which make Belgium unique. Their splendour often exceeds that of contemporary ecclesiastical foundations, while their decorative language was not without influence on churches such as Antwerp cathedral.

The classic type was established in the town hall of Aalst of c. 1225, with its four corner towers and long façade pierced with uninterrupted horizontal bands of windows. This was echoed in the thirteenth-century Cloth Hall at Bruges, now dominated by the immense octagonal belfry added in the fifteenth century; and in the Cloth Hall at Ypres (fig. 223), begun in 1304 as the largest in Europe with a 49-bay front, 440 feet (134m) long. The town halls at Bruges and Brussels of the late fourteenth to mid-fifteenth centuries develop the type

by articulating the façades with rich Late Gothic decoration. Similar splendour governs the town halls at Mons (1458) and Ghent (1518), but the most ambitious of all are the towering shrine-like Louvain (1448) and the sumptuous Oudenaarde (1526–36), a final defiant Gothic statement by the merchants of the north against the new Renaissance style of the south.

Early Gothic in Italy

Like Germany, Italy took late to the Gothic style, but in the strongly classical soil of Italian culture it could not set down such strong roots as it did further north, so that Italy is far less important than Germany in the history of Gothic ecclesiastical architecture. Moreover the fifteenth century, which was such a productive period for Gothic in Germany and Spain, was in Italy dominated by the return to classicism known as the Renaissance. However, the separate city states of Italy between the thirteenth and the fifteenth centuries sought to emphasize their identity with secular buildings which, though Gothic, lacked the aspiring verticality of the northern cathedrals.

The first important Gothic buildings in Italy, after the early French-inspired attempts of the Cistercians at Fossanova and Casamari, are the two Franciscan churches of S. Francesco at Assisi of 1228–39, and of S. Francesco at Bologna of 1236–50. St Francis of Assisi (c.1181–1226), a preacher but not a priest, founded a new religious order which called for a renewal of faith by a return to Christian poverty. His example was echoed at the same time by the Spanish St Dominic (1170–1221), who founded the Dominican order with a view to suppressing heresy. The concern of these two new mendicant orders of preachers for the moral and spiritual welfare of the laity, as opposed to that of the clergy, whether monks or secular priests, had enormous influence throughout the parishes and universities of Europe. As we have already seen on p. 162, they were particularly associated with the hall church as a convenient setting for sermons. The emphasis on plain wall surfaces in their church at Assisi is a measure of the debt to the antique Roman and Romanesque stress on the mass of the wall, but it was also found to provide suitable surfaces for the frescoes depicting the lives of the saints which adorn the walls of so many Italian churches. The upper church at Assisi was frescoed by the leading Gothic painter Cimabue (active 1272–1302). The hymns and sermons of St Francis and his followers not only influenced the subject-matter of Italian painting, but may also be said to have given birth to Italian vernacular literature, which produced an early flowering in the writings of Dante (1251–1321).

Built on a sloping site with a substantial crypt forming a lower church, S. Francesco at Assisi is a simple aisleless Latin cross with none of the complexity of detail or aspiring verticality of French Gothic. S. Francesco at Bologna, though still with a largely Romanesque façade, has an interior which shows more understanding of Gothic with its aisled basilican plan, ambulatory with radiating chapels, and flying buttresses. Its simplicity and clarity, which seem related to its materials, local red brick mainly plastered internally, set a pattern for churches in Bologna for nearly two centuries. More significant was the leading Dominican church in Florence, Sta Maria Novella, begun in 1279, which is lighter, airier and more aspiringly Gothic than S. Francesco, though at the same time it is fully open to the aisles through broad arcades. S. Croce, the rival Franciscan church in Florence, was designed in 1294 by Arnolfo di Cambio (c.1245–c.1310), who had originally been trained as a sculptor. Like Sta Maria Novella, it is another monument of transparent clarity, yet retains the flat open-trussed wooden roof of Early Christian and Romanesque Italy.

The Gothic cathedrals of Siena, Orvieto and Florence show in different ways a similarly hesitant acceptance of

282 *Top right* The upper church of S. Francesco at Assisi (1228–39), with later frescoes by Cimabue

283 *Bottom right* Plans of the upper and lower churches, St Francesco, Assisi

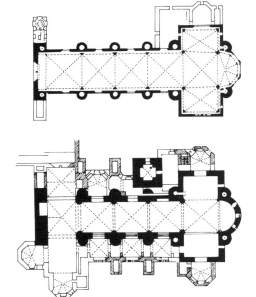

the Gothic style. At Siena cathedral, begun in the mid-thirteenth century and continued in the same style for a century and a half, the numerous Gothic elements are cancelled out by Romanesque features such as the domed crossing tower and, above all, by the insistent horizontal banding in polychrome marble which, according to one art historian, makes one feel 'as if one were in the belly of a gigantic zebra'. The most Gothic feature is the richly decorated screen façade at the west end, of which the lower parts were designed and partly carved by the sculptor Giovanni Pisano in 1284–c.1320. It influenced the sumptuous west front of Orvieto cathedral, begun in 1310 from designs by the Sienese architect Lorenzo Maitani. This neatly articulated Gothic façade is treated like a giant reredos as a background for a polychromatic display of sculptured reliefs, figures in marble and bronze, and mosaics.

Florence and Milan cathedrals

Florence cathedral, designed in 1296 by Arnolfo di Cambio, has the same calm spaciousness as Sta Maria Novella, with nave and aisles tending to be read together as a single broad vessel. Work proceeded slowly and attention was transferred to the adjacent campanile, designed in 1334 by the painter Giotto. Continued after his death in 1337 by Andrea Pisani and completed to a variant design by Francesco Talenti in the 1350s, the fine campanile, square in plan and ornamented in marble with a rectilinear panelled veneer, is rooted in a Florentine Romanesque tradition which owes little to Gothic. It picks up its style from the nearby Baptistery (c.1060–1150), then thought to be a converted Roman temple.

Talenti went on to continue work on the cathedral, where Arnolfo's design was modified in 1357–68 by an astonishing number of committees of painters, sculptors and goldsmiths, including Taddeo Gaddi and Andrea Orcagna. Debate of this kind indicates the increasing attention which was paid to the views of artists, especially in the Renaissance, and the decreasing significance of the full-time master-masons who had

284 *Above* The west front of Orvieto cathedral (begun 1310), designed by Maitani

285 *Opposite* Florence cathedral: the exterior of the east end, original design of 1296 by Arnolfo di Cambio; revised 1366; dome by Brunelleschi (see Chapter 6)

been trained in the lodges of medieval Europe. It is also a sign of the seriousness with which Florence cathedral was regarded as a civic symbol. It was essentially a public monument financed by a subsidy from the city treasury and by a tax on all male inhabitants. By an ordinance of 1339 the levels of the surrounding streets were lowered so as to allow the height of the rising new building to have the full visual impact.

The scheme of 1366 for the cathedral which was adopted in 1368 provided for a giant dome, as wide as the nave and aisles together, on an octagonal base open to three apses. The idea for this went back to Arnolfo, but neither in his time nor in the 1360s could anyone have had any idea how to construct what would have been the largest dome and cupola since antiquity. It is often supposed that new materials and constructional techniques lead to the development of new styles. However, the aesthetic impulse for a new kind of architecture often, as in Florence, precedes the necessary techniques. It was thus not until the fifteenth century that, thanks to the genius of Brunelleschi, the dome of Florence cathedral could be erected.

The mendicant orders in Venice in the fourteenth century produced two large red-brick churches, both begun in the 1330s, which derive ultimately from S. Francesco at Bologna: the Dominican SS. Giovanni e Paolo, and the Franciscan Sta Maria Gloriosa dei Frari. In both churches the prominent use of tie beams across the nave and aisles is an indication of Italian lack of interest in the system of abutment involving flying buttresses which made French Gothic possible. However, at Milan at the end of the fourteenth century a serious, if unsuccessful, attempt was made to produce a building in conformity with French practice. At Milan the kind of debate which had raged at Florence was repeated, though here on an international basis, following the acceptance of an initial plan for a cathedral in 1387. To assist them in the construction of a vast basilican double-aisled cathedral, inspired by Bourges and Le Mans though with the broader proportions favoured in Italy, the Milanese called on the assistance between 1387 and 1401 of several architects from Campione and Bologna; Nicolas de Bonaventure and Jean Mignot from Paris; Johann von Freiburg and Hans Parler from Germany; and a mathematician, Gabriele Stornaloco, from Piacenza. The fascinating debates at Milan remind us that since no one in the Middle Ages, not even the French, could fully understand or predict the structural forces involved in their buildings, the choice between one geometrical system and another was dictated by aesthetic choice or traditional practice.

286 The nave of Milan cathedral (begun 1387)

The interior has an overwhelming grandeur to which the piers, with their strange tabernacled capitals containing statues, contribute an almost antique resonance, since they are somehow reminiscent of the figured columns of the Temple of Artemis at Ephesus (p. 32). This rich solemnity is underlined by the pink marble with which the exterior and interior is faced. Work was carried on almost continuously until its completion in 1858. The pinnacled luxuriance of the exterior is a Late Gothic fantasy without equal in Italy.

Italian secular architecture

Italy was richer than other parts of Europe in the Middle Ages in secular buildings in an urban context. In towns such as Siena, Florence and Venice, these have survived to a remarkable degree. This tremendous building activity was related to the increasing prosperity associated with Italy's emergence as the banking centre of Europe, and to the growing sense of civic identity which was heightened by the endless warring of the factions in the struggles for internal and external power. Both the climate and increasing confidence encouraged a fondness for buildings opened to the outside world through ground-floor loggias and large upper windows, balconies and outside staircases. The first floor often contained a large hall suitable for fresco painting. From the second half of the thirteenth century we find imposing civic buildings associated with the newly created office of the Capitano del Popolo, a body representing the guilds and the bourgeoisie: for example the Palazzo del Capitano del Popolo at Orvieto, the Palazzo Comunale at Piacenza, the Palazzo dei Priori at Perugia, and the more fortress-like Palazzo del Capitano (Bargello) at Florence. At Todi a single square contains the thirteenth-century cathedral and three civic buildings including the Palazzo del Capitano, begun in the 1290s, and the adjacent Palazzo del Popolo (1213–67).

The creation during the fourteenth century of the celebrated fan-shaped square at Siena, the Campo, marks the beginning of coherent town planning along aesthetic lines, perhaps for the first time since antiquity. Established by municipal ordinances of 1298 which governed the size and style of houses, the Campo is dominated by the Palazzo Pubblico (1298–1348), over which soars the Torre della Mangia, tallest of all the municipal towers in Italy. Inside this magnificent seat of local government is a complex network of council chambers, offices and living quarters, many frescoed by the leading artists of the day, including Simone Martini, Ambrogio Lorenzetti and Spinello Aretino. The corresponding municipal building in Florence, the monumental Palazzo della Signoria or Palazzo Vecchio (1299–1310), probably designed by Arnolfo di Cambio, has not yet made the leap forward from fortress to palace. Harmonious, almost classical restraint is the keynote of much fourteenth-century Florentine architecture, as can be seen in private palaces such as Palazzo Davanzati (c.1350) and in the Loggia della Signoria, built in the late 1370s from designs by Simone Talenti and Benci di Cione. Standing next to the Palazzo Vecchio in the Piazza della Signoria, this loggia approaches Renaissance ideals in the forms of its round arches and horizontal skyline as well as in its visual and

287 Aerial view of Siena showing the fan-shaped Campo and the Palazzo Pubblico (first half of 14th century)

288 Plan of the Campo at Siena

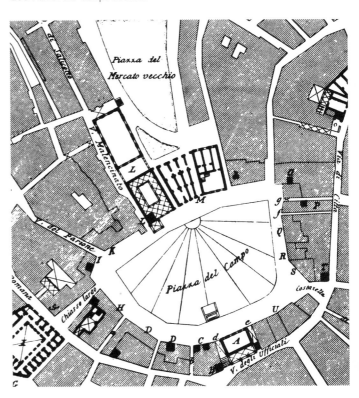

functional contribution to the amenities of a public square.

Castle building reached a peak of architectural sophistication in the 1230s and 1240s in southern Italy with the castles of the Holy Roman Emperor, Frederick

289 *Above* Venice: the Piazzetta with the Doges' Palace (façade of 1420s) and S. Marco in the background

290 *Left* The Ca' d'Oro in Venice (1421–40)

II of Hohenstaufen (1212–50), for example at Castel del Monte, and Castel Ursino in Sicily. The regularity of the octagonal Castel del Monte combines French Gothic with antique Roman details in a way that is unique in Europe at that moment and that undoubtedly reflects Frederick's own taste for the classical. While in Tuscany the republican city-states took over the functions of the castle, in northern parts of Italy, especially Lombardy, we find elaborate castles built well into the fourteenth century. The castle strung out along the shore at Sirmione on Lake Garda, built around 1300 by the Scaliger family, recalls the contemporary Caernarvon Castle in Wales, which also relied for protection on massive curtain walls rather than on a keep. The castle of Fenis, built in c.1340 in the Val d'Aosta with a pentagonal plan, combines defensible towers with the comfortable living quarters which were required.

The most attractive Italian contributions to late-medieval domestic architecture are those in the glorious city of Venice. In the fifteenth century the Most Serene

Republic was at the height of her prosperity, especially following the fall of the Byzantine Empire in 1453 when she took over responsibility for the eastern Mediterranean. The Doges' Palace, besides containing the apartments of the Doge (Duke), houses council chambers, law courts, prisons and the colossal Sala del Maggior Consiglio, seat of the elected lower house of the Venetian parliament. The palace has a mid-fourteenth-century core but was given its present character in the 1420s, with the graceful double colonnade occupying the ground and first floors and the contrastingly static upper storeys hung with pink and white marble patterned like a silk damask cloth. The latticework tracery may have an Islamic feel, but the opening of the façade through arcades was a long-established Venetian tradition which reached a climax in the fifteenth century in numerous Late Gothic palaces such as the Pisani-Moretta, Foscari and Sanudo, of which the earliest is the most striking, the Ca' d' Oro (House of Gold), built in 1421–40 for Marco Contarini, Procurator of S. Marco. It derived its name from the fact that its lacy web of ogee tracery and rich carving was originally brightly painted in red and blue and gilded. Further animated by the dappled reflections of the constantly moving waters of the Grand Canal, it encapsulated the glittering luxury which late-medieval man was willing and able to apply to his private habitation.

Gothic in Spain in the thirteenth and fourteenth centuries

Spain is far richer in Gothic ecclesiastical architecture than Italy though, for a range of cultural and political reasons, it has been far less visited by modern travellers. Although most of the Iberian peninsula had been liberated from Muslim occupation by 1150, the following century saw the capture from the Moors of the key cities, Córdoba in 1236, Murcia in 1241 and Seville in 1248. So from the earlier thirteenth century the Christian kingdoms, above all Aragon and Castile, were ready to launch a building programme intended to rival that of France.

Inspiration from early French cathedral Gothic appeared hesitantly around the year 1200 in aspects of the plans and elevations of the cathedrals of Ávila, Tarragona, Cuenca and Lérida. However, Spanish Gothic, or rather French Gothic in Spain, really begins in the 1220s with the two great cathedrals of Burgos and Toledo. These echo the broad spread of Bourges, but the cathedral of León, apparently begun in the mid-1250s, is a very different essay in the most up-to-date Rayonnant style, incorporating features such as the linked clerestorey and triforium, the latter glazed in its outer plane. León survives in something like its original form with much early glass, predominantly green, yellow and purple in hue unlike the reds and blues of France. The original lines of Burgos and Toledo, on the other hand, have been smothered over the centuries by additional chapels and sacristies, in a process of accumulation which is also reflected in the elaborate screens and other fittings which have silted up their interiors down the centuries. All this is part of the rich cultural deposit which gives Spanish architecture its characteristically heady flavour.

The province of Catalonia, which belonged to the kingdom of Aragon, and the island of Mallorca, which was a short-lived kingdom from 1262 until it was absorbed by Aragon in 1393, developed a recognizable architectural form in opposition to the Rayonnant style. In fact it was part of a widespread Mediterranean type especially associated with the single-nave churches of the mendicant orders flanked by chapels inserted between abutments. This type, of which Albi is the classic example, is represented by the superb cathedrals at Barcelona, begun in 1298, Palma de Mallorca, begun in 1306, and Gerona, begun in 1312. The staggering scale of Palma cathedral and the unique drama of its sea-front setting make it one of the most memorable buildings of Gothic Europe. The forest of piers, abutments and flying buttresses which form its lateral façades is an uncompromising display of engineering which supports the audacious interior, with vaults higher than Amiens and a nave approaching twice the width of York, the

291 *Above* The south façade of the cathedral at Palma de Mallorca (begun 1306), from the south-east

292 *Right* The interior of Seville cathedral (begun 1401)

widest nave in England. The French chevet and triforium of Barcelona have been abolished so that nothing interrupts the luminous spatial flow. Light floods in from all sides and especially from the vast rose window set high in the east wall of the nave. The great mesh formed by its intersecting tracery of equilateral triangles recalls the ornament of Moorish buildings in Spain.

The size of Palma cathedral was eclipsed by that begun at Seville in 1401, which was to cover the largest area of any in Europe. A vast parallelogram of five aisles with the Catalan feature of side chapels between the internal buttresses, it seems to echo the square mosques of Islam. Indeed, it replaces a mosque of which all that was allowed to survive was the late-twelfth-century tower, known as La Giralda after it was heightened in 1568. The Late Gothic nave at Seville lacks a full triforium so that the tremendously high arcades soar up to meet the Flamboyant balustraded gallery at the base of the clerestorey windows. The simple quadripartite vaulting gives way round the crossing to a Flamboyant pattern of decorative cusped ribs designed by Juan Gil de Hontañón when he added the crossing lantern in 1524–6. Like many Spanish buildings, both Moorish and Christian, Seville is destined to be admired more from inside than out, for the dazzling brilliance of the southern sun does not always make it easy to concentrate on external effect. A favourite Spanish trick is to contrast bare walls with sudden concentrations of encrusted ornament, especially round doors and windows. The external coherence of Seville cathedral was especially compromised by the addition of sumptuous sacristies and a chapter-house in the sixteenth century, when Seville became the chief port of a country enormously enriched by wealth acquired from America.

Juan Guas and the Isabelline style

The unification of Spain following the marriage of Ferdinand of Aragon and Isabella of Castile in 1469; the conquest of Granada, the last stronghold of the Moors, and the discovery of America, both in 1492; and the ascent of Charles I of Spain to the throne of the Holy Roman Empire, as Charles V, in 1519, all gave the country a basis of power and wealth which can rarely have been equalled, on which to build its architectural programmes. The remarkable chain of major cathedrals which were built in the Gothic style until the late sixteenth century is a powerful symbol of the wealth, Catholicism and conservatism of Spain at this time: for example, Astorga (1471–1559); Palencia transept and nave (1440–1516); Salamanca (1512–c.1590) and Segovia (1525–91), both designed by Juan Gil de Hontañón and his son Rodrigo.

Architects and craftsmen from Germany, Flanders and France joined with Spaniards to create a distinctively Spanish Late Gothic style, sometimes known as Isabelline after the queen, albeit with certain Islamic elements derived from the *mudéjar* style indigenous to Toledo. One of the most significant architects was Juan Guas (c.1433–96), who designed the Franciscan monastery church of S. Juan de los Reyes at Toledo

(1477–96). This was commissioned by Ferdinand and Isabella, the Catholic Sovereigns, to commemorate their victory at Toro over the king of Portugal in 1476, and was intended, until the conquest of Granada, to serve as the royal burial-place. The profusion of carved ornament including Flemish fringed arches, nodding ogees, star vaults, Islamic stalactite cornices, ostentatious heraldry in the transepts, balconies opening from the royal apartments in the adjacent monastery, and blank cusped panelling on the exterior containing decoratively hung chains from which Christian prisoners were freed by Ferdinand and Isabella, all make the church a place of compelling strangeness and conspicuous display which is somewhat incongruous in a Franciscan monastery. A feature common in Spanish Gothic but rare elsewhere in Europe is the octagonal *cimborio* or lantern over the crossing tower, supported here by a star vault of double-curved ribs. The ornamental treatment of the building

293 S. Juan de los Reyes, interior (1477–96) by Guas

should be compared with that of the final building phase of King's College Chapel, Cambridge, in 1508–15, under Henry VIII, when large-scale heraldic ornament was added at the west end. Not only is the architectural use of heraldry itself a Spanish characteristic, but at King's identical coats were repeated in adjacent bays exactly as at S. Juan de los Reyes. It should not be forgotten that the successive marriages of Catherine of Aragon in 1501 and 1509 to Henry VII's sons, Prince Arthur and Henry VIII, had brought the upstart Tudor court of England into contact with the greatest world power.

A further example of this exotic court art in which Catholicism is tinged with worldliness is the octagonal Capilla del Condestable at Burgos Cathedral, built in 1482–c.1494 for Pedro Fernández de Velasco, hereditary Constable of Castile. The architect, Simon of Cologne (c.1440–1511) or Simon de Colónia, was the most important Isabelline architect after Juan Guas. In the Capilla del Condestable the intricate cusping of the ogee-headed wall arches, the Flamboyant tracery and the colossal coats of diagonally set arms are somehow united in a symphony of controlled ornament which reaches a triumphant climax in the star vault where the central star formation contains pierced openwork tracery, possibly of Islamic inspiration.

Simon of Cologne was also reponsible for the west front of S. Pablo, Valladolid (c.1495–1505) which, with its repeated ogee arches, influenced Juan Gil de Hontañón at Salamanca cathedral in 1512. We can also safely attribute to Simon and to the sculptor Gil de Siloe the carved heraldic *trascoro* or choir screen of c.1499–1519 at Palencia Cathedral, and the west front of Sta María la Real at Aranda de Duero (c.1506), which resembles a huge stone *retablos* or reredos. The same resemblance is even more marked in the façade at the Dominican College of S. Gregorio at Valladolid (c.1494), the design of which is attributed to Gil de Siloe and Diego de la Cruz.

Encrusted with seaweed-like ornament threatening to engulf the royal coat of arms above the triple ogee arch, this overblown gateway is the prelude to a lavish cloister in which twisted columns support a traceried gallery of *mudéjar* inspiration. More restrained is the Capilla Real (Royal Chapel) at Granada cathedral, built in 1506–21 by Juan Guas's pupil Enrique Egas (died 1534), though not necessarily designed by him. This tomb chapel of the Catholic Sovereigns is entered through an elaborate portal which echoes the Flamboyant ornament of the church and ducal tombs at Brou in Burgundy. Built by a Belgian architect for Margaret of Austria, Brou is often compared with the Isabelline style, though its date of 1513–23 makes it too late to have exercised much influence in Spain.

Secular architecture in Spain

Spain, like Italy, is astonishingly rich in largely undisturbed medieval towns and villages, of which Ávila and Toledo are among the best known. It is much less well provided than Italy or Flanders with medieval civic buildings, except perhaps in fifteenth-century Catalonia and neighbouring Valencia, where the Flamboyant style produced such splendid works as the Parliament House (*Generalidad*) at Barcelona, and the Exchange (*Lonja*) at Palma and at Valencia, both of which boast great halls supported by twisted piers. However, no European

294 The castle and palace of Bellver, near Palma de Mallorca: the circular court (1300–14; designed by Silva)

country can rival Spain in the number and excellent state of preservation of its castles. The most numerous and spectacular of these date from the fifteenth century, but one of the earliest and most unusual is the royal castle-palace of Bellver, crowning a hill on the edge of Palma de Mallorca. This was built for King Jaime of Aragon in 1300–14 from designs by Pere Silva. It is completely circular, with the king's apartments built in the form of a drum round the circumference of the circular open court. This is elegantly surrounded by a two-storeyed arcade with cusped pointed arches in the upper tier. Standing outside and connected by a high bridge is the much smaller keep, also circular, containing the guard-rooms and dungeons. The poetic geometry of Bellver is an echo of Frederick II's octagonal Castel del Monte in southern Italy, but the remarkable attempt at Bellver to solve the problem of separating residential from military quarters was never imitated.

The royal castle of Olite built by Charles the Noble of Navarre in c.1400–19 is a rambling fortified palace like that of the popes at Avignon, but decorated internally by *mudéjar* craftsmen and boasting a roof-garden like the hanging gardens of Babylon, an aviary with a pool, and a lions' den. However, the internecine struggles of fifteenth-century Spain produced a series of fortresses which are works of military engineering without the aesthetic or luxurious elements of Bellver or Olite. Rising from the hot dusty plains, the pristine stone walls of fifteenth-century castles like Montealegre, Torrelobatón or Barco de Ávila are not charming like their ruined English counterparts set in green valleys, but terrifying with their resolutely unornamented round or square towers and their daunting walls almost totally unpierced with windows.

Town houses preserved the Moorish disposition of the patio or courtyard, often with richly decorated arcaded galleries but with façades of great severity. Towards 1500 the façades themselves began to be treated ornamentally, as in the Casa de la Conchas at Salamanca, prettily peppered with carved scallop-shells since it was built for a Knight of the Order of Santiago which had adopted the shell as its emblem. A similar theme recurs in the palace of El Infantado at Guadalajara, built in 1480–3 for the second Duke of Infantada by Juan Guas with the assistance of the decorative carver Egas Cueman (fig. 246). The façade is studded with diamond-shaped bosses and rises to an Islamic stalactite cornice surmounted by an open arcaded gallery with projecting semi-circular *miradores* or loggias. No less exotic is the Court of Lions within, mingling in its frilly arcades Gothic and *mudéjar* motifs, heraldic lions and twisted columns.

Gothic in Portugal

Portugal is especially associated with the Manueline style, named after King Manuel I (reigned 1495–1521), an undisciplined Flamboyant contemporary of the finer Isabelline style of Spain. However, the austere Gothic of the twelfth century arrived early in Portugal through the medium of the Cistercians, whose impressive abbey-church at Alcobaça was built in 1178–1223 in the Burgundian Cistercian style. In the fourteenth century the key monument is the Dominican church of Sta Maria de Vitória, founded in 1387 on the battlefield of Batalha by King João I to commemorate his victory over King Juan of Castile. This victory led to the re-establishment of Portugal as a nation independent of Spain, and the extraordinary richness and eclecticism of the church at Batalha can be seen as an attempt to assert that Portugal could rival the best buildings in Europe. Thus what began as a conventional friars' church developed, with the arrival of a new architect in 1402, into a Flamboyant medley with a façade inspired by English Perpendicular; English rib-vaults but French Flamboyant tracery; eastern chapels following a Cistercian plan; and a spire based on German open-work steeples such as those at Esslingen or Strasbourg. Not surprisingly, this unique building exercised no influence on Portuguese architecture.

The royal burial-place of João and his successor, Batalha was elaborated with additional funerary chapels and cloisters during the course of the fifteenth century

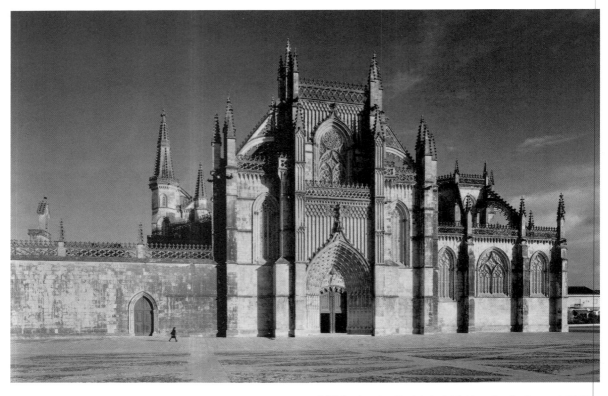

in the same over-elaborate style as the church. King Manuel the Great resumed work in c. 1500 on the never-to-be-completed funerary octagon at the east end with its seven radiating chapels, providing it with an extravagant doorway designed by Mateus Fernandes. Layer upon layer of ogee and trefoil-headed arches, intricately carved with lace-like profusion, create the characteristic Late Gothic continuity in depth. The doorway recalls the much earlier one in the porch of St Mary Redcliffe at Bristol, a port in constant touch with Portuguese trading fleets.

King Manuel effectively became head of an international trading company, for it was during his reign, which began in 1495, that Vasco da Gama opened a sea-route to India; Cabral established contact with Brazil; and Goa and Malacca were captured. The sense of riches pouring into Portugal by sea from exotic places is a defining characteristic of the Manueline style in which monuments commissioned by the king were designed. It seems to reflect his personal taste and largely comes to a halt with his death in 1521. Apart from the

work at Batalha by the French architect Diogo Boytac, the principal monuments are the church of Jesus at Setúbal; the Jeronymite monastery founded by Manuel at Belém, the site of Vasco da Gama's landing on his return to Portugal; the church and cloister of Sta Cruz at Coimbra, both by Boytac; the chapter-house and nave of the Templar monastery at Tomar, by Diogo de Arruda; the Tower of Belém, built opposite the monastery; and the sacristy door at Alcobaça, framed by tree trunks with roots, knots and leafy branches forming an ogee arch. The Manueline style with its columns like twisted ropes, its cusping like the fringed leaves of banana trees, its ubiquitous succulence and opulence, finds its most bizarre expression in the window of Diogo de Arruda's undercroft of 1510–14 below the choir of the Cristo Monastery at Tomar. The frame of this rectangular window, conceived as a monument to Vasco da Gama, is overlaid with a seething growth of marine vegetation incorporating tree roots, ropes, cork floats, chains, shells and astrolabes. The upper window is circular, with a deep surround carved with forms resembling a whirlwind or billowing sails restrained by ropes. It is set in a building which rises like a ship dredged up from the ocean, its buttresses encrusted with coral growth, barnacles and petrified seaweed.

Town planning

The rise of civic identity

After the fall of the Roman Empire, the Roman cities in Europe shrank in size, to become small settlements following the rise of the German kingdoms in the fifth century. The typical rectangular street network of the Romans was gradually abandoned, especially north of the Alps, the towns often becoming dominated by monasteries as centres of culture. However, at the end of the Dark Ages, the twelfth century saw the revival of the kind of urbanism that had been neglected since the end of Roman civilization.

As a result, the ambition of medieval cities throughout Europe was to become self-governing, leading to the widespread creation of city councils. The towns in northern Italy that were the seats of bishops led the way, from the eleventh century, in the transition from feudal to popular government. The growing power of the commune was increasingly expressed in the erection of town halls, guild halls, storehouses, market buildings and shops, which represented a challenge to the long-established authority of bishops, religious orders and lay lords.

The development of trade was a vital tool in the growth of this secular independence. Towns were positioned along trade routes through the Low Countries in the north, through the Rhineland and down the Rhône to cities in northern Italy such as Pisa, Genoa and Venice. Even in Rome, despite the power of the papacy, premises for a senate were established in a remodelled Roman building on the historic Capitoline hill in the mid twelfth century. In Tuscany, well known for its free cities and republican communities, a programme of urban improvement was begun in Florence in 1284 which led to the linking of the cathedral and Baptistery to the grain market and Town Hall by a new street.

In northern France and Flanders, as at Antwerp, Arras, Brussels and Bruges, the open space for the market would be surrounded by a town hall, guild premises and houses for the wealthier citizens. An international port and the centre of the cloth trade, Bruges is one of the best preserved medieval cities. Its surviving buildings, dating mainly from the thirteenth to the fifteenth centuries, follow an irregular town plan featuring houses of brick and timber.

It is impossible to exaggerate how greatly the life and the form of medieval towns were dominated by the church. Holidays were based on religious festivals which grew into fairs, while all aspects of communal activity such as the guilds and archery companies had a religious content. We should therefore not suppose that there was always a separation between bishops and the secular arm. For example, Ulm is a powerful example of the connection between politics and church building. The

297 View of Bruges, Belgium

gigantic new cathedral was seen from the moment of its foundation in 1377 as the creation of the city council, paid for by the citizens, and serving as a symbol of their independence. In the thirteenth century Siena had initiated a parallel political course in which power was transferred from aristocratic families to leading merchant families.

Building regulations

The growth of these beautiful towns was not left to chance. In Florence, there were laws to control maximum height, while in Siena the inhabitants devised an extraordinarily comprehensive building code to help unite the three geographically separated communities that made up the city. The city council met annually to issue regulations which governed the erection of public buildings, churches, houses, streets and fountains. As a result, it is known today as one of the most enthralling medieval towns of Europe.

Parallel regulations grew up in other cities, though generally concerned with civic amenities rather than with what we would now understand by town planning. Thus, by 1300 in large cities such as London and Paris householders were obliged to clean their pavements, while the removal of waste was subject to control. In London there were fire and drainage regulations, and in major Italian and Spanish towns control was exercised over the width of streets and the projection of roofs. It has been calculated that in Venice there were eventually as many as 35 categories of control, rooted in concepts of public order and morality, which affected many aspects of life from minor details of dress, through feasting and the design of gondolas, to decoration of palaces.

The response to Roman monuments and to landscape

Despite these constant attempts at regulation, planning was rarely coherent. Moreover, medieval towns often derive much of their individuality and charm from their relation to the natural landscape setting. At Laon, the

298 Cloth Hall, Bruges

299 Segovia, Spain

cathedral and upper town are on a plateau, 650 feet (c.200m) high. The rocky defensible promontory at Segovia is similarly dominated not by a castle but by a gigantic cathedral. The Old Town of Edinburgh runs up its precipitous rock, whereas the strung-out town of Rothenburg-an-der-Tauber follows the line of a long hill. The irregular setting of Siena on its Y-shaped ridge led to its development in a unique way which culminated in its celebrated fan-shaped Campo, on the site of the Roman forum.

This recalls the principle that a determining factor was frequently the survival of Roman planning or monuments. At Verona, where the Roman amphitheatre is still the largest building in the city, many of the

300 Aerial view of Verona

medieval buildings follow the Roman grid plan, the main market-place, the Piazza delle Erbe, occupying the site of the Forum. At Lucca the existence of the amphitheatre is eloquently preserved in the oval form of the Piazza dell'Antifeatro. At Arles, in southern France, a Greek settlement refounded as a military city by Julius Caesar in 46BC, the Roman amphitheatre was fortified in the ninth century and subsequently adapted as residential accommodation with two parish churches.

New towns

We should note that there were basically two types of medieval town. The majority, those we might describe as 'historic', had grown over a long period in a largely haphazard way. Those we have seen so far belong to this category. However, there were, by contrast, a considerable number of planned towns on new sites such as Salisbury or Lübeck, sometimes known as 'planted' towns, or as 'bastides' in France. These were laid out on a grid, unrelated to the site, with rectilinear plots following predetermined units of measurement. This system went back to Hippodamus of Miletus, the Greek architect and town planner.

At Lübeck, founded in 1158, much survives from the thirteenth and fourteenth centuries, mainly brick-built. Salisbury, Wiltshire, was moved down by the Bishop of Sarum in c.1218 from the nearby inconvenient hill known as Old Sarum. On its new flat site, it became a famous under the patronage of its bishop as the most successful of the new towns of medieval England. Principally a textile town, increasing the bishop's revenue, its wide streets formed an irregular grid round the great market-place. However, in common with many planned towns, Salisbury eventually expanded from its original core.

In 1246, St Louis, King of France, founded Aigues-Mortes, on the mouth of the Rhône in Southern France, to serve as a secure base from which to launch Crusades and as a commercial centre for the promotion of trade between Levant and northern France. A walled city on a relentless grid plan, it is one of the largest surviving medieval fortified towns. In 1296–7, Edward I, King of England, Duke of Aquitaine and nephew of St Louis of France, established a colloquium to discuss how to plan and administer towns. Though numerous planned towns already existed in England, he had doubtless been influenced by seeing Aigues-Mortes from which he set out on the Crusades in 1270. As a result of summoning what must have been one of the first town-planning conferences, he ordered 24 new towns in 1296 in Gascony, England and Wales. These fortified towns such as Beaumaris and Caernarvon, often port towns on coasts, were as much for military as for commercial purposes. With their grid plans, centring on a market, they were intended for merchants, free burgesses who were no longer subject to feudal dues.

Many of the purpose-built bastides, which could not survive without outside subventions, never developed. Within their fortified walls, the great 'historic' cities of medieval Europe expanded in a tightly packed way, with narrow winding streets, little wider than lanes. In Britain, the castle was often the most important element, as at Lincoln or London, while in Italian and French cities the bishop's palace and adjacent cathedral,

301 Aigues-Mortes (founded 1246)

were often the dominant elements. Without the benefit of any overall systematic planning, many major medieval cities had acquired by the end of the twelfth century the basic formation that was to survive until at least the Industrial Revolution.

6 Renaissance Harmony

MEDIEVAL SCHOLARS READ WIDELY IN CLASSICAL LITERATURE. As priests and monks they did so largely with theological or philosphical ends in view. With the growth of the city-state in Italy came a new class of professional administrators, not necessarily in holy orders, who taught Latin, philology, grammar and rhetoric. Reading the classics for literary purposes, these humanists provided an intellectual climate in which it was increasingly believed that not only were the classical literary texts valuable in themselves, but that the civilization which had produced them should serve as a model for a modern cultural rebirth or Renaissance. Gothic, with its northern focus, had never been fully acclimatized in Italy where it seemed natural to seek inspiration in the indigenous classical architecture surviving as a constant reminder of the ancient Roman world.

Humanist scholars promoted 'humane' studies: that is, worthy of the dignity of humankind. We should not interpret humanism as hostile to Christianity, for it was still universally believed that humans were made in the image of God. The belief that mankind could rival God in bringing rational order and harmony to the world was given expression in painting at the beginning of the fifteenth century by the invention of linear perspective, attributed by his contemporaries to the architect Brunelleschi. The new emphasis on human capabilities led to the growth of the many-sided man who might be at once a scholar, soldier, banker and poet. The architect Alberti, the most important of these 'universal men' in the fifteenth century, was followed by artists such as Leonardo, Raphael and, above all, Michelangelo, architect, sculptor, painter and poet, whose talents caused him to be known as 'divine' in his lifetime.

The brilliant Renaissance culture of Italy was influential throughout Europe, though at first often confined to ornamental details and spreading only slowly in view of the vitality of the Late Gothic tradition. In England, for example, it did not flower in a pure architectural form until the early seventeenth century, by which time Italian architects were already moving on to the different phase of classicism we know as Baroque.

The birth of the Renaissance

Florence and Brunelleschi

Florence was a city which had never forgotten the classical past of Italy. The so-called proto-Renaissance of the eleventh and twelfth centuries produced buildings such as San Miniato al Monte (fig. 209), designed in a seductively elegant classical style which continued to influence Florentine architects for nearly three centuries. Even the octagonal crossing of Arnolfo di Cambio's cathedral at Florence in 1294 may have been inspired by the adjacent octagonal baptistery which, as we saw in the last chapter, was then believed to be a Roman temple in origin. The problem of raising a dome over this crossing, nearly 140 feet (42m) wide, was aggravated in 1410–13 by the addition of the thin-walled octagonal drum which brought the total height from the floor to the top of the drum to about 180 feet (55m). The expected solution of raising the dome on a wooden framework known as centering, used in the construction of vaults and arches, would be impossible here because of the width of the span.

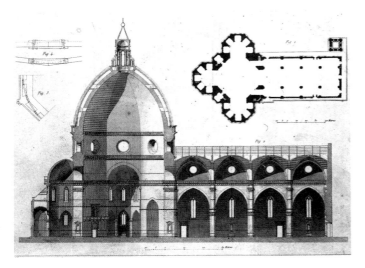

302 Plan and section of the cathedral, Florence, by Brunelleschi (and A. di Cambio) (dome 1420–36)

In the end the answer came from Filippo Brunelleschi (1377–1446), the son of a prosperous Florentine notary and diplomat, who had received a good classical education and had trained as a goldsmith. Turning to sculpture, he entered the competition for the new doors for the baptistery in 1401. When this was won by Ghiberti he visited Rome with the sculptor Donatello to study antique sculpture This was the first of several visits, during which he also investigated the Roman ruins and especially their constructional principles. We know from a near-contemporary what an impact Rome had on him because, such was his fame, he was made the subject of a biography in c.1480 by Antonio Manetti. Here we learn that:

> while he was studying the sculptures [in Rome] with a perceptive eye and an alert mind, he observed the ancient way of building and their laws of symmetry. It seemed to him that he could recognize a certain order in the disposition, like members and bones, and it was as though God had enlightened him. . . . He was the more struck by it, since it seemed to him very different from the methods usual in those times.

In 1418 both Brunelleschi and Ghiberti produced brick models for the dome, but it was Brunelleschi's proposal which was eventually adopted and erected in

1420–36, to the wonder of the world, since it was a man-made mountain equalled only by Hagia Sophia and the Pantheon. Brunelleschi's genius was to substitute for centering a system of which the four most important features were, first, building up the dome in a succession of horizontal courses as in the concrete dome of the Pantheon; second, giving it a double shell so as to reduce the weight as much as possible, a device borrowed from the baptisteries of Pisa and Florence; third, echoing Gothic rib construction by stretching the outer skin of the dome over a frame of twenty-four ribs; and, finally, because a pointed arch exerts less side-thrust than a round one, giving the dome a pointed profile rather than the Pantheon-like hemisphere he would have preferred. He further bound the dome together by burying into it a succession of continuous rings of stone and iron chains. The constructional technique, involving the use of bricks and masonry laid in herringbone formation, makes it clear that he had studied not only the Pantheon (p. 76), but vaulting in other Roman buildings such as the so-called Temple of Minerva Medica. His interest in the construction rather than the visual appearance of Roman buildings sets him apart from many Renaissance architects, from Alberti onwards.

Brunelleschi's subsequent buildings, though more classical in form than the swelling half-Gothic dome of Florence cathedral, derive almost as much from the Tuscan proto-Renaissance as from ancient Rome itself. However, at the time Brunelleschi was hailed, indeed 'blessed' as the architect Filarete put it, for restoring 'in our city of Florence the ancient style of building in such a way that today in churches and private buildings no other style is used'. How did Florence come to be such an architecturally active centre? During the last quarter of the fourteenth century Florence had been struggling to establish supremacy over territories such as Lombardy, Venice, the papal states and Naples-Sicily. Her ambition was to dominate Tuscany so as to create a regional rather than a city state. Her cathedral, essentially a civic enterprise, was a potent symbol of that ambition, while its dome, brooding magnificently over the city today as then (fig. 348), proclaimed the wealth and power of the Wool Guild who were charged with responsibility for its execution. In the fifteenth century the political and economic success of Florence gave continuing encouragement to those who wished to make it the most beautiful city in Europe, an ambition especially associated with the Medici family of international bankers. The lead in patronage given by Cosimo the Elder, virtual ruler of Florence from 1434 till his death thirty years later, and by his grandson Lorenzo the Magnificent (d. 1492), was followed by the great merchant families such as the Strozzi, Rucellai and Pitti. But economics do not explain style, and we still have to ask why it was that, while wealth on this scale was being used in Flanders, England and Spain to subsidize buildings in Late Gothic styles, Florentine artists had already rejected Gothic in favour of the classical style we know as Renaissance.

In trying to understand this phenomenon we should emphasize once more that Gothic had never become indigenous to Italy as it had elsewhere in Europe, that the survival of ancient Roman ruins in Italy continually recalled her glorious past, and that the study of classical literature by humanist scholars was likely to encourage a revival of classical art. Tuscan architects had already in the eleventh century begun to revive classical ideals; Petrarch (1304–74) imitated every style of Latin poetry; while in the *Divine Comedy* Dante (1265–1321) was the first to treat the classical and Christian worlds as parallel and equal. Moreover it was not unreasonable for Florentines to regard Gothic as a wild northern style associated with the descendants of the Germanic chiefs who had vanquished Rome, and to celebrate, by contrast, the uniqueness of the mercantile republic of Florence by renewing its claims to have originated as a colony of republican Rome. The creation by architects, sculptors and painters like Brunelleschi, Michelozzo, Ghiberti, Donatello and Masaccio of a grave and lucid *all'antica* style, comparable to Roman antiquity, gave tangible expression to the Florentine sense of its own history and destiny, both cultural and political.

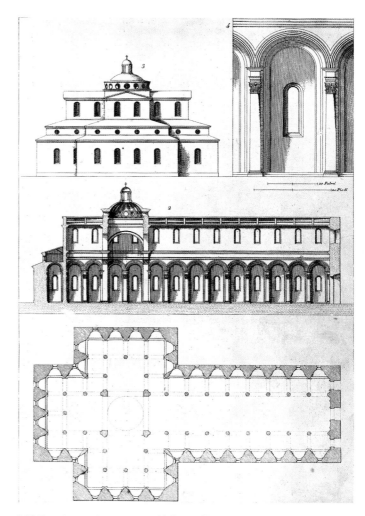

303 Elevation, section and plan of S. Spirito, Florence, by Brunelleschi (begun 1436)

Most of Brunelleschi's commissions came from the guild and banking circles of Florence. For the Guild of Silk-Merchants and Goldsmiths, to which he belonged himself, he designed the Foundling Hospital in 1419, the first in Europe, with its elegantly arcaded loggia. It was Giovanni di Bicci de' Medici who commissioned the sacristy at S. Lorenzo in 1421, and his friend the banker Andrea de' Pazzi who commissioned the chapter-house or Pazzi chapel at S. Croce in 1429. Brunelleschi's two large basilical churches in Florence, S. Lorenzo (begun in 1421) and S. Spirito (begun in 1436), were designed to create an ordered harmonious balance which is a

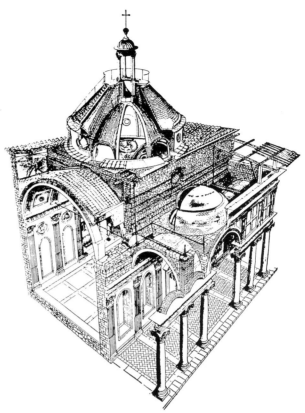

304 *Above* Interior of the Pazzi Chapel, Florence, by Brunelleschi (begun c.1430)

305 *Right* Sectional diagram of the Pazzi Chapel

306 *Opposite* Interior of S. Spirito, Florence, by Brunelleschi

parallel to the discovery of the laws of perspective by Florentine painters at that moment. The churches became models of proportional planning, since the square of the crossing is the basic module for the whole composition. Thus at S. Spirito this square is repeated three times to form the choir and transepts; the nave is four squares long and is twice as high as it is wide; the clerestorey and arcade are of equal height; and the aisles consist of square bays, also twice as high as they are wide. All the parts are harmoniously related to each other in a series of architectural perspectives which are given an imperial Roman grandeur by the powerful Corinthian colonnade marching all round the interior.

The Pazzi chapel (begun c.1430), a building of great delicacy and subtlety, is not, strictly speaking, centrally-planned since the central domed square is flanked by tunnel-vaulted side bays. It is preceded by an entrance loggia which also has a central saucer-domed space neatly balancing the small domed choir in axis with it on the other side of the chapel. The interior is articulated with a linear pattern produced by the structural and decorative members which, made from *pietra serena* (local grey stone), stand out against the white plastered walls as though they were the lines of the newly

discovered laws of perspective drawn on the architecture. His later work became heavier and more moulded, as in the lantern of the cathedral and the exedrae in the drum of its dome, and in the uncompleted church of S. Maria degli Angeli (1434–7). This was the first fully centrally-planned Renaissance building, a type which was to fascinate all fifteenth- and sixteenth-century architects. The central domed octagon of this church is defined by a ring of eight piers which support the drum and form the dividing walls of the eight radiating chapels or apses. Thus the whole building is treated as a sculptural unit based on the concept of the moulded wall-mass, which must derive from his study of the centrally-planned domed interiors of ancient Rome.

Alberti

The other towering genius of the fifteenth century in architecture was Leon Battista Alberti (1404–72), though he had not been trained as an architect or in any craft. In fact he represents the new type of genius described at the beginning of this chapter, a scholar, author, mathematician and athlete, with a profound knowledge of all the arts. Equipped with one of the most brilliant minds of the entire Renaissance period, he was determined to leave his mark on the culture of his day. This meant studying the remains of antique Roman architecture, as his friend Brunelleschi had done, to provide a sure basis for modern design. However, whereas Brunelleschi had concentrated on the methods of construction and scarcely troubled to distinguish between the orders, Alberti was more interested in the supposed principles of designs and in the models they provided for the decorative handling of the orders. He enshrined his conclusions in the first of the many architectural treatises to be produced in the Renaissance, *De re aedificatoria*, of which the first version was presented to Pope Nicholas V in 1452. Written in Ciceronian Latin, it was modelled on the Roman Vitruvius' treatise and even referred to churches as 'temples' and to God and the saints as 'the gods', though it should not be doubted for a moment that his whole classical cultural vision was conceived entirely within a Christian framework: he was, for example, a Catholic priest.

In his book Alberti does not see architecture as rooted in the crafts, but as an intellectual discipline and a social art in the practice of which two of the most necessary skills are painting and mathematics. He thus implied that architectural knowledge was not any longer to be acquired in the lodges of medieval Europe where the Gothic master-masons had learned their trade, but was open through study to all scholars, patrons and dilettanti who were men of education and taste. Though he was by no means impractical, it seems that Alberti did not have any great technical knowledge of architectural construction; he simply designed buildings and left their erection to others. As many commentators have done, he found Vitruvius' text muddled and made sure that his own book was much better ordered.

Though he organizes it round Vitruvius' dictum that good architecture consists of three parts, *Utilitas*, *Firmitas* and *Venustas* (function, structure and design or beauty), he adds that beauty in an individual building depends on the combination of three qualities: *Numeros* (number); *Finitio* (proportion, inspired by both the Vitruvian doctrine of the relation of the various parts of the human body to the whole, and by the application to architecture of the Pythagorean harmonic ratios that have been established for music – see below, p. 244); and *Collocatio* (location, disposition, or arrangement). These unite to produce *Concinnitas* (a well-adjusted whole). He did not believe that there were absolute rules for beauty but, echoing Socrates, defined it in a famous phrase as 'the harmony of all the members, so that nothing can be taken away or added or changed, except for the worse'. Beauty needed the addition of ornament for its full effect, and 'in all architecture, the fundamental ornament is undoubtedly the column'. Explanation of the correct use of the five orders thus occupies a substantial part of Alberti's text, though many modern scholars would claim that it was only in Roman architecture, not Greek, about which Alberti knew nothing, that the column played a decorative as opposed to a functional role.

Not surprisingly for someone living and working in fifteenth-century Florence, he saw architecture as a civic art in which the ordered hierarchy of social and religious ideals would be expressed with clarity and dignity. He divided the buildings in a town into sacred and secular, the former including the basilica (law court), since justice emanates from God. The most important building should be the temple (church), fronted with a portico and raised on a high podium. How far was he able to put his ambitious ideals into practice? His principal works are few: three churches, the façade of a fourth, and the façade of a Florentine palazzo, yet in their boldness and imagination they set precedents which have inspired architects ever since. In the façade of the Palazzo Rucellai in Florence, built for the banker Giovanni Rucellai some time between 1446 and c.1470, Alberti applied for the first time to domestic architecture the pilaster system of Roman public buildings such as the Colosseum. The Tempio Malatestiano at Rimini was begun by Alberti in c.1450 for Sigismondo Malatesta, soldier and patron of the arts, who had wrested the lordship of Rimini from his uncle and brothers at the age of fourteen. The original medieval church, dedicated to S. Francesco, was transformed into an imposing neo-antique temple of glory to Sigismondo as well as a burial place for him, his wife and sometime mistress Isotta, and his court. Condemned as 'full of pagan images' by Pope Pius II, who excommunicated Sigismondo, the church has long been known not as S. Francesco but by its more classical, pagan name.

It is the first application to the entrance façade of a Christian church of the classical triumphal arch, inspired in this case by the Arch of Augustus in Rimini itself and by the Arch of Constantine in Rome. The tombs of Sigismondo and Isotta were to be housed in the niches on this façade so that its form would symbolize Christian triumph over death rather than the purely military triumph of its antique models. Forming a composition derived from the Mausoleum of Theodoric at Ravenna, the austerely moulded arches on the side front of the Tempio Malatestiano each contained the sarcophagus of one of the humanist poets and philosophers at Sigismondo's court. Despite the undoubted majesty and originality with which antique elements were revived at the Tempio, it scarcely provided a model for the application of classical principles to the design of the ordinary parish church. Alberti provided a brilliant and influential solution to that problem at Mantua in the second of the two churches he built there: S. Sebastiano, begun in 1460, and S. Andrea, begun ten years later. Both were commissioned by Ludovico Gonzaga, Duke of Mantua, whose court painter, Andrea Mantegna, worked in a style as strongly influenced by Greek and Roman sculpture as Alberti's was by Roman architecture.

S. Sebastiano is the first in a line of domed churches on a Greek cross plan, but the more influential S.

307 Exterior of Tempio Malatestiano, Rimini, by Alberti (begun c.1450)

308 The west front of S. Andrea, Mantua, by Alberti (begun 1470)

309 Interior of S. Andrea, Mantua, by Alberti

domed chapels alternating with large barrel-vaulted chapels which fill the space between the piers. This grandiose interior is the parent of most of the finest Italian churches of the sixteenth century from St Peter's to the Gesù. Its west front is a similarly powerful variant on antique themes though, surprisingly, it turned out to be less influential. Its great arched opening flanked by smaller openings echoes the alternating rhythm of large and small chapels in the internal nave elevation. The façade is further organically linked to the interior by the central arch with its deep shadowy soffit, since its form echoes and prepares the spectator for the great barrel-vaulted nave within. Moreover, the whole façade manages to combine references to both the triumphal arch and the temple front, since the central arch is flanked by four pilasters surmounted by a pediment.

Palaces and town planning in Pienza, Urbino and Florence

Alberti's influence can be felt at Pienza, near Siena, built from 1460 as the first ideal city of the Renaissance at the behest of the humanist Pope Pius II, Aeneas Silvius Piccolomini. This enchanting town, surviving today in untouched fifteenth-century form, centres on the piazza containing the cathedral, bishop's palace, Piccolomini palace and town hall, all built by the Florentine architect Bernardo Rossellino (1409–64) under Pius's supervision. The piazza is a carefully planned piece of optical perspective in which the palaces flanking the cathedral are set at canted angles like the wings of a stage set. The Piccolomini palace is directly inspired by Alberti's Palazzo Rucellai but boasts a novel three-storeyed garden front, consisting of three tiers of open porticoes expressly built so that Pius could enjoy the views from them of the countryside. This must be one of the first buildings since Pliny's villa (p. 71) with a site and a disposition which had been determined by the views from it.

Pienza is recalled in a beautiful architectural painting showing the piazza in an ideal town, which is often attributed to Piero della Francesca. This survives in the

Andrea, Alberti's finest work, created a new type of church at a stroke by replacing the traditional aisles of the Gothic and basilican church with a series of side-chapels. This gave all the pilgrims who flocked to the church an uninterrupted view of the domed crossing, where two vases, said to contain the blood of the crucified Christ, were displayed annually on Ascension Day. The architectural precedent for such a plan was to be found in Roman buildings like the Baths of Diocletian and the Basilica of Constantine, where the weight of the vault was carried by enormous abutments which could be hollowed out to form openings at right angles to the main axis. Alberti's huge coffered barrel-vault, nearly 60 feet (18m) wide and the largest erected since Roman times, is supported by piers containing small square

Galleria Nazionale at Urbino and may have been painted for Federico da Montefeltro, Duke of Urbino, who transformed the capital of his tiny principality into one of the most beautiful Renaissance towns in Italy and one of the most civilized courts in Europe. He concentrated his attention on the creation between 1455 and 1480 of the Palazzo Ducale, which has been described as 'a curious combination of military academy and institute of Classical studies'. It demonstrates a feeling for spatial composition which we can also find in a line of painters from Piero della Francesca to Raphael, born in Urbino in 1483. This quality is most apparent in the broad arcaded courtyard of the Palazzo Ducale, almost certainly designed by the Dalmatian architect Luciano Laurana (c.1420–79) in c.1464. He had evidently studied Florentine buildings such as Brunelleschi's Foundling Hospital and the Medici Palace (1444–59) designed by Michelozzo di Bartolommeo (1396–1472), though he turns his arcade round the corners more neatly than Michelozzo by adopting L-shaped angle piers. From the courtyard a monumental staircase, one

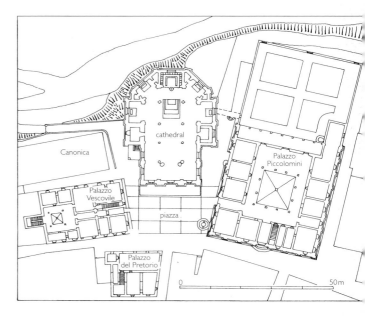

310 Plan of the piazza, Pienza, by Rossellino (begun 1460)

311 The piazza, Pienza, showing the cathedral and Palazzo Piccolomini, by Rossellino

of the first of its kind, leads to the rooms of the ducal apartment with the delicately classical carvings of their door and window surrounds, capitals and chimney-pieces. In the tiny neo-antique Cappella del Perdono (chapel of forgiveness), barrel-vaulted, apsed and richly decorated, and in the adjacent Tempietto delle Muse (temple of the muses), the Duke celebrated his equal veneration for the Christian and pagan religions, apparently without any sense of incongruity. Over these on the first floor was his exquisite Studiolo (study), lined with inset portraits of classical and Christian philosophers and poets, where he kept his rarest manuscripts. This led into the enchanting open-air loggia, placed to capture the best view of the surround-

ing countryside. Here love of classical scholarship at last gave way to a new-found love of nature.

Michelozzo's Palazzo Medici in Florence was influential not only for its elegant courtyard, a secular version of the monastic cloister, but for its façade and general architectural disposition. Humbly born in Florence in 1396, Michelozzo worked with Ghiberti and with Donatello before winning the prestigious commission from Cosimo de'Medici for a monumental new palace in 1444. The massive building, filling a city block, was designed with a new emphasis on symmetry and balance, presenting a face of power to the outside world with its heavily rusticated blocks, which were to become a status symbol in Florentine palaces. Such novel features, including the enormous classical cornice nearly 10 feet (3m) high which crowns the whole building, exercised powerful influence over buildings such as the Palazzo Pitti (begun in 1548) and the Palazzo Strozzi and Palazzo Gondi, both designed in c.1490 by Giuliano da Sangallo (1443–1516).

Filarete and Leonardo

In Milan, Michelozzo, Filarete, Leonardo da Vinci and Bramante all worked for those great patrons, the Sforza Dukes of Milan. Antonio Averlino (c.1400–69), the Florentine sculptor known as 'Filarete', Greek for 'lover of virtue', designed the Ospedale Maggiore in Milan (c.1460–5), with eight square courtyards defined by wards forming crosses, and a central rectangular courtyard containing a centrally-planned church. The

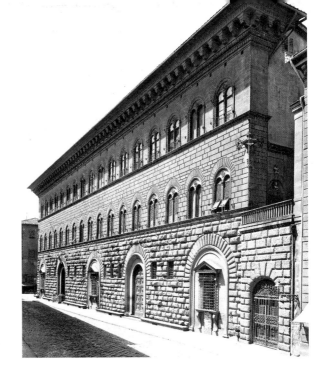

312 *Opposite above* Circle of Piero della Francesca: *An Ideal Town*, Galleria Nazionale, Urbino (15th century)

313 *Opposite below* Exterior of the Palazzo Ducale, Urbino, by Laurana (c.1464)

314 *Above right* Exterior of Palazzo Medici-Riccardi, Florence, by Michelozzo (1444–59)

315 *Right* Interior of the Cappella del Perdono, Palazzo Ducale, Urbino, by Laurana

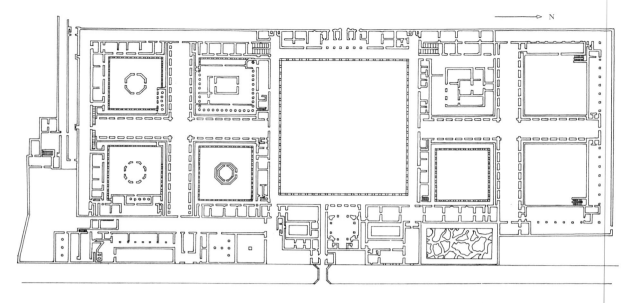

316 Plan of the Ospedale Maggiore, Milan, by Filarete (c.1460–6)

first modern hospital, it was also the earliest instance of the sweeping cross-in-square courtyard planning which was to be so influential on public buildings of all kinds. Though it brought the ordered spirit of the Tuscan Renaissance to Milan, it was designed with typically Lombard rich decoration and high angle towers like the Portinari Chapel at S. Eustorgio, Milan (c.1460), which is often attributed to Michelozzo.

Filarete wrote a *Trattato d'architettura* ('Architectural treatise') in c.1455–60, in which he proposed an ideal town called Sforzinda after the Dukes of Milan. There is a romantic fairy-tale quality in Filarete's writing so that Sforzinda, for example, was to boast a ten-storey tower of Vice and Virtue with a brothel at its foot and an observatory at the top. However, the star-shaped plan of Sforzinda with radial streets made it the first ever symmetrically designed city. This dynamic centralized concept demonstrates Filarete's ability to think on a large scale, and is also a parallel to Niccolò Machiavelli (1469–1527) whose book, *The Prince*, saw the state as a work of art, glorifying the will of man.

Filarete's interest in central planning seems to have fired both Leonardo and Bramante. Leonardo's numerous architectural drawings of c.1490–1519

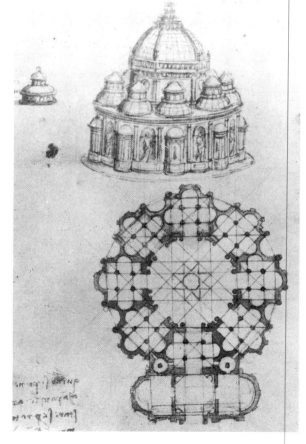

317 Leonardo: Plan and drawing of a centrally planned church (c.1490–1519). (Ms 2037 5 v. Codex Ashb. II, Institut de France)

include town-planning schemes as well as projects for centrally-planned and longitudinal churches, often with multiple domes. Shown in plan, perspective and elevation, these are virtually the first architectural drawings of their kind, and were prepared for his never-completed *Treatise on Architecture*. An imaginative synthesis of the Early Renaissance ideals of his contemporaries such as Alberti, Filarete and Francesco di Giorgio, this astonishing corpus of drawings also anticipates High Renaissance practice.

High Renaissance

Rome: Bramante

It seems that Leonardo never built anything, so it was his friend Donato Bramante (1444–1514) who made the step from design to built form, thus influencing the course of western architecture for centuries. Born near Urbino and probably trained as a painter by Piero della Francesca and Mantegna, he was called to Milan in c.1480 by Ludovico Sforza. His early works in Lombardy are a synthesis of the architectural language of Laurana and Francesco di Giorgio in Urbino; of Alberti in Mantua, which he visited on his way to Milan; of Lombardic Romanesque buildings such as the façade of the Certosa at Pavia and of the Late Roman and Early Christian monuments of Milan itself. His earliest architectural work, the rebuilding from 1478 of the ninth-century church of S. Maria presso S. Satiro, includes an east end echoing the interior of Alberti's S. Andrea in Mantua but constructed in flat relief as a painted perspective illusion: a tribute to his training as a painter. The original Early Christian church of S. Satiro, which Bramante did not destroy but elegantly remodelled, was in plan a Greek cross in a square inside a circle. It thus contained the seeds of Bramante's design for St Peter's in Rome. Its plan also inspired the richly ornamented sacristy which Bramante added to S. Satiro. His next work in Milan, the magnificent domed chancel of S. Maria delle Grazie, begun in 1493 as the Sforza

memorial chapel, is also centrally planned, this time echoing Alberti's S. Sebastiano in Mantua.

Bramante's move to Rome in 1499, following the French occupation of Milan and the overthrow of the Sforzas, exercised a profound influence on his style. The popes had been generally absent from Rome in the first half of the fifteenth century and the city had been of little political importance, but after the death of Lorenzo de' Medici in Florence and the fall of Ludovico Sforza in Milan in the 1490s, it became a centre of cultural and political influence which culminated in the extraordinary pontificate of Julius II (1503–13). A soldier busy extending the temporal power of the papacy, he was also a patron of rare discernment, giving simultaneous employment to Bramante, Michelangelo and Raphael. Already in the later fifteenth century two major palaces for cardinals, the Palazzo Venezia and the Palazzo della Cancelleria, both by unknown architects, had brought

318 S. Maria delle Grazie, Milan, with Bramante's chancel (begun 1493)

319 Courtyard of the Palazzo della Cancelleria, Rome, by Bramante's circle (begun c.1485)

320 Bramante: The Tempietto at S. Pietro in Montorio, Rome (1502)

the style of Alberti to Rome and expressed it with a characteristically Roman monumentality and weight. The noble colonnades of the uncompleted courtyard built in the 1460s at the Palazzo Venezia have piers set with half-columns like those of the nearby Theatre of Marcellus or of the Colosseum, while the Cancelleria (begun c.1485), is a sumptuous development of Albertian and Urbinesque themes such as the colonnaded courtyard, the rusticated pilaster-façade, and the running frieze with Latin inscription, the first of its kind in Renaissance Rome.

On his arrival in Rome Bramante set about preparing measured drawings of its antiquities. These attracted the attention of the Cardinal of Naples who invited him to design a new cloister at S. Maria della Pace in 1500. The first work in Rome of such thoroughgoing neo-antique character since the courtyard of the Palazzo Venezia, this cloister was surpassed in importance and influence by the Tempietto he built at S. Pietro in Montorio, a convent of Spanish Franciscans. This was commissioned in 1502 by Ferdinand and Isabella of Spain to mark the spot in Rome where St Peter had traditionally been

crucified. Bramante erected – for the first time since Roman days – a domed peripteral rotunda, that is a circular cella completely surrounded by a colonnade in the manner of the so-called Temples of Vesta at Tivoli and near the Tiber in Rome.

Like Raphael's paintings of pagan Greek philosophers and modern Catholic theologians in the Vatican (1509–11), the Tempietto is an attempt at reconciling Christian and humanist ideals, for its small centrally-planned form echoes the Early Christian *martyria* which had been erected not to serve as parish churches but to mark places with holy associations. The Tempietto is thus a monument of exceptional artistic gravity and with no practical function, yet charged with a profound Christian significance. To underline this, the peristyle is composed of genuine antique Roman Doric columns while the metopes in the triglyph frieze which they support are carved with the keys of St Peter and the liturgical instruments of the mass: a parallel to the frieze of the Temple of Vespasian which, carved with sacrificial instruments, is known to have been above ground in the sixteenth century. Moreover, as a circular building

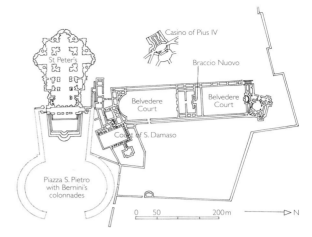

321 Bramante: Exterior of the Belvedere Court, Vatican, Rome (begun 1505)

322 Plan of the Belvedere Court, Vatican, Rome

intended by Bramante to stand in the centre of a circular colonnaded court, its form was regarded as representing the world and divine reality, a concept dear to medieval and Renaissance thinkers. Palladio, to whom the circular Pantheon was significant as 'an image of the world', paid the Tempietto the exceptional tribute of including it among the 'ancient temples' which formed the subject of the fourth book of his *Quattro Libri dell'Architettura* (1570). The building thus became in its own century what it has remained ever since, a norm by which the whole High Renaissance achievement in architecture can be measured.

Bramante set a similar pattern for palace architecture in c.1512 with the design of the now destroyed Palazzo Caprini, better known as the House of Raphael, since it was acquired by that artist in 1517. The articulation of the wall was given dignity, solidity and depth by the application for the first time of Roman half-columns to the upper storey. He deployed this theme even more forcefully in the side elevations of the Belvedere Court at the Vatican, begun for Pope Julius in 1505. Never completed and now much altered, this Court was an essential part of Julius's intended rebuilding of the Vatican Palace and of St Peter's itself to form an imperial palace and church appropriate for his role as a new Julius Caesar, as *imperator* and *pontifex maximus* (emperor and chief priest) – not for nothing had he taken the name Julius at his coronation. Under his reign the papal states

became a European power for the first time in centuries, while Rome became the artistic capital of Europe for the first time since late antiquity. Bramante's Belvedere Court, with its terraces, loggias, sculpture courtyard, open-air theatre, orange trees and fountains is a conscious attempt to echo the ancient imperial palaces on the hills of Rome, such as the Golden House of Nero, Hadrian's villa at Tivoli, and the palace on the Palatine with a hippodrome which inspired the shape of the Belvedere Court.

St Peter's from Bramante to Maderno

The project for rebuilding Old St Peter's which Julius entrusted to Bramante in 1506 was monumentally daring. We can reconstruct Bramante's scheme from two principal sources, the image on a medal struck in 1506, and a drawing in his hand showing part of the plan. Though St Peter's was the greatest church in Christendom, especially since Hagia Sophia had now become a mosque, it was still essentially the *martyrium* for the tomb of the Prince of the Apostles. Bramante thus provided a centrally-planned building like his Tempietto, though now enlarged to a superhuman scale. It is fundamentally a Greek cross with each arm terminating in an apse and with a gigantic Pantheon dome on a colonnaded drum over the crossing. There were minor domes on the corners of the cross and tall campanili flanking the main façade. All this echoes the projects of Leonardo and Filarete in Milan around 1500. However, the plan is further complicated by the transformation of the four corner chapels into subsidiary Greek crosses, thus creating a square ambulatory round the central domed space. What had been completed of this scheme on Bramante's death in 1514 was the lower part of the great crossing piers and the setting out of the coffered arches connecting them and supporting the dome. The present dome of St Peter's still rests on Bramante's piers and crossing arches, despite the rejection of his design for the rest of the church. The massive modelling of his work was on a scale unequalled since antiquity. Rejecting the fifteenth-century concept of the wall as a plane, he returned triumphantly to what Brunelleschi had hinted at in his uncompleted S. Maria degli Angeli in Florence: the moulded wall of the Roman baths constructed from brick-faced concrete.

The striking effect which Bramante's single-minded Greek-cross plan would have created can be appreciated in a number of singularly lovely churches closely inspired by his design, notably S. Maria della Consolazione at Todi in Umbria, begun in 1508 by Cola da Caprarola, and S. Biagio at Montepulciano in Tuscany (1518–45) by Antonio da Sangallo the Elder (1455–1534). Both, significantly, were not designed as working parish churches but as beautiful shrines or places of pilgrimage. They stand on open hillsides commanding views of lovely countryside to which they are obviously designed

323 Exterior of S. Maria della Consolazione, Todi, by Caprarola (begun 1508)

324 Plans for St Peter's, Rome, by Bramante (1506), Bramante and Peruzzi (before 1513), Sangallo (1539) and Michelangelo (1546–64)

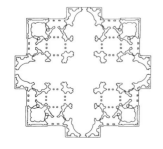

as a complement. The inadequate provision for large congregations in centrally-planned or Greek-cross churches, in comparison with that provided by basilican or Latin-cross churches, led to proposals to modify Bramante's design for St Peter's after his death by the addition of a nave. One of the most ambitious of these schemes, which include submissions by Raphael and Peruzzi, can be seen in the wooden model made in the 1540s from designs by Antonio da Sangallo the Younger (1485–1546). However Sangallo's numerous storeys, repetitively ornamented with the orders on a small scale, recall Geoffrey Scott's criticism of the Victoria and Albert Museum in London that 'while we perceive this building to be large, it conveys a feeling not of largeness but of smallness multiplied'.

Perhaps the only architect who could think on Bramante's heroic scale was Michelangelo, who succeeded Antonio da Sangallo as architect in 1546. By the time of his death in 1564 he had brought much of St Peter's to completion following a modified version of Bramante's centralized plan. His work, which we shall describe in due course, included the construction of the drum up to the springing of the dome, which he proposed to execute with an aspiring slightly pointed profile. This was executed in the 1580s by Giacomo della Porta and Domenico Fontana, while the long nave and west front were added by Carlo Maderno in the first half of the seventeenth century as the final triumph of the Latin-cross plan (fig. 354).

Raphael, Peruzzi and Antonio da Sangallo the Younger

If Michelangelo was the heir to the superhuman quality of Bramante's project for St Peter's, Raphael (Raffaello Sanzio, 1483–1520), trained as a painter in Umbria, responded to the sweeter classical harmony of Bramante's earlier work. We can see this in paintings such as *The School of Athens* in the Vatican Stanze. His Palazzo Pandolfini, Florence, begun in c.1518, is an elegant blend of the Florentine type, as represented by the Palazzo Strozzi, with the Roman type of Bramante's

House of Raphael. In form it is something of a cross between a palazzo and a villa, for when built it stood on the outskirts of the town. In 1515 Raphael was appointed Superintendent of Roman Antiquities by the Medici Pope Leo X. The Villa Madama, which he began building near Rome in c.1516 for Cardinal Giulio de' Medici, the future Pope Clement VII, reflects this fresh wave of interest in the antique. This is demonstrated with especial brilliance in the garden loggia, which Raphael and his pupils adorned with sumptuous brightly painted stuccowork in imitation of the recently discovered vaults of the Golden House of Nero and so-called Baths of Titus. The apsed plan of the loggia and the central circular courtyard, of which only one half was completed, derive from the formal planning of the baths, although the complex disposition of this hillside villa on different levels was a response to the pictorial grouping of Roman villas such as Hadrian's at Tivoli. It involved a succession of elements which could not all be seen at once, such as terraced garden, hippodrome and open-air theatre.

A palace in which the order is unusually, though not illogically, transferred to the ground floor is the Palazzo Massimi alle Colonne, built for the brothers Pietro and Angelo Massimi in 1532 from designs by the Sienese-born architect Baldassare Peruzzi (1481–1536). In fact there are two adjacent palaces with contrasting plans cleverly contrived on an irregular site, the more ambitious being that of Pietro Massimi on the eastern side. The rusticated façade of his palace follows the gentle curve of the street line, a surprisingly unconventional touch, and contains a shadowy entrance porch *in antis*. The stone beams which span this portico may be the earliest revival of this antique practice. It leads into a colonnaded atrium with a richly ornamented first floor loggia. The main courtyard of each palace was designed as a neo-antique atrium, perhaps in allusion to the supposed Roman origin of the Massimi family who claimed descent from Fabius Maximus. In the third century BC he had been five times Consul, one of the most important officials in the Roman Republic.

325 *Above* Interior of the garden loggia at the Villa Madama, Rome, by Raphael (begun c.1516)

326, 327 *Below and right* Exterior and plan of the Palazzo Massimi, Rome, by Peruzzi (1532)

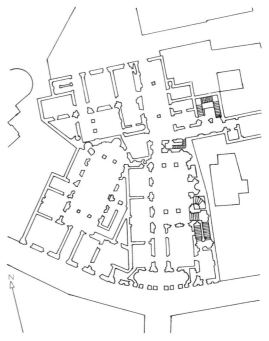

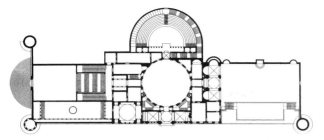

Delicacy, variety and ingenuity are the keynotes of this unique classical masterpiece, as they are of Peruzzi's first important work in Rome, the Villa Farnesina (1509–11), a building which similarly had no precise imitators. With its two open ground-floor loggias and its exquisitely frescoed interiors by Raphael and his

330 *Above left* Plan of the Villa Madama, Rome

331 *Below* Plan of the Palazzo Farnese, Rome

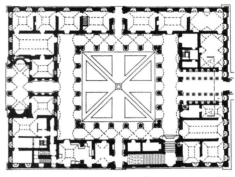

328 *Above* Exterior of the Villa Farnesina, Rome, by Peruzzi (1509–11)

329 *Below* Exterior of the Palazzo Farnese, Rome, by Sangallo (begun 1517)

pupils including, by Peruzzi himself, one of the finest Renaissance examples of illusionistic architectural painting in perspective, the Villa Farnesina is an early attempt at recreating a *villa suburbana* of the type described in antiquity by Pliny the younger (p. 70).

The most celebrated Renaissance palace in Rome, the Palazzo Farnese, was rising from designs by Antonio da Sangallo the Younger in 1517, soon after Peruzzi's Villa Farnesina. Whereas the latter was built for a Sienese banker and collector, Agostino Chigi, the Palazzo Farnese was the seat of one of the most powerful men in Rome with a retinue of over three hundred persons, Cardinal Alessandro Farnese. On his election to the papacy in 1534 as Paul III he had the design of the palace completely remodelled by Sangallo to reflect the grandeur of his new status. Its cliff-like elevations, nearly 100 feet (30m) high, its imposing barrel-vaulted and colonnaded entrance tunnel, its courtyard articulated with superimposed arcades like the Colosseum or Theatre of Marcellus, show that its architect was for once capable of echoing the antique heroic grandeur of late Bramante and Michelangelo. Indeed the gigantic crowning cornice and the powerfully modelled second storey of the courtyard were added by Michelangelo in the 1540s.

Divergencies in Mantua: Giulio Romano

After Raphael, Peruzzi and Antonio da Sangallo the younger, the other major architect of palaces and villas was Giulio Romano (c.1499–1546) who, as his name implies, was a true Roman, indeed the first leading artist to have been born in the city for centuries. His subtle and virtuoso style of architecture reflects the self-conscious pursuit of neo-antique scholarship and refinement within a small inward-looking circle of connoisseurs. His principal patron was Federigo Gonzaga (1500–40), 2nd Duke of Mantua, who summoned him to his court in 1524; there he was treated with unparalleled generosity in view of the status he had acquired in Rome as Raphael's principal assistant.

332 Courtyard of the Palazzo del Tè, Mantua (1525–34), by Giulio Romano

333 Plan of the Palazzo del Tè, Mantua

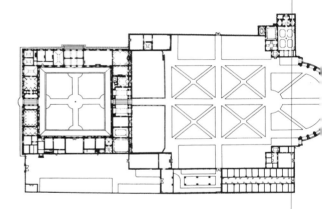

On the outskirts of Mantua where he had a famous stud the Duke decided to recreate an antique *villa suburbana*, not for residence but for relaxation, refreshment and entertainment. The Palazzo del Tè, built from Giulio's designs in 1525–34, was an experiment in classicism which had already been tried at the Villa Madama, in the decoration of which Giulio had been employed. Like an antique Roman villa the Palazzo del Tè consists of four low ranges enclosing a square courtyard but, in a departure from High Renaissance harmony, the architectural treatment of the western, eastern and entrance fronts is quite different, while the garden front has an axis at right angles to that of the entrance front, which is not even symmetrical. Inside the courtyard the differently articulated façades collide at the corners and there are further clashes between aggressive rustication and flat ashlar side by side, while the famous dropped triglyphs and keystones suggest that the building is still in the process of adjustment for functional or, more likely, aesthetic reasons. This is aesthete's architecture, devised to flatter and entertain patrons so gifted that they can not only understand but even participate in the process of design.

The same vivid artistry governs the stuccoed and frescoed interiors, some developing erotic themes, others featuring *trompe l'oeil* decoration: for example the Sala dei Cavalli where the Duke's favourite horses stand incongruously but realistically in front of elegant fluted pilasters, or, more spectacularly, the Sala dei Giganti, a dark room with its corners smoothed over as a background for a *trompe l'oeil* riot in which the giants rebelling against Olympus are being crushed beneath collapsing columns, falling rocks and blocks of stone which also threaten to engulf the spectator. From here he

passes with relief into the contrasting barrel-vaulted loggia on the garden front, a symphony of classical grace and order with its harmonious clusters of columns supporting a trio of arches framing views of the formal garden. The garden front forms an unprecedented spectacle of light and shadow, since it is fronted with a continuous open screen of arches on the so-called Venetian window pattern. This consists of three openings, the central one arched and wider than the others. Much used by Palladio, it is also often known as a Serliana or Serlian motif, since it was first illustrated by Serlio in his *Architettura* (1537).

Similarly mannered display is found in the courtyard which Giulio Romano built in 1538–9 in the Palazzo Ducale of the Gonzagas in Mantua. Here overscaled elements clash against each other in a series of façades

334 Courtyard of the Palazzo Ducale, Mantua, by Giulio Romano (1538–9)

335 Giulio Romano's house, Mantua (1538–44)

which are set in dynamic motion by spirally twisting engaged columns, inspired by those on the High Altar of Old St Peter's but used here for the first time in full-scale external architecture. In remodelling Mantua cathedral in the 1540s with a flat-ceilinged nave and Corinthian colonnades, he chose to recall the old-fashioned Early Christian source of Old St Peter's. However, in his own house in Mantua, an imposing palazzo reflecting his high standing in the city, he returns to the caprice of the Palazzo del Tè. It has been interpreted as a kind of parody of Bramante's House of Raphael, marked by a precious quality which is typified by details like the string courses, one of which disappears behind the voussoirs on the ground-floor windows, while the other is wittily bent upwards to form the pediment over the main entrance. Liberties of this kind form part of the style often known today as Mannerism which can be found in the work of Michelangelo, Vasari and Amanati, as well as in that of Giulio Romano. Its complex surface modelling, ambiguous rhythms and disortion of classical motifs have been interpreted as signs of spiritual unrest, but should more probably be explained in internal artistic terms as a reaction against High Renaissance repose.

Michelangelo

Giulio Romano's architecture remained for the most part a sophisticated private game, but the liberties taken by Michelangelo were developed much later by Bernini and Borromini in the new style of classical architecture we know as Baroque. Michelangelo Buonarroti (1475–1564) always regarded himself primarily as a sculptor, a fact which already tells us much about his architecture. Trained as a painter in Florence, his talents were spotted by Lorenzo de' Medici (the Magnificent), in whose stimulating household he lived from c.1489 to 1492. His first major commission came in 1505 for an enormous tomb for Julius II with forty marble figures, but when the pope transferred his interest to Bramante's St Peter's he forced a reluctant Michelangelo to paint the ceiling of the Sistine Chapel instead. During the reigns of two Medici popes whom he had known from boyhood, Leo X (1513–21), younger son of Lorenzo de' Medici, and Clement VII (1523–34), Michelangelo worked on the family church of the Medici in Florence, Brunelleschi's S. Lorenzo. His project of 1517 for the façade in the form of an elegant linear frame to be hung with sculpture was never executed, but his New Sacristy or Medici Chapel was built at the same church in 1519–34. The novelty of this interior is best described by the artist and historian Giorgio Vasari, who joined Michelangelo on this project as a pupil in 1525:

> And since he wished to make it in imitation of the Old Sacristy that Filippo Brunelleschi had built, but with another kind of ornament, he made a composite ornament, in a more varied and more original manner than any other master at any time, whether ancient or modern, had been able to achieve, for in the novelty of the beautiful cornices, capitals, bases, doors, tabernacles, and tombs, he made it very different from the work regulated by measure, order, and rule, which other men did according to normal usage and following Vitruvius and the antiquities, to which he would not conform . . . Therefore the craftsmen owed him an infinite and everlasting

obligation, because he broke the bonds and chains of usage they had always followed.

The peculiar design of the tabernacles pressing down on the doors below them, the strange omissions of expected classical motifs, and the linear weave of overlapping planes, all tend to dissolve the certainties of a wall clearly articulated with functional columns into a piece of linear abstract sculpture. Moreover, as Vasari himself explains, 'Afterwards he demonstrated his method even more clearly in the library of S. Lorenzo . . . where he departed so much from the common use of others, that everyone was amazed.' The entrance vestibule to the library was begun in 1524, though the strange staircase which fills half the floor space was not executed until the 1550s, under the supervision of Ammanati, who based its design on a clay model sent by Michelangelo from Rome in 1550. The visitor is dwarfed by the excessive height of the room with its forbidding blank windows and thwarted by the staircase which seems to impede rather than encourage ascent, flowing downwards like gradually congealing lava. The convex steps of the central flight, widening as they descend, curve outwards at each end into small globular formations seemingly the result of strange internal pressures, while the straight flanking flights, lacking an outer balustrade to provide protection, suggest new hazards. The surrounding walls, left largely blank in their lower sections, are punctuated with over-scaled console brackets which would normally function as supporting members but here hang downwards bearing nothing but their own weight. Above each of them, but deliberately insulated from them, are coupled columns perversely made to appear non-load-bearing by being unconventionally buried in recesses in the wall. Perhaps it is not too fanciful to see these columns, thus constrained within their oppressive niches, as a parallel to Michelangelo's carved figures of captives struggling to emerge from the unworked stone. Michelangelo, one of the first artists who saw himself as a romantic genius, had an inner life full of painful spiritual conflicts, for example between

336 Michelangelo: interior of the Medici Chapel, Florence (1519–34)

337 Vestibule (begun 1524) and staircase (1550s) of the Laurentian Library, Florence, by Michelangelo

his profound Catholic piety and his profound homo-sexuality, and between his obsession with the nude in painting and sculpture and the hostility to the nude of the Counter-Reformation church.

He spent the last thirty years of his life in Rome where his most important works were the Capitoline palaces, the eccentric and theatrical Porta Pia, the church of S. Maria degli Angeli, and the continuation of St Peter's for which he refused to accept any salary. The plateau known as the Campidoglio, on top of the Capitoline hill, had been the centre of Roman political life throughout the Middle Ages. Michelangelo's transformation of the Campidoglio for Pope Paul III from 1538 was the most brilliant of all Renaissance town-planning schemes. It was to be widely influential during the ensuing centuries on the spatial manipulation of voids and masses in urban design as well as on the organization of palaces and villas. Finding a disorderly group of medieval buildings, he left a coherent piazza with five entrances and three palaces. The medieval Senators' Palace on the east side and fifteenth-century Conservators' Palace on the south were not at right angles to each other but at an angle of 80 degrees. Michelangelo exploited this accidental orientation so as to create a trapezoidal piazza with an inlaid pavement forming a raised oval pattern in the centre. The oval, still a novel form in architectural design, was to play a vital part in Baroque planning. In the centre of the oval, on an oval-ended pedestal designed by Michelangelo, stands an equestrian statue of the emperor Marcus Aurelius, brought to the Campidoglio by the pope in 1538. Behind this, at the climax of the whole carefully organized composition, is Michelangelo's great double-ramped staircase in front of the remodelled Senators' Palace. The first staircase of its type to be adapted to the

façade of a palace, this was conceived as a theatrical focus for civic ceremony.

The design of the flanking palaces on either side of the piazza was equally influential. In a popularization of what is known as the 'giant order', Corinthian pilasters rise the full height of the two-storey buildings, with the columns and entablatures of the subsidiary ground-floor order on a separate plane behind them. Once again Michelangelo dissolved the flat wall into a complex grid of interlocking and overlapping planes.

We have already touched on Michelangelo's work at St Peter's where, following his appointment as architect

338 *Right* St Peter's, Rome: the liturgical east end by Michelangelo (1549–58), with the dome and lantern by Giacomo della Porta (1588–93)

339 *Opposite* Michelangelo: Palace on the north side of the Capitol, Rome, designed 1538 (executed 1644–54 by Gerolamo and Carlo Rainaldi), showing the 'giant order'

in 1546, he abandoned Sangallo's plan in favour of a scheme closer to Bramante's. However, he did not resurrect Bramante's subsidiary domes and campanili, but instead carried the outer walls to the same height all round and articulated them with the massive coupled Corinthian pilasters devised by Bramante for the piers supporting the dome inside the church. What is Michelangelo's own contribution is the way that they and the pilaster strips behind them seem to exert pressure on the narrow spaces between them, where oddly-placed little windows and niches seem in danger of being squeezed out of existence. The dynamic verticality of these patterns of movement leads the eye naturally on to the great dome with its near-Gothic system of buttresses and ribs.

Bramante's St Peter's had been conceived by the confident Julius II as a monument which would outshine the baths of ancient Rome. One of Michelangelo's last commissions, from Pope Pius IV in 1561, was to convert the great hall or tepidarium of the Baths of Diocletian (see p. 81) into the church of S. Maria degli Angeli. The adjacent ruins were to become a Carthusian monastery, the most austere of the orders of contemplative monks. In the interval of over half a century between the two popes, Julius and Pius, the church had been confronted

340 Michelangelo: Interior of S. Maria degli Angeli, Rome (begun 1561)

with the spiritual and material threats of the Reformation, initiated by Luther who posted his ninety-five propositions concerning Indulgences to the door of the university church at Wittenberg in 1517, and the Sack of Rome ten years later by the mercenary troops of the emperor Charles V. The humanism and neo-Platonism in which Bramante, Julius and the young Michelangelo indulged had been replaced by a hostility to pagan culture and a reassertion of the strictest Catholicism in the form of the founding of the Jesuit order by Michelangelo's friend, St Ignatius of Loyola, in 1540, the reintroduction of the Inquisition in 1542, and the decrees of the Council of Trent in 1545–63. For a few years in this Counter-Reformation period it seemed that the church might be permanently hostile to pagan, that is classical, forms.

The project of S. Maria degli Angeli was not, however, initiated by a pope as a gesture of triumphalism but was pressed on Pius IV by a Sicilian priest who had had visions of angels. It was in this spirit of piety that the 86-year-old Michelangelo undertook the remodelling of the baths into an austere Carthusian church with simple white walls. The mood was not to last long. The splendour of the ancient world soon captivated the imagination of architects once again, so that in the late Baroque period the architect Vanvitelli buried Michelangelo's work beneath coloured marble decoration closer to the mood of imperial Rome than to Michelangelo's monochrome interior of the 1560s.

High Renaissance in Verona and Venice: Sanmicheli and Sansovino

Though the impact of the Sack of Rome reduced the number of architectural commissions available in Central Italy, the Venetian state remained as powerful as ever. Following the Sack of Rome the sculptor Sansovino (Jacopo Tatti, 1486–1570) left Rome for Venice, then by far the richest city of Italy, where in 1529 he was appointed chief architect. Michele Sanmicheli (1484–1559) was born in Verona, part of the Venetian territory, and was probably trained as an architect in

341 Sanmicheli: Cappella Pellegrini, Verona (begun 1527), with the altarpiece of 1579 by Bernardino India of *The Virgin and Child with St Anne and Angels*

Rome, but by 1530 was in the service of the Venetian Republic to which he subsequently became principal military engineer. His city gates at Verona, the Porta Nuova (1533–40) and the Porta Palio of twenty years later, are defensible buildings where the Doric order has been used symbolically to give an atmosphere of strength. They echo the expressive language of Giulio Romano. Sanmicheli's delectable Cappella Pellegrini, begun in 1527 at S. Bernardino, Verona, is a miniature version of the Pantheon, while his Madonna di Campagna (begun in 1559), a circular pilgrimage church on the outskirts of Verona containing a miraculous image, is less happily proportioned. It is one of the few attempts to follow Alberti's call for a modern church in the form of a free-standing round 'temple', though the interior is octagonal and the choir is a separate centrally-planned unit on a Greek cross plan.

342 *Above* Exterior of Sansovino's library of S. Marco, Venice (begun 1536), with the Campanile

343 *Left* Sansovino: The Loggetta at the foot of the Campanile, Venice (1537)

In Venice state and private patronage was more important than ecclesiastical patronage, so that Sansovino's most important work consists of public buildings and palaces. He is best known for the library of S. Marco, Venice, an L-shaped composition begun in 1536 in a brilliant stroke of town planning which gave their present form to the Piazza S. Marco and the adjacent Piazzetta at right angles to it. The first fully classical building in Venice in which the orders were correctly used, the library was to Palladio in 1570 simply 'the richest and most ornate building that has been put up, perhaps, since the time of the ancients'. Despite its solidly Bramantesque origin, derived from the superimposed orders of the Theatre of Marcellus, the library becomes more festive as it rises. Its increasing richness of surface texture incorporates on the first floor two sets of engaged Ionic columns of contrasting sizes, an abundance of swagged ornament in the frieze, and a dancing skyline of statues and obelisks. The interiors were sumptuously decorated by the painters and sculptors whose splendour, chiaroscuro and colour are precisely analogous to Sansovino's style: Titian, Tintoretto, Veronese, Vittoria and Cattaneo.

Exuberant ornament is the keynote of the opulently decorated Loggetta, which Sansovino built in 1537 next to his library at the base of, and in daring visual contrast to, the medieval campanile. This little building with its triumphal-arch theme was built as an assembly room for the noblemen attending the Councils of State. At about the same time, at the opposite end of the library, he built the Zecca, the mint and treasury in which the bullion of the Republic was stored. It had to look reassuringly strong so Sansovino used the Doric order expressively, as Giulio Romano and Sanmicheli had before him, to convey a striking impression of power, even of brute force. In so doing he introduced rustication, according to Vasari, to Venice.

Giulio Romano again seems to lie behind certain details of Sansovino's incomparably magnificent and influential Palazzo Corner della Ca' Grande (fig. 365), begun after 1533, where the triple-arched entrance loggia derives from the entrance front of the Palazzo del Tè. From the loggia a long gallery leads to a handsome courtyard, unusually large for Venice, with richly modelled rusticated elevations.

In a different mood is Sansovino's Villa Garzoni at Pontecasale near Padua, designed in c.1540 as one of the most serene and harmonious of all High Renaissance buildings. Its U-shaped plan with a loggia in the centre of the entrance front is derived from Peruzzi's Villa Farnesina, but the loggia is duplicated on the first floor and a cloister court opens up at the rear. The villa is a self-contained work of art and it is hard to imagine it as the centre of a working farm. For that transformation we have to turn to the villas of the most famous sixteenth-century architect in the Veneto, Palladio.

Vignola and the origins of Baroque

Before doing so we should investigate villa and palace design in Rome and northern Italy in the second half of

344 Exterior of the Villa Garzoni, Pontecasale, by Sansovino (c.1540)

the sixteenth century. The most important Roman figure is Giacomo Barozzi da Vignola (1507–73), whose first major commission was the Villa Giulia, begun in 1551 as an elegant retreat for Pope Julius III on the edge of Rome. A comparatively plain entrance front is unexpectedly backed by a hemispherical wing with colonnades forming one end of a court which is obviously a reflection of the Belvedere Court at the Vatican. This court is terminated by an open loggia which looks into the second court, a semi-circular nymphaeum flanked by quadrant staircases and terminating in yet another open belvedere. With assistance from Ammanati, Vasari, Michelangelo and the pope himself, Vignola blended buildings, gardens, terraces, fountains, staircases and sculpture into a paradise where Julius would dine out of doors to the accompaniment of minstrels and dancers, before returning via the river Tiber to the Vatican in a flower-decked boat.

The Palazzo Farnese at Caprarola, where Vignola worked from 1552 to 1573, is a very different affair, half palace, half castle, on a pentagonal plan established by Antonio da Sangallo the younger and Peruzzi in the 1520s. Its operatic setting at the head of vast flights of external staircases and ramps is reflected in its dramatic internal disposition round a great circular courtyard ringed with colonnades giving access to the principal rooms, all richly frescoed. No less dynamic is the layout

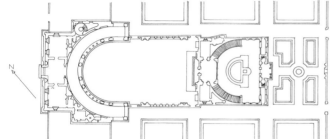

of the formal gardens which culminate in a secret garden, reached through a wood. This is presided over by Vignola's Villa Farnese, where Cardinal Alessandro Farnese could escape from the public ceremonies surrounding a prince of the church.

The same cardinal was the patron and benefactor of the Gesù, mother church in Rome of the Jesuit order, which Vignola began in 1568. It was destined to be an influential type, since the Jesuits imitated it throughout the world. Cardinal Farnese wrote to Vignola in 1568: 'The church is not to have a nave and two aisles, but is to consist of one nave only with chapels down each side. . . . The church is to be entirely vaulted over . . . [so as to be] well adapted to the voice.' The Jesuits needed a preaching hall in which everyone also had a

345, 346 *Left above and left* View of the hemicycle and plan of the Villa Giulia, Rome (begun 1551) by Vignola

347 *Below* Exterior of the Palazzo Farnese, Caprarola, by Vignola (1552–73)

348 A general view of Florence and the cathedral

clear view of the High Altar. Vignola returned to the broad, aisleless, tunnel-vaulted nave devised by Alberti at S. Andrea, Mantua, though his side chapels are far lower and less important visually than Alberti's. Originally the twin pilasters in the nave were plain grey and the vault was stuccoed in white. This austerity was in accordance with the artistic ideals of the Council of Trent (1545–63), which was called to renew discipline and spiritual life within the Roman Catholic church. The richly Baroque illusionistic frescoes and coloured marbling with which the interior was subsequently overlaid would not have been welcomed by Vignola,

241

349 Façade of the Gesù, Rome, by Giacomo della Porta, from a design by Vignola (begun 1571)

350 Plan of the Gesù by Vignola

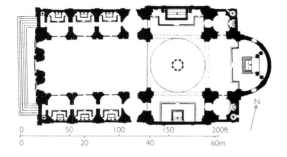

though it must be said that the way in which he contracted and darkened the last bay of the nave, so as to contrast with the burst of light flooding down from the dome, is already a Baroque device. Similarly, in introducing the oval plan to church design for the first time in S. Andrea in Via Flaminia and S. Anna dei Palafrenieri, two Roman buildings of the 1550s, he pioneered a plan which was to be fundamental to much Baroque architecture. The two-storeyed façade of the Gesù, also influential, was begun in 1571 by Giacomo della Porta (1533–1602), who chose to complicate

unnecessarily a design by Vignola. With its large scrolls smoothing the transition to the higher central portion, it is derived from another pioneering work of Alberti, S. Maria Novella in Florence.

Among those whom Vignola influenced in Rome none was more famous than Domenico Fontana (1543–1607), best known for re-erecting the Egyptian obelisk in the Piazza di S. Pietro in 1586. He did this in his capacity as architect to Pope Sixtus V (1585–90), who began replanning the city of Rome with gusto, forming new streets marked at their intersections by obelisks and fountains. Fontana's independent buildings are far less lively, as can be seen from the vast papal palace of the Lateran, begun in 1586, and indeed from the Vatican itself, which is largely his work.

The town planning which we have noted as characterizing High Renaissance ambition at Venice and Rome found equally splendid expression in the republic of Genoa. Here Galeazzo Alessi (1512–72), trained in Rome where he was influenced by Michelangelo, was involved in the layout from 1550 of a grand new street of patrician palaces, the Strada Nuova (now Via Garibaldi). His largest palace, not in Genoa but in Milan, is the Palazzo Marino, begun in 1558 for a newly wealthy Genoese merchant on the scale of, and with something of the florid decoration of, a mid-nineteenth-century government building, while his domed centrally-planned church of S. Maria di Carignano, begun on a hilltop in Genoa in 1549, is a bold echo of the early designs for St Peter's of Bramante, Michelangelo and Sangallo.

Charles Borromeo, the Archbishop of Milan (later canonized) who produced a book of instructions for church builders in 1577 in conformity with the decrees of the Council of Trent, gave employment both to Alessi and to Pellegrino Pellegrini (or Tibaldi, 1527–96). Pellegrini's Collegio Borromeo at Pavia (1564), with its arcaded courtyard, echoes Alessi's Palazzo Marino. Another major Milanese project initiated by Borromeo was the rebuilding by Martino Bassi (1542–91) of the Early Christian church of S. Lorenzo after its collapse in 1573. It is astonishing to see this *cinquecento* edifice rising

from a late-antique quatrefoil plan, which Borromeo insisted should be retained.

A larger and later centrally-planned building in north Italy was begun for Duke Carlo Emanuele I of Savoy in 1596 from designs by Ascanio Vitozzi (c.1539–1615). This is the pilgrimage or sanctuary church of S. Maria at Vicoforte di Mondovi in Piedmont. Housing a miraculous image beneath its high dome, which was flanked by corner towers, and providing chapels for family tombs, since this was also a dynastic funerary church, S. Maria has a dynamic oval plan which contained the seeds of Piedmontese Baroque. The elongated oval plan is typical of Baroque with its dynamic directional movement, in contrast to the static circular plan which is characteristic of High Renaissance calm and harmony.

Palladio and High Renaissance harmony

The work of Andrea Palladio (1508–80) has been valued for centuries as the quintessence of High Renaissance calm and harmony. Indeed, there is probably no architect whose work has been so widely imitated in so many countries for so long a period. This is partly because most of his buildings survive, and also because he publicized his ideals in a lucid illustrated treatise, *I Quattro Libri dell' Architettura* ('The Four Books of architecture') (Venice, 1570). This book provides illustrations of the classical orders, of some of the most important buildings of Roman antiquity, and of a range of Palladio's own works in plan, elevation and section with measurements and descriptive text. His own buildings thus appear on a par with those of antiquity.

The belief that the harmonic proportions of Palladio's designs were divinely inspired lent them further authority. The identification of musical and spatial ratios in the Renaissance went back to the Greeks, supposedly including Pythagoras himself. When plucking strings of different lengths to produce different notes, they observed that a string half the length of another will result in a difference in pitch of an octave, two thirds of

351 The Strada Nuova, Genoa, by Alessi (begun 1550)

352 Vitozzi: Plan of S. Maria, Vicoforte di Mondovi (begun 1596)

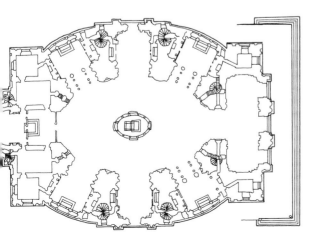

the length a fifth, and three-quarters of the length a quarter. It was thus supposed that solids and voids with similar ratios, i.e. of 1: 2, 2: 3 or 3: 4, would acquire a visual harmony analogous to musical harmony. Hence the care with which Palladio published the measurements of his buildings and their interior spaces, sometimes showing, in the case of rooms that measure 18×20 units or 12×20, that he used ratios of 3: 5 in addition to the Greek musical scale, or elsewhere major and minor thirds such as 5: 6 and 4: 5. Investigation of Palladio's buildings does not always bear out the accuracy of the measurements shown in his plans, and doubtless in designing his buildings he was initially guided by his eye rather than by an abstract ratio in his mind. Nonetheless, we cannot appreciate all the allusions in his work without being aware of his belief in mathematical harmonies and in their reflection of the divine order of the cosmos.

He was trained as a stonemason and sculptor, but his talents were not spotted until he was taken up at about the age of thirty by Count Giangiorgio Trissino, a humanist scholar in Vicenza. Trissino accompanied him to Rome, where he studied the monuments of antiquity, and even provided him with a neo-antique name, Palladio, an allusion to the Greek goddess of wisdom Pallas Athene, in place of his more mellifluous family name, Andrea di Pietro della Gondola. His first commission was for the refronting of the medieval basilica or town hall in Vicenza in 1549. Here he adopted the Venetian-window openings of Sansovino's library in Venice in a dramatic way. There followed a succession of town palaces in Vicenza of which often little more than the street block was built, though the plans in *I Quattro Libri* tend to equip them with full-scale neo-antique peristyles. The rusticated Palazzo Thiene (c. 1550) shows him in a heroic mood derived from Giulio Romano, while the Palazzo Valmarana (1566) has an order of giant pilasters derived from Michelangelo's Capitoline palaces incorporated into a linear pattern of overlapping planes with liberal use of sculpture, forming a pattern which is often interpreted as Mannerist.

A certain Mannerist strangeness colours two late works of c. 1570, the Villa Sarego with its blocky rusticated columns like piles of cheeses, and the Loggia del Capitaniato opposite his basilica in the Piazza dei Signori in Vicenza. Begun in 1571 for the Venetian *capitano* (captain or governor) of the city to contain an assembly hall and a balcony from which proclamations could be made, the Loggia was abandoned unfinished in 1572. Though it was complete as a design in itself, it is possible that the façade would have been extended by another two bays. The form of the building was an echo of the open arched loggias which in most Italian communes from the early Middle Ages served as a background for civic ceremonies. However, the side elevation takes the form of a triumphal arch with an accompanying relief in honour of the Battle of Lepanto

353 Palladio: Loggia del Capitaniato, Vicenza (begun 1571)

354 *Opposite above* The nave of St Peter's, Rome, by Carlo Maderno (1607–c.1614), showing the baldacchino by Bernini (1624–33)

355 *Opposite below* Michelangelo: The Medici Chapel or New Sacristy (1519–34)

356 Exterior of the Villa Barbaro, Maser, by Palladio (c.1560)

of 1571, and is oddly related to the main front, where the giant columns seem to have survived from an antique building into which later work has been embedded. The windows break into the entablature; triglyphs, strayed from a non-existent Doric frieze, act as brackets supporting the balconies; the walls are covered with stuccoed ornament. This polychromatic sculptural building has few parallels in Palladio's oeuvre.

Among Palladio's numerous villas in the Veneto the Villa Barbaro at Maser (c.1560) is closest to the Loggia del Capitaniato. Its façade is crowned by a pediment like that of a temple, but the columns are engaged to the wall and the entablature is abruptly broken into by a round-headed window, the head of which is smothered with stucco swags. It was built for Palladio's friends, the Barbaro brothers, of whom Daniele was a humanist scholar and author of a translation of Vitruvius for which Palladio provided the illustrations. In the course of this book Barbaro praises the work of Pirro Ligorio (c.1510–83) whose miniature masterpiece, the Casino del Pio IV in the Vatican (begun 1559), has a Mannerist façade smothered with stuccoed ornament. Perhaps certain elements of the Villa Barbaro derive from Daniele's enthusiasm for Ligorio, while he may also have selected the themes of Roman ruins, landscapes and

figures with which Veronese illusionistically frescoed the cruciform hall and garden room.

The latter leads into the semi-circular nymphaeum around a pool at the back of the villa where niches contain stucco statues by Alessandro Vittoria representing the deities of Olympus. Palladio took the trouble to describe this garden in *I Quattro Libri*, making it clear that the water from the fountain pool first fed the kitchen, then two fishponds, and finally irrigated the kitchen garden. Indeed the whole classical allusion contrived by Barbaro, Palladio, Veronese and Vittoria is disarmingly contained within the confines of a working farm, the body of the villa being flanked by arcades housing animals, dovecots and farm equipment. This pattern is repeated in Palladio's other villas because the Venetian and Vicentine aristocrats for whom they were built, facing a decline in Venetian overseas trade, found it profitable to develop commercially their holdings on dry land, as well as to live on them from time to time.

His earlier villas have considerable variety of form, often based on themes from the Roman baths, but in the absence of information about what ancient Roman houses were really like he came, wrongly, to assume that, like temples, they would have sported porticoes. Thus the villas Pisani (at Montagnana), Badoer, Chiericati, Emo, Foscari (the Malcontenta), Cornaro and Rotonda, all dating from the 1550s and 1560s, form a delightful set of variations on the theme of the temple front with

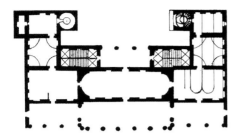

357 Plan of the Palazzo Chiericati, Vicenza (1550s/60s) by Palladio

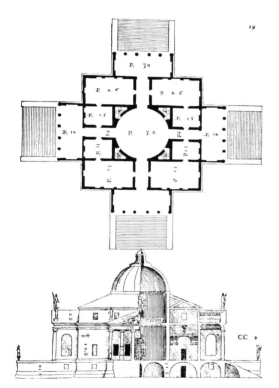

358 *Above right* Exterior of the Palazzo Chiericati, Vicenza, by Palladio

359 *Above* Plan and section of the Villa Rotonda, near Vicenza (c.1566–70) by Palladio

360 *Right* Exterior of the Villa Rotonda

361 *Overleaf* The Château de Chambord, begun in 1519 by Domenico da Cortona

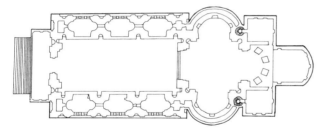

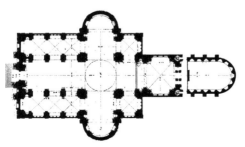

362 *Top* Interior of Il Redentore, Venice, by Palladio, showing the screen of columns at the east end (1576–7)

363 *Centre* Plan of Il Redentore, Venice, by Palladio

364 *Above* Plan of San Giorgio Maggiore, by Palladio

portico and of the two-storeyed villa with superimposed colonnades or loggias. They gain additional variety by the different placing of the outbuildings and the wings, sometimes quadrant, which link them to the villa itself. The most celebrated is one of the most formal, perhaps because it was near Vicenza and so a *villa suburbana*, lacking service buildings, rather than a *villa rustica*. This is the Villa Rotonda, built in c.1566–70 for Paolo Almerico, a retired Monsignor and officer of the papal court. It is intended to demonstrate the beauty of pure form with its geometrical plan composed of square, circle and rectangle, and its four symmetrical porticoed faces. Palladio himself describes it as a pure work of art whose only function was to serve as a belvedere: 'It is upon a small hill of very easy access . . . and is encompassed with most pleasant hills, which look like a very great theatre, and are all cultivated . . . and therefore, as it enjoys from every part most beautiful views, some of which are limited, some more extended, and others that terminate the horizon, there are loggias made in all the four fronts.' Such a combination of classic harmony with an appreciation of natural scenery was high among the qualities which endeared Palladio to the Whig noblemen landowners of eighteenth-century England, for whom no less than four variants of the Villa Rotonda were erected between the 1720s and 1750s (see pp. 374–6).

The countryside is visible not only from the porticoes at the Villa Rotonda but even from the central circular hall or saloon. This richly stuccoed and frescoed room is surmounted by a dome, perhaps the first application to domestic architecture of a form especially associated with churches. It is indeed stylistically close to his little chapel of 1579–80 in the grounds of the Villa Barbaro at Maser. In Venice his two major churches, S. Giorgio Maggiore (1565) and Il Redentore (1576–7), are both domed but both reject the central plan so dear to Alberti. However, they develop Alberti's attempts to find an appropriately classical solution for the west front of a Christian church, by devising a subtle method of interlocking two separate pedimented temple fronts with engaged columns. Both churches have unusual plans which related to the need to house two choirs on special liturgical occasions attended by the Doge. In each case the monastic choir, which is Benedictine at S. Giorgio and Capuchin at the Redentore, is placed behind a screen of columns. At the Redentore this screen takes a boldly segmental form, perhaps inspired by the great halls of the baths which Palladio had begun his career by studying. The structure of the Redentore, too, is imperial Roman. It reverts to a method of supporting the vault by means of the wall mass, hollowed by niches and hung with purely decorative columns. In this serene white and grey interior, which realizes with such grace and poetry so many of the ambitions of Alberti and Bramante, we may appropriately terminate our survey of one of the greatest phases of western classical architecture.

The Renaissance outside Italy

France under François I

In no other European country do we find so consistent a tradition as in Italy of harmonious classical architecture in a High Renaissance style. Outside Italy, Gothic persisted throughout the fifteenth century, knowledge of the Renaissance arriving after 1500 largely in the form of ornamental details. Of the various European countries France produced the most ambitious and extensive Renaissance architecture, partly because of the direct contact with Italy which had been established by the Italian campaigns of the French kings in the late fifteenth and early sixteenth centuries. Charles VIII's invasions of Naples and Milan in 1494 and the re-establishment of French power in Milan and Genoa by Louis XII and François I in 1500–25 introduced medieval Frenchmen to the fullness of Renaissance culture. The French returned to France eager to imitate the sophisticated classicism of Italian courts, not only in architecture, painting and sculpture, but in dress, furniture, interior decoration, indeed in the whole way of life associated with the Renaissance palace.

One of the leading patrons was Cardinal Georges d'Amboise, Archbishop of Rouen, chief minister to Louis XII and viceroy of Milan, who built the château of Gaillon near Rouen in 1502–10 with the assistance of craftsmen from Tours and of artists brought back from Italy. All that survives is the gateway of c.1508 which, though medieval in form, boasts classical pilasters and friezes decorated in the Lombardic Renaissance style. The châteaux of Bury (1511–24), Chenonceaux (1515–24) and Azay-le-Rideau (1518–27), all built for wealthy financiers, echo this kind of ornament and also introduce a new regularity of plan. However, they combine these features with skylines of gabled dormers, high roofs, chimneys and turrets, producing a romantic effect which it is tempting to describe as self-consciously medievalizing.

The same combination is found on a grander scale in the royal palaces of Blois and Chambord in the Loire district, where François I indulged his passion for building in a spectacular manner. At Blois in 1515–24 he constructed a new wing on medieval foundations with an old-fashioned plan but sporting a three-storeyed open arcaded loggia on its outer façade. Though inspired by the contemporary *logge* of the Vatican, this rather misses the point because, except on the top storey, there is no internal communication between one bay and the next. On the court façade the famous open staircase brings Renaissance detailing and a new monumentality to the traditional stone spiral staircases of fifteenth-century France. The same qualities appear at Chambord, essentially a moated medieval castle dominated by a square keep which is flanked with round conically-roofed towers. However, the keep is built, unusually, on a Greek cross plan of Renaissance origin. Indeed, the architect was Domenico da Cortona, a pupil of Giuliano da Sangallo in whose pioneering Villa Medici at Poggio a Caiano near Florence (c.1480) groups of rooms are arranged to form suites as at Chambord. *Appartements* of this kind were to become the norm in French château

365 *Opposite* The Palazzo Corner della Ca' Grande, Venice, by Sansovino (mid-16th century)

366 *Above* The François I gallery at Fontainebleau, with stuccowork and painting by Rosso and Primaticcio (1530s)

architecture. At the centre of the Greek cross plan at Chambord is the celebrated double spiral staircase which may have been inspired by designs by Leonardo da Vinci, whom François I had lured to France in 1516. The fantastic skyline of Chambord is a unique example of

Flamboyant Gothic exuberance combined with surprisingly pure classical details (fig. 361).

François I also built numerous palaces in the Ile de France, notably the châteaux of Madrid and Fontainebleau. The former, begun in 1528 with a plan inspired by Poggio a Caiano and elaborate terracotta decoration by Girolamo della Robbia, no longer survives, but the additions at Fontainebleau of 1528–40 constitute the most complete early Renaissance ensemble in France. The architect Gilles le Breton (d. 1553) extended the medieval buildings in a haphazardly planned way of which the principal survivals are the Porte Dorée, with superimposed *logge* like those at the Ducal Palace at Urbino, and the simpler north side of the Cour du Cheval Blanc.

The Long Gallery at Fontainebleau, later known as the Galerie François I (fig. 366), is the earliest example of a type of room which became popular in France and England, though its architectural origin and even its function remain unclear. Its elaborate but refined interior decoration of c.1533–40 is by Giovanni Battista Rosso (1494–1540), a Florentine artist who had left Rome following the Sack in 1527 and was summoned to the court of François I in 1530. He was joined in 1532 by Francesco Primaticcio (c.1504–70), who had worked from 1526 under Giulio Romano on the interiors of the Palazzo del Tè in Mantua. The combination of stucco work and mural painting completely concealing the wall surface, which makes the gallery so memorable, is derived from the decorative treatment of the façades of Raphael's Palazzo Branconio dell' Aquila, Rome (1516–17), as well as from Giulio Romano, while the carvings of mannered long-limbed young men are frankly Michelangelesque. An especially dominant feature of the plasterwork is strapwork decoration, used here for the first time on this scale and later featuring excessively in English, German and Flemish ornament.

The course of French architecture was further influenced by the arrival at Fontainebleau in 1540 from Venice of Sebastiano Serlio (1475–1554), who had worked under Peruzzi from 1514 until the Sack of

367 The court façade at Blois (1515–24), showing the open staircase

Rome. At Fontainebleau he built the now demolished 'Grand Ferrare' in 1541–8 for Ippolito d'Este, Cardinal of Ferrara and papal legate to France. A town house or *hôtel* round three sides of a courtyard, this established the typical French plan for such houses for over a century. His principal building in France is the château of Ancy-le-Franc in Burgundy (c.1541–50) with courtyard elevations in which the rhythm of coupled pilasters and niches is derived from Bramante's Belvedere Court at the Vatican.

Serlio illustrated the Belvedere Court in his *Regole generali di architettura* ('General rules of architecture'), an architectural treatise which, published in six parts in 1537–51 with a posthumous seventh part in 1575, was to be more influential than his few executed buildings.

368 *Above* Serlio: Courtyard of the Château of Ancy-le-Franc, Burgundy (c.1541–50)

369 *Below* Plan of the Château de Chambord (begun 1519) by Domenico da Cortona, from a drawing by Androuet du Cerceau

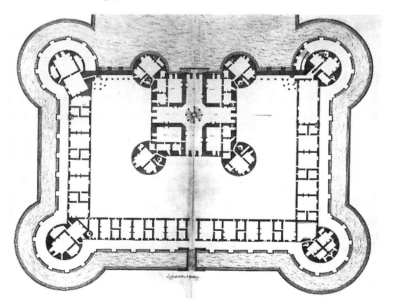

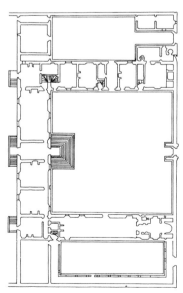

370 *Above* Plan of 'Le Grand Ferrare', Fontainebleau, by Serlio (1541–8)

371 The Queen's House, Greenwich, by Inigo Jones, begun 1616; extended 1661 by John Webb

A practical compendium, avoiding the theory so dear to Alberti, its popularity perhaps depended partly on its lack of intellectual or conceptual content. Also, it was not written in Latin, like Alberti's, but in the Italian vernacular, from which it was translated into French, Flemish, German, Spanish, Dutch and English. The first book to codify the five orders, it also contained information on how to construct the orders as well as illustrations of the antique and Renaissance buildings of Rome, and designs for churches, houses, chimney-pieces, windows and gateways incorporating a wealth of ornament, often marked by Mannerist licence. This ornament was eagerly taken up by builders and craftsmen who tended to superimpose it on buildings of fundamentally Gothic character.

The establishment of French classicism: Lescot, de l'Orme and Bullant

The building which established French classicism was not by Serlio, but was the Square Court of the Louvre in Paris, begun in 1546 for François I by Pierre Lescot (1510/15–1578). The façades are bold and richly modelled with a great variety of window treatment and with accurately detailed columns and pilasters of the richest of orders, Corinthian and Composite. The sculptural richness is heightened by the figures and reliefs inside and outside the building, carved by the sculptor Jean Goujon whose work can also be seen at Lescot's Hôtel Carnavalet, Paris, begun in c.1545. Lescot was a very different figure from the master-masons of medieval France or even from an architect like Gilles le Breton. Born into a noble and prosperous legal family, he was well educated in mathematics, geometry and painting as well as in architecture.

372 Square Court of the Louvre, Paris, by Lescot (begun 1546)

More distinguished though more capricious than Lescot was Philibert de l'Orme (1505/10–1570), a brilliant enigmatic architect most of whose work has been destroyed. Born in Lyons, the son of a master-mason, he was in Rome in the 1530s studying the antiquities and forming a friendship with the collector and excavator Cardinal du Bellay and his secretary, the humanist author Rabelais. In c.1540 he designed for the cardinal the château at St-Maur-les-Fossés near Charenton, which was an echo of the Palazzo del Tè. In 1547–52 he built the château at Anet near Dreux in Normandy for Diane de Poitiers, mistress of Henri II, whom he had met through du Bellay.

His inventive and experimental style can be well appreciated at Anet in the beautifully grouped entrance gateway. This is a novel variant of the triumphal arch motif, treated in an abstract sculptural way which is emphasized by the unusual chimneys in the form of antique sarcophagi. The nearby chapel is an arresting version of the circular form recommended by Alberti, adopted by Bramante at the Tempietto, and continued

by Sanmichele in the Cappella Pellegrini at S. Bernardino, Verona, a building which de l'Orme seems to have studied closely. The ingenious coffering of the dome at Anet produces a spiralling network of diamond-shaped panels which is echoed in the design of the black and white marble floor. Both coffering and floor have antique sources in the Temple of Venus and Rome (fig. 97) and in certain Roman mosaic pavements, but are deployed here in an animated and utterly novel way. The west front is flanked by towers capped with tall pyramidal roofs which have a curiously antique flavour.

Unfortunately, the château at Anet has been largely demolished, though the frontispiece from the main block was re-erected in the courtyard of the Ecole des Beaux-Arts in Paris. A tower of the orders with Doric, Ionic and Corinthian on its three storeys, this frontispiece has a severity and monumentality which contrast with the richer work of Lescot at the Louvre.

In his capacity as superintendent of buildings to Henri II de l'Orme designed the superb tomb of François I at St-Denis in 1547. This is inspired by the Arch of Septimius Severus in Rome, though an elegant

PLANVM SACELLI INTRA
ÆDIFICII PROXINTVM
CONSTITVTI DANET

LE PLAN DE LA
CHAPPELLE DEDANS
LE LOGIS DANET.

373 *Left* Plan of the Château of Anet, near Dreux
(1547–52), by de l'Orme

374 *Below* Entrance gateway of the château at Anet

Ionic order has been substituted for the more florid Corinthian of the Roman original, and the central arched bay has also been brought dramatically forward. The base of the tomb and the barrel-vault within are exquisitely adorned with bas-reliefs by the sculptor Pierre Bontemps. These and the use of coloured marbles provide a surface richness which contrasts effectively with the sobriety of the actual architecture. In 1567 de l'Orme published *Le Premier tome de l'Architecture* ('First volume of architecture'), in which his independence, ingenuity and determination to avoid slavish imitation of Italian models led him to invent a French order of classical architecture in addition to the five Italian orders. The book was to have been followed by another which would have included an exposition of his theory of Divine Proportion, based on the accounts given in the Old Testament of the buildings of which the design was dictated by God to the Jews.

Philibert de l'Orme is of central importance for having established an essentially French version of classicism which can be said to have survived until the eighteenth century. His gravity and fire, as well as many specific architectural features, recur in the work of Jean Bullant, Salomon de Brosse and, above all, in his most distinguished disciple, François Mansart. At the château of Ecouen, Seine-et-Oise, Jean Bullant (c.1515/20–1578) provided a now destroyed frontispiece in c.1555–60 which was inspired by Philibert de l'Orme's at Anet, but his surviving entrance portico of c.1560 on the south side introduces the giant order for the first time in France. This taste for monumentality recurs in the remarkable gallery he built at Fère-en-Tardenois for his patron at Ecouen, Constable Anne de Montmorency, to connect the fortified thirteenth-century château with its dependencies. A series of giant arches carries the gallery dramatically across the valley, creating an impression of a Roman aqueduct which is fortuitously heightened by the present ruinous state of the building. In about 1560 Bullant built the small château at Chantilly, again for Montmorency. It features a monumental arch supported by coupled columns, perhaps inspired by Bramante's

work of the 1490s, though used at Chantilly with Mannerist freedom not to mark an entrance but simply as an applied decorative device to enliven a façade containing windows but no doors. Syncopated Mannerist rhythms recur in the gallery he built in the 1570s for the Queen Mother, Catherine de' Medici, over Philibert de l'Orme's bridge at Chenonceaux, one of the loveliest of all the Loire châteaux.

375 View of the Petit Château at Chantilly, with Bullant's frontispiece of c.1560 in the centre

376 De l'Orme and Bullant: Château de Chenonceaux (1556–c.1576)

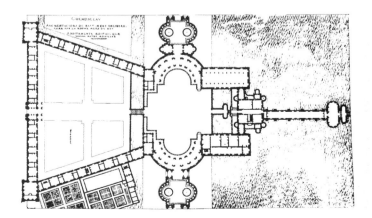

Bullant's shift from de l'Orme's gravity to Mannerist caprice brought him close to the style of Jacques Androuet du Cerceau the Elder (c.1515–c. 1585), the founder of a dynasty of French architects and decorators. He is best known for his books of engravings, which included many extravagant decorative details often based on Italian *grotteschi* (p. 227). Beginning with his *Livre d'Architecture* ('Book of architecture', 1559), he published numerous designs for town houses and châteaux as a guide to builders, while his *Les plus excellents Bastiments de France* ('The finest buildings in France', 2 vols., 1576 and 1579), is a proud record of the Frenchness of French classical architecture, though he could not resist adding ornamental features of his own fantastical invention to his records of existing buildings.

Pride in French achievement combined with emphasis on domestic comfort at a bourgeois level also mark the town-planning schemes with which Henri IV gave new heart to the capital of a country worn out after the Wars of Religion (1560–98). In 1599–1610 he completed the Pont Neuf, built the Hôpital St Louis, began the Collège de France and, most importantly, created the rectangular Place Royale (now Place des Vosges), the triangular Place Dauphine and the semi-circular Place de France. While the squares of Italian towns were dignified by public buildings, Henri's squares were important for providing the regularity of Italian Renaissance design as a background to the private houses of the prosperous bourgeoisie. With its dignified but homely architecture of sensible red brick with stone quoins, the Place des Vosges, begun in 1605, survives largely intact as an attractive souvenir of Henri IV's urban ideals. It was to prove influential in France and beyond, one of its notable descendants being Inigo Jones's Covent Garden in London of c.1630.

The development of classicism by de Brosse, Lemercier and Mansart

French classical architecture in the seventeenth century before the adoption of Baroque ideals is dominated by three architects, Salomon de Brosse (c.1571–1626),

377 *Above* The Place des Vosges, Paris (begun 1605)

Jacques Lemercier (c.1582–1654) and François Mansart (1598–1666). Though he was the grandson of Jacques Androuet du Cerceau, Salomon de Brosse rejected his emphasis on ornament and detail and conceived his buildings in the round. This sculptural sense of mass is immediately evident in all his principal works, including the château of Blérancourt (1612–19), now demolished; the Palais du Luxembourg in Paris (c.1614) for the Queen Regent, Marie de' Medici; and the palace for the *parlement* of Brittany at Rennes (1618). Blérancourt was significant as the first free-standing symmetrical château built in France since Philibert de l'Orme's pioneering Château Neuf at St-Germain. Unencumbered by subsidiary service wings, Blérancourt could be admired from all four sides as a pure work of art. Salomon's characteristically clear architectural masses articulated with crisp classical detail, shown even on a small scale in his surviving Vignolesque pavilions in the forecourt of Blérancourt, make him the true forerunner of the greatest architect in seventeenth-century France, François Mansart (1598–1666).

Jacques Lemercier, who had studied in Rome in c.1607–14, brought to Paris the academic taste of contemporary Rome as expressed in the language of Giacomo della Porta and Vignola. We can see this in his domed church of the College of the Sorbonne (begun in 1626) with its plan based on that of Rosato Rosati's S. Carlo ai Catinari, Rome (1612). The Sorbonne was commissioned by Cardinal Richelieu, Louis XlII's chief minister, for whom Lemercier also built the château and adjacent new town of Richelieu, Indre-et-Loire, from 1631. The now demolished château was less interesting than the town, which survives as a striking example of the impact of Henri IV's Parisian *places*. With its grid plan containing two squares, of which the larger is flanked by the church and the market hall, Richelieu reflects the French aptitude for centralized planning which might also be seen as the basis of Cardinal Richelieu's success as a statesman.

The château of Balleroy, Calvados, begun in c.1626 as an early work of François Mansart, is also a variant on the brick and stone domestic architecture of Henri IV, though it also demonstrates Mansart's brilliant grouping of masses. Also memorable is his lively connection of the château with the approach from the village in a series of different levels connected with staircases and terraces. The first work of Mansart's maturity is the Orléans wing at Blois, built in 1635–8 for the brother of Louis XIII, Gaston, Duc d'Orléans, whose chancellor was the son of Mansart's patron at Balleroy. Mansart was humbly born, the son of a master carpenter, and was trained by his brother-in-law, Germain Gaultier, who had worked with Salomon de Brosse at Rennes. The later work at Blois is derived from buildings by de Brosse such as Blérancourt and the Luxembourg Palace, but is marked by increased purity of detail, producing a grave classic lucidity which has been compared to the tragedies of Pierre Corneille (1606–84), the classical paintings of Nicolas Poussin (1593/4–1665) and the philosophy of René Descartes (1596–1650). Mansart's subtle planning at Blois conceals the difference in axis and in ground level between the entrance front and the garden front.

In later work Mansart modelled his surfaces more richly, as in his masterpiece, the château of Maisons (today Maisons-Lafitte) near Paris, begun in 1642 for the wealthy financier René de Longueil, who gave him a free hand. It is conceived as a free-standing block on an imposing moated stone terrace with only the smallest projections in the form of one-storeyed wings on the

378 Exterior of the church of the College of the Sorbonne, Paris, by Lemercier (begun 1626)

entrance front; the walls are a rectilinear grid modelled in depth with a series of sharply cut panelled planes defined by pilasters, free-standing columns, entablatures and window surrounds. It is a hymn in praise of the orders. The variety and subtlety of this essentially architectural ornamental treatment are reflected in the interior, in the oval rooms in the wings and especially in the entrance vestibule and adjacent staircase where the carved Doric order and the allegorical reliefs are left in plain stone with neither colour nor gilding.

In ecclesiastical architecture Mansart was less significant, but his Ste Marie de la Visitation in Paris of 1632–3 is a circular domed church surrounded by small chapels on three sides as at de l'Orme's chapel at Anet. The oval, cut-off domes dramatically silhouetted against light flooding in from tall lanterns introduce a note of almost Baroque complexity into a building of fundamentally High Renaissance character. The same

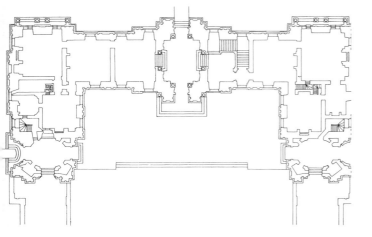

379, 380 *Above and below* Mansart: Plan and exterior of the château of Maisons-Lafitte, near Paris (begun 1642)

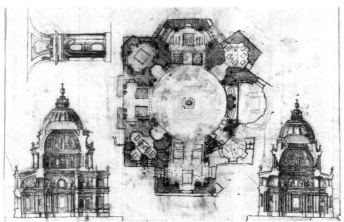

381 *Above* Mansart: Plan and sections for the Bourbon chapel at St-Denis (1665)

spatial interest colours the Parisian church of the Val-de-Grâce, begun in 1645 by Anne of Austria in fulfilment of a vow made before the birth of the Dauphin, the future Louis XIV. Mansart was a vain and difficult man, a perfectionist accustomed to change his designs constantly while they were in process of execution. Not all patrons were as accommodating as René de Longeuil, so that the building of the Val-de-Grâce was removed from his hands and entrusted to Lemercier in 1646. His indecisiveness or, as it might equally be called, endless fertility of invention, lost him the commission for the east front of the Louvre for which, at the invitation of Louis XIV's chief adviser Colbert, he had produced numerous monumental projects in 1664. For Colbert he also prepared designs in 1665 for an immense chapel for the tombs of the Bourbon dynasty at St-Denis. Echoing designs by Leonardo da Vinci, the central domed space was surrounded by smaller chapels but these were to be surmounted by cut-off domes through which the spectator could see the outer shell dome. This Baroque device, which he had hinted at in the staircase at Blois, was to influence the dome of the Invalides designed by his great-nephew, J. H. Mansart, in the 1680s.

Spain

The arrival of Renaissance forms in Spain was fostered, as it was in France, by the country's political links with Italy. Even before Spanish rule in Naples under Charles V from 1526 and Philip II from 1555 ensured close artistic contact we can see Italian influence in early buildings like the Royal Hospital at Santiago de Compostela, designed in 1501 by Enrique Egas (d.1534) for the Catholic Monarchs, Ferdinand and Isabella, who at the same time were commissioning the Tempietto in Rome from Bramante. The hospital at Compostela has a cruciform plan echoing those of Filarete's Ospedale Maggiore at Milan and of Sangallo's S. Spirito Hospital in Rome. The elaborate but delicate ornament round the doors and windows, blending Gothic form with Lombardic Renaissance detail, is in the style known as Plateresque from a supposed affinity with silversmiths'

382 *Above* Siloe: Dome of the rotunda at the east end of Granada cathedral (begun 1528)

383 *Above right* The Royal Hospital at Santiago de Compostela (1501–11) by Egas, with the portal of 1518

384 *Right* Circular courtyard of the palace built by Machuca (1527–68) for Charles V at the Alhambra, Granada

work. One of the most stylish products of the last phase of this style is the College of S. Ildefonso at Alcalá de Henares of 1537–53 by Rodrigo Gil de Hontañón (1500/10–77), while the main north façade of the Alcázar at Toledo (designed 1537, executed 1546–52) by Alonso de Covarrubias (1488–1570) is perhaps closer to Italian architecture, though Renaissance forms are still essentially employed as decoration.

Strikingly different is the unfinished palace built in 1527–68 for the Emperor Charles V inside the Alhambra

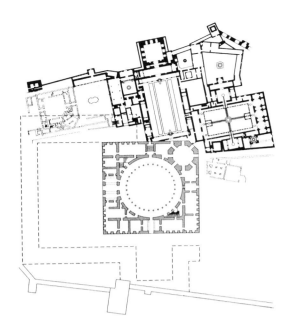

385 *Above* Plan of the Alhambra, with Machuca's circular courtyard

386 *Above right* The Portal of Pardon, Granada cathedral, by Siloe (begun 1536)

387, 388 *Below and opposite* Toledo and Herrera: Plan and exterior of the Escorial (1563–82)

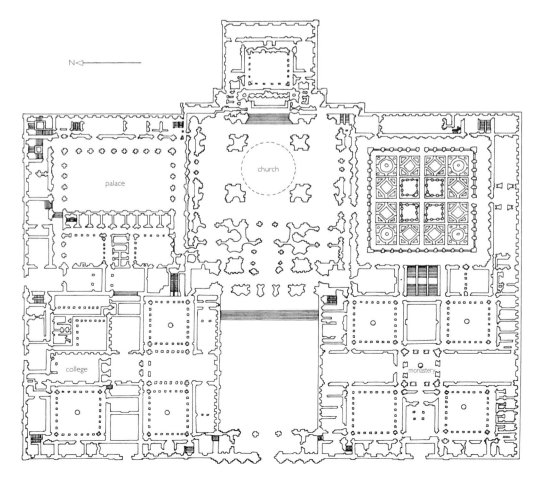

at Granada from designs by Pedro Machuca (c.1485–1550), a Spanish painter trained in Italy. Inspired by the palace designs of Bramante and Raphael, it would have been the finest High Renaissance palazzo in Europe. Its circular courtyard surrounded by a two-storeyed, free-standing colonnade of Doric and Ionic columns echoes Raphael's uncompleted court at the Villa Madama and anticipates Vignola's at Caprarola. So Roman a building found no imitators in Spain, though Diego de Siloe (c.1495–1563) designed the lavishly ornamented Escala Dorado (gilded staircase) (1519–23) in Burgos cathedral, probably derived from Bramante's staircase connecting the terraces in the Belvedere Court at the Vatican. The leading Plateresque architect in Spain, Siloe, who is known to have been in Italy in 1517, was the son of a French sculptor who had settled in Burgos. His masterpiece is Granada cathedral, begun in 1528 on the site of the former mosque. Its majestic domed rotunda at the east end was intended for the perpetual exposition of the Blessed Sacrament as an act of expiation for the Moorish past of Granada. This inspired design recalls the Early Christian Anastasis Rotunda at the church of the Holy Sepulchre at Jerusalem, as well as Bramante's designs for St Peter's. At the same time the building has a strongly Plateresque character, noticeably,

for example, in the ornament of the handsome triumphal arch on the exterior of the north transept, known as the Portal of Pardon.

By far the most important product of the Renaissance in Spain was the monastery-palace of the Escorial, built in 1563–82 in the mountains 30 miles (48km) from Madrid. It was commissioned by Philip II to house the mausoleum of his father, Charles V, in a manner which would adequately symbolize Spanish imperial might and Spanish Catholic piety. The plan of this vast edifice was drawn up by the architect Juan Bautista de Toledo, an assistant of Michelangelo's at St Peter's from 1546–8 whom Philip II called to Madrid from Naples in 1559. The great cross plan echoes Filarete's hospital in Milan, as well as late antique sources such as Diocletian's Palace at Spalato and his Baths in Rome. The austerity of the elevations, in a simple style reduced from that of Giacomo della Porta and Vignola, is related both to the hard material, the local grey granite, and also to the Counter-Reformation spirituality which made so great an appeal to Philip II. Even so, Toledo's design for the church failed to impress the king, who was passionately interested in architecture, so that he sought alternatives from Alessi, Tibaldi, Palladio, Vignola and other architects. In the end Juan de Herrera (c.1530–97), who had been Toledo's assistant from 1563 and successor from 1572, reworked Toledo's designs for a domed Greek-cross church with an extra eastern bay for the choir. Showing knowledge of churches by Alberti, Alessi and Tibaldi as well as of Bramante's designs for St Peter's, its cold grandeur harmonizes with the mood of the entire complex which, with its seventeen courtyards incorporating a Jeronymite monastery, seminary, hospital, royal palace and dynastic mausoleum, is surely one of the wonders of the modern world. Here Philip II, half king, half monk, ruler of one of the greatest empires in history, died in 1598 in a tiny bare room designed to command a view down to the High Altar. As royal inspector of buildings Herrera was able to ensure that his rather daunting manner became the official architectural style of Spain for the rest of the century and beyond. It can be seen in numerous palaces, public buildings, town halls and churches throughout the country.

Germany

France and Spain, Catholic countries with easy and obvious access to Italy, adopted Renaissance architecture in a coherent manner in marked contrast to England, Germany and the Low Countries, where the greater impact of the Reformation prevented the full adoption of Renaissance ideals. Germany was to be important for its Baroque rather than its Renaissance architecture. Renaissance forms arrived in Germany in the chapel added at the west end of the church of St Anne in Augsburg, Swabia, in 1510–12 by the Fugger banking family. The Fugger Chapel is an essay in the North Italian or Venetian *quattrocento* manner but contains an incongruous Late Gothic German net-vault. For Germany during much of the sixteenth century the Renaissance was simply a system of ornament, derived from north Italian *quattrocento* buildings in Como or Pavia, and applied to Late Gothic structures. We can see this in the 1530s in the Georgenbau in the Schloss at Dresden, though the contemporary Johann-Friedrichs-Bau at Schloss Hartenfels, Torgau, also in Saxony,

389 The arcaded court at the Altes Schloss, Stuttgart, by Tretsch (1553–62)

390 The court façade of the Ottheinrichsbau of the Schloss at Heidelberg (1556–c.1560)

391 West front of the Jesuit church of St Michael, Munich, by Sustris (begun 1583)

designed by Konrad Krebs (1492–1540), is a more ambitious monument. It boasts an astonishing open staircase in a huge stone cage, a kind of Lombardo-Germanic parallel to the staircase in the François I wing at Blois.

An exception is provided by the Stadtresidenz at Landshut, Lower Bavaria, built for Ludwig X, Duke of Bavaria-Landshut, in 1536–43 with the assistance of masons and stuccoists brought from Mantua, where he had admired the Palazzo del Tè on a visit in 1536. With its vaulted loggias the Landshut Residenz is architecturally an unimpressive reflection of the Palazzo del Tè, but its frescoed and stuccoed interiors are more convincingly Italianate. Far more typical are buildings dominated by gables adorned with Flemish decoration and stubby columns, and courtyards lined with superimposed arcades. Typical of the numerous town halls in this style are those in Saxony, at Leipzig (1556–64) and Altenburg (1562–4). A fine example of an arcaded court is that in the Altes Schloss at Stuttgart, built in 1553–62 by the

architect Alberlin Tretsch (d.c.1577) for Duke Christoph of Württemberg. The high point of Flemish-inspired ornamental exuberance is reached with the Ottheinrichsbau of the Schloss at Heidelberg, built in 1556–c.1560 for the collector and patron Ottheinrich, who became Elector Palatine in 1556. Though it presents an austere face to the outside world, the court façade of the now ruinous Ottheinrichsbau is an outrageously showy composition completely smothered in sculptural ornament. The design owes something to Serio's treatise, while details such as the three-dimensional scrolled strapwork probably derive from Cornelis Floris (c.1514–75), who published two influential books of engravings in 1556 and 1557.

Munich, a profoundly Catholic city, enjoyed close links with Rome which are commemorated in the church of St Michael, begun in 1583 as the first major church built by the Jesuits in northern Europe. It was paid for by Wilhelm V, Duke of Bavaria, who had already remodelled Burg Trausnitz at Landshut in 1573–8 with an arcaded court designed by the Dutch architect Frederick Sustris in an international Late Renaissance style. The interiors at Trausnitz were richly painted with arabesque work and figures by a team of artists brought by Sustris from Italy. In 1569–73 this team, with Sustris's help, had decorated interiors for Hans Fugger in the now destroyed Fuggerhäuser in Augsburg in a rich Mannerist style rivalling the work of Giulio Romano and Giorgio Vasari (1511–74) in Italy. Sustris, trained as a painter, seems to have been the original architect of the Munich church, and it was certainly he who provided the new crossing and choir in 1593–7 following the collapse of the tower. After the Roman nave with its barrel vault and side chapels, the west front echoes Vignola's Gesù only very remotely, for it turns as it rises into an echo of the characteristic gabled town house of the Northern Renaissance.

In the meantime Wilhelm V was turning the Munich Residenz, the old fortified seat of the Wittelsbach princes, into a Renaissance palazzo. His most striking contribution was the Antiquarium, remodelled for him

392 Antiquarium, Munich Residence (1586–1600)

393 Exterior of Schloss Johannisburg, Aschaffenburg, by Ridinger (1605–14)

by Sustris in 1586–1600 out of a long low room built as the first museum in Germany in 1569–71 for Duke Albrecht V of Bavaria from designs by the Milanese antiquary Jacopo Strada. To gain height Sustris lowered the floor of Strada's barrel-vaulted crypt-like room, perhaps inspired by antique Roman semi-subterranean interiors. Sustris covered every inch of the broad vault with frescoes, including illusionistic figures and polychromatic arabesques in a late Mannerist style close to Vasari's. The decorative team included Netherlandish, German and Italian artists.

Far more typical is the gabled Germanic exuberance of the great south wing added in the late 1590s to the already extensive Schloss Hämelschenburg. One of the most ambitious secular buildings of late-sixteenth-century Germany, this vies in grandeur with the 'prodigy houses' of England such as Wollaton and Hardwick (p. 276), though it lacks their emphasis on harmony and symmetry. Those ideals are achieved in the enormous quadrangular Schloss Johannisburg at Aschaffenburg, built at one go in 1605–14 by Georg Ridinger (1568–after 1616) for the archbishop-elector of Mainz, Johann Schweickhardt von Kronberg, whose territory and architectural ambitions exceeded those of any of the lay electors. Its scale and power may anticipate the great palaces of later-seventeenth-century Germany but, with the fantastic Mannerist decoration of its high gables, derived from plates published by Wendel Dietterlin in the 1590s, it is more appropriately regarded as a culminating point of the German Renaissance. Another is reached at the castle at Heidelberg, which saw the erection in 1601–7 of the Friedrichsbau from designs by Johann Schoch, who had evidently not shaken off the influence of the adjacent Ottheinrichsbau with its crowded ornament. The exact ecclesiastical equivalent of this work is the sumptuous west front of the Protestant Stadtkirche at Bückeburg of 1610–15, probably designed by Hans Wulff, though the interior is still in a predominantly Late Gothic style.

Calm was bound to return after such fantasy. The architect who is above all associated with its introduction is Elias Holl (1573–1646), a Protestant who came from a family of Augsburg master-masons employed by the Catholic Fuggers. After a visit to Venice in 1600–1 he succeeded his father as city architect of Augsburg in 1602. His austerity is immediately recognizable in his Schloss Willibaldsburg at Eichstätt, Bavaria, of c.1609–19, and in two Augsburg buildings, the Slaughterhouse (1609) and Gymnasium St Anna (1613–15). Stylistically close to Willibaldsburg is the Englischer Bau (English building) at the castle of Heidelberg, built in 1613–15 by the Elector Palatine

Friedrich V. Its chaste design has sometimes been connected with the name of Inigo Jones who almost certainly visited Heidelberg in 1613 with Lord Arundel following the marriage of Friedrich V to Princess Elizabeth, daughter of James I of England.

Holl's masterpiece is the Rathaus (town hall) at Augsburg, built in 1515–20 as a kind of Counter-Reformation skyscraper with a central block of six storeys plus a tall pedimented attic. Its simplicity of detail recalls the work of Giacomo della Porta and Domenico Fontana; its octagonal domed towers are more Germanic; while its complex massing and cubic clarity are Holl's own. The interiors, with which Holl was not involved, reached a climax in the vast sumptuously decorated Goldener Saal of 1620–3, unfortunately largely destroyed in the Second World War. The imposing austerity of the Rathaus influenced the new wing of the Rathaus at Nuremberg of 1616–22 by Jakob Wolf the Younger (1571–1620). The cold grandeur of this building and the almost industrial bands of repetitive fenestration seem a distant echo of Herrera's Escorial (p. 264). Despite their enthusiasm for the work of the painter and draughtsman Albrecht Dürer, the inhabitants of Nuremberg had been slow to adopt Renaissance forms in architecture, as can be gathered from the Pellerhaus, erected as late as 1602–5 from designs by Jakob Wolf the Elder, with its gabled front and arcaded courtyard overlaid with ornament. Both the Rathaus and the Pellerhaus at Nuremberg were destroyed in the Second World War but have since been largely rebuilt.

Eastern Europe

Countries in eastern Europe such as Hungary, Russia, Poland, Bohemia and Austria took earlier to the Renaissance than the countries at which we have already looked. If we have not yet considered this work, it is because it follows a random path which is difficult to plot. In Moscow, the Italian architect Alevisio Novi built the cathedral of St Michael in the Kremlin (1505–9), incorporating Renaissance detail but retaining a

394 Exterior of Holl's town hall at Augsburg (1515–20)

traditional Russo-Byzantine plan. Hungary since the fourteenth century had established itself as an isolated outpost of Italian Renaissance humanist scholarship, a cultural efflorescence which continued during the fifteenth century only to be suppressed by the invading Turks in the sixteenth century. The key figure was King Matthias Corvinus (reigned 1458–90), a patron of Mantegna, Verrocchio and Benedetto da Maiano, who employed a Florentine architect, Chimenti di Leonardo Camici, at Buda where his now destroyed rebuilding of the castle almost rivalled the ducal palace at Urbino. One of the first fully Renaissance monuments in Hungary is the distinctly Florentine chapel erected on a domed Greek-cross plan in 1507–10 near the cathedral at Esztergom, seat of the primate of Hungary. Constructed of local red marble, this was commissioned by Cardinal Archbishop Tamas of Bakócz as a sepulchral chapel for himself. Matthias Corvinus was, however, also content to commission buildings in the Gothic style, which suggests

395 The arcaded loggia of the Belvedere, Prague, by Paolo della Stella (begun 1534)

396 Wawel cathedral, Cracow (1519–33). The Sigismund Chapel by Berrecci is on the right

that the Renaissance style was not yet universally accepted for all purposes.

In 1502 the future King Sigismund I of Poland, who had been brought up in Matthias Corvinus's palace, brought with him from Buda to Cracow the Florentine architect Franciscus Florentinus. For Sigismund, crowned in 1506, Franciscus began the conversion of the castle on the Wawel in Cracow into a Renaissance palazzo, a process which was continued in 1516–35 by another Florentine architect, Bartolommeo Berrecci (c.1537). The principal feature is the courtyard with superimposed round-arched colonnades of the type which were to be popular later in Germany. Berrecci, who arrived in Poland via Hungary, had evidently been trained in the circle of Bramante. His most distinguished achievement is the Sigismund Chapel in the Wawel Cathedral at Cracow, commissioned by Sigismund in 1517 as a royal mausoleum after the death of his first wife. Replacing an existing Gothic side chapel, it was built in 1519–33 with the assistance of Italian artists brought from Hungary by the king. Constructed of white sandstone and red Hungarian marble, it consists of a cube surmounted by pendentives carrying a cylindrical drum expressed as an octagon on the exterior, crowned by a high lantern. Architecturally and decoratively it is one of the finest expressions of Italian early Renaissance ideals of a type not exactly paralleled in Italy and certainly nowhere in France or Germany. Its interior is covered with sumptuous carved ornament following a programme which may have been influenced by humanist circles at Cracow University. Sigismund's marriage in 1518 to Bona Sforza of the Milanese ruling family may perhaps explain the Lombardic flavour of this chapel, which might have been considered too highly ornamented by Raphael or the Sangallos. It exercised considerable influence on other centrally planned chapels in Poland, including one at the Wawel cathedral itself, though they lacked its brilliance.

Sigismund's brother Vladislav, King of Bohemia, employed Benedikt Ried to build the Vladislav Hall in 1493–1502 at the castle in Prague. The Late Gothic vaults we have admired in Chapter 5 were oddly combined with Renaissance features, such as windows framed by Corinthian pilasters and half-columns. By the time this part of the palace was finished in 1510, its increasingly classical forms made it one of the earliest Renaissance buildings north of the Alps. Ferdinand II, brother of the Emperor Charles V and the first Habsburg ruler of Bohemia, was responsible for another remarkable early Renaissance addition to the architecture of Prague, the Belvedere (Letohrádek), begun as a garden pavilion for his wife in 1534. The architect of this arcaded loggia of Venetian *cinquecento* character was Paolo della Stella (d.1552), a sculptor trained by Andrea Sansovino. Work was halted after a fire in 1541 and the S-curved copper roof was not completed until 1563 by the Viennese-trained architect Bonifaz Wolmut (d.c.1579). Nearby is the tennis-court of 1567, also by Wolmut, with a heavy arcade adorned with *sgraffito* decoration. Such Italianate monuments are exceptional; in general Bohemian architecture conforms to the German pattern of gabled exteriors and court-yards with superimposed arcades.

Netherlands

In c.1512 Pope Leo X commissioned from Raphael a set of tapestries to hang in the Sistine Chapel. In 1517 Raphael's cartoons for these tapestries arrived in Brussels where they were to be woven, thus bringing the Renaissance to the Netherlands in decisive fashion. In the same year the Regent, Margaret of Austria, made additions in the new style to the palace at Mechelen (Malines), but it was not until the building of the town hall at Antwerp in 1561–66 that the Renaissance in Flanders came of age. Its architect, Cornelis Floris (c.1514–75), a native of Antwerp, studied sculpture under Giambologna and visited Rome in 1538. His town hall is a grave and monumental work, nineteen bays long, dominated by a towering gabled frontispiece which is in fact just a showpiece with nothing behind it.

397 Exterior of Floris's town hall at Antwerp (1561–6)

398 Exterior of the Huis Ten Bosch at Maarssen, near Utrecht, by Van Campen (1628)

399 Exterior of the Mauritshuis, The Hague, by Van Campen (1633–5)

400 Exterior of the Meat Hall, Haarlem, by De Key (1601–5)

Ornamented with features derived from Bramante and Serlio such as coupled columns and pilasters flanking niches, scrolls and obelisks, it influenced many town halls in Germany and the Netherlands, beginning with the more modest imitation at The Hague, built in 1564–5 by an unknown architect. Equally influential was its exuberant strapwork ornament which, though not a dominant feature either here or at Floris's magnificent marble rood screen of 1572 at Tournai Cathedral, was an important element of the arches and other ceremonial constructions erected by him for the entry of the Emperor Charles V and his son, the future Philip II of Spain, into Antwerp in 1549. Engravings of these were published in 1550 and were followed by Floris's *Veelderleij niuwe inventien van Antychsche* in 1556–7, by Hans Vredeman de Vries's *Architectura* (Antwerp 1563) and *Compertimenta* (1566), and by Wendel Dietterlin's even more florid *Architectura* (Nuremberg 1594–8).

Gables covered with ornament of this kind are the hallmark of the town halls, guild halls and private houses of the Netherlands well into the seventeenth century. None is more spectacular than the Meat Hall at Haarlem (1601–5) by the leading Haarlem architect Lieven de Key (c.1560–1627). His opposite number in Amsterdam is the architect and sculptor Hendrick de Keyser (1565–1621). Keyser's two major works are the Zuiderkerk (1606–14) and the Westerkerk (1620–38), with their ambitious towers dominating the skyline of Amsterdam. The Zuiderkerk is the first large Protestant church in Holland planned with an emphasis on the pulpit rather than on the altar. Both churches have simple round-arched arcades but in general remain in a style transitional from Gothic.

The last vestiges of florid Flemish ornament and of transitional Gothic were ruthlessly swept away by Jacob van Campen (1585–1657), architect, painter, landowner and wealthy bachelor. He introduced Palladianism into Holland in buildings like the Coymans house of 1625 in the Keizergracht at Amsterdam, and the lovely Huis Ten Bosch of three years later in the woods near The Hague, which boasts the first pedimented giant order in Dutch architecture, evidently inspired by Scamozzi's *Dell'Idea dell'Architettura Universale* (Venice 1615). His masterpiece is probably the Mauritshuis, built for Prince Johan Maurits van Nassau at The Hague in 1633–5 of homely red brick enlivened with closely-set giant Ionic pilasters of sandstone: a style not unlike that of the Henri IV period in France. Gracious and dignified, but undemonstrative for a princely palace, it was in a manner which had a considerable influence on the course of domestic architecture in England. Jacob van Campen went on to design the imposing stone-built Town Hall (now Royal Palace) at Amsterdam where the superimposed giant orders achieve a Baroque grandeur. Built in 1647–65, the unparalleled scale of this town hall seems to reflect the mood engendered by the Peace of Munster when, following eighty years of war with Spain, the independence of the Dutch Republic was formally recognized.

England and the growth of the 'prodigy house'

The Reformation under Henry VIII, followed by the insular nationalist policy of his daughter, Elizabeth I, ensured that England was largely isolated from the sources of Renaissance thought and design in Italy. England, for example, was the only significant country in Europe to which no Italian architect was called to design a building. Henry VIII's palace of Nonsuch in Surrey, begun in 1538 and demolished in the 1680s, was architecturally a failure in comparison with François I's Chambord which may have been its model. The stuccoed interiors recalling those by Rosso at Fontainebleau were more successful, but only because foreign craftsmen were employed. The first fully classical building was the now demolished Old Somerset House in London, built in 1547–52 by the Lord Protector Somerset who acted as Regent for two years during Edward VI's minority from 1547. Its frontispiece with a triumphal arch motif on the ground floor recalled contemporary French buildings by Philibert de l'Orme and Jean Bullant. Somerset's successor as Lord Protector, the Duke of Northumberland, sent John Shute to Italy in 1550 to study both antique and modern architecture. The result was the first book on the classical orders in the English language, Shute's *The First and Chief Groundes of Architecture* (1563), evidently derived from a study of Serlio and Vignola. The origin of two great houses can be traced to the circle round Lord Somerset: Burghley, built by his secretary William Cecil, and Longleat, built by his steward, Sir John Thynne, who had been in charge of the building of Old Somerset House.

Burghley House, Northamptonshire, was erected between the 1550s and 1580s by Queen Elizabeth's first minister, the Lord High Treasurer, William Cecil, 1st Lord Burghley (1520–98), the man who, as much as any other, was responsible for establishing the power, peace and prosperity of the newly Protestant kingdom. The vast mansion which reflects his national prestige is the classic 'prodigy house', conceived as a setting in which to entertain the queen and her court. Built over a long period with gradual changes of style, it combines traditional features, such as the turreted entrance gateway, with the most up-to-date French classicism, such as the barrel-vaulted stone staircase and the tower of the orders in the court, dated 1585, with its triumphal arch theme and its crowning pyramidal obelisk. We know that Burghley ordered architectural books from Paris, including Philibert de l'Orme's, though the tower also shows the influence of Flemish decoration.

A similar source appears at the charming Gate of Honour (1572–3) at Gonville and Caius College, Cambridge, built for Dr Caius, a Renaissance scholar and doctor who had studied and taught at Padua. With its obelisks, engaged columns and domed hexagonal top, this fetching toy is derived from one of the festive gateways erected at Antwerp for Prince Philip's entry in 1549, itself based on a design published by Serlio. Designed by Caius with the help of a Flemish architect, Theodore de Have, who had settled in England in 1562, the Gate of Honour is preceded by the Gates of Humility and of Virtue. Thus the plan of Dr Caius's college symbolizes the progress of the undergraduate in the kind of allegorical image which was dear to the Elizabethan mind.

The great house of Longleat, Wiltshire, though incorporating earlier work, dates substantially from 1572–80. The master-mason and doubtless the designer was Robert Smythson (c.1536–1614), the most brilliant architect of his day. The absolute symmetry of the façades is new, as are the harmonious classical balance, the rectilinear grid of the giant windows and the reticent skyline. Smythson went on to build Wollaton Hall, Nottinghamshire, in 1580–88 for Sir Francis Willoughby, who wanted a suitably magnificent setting in which to entertain the queen. It is a more animated version of the Longleat formula enlivened with decorative details from Serlio and de Vries. Hardwick Hall, Derbyshire (1590–6), doubtless also designed by Smythson, is the dynamic climax of the vertical glass cage motif. Its plan introduces a new Italianate symmetry by placing the hall for the first time in the centre, at right angles to the main body of the house, whereas the medieval great hall was generally placed asymmetrically. Indeed, the hall seems no longer to have been used for dining, for there was a large dining-room on the first floor which housed the

401 *Below* Exterior of Burghley House, Northamptonshire (1550s–1580s)

402 *Opposite* Caius and de Have: The Gate of Honour, Gonville and Caius College, Cambridge (1572–3); on the right the contemporary Gate of Virtue

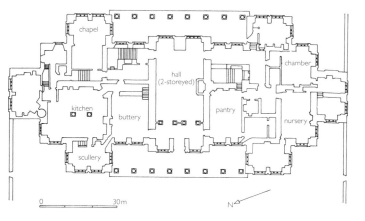

403 *Top* Exterior of Longleat, Wiltshire, by Smythson (1572–80)

404, 405 *Above and left* Exterior and plan of Hardwick Hall, Derbyshire, by Smythson (1590–6)

impressive apartments of the owner, the colourful Countess of Shrewsbury. Above these, on the second floor, were the state apartments, where the Long Gallery and High Great Chamber commanded magnificent views. The provision of two independent suites of living quarters, public and private, which was to be extremely influential, probably derives from the late-medieval

English custom of providing separate suites for the king and queen in royal palaces.

Another great Elizabethan house of striking and unusual disposition is Longford Castle, Wiltshire, built in the 1580s by a courtier, Sir Thomas Gorges. It has a triangular plan presumably intended to symbolize the Trinity and a five-bay open loggia of two storeys, perhaps derived from François I's Château de Madrid, begun in 1528. This is the only two-storeyed loggia in English Renaissance architecture though, as we have seen, the form was especially popular in Germany and Central Europe. Even one-storeyed loggias are not common before c.1600: one of the finest and earliest is that at Hatfield House, Hertfordshire (1607-12), the seat of Robert Cecil, 1st Earl of Salisbury (1563–1612), who filled the same high offices of state under James I as had his father, the 1st Lord Burghley, under Elizabeth I. Like his father he was also a passionate builder who took a great interest in design. Thus, though the carpenter-cum-architect Robert Lyming designed much of Hatfield, Lord Salisbury also consulted the architect Simon Basil, Surveyor-General of the King's Works, as well as his successor in that office, Inigo Jones. Indeed Jones's hand has sometimes been seen in the design of the south front with its nine-bay loggia and central tower of the orders. A Jonesian origin for these features seems unlikely in view of the extent of Flemish strapwork ornament, though this is nothing compared with the barbaric profusion of such ornament on the monumental screen in the Great Hall and on the Grand Staircase, both carved by John Bucke.

Inigo Jones and High Renaissance clarity

It was Inigo Jones (1573–1652) who put an end to the kind of applied decoration which is so dominant at Hatfield by introducing England for the first time, however belatedly, to the ideals and not just to the ornamental language of the Italian Renaissance. A contemporary wrote in 1606 that it was Jones 'through whom there is hope that sculpture, modelling, architecture, painting, acting and all that is praiseworthy

406 Interior of the Great Hall, Hatfield House, Hertfordshire, by Lyming *et al.* (1607–12)

in the elegant arts of the ancients, may one day find their way across the Alps into our England'. Inigo Jones's role was akin to that of Alberti in that he believed that architecture was a liberal art, not just a craft, and that the architect needed to travel in Italy, to study and to think. Indeed he virtually invented the office of architect in England, where previously buildings had been designed by master-masons and surveyors.

Though modestly born, Jones had made his way to Italy before 1603 where he may have studied masque design at the Medici court in Florence, for he was employed from 1605 as a masque designer by James I's queen, Anne of Denmark. The masque, a musical entertainment with political or allegorical dialogue and elaborate scenery, was an essential feature of Renaissance courts and obviously made a deep impression on Jones. In 1613–14 he visited Italy once again, this time in the company of Thomas Howard, 14th Earl of Arundel (1586–1646), the first connoisseur in England to collect systematically in the Renaissance manner, and one of the most distinguished collectors and patrons in the history of English art. Jones admired the masterpieces of sixteenth-century architecture in centres such as Vicenza, Venice, Padua, Genoa and, above all, Rome where he studied the antique buildings with the fourth book of Palladio's *Quattro Libri* in his hand. He not only managed to acquire Palladio's drawings for public and private buildings, a purchase of profound consequence for the future of English architecture, but also met Scamozzi whose own buildings had eliminated the Mannerist element in Palladio's style. Jones imitated Scamozzi in this as in much else, summarizing the purity at which he aimed in the following words, written in his Italian sketchbook on 20 January 1615:

> And to say true all these composed ornaments the which proceed out of the abundance of designers and were brought in by Michelangelo and his followers in my opinion do not well in solid architecture and the façades of houses, but in gardens, loggias, stucco or ornaments of chimney pieces or in the inner parts of houses those compositions are of necessity to be used. For as outwardly every wise man carrieth a gravity in public places, where there is nothing else looked for, yet inwardly hath his imagination set on fire, and sometimes licentiously flying out, as nature himself doth often times extravagantly, to delight, amaze us, sometimes move us to laughter, sometimes to contemplation and horror, so in architecture the outward ornaments [ought] to be solid, proportionable according to the rules, masculine and unaffected.

Just these qualities characterize the first major work which he designed in his capacity as Surveyor-General of the King's Works, to which he was appointed in 1615:

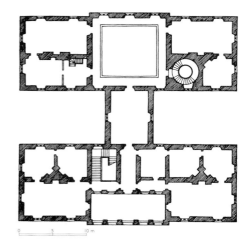

407 Plan of the Queen's House, Greenwich (begun 1616) by Jones

the Queen's House at Greenwich, begun in 1616 for Queen Anne of Denmark (fig. 371). The plan may owe something to that of Giuliano da Sangallo's villa of the 1480s at Poggio a Caiano, but the source for the south front with its open loggia is Scamozzi's Villa Molini, near Padua, of the 1590s. The stark white elevations of the Queen's House, relying for their effect not on ornament but on the perfect proportional relationship of window to wall, must have been shocking in the same way that Holl's work was in Germany and van Campen's in Holland. In fact, work on the building was halted on the queen's death in 1618 and was not resumed until 1630–5 when it was completed for Charles I's wife, Henrietta Maria. In the meantime Jones was at work on James I's new Banqueting House, built in 1619–22 in the rambling Tudor Palace of Whitehall to which its sophisticatedly classical façade, inspired by Palladio's town palaces in Vicenza, was a breathtaking contrast. The interior was planned to resemble an antique Roman basilica deriving from Vitruvius via Palladio, with the perfect proportions of a double cube, 110 by 55 feet (33.5 × 16.75m).

The same proportions recur in the Catholic chapel which Jones added to the red-brick Tudor St James's Palace in 1623–7 for the proposed Spanish bride of the Prince of Wales, who succeeded as Charles I in 1625. Known as the Queen's Chapel, since it was first used by Charles' French wife, Queen Henrietta Maria, its design seems a cross between the cella of a Roman temple and

408 *Above* Aerial view of Palmanova (1590s)

409 *Left* Drawing showing Jones's portico (1634–40) on the west front of Old St Paul's cathedral

a house by Palladio. Certainly neither its exterior nor interior resembled any ecclesiastical building in the country. Jones's Protestant church of St Paul, Covent Garden (1631–3) is, by contrast, an austere essay in the Vitruvian Tuscan order, with a stark portico and a somewhat archaic air which anticipates that of certain neo-classical architects of the eighteenth century. Jones also designed the surrounding square, known as the Piazza, as part of speculative development for the 4th Earl of Bedford. Jones's houses, with their vaulted ground-floor loggias and red-brick façades enlivened with stucco pilasters, echo those in Parisian squares such as the Place des Vosges. Sadly for us, not one survives.

One of Jones's most startling achievements was the erection in 1634–40 on the west front of Old St Paul's cathedral of the largest portico north of the Alps. He based the sumptuous Corinthian order on that of the Temple of Antoninus and Faustina in Rome, while he took the idea of a giant unpedimented portico, half the height of the building to which it is attached, from Palladio's reconstruction of the Temple of Venus and Rome (p. 78). Built of carefully selected Portland stone, the portico was conceived on a scale which astonished contemporaries. One of them, the architect John Webb,

Jones's nephew by marriage, claimed that it 'contracted the envy of all Christendom upon our Nation, for a Piece of Architecture, not to be parallel'd in these last Ages of the World'. Here at last was the first English building since before the Reformation which could claim European standing. It represented the first true renaissance of the splendour of the ancient world.

Town planning

Ideal towns

We have already noted the origin of Renaissance town planning in the mid-fifteenth century at Pienza, where a theatrically designed square was imposed on a modest Tuscan hill town, and at Filarete's unexecuted ideal town of Sforzinda with its radial street plan. Though an invention of the Renaissance, radial planning may have been inspired by a misunderstanding of Vitruvius' discussion of the orientation of towns in relation to the winds (*Ten Books of Architecture*, Book 1, ch.6). The radial plan also seems to have been thought aesthetically superior to the grid layout of most planned towns.

A surviving grid town of the Italian Renaissance is Sabbioneta in the Po valley in north Italy. The capital of a small Gonzaga Duchy, this was a model city built by the duke from 1560 to 1584. It was a well-balanced town of 30 rectangular blocks with provision for military, civic, cultural and domestic functions. With its remarkable theatre by Scamozzi, Sabbioneta can be seen as an attempt to recreate the Vitruvian city on the basis of the illustrations in translations of Vitruvius such as that by Cesariano of 1521. The only complete example of radial town planning built in Italy in the sixteenth century is the town of Palmanova of the 1590s. Possibly designed by Scamozzi, this was primarily a fortress constructed by the rulers of Venice to protect their rural neighbourhood from attacks by the Ottoman Empire.

410 The Piazza SS. Annunziata, Florence

411 Bramante: Vigevano, main square (1492–4)

The creation of the square

The central achievement of Italian urban designers is, for many, the square rather than geometrically planned towns like Palmanova. In medieval planned towns the market square was not necessarily surrounded with coherently designed buildings. An important step was taken in Florence in 1421 where Brunelleschi cleared an area in order to create the rectangular Piazza S. Annunziata, flanked by the porticos of the church on one side and of the new hospital at right angles to it. Opposite the church a new street was formed to continue the axis of the piazza.

Alberti was significant for his stress on the city square, colonnaded and entered through triumphal arches, the inspiration for which he took from Vitruvius' account of the Forum. This humanist ambition to revive the Roman idea of the Forum clearly influenced Bramante, who remodelled the centre of the silk-weaving city of Vigevano in 1492–4 to create the large, arcaded Piazza Ducale. Though still attractive today, the Piazza has been altered by the removal of the great staircase connecting it with the Sforza castle, and by the addition of a monumental Baroque façade to the cathedral. The Piazza thus states less clearly the delicate balance that Bramante created between the power of the prince, the Sforzas of Milan; the church, in the form of the cathedral; and the civic power, in the form of the Palazzo del Commune.

Michelangelo's Piazza del Campidoglio, Rome, conceived in the 1530s as a transformation of earlier buildings, has already been noted for its influence in the history of civic planning. It is exceeded as urban scenery only by Sansovino's contemporary creation of the linked Piazza S. Marco and Piazzetta in Venice.

The monumental street

Monumental street improvements were, architecturally, as important as the square. In Florence, Vasari created a street vista between the two wings of his Uffizi from the 1560s. This scenic piazzetta may have owed something to Scamozzi's urban stage-sets for the Teatro Olimpico

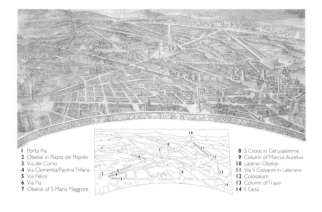

1	Porta Pia	8	S Croce in Gerusalemme
2	Obelisk in Piazza del Popolo	9	Column of Marcus Aurelius
3	Via del Corso	10	Lateran Obelisk
4	Via Clementia/Paolina Trifaria	11	Via S Giovanni in Laterano
5	Via Felice	12	Colosseum
6	Via Pia	13	Column of Trajan
7	Obelisk of S Maria Maggiore	14	Il Gesù

412 *Above* Plan of Rome under Sixtus V (fresco in the Salone Sistino, Library, Vatican, Rome)

413 *Right* Mexico City aerial view (begun 1524)

in Vicenza. However, in the development of street architecture in the Renaissance it was Rome which played the vital role.

Rome, of course, had a classical model, the Via del Corso, the Via Lata of antiquity, which still marches across the centre of the historic city. On the day of his election as pope in 1585, Sixtus V commanded Domenico Fontana to construct the Acqua Felice, an aqueduct which brought water to the hills of Rome for the first time since antiquity. This enabled him to expand the habitable area of Rome, beginning with the Via Felice in 1585 which connected S. Maria Maggiore with S. Trinità dei Monti. He went on to link the pilgrimage churches with further roads which were needed for the vast numbers of pilgrims who came to Rome every twenty-five years from 1450 to celebrate Holy Year. He punctuated these roads with obelisks serving as visual connections and as powerful symbols of the triumph of Christianity over paganism. The impact of the new planning in Rome led to the formation of similar streets in other Italian cities, notably the Via Toledo (1536–43) in Naples and the Strada Nuova (1548–71) in Genoa.

Town planning in Spain and France

We have seen the imaginative recreation of classical antiquity as a guiding force of the Renaissance, but this was also the age of another exploration, that of America. The Spanish were the first to lay out true cities in their colonies. Thus, when they took possession of Mexico City in 1519–21, they destroyed the great Aztec temple, the Templo Mayor, but built a cathedral on part of its site and turned the temple courtyard, the ritual centre of the Aztec city of Tenochtitlàn, into the main arcaded square of a new Spanish colonial city. It was a larger echo of the arcaded or porticoed market squares that were frequently found at the centre of Spanish towns. Regulations for the building of cities, often known as the Laws of the Indies, were formalized by Philip II of Spain in 1573. Probably written by his architect, Juan de Herrera (1530–97), they were ultimately of Vitruvian origin. Incorporating European grid-planning, they required a central square used for markets as well for all kinds of festivities including tournaments.

From the 1560s to 1580s Juan de Herrera was in charge of the major programme of public works and urban renewal in both Spain and the colonies initiated by Philip II. These included the first Renaissance squares of their kind outside Italy, intended for ceremonial functions as well for the purposes of trade. In Madrid, which had been a far less important town than Valladolid until Philip II moved his court there from Toledo in 1561, Herrera applied the principles of the Laws of the

414 Madrid, Plaza Mayor (1617–19)

Indies to the layout of the arcaded Plaza Mayor, intended for fairs and celebrations as well for trade. It was finally built in 1617–19 in red brick and stone by Juan Gómez de Mora (c. 1580–1648).

The Plaza Mayor in Madrid had been preceded by the similar Plaza Mayor in Valladolid, the scene of the executions of the Inquisition. It was built by the city architect, Francisco de Salamanca (d.1573), as part of the reconstruction of the town after a fire in 1561 from designs by Juan Bautista de Toledo (c. 1515–67), architect of the Escorial. The town emerged with new public and private buildings arranged according to strict zoning of functions.

In France, major town planning is due to Henri IV who in the five crowded years before his assassination in 1610 transformed Paris from a medieval city, suffering from war and neglect, into a modern capital. This was a true Renaissance in which he drew on the Italian models with which his wife, Marie, a Medici and a daughter of the Duke of Tuscany, was familiar. His principal achievements in Paris were the Grande Galerie of the Louvre, the Pont Neuf and Place Dauphine, the Hôpital St Louis and the Place Royal (today des Vosges; fig. 377). He boldly placed an equestrian statue of himself, made in Florence, in a commanding position on the Pont Neuf at the point where it crossed the Ile de la Cité. The statue also commanded a view towards a new triangular square, the Place Dauphine, which he created immediately to the east.

The arcaded Place des Vosges, which survives intact, was inspired by Italian models such as the piazza of c.1600 at Livorno, the Medici port of Tuscany, which had uniform façades and closed corners. The objective of Henri IV in all these works was not only, as is often thought, 'the expression of royal power', or even of aesthetic ideals, but the promotion of domestic manufacturing which would link the court to commerce and establish Paris as the focal point of the newly unified French state.

7 Baroque Expansion

Italy

The exuberance and splendour of Baroque architecture, especially in Italy and south Germany, represent the climax of the power of the Catholic church and of Catholic princes before both were submerged by the rising tides of rationalism and nationalism. The Council of Trent (see p. 241) had given the church renewed confidence in her traditional doctrines and, once the austerities associated with the initial years of the Counter-Reformation were over, she threw herself with a vigour unparalleled since the Middle Ages into the task of representing eternal truths as compellingly as possible in temporal forms. Architecturally these forms were the classical ones established by the pioneers of Renaissance design in Italy. However, they were now articulated in a more three-dimensional and forceful manner so as to create dynamic spatial effects involving an openness of structure and an imaginative control of light which can seem close in spirit to Gothic. In Chapter 5 we have seen the recurring emphasis of Gothic architects on the 'multiple image' and on diaphanous structure involving diagonal vistas. These effects were paralleled by Baroque architects, though their buildings are too massive to be called diaphanous. The leading late-Baroque architect Bernardo Vittone wrote in 1766 that the 'perforated and open' vaults of his churches 'remain open so that light can be diffused from the cupola down through them and illuminate the church more visibly', words that are strongly reminiscent of those of Abbot Suger (p. 151).

The creation of Baroque: Bernini

The architect who first gave full expression to the style we know as Baroque was Gianlorenzo Bernini (1598–1680). He did so in the baldacchino of 1624–33 at St Peter's, Rome, a monument which transcended the boundaries between architecture and sculpture, like so many of its successors in the Baroque period. Erected over the site of St Peter's tomb, it is a monumental altar, protected by a bronze canopy supported by dynamically twisted 'Salomonic' columns, and was a triumphant assertion of the authority and splendour of the Roman Catholic faith. This glittering extravaganza, over 95 feet (29m) high, was a symbolic celebration of the ascendancy of the church over paganism and Judaism, since the columns were partly made fiom bronze originally used in the portico of the pagan Pantheon, while their spiral form echoed the columns of the high altar of Old St Peter's, which were supposed to have come from the Temple of Jerusalem.

Bernini was born in Naples, the son of a Neapolitan mother and a Florentine father who was a sculptor in a late Mannerist style. In about 1605 the family moved to Rome, a city in which Bernini was to spend his entire career and which he was to do much to transform. Like Michelangelo, he saw himself primarily as a sculptor, though he was also an architect, painter and poet, a dynamic and dedicated worker and a man of deep Catholic piety. But in contrast to Michelangelo he was untroubled by doubt and introspection; he was a happy family man with aristocratic manners and an air of high distinction. This mood of stylish buoyancy and prosperous ease was to be reflected in Baroque art throughout Europe. Like Michelangelo, Bernini owed his most significant commissions to the patronage of popes. In his close friend Maffeo Barberini, who reigned as Urban VIII from 1623 to 1644, and in Fabio Chigi, Alexander VII from 1655 to 1667, Bernini found enthusiastic patrons who were determined to stamp Rome with a spirit of festive splendour.

The erection of the eye-catching baldacchino in St Peter's led to the creation of an altar of commensurate splendour in the apse at the focal point of the church, the (liturgical) east end (fig. 354). Though impressive as a composition in its own right, the new altar was also designed to be seen from a distance framed by the columns of the baldacchino, a scenographic consideration which was to be typical of Baroque designers. The project, not realized until 1658–65 in the reign of Alexander VII, incorporated an appropriate setting for the Cathedra Petri, long venerated as St Peter's chair, though now believed to be the coronation chair of the Emperor Charles the Bald, dating from 877. Bernini enshrined the chair within a gorgeous bronze throne supported by figures representing the four Fathers of the Church, over twice life-size, and lit from above by an oval window of intense yellow glass containing an image representing the Dove of the Holy Spirit, the divine source of papal infallibility. Gilded rays shoot out in all directions from this image, piercing billowing clouds of stucco inhabited by putti. This sculptural blend of fantasy and reality, of real light, concealed light and imitation light, had been invented by Bernini in his theatrical Cornaro chapel of 1645–52 at S. Maria della Vittoria, Rome.

Bernini's celebrated colonnades, begun in 1656 to form a vast oval piazza in front of St Peter's, were symbols as compelling as the baldacchino and Cathedra Petri of the all-embracing might of the church. In language which epitomizes the fundamentally Catholic nature of most Baroque art, Bernini himself described how his colonnades were designed 'to receive Catholics in a maternal gesture in order to confirm their belief, heretics in order to reunite them with the Church, and infidels in order to reveal to them the true

415 Bernini's Scala Regia (1663–6) in the Vatican, Rome

Faith'. Though the colonnades have a swinging movement which is an essential part of what we understand by Baroque, the emphasis on the freestanding load-bearing column recalls the spirit of the Greek temple rather than ancient Roman or Renaissance architecture, which had stressed the wall (fig. 500).

The Scala Regia of 1663–6, the ceremonial staircase leading from the colonnade to the papal apartments, is one of Bernini's most brilliant concepts. Exploiting the fact that the existing walls within which it had to be inserted were not parallel, he dramatized the perspective effect by making the two rows of Ionic columns which flank the staircase converge and gradually diminish in height as they rise. Light falls from a concealed source at the half-landing and from a window at the top of the lower flight. At the bottom landing Bernini placed an equestrian statue of the Emperor Constantine at the moment of his conversion, looking up in amazement at the golden cross which is over the entrance arch to the stairs. This extension of

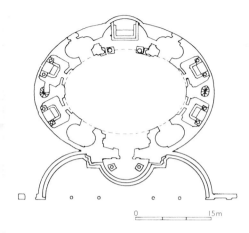

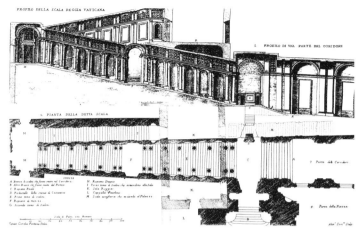

418 *Above* Plan of Bernini's Scala Regia, Vatican, Rome (1663-6)

dramatic action across an architectural space recurs in the church of S. Andrea al Quirinale (1658–70), the finest of three churches which were Bernini's essays in central planning: oval at S. Andrea, Greek-cross at Castelgandolfo, and circular at Ariccia.

At S. Andrea al Quirinale the altar-painting of St Andrew's martyrdom is lit from a dome which is invisible from the nave, while there is also a stucco figure of the saint rising to heaven on a cloud of glory from the concave pediment over the columns framing the entrance to the altar niche. The whole movement of the oval interior seems to reach a climax in this energetic but ethereal figure. The building was designed as a chapel for novices in the Jesuit order, whose priests had educated Bernini and trained him in the Spiritual Exercises of St Ignatius Loyola. The exterior of this comparatively small church is equally charged with energy, though it was less influential than the interior. The façade is flanked on each side by low quadrant walls which create a miniature piazza. The whole composition forms one of the supreme examples of the Baroque use of curved forms to create new spatial configurations. The horizontal segmental entablature of the projecting porch sets up a counter-rhythm to the vertical semicircle of the arch on the entrance wall behind. This

416, 417 *Top and above* Bernini: Plan and Interior of S. Andrea al Quirinale, Rome (1658–70)

419 Bernini: Sta Maria dell'Assunzione, Ariccia (1662–3)

dynamic motion is held in check by the restraining power of the pedimented frontispiece supported on giant Corinthian pilasters.

Bernini's church of S. Maria dell'Assunzione (1662–3) at Ariccia comes, by contrast, as a great surprise, for its exterior is an austere recreation of the Pantheon. It is a neo-antique exercise of the kind which would be called neo-classical were it built a century

later. This should make one wary of attaching too much significance to modern stylistic labels like Baroque and neo-classical, though the interior with its realistically carved angels and putti round the base of the dome, holding garlands in honour of the Assumption of the Virgin Mary, is closer to the sculptural liveliness we associate with the Baroque.

In secular architecture Bernini was important for establishing in the Palazzo Chigi-Odescalchi, begun in 1664, a monumental type of palace façade articulated by giant pilasters above a rusticated ground floor. He developed this influential form in the gigantic project for the completion of the Louvre in Paris which he prepared in 1664–5 for Louis XIV. Despite Bernini's triumphal visit to Paris in 1665 as the guest of the king, the building was never even begun, though it influenced numerous eighteenth-century royal palaces including those in Madrid and Stockholm.

An individual voice: Borromini

The other great master of Roman Baroque was Bernini's contemporary Francesco Borromini (1599–1667), whose real surname was Castello and who was born at Bissone on Lake Lugano into a family of masons. Unstable and neurotic, a gloomy eccentric bachelor who eventually committed suicide, he was wholly different in character from Bernini. It is tempting to see an echo of this difference in his architecture, which Bernini condemned as fantastic ('chimerical'), claiming that he

420 Bernini's first project for the Louvre (1664–5)

had been 'sent to destroy architecture'. Borromini rejected the serene conception of architecture as a reflection of the proportions of the human body, an idea which had been accepted by all classical architects from Brunelleschi to Bernini. Instead, Borromini said that his architecture was based on nature, Michelangelo and the antique. Michelangelo, as we have seen, was a source of strange architectural licence. The antique sources Borromini used were not standard models like the Colosseum or the Pantheon, but inventive curvilinear buildings such as the pavilion of the Piazza d'Oro at Hadrian's Villa at Tivoli (see p. 74). He must also have known the fanciful drawings of such buildings by Giovanni Battista Montano (1534–1621). Borromini's idea of nature, which he never fully clarified, seems related to his deep interest in geometry. He may have inherited this from the late-Gothic masons whom he met in his youth working on the continuation of Milan cathedral.

Although he began his career at St Peter's in c.1620 as a decorative stonecutter under his kinsman Carlo Maderno, and also worked on the baldacchino under Bernini's direction, he did not owe his principal commissions to the papacy, as Bernini did, but to humbler or more specialist institutions such as the poor Spanish order of the Discalced Trinitarians, the order of the Oratorians, and the University of Rome. His first independent commission in 1634, the tiny church and monastery for the Discalced Trinitarians, S. Carlo alle Quattro Fontane, shows the three sources of his new architecture. Thus he echoed Michelangelo's essentially plastic handling of architectural members; he had obviously studied antique centrally-planned buildings; while he may have seen justification in nature for his flowing organic lines.

The remarkable plan of S. Carlo alle Quattro Fontane is based on two equilateral triangles forming a lozenge within which are inscribed two circles joined by arcs so as to create an oval. With its undulating periphery, this plan is a combination of a Greek cross and an elongated lozenge, and only becomes oval at the level of the cornice of the dome (fig. 501). The deep honeycomb coffering is probably inspired by that at the fourth-century mausoleum of S. Costanza. However, the attenuated proportions of the sixteen columns with

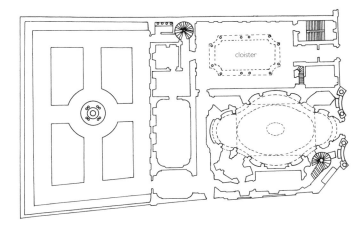

421, 422 Borromini: Exterior and plan of S. Carlo alle Quattro Fontane, Rome (1637–41; façade begun 1665)

423 Façade of the Oratory of the Congregation of St Philip Neri, Rome (1637–40), by Borromini

completely that, with its swinging rhythms, it is a supreme example of what we understand by High as opposed to early Baroque. Its use of two giant orders of equal height on each storey is an ambitious development from Michelangelo's Capitoline palaces, while the bizarre canopy over the statue of St Charles Borromeo, which is actually formed by the wings of cherub-herms, shows how far Borromini had moved from Bernini. To Bernini figure sculpture was essentially narrative and not to be subordinated to or blended with architecture. At the same time, Borromini relied far more than Bernini on architectural forms and generally avoided concealed sources of illumination.

The façade of S. Carlo had been anticipated in Borromini's extraordinary curved frontage of 1637–40 at the Oratory of the Congregation of St Philip Neri, one of the leading orders of the Counter-Reformation church. The delicacy of this façade, perhaps the first curved front in Rome, is underlined by the finely-laid brick of which it is constructed, following the techniques originally employed in the architecture of imperial Rome. The small oratory behind this façade is articulated with giant pilasters which are continued through the clerestorey to the coved ceiling and form webbed intersecting patterns closely resembling the ribs in a Gothic vault. Despite this Gothic flavour we should note that Borromini himself claimed the concrete vaults of ancient Rome as the precedent for this kind of skeletal structure. In his *Opus Architectonicum* (c.1647) he wrote:

> I wanted to follow in some measure the practice of the ancients, who would not dare to rest a vault directly on a wall, but who instead rested its entire weight on columns or piers which they planted in the corners of the room, so that the adjacent walls served only to buttress these piers, as one can observe in Hadrian's Villa, in S. Maria degli Angeli in the Baths of Diocletian, and elsewhere, and as I observed in a recent excavation for the Marchese del Bufalo near the Lateran hospital, where corner piers

which the little interior is crowded add a note of almost Gothic verticality to this complex and poetic building. Borromini concentrates our attention on the novel form by refusing to colour the interior of the church, which is predominantly grey. Sumptuous polychromy was not characteristic of his aesthetic. The originality of the church struck contemporaries, the Procurator General of the Discalced Trinitarians boasting that architects all over Europe were asking for copies of its plan and that 'in the opinion of everybody nothing similar with regard to artistic merit, caprice, excellence and singularity can be found anywhere in the world'.

The church was built in 1637–41 and the undulating façade, though designed in the 1630s, was not begun till 1665 and was completed after Borromini's death in 1667. The contrast of concave and convex forms determines the composition of the whole façade so

424 Borromini: Ceiling of chapel at the Collegio di Propaganda Fide, Rome (1662–4)

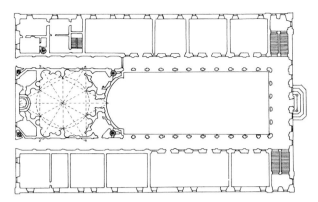

426, 427 *Above and below* Plan and exterior of S. Ivo della Sapienza, Rome

425 Interior of dome of S. Ivo della Sapienza, Rome (1642–60), by Borromini

were found supporting the vault of an underground temple.

The entrance wall of the Oratory is a perforated screen formed by three arched openings on the ground floor below the corresponding openings of the cardinal's loggia on the first floor. Borromini here moved towards a kind of open structure that was later developed by Guarini.

Borromini adopted this theme even more strikingly in the chapel he built in 1662–4 at the Collegio di Propaganda Fide (Propagation of the Faith), where the pseudo-ribs are not confined to the cove but connect diagonally across the entire ceiling. Moreover, the wall space between the pilasters has been almost entirely dissolved, creating a skeletal effect akin to that of the Gothic church. Borromini provided an arrestingly different demonstration of his inventive imagination at S. Ivo della Sapienza (1642–60), the chapel attached to Rome University or the Sapienza (literally 'Wisdom'). The plan consists of two equilateral triangles interpenetrating so as to form a six-pointed star, symbol of Wisdom, with a hexagonal central space. The hexagon is flanked by three semi-circular apses so that the plan resembles a triangle with three apses. This unique form

is emphasized by the breathtaking way in which the profile of the interior cornice is silhouetted against the dome rising directly from it, uninterrupted by the customary drum. Though the details are all classical, the total effect is one of almost Gothic dynamism as, for example, in the octagon at Ely (p. 176). Following, as it does, the ground-plan of the church, the dome has a faceted surface without precedent in Renaissance buildings but, as Borromini well knew, present in late antique buildings such as the serapaeum and the pavilion of the Piazza d'Oro at Hadrian's villa at Tivoli.

428 Piazza Navona, Rome (begun 1652), with Bernini's Fontana del Moro (1653–5) in the foreground and his Four Rivers fountain (1648–51) beyond; S. Agnese on the left

Contemporaries saw the plan of S. Ivo as resembling the shape of a bee, dynastic symbol of the Barberini pope, Urban VIII, who had appointed Borromini architect to the university in 1632. The church also contains references to the Temple of Solomon, proverbial for his wisdom, such as the carved cherubim, palms, pomegranates and stars in the dome. The symbolical justification for the eccentric form of the cupola and lantern on the exterior of the building is harder to fathom. Above the drum is a stepped pyramid crowned by the lantern, which is surrounded by coupled columns flanking concave bays exactly as in the late Roman Temple of Venus at Baalbek in Syria. This proto-Baroque temple can hardly have been known to Borromini but perhaps he had seen some now lost antique funerary monument of similar form near Rome. The lantern is capped by an even more baffling form, a spiral ramp like a tower of Babel or a Babylonian ziggurat. This terminates in a flaming laurel wreath supporting a curved iron cage, a flame of truth, below a cross and orb. Nothing like this eclectic configuration had been seen from any other architect before.

The last of Borromini's commissions in Rome which we shall examine is the church of S. Agnese in the Piazza Navona, one of the finest squares in Europe. Giovanni Battista Pamphili, who reigned as Pope Innocent X from 1644 to 1655, wanted to turn this square, in which his family palace was situated, into the noblest in Rome. It owed its elongated form to its origin as the Stadium of Domitian in the Campus Martius, and it may have been the pope's intention to recreate in Christian terms the relationship between Domitian's imperial residence on the Palatine, the Domus Augustana, and the Circus Maximus which it overlooked. Augustus had set up on the axis of this circus an Egyptian obelisk of red granite, and in 1647 Borromini provided Innocent X with designs for a fountain featuring an obelisk in the Piazza Navona. The commission was transferred to Bernini, who executed the celebrated Four Rivers Fountain in 1648–51 with its central obelisk crowned by a dove as a symbol of peace and of papal inspiration. The pope also wanted the square to be dominated by a new church of S. Agnese, the design of which he entrusted in 1652 to Carlo Rainaldi (1611–91) and his father Girolamo. Work proceeded for a year on the construction according to their designs for a Greek-cross-plan church which is a High Baroque version of the centralized plans for St Peter's. Borromini took over from the Rainaldis in 1653 and completely remodelled their façade so as to create a broad concave front forming a deliberate counter-curve to the drum of the dome immediately behind. The composition is flanked by two powerful campanili, and thus pays tribute to the west front of medieval churches. Borromini was himself replaced in 1657 by a committee of architects so that all above the cornice line is the work of Carlo Rainaldi and Bernini. The rich encrustation of the interior with marble reliefs, gilded stuccowork and frescoes was carried out during the rest of the century in a way which, though characteristically Baroque, did not reflect Borromini's more austere and architectonic taste.

Pietro da Cortona

The third in the great trio of artists in High Baroque Rome is Pietro Berrettini (1596–1669), known as Pietro da Cortona after his native town in Tuscany. Unlike his two contemporaries, Bernini and Borromini, he was primarily a painter. His frescoed interiors of the 1630s and 1640s at the Palazzo Barberini, Rome, and Palazzo Pitti, Florence, with their rich blend of trompe l'oeil architecture, allegorical figures and stuccowork, are among the most magnificent examples of Baroque illusion in Europe. As a young man in Rome Cortona had studied antique statues and reliefs as well as the architecture of Michelangelo and the paintings of Caravaggio and Raphael. His architecture was to be lively and eclectic with a strong neo-antique inspiration. This is clearly demonstrated in his first major work, the Villa Sacchetti del Pigneto near Rome, built in the mid-1630s but now destroyed. Set into the hillside, it was approached through a system of ramps and terraces leading up to the entrance exedra, an arrangement

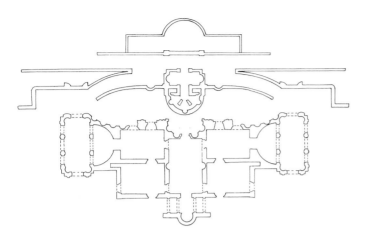

429 *Above* Plan of Villa Sacchetti del Pigneto, near Rome (mid-1630s), by Cortona

430, 431 *Above and below* Interior and exterior of SS. Luca e Martina, Rome (1634–69) by Cortona

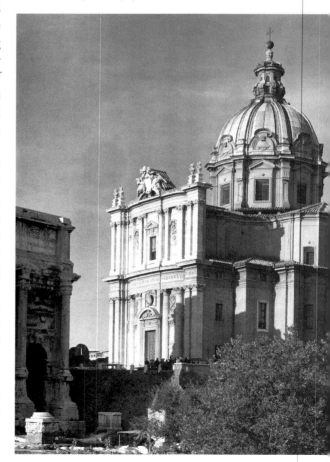

inspired by the Roman Sanctuary of Fortuna Primigenia at Praeneste (Palestrina) (p. 62), of which Cortona made a restoration on paper in 1636. Features of the planning such as the two rooms containing large semicircular apses screened by columns derive from the solaria of the Roman baths. The giant entrance niche echoes that at the Belvedere in the Vatican and is flanked by curved wings, vying with Borromini's Oratory of St Philip Neri as the earliest curved façade in Rome.

Cortona's major architectural work, commissioned by Cardinal Francesco Barberini, the pope's nephew, is the church of SS. Luca e Martina (1634–69), on a prestigious site in the Roman Forum next to the Arch of Septimius Severus. The two-storeyed central section of the façade follows a convex curve which seems the result of pressure from the rectangular blocks flanking it. Columns are embedded into the convex wall in the manner devised by Michelangelo in the vestibule of the Laurentian Library in Florence. Florentine Mannerism was always a strong influence on Cortona's architectural language. The interior, in plan a Greek cross with rounded ends to all four arms, is moulded in a similarly flexible way with complex wall planes articulated with inset and freestanding giant Ionic columns. Cortona, like Borromini, did not enrich his interior with colour and figure sculpture in the way that Bernini would have, so that below the entablature all is white travertine and stucco, emphasizing the architectural character of the design. The crypt or lower church is more richly coloured and is perhaps intended to convey something of the mysterious atmosphere of the Early Christian catacombs. During the excavations for the church in 1634 the body of S. Martina was discovered with much excitement, and Cortona housed her relics in a sumptuous altar-shrine in the crypt.

In the 1640s and 1650s Cortona created a number of dazzlingly illusionistic frescoed and stuccoed interiors, such as the long gallery linking the Palazzo Pamphili to the church of S. Agnese in the Piazza Navona. However, with the accession of Alexander VII Chigi to the papacy in 1655, he returned to architecture to produce two of the most fascinating church façades in Baroque Rome. The church of S. Maria della Pace, containing the Chigi family chapel, had been built in the fifteenth century by Pope Sixtus IV to mark the peace which followed a war

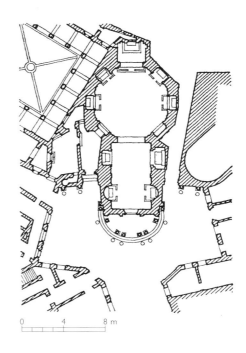

433, 434 *Above and below* Exterior and plan of S. Maria della Pace, Rome (1656–9), by Cortona

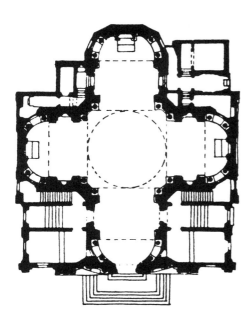

432 Plan of SS. Luca e Martina, Rome by Cortona

293

between the Medici and the papacy. Cortona's new façade of 1656–59, commissioned by Alexander VII, celebrates the church as a temple of peace with its projecting half-oval porch of Tuscan columns. Resembling a section of a temple, this may equally have been inspired by a reconstruction of the Baths of Diocletian. The recessed upper storey, though flanked by concave wings, is convex like the porch, and with its embedded columns has a malleable Michelangelesque quality. Indeed the crowning feature of the façade, the triangular pediment enclosing a segmental one, is probably derived from Michelangelo's Laurentian Library. What is new is the way in which Cortona extended the façade of the church over the adjacent buildings so as to create a miniature open-air theatre

435 Cortona: Exterior of S. Maria in Via Lata, Rome (begun 1658)

with the church façade as the backdrop, the little piazza as the auditorium and the flanking houses as the boxes. This impression is heightened by the fact that the wings actually contain openings like stage doors leading to the adjacent streets. Cortona had to demolish a number of houses to create this little piazza, which had to be just wide enough to accommodate the turning of a carriage. His achievement, which can be seen as a development from Bernini's theatrical Cornaro Chapel, is one of the most exhilarating of all examples of the Baroque principle of 'extended action'.

Scarcely less memorable, in a totally different manner, is Cortona's façade begun in 1658 at the church of S. Maria in Via Lata on the Corso, the narrow principal thoroughfare of ancient as well as of Baroque Rome. Built over an early Christian chapel supposedly incorporating a house or hostelry in which St Peter himself had stayed, this church had been rebuilt many times but Cortona, with unusual respect for its archaeology, restored the crypt as a shrine to St Peter. On the entrance front he provided a ground-floor portico *in antis* like that at Peruzzi's neo-antique Palazzo Massimi and, seeing that the church was in danger of being dominated by the new buildings that were rising round it, persuaded Alexander VII to allow him to add a huge upper storey in 1662. Technically functionless, this eye-catching belvedere can perhaps be seen as an echo of the imperial viewing-boxes overlooking the circuses of ancient Rome. Certainly its dominant motif of an arcuated lintel, that is an entablature bent up to form an arch projecting into the pediment, is a specific echo of proto-Baroque elements in late-imperial Roman architecture at Baalbek and Spalato (pp. 85, 86).

Cortona's monumental but animated, assertive architecture was strongly coloured by his passion for antiquity. We find him in old age climbing Trajan's column to make drawings of the figured reliefs and descending into excavations to investigate newly discovered ancient frescoes. Perhaps this interest in the classical world is inescapable in Rome; it should certainly prevent us from making the mistake, common in the eighteenth and nineteenth centuries, of thinking that Baroque architecture is anti-classical. For example, the twin churches begun in 1662 in the Piazza del Popolo, Rome, S. Maria di Monte Santo and S Maria dei Miracoli, have freestanding pedimented porticoes which deliberately recall antique temples. They were designed by Carlo Rainaldi and Bernini as part of a brilliant town-planning scheme in which Rainaldi created a memorable entrance to Rome for the visitor arriving through the Porta del Popolo. The side façades of the churches are blended into the street architecture in a novel way so as to forge piazza, streets and churches into a single urban unity.

Contrasting currents in late-Baroque Rome

In later seventeenth-century Rome two currents of Baroque architecture and decoration emerged, the more stylistically exaggerated including Andrea Pozzo and Antonio Gherardi, the more conservative led by Carlo Fontana. Andrea Pozzo (1642–1709), a Jesuit lay-brother, was the leading *quadraturista* or painter of perspective illusion. His most important works were at the two principal Jesuit churches in Rome, the Gesù where he provided the sumptuous altar of S. Ignazio, and the church of S. Ignazio where he painted the nave vault, dome and apse in 1685–94 with frescoes depicting the

436 Frescoes by Pozzo on the nave vault of S. Ignazio, Rome (1685–94)

437 De Sanctis: The Spanish Steps, Rome (1723–8). At the top is the church of SS. Trinità dei Monti with its late-16th-century façade

438 Fontana: S. Marcello, Rome (1682–3)

missionary work of Jesuits throughout the world. In 1693–8 he published a two-volumed treatise, *Perspectiva Pictorum et Architectorum* ('Perspective of paintings and architecture'), with elaborate illustrations including curvilinear altars and temporary structures which influenced architects all over Europe.

The most compelling work of Carlo Fontana (1638–1714) is the façade of S. Marcello in the Via del Corso (1682–3), which brought a new classical sobriety and harmony to the curved frontage associated with Borromini and Pietro da Cortona. Fontana became a successful but cautious establishment architect, designing rather dull buildings like the Jesuit church and college at Loyola in Spain. Far livelier was his pupil Alessandro Specchi (1668–1729), who built the now destroyed Porta di Ripetta (1703–5), a dock on the banks of the Tiber opposite the church of S. Girolamo degli Schiavoni. With their Borrominiesque double S-

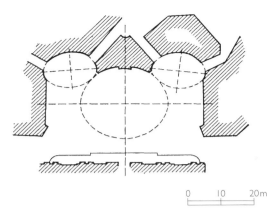

439 Piazza di S. Ignazio, Rome

440 Façade of S. Maria Maggiore, Rome (1741–3), by Fuga

curves, the steps leading to the river anticipated the vaster but looser composition of the celebrated Spanish Steps mounting from the Piazza di Spagna to the church of SS. Trinità dei Monti. Specchi was initially concerned with the design of the Spanish Steps but he was replaced by Francesco de Sanctis (1693–1740), who created in 1723–8 one of the most enthralling pieces of scenographic town-planning in Europe. Something of its spirit is found in a smaller scale in the rippling motion of the charming Piazza di S. Ignazio, Rome (1727–8), by the Sicilian-born architect Filippo Raguzzini (c.1680–1771). Houses with convex curved façades separated by diagonally-set streets confront the earlier church of S. Ignazio like the wings of a stage set.

These curvilinear effects were generally given up in Rome, partly through the impact of the classical tastes of the Florentine Cardinal Lorenzo Corsini who, after his election to the papacy as Clement XII in 1730, called to Rome two Florentine architects, Alessandro Galilei (1699–1736) and Ferdinando Fuga (1699–1781). In 1733–5 Galilei provided the Early Christian basilica of St John Lateran with a monumental façade which is more like that of a palace than a church. Indeed, with its giant order and smaller order inset on the ground floor, it may be regarded as the grandiloquent apotheosis of Michelangelo's Capitoline palaces. Inside the church Galilei added the Cappella Corsini, a family chapel for Clement XII in a gravely classical style. It contained Clement's tomb which, in conformity with his tastes,

was a re-used ancient Roman sarcophagus brought from the portico of the Pantheon. Ferdinando Fuga remained closer to Baroque ideals, as in the staircase of his otherwise rather dull Palazzo Corsini, built for Clement XII in 1736–c.1750, and in his splendid façade of 1741–3 at the Early Christian basilica of S. Maria Maggiore. Here he exploited the requirement of a benediction loggia for the pope (a balcony from which he could give his blessing) by providing a more sculptural version of the typical two-storeyed church façade of the sixteenth century as established at the Gesù, but hollowed out with deep shadowy arcades on both storeys.

The last great monument of eighteenth-century Baroque Rome, and in some ways the most remarkable, is the Trevi Fountain of 1732–62 by Nicola Salvi

(1697–1751). Salvi concealed the façade of an existing palace behind a triumphal arch so as to create the most grandiose of the many architecturally designed fountains which had been a feature of Rome from classical times. Baroque in its heroic grandeur of scale and exuberant figure sculpture, Rococo in its romantically naturalistic rocks sprouting into carved foliage, and neo-antique in its reference to the triumphal arch, it is a masterpiece of classical design which transcends all stylistic boundaries.

Piedmont: Guarini, Juvarra and Vittone

Though Rome was the undoubted artistic centre of what we now call Italy, and, in the early eighteenth century, of Europe, the other independent states on Italian soil developed their own versions of Baroque. The most important of these territories was Piedmont which, under the House of Savoy, rose to the status of a European power between the mid-sixteenth and mid-eighteenth centuries. Turin, the capital from 1563, was remodelled along Baroque lines during the seventeenth century, though retaining the grid-plan of its Roman origins. In 1663 Duke Carlo Emanuele of Savoy (1638–75) called to Turin Guarino Guarini (1624–83), one of the most brilliant and original architects of the entire Baroque period.

Like countless distinguished architects Guarini had received no formal architectural training. He was a priest of the Theatine order, one of the new Counter-Reformation orders like the Jesuits and the Oratorians which, unlike them, has since died out. From 1639 to 1647 he studied theology, philosophy and mathematics at the Theatine house in Rome, where he was appointed professor of philosophy in 1650. It is evident that he also looked closely at the work of Borromini, whose influence can be traced in his early designs for churches at Lisbon, Messina and Paris. His church of S. Maria Divina Providencia, Lisbon (c.1656), which collapsed in the great earthquake of 1755, boasted a nave consisting of a series of interlocking ovals in which the transverse arches were three-dimensional, that is, they swung forwards as well as upwards. This rhythm was echoed in the Salomonic or twisted pilasters which lined the nave walls, and in the amazing kidney-shaped windows in the lunettes. Guarini's unexecuted project of 1660 for the church of the Somaschian order at Messina, Sicily, and his never fully realized and now destroyed Theatine church of Ste-Anne-la-Royale, Paris (1662), hint at his love of replacing the solid dome with an openwork system of intersecting ribs. The origins of the device of the ribbed dome may lie in the ceilings of Borromini's Oratory and Propaganda Fide chapels, but Guarini transforms it in a way which is paralleled only by some of the Late Gothic vaults we saw in Chapter 5.

At Turin cathedral Guarini took over from Amadeo de Castellamonte the building of the Cappella della SS. Sindone, which was to house one of the best-known relics in Europe, the Holy Shroud, a much prized possession of the House of Savoy. Believed to be miraculously imprinted with the image of Christ's dead body, this has even today lost nothing of its ability to stir the imagination. Modern scientists, still at a loss to account for the phenomenon, have sometimes spoken of a kind of instant electric radiation, and certainly Guarini's dome over this chapel quivers with a vibrant electric force. The upper stages of this uniquely

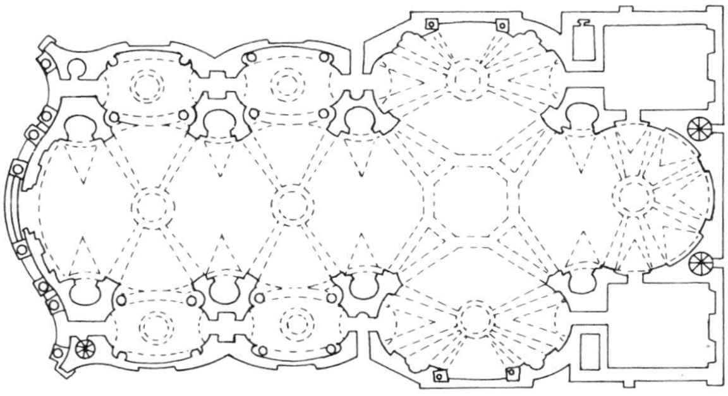

441 *Opposite* Salvi: The Trevi Fountain, Rome (1732–62)

442 Plan of S. Maria Divina Providencia, Lisbon (c.1656), by Guarini

443 Interior of dome of the Cappella della SS. Sindone, Turin Cathedral (1667–90), by Guarini

audacious openwork dome, built in 1667–90, are composed of diminishing tiers of flattened rib-like arches stacked above each other like a house of cards, each framing a segmental window. This skeletal cone-shaped hexagon is surmounted by a circular lantern, containing an image of the Holy Dove, rising from a ring supported by ribs forming a star pattern which is boldly silhouetted against light from the oval windows in the lantern above. This transcendental architectural poetry is conceived without colour and depends for its mysterious effect on marble ranging from black in the dark lower parts of the building to grey in the brighter cupola, where light filters diaphanously through the honeycomb of segmental windows. The sepulchral mood of the body of the chapel, in contrast to the luminosity of the dome, is appropriate to the function of the building as a shrine for a shroud. On the equally bizarre exterior the ribs over the segmental windows are like the zig-zag steps of a ziggurat or tower of Babel,

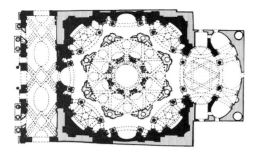

444 Plan of S. Lorenzo, Turin

while the surmounting lantern also diminishes in three stages like a pagoda or a Buddhist *stupa*.

Guarini's church of S. Lorenzo, Turin (1668–80), is square in plan but has an octagonal central space in which each side curves inwards in the form of a wide, open arch of the 'Palladian' – also called 'Venetian' or 'Serliana' – type. In the four diagonal axes these column-framed openings lead into chapels of a curious near-oval plan defined by two arcs of circles. In the zone above this, Serlian windows alternate with pendentives supporting the cone-shaped tower-like dome, which consists of eight semi-circular ribs disposed so as to create an eight-pointed star with an open octagonal space in the centre. Above this space rises a tall lantern covered by a small dome which is itself constructed of ribs. The octagonal nave opens into an oval choir, vaulted with a second circular ribbed dome, which leads through a Serlian arch into a further oval space containing the high altar. The only parallel to these networks of intersecting ribs is in Hispano–Moresque buildings which Guarini may have seen, such as the domes of the mosque at Córdoba or of the cathedral at Saragossa. However, these domes are not diaphanous like Guarini's, for he hollowed out the space between the ribs and raised lanterns at their intersections.

The effect is in the end closer to late Gothic than to Moorish architecture. It therefore comes as no surprise that Guarini's architectural treatise, *Architettura civile* (published in 1737 though some of the plates had appeared in 1686), contains one of the earliest and most spirited defences of Gothic architecture. He confessed

himself amazed by Gothic builders who constructed arches 'which seem to hang in the air; completely perforated towers crowned by pointed pyramids; enormously high windows and vaults without the support of walls. The corner of a high tower may rest on an arch or on a column or on the apex of a vault'. Guarini's brilliant treatise concentrates on the application of geometry to architecture, as in the plane projection of spherical surfaces and in stereotomy, the art of cutting and dressing stones to fit vaults. The French, who had invented Gothic architecture, were masters in stereotomy which they regarded as an essential part of the architect's understanding of his art. Guarini, who had visited Paris to teach theology, drew on Philibert de l'Orme's *Premier tome de l'architecture* ('First volume of architecture') (1626), Desargue's *Projective Geometry* (1639), and François Derand's *L'architecture des voûtes* ('Architecture of vaults') (1643), all of which contained information on the art of stereotomy.

After Guarini's death there was a lull in building activity in Turin until the accession of Vittorio Amedeo II of Savoy, who became King of Sicily in 1713 but was obliged to exchange this in 1720 for Sardinia whilst retaining his royal title. He appointed as royal architect the Sicilian-born Filippo Juvarra (1678–1736), who had acquired an international reputation during his ten-year period in Rome from 1704, where he had been a pupil of Carlo Fontana. Juvarra took minor orders in the Catholic church, like Borromini and Guarini before him. He was an unbelievably prolific architect of royal palaces as well as of town mansions, churches and new streets in Turin. He completed the transformation of Turin from a ducal to a royal capital, building or remodelling as many as sixteen palaces and eight churches in a fluent international Baroque style. His church of S. Cristina (1715–28) echoes Carlo Fontana's S. Marcello in Rome, while in 1718–21 he rebuilt the Palazzo Madama for the Queen Mother, Maria Giovanna Battista, creating for her one of the grandest staircases in Italy. The opportunities for spatial play provided by

445 *Above* Juvarra: The staircase at the Palazzo Madama, Turin (1718–21)

446 *Opposite* View towards the dome of S. Lorenzo, Turin (1668–80), by Guarini

staircase-design made it especially popular with Baroque architects. The grandiose staircase was also welcomed by royal or princely patrons, since an important part of contemporary social ritual was how far a host descended such a staircase to meet his guest.

447 Juvarra: The Superga, near Turin (1717–31)

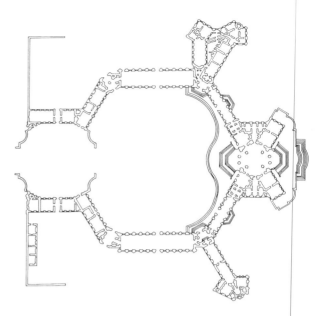

448 Juvarra: Plan of the palace at Stupinigi, near Turin (1729–33)

The play with light and with scenographic effect which was essential to Juvarra's architecture was the fruit of his extensive work as a stage designer for Cardinal Ottoboni in Rome from 1708. Juvarra's novel church of the Carmine, Turin (1732–5), is a striking example of his control of light in a daringly skeletal structure. It is a wall-pillar church, that is to say a northern late-Gothic type, like St Barbara at Kuttenberg (Kutná Hora) (p. 192), in which the walls dividing the side chapels are carried to the full height of the church, allowing for galleries over the chapels. Unusual oval apertures in the vaults of these chapels allow light to descend into them from the windows in the gallery.

Juvarra's masterpiece is the Superga (1717–31), a royal burial church for the House of Savoy and a monastery superbly placed on a high hill outside Turin, near the site of the Battle of Turin (1706) in which Vittorio Amedeo II and Prince Eugene of Savoy defeated the French and regained their duchy. The church is a re-splendently Baroque echo of the Pantheon with a gigantic square portico boldly juxtaposed against the high domed cylinder of the nave. It is flanked by a pair of campanili, as in Borromini's S. Agnese, while the curved windows round the inside of the drum of the dome are also Borrominiesque. However, the helms of the towers are

449 Interior of the main salon of the Royal Palace at Stupinigi

distinctly Austrian, and it is probable that Juvarra's inspiration for the combination of pedimented portico, towers and dome also owed something to its near-contemporary as a votive church, the Karlskirche in Vienna, erected by Vittorio Amedeo's imperial ally (see p. 324).

The expansive mood, lively detail and vigorous eclecticism of Juvarra is nowhere better expressed than in his royal palace, technically a hunting-lodge, at Stupinigi, built in 1729–33 for Vittorio Amedeo II a few miles from Turin. The X-shaped plan of the main block, with diagonal wings radiating from a central rotunda, echoes a design by Serlio (Book VII, chapter XIII) which had been adapted by Fontana in a design for a villa of 1689.

To this concept Juvarra added the notion of extending wings in front of the palace so as to form a vast hexagonal forecourt. In short, Stupinigi is a dream of a French hunting château as realized by an Italian scene-painter. This visionary scenographic drama reaches its climax in the main saloon, which is a domed ballroom of such height that it incorporates balconied galleries for musicians and spectators. Richly frescoed and stuccoed, the interior recalls a piece of festival architecture or a stage-set. Its central domed space surrounded by four freestanding piers is flanked by four high apses, two large and two small.

Juvarra was an international figure working in an international style. He had stayed in 1720 as the guest of the Portuguese ambassador in London; there he seems to have met Lord Burlington, to whom he dedicated a volume of imaginative architectural sketches. He died in Madrid, the guest of Philip V of Spain for whom he was designing the gigantic royal palace which still dominates the capital. Fluent and sophisticated as a personality and as a designer, Juvarra was the heir to a long tradition of classical design from the fifteenth century down to his own day. He approached this tradition synthetically and eclectically in a manner similar to Johann Fischer von Erlach, whose *Entwurff einer historischen Architectur* (Vienna 1721) was the first comparative study of world architecture (p. 324).

The true successor to Guarini and Juvarra was Bernardo Vittone (1702–70) who, following his architectural training at the Accademia di S. Luca in Rome in 1731–3, edited Guarini's papers, published by the Theatines in 1737 as the *Architettura civile*. Like Borromini, Guarini and Juvarra, by all of whom he was powerfully influenced, he remained a bachelor, devoted perhaps less to sensual pleasure than to the sensuous thrills of architecture. His earliest recorded work of significance is the little Sanctuary of the Visitation (1738–9) at Vallinotto near Carignano, a rural wayside chapel built for farmworkers on the estate of Antonio Faccio, a banker from Turin. Vittone crowded into a hexagonal space with a diameter of about 50 feet (15m) many of the exotic forms which characterize his later buildings. From the six piers of the central hexagonal space, flanked by six segmental chapels, spring six ribs which intersect to form a dome of Guariniesque character. However, Vittone went beyond Guarini in spatial complexity by raising two further domes or shells over this, both frescoed with the hierarchy of angels. The first, without windows, contains a wide hexagonal aperture in the centre which opens into the second dome, lit by concealed circular windows and surmounted by a lantern with a symbol of the Trinity painted on its vault. The double-shell dome is probably derived from J. H. Mansart's at the Invalides, Paris, while the vaults of the side chapels, which are pierced with oval apertures, are inspired by those at Juvarra's Carmine church in Turin. The complex vistas, the plunging light, the false, i.e. inaccessible, balconied galleries over alternate chapels, the sense of a structure within a structure, all produce an operatic effect not far from the visionary sketches for scenery of the Galli-Bibiena family of stage designers who worked in Bologna (p. 307).

Vittone's brick-built church of S. Chiara at Brà (1742) is a sophisticated variant on the same theme, probably inspired by Juvarra's saloon at Stupinigi. Here, although the ribs of the first dome are not freestanding, the solid surface of the dome is pierced with four

450 Vittone: S. Chiara, Brà (1742)

curvilinear openings through which can be seen the second dome painted with a sky inhabited by angels and saints. At S. Bernardino, Chieri (1740–4), the octagonal dome hangs in a square space which flows round it in the form of light chambers. Both the vaults of the surrounding apses and the pendentives of the dome are perforated so as to be open to this source of light, the openings in the pendentives resembling in shape giant keyholes. Vittone built over twenty-five churches, of which the majority are more conventional than Vallinotto or Brà, but there is one group in which he introduced highly individual structural and lighting effects through the use of gouged-out pendentives so as to dissolve the distinction between drum, pendentive and dome: these are the chapel of the Ospizio di Carità at Carignano (1744), S. Maria in Piazza, Turin (1751–4), SS. Pietro e Paolo, Mondovì (1755) and, most strikingly, S. Croce, Villanova di Mondovì (1755).

Like Guarini, Vittone thought deeply about architecture and published two treatises, the *Istruzioni*

elementari (1760) and *Istruzioni diverse* (1766). They are the last in a line reaching back to Alberti in which spiritual beauty is equated with mathematical, geometrical and musical harmony. Surprisingly, they contain little that is revealing about the most unforgettable aspects of his own buildings, the miraculous open domes and vaults through which he allowed a little of heaven to illuminate the world below.

Genoa, Milan, Bologna and Venice

Nowhere else in north Italy was Baroque developed so extensively as in Piedmont. The principal building phase in Genoa had been in the late sixteenth century, and the heir to that tradition was Bartolommeo Bianco (before 1590–1657), the city's leading early Baroque architect. His masterpiece is the Jesuit College of 1630, today the University, which draws on the experience of architects such as Galeazzo Alessi (1512–72) in constructing palaces on sloping sites. In Bianco's brilliant spatial composition the entrance vestibule contains a grand staircase leading up to the colonnaded cortile which is on a higher level. Visible through the open arches at the far end of the cortile is a great double staircase rising the full height of the building. Genoa was developed during the eighteenth century with numerous richly Baroque churches, palaces and villas. In Milan the principal Baroque architect was Francesco Maria Ricchino (1583–1658). Many of his churches have been destroyed, but the concave façade which he added in 1627 to the Swiss College, built in 1608 from designs by Fabio Mangone (1587–1629), survives as probably the first of its kind in Italy. It was not a theme which Ricchino or his north Italian contemporaries developed, but it is tempting to imagine that Borromini, who had left Milan by 1618, may have seen a drawing of Ricchino's remarkable façade.

In Bologna we should single out Carlo Francesco Dotti (1670–1759), who is best remembered for his Sanctuary of the Madonna di S. Luca (1723–57), a pilgrimage church crowning a hill on the edge of the city. Memorable in itself, this domed elliptical Greek-

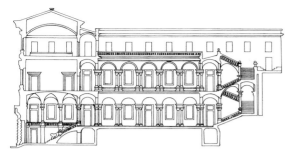

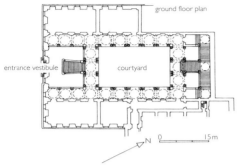

ground floor plan

entrance vestibule

courtyard

N 0   15m

451 *Above* Bianco: Section and plan of the University, Genoa (1634–6)

452 *Below* Dotti: Plan of the church of Madonna di S. Luca, Bologna (1723–57)

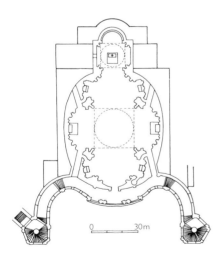

0   30m

of the Road to Calvary, merges with the façade of the church which is fronted with a double-S-curved arcade. The Arch of Meloncello, designed by Dotti in 1722 with an asymmetrical curved colonnade leading away from one side, is itself a strikingly theatrical piece of urban Baroque architecture.

Dotti's other works include the splendid double-return staircase of c.1730 in the Palazzo Davia-Bargellini which grew out of the Bolognese tradition of scenographic staircases. Another spirited example is that of 1695 by Giovanni Battista Piacentini in the Palazzo di Giustizia. Perhaps the most significant Bolognese contribution to Baroque architecture was made by the Galli-Bibiena family of stage-designers and architects, who carried *quadratura* painting to its limits. Between the 1670s and 1770s Ferdinando (1657–1743), his sons Alessandro (1687–1769), Giuseppe (1696–1757) and Antonio (1700–74), and his brother Francesco (1659–1731) worked in many of the German- and Italian-speaking courts of Europe in a heady language which influenced the creative imagination of Juvarra, Vittone and, perhaps even more significantly, that of Piranesi.

In Venice the continuing influence of Palladio and Scamozzi discouraged any very extensive Baroque development in architecture except in the case of Baldassare Longhena (1598–1682), a pupil of Scamozzi. His most brilliant work is S. Maria della Salute, a commission which he won in a competition following a vow to erect a church made by the Doge and Senate during the plague of 1630. This great centrally-planned octagonal church with its huge billowing dome, weighed down by twelve massively Baroque scrolls, was seen by Longhena as a symbolic crown. In the explanatory notes with which he accompanied his model in April 1630, he wrote that 'The mystery contained in the dedication of this church to the Blessed Virgin made me think, with what little talent God has bestowed on me, of building the church in *forma rotonda*, i.e. in the shape of a crown.' The church thus celebrates Mary as Queen of Heaven. Her statue with a crown of stars surmounts the dome

cross-plan church is rendered absolutely unforgettable by means of its uniquely scenic method of approach: a long arcaded passageway which ascends the hill in a great series of curves and zig-zags from the Arch of Meloncello marking the entrance to the city. On arrival at the summit of the hill this dramatic passage, a symbol

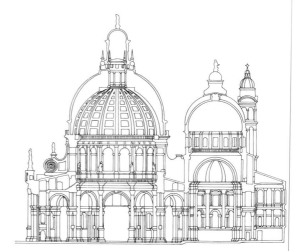

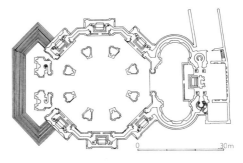

453, 454 *Above and right* Longhena: Interior, section and plan of S. Maria della Salute, Venice (begun 1630)

and reappears over the high altar beneath a huge crown hanging from the vaulting.

The architectural form in which Longhena chose to express his image of a celestial crown is a regular octagon surrounded by an ambulatory, a form which had not been adopted in Renaissance or Baroque architecture but which featured in both Late Antique and Byzantine buildings in Italy such as S. Costanza, Rome, and S. Vitale, Ravenna. Carefully contrived theatrical or scenographic vistas radiate through the arches which surround the central octagonal space. This disposition doubtless depends on Longhena's knowledge of stage scenery, such as that in Palladio's Teatro Olimpico at Vicenza where a triumphal-arch proscenium frames a perspective vista up a street of festive palaces. The triumphal arch motif also dominates the central section of the façade of the Salute so that when the doors are open the view which opens up towards the high altar is indeed close to Palladio's theatre. In the impressive vista from the domed sanctuary to the rectangular monks' choir behind the

high altar, the control of illumination is as subtle as on a stage.

Palladio lies behind many features of the church including the Diocletian windows, the columns on high pedestals, the colour scheme of a whitewashed background contrasting with structural features in grey stone, the harmonically proportioned relationship between the three parts of the church, and the façades of the two side chapels receding diagonally from the entrance front which are inspired by Palladio's little church of Le Zitelle on the Giudecca in Venice. Moreover, the profile of the small dome over the sanctuary, with a stilted profile over a high drum flanked by two campanili, follows a Byzantine-Venetian model which Palladio had already adopted at the Redentore. S. Maria della Salute is thus a dazzlingly successful blend of Venetian and Palladian types given a new visual coherence by means of Longhena's individual approach to the scenographic qualities of the Baroque. The undeniably Picturesque relationship of its domes to the skyline of Venice is also evidence of a painterly approach to urban composition which goes beyond Renaissance ideals.

Longhena's theatrical talent emerged once more in his staircase-hall (1643–5) at the Monastery of S. Giorgio Maggiore, Venice. This is of the so-called imperial type, with a single central arm breaking into two flights which follow the outer walls. With Bianco's staircase at Genoa University of 1630, this is one of the first Baroque staircases in Italy. Longhena's domestic architecture, in particular his Palazzo Rezzonico (begun 1670) and Palazzo Pesaro (begun 1676), is characteristic of seventeenth- and eighteenth-century Venetian palazzi in echoing Sansovino's Palazzo Corner, though with increasing sculptural richness. This richness reaches its height in Longhena's little church of the Ospedaletto (1670–8), smothered in carved lions' masks, shields, bunches of fruit, and atlantes (male figures used as supports).

The most enthralling Baroque church in Venice is the Gesuiti, built for the Jesuits in 1715-28 from designs by Domenico Rossi the Younger (1652–1737), though the riotous façade of 1729 is by Giovanni Battista Fattoretto. The almost outrageously sumptuous interior appears to be upholstered throughout with green and white damask, an effect created by an astonishing virtuoso use of inlaid marble. The high altar with figure sculpture and a tabernacle of lapis lazuli beneath a curvilinear domed baldacchino supported on twisted columns was designed by Andrea Pozzo's brother, Jacopo Antonio (1645–1725). The rich use of coloured marbles in this church leads us to southern Italy, where it was a technique especially favoured by Neapolitan and Sicilian architects.

Naples and Sicily

Naples, in the seventeenth century a province of Spain governed by a viceroy, was richly developed with Baroque buildings for patrons dedicated to the pursuit of both pleasure and piety. The leading architect was Cosimo Fanzago (1591–1678), trained as a sculptor and marble-worker and noted above all for his decoratively

455 Rossi the Younger: Interior of the Gesuiti, Venice (1715–28), showing the high altar by Jacopo Antonio Pozzo

456 Fanzago: Exterior of the uncompleted Palazzo Donn'Anna, Posilipo, near Naples (1642–4)

inlaid marble interiors as in the chapels of 1637–50 at the Gesù Nuovo and of 1643–5 at S. Lorenzo Maggiore. His more strictly architectural skills emerged in churches such as S. Giovanni degli Scalzi at Pontecorvo (1643–60), where a dramatic western vestibule contains a double staircase leading up to the nave which is on a higher level than the street. His most remarkable building is the uncompleted Palazzo Donn'Anna (1642–4), built at Posilipo near Naples for the Spanish Viceroy, the Duke of Medina, and his wealthy Italian wife. Rising out of the sea like Diocletian's palace at Spalato (Split), its sea-front is dominated by a monumental belvedere of three storeys or super-imposed loggias. The building has astonishing bevelled corners and incorporates real rocks as an irregular rusticated basement, an idea taken up by Bernini in one of his unexecuted projects for the Louvre.

457 The Piazza del Gesù, Naples, with the Guglia dell'Immaculata, by Genuino (1747–50)

458 Vaccaro: The majolica cloister at S. Chiara, Naples (1739–42)

Among the most exuberant expressions of Neapolitan gaiety and ebullience are the *Guglie*, columns or obelisks surmounted by commemorative statues and richly adorned with sculpture. Fanzago designed the Guglia di S. Gennaro in 1637, but the most extravagant is the Guglia dell' Immaculata (1747–50) by Giuseppe Genuino, rising in Rococo flamboyance in the square outside the Gesù Nuovo church. Fanzago's principal followers, working in a spirited Late-Baroque manner, both pupils of the Neapolitan painter Francesco Solimena, were Domenico Antonio Vaccaro (1681–1750) and Ferdinando Sanfelice (1675–1750). Vaccaro's most interesting churches are those exploiting the combination of octagonal and rectangular spaces, in plans which seem centralized though they have a longitudinal emphasis. These include his Concezione at Montecalvario (1718–24), and especially his S. Maria delle Grazie at Calvizzano (c.1743), near Naples. Here structural divisions between drum and cupola are dissolved beneath a froth of stuccowork which, by the time it reaches the opening into the lantern, resembles a cloud-flecked sky. Vaccaro's most cheerful work is the enchanting majolica cloister at S. Chiara, Naples, of 1739–42, where he filled the centre of a Gothic cloister with pergolas. These are supported by octagonal piers of coloured majolica painted with vine clusters which blend with the real vines. The piers are linked by benches, also of majolica, ornamented with painted landscapes and pastoral scenes.

Ferdinando Sanfelice, who came from a prominent and wealthy Neapolitan family, was celebrated for his open staircases. The most elaborate of these is at the Palazzo Serra di Cassano (1720–38), an immense double staircase the size of a small courtyard. Approached through a huge archway from an octagonal courtyard, the staircase consists of two halves in oval vestibules, in between which are semicircular landings forming a pair of bastions confronting the visitor as he approaches the staircase. The two flights converge at an imposing bridge from which access is gained to the main apartments. Sanfelice's other principal contribution was in the design of the extravagant temporary structures which were

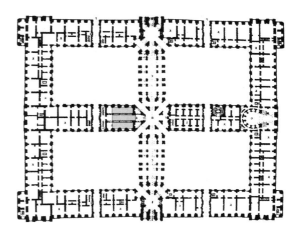

459 Plan of Vanvitelli's palace at Caserta (1752–74)

erected throughout Baroque Europe on festive occasions. One of the most extraordinary, marking the birth of a daughter to the King of the Two Sicilies in 1740, was the transformation of the square outside the Viceroy's palace into a giant arcaded hemi-cycle approached through triumphal arches and dominated by a central pagoda-like tower of great height with a double staircase running round it.

Charles Bourbon, who reigned as first King of the Two Sicilies from 1734 until 1759 when he succeeded his father as Charles III of Spain, summoned to Naples in 1750 two Roman-trained architects, Ferdinando Fuga (1699–1782) and Luigi Vanvitelli (1700–71). At Caserta, about 20 miles (32km) north of Naples, Vanvitelli began building a palace for the king in 1752. With four courtyards, 1,200 rooms and the largest staircase in Italy, it is one of the most impressive palaces in the world and the last of its kind in the country. Its façades, 34 bays long, are somewhat cold and monotonous but the breathtaking vistas through the central axis of the entire complex, incorporating three huge octagonal vestibules, are the most magnificent realization of the visions of Longhena and the Galli-Bibiena family.

Sicily in the eighteenth century produced a group of architects whose energy and imagination resulted in a

460 *Above left* The ballroom at the Palazzo Gangi, Palermo (1750s)

461 *Above* Syracuse cathedral: the west façade (1728–54) and the side elevation with Greek Doric columns of the 5th century BC

462 *Opposite* Vaccarini: Exterior of S. Agata, Catania (1735–67)

vast number of captivating buildings in the ornate final phase of Baroque, known as Rococo, though the term is probably best used to describe interior decoration. Among the most distinguished of these Sicilian architects was Tommaso Napoli (1655–1725), a Dominican monk, who produced two extravagant villas for Sicilian noblemen at Bagheria about ten miles (16km) east of Palermo, the Villa Palagonia (begun 1705) and the Villa Valguarnera (1709–39), both with curvilinear and ingenious external staircases.

The seventeenth-century churches of Palermo are conspicuous for their sumptuous decoration in coloured inlaid marble, but around the opening years of the eighteenth century Giacomo Serpotta (1656–1732), working in an indigenous tradition of plasterwork, was responsible for three oratories with lavishly stuccoed interiors of unsurpassed fertility of invention: the Oratories of the Rosary at S. Zita (1687–1717) and at S. Domenico (1720), and the oratory at S. Lorenzo (1706–8). Serpotta also decorated S. Spirito, Agrigento, in the 1690s with a high altar smothered beneath stucco clouds, while his son Procopio decorated the oratory of S. Caterina at Palermo (1719–26) in a similarly exuberant fashion.

Among the numerous Baroque palaces of Palermo we should note the Palazzo Cattolico (1719–26) by Giacomo Amato, the Palazzo Bonagia (c.1760) by Andrea Giganti (1731–87), and the Palazzo Gangi, perhaps of the 1750s. The arcaded courtyard of the Palazzo Cattolico is theatrically divided by an open-arched bridge, a device echoed in the courtyard of the Palazzo Bonagia which is dominated by an open staircase beneath a gigantic arch. At the Palazzo Gangi, perhaps the best-preserved palace in Palermo, the ballroom is one of the finest examples in Europe of Baroque forms set into the fluttering motion which is characteristic of the Rococo style. The walls are lined with huge triple mirrors in delicately curled frames; the unique double ceiling consists of two layers, the lower one resembling coving from which the panels have been removed, leaving only the ribs, thus forming openings through which we see the frescoes on the vaulted ceiling above.

This magical interior encapsulates the heady luxury of Giuseppe di Lampedusa's novel of Sicilian life, *The Leopard* (*Il Gattopardo*, Milan 1958). It was appropriately chosen by Visconti as the setting for the ball-scene in his film of the prince's novel.

Sicily was devastated by an earthquake in 1693, after which the eastern part of the island was reconstructed in a lavish manner. One of the most striking products of this was the façade of the cathedral at Syracuse. This effervescent creation was added in 1728–54 by Andrea Palma (1664–1730) as a startling termination to the body of the church, which is no less than a fifth-century Greek Doric temple converted into a church in the Early Christian period. At Syracuse cathedral the history of western architecture unfolds before the eyes. The hillside towns of Noto, Ragusa and Modica, all completely rebuilt after the earthquake, are dominated by the memorable churches of Rosario Gagliardi of the 1730s and 1740s. Rising dynamically above imposing flights of steps, the west façades of these churches consist primarily of oval belfry towers, a disposition unknown elsewhere in Italy though paralleled in northern Europe by architects such as Neumann and Hawksmoor, who can scarcely have known them.

Finally we should turn to Catania, which was transformed from 1730 onward by G. B. Vaccarini (1702–68), a canon of Catania cathedral, born in Palermo but trained in Rome under Carlo Fontana in the 1720s. In the Piazza del Duomo he completed the town hall (1735) and built the façade of the cathedral (1733–57). His town fountain (1735) is in the form of an elephant bearing an Egyptian obelisk. These works abound with Borrominiesque touches, as do his brilliant churches. These include his masterpiece, the convent church of S. Agata (1735–67) where the façade, inspired by S. Carlo alle Quattro Fontane (p. 287), boasts huge pilaster capitals carved with palms, lilies and crowns, symbols of St Agatha's martyrdom. At Vaccarini's S. Giuliano (1739–51), also with a curved façade, the dome terminates in an octagonal belvedere in which nuns relaxed or watched religious processions, a common feature of Sicilian convents. In later works, such as the Palazzo del Principe di Reburdone (c.1740–50) and the Collegio Cutelli (1748), he turned towards the more austere classical manner then being introduced at Naples by Fuga and Vanvitelli. In the work in Palermo of his gifted follower, Stefano Ittar (d.1790), there is, however, scarcely any acknowledgement of the classicism which had by then overtaken northern Europe. Ittar's Chiesa Collegiata (c.1768) and S. Placido (finished 1769), with their concave façades and lively Rococo ornament, are a late and lovely flourish at the end of a long line of curvilinear designs.

Baroque outside Italy

France

Though France never took to Baroque as whole-heartedly as either Italy or Germany, the development of the style was influenced more by France than by any other country except Italy. This was because the image of the Sun King's palace of Versailles, in its spectacular Le Nôtre gardens, proved seductive throughout Europe, while it was also French designers who gave birth to the Rococo, the last phase of Baroque.

The architects chiefly responsible for creating the dazzling setting for Louis XIV and his court were Louis Le Vau (1612–1670) and Jules Hardouin-Mansart (1646–1708). The first important work of Le Vau, son of a Parisian master-mason, was the Hôtel Lambert, begun in 1640 on the eastern tip of the Ile St-Louis in Paris for the flamboyant financier J.-B. Lambert. This brilliant demonstration of Le Vau's gift for dramatic display is built round a courtyard in which the range, with its curved façade opposite the entrance, is entirely devoted to a magnificent staircase exploiting contrasts of light and darkness in a characteristically Baroque manner. The upper landing is flanked on one side by an octagonal vestibule and on the other by an oval vestibule from which one can look down a long gallery projecting from the house like a finger and terminating in a great curved

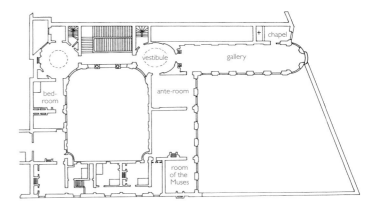

bow commanding a view of the river Seine. This gallery wing is an unusually early example of asymmetrical planning in order to catch a view of a natural object. The principal interiors are richly decorated with bronzed and gilded stucco reliefs by Gerard van Obstal, and wall and ceiling paintings of mythological and landscape subjects by Eustache Le Sueur, Charles Lebrun, and others.

The nearby Hôtel Lauzun, which is also richly decorated, is generally attributed to Le Vau and the team of artists responsible for the Hôtel Lambert. This magnificent house was built in the mid-1650s for Charles Gruyn des Bordes. Like Lambert he was one of the group of financiers who accumulated huge fortunes while raising equally large sums for the Italian-born Cardinal Mazarin, the effective ruler of France from 1641–60 during Louis XIV's minority and earliest adult years. It was at this time, when cultural crosscurrents between France, Italy and the Low Countries were at their most productive, that Le Vau and his associates created the style and the mood which the Sun King subsequently adopted for himself. The interiors of the Hôtel Lauzun positively drip with gold, so that it is no surprise to learn that its patron was brought before the Chambre de Justice set up by Jean-Baptiste Colbert in 1662 to investigate the activities of the financiers, and that his property should subsequently have been confiscated.

The same fate overtook another leading financier, Nicolas Fouquet, the Overseer of Finance, for whom Le Vau created what was at the time the most magnificent château in France, Vaux-le-Vicomte near Paris, built in 1657–61 as the climax of the earliest formal garden designed by André Le Nôtre (1613–1700). The most arresting feature of the château, the domed oval saloon projecting from the garden front, had already been introduced by Le Vau in his now demolished château of Le Raincy (c.1645). The plan of Vaux-le-Vicomte provided grand *appartements*, one for Fouquet and one for the king, on either side of the central vestibule and saloon. The king's bedroom, the most sumptuous

463, 464 *Top and above* Plan of principal floor and courtyard entrance of Hôtel Lambert, Paris, by Le Vau (begun 1640)

interior in the château, was decorated by Charles Lebrun (1619–1690) with rich stuccowork, gilding and painting in a style then current in Italy. The royal bed was placed behind a kind of proscenium arch in an alcove separated from the body of the room by a low balustrade like altar rails in a church. This followed a

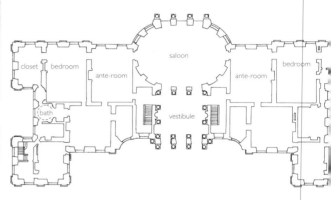

465, 466 *Top and above* Le Vau: Garden front and plan of Vaux-le-Vicomte, near Paris (1657–61)

467 *Left* Interior of the domed oval saloon at Vaux-le-Vicomte

custom which had been established by the 1640s in French royal bedchambers, or in state bedchambers in private houses designed to be used by visiting royalty. People of high birth were accustomed to receive in their bedchambers, and it was necessary to keep all but the most favoured from contact with the royal person. Courtiers who had the right of access within the balustrade were known as *seigneurs à balustrade*.

This tradition was deployed with special brilliance by Louis XIV, who saw himself as the greatest monarch in Europe. Indeed, on Mazarin's death in 1661, he decided that he would govern France himself without the aid of a First Minister. Following a sumptuous entertainment given in August 1660 by Fouquet to the entire court at Vaux-le-Vicomte, including a ballet by Molière with music by Jean-Baptiste Lully and décor by

468 *Above* Perrault: East front of the Louvre, Paris (1667–74)

Lebrun, followed by a firework display, Fouquet was arrested for embezzlement. Colbert, Louis XIV's chief adviser, took into the royal service the whole team of artists who had helped create Vaux-le-Vicomte. The creation of a centralized design machine for the glorification of an absolute monarch was one of Colbert's most remarkable achievements. His ambitions included the completion of the Louvre in Paris as an expression of national glory.

Le Vau and Lebrun had designed the Galerie d'Apollon at the palace of the Louvre in 1661–3 in the sumptuous manner they had adopted at Vaux-le-Vicomte. Colbert's lust for grandeur now led him to seek designs from Bernini, regarded as the greatest artist in the world. He arrived in Paris in June 1665 with something of the pomp of a visiting monarch, but his boldly Baroque designs for the Louvre (p. 286) were rejected and in 1667 Louis XIV appointed a committee of three men to prepare alternative designs. These were his First Architect, Le Vau, his First Painter, Lebrun, and Claude Perrault, an anatomist and amateur architect with one of the most brilliant minds of his day. Perrault's edition of the treatise of Vitruvius, first published in 1673, was a polemical work with illustrations of restored antique buildings intended to serve as models

for modern architects. This massive, grave and lucid trabeated architecture, with its stress on the load-bearing column of the Greeks rather than on the moulded wall-mass of the Romans, was given imposing expression in the east front of the Louvre, built in 1667–74 almost certainly from Perrault's designs. The gravity and nobility of this building, the associated refusal to build up to an obvious or showy climax in the centre, and the antique flavour imparted by the peristyle, made it particularly admired not only at the time of its erection but for the next hundred or so years when it was seen as representing all that was best in the 'great century', an ideal that it was feared would be impossible to repeat. Classical yet modern, rational yet grandiose, and French yet universal in its air of authority and detachment, it is the perfect example of the classical Baroque style of seventeenth-century France.

Versailles

In the meantime Louis XIV had transferred his interests from the Louvre to Versailles, a few miles outside Paris, where he had a freer hand on a larger site to give expression to his own image of the monarchy, and where he was safer from subversive elements among the Paris mob. In 1669 he employed Le Vau to expand and remodel the comparatively modest hunting-lodge built at Versailles by his father, Louis XIII, in 1623 and 1631. Le Vau left much of the old château exposed on the court side, the Cour de Marbre, but provided the garden front with a handsome new twenty-five bay front of which the central eleven bays were recessed on the first and second floors behind a terrace. The uncompromising cubic mass of this façade, its horizontal skyline and severe applied order of Ionic columns, coupled in the side pavilions, reflected something of the weightiness of Perrault's Louvre. Le Vau's Versailles was a taut and forceful exercise steeped in French classicism, though from 1678 it lost its compact vigour when J. H. Mansart filled in Le Vau's terrace with the Galerie des Glaces and more than trebled the length of his garden front by the addition of north and south wings.

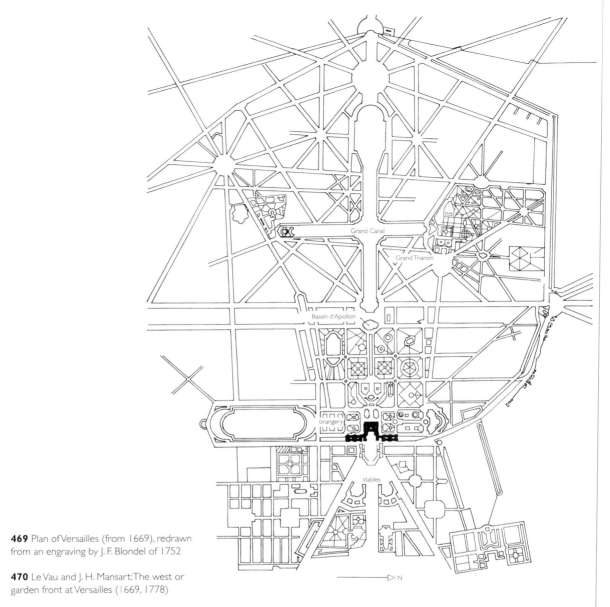

Grand Canal

Grand Trianon

Bassin d'Apollon

orangery

stables

N

469 Plan of Versailles (from 1669), redrawn from an engraving by J. F. Blondel of 1752

470 Le Vau and J. H. Mansart: The west or garden front at Versailles (1669, 1778)

The iconography of Lebrun's decoration of the seven rooms of the king's apartments was based on Apollo, the Sun God, of whom Louis XIV saw himself as a living embodiment. The decorative treatment of the walls, for example in the celebrated but now destroyed Staircase of the Ambassadors, not only included illusionistic painting but also panelling in polychromatic marbles, arranged in far more rigid and geometrical patterns than those of Baroque Italy. Something of this geometrical ordering governed the layout of the gardens by Le Nôtre, done in 1662–90 and featuring a similar iconography which culminated in the *bassin d'Apollon* (pool of Apollo). Here a magnificent sculptural group by Jean-Baptiste Tuby showed the Sun God at the start of his daily journey, rising in his chariot from the water amid the spray of fountains and accompanied by tritons and dolphins announcing the return of day.

The organic relationship of the château of Versailles to a vast landscape, to which it is united by means of a principal axial vista, had been the keynote of the layout of François Mansart's imposing château at Maisons (p. 262). Le Nôtre enriched and complicated this theme with numerous subsidiary diagonal axes, thus creating frequent compartments in the gardens which were separated by clipped topiary and geometrically disposed clumps of trees, terraces, canals, and extravagant fountains. These compartments served as a backdrop for a variety of court spectacles, plays, concerts and firework displays.

Jacques Lemercier's linked château and town of Richelieu of the 1630s for Cardinal Richelieu provided a model for the formal layout of the town serving the château at Versailles. The town of Versailles continued the axis of the garden, providing an eventual total length of eight miles (13km). In 1701 the king moved his bedroom to a position in the centre of this axis, thus symbolizing the monarch as the source of all power and order. The growth of the gardens during the 1660s echoed that of the king's power, when the great central canal was extended westwards in 1669 following the signing of the Treaty of Aix-la-Chapelle in 1668 which ended the Dutch War of Devolution. After the Peace of Nijmegen in 1678, finally settling Louis's claims in the territory of the Spanish Netherlands, the king decided to extend the château on a megalomaniac scale, entrusting the commission to Jules Hardouin-Mansart (1646–1708), whom he had appointed as Royal Architect in 1685.

J. H. Mansart was a great-nephew and pupil of the great François Mansart, though he had also learned much from Le Vau, including how to create dramatic architectural display as well as a successful professional career. The giant wings he added to the garden front of Versailles, in which he simply repeated the bay design established by Le Vau for the much smaller central block, impress through sheer size rather than detail. More successful is the sequence of the centrally placed Galerie des Glaces or Hall of Mirrors, opening in a scenographic way through archways into the Salon de la Guerre at the north end and the Salon de la Paix at the south (fig. 508). The decorative and iconographical treatment of these rooms is that established by Le Vau and Lebrun, but handled in an increasingly sumptuous manner. With its long line of arched mirrors echoing the shape of the windows opposite and reflecting the light, the sky and the gardens outside, and its glittering silver furniture (today convincingly reproduced in fibre-glass), the Galerie des Glaces is, as Louis XIV intended it to be, one of the great rooms of Europe.

The chapel at Versailles, begun by J. H. Mansart in 1698 and completed by Robert de Cotte in 1710, is equally spectacular. Like the Sainte-Chapelle in Paris and other medieval royal chapels, this is two-storeyed with a gallery reserved for the king and his suite. The tall upper storey is completely surrounded by an imposing colonnade of freestanding Corinthian columns, an idea possibly suggested by Claude Perrault, who may have had a hand in the first designs for the chapel in 1688–9. Though it reflects the interests of Perrault and his circle in an ideal classical architecture of load-bearing columns, the colonnade and its associated lighting effects echo the piers in a Gothic church. This

471 J. H. Mansart and R. de Cotte: Interior of the chapel at Versailles (1698–1710)

Gothic parallel is underlined both by the extreme height of the chapel in relation to its breadth and also by the use of flying buttresses externally. As we shall see in the next chapter, the belief that Gothic architecture enshrined rational structural principles, akin to those of Greek architecture, was to colour some of the radical neo-classical theories proposed by French writers in the first half of the eighteenth century.

Other works by Mansart at Versailles include the magnificent stables (1679–86); the rusticated orangery (1681–6), conceived on an amazingly grandiose scale; and the Grand Trianon (1687). Designed as a retreat for the king from the formality of court life, the Trianon is a rambling one-storeyed building with a U-shaped centre and an informal open-air atmosphere emphasized by the unusual entrance range, which consists of a broad open colonnade.

Novel, again, especially in terms of its relation to its garden, was another and larger retreat built for Louis XIV, the now destroyed château of Marly, begun from Mansart's designs in 1679. Here a miniature palace, two-storeyed and nine bays square, commanded a view down a water-garden which was flanked by a series of twelve small pavilions, six on each side of the central canal. Just two bays square, each of these extraordinary little buildings, like enlarged sentry boxes, housed two married couples for short visits as the king's guests. These invitations were much sought after, so that when it became known that the king was about to visit Marly, he was greeted by courtiers with the request, 'Sire, Marly?', as he passed down the Galerie des Glaces at Versailles on his way to mass in the chapel. Nothing like Marly has been seen before or since. It was the unique expression of the combination of splendour and sycophancy in which, perhaps disastrously for the long-term future of the French monarchy, the entire organization of the country focused on the person of Louis XIV.

For another expression of this we can turn to the circular Place des Victoires in Paris, laid out by Mansart from c.1685 round a statue of the king before which four massive lamp standards were always kept burning, exactly like the votive lamps at a shrine in a Catholic church. Little exists of this Place today but Mansart's Place Vendôme, begun in 1698, survives intact as a commanding product of his ability as a town planner. With its unified palatial façades articulated with giant pilasters and pediments, its canted corners and two carefully contrived axial exits, it is a triumph of Baroque organization on the grand scale. The desire for a magnificent display of uniform façades came first, while the plans of the various houses behind them, often designed by other architects, were a secondary consideration. This was partly because the Crown could not afford the original plan and so had to sell off lots piecemeal.

Baroque grandeur similarly characterizes Mansart's great church of the Invalides (c.1679–91), commissioned by Louis XIV at the military hospital of the Invalides probably as a burial-place for himself and the Bourbon dynasty. The domed Greek cross plan is taken from François Mansart's unexecuted Bourbon chapel at St-Denis, as also is the most Baroque feature of the interior, the cut-away dome, through which is visible a heavenly glory painted on an outer shell dome and lit from a ring of concealed windows. Moreover, these two inner domes are surmounted by the outer dome of lead-covered timber.

French Rococo

Despite the Baroque magnificence of the Invalides and the Place Vendôme, Mansart or his assistants such as Pierre Cailleteau, called Lassurance, and Pierre Le Pautre, took a number of decisive moves from the 1680s and 1690s towards the more intimate and delicate style of interior decoration we know as Rococo, the last phase of the Baroque. Characteristic examples include a number of private rooms at Versailles, the Trianon and Marly, such as the Salon de l'Oeil de Boeuf of 1701 next to the king's bedroom at Versailles. The tendency here was to lessen the impact of architectural features such as pilasters and cornices in favour of lighter panelling enlivened by pilasters decorated with arabesques, and tall arched mirrors. Houses were planned more and more for convenience and comfort than for the ceremonial display of their owners' rank. The plan of J. H. Mansart's Château Neuf at Meudon (1706–9), designed as a guest-house for the dauphin, contained numerous small suites or apartments of engaging intimacy and charm. A similar though even more imaginative plan was adopted by Boffrand for his château of Saint-Ouen, built in c.1710 for the Prince de Rohan. Germain Boffrand (1667–1754) was the most important of the group of designers, including Lassurance, Jean Aubert, Gilles-Marie Oppenord and

472 Boffrand: Salon de la Princesse, Hôtel de Soubise, Paris (1735–9), with paintings by Natoire

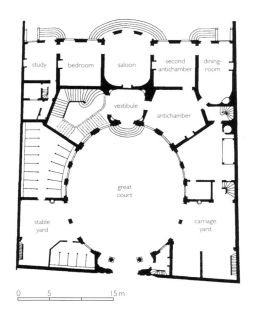

473 Plan of the Hôtel d'Amelot de Gournay, Paris (1712) by Boffrand

321

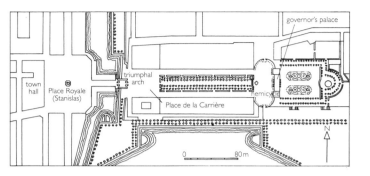

474 Héré de Corny: Plan of the three linked squares – Place Royale (now Stanislas), Place de la Carrière and the Hemicycle – at Nancy (1752–5)

Juste-Aurèle Meissonnier, responsible for developing the Rococo decorative style associated with this new way of living.

The first phase from c.1710 to c.1730 was known as the Régence, after the regency of Philippe d'Orléans during the minority of Louis XV, 1715–23. This subsequently developed into the full Rococo style, known as 'le genre pittoresque', which flourished well into the 1750s. Trained as a sculptor but subsequently the pupil and collaborator of J. H. Mansart, Boffrand built the Hôtel Amelot de Gournay (or de Montmorency) in Paris in 1712, not for a specific client but simply as a speculation. Organized round an oval courtyard with bizarre pentagonal, trapezoidal and apsed rooms, it is equalled as an astonishing product of Rococo fantasy and lightheartedness only by the lovely interiors in the two-storeyed pavilion which he added in 1735–9 for the Prince de Soubise at the Hôtel de Soubise (today Archives Nationales), Paris. The Salon de la Princesse is a riot of fluttering asymmetrical decoration in carved and gilded plasterwork, running over the edge of inset paintings by Charles-Joseph Natoire and round-headed mirrors. The articulation of the room is similar to that of the principal oval-ended saloon at the short-lived château of Malgrange, near Nancy, begun in 1712 for Duke Leopold I of Lorraine

by Boffrand, whose chief architect he had become in the previous year. Boffrand's alternative unexecuted project for Malgrange on an X-plan with a central circular colonnaded hall was a dynamic Baroque extravaganza which anticipated Juvarra's Stupinigi.

In contrast, the chapel which Boffrand built at Duke Leopold's château of Lunéville, 20 miles (32km) from Nancy in eastern France, is a radical neo-antique essay emphasizing the structural honesty of load-bearing columns and horizontal entablatures. Designed in 1709 and built in 1720–23, this was reconstructed in 1744 by the architect Emmanuel Héré de Corny (1705–63) after a fire. Boffrand is a difficult architect to classify, since he contrives to be Baroque, neo-classical and Rococo. There is also a strong neo-Palladian element in his work as, for example, in the courtyard of the uncompleted town palace for Duke Leopold at Nancy (begun 1717; demolished 1745). The entrance front of this building featured curved wings inspired by Bernini's first Louvre project. The style of this palace, and of the Hôtel de Beauvau (or de Craon) which Boffrand built in 1712–13 in the nearby Place de la Carrière, set the pattern for the remarkable development of Nancy in 1752–5 by Emmanuel Héré de Corny for King Stanislas, ex-king of Poland, father-in-law to Louis XV, and tenant from 1737 of the Duchy of Lorraine until, by agreement, it lapsed to the French crown on his death. Héré created a series of three linked squares, the Place Royale (now Stanislas), dominated by his town hall, leading through a triumphal arch modelled on the Arch of Septimius Severus in Rome, to the long Place de la Carrière, and finally into the elliptical Hemicycle where semicircular colonnades flank the Hôtel de l'Intendance, marking the end of the whole axis. The elements of variety and surprise, of enclosure and release, of contrasting building heights, and especially the curved openwork grilles of gilded wrought iron by Jean Lamour sheltering fountains in the corners of the Place Stanislas, create a Rococo liveliness in what is in essence one of the grandest pieces of formal Baroque town planning in Europe.

Austria and Germany

The arts in Germany suffered enormously from the Thirty Years War of 1618–48. Recovery, which took nearly half a century, involved an attempt to replace the itinerant Italian architects, largely responsible for introducing the Renaissance, with native artists. The ideal was now represented by Austrian or German architects who had studied in Rome, such as Fischer von Erlach and Hildebrandt in Austria, Schlüter in Prussia, and the Asam brothers in Bavaria. The position of Vienna, capital city of the Habsburg emperors who ruled Austria, Bohemia and Hungary, had been enormously strengthened by the final victory over the invading Turks in 1683 with the Relief of Vienna, and the recovery from Turkish domination of Hungary and of much of the Balkans by treaty in 1699 and 1718

475 Fischer von Erlach: The Ancestral Hall at Schloss Frain, Moravia (now Vranov nad Dyjí, Czech Republic) (1690–4)

respectively. Austria, with its growing sense of national identity, was the first of the German-speaking countries to establish a native Baroque style.

Fischer von Erlach

The leading architect in this newly confident phase was Johann Bernhard Fischer von Erlach (1656–1723), one of the most original architects of his day in Europe. The son of a sculptor from Graz, he was sent to study in Rome where he probably became a pupil of the painter-decorator Johann Paul Schor and moved in the circle of Bernini and Fontana. After over twelve years in Italy he settled in Vienna in 1687, where he was appointed court architect in 1705 by his former pupil, Emperor Joseph I, a ruler anxious to emulate the splendour of his rival, Louis XIV of France.

One of the earliest works of Fischer von Erlach was Schloss Frain, Moravia (now Vranov nad Dyjí, the Czech Republic), of 1690–4, for Johann Michael, Count Althan. Here he raised a great oval structure, the Ancestral Hall of the Althan family, towering dramatically over the sheer precipice above the river Thaya. It is decorated with frescoes celebrating the history of the Althans by the Venetian-trained painter Johann Rottmayr, the first instance of what was to be a fruitful collaboration between him and Fischer. The oval space was, of course, derived from Roman Baroque architecture, while the huge oval dormer windows cutting deeply into the mass of the dome produce a shadowy contrast of mass and hollowed-out space. Fischer von Erlach's unexecuted plan of c.1690 for a gigantic palace for the emperor at Schönbrunn outside Vienna similarly united themes from French and Italian Baroque and from Roman antiquity: Trajan's Column, the Temple of Fortune at Praeneste, Bernini's project for the Louvre, and J. H. Mansart's Versailles. Several of his earliest masterpieces were built at Salzburg for its prince-archbishop, Johann Ernst von Thun-Hohenstein (1687–1709), in particular the Dreifältigskeitkirche (Trinity church, 1694–1702), and the Kollegienkirche (1696–1707) of the Benedictine University, the former with a concave front between two towers as at Borromini's S. Agnese, and the latter with a convex front which was to be reflected in many of the great Benedictine churches of the eighteenth century in south Germany.

Fischer von Erlach's most fascinating work is the Karlskirche in Vienna (1716–33), a votive and dynastic church which was built for the Emperor Charles VI (1711–40) in fulfilment of a vow he made to his patron saint, Charles Borromeo, should Vienna be relieved from the plague of 1713. Since the site was very wide, the extraordinary plan of this church incorporates a long western front with a loggia and flanking pavilions in the form of a screen. The central Corinthian portico recalls that of the Pantheon (p. 76) or of the Templum Pacis, in an attempt to invest the Holy Roman Empire of Charles VI with Roman imperial grandeur. This is underlined by the two imposing versions of Trajan's column which flank the portico, resembling the minarets at the corners of a mosque or of Hagia Sophia in Constantinople, the second Rome (p. 95). Without predecessors or successors in such a position, these columns are not purely ornamental but have a complex iconographical justification. Besides endowing Vienna with powerful souvenirs of the might of Trajanic Rome, they also recall the twin pillars which stood in the porch of the Temple of Solomon, as well as the Pillars of Hercules, used as a heraldic emblem by Charles VI. Since the Straits of Gibraltar were also known as the Pillars of Hercules, the columns thus refer to Charles VI's brief occupancy of the throne of Spain. Moreover the columns are completely Christianized, being carved with scenes from the life of St Charles Borromeo though topped by imperial eagles and by cupolas surmounted by the crowns of Spain. The iconographical programme was devised with assistance from scholars such as the antiquary Heraeus and the philosopher Leibniz, and culminates inside the church with the apotheosis of St Charles Borromeo depicted not only in Rottmayr's fresco in the dome but also sculptured over the high altar beneath stucco clouds pierced with gilded rays.

476, 477 *Above and below* Fischer von Erlach: Plan and exterior of the Karlskirche, Vienna (1716–33)

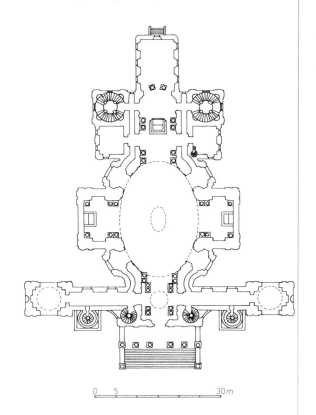

478 Fischer von Erlach: Interior of the Imperial Library at the Hofburg, Vienna (designed c.1716–20; built 1723–26)

Babylon, Stonehenge, pyramids, obelisks, Roman ruins, mosques and pagodas, intended 'to inspire the artist to inventions', as Fischer himself put it, were almost as important as a stimulus to architects as were the engravings of Piranesi (see p. 371).

In his *Entwurff* Fischer also illustrated some of his own buildings, which he justly regarded as rivalling the great monuments of the past. These included the palace for Prince Eugene of Savoy (1695–8) in Vienna, and the Gallas Palace in Prague (1713–19), both of which were remarkable for their dynamic sculptural handling, especially in the use of caryatids or atlantes in staircases or portals. This grandiose style reached its climax in the Imperial Library at the Hofburg in Vienna, which he designed for Charles VI in c.1716–20 but which was largely built posthumously by his son, Joseph Emanuel Fischer von Erlach (1693–1742), in 1723–6. Never have the fruits of scholarship and literature been given a more sumptuous repository than in this library with its oval, domically vaulted central space, frescoed by Daniel Gran in 1726–30 and flanked by giant columnar screens.

Hildebrandt

An intellectual and eccentric figure, Fischer von Erlach was succeeded as Surveyor General of Imperial Buildings in 1723 by his rival, the worldly and genial Johann Lucas von Hildebrandt (1668–1745). Born and brought up in Genoa, the son of an Italian mother and a German-born father who was a captain in the Genoese army, he studied civil and military architecture in Rome under Carlo Fontana. He accompanied Prince Eugene of Savoy on his Piedmontese campaigns as a military engineer in 1695–6, after which he settled in Vienna. Here he worked not so much for the Habsburg court itself but for Austro-Hungarian noble families such as the Schönborns, Harrachs, Starhembergs and Dauns, as well as for Prince Eugene himself for whom he built his masterpiece, the Belvedere Palace in Vienna. This extravagant complex comprises a double garden-palace, the Lower and Upper Belvedere, built on a sloping site in 1714–16 and 1721–2 respectively. Palaces on sites

Fischer von Erlach's dynamic Karlskirche, brimming with artistic and intellectual vigour, can be interpreted as a deliberate synthesis of sacred and imperial architecture, replete with pagan, Jewish and Christian resonances, in which Charles VI is seen as a second Solomon and a second Augustus. In fact it is the analogy in stone to the engravings in Fischer's *Entwurff einer historischen Architectur*, published in Vienna in 1721 with a text in both German and French, and translated into English in 1730 as *A Plan of Civil and Historical Architecture*. This remarkable compilation of world architecture is a forerunner of the voracious, encyclopedic and eclectic mentality of the eighteenth-century Enlightenment. Its ninety captivating plates of

479 Hildebrandt: Exterior of the Upper Belvedere, Vienna (1721–2)

outside the city walls were much in demand by the Viennese nobility at this moment; none of them, however, rivalled what Hildebrandt created for Prince Eugene who, as commander-in-chief of the imperial army, governor of the Spanish Netherlands and a prince of the ruling house of Savoy, was almost a second emperor in Vienna.

The comparatively modest Lower Belvedere was built as a summer residence for the bachelor Prince Eugene, while the far more splendid Upper Belvedere was added to house his art collection and library and to serve as a setting for princely entertainment and full court ceremonial. The entire layout is a perfect expression of the Baroque genius for scenographic spatial organization, in which the architecture is an incident in an enclosed environment defined by formal gardens, terraces, steps, avenues, fountains and artificial lakes. Inventive architectural detail in which Mannerist elements like strapwork and tapering pilasters are transmuted into a flexible Baroque language reveals Hildebrandt as a formal innovator rivalling Michelangelo or Borromini. The masterly play with spatial levels in the Upper Belvedere begins, for the visitor approaching from the garden front, with a flight of steps leading surprisingly down from the entrance to the *sala terrena*, dominated by straining atlantes, whence a second flight leads up to the main saloon. Among Hildebrandt's most brilliant sculptural staircases are those in the Daun Kinsky Palace, Vienna (1713–16), and in Schloss Mirabell, Salzburg (1721–7), for Franz Anton von Harrach, prince-archbishop of Salzburg.

Hildebrandt was also involved in the design of two of the most magnificent products of Franconian Baroque, the Schloss at Pommersfelden and the Residenz at Würzburg, which we will describe when dealing with their principal architects, Dientzenhofer and Neumann respectively.

Prandtauer

Jakob Prandtauer (1660–1726), the third in the great trio of Austrian Baroque architects, worked almost exclusively on ecclesiastical buildings. Like Guarini and Juvarra, he was a man of deep piety and a member of a religious confraternity. He was also a traditional master-mason, unlike Fischer von Erlach or Hildebrandt, painstakingly supervising the entire building work of every project. His masterpiece is the Benedictine monastery of Melk in Lower Austria, rebuilt by him for the dynamic Abbot Berthold Dietmayr from 1702 to 1727. Set superbly on a cliff above the river Danube, Melk vies with the cathedral and fortress of Durham, crowning their acropolis above the river Wear, as one of the great set-pieces of western architecture. Its twin-towered silhouette is the Baroque answer to the west front of a Gothic church, but Prandtauer has organized the buildings in the forecourt before the west front in a dramatic way which is quintessentially Baroque. The side wings, containing the library and Imperial or Marble Hall, are linked by a lower curved entrance range punctuated by a huge arch like a Serlian or Venetian window. This acts as a proscenium arch dissolving the distinction between outside and inside: thus it not only focuses the attention of the traveller down the Danube, but acts simultaneously as a window on the world for the monks who, in a medieval monastery, would have been more inward-looking. Benedictine monasticism has always been noted for its emphasis on learning and on hospitality, and nowhere have those qualities been given fuller expression than in the Baroque monasteries of eighteenth-century Germany and Austria. Here the provision of a library and a splendid room in which to receive the Emperor was as important as the abbey church itself.

480 Prandtauer: Exterior of the monastery of Melk, Lower Austria (1702–27)

Having already mentioned the affinities of Baroque with Gothic, we should note in passing one remarkable architect, Johann Santini Aichel (1677–1723), born in Prague of Italian extraction and trained in Italy. Though he worked in a style derived from Borromini and Guarini, he also developed an individual Gothic Baroque which is best shown in a number of churches in Bohemia such as his pilgrimage church of Zelená Hora (1720–2), near Žd'ár (Saar). This style looks back to the poetic Late Gothic of Benedikt Ried at Kuttenberg (p. 192) and is related to Aichel's sense of certain aesthetic similarities between Gothic and Baroque. The growing cult of Bohemian saints such as St John Nepomuk found original expression in the church at Zelená Hora, where his incorrupted tongue was preserved as a relic. Santini designed the church in the shape of a five-pointed star, in allusion to the five stars that appeared around the martyr's head when he was thrown into the river Vltava (Moldau), while further symbolical details include tongue-shaped door and window openings.

The leading Baroque architects in Prague and Bohemia were the Dientzenhofer family of Bavarian origin. They included Christoph Dientzenhofer (1655–1722), his brother Johann (1633–1726), and his son Kilian Ignaz (1689–1751). Johann Dientzenhofer was important for bringing the inventive spirit of Bohemian Baroque to the central province of Franconia, where his masterpieces are the Benedictine abbey of Banz (1710–19) and Schloss Weissenstein at Pommersfelden, begun in 1711 for Lothar Franz von Schönborn, prince-archbishop-elector of Mainz and prince-bishop of Bamberg. The plan of the church at Banz consists of interlocking transverse ovals, vivaciously expressed in the vaulting by means of huge three-dimensional ribs. The magnificent Schloss at Pommersfelden is chiefly memorable for its staircase, occupying a projecting pavilion of its own which forms the central stroke of the whole E-shaped building. This extravagant devotion of so much space to a staircase was the Elector's own idea, as was the dramatic notion of making the flights

481 Dientzenhofer: Staircase at the Schloss at Pommersfelden (begun 1711)

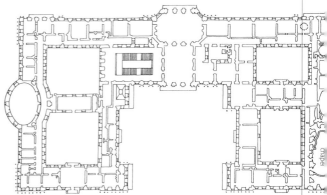

482 Von Erthal and von Welsch: Plan of the Residenz at Würzburg (c.1720)

freestanding rather than attached to the outer walls. For help in the design of the staircase he turned to Hildebrandt, who introduced the surrounding three-storeyed gallery with its arcades of columns and herms. This produces a magical effect worthy of the designs of the Galli-Bibiena (p. 307), and makes ascent of this staircase one of the most exhilarating possible of architectural experiences. Among the principal interiors by Dientzenhofer is the Marble Saloon or Imperial Hall, approached from the staircase gallery, and, below this room, the *sala terrena*. This low vaulted room leading from the ground floor to the garden is treated like a grotto, encrusted with rococo stuccowork by Georg Hennicke. The arrangement at Pommersfelden of a low

sala terrena, leading via a grand staircase to a principal saloon, was standard in many German Baroque palaces.

Neumann and Asam

Ceremonial staircases of the utmost splendour are also the hallmark of the greatest German architect of the late Baroque or Rococo period, Balthasar Neumann (1687–1753). They form the principal accents of the Würzburg Residenz, Schloss Bruchsal, Schloss Werneck and Schloss Brühl. Neumann moved to Würzburg in 1711, where he became a military engineer and in 1720 was appointed surveyor, with Dientzenhofer, for the proposed episcopal palace of the prince-bishop, Johann Philipp Franz von Schönborn, nephew of the builder of Pommersfelden. The initial plans for the Residenz at Würzburg, one of the grandest Baroque palaces in Europe, were drawn up by two amateur architects from Mainz, Philipp Christoph von Erthal and Maximilian von Welsch, but construction proceeded slowly and it was not until 1737–42 that, for a new bishop, Neumann's breathtaking staircase was designed and constructed. High above the flights of the staircase,

483 *Opposite* Neumann: The staircase at the Residenz at Würzburg (1737–42), showing the frescoes (1752–3) by Tiepolo

484 Neumann: Interior of the pilgrimage church at Vierzehnheiligen (begun 1743)

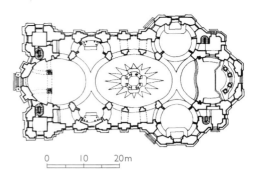

485 Plan of the pilgrimage church of Vierzehnheiligen

supported on high open arcades, floats the ceiling in which, unusually, a single vault is made to cover the whole area of the staircase hall. The ceiling was frescoed by Giambattista Tiepolo in 1752–3 with a representation of the Four Continents which is perhaps the climax of Rococo art. The staircase at Würzburg leads to ceremonial apartments of incomparable magnificence such as the Kaisersaal (Imperial Hall) and the Weisser Saal (White Saloon). However, Welsch's plan to incorporate an oval chapel in the centre of the south garden front was abandoned by Neumann, who removed it to the south-west corner of the palace so that it could rise to the full height of the building. Built and decorated in 1732–44, the chapel has an interior of startling opulence which adopts Dientzenhofer's intersecting vaults at Banz with their three-dimensional arch ribs, and places them over a ground plan of interlocking ovals (fig. 509).

Neumann's chapel at Würzburg is related to numerous churches of similarly arresting poetry, in which he devised complex vaulting in a series of mathematical variations likened to those of a Bach fugue, for example, the chapel of Schloss Werneck (1734–45) for Friedrich Carl von Schönborn, prince-bishop of Würzburg, the Benedictine abbey-church of Neresheim (1747–92), and, above all, the astonishingly lovely pilgrimage church of Vierzehnheiligen, begun in 1743 on the hilltop site above the river Main where a shepherd in 1445 had a vision of the Christ Child surrounded by fourteen saints in the form of children. The dynamic verticality of its twin-towered façade, not rich in ornamental detail, leads to a rippling interior apparently designed as a radiant expression of divine gaiety. This fairy-tale atmosphere is made concrete in the heart-shaped centrally-placed altar of the fourteen saints, a riot of curvilinear ornament as fantastic as Cinderella's coach which, like all the best coaches, is simply an example of Rococo survival!

In concept the church is a basilica with a Latin cross plan consisting of three longitudinal ovals, the central and largest of the oval vaults being placed not over the crossing but over the saints' altar to its west. Over the crossing, where one might expect a dome, the vault is dissolved and is represented by four interpenetrating spaces defined by three-dimensional arches. Further spatial complexity derives from the carrying of the complex vaults not on the outer walls but on piers which separate the nave from open galleried aisles. Light thus floods in through these openings from the three storeys of windows in the outer walls, giving a diaphanous effect. Lightness is the theme of the whole interior, including the delicate plaster decoration in grey and white by Johann Michael Feuchtmayer and Johann Georg Übelhör, and the frescoes by Giuseppe Appiani. This dancing lightness is the essence of the Rococo, the term by which, as we saw in our survey of French design around 1700, we know the last phase of the Baroque. We have arrived at the Rococo by following Neumann's career chronologically, but in shifting now to Bavaria we return to the fuller and richer Baroque in the work of his contemporaries, Cosmas Damian Asam (1686–1739) and his brother, Egid Quirin (1692–1750).

486 *Above right and right* Façade and interior of the Asamkirche or St John Nepomuk, Munich (1733–46), by the Asam brothers

487 *Below* Asam Brothers: The high altar at the abbey church of Weltenburg (1716–21), with the statues of St George and the Dragon

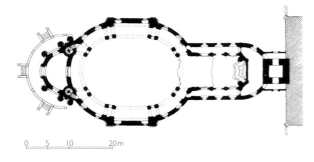

488 Plan of the church at Weltenburg, by the Asam Brothers

Cosmas Damian Asam was trained as a fresco painter in Rome in c.1711–14, while his brother was a pupil in Munich of the Austrian-born sculptor Andreas Faistenberger. Both brothers were sent to Rome by the Abbot of Tegernsee, a Benedictine abbey where their father had been employed as a painter. It is characteristic of Bavarian art and patronage at this point that their architectural work was to be exclusively ecclesiastical. Though they collaborated as architects on the design of four new churches, their commissions were principally for interior decoration and transformation of existing buildings. Their finest independent buildings are the Benedictine abbey of Weltenburg (1716–21) near Kelheim; the nearby Augustinian priory church of Rohr (1717–23); and the church of St John Nepomuk, Munich (1733–46), known as the Asamkirche since it was entirely paid for by the pious Egid Quirin Asam.

At the small and isolated monastery of Weltenburg, on the edge of the Danube, the interior of the church provides one of the most enthralling experiences in Baroque architecture. Like Bernini's S. Andrea al Quirinale, it is oval in plan, richly decorated with marbles and is dominated by the theatrical *tableau vivant* behind the high altar. In the Bavarian church an equestrian sculptural group of great emotional intensity, depicting St George rescuing the princess from the dragon, is silhouetted against the frescoed apse illuminated with concealed lighting. The oval vault over the nave is, moreover, cut away in the centre to expose an upper vault, frescoed by Cosmas Damian and, again, lit by concealed windows. Egid Quirin's high altar at Rohr boasts a dynamic sculptural composition depicting the Assumption, in which astonished apostles surround an empty sarcophagus while the Virgin accompanied by angels floats above their heads. His masterpiece, the Asamkirche, has an astonishingly mobile narrow entrance front forming part of the street façade and, indeed, flanked by the façades of his own house and of the priest's. The interior is two-storeyed, as in a palace chapel, so that Asam could enter it from the *piano nobile* of his own home. With its undulating walls, curvilinear entablatures, twisted columns, balustraded gallery and sumptuous ornament dripping down like long stalactites, this high narrow interior resembles a kind of sea-grotto seen through rippling translucent water.

The interiors of Weltenburg and the Asamkirche, with their lustrous marbling and gilding which ultimately depend on the Roman work of Bernini, are untypical of German Late Baroque and Rococo interiors. These are characterized by white and gold or pastel-coloured stuccowork combined with frescoes in a riot of joyous confectionery. This lighter style was adopted by the Asam brothers, as can be seen in Bavaria in the enchanting interiors they created in churches designed by other architects, for example at Weingarten (1719–20), Freising (1723–24) and St Emmeram, Regensburg (1732–3). In the last two churches, both fundamentally Romanesque buildings, the sense of Rococo plasterwork as a vast confection is eloquently underlined by the survival beneath it of the massive medieval structure.

German Rococo

The move away from the rich Roman-inspired language of the Asam brothers to the more light-hearted Rococo is especially associated with Dominikus Zimmermann (1685–1766), trained as a stuccoist at Wessobrunn. In 1728–33 he built for the Premonstratensian order the parish church and pilgrimage shrine at Steinhausen, with an oval nave separated from an outer ambulatory by a ring of freestanding piers. Since the vaults of the nave and ambulatory rise to the same height, the interior might be said to be a Rococo version of the Gothic hall church. The fantastic stuccowork in the upper regions

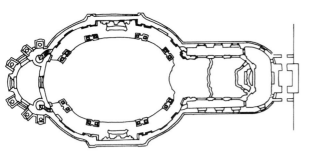

489 Plan of the Wieskirche (1746–54), by Dominikus Zimmermann

490 J. M. Fischer: Entrance façade of the abbey church at Ottobeuren (1748–54)

of the church begins to take on a life of its own, as opposed to serving merely as a framework for the lively fresco paintings on the nave vault. These are by Dominikus Zimmermannn's brother, Johann Baptist, with whom he was frequently associated.

The hall-church system of Steinhausen was brilliantly developed by Dominikus at the Wieskirche (the church in the meadows), built and decorated in 1746–54 as the loveliest and most moving of all South German Rococo churches (fig. 513). The arcade separating the oval nave from the ambulatory is more open and diaphanous than at Steinhausen, the rococo stuccowork more sensational, and the colouring more brilliant, while the lath and plaster vaults are penetrated with openings revealing partial views of Johann Baptist Zimmermann's frescoes on a plane behind. The vast fresco over the nave shows the moment before the Last Judgement, a solemn Byzantine theme which contrasts movingly with the lyrical gaiety of the architecture. The building is a work of art which touches all human sensations, spiritual and artistic. Set far from any village in the midst of lush fields at the foot of the Bavarian Alps, it is a pilgrimage church, built as an expression of peasant piety to house a primitive but miraculous image of the Scourging of Christ at the Pillar. Like the other German churches in this chapter, it is as popular today with religious and artistic pilgrims as it was in the eighteenth century. These buildings have survived every change in architectural fashion and have even been untouched by the liturgical reordering which has wrecked so many churches since the Second Vatican Council.

Though the Asam and Zimmermann brothers were the most distinguished late-Baroque architects at work in Bavaria and Swabia, we should not ignore their numerous lesser contemporaries such as Peter Thumb (1691–1766), Joseph Schmuzer (1683–1752), and especially the prolific Johann Michael Fischer (1692–1766). Effervescent works by these architects include Thumb's pilgrimage church at Birnau (1746–58) on Lake Constance; Schmuzer's parish church at Oberammergau (1736–41); and J. M. Fischer's Imperial Free Abbey of Ottobeuren (1748–54), where his palatial monastic buildings, culminating in a spectacular Kaisersaal, provide a Baroque answer to the splendours of medieval Cluny.

It was in secular architecture that the Rococo language was first developed. The element of fantasy and exaggeration which Rococo designers extracted from Baroque design surfaces strikingly in the remarkable Zwinger at Dresden, the only executed part of the proposed new palace designed for Augustus the Strong, Elector of Saxony and King of Poland, by Matthäus Daniel Pöppelmann (1662–1736). The Zwinger, a large courtyard intended for tournaments and festivities, was

491 Pöppelmann: The Zwinger, showing the Wallpavillon, Dresden (1716–18)

492 Knobelsdorff: Sans Souci, Potsdam (1745–7)

described by Pöppelmann as resembling an antique Roman theatre. Its articulation is astonishingly varied with long, low, one-storeyed flanking galleries or orangeries interrupted by four corner pavilions, including the elaborate Wallpavillon (1716–18), and the towering gateway, the Kronentor, built in 1713. Pöppelmann's curvaceous and sculptural architecture blends perfectly with the dynamism of the mythological figure sculpture carved by Balthasar Permoser (1651–1732).

The Zwinger is partly inspired by Hildebrandt's garden palaces in Vienna, but the impact on German kings and princes of Louis XIV's court at Versailles led to an increasing adoption of French styles and even architects. The most important architect was the diminutive François Cuvilliés, born near Brussels, who in 1708 entered the service of Max Emanuel, Elector of Bavaria, then in exile in the Spanish/Austrian Netherlands. Having studied architecture in Paris in 1720–4 under J.-F. Blondel, Cuvilliés provided up-to-date French Rococo interiors from 1728 at Schloss Brühl for Clemens August, Elector of Cologne, and at Schloss Nymphenburg, Munich, for his brother, Carl Albert, the new Elector of Bavaria. His most brilliant independent work is the one-storeyed Amalienburg pavilion (1734–9) in the grounds of Nymphenburg, combining subtle French planning with Viennese-inspired façades. The principal interior is the circular saloon surrounded by mirrors, where Cuvilliés went beyond French Rococo sources in dissolving the traditional cornice above the boiseries into a fluttering play of stucco foliage by Johann Baptist Zimmermann sheltering birds, animals, trees, cherubs and cornucopiae. The animated movement is made more three-dimensional by the mirrors with which the room is surrounded, while the precious jewel-box quality is heightened by the colouring in blue and silver, the heraldic colours of the Wittelsbach family, Electors of Bavaria (fig. 503). The exterior of the dome over this room served, somewhat incongruously in view of the frail elegance within, as a stand from which to shoot pheasants.

As well known as the Amalienburg is Cuvilliés's Theatre at the Munich Residenz (1750–3), enlivened with gilded swags, drapery, caryatids, musical trophies and extravagant cartouches. Cuvilliés exercised enormous influence on German Rococo, not only through the captivating brilliance of his work at Munich and Schloss Brühl but through the engravings of ornament and architecture which he published from 1738 onward. In north Germany, Rococo interiors of scarcely less elaboration were provided in the 1740s by Georg von Knobelsdorff (1699–1753) for Frederick the Great of Prussia. Knobelsdorff's finest work for this eclectic patron was the little pink and white palace at Potsdam known as Sans Souci. This stands at the head of sloping ground laid out with terraces lined with greenhouses, creating the impression of a frozen cascade. In these Frederick could grow his favourite Mediterranean flowers and fruits, in defiance of the Prussian climate.

England

We have seen the Baroque in France and Germany as a style especially associated with such building types as Catholic pilgrimage churches and the palaces of absolutist or would-be absolutist monarchs and princely rulers. England during the seventeenth century was for the most part fiercely anti-Catholic, while first the Civil War and finally the Revolution of 1688 put an end to the concept of the divine right of the monarch and instead vested power in the hands of the Whig oligarchy. How far could the Baroque style flourish in such a setting? Though we will find nothing as extreme as in southern Italy or Bavaria, there is a surprising amount of architecture and decoration in Protestant England for which no other name can be found than Baroque.

Wren

Charles II, who reigned from 1660 to 1685, had a deep admiration for Louis XIV which he clearly expressed in the buildings he commissioned from Sir Christopher Wren, for example a new palace at Winchester, echoing the layout of Versailles, and the Royal Hospital at Chelsea, inspired by the Invalides. Moreover, the state apartments at Windsor Castle which Hugh May, Antonio Verrio and Grinling Gibbons created for Charles in 1675–84 were among the most extravagantly Baroque interiors ever executed in England. Designs by Wren for three major buildings helped determine the bold architectural language developed by Sir John Vanbrugh and Nicholas Hawksmoor: these are the rebuilding of Hampton Court for King William III and Queen Mary, where Wren's first unexecuted designs echoed projects for the Louvre by Bernini, François Mansart and Le Vau;

493 Interior of the Sheldonian Theatre, Oxford (1664–9) by Wren

the unexecuted palace of Whitehall which Wren designed in 1698; and his first design for Greenwich Hospital. Sir Christopher Wren (1632–1723) was a towering genius of enormous influence whose career we should investigate in some detail.

Wren was born into a royalist, conservative, High Anglican and High Tory family, and his architectural commissions were to come almost exclusively from the Crown and the church. His father became the Dean of Windsor while his uncle was the Bishop of Ely (he was taken from his palace by the Puritans who in 1641 imprisoned him in the Tower of London for eighteen years). Wren did not begin as an architect but as an experimental scientist of brilliantly inventive imagination. Like Claude Perrault he was distinguished as an anatomist, but he was best known as an astronomer, occupying the Savilian Chair of Astronomy at Oxford from 1661 to 1673. It was probably in about 1660 that he first took a serious interest in architecture, partly as a result of his skill in mathematics and model-making. There was as yet no separate profession of architecture so that any educated man of taste could try his hand at it. In 1663, Wren was consulted by the Royal Commission for repairing Old St Paul's Cathedral and in the same year was invited by his uncle to design a new chapel at Pembroke College, Cambridge. The result was the first non-Gothic chapel in Oxford or Cambridge, a neat if uninventive exercise inspired by Serlio (p. 231). It was followed by the much more original Sheldonian Theatre (1664–9) at Oxford, a building for university ceremonies which echoes in plan Serlio's reconstruction of the D-shaped Theatre of Marcellus in Rome. Instead of the *velarium* or awning which protected Roman audiences from the sun, Wren devised an ingenious system of triangulated timber trusses concealed by a painted sky with allegorical figures showing the Triumph of Truth and the Arts.

In 1665–6 Wren paid a long visit to Paris in order to inspect the buildings by modern architects, whose reputation must have been well known in London and court circles. He met Bernini, who gave him an all too brief glimpse of his designs for the Louvre, and he also saw François Mansart's designs for the same palace. He doubtless visited the major domed churches of Paris — the Sorbonne by Lemercier, the Val-de-Grâce by Lemercier and Mansart, and the smaller Ste-Marie de la Visitation, also by François Mansart — though the buildings he most praised were Mansart's château at Maisons and Le Vau's at Le Raincy and at Vaux-le-Vicomte. Surprisingly, he never travelled abroad again, and in his architecture drew constantly on his first-hand experiences of the late-sixteenth- and seventeenth-century French classical tradition. This must have come as a revelation to him, for in England at that time there were no domed churches and no classical palaces on anything like the scale of those by Le Vau and Mansart. The Great Fire of London of September 1666 must have seemed to Wren like a heaven-sent opportunity to rebuild the city on the grandiose classical lines that he had admired on his visit to Paris. His famous plan in which the tortuous thoroughfares of the medieval city were replaced with straight broad streets radiating from piazzas, as in Sixtus V's Rome, was rejected as too radical. However, it was partly as a result of this broad-ranging scheme that he was appointed Surveyor General of the King's Works in 1669.

494 Wren: Tower and spire of St Bride, Fleet Street, London (1670–84)

The Act for rebuilding the city was passed in 1670 and during the next 16 years Wren designed fifty-two new city churches. There had been very little church-building in England since the Reformation, and no one had given any thought to what a Protestant church of the Anglican communion ought to look like. Wren went back to first principles and in a celebrated document argued that 'in our reformed Religion, it should seem vain to make a Parish church larger than that all who are present can both hear and see. The Romanists, indeed, may build larger Churches, it is enough if they hear the murmur of the Mass, and see the Elevation of the Host, but ours are to be fitted for Auditories.' Another challenge was that the sites for the city churches were medieval and irregular so that all Wren's ingenuity was

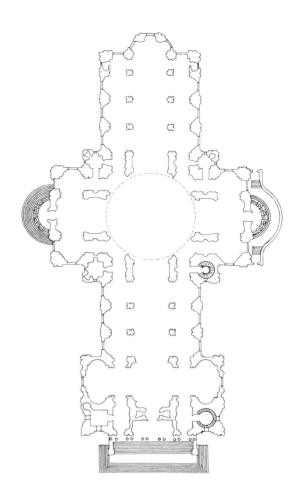

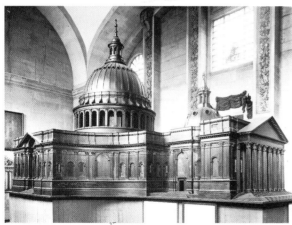

495 *Top* Interior of St Stephen Walbrook, London (1672–7), by Wren

496 *Above* Wren: Great Model for St Paul's Cathedral, London (1673)

497 *Above right* Plan of St Paul's Cathedral (1673)

needed to dispose handsome classical buildings on them. In fact the variety he achieved is enormous, ranging from those with antique sources such as St Mary-le-Bow, inspired by the Basilica of Maxentius, and St Bride, Fleet Street, inspired by Perrault's illustration of Vitruvius's basilica at Fano, to those with centralized plans echoing seventeenth-century Dutch churches by Jacob van Campen, such as St Mary at Hill and St Martin Ludgate. There is even one, St Dunstan in the East, which has an elaborate neo-Gothic steeple.

The steeples are perhaps the most arresting feature of the churches, though they were often built or designed fifteen or twenty years later. These poetic extravaganzas, like temples in the sky, include the multi-storeyed spires of St Bride, Fleet Street, and St Mary-le-Bow, Cheapside, which are indebted to Antonio da Sangallo's model for St Peter's, and those of St Michael, Crooked

498 The colonnade by Bernini in the Piazza S. Pietro, Rome (begun 1656)

499 *Opposite* The interior of the dome of S. Carlo alle Quattro Fontane, Rome, by Borromini (1637–41)

Lane, and St Vedast, Foster Lane, which have a Borrominiesque sculptural play with concave and convex curves. The spire of St Stephen Walbrook is an intricate and playful composition but it is the interior of this church which is its loveliest and most complex feature. In this brilliant and spatially ambiguous combination of the aisled nave plan and the centralized plan, the large dome floats gracefully not on massive piers but on eight slender columns and eight arches. The idea of a dome resting on eight equal arches was realized in an even more ambitious scale at St Paul's cathedral.

Wren's first scheme for a total replacement of the burnt and decayed Old St Paul's is known as the Great Model design, after the wooden model made of it in 1673 which survives at the cathedral. This is centrally planned with a dome of great beauty inspired by that at St Peter's, the drum being Bramantesque and the surmounting ribbed section Michelangelesque. The body of the church is preceded by a domed entrance vestibule inspired by that in Sangallo's design for St Peter's, while the linking of the arms of the Greek cross

plan by concave walls echoes a fantastic design for a palace in Antoine Le Pautre's *Oeuvres d'architecture* (1652). This, Wren's favourite scheme for St Paul's, was rejected by the Dean and Chapter as impractical. They wanted a traditional Latin cross plan with a large choir for the sung daily services and a nave for the congregation on special occasions. Thus in 1673 Wren produced the so-called Warrant Design with a long nave, choir and transepts. This was executed in 1675–1710, with the exception of its rather odd spire which Wren replaced early on with a dome echoing that in his Great Model design, altering at the same time the design and construction of the outer nave walls. As a result they were carried up as false walls many feet in front of the clerestorey windows in the nave and choir. These walls help counteract the thrust of the dome, while to carry the extra weight of the heightened walls they were made two feet thicker than in the Warrant Design. In the gap between the clerestorey of the choir and these false outer walls he hid the flying buttresses that help carry the weight of the choir vault.

The willing adoption of deception on this scale shows the essentially Baroque freedom of Wren's approach. A High Renaissance architect would scarcely

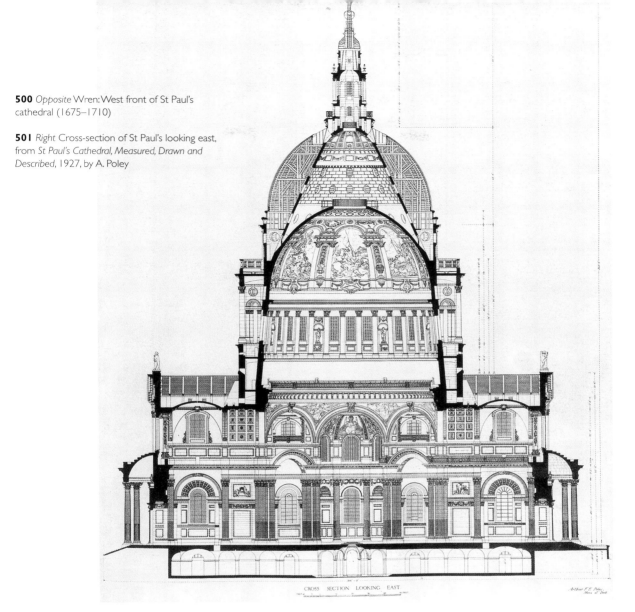

500 *Opposite* Wren: West front of St Paul's cathedral (1675–1710)

501 *Right* Cross-section of St Paul's looking east, from *St Paul's Cathedral, Measured, Drawn and Described*, 1927, by A. Poley

CROSS SECTION LOOKING EAST

Arthur F.E. Poley
Mens et Sens

have allowed such expedients. They are, moreover, continued in the design of the dome itself, which follows Michelangelo's device at St Peter's of an inner dome of a height which will impress from within the church and an outer dome which is much higher in order to tell in distant views. Wren's inner dome is left open in the middle, like those designed by the two Mansarts, so as to allow light to stream dramatically through from the crowning lantern far above. This heavy stone lantern could not be carried on the outer dome, which is simply a timber frame covered with lead, so, to perform this function, Wren introduced a unique third layer consisting of a tall brick cone which is invisible from both inside and outside the cathedral. It is a stroke of audacious invention, taking us back to the Wren who as a young scientist invented a double telescope and a transparent beehive.

Though we have pointed out some of the Baroque elements in St Paul's it should be remembered that the outer dome does not have the aspiring or thrusting verticality of Baroque domes, but the calm, almost hemispherical profile of Renaissance domes such as that projected by Bramante for St Peter's. The two-storeyed disposition of the façades also lacks Baroque dynamism but is derived from Inigo Jones's Banqueting House (p. 278), and is enlivened with much crisp small-scale carving of flowers and foliage by Grinling Gibbons and others, echoing the decoration of sixteenth- and early seventeenth-century buildings Wren had seen in Paris On the other hand, there are positively Baroque features such as the curved porticoes on the transept fronts,

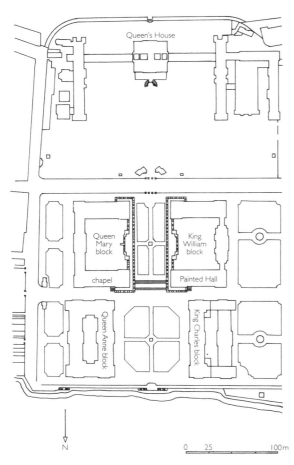

502 *Above* Wren: Plan of the Royal Hospital, Greenwich (1696–1716), incorporating the earlier Queen's House by Jones (see p. 278)

503 *Right* The Mirror Room of the Amalienburg, Munich, by Cuvilliés (1734–9), with stuccowork by Johann Baptist Zimmermann

504 Wren: Interior of the Painted Hall, the Royal Hospital, Greenwich, with carved detail by Hawksmoor and painting by Thornhill

derived from Pietro da Cortona's S. Maria della Pace in Rome, the Borrominiesque west towers with their clashes of concave and convex forms, and the use of false perspective in the window surrounds on the west front, again a feature derived from Borromini.

We have already touched in passing on the significance of Wren's monumental public buildings and palaces, the first of their kind in England, at Chelsea, Winchester, Hampton Court, Whitehall and Greenwich. The grandest of those carried into execution is the Royal Hospital at Greenwich, where in 1696–1716 he completed what John Webb had begun in 1664–9 in his Charles II Block, a pioneering Baroque masterpiece. Wren produced a grandiose vista flanked on each side by long colonnades of coupled columns inspired by Perrault's at the Louvre and terminating in the balancing domes of the chapel and the Painted Hall. The Painted Hall consists of a domed vestibule resembling a church, the long dining-hall proper, and the upper hall containing the High Table. All three spaces open into each other through great archways and are on different levels. With its carved detail by Nicholas Hawksmoor and flowing figure paintings by Sir James Thornhill with their complicated royal iconography, this magnificent spatial sequence is one of the finest Baroque ensembles in Europe.

Talman, Vanbrugh, Hawksmoor

Wren's role as a royal architect left him virtually no time for, or interest in, private country-house commissions. Chatsworth in Derbyshire was the first of the great Whig palaces which by their size and splendour symbolized the changed relationship between Whig landowners and their monarch, a consequence of the Revolution of 1688 and of the offering of the throne to the Dutch Protestant, William of Orange. At Chatsworth the south and east fronts were built by William Talman (1650–1719) in 1687–96, in a style echoing Bernini's designs for the Louvre. Though his patron, the 1st Duke of Devonshire, had played an important part in the Revolution, he was content to express his own power and glory by adopting the Baroque style of architecture and ornament associated with the former Stuart court. This Franco-Italian style, with its gilded interiors enriched with florid murals, had first appeared in England in Webb's Double Cube Room of 1648–50 at Wilton House, Wiltshire. It was then taken up by Hugh May at Windsor Castle in 1675–84, and reappeared at Chatsworth in a sequence of sumptuous interiors painted and carved by continental artists such as Antonio Verrio and Louis Laguerre.

In 1702 Talman was succeeded as Comptroller of His Majesty's Works by John Vanbrugh (1664–1726), a romantic adventurer who began his career as a soldier, was imprisoned in France as a spy, and subsequently became a playwright, producing a number of popular and licentious comedies. What made him turn to

505 *Above* The west front (1700–3) of Chatsworth, Derbyshire, with Archer's north front (1705–7) on the left

506 *Left* Hawksmoor: The Mausoleum at Castle Howard, Yorkshire (1729–36)

507 *Below* Vanbrugh: Plan of Castle Howard, Yorkshire (1699–1726)

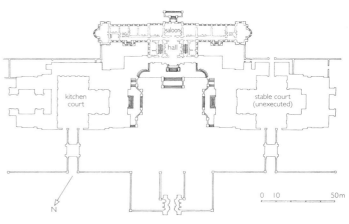

508 *Above* The Salon de la Guerre, Versailles (begun 1678), with the relief of Louis XIV by Coysevox and on the right the Galerie des Glaces

509 *Opposite* The chapel of the Würzburg Residenz (1732–44), by Neumann

architecture we do not know, but by 1699 he was able to produce a design for Castle Howard, Yorkshire, of such brilliance that the 3rd Earl of Carlisle immediately chose it in favour of plans already prepared by Talman. Vanbrugh's Castle Howard was an imaginative culmination of the monumental tradition begun by Webb at Greenwich, continued there by Wren, and introduced to country-house design by Talman at Chatsworth. For help in preparing the detailed drawings for Castle Howard and in supervising its construction in 1700–26, Vanbrugh turned to the brilliant architect Nicholas Hawksmoor (1661–1736), who had worked in Wren's office for about twenty years.

Vanbrugh's flamboyant domed palace, which almost rivals in megalomaniac splendour the palaces erected by reigning prince-bishops in Germany, was built simply as a symbol of the wealth and the pride in landownership

510 *Above* Vanbrugh: southwest exterior of Castle Howard, Yorkshire (1699–1726)

511 *Below* Aerial view of Blenheim Palace, Oxfordshire (1705–25), by Vanbrugh and Hawksmoor

512 St George's, Bloomsbury, London (1716–30), by Hawksmoor

of a Yorkshire squire who retired to his estates in 1702 after a brief period as First Lord of the Treasury to William III. Castle Howard had no ceremonial function and, indeed, no interiors of any great size or special consequence other than the spectacular domed entrance-hall, flanked by staircases visible through open arches. The magnificent park contains equally extravagant monuments to the art of architecture and to dynastic pride: the great Pyramid built in 1728 from designs by Hawksmoor to commemorate the founder of the Carlisle family estates; the Mausoleum (1729–36), also by Hawksmoor, an enormous tholos of stern Doric columns; and the Belvedere Temple (1725–8), an ambitious souvenir of Palladio's Villa Rotonda.

As the creator of a monument of such conspicuous display as Castle Howard, Vanbrugh was a natural choice

of architect in 1704 for Blenheim Palace, Oxfordshire, intended primarily as the national memorial to the Duke of Marlborough in gratitude for his victories over Louis XIV, and only secondarily as a convenient dwelling-house. Built in 1705–25 as the joint work of Vanbrugh and Hawksmoor, Blenheim is a development of ideas first expressed at Castle Howard. The theatrically managed approach through a gradually narrowing forecourt is evidently inspired by Versailles, while the sculptural treatment of the extraordinary lanterns or arcaded belvederes which surmount the four corner towers has a positively Borrominiesque flavour.

Hawksmoor is best known for his six London churches, designed in 1712–16 as a consequence of the Act for Building Fifty New Churches of 1711. This was passed by the Tory government of 1710–14 as part of a call for religious and social order in conformity with the ideals of the High Church party within the Church of England. In these striking buildings, especially in their highly idiosyncratic steeples, Hawksmoor's gift for abstract sculptural design found an ideal expression. At St-George-in-the-East, Stepney, Hawksmoor invents a uniquely personal architectural language which achieves Baroque dynamism through the use of blocky or geometrical, not of curvilinear, forms. It should not be thought, as it often was in the later eighteenth and nineteenth centuries, that Baroque architects were bent on creating an extravagant language far removed from the central tradition of classical architecture reaching back to antiquity. On the contrary, architects like Borromini and Pietro da Cortona, as we have seen, were deeply concerned with antique architecture and archaeology. So, too, was Hawksmoor who made an audacious attempt to apply the sacred architecture of the ancient world to the purposes of the Protestant Church of England. His church of St George,

513 *Overleaf left* The Wieskirche (1746–54) by Dominikus Zimmermann

514 *Overleaf right* The Trasparente (1721–32) in Toledo cathedral, by Narciso Tomé

515 Hawksmoor: West front of St George-in-the-East, Stepney, London (1715–23)

516 Archer: The domed garden pavilion at Wrest Park, Bedfordshire (1709–11)

Bloomsbury, thus boasts not only a giant Corinthian portico inspired by that of the Pantheon, but also a strange pyramidal steeple with a stepped profile, designed as a reconstruction of the Tomb of Mausolus at Halicarnassus (p. 46).

Archer and Gibbs

Almost the only English architect to adopt, on an extensive scale, the language of Bernini and Borromini was Thomas Archer (c.1668–1743) who, rarely for an English architect at this time, had travelled in Italy, Holland and probably Germany and Austria. The rhythmic confrontation of concave and convex forms occurs in all his major works, for example St Philip, Birmingham (1710–15), St John, Smith Square, London (1713–28), the Cascade House at Chatsworth (1702) and, above all, the domed garden pavilion at Wrest Park, Bedfordshire (1709–11), a substantial building resembling a miniature church with features inspired by Bernini's S. Andrea and Borromini's S. Ivo. Archer found an ideal patron in the 1st Duke of Shrewsbury, who had lived in Rome from 1700 to 1705, had commissioned there a design for a house from Paolo Falconieri, and had married an Italian wife. Like the 1st Duke of Devonshire, for whom Archer designed the bowed north front of Chatsworth, Shrewsbury was one of the seven signatories who invited William of Orange to England. Heythrop House, Oxfordshire, which Archer built for Shrewsbury in 1707–10, was a clear reminder to the king of the powerful status of the Whig oligarchs to whom he owed his throne. It was inspired in general form and vigorous massing by Bernini's final design for the Louvre and featured perversely complicated windows taken direct from Bernini, but its most striking internal feature was unfortunately not reinstated after a fire in 1831: an apsed vestibule on a quatrefoil plan at the heart of the building, a Baroque space unique in English domestic architecture.

In view of the irony that the Italian Baroque Heythrop should have been commissioned by an avowed enemy of Catholicism and absolute monarchy, the

517 Gibbs: The west front of St Martin-in-the-Fields, London (1720–6)

518 Gibbs: Exterior of the Radcliffe Library, Oxford (1737–48)

architect James Gibbs (1682–1754) was unlucky at suffering professionally through being a Catholic, a Tory and, probably, a Jacobite, i.e. someone rejecting the title to the British throne of the Hanoverian George I in 1714. In 1703 Gibbs went to the Scots College in Rome to train for the Catholic priesthood, but abandoned his studies to become a pupil of Carlo Fontana (1638–1714), the leading Baroque architect in Rome. This first-hand continental training, which made him unique in the insular Britain of his day, was put to good use in his first building, St Mary-le-Strand, London (1714–17). Designed in his capacity as joint surveyor with Hawksmoor to the Commissioners for Building Fifty New Churches, this is a vigorous and original

composition drawing on the seventeenth- and early-eighteenth-century buildings which he had admired in Rome. Thus it is preceded by a semi-circular portico recalling Cortona's at S. Maria della Pace, while the sculpturally modelled side elevations with their tabernacles along the ground floor echo the façades and window treatment of Borromini's Palazzo Barberini. The exuberant stuccowork in Gibbs's ceiling recalls that in two more Roman churches, Cortona's SS. Luca e Martina, and Fontana's SS. Apostoli.

Gibbs's other principal church, St Martin-in-the-Fields, London (1720–6), was one of the most influential churches of the eighteenth century, for its combination of a steeple rising above a temple portico

519 Interior of the octagonal pavilion at Orleans House, Twickenham (c.1716–21), by Gibbs

Gibbs's favourite Italian stuccoists, Artari and Bagutti, produced vivid flowing ornament of continental effusion. One of the happiest examples of their work is in the octagonal pavilion which Gibbs built on the riverside at Orleans House, Twickenham in c.1716–21, a near-Rococo extravaganza intended by its owner as a room in which to entertain the Princess of Wales.

In his last major public building, the Radcliffe Library (1737–48) at Oxford, Gibbs returned to something of the inventiveness he had shown in St Mary-le-Strand. This great domed rotunda, actually a polyhedron of sixteen sides, is wrapped round with a colonnade of engaged coupled Corinthian columns inspired, according to Gibbs, by the Mausoleum of Hadrian in Rome. The aspiring dome has a Michelangelesque profile while the ring of curved buttresses supporting its drum echoes Longhena's S. Maria della Salute of the 1630s. Eclectic but original, powerful yet perfectly balanced, the Radcliffe Library is Gibbs's masterpiece. He was a chameleon architect: Rococo as in the saloon at Ragley Hall, Warwickshire (1750–4); Palladian as in his designs for Whitton Place, Middlesex (1725–8); and neo-Gothic as in the Temple of Liberty at Stowe, Buckinghamshire (1741–7), the first monument of its kind in Europe. This kind of versatility in a fundamentally Baroque architect should not surprise us, for we have already seen it in Germain Boffrand who died in the same year as Gibbs, 1754.

Spain

Spain has in many ways been a law unto herself for centuries from a cultural and religious point of view. What, for example, are we to make stylistically of the tremendous west front designed in 1664 by the painter-architect Alonso Cano (1601–67) for the already highly idiosyncratic cathedral of Granada, begun in the 1520s by Diego de Siloe? The west front as executed from 1667 rises like a huge triumphal arch which, with its two storeys and great height, is less reminiscent of ancient Rome than of early Romanesque attempts to recapture Roman grandeur like the west front of

was imitated throughout the British Isles as well as in the American colonies and the West Indies. Earlier designs by Gibbs for the church included one in which a Pantheon-like portico leads to a spectacular circular nave, apparently inspired by a design of 1693 by Pozzo, the master of Baroque illusionistic painting.

In 1716 Gibbs was dismissed by the Whigs from his Surveyorship and, unable to hold public office in view of his political and religious sympathies, he turned to country-house design, especially for Tory peers and squires. Debarred from inclusion by the Whig Colen Campbell in his influential *Vitruvius Britannicus* (3 vols., 1715–25), Gibbs published 150 of his own designs as *A Book of Architecture* (1728), which became one of the most widely used architectural books of the century. Gibbs's country houses, for example Ditchley House, Oxfordshire (1720–31), have somewhat unadventurous exteriors. Baroque fireworks are reserved for their interiors, where

520 Cano: West front of Granada cathedral (designed 1664; begun 1667)

Lincoln cathedral (p. 128). Its bony linear strength makes it difficult to relate it to contemporary work elsewhere, though it incorporates decorative details borrowed from sixteenth-century North European Mannerist sources which often recur in later Baroque buildings in Spain, for example in the work of the prolific Leonardo de Figueroa (c.1650–1730), who established Baroque in Seville. A late work such as his chapel in the College of S. Telmo, Seville (1724–34), is basically a three-storeyed frontispiece of the orders in a tradition going back to Philibert de l'Orme at Anet, but it is smothered in exuberant seething ornament, some of which recalls the work of the late-sixteenth-century German architect and engraver, Wendel Dietterlin. The plates of architectural decoration which

he published showed the northern concept of Mannerism at its most ornamental, with complicated patterns of interlaced strap-work and grotesque classical figures.

This rich style of surface decoration which, as we have already seen, characterized Plateresque architecture in the sixteenth century, thus recurs in Spain around the start of the eighteenth century. This Spanish Baroque style is often known as Churrigueresque, though the Churriguera brothers were among its less interesting practitioners. It might be described as a kind of Mannerist-Rococo, considerably removed from the Baroque of Italy, Austria or South Germany. Perhaps the most celebrated monument of this period is the west façade of the Romanesque cathedral of Santiago de Compostela. Faced, during the seventeenth century, with rivals to its status as the most popular pilgrimage church in Spain, the authorities chose to renew its appeal by modernizing its exterior while at the same time preserving its Romanesque interior and even its sculptured portals: a characteristically Spanish gesture of piety towards the national past. The remodelling of the cathedral was a slow process which culminated in the ornate west front known as El Obradoiro (the work of gold). Built in golden granite in 1738–49 from designs by Fernando de Casas y Nova, it has a twin-towered silhouette which underlines the affinities between Gothic and Baroque. It is an intensely sculptural composition, rich in surface relief of a most unusual kind, including the composition of the spires from superimposed volutes like those at Longhena's Salute. The constant breaks and recessions of the façade produce a fluttering staccato effect which is a hallmark of the Churrigueresque style.

The most astonishing creation of Spanish Baroque is the Trasparente of 1721–32 in Toledo cathedral, by Narciso Tomé. This is the pinnacle of the Baroque concern for the welding of architecture, painting and sculpture into a total spatial illusion. In order to allow for adoration of the Blessed Sacrament in the tabernacle over the high altar from both the choir and the

ambulatory behind, the tabernacle was fitted with glass doors. Further to direct the attention of the devout to the Sacrament in the Gothic gloom of the ambulatory, Tomé constructed round it a towering confection sprouting with figures of the Virgin, angels and putti caught up in golden rays. This builds up to a three-dimensional representation of the Last Supper, at which the Blessed Sacrament was instituted. It is surmounted by a figure of St Longinus holding the spear which pierced Christ's side, thus drawing the blood which becomes the sacramental wine. This extraordinary reredos is set in a concave bay flanked by columns with downward-curving entablatures in order to heighten the false perspective. But this is only half the story, for the visitor is himself on the stage, following a tradition established by Bernini. The whole amazing sculptural group is dramatically lit by a golden light from a concealed source behind the visitor. When he turns to look back at this source he is confronted with a celestial vision contrived in the space created by the removal of one whole rib vault in the ambulatory. Above this Tomé constructed a large high dormer containing a window invisible from below. Carved angels frame the mouth of this bizarre opening, the interior faces of which are painted with further members of the heavenly host, the 24 Elders of the Apocalypse and the Lamb of the Seven Seals (fig. 516).

The Trasparente began as a unique solution to a unique problem, though its fame led to imitations. Its spirit of fantasy also recurred in the work of the architect Francisco Hurtado Izquierdo (1669–1725), for example his chapels of S. José in Seville (1713) and at El Paular near Segovia (begun 1718). El Paular, his last and most complex work, is as complex in form as it is sumptuous in materials. It comprises a dark passage leading from the High Altar to the *camarin* (a small holy room, a type unknown outside Spain), which in turn is separated from the larger *sagrario* (sacristy) by an almost Moorish red

and gold lacquer screen. Both *camarin* and *sagrario* are on a Greek cross plan; the former, which is a domed octagon called the Trasparente, is dominated by the centrally-placed circular tabernacle surmounted by a baldacchino of twisted columns of bright red marble.

One of the prettiest *camarines* is the Rosary Chapel of 1726–73 at Sta Cruz la Real at Granada, a former Dominican church now known as Sta Escolástica. This three-apsed domed shrine is inlaid most attractively with varied mirrors, plane, convex and concave. This characteristically Baroque play of convex and concave forms first appears architecturally in Spain in the startlingly Borrominiesque façade of Valencia cathedral, begun in 1703 by Conrad Rudolph, a German architect supposedly trained in Rome by Bernini. In similar vein is the west front of the Gothic cathedral of Murcia, built in 1736–49 from designs by Jaime Bort Miliá. This ample theatrical composition, centred on a deep concave frontispiece with a flowing curved pediment, has a dazzling Rococo exuberance like a realization of one of Meissonnier's fantastic engraved projects.

Exotic fantasy is the keynote of another Rococo masterpiece in Valencia, the palace of the Marques de Dos Aguas as remodelled in 1740–44 by Hipólito Rovira y Brocandel. In its flowing sculptured portal the two rivers of the city are symbolized by river-gods and water-nymphs, almost smothered by trees, clouds and scrolls. This extraordinary composition, two storeys high, is set against walls painted in simulation of watered silk, a reminder that Valencia, on the east coast of Spain, was the centre of the silk industry and consequently in close touch with French textile centres such as Lyons.

The leading late-Baroque architect in Spain is Rodríguez Tizón Ventura (1717–85), who has some of the chameleon qualities of Boffrand in France or Gibbs in England. His earliest major work is the church of S. Marco, Madrid (1749–53), with a curved façade echoing Bernini's S. Andrea al Quirinale and an astonishing Guariniesque plan consisting of a succession of no less than five intersecting ellipses. In 1750, at the church of El Pilar at Saragossa, he provided the oval

521 *Opposite* Fernandon de Casa y Nova: The west front of the cathedral of Santiago de Compostela (1738–49)

522 Jaime Bort Miliá: West front of the cathedral at Murcia (1736–49)

523 Churriguera: The Plaza Mayor, Salamanca (1729–33)

chapel that houses the sacred pillar on which the Virgin appeared to St James. This is an interior of tremendous richness and complexity, combining references to Bernini and Borromini beneath a perforated dome inspired by Guarini. In Andalusia the architect Francisco Xavier Pedraxas (born 1736) built the parish church of the Ascension at Priego in 1771–86, which is dominated by its ambitious domed octagonal *sagrario*. This two-storeyed and galleried interior with an undulating cornice supporting the balcony contains much Rococo ornament, handled with that repetitive fluttering multiplicity which was given its fullest expression by Spanish architects in Mexico.

The passionate Catholicism of the Spaniards has meant that our story has been one mainly of ecclesiastical architecture. Indeed, the best way to appreciate the heady magnificence of these exotic interiors is to visit southern Spain in Holy Week. The sumptuous churches and glittering shrines, like those in south Germany, still function today as in the Baroque period: in the colourful and dramatic processions of hooded penitents silver-columned Baroque canopies sheltering richly garbed figures of the Virgin and scenes of the Passion are carried to the churches through crowded streets.

Secular architecture has been less studied than ecclesiastical but, in the field of town planning, we should glance at the Plaza Mayor at Salamanca. This closed arcaded square was laid out in 1729–33 by Alberto de Churriguera but, delightful though it is, it lacks Baroque energy – indeed the surrounding façades are neo-Plateresque. Spanish culture, unlike Portuguese, is essentially urban, and in every town the Plaza Mayor, rather than a park or garden, serves as an open-air drawing-room where the populace promenades and converses once the great heat of the day has lifted.

Thanks to the wars with France in the seventeenth century, the consequent economic decline and the War of the Spanish Succession, there was little royal building, elsewhere such a fruitful field for Baroque expression. However, once the Bourbon King Philip V, grandson of

Louis XIV, had been settled on the Spanish throne by the Treaty of Utrecht in 1713, work was begun on the royal country palaces of La Granja and Aranjuez, both with charming French gardens, and, more importantly, on the vast royal palace in Madrid. The first plan, by Juvarra in 1735, was for a palace larger than Versailles and built round four courts, but this was replaced in 1738 by his pupil Giovanni Battista Sacchetti with the scheme as executed containing a single large court, similar to Bernini's third project for the Louvre. Of the many tributes to Bernini made in designs for palaces through Europe the colossal urban edifice in the centre of Madrid comes closest to realizing the ambitions of the greatest of all Baroque architects.

Portugal

In Portugal the efflorescence of Baroque occurred in the reign of João V (1706–50), when wealth poured into the country from the gold and diamond mines of Brazil. This new-found wealth encouraged the tendency for extravagantly gilded interiors already established in late-seventeenth-century churches, for example in the remodelling of the Gothic churches of Santa Clara and São Francisco in Oporto. The magnificent symbol of this flush of confidence, though combined with characteristic Iberian piety, was the palace-convent of Mafra near Lisbon, a gigantic building larger than the Escorial. This was built for João V from 1717 onwards from designs by the German-born Johann Friedrich Ludwig (1670–1752), known as Ludovice in Portugal. Ludovice, who had worked as a goldsmith in Rome under Andrea Pozzo, provided a building reminiscent in

524 Ludovice: Exterior of the palace-convent of Mafra, near Lisbon (begun 1717)

its organization of a great German monastery such as Weingarten, with German corner pavilions surmounted by bulbous towers. However, the architectural and decorative treatment is an eclectic assembly of motifs from Roman Baroque architects, especially Carlo Fontana and his school. If this glorious building were in Italy or France rather than in a country which, like the whole Iberian peninsula, has been outside the ordinary Grand Tour route, it would be as well known as it deserves to be.

The design of the ornate Royal Library, presented to the University of Coimbra by João V and built in 1716–28, has sometimes been attributed to Ludovice, though it may be the work of the local architect Gaspar Ferreira. The most important contribution was made by Claude de Laprade, a French-born craftsman to whom is due the lavishly carved and gilded interior decoration.

525 *Right* Interior of the Royal Library at the University of Coimbra (1716–28)

526 *Below* Oliveira: Garden front of the royal palace at Queluz (1747–52), showing one of the flanking wings (1758–60) by Robillion

527 Amarante: Exterior of Bom Jesus do Monte, near Braga (begun 1780s), showing the cascade of steps (begun 1727)

Spread through three rooms open to each other through two high arches, this lustrous and opulent work in a style derived from the Régence of contemporary France includes elaborate bookcases in red and gold Chinese lacquer.

João V's passion for Baroque Italy and his lack of confidence in Portuguese architects led him to commission a chapel in 1742 from two leading Roman architects, Luigi Vanvitelli and Nicola Salvi. This,

amazingly, was constructed in Rome, blessed by the pope, and then shipped to Lisbon where it was erected under Ludovice's supervision as the chapel of St John the Baptist, the king's patron saint, in the Jesuit church of São Roque. A miniature Baroque jewel, just 17 feet by 12 (6×4m), it is encrusted in a characteristically Portuguese way with lapis lazuli, amethyst, agate, onyx, gilt bronze, silver and mosaic.

The only other major royal building project in the period covered by this chapter, the palace at Queluz, was commissioned by João's son, Dom Pedro. Directly inspired by the château of Marly, this was erected in

1747–52 by Mateus Vicente de Oliveira (1706–86), a pupil of Ludovice, while the garden front was extended with one-storeyed flanking wings in 1758–60 by the French engraver and decorator, Jean-Baptiste Robillion. The Rococo richness and variety of Queluz and its interiors are reflected in the exquisite gardens, where great play is made of the different levels. A particularly delightful feature is the canal lined with blue and white figured tiles and crossed by a bridge of the same material.

The theme of pleasure pavilions in well-watered gardens is one which the Portuguese, gayer in their approach to Catholicism than the Spaniards, applied to the earthly dwelling-places of the Almighty himself. Entrancing popular expressions of this mood include two pilgrimage churches in northern Portugal, Bom Jesus do Monte near Braga and Nossa Señhora dos Remédios at Lamego, set in a kind of sacred garden architecture. Both churches on steep hills are approached by dramatic sacred staircases, flanked by chapels containing the Stations of the Cross but festively decorated with fountains, statues, urns, obelisks, potted plants and clipped bushes. The cascade of steps at Bom Jesus was begun in 1727 but the twin-towered church, designed by Cruz Amarante, dates from the 1780s. The similar church at Lamego (1750–61) is inspired by the buildings of the Tuscan-born architect Niccoló Nasoni, who lived and worked in Oporto from 1725–73. He introduced the extravagant forms of the late Baroque and Rococo of southern Italy, his masterpiece being the church of São Pedro dos Clérigos (1732–50), a design quivering with electric energy and originality.

The earthquake of 1755 destroyed the whole centre of Lisbon, so that it is difficult now to assess the merit and extent of the Baroque contribution to the capital up to that time. The rebuilding of Lisbon on a grid plan, directed by the king's energetic minister, the Marques de Pombal, was carried out until 1763 by Eugénio dos Santos de Carvalho (1711–60) and Carlos Mardel. The architectural language adopted was a simplified mid-eighteenth-century Roman Baroque which became known as 'Pombaline', and it was not in Lisbon or Oporto but in the Portuguese colony of Brazil that the gilded extravagance of Portuguese late-Baroque and Rococo found its fullest expression.

Town planning
The contribution of Rome

The father of Baroque town planning was Pope Sixtus V who, as we have seen, replanned Rome in the sixteenth century with great streets that fulfilled theatrical as well as functional roles. Seventeenth-century Baroque art suggests the metaphor of 'the world as a stage' in which earthly flamboyance expresses a God-given order. Art and architecture make a sensual appeal to the viewer, combining all the arts into a totality through the use of illusionistic devices. Designers adopted the various theatrical devices associated with processions and festivals, whether they were celebrating religion or the state.

Indeed, engravings made of Rome for Pope Alexander VII in 1665 were published as *Il nuovo teatro . . . di Roma moderna* (The New Theatre of Modern Rome). It was Alexander VII who commissioned Bernini in 1656 to create the vast, colonnaded Piazza di S. Pietro in front of St Peter's as a stage for papal spectacle. Alexander VII also revitalized an existing commission which had authority to straighten and enlarge roads as well as to clear streets and squares. His other notable planning achievement was to commission Carlo Rainaldi (1611–91) in 1658 to make the Piazza del Popolo scenically memorable by flanking the entrance into it of the Corso with two churches. These formed a theatrical composition to impress visitors arriving in Rome from the north. Roman planning of this kind survived as a model until the end of the nineteenth century. Indeed the streets of papal Rome were the grandest before those of Haussmann in nineteenth-century Paris.

A more intimate Roman square than the Piazza del Popolo, but no less scenic, is the Piazza di S. Ignazio, created in 1727–35 by Filippo Raguzzini (c.1680–1771)

(p. 297). The elliptical façades of the five apartment blocks which form the square appear as wings in stage scenery, introducing a note of mystery and illusion by concealing the street entrances. No less poetic was the now demolished Porta di Ripetta, Rome, commissioned by Pope Alexander XI and built in 1703–5 from designs by Alessandro Specchi (1667–1729). This was a port or docking area to facilitate the loading and unloading of goods on the barges which came down the river Tiber from Tuscany and Umbria. Specchi solved a seemingly mundane problem with much imagination by creating a hemicycle with elaborate ramps and curved, wave like steps rising to an elliptical piazza with a fountain in front of the church of S. Girolamo. A miniature masterpiece of city planning, designed so as to function at whatever the level the water reached, this was also one of the few urban schemes in Roman history to incorporate the river as part of the scenery.

In 1723 Specchi entered unsuccessfully the competition for the so-called Spanish Steps in Rome, leading from the Corso and the Piazza di Spagna to the area of SS Trinità dei Monti and the Via Sistina. Once more a commission from the visionary Pope Clement XI, this was the product of an ancient rivalry between the papacy and the French monarchy, for the church of SS Trinità dei Monti was a French foundation. Specchi's work influenced the winning architect, Francesco de Sanctis (1693–1740), who built the Spanish Steps in 1723–5. More than a staircase of over 100 steps, it resembles a sloping piazza with a scenic effect like that of a giant frozen waterfall.

The Piazza di S. Ignazio, Porta di Ripetta and Spanish Steps were all too individual in character to be of great influence. It was the cutting of new streets through papal Rome in the sixteenth and seventeenth centuries that established the expectation that new streets would be straight, lined with uniform buildings, and terminate in an eye-catching monument. The creation of straight, open streets in old town centres spread throughout Europe, the most impressive being the avenue laid out in Berlin in 1647 by Friedrich Wilhelm, the Great

528 Rome from the Piazza del Popolo

529 Specchi: The Porta di Ripetta, Rome (1702–3)

530 Unter den Linden, Berlin

Elector (reigned 1640–88). Known as Unter den Linden (under the limes), this great avenue of parade links the palace with the western entrance to the city and the Tiergarten, the hunting grounds of the Electors of Brandenburg. Nearly a mile (1.5km) long and

65 yards (60m) wide, it was lined with three rows of trees as possibly the earliest tree-lined road. It was probably inspired by the avenues in the landscaped parks recently laid out at Cleve, today a German town in North Rhine-Westphalia, by the Count of Nassau-Siegen, the Stadtholder of Cleve.

Unter den Linden is still the core of Berlin, as the Cours à Carrosses (today Cours Mirabeau) is of Aix-en-Provence in southern France. This broad, tree-shaded avenue was built in 1650 to connect the old town with the new Quartier Mazarin.

Versailles and its influence

The meeting of three streets diagonally at a piazza, a novelty in town planning when it was first achieved in the Piazza del Popolo, was adopted strikingly in the planning of the town of Versailles by Le Nôtre and Le Vau, echoing the garden designs with which they had been involved at Vaux-le-Vicomte and Versailles. By 1668–9, three great tree-lined roads converged at the parade ground (Place d'Armes) in front of Louis XIV's vast château at Versailles to which he transferred the seat of the court and government from Paris in 1682. In 1701 he moved his bedroom, where the ritual which accompanied his rising and retiring took place, to the exact centre of the palace. Thus, the symbolism of life-giving rays emanating from the Sun King was given a total urban expression.

This imagery was developed further in the city of Karlsruhe (Charles' peace), the capital of Baden, as laid out from 1715 by Karl Wilhelm, Margrave of Baden-Durlach, by his military architect, Johann Friedrich von Batzendorf. At the core was an octagonal tower, later extended into a palace, from which the town stretched out in no less than thirty-two radiating streets like the spokes of a wheel or the rays of the sun. Aranjuez, near Madrid, was laid out in 1748–78 for Philip V of Spain by two French military engineers who adopted the radiating avenues of Versailles. These recur on an even more magnificent scale at St Petersburg, though here the three great boulevards, first conceived in 1737 for

531 Aerial view of Karlsruhe (laid out from 1715)

Peter the Great, centre on the Admiralty Building not on the royal palace.

Versailles was also the model for the creation of the princely residence with its own town laid out on a grid, as at Ludwigsburg, near Stuttgart, built from 1709 for Duke Eberhard Ludwig of Württemberg by the military engineer Johann Nette (1672–1714) and later by the North Italian architect and stuccoist Donato Frisoni (1683–1735). More impressive is Mannheim, Baden, founded in 1606 by Elector Palatine Friedrich IV as a fortified decagonal town with streets on a grid plan to serve as a bastion of Calvinism against the Catholic powers. When it became the court of the Electors Palatine of the House of Wittelsbach in 1721, the citadel, adjacent to the town, was replaced by a palace designed by Louis Rémy de la Fosse (1666–1726) as the largest in Germany, while the town was newly laid out on a vast square grid, one of the most ruthless of all, relieved only by a few small squares.

There was no political theory or terminology to distinguish between a capital city and a princely seat. Sometimes they coincided but sometimes they were widely separated as in the Netherlands, where Amsterdam was the capital, and The Hague was the seat of the court. A similar dualism existed in France between Paris and Versailles, while the complementary roles of Washington and New York might be seen as a modern parallel.

Vauban and the fortified town

Sébastien le Prestre, Maréchal de Vauban, (1633–1707) was a French military engineer who designed over one hundred and twenty fortresses in which for the first time French defences were considered on a national basis. He also has an important place in town planning for designing new towns on the French frontiers such as Sarrelouis, Longy and Montlouis in the Pyrenees. Typical is Neuf-Brisach, founded in 1697 south east of Colmar to guard the crossing of the Rhine. This features Vauban's characteristic geometrical, star-shaped fortifications with the grid pattern of the town streets centring on a great open square which could also be used as a parade ground. Vauban, as well as Versailles, was doubtless an influence on the town of Karlsruhe.

The Place Royale

The Place Royale, dominated by a statue of the monarch, was especially associated with seventeenth-century France with its strong centralized monarchy.

532 Aerial view of Neuf-Brisach by Vauban (1697)

In Paris, the Place des Vosges and Place des Victoires, were followed by the Place de Louis-le-Grand (Vendôme), projected by Louis XIV in 1685 as the largest square in Paris. Flanked by royal academies, royal library and mint, this was intended to celebrate French military and cultural achievements. Though work had begun, it was abandoned in 1691 as too ambitious and the square was reconceived by the architect J. Hardouin-Mansart as a residential ensemble

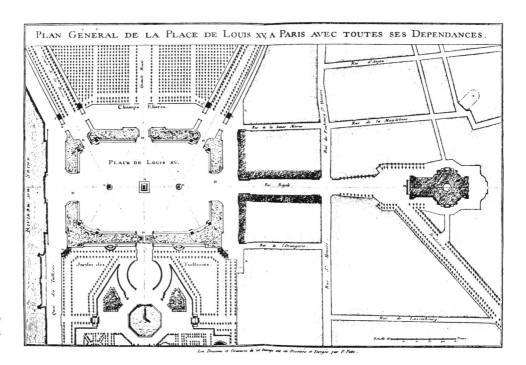

533 Gabriel: Plan of Place Louis XV (today de la Concorde), Paris (1753)

365

in c.1700 for members of the most socially mobile elite in France, the financiers of Paris.

It was followed in 1753 by Gabriel's unusually planned Place Louis XV. Originally dominated by Bouchardon's equestrian statue of the king, this was bounded on the south by the river Seine and on the east and west by the trees of the Champs-Elysées and the Tuileries as well as by a curious system of moats, since filled in. The only buildings are the twin palaces along the north side, the Hôtel de Coislin (today Hôtel de Crillon) on the west, and the Gardemeuble (today Ministry of Marine) on the east. With their giant colonnades rising through the first and second floors, these pay eloquent tribute to Perrault's east front of the Louvre, built for Louis XIV in 1667–74 (p. 317).

Gabriel was also indebted to his father, Jacques Gabriel (1667–1742), who had laid out royal squares at Rennes and Bordeaux in the 1730s. Similar town-planning schemes were carried out in the 1750s at Reims by Legendre, at Rouen by A.-M. le Carpentier and, as we saw in the last chapter, most spectacularly of all at Nancy by Emmanuel Héré de Corny. These schemes, which were a public and political statement of royal supremacy, were made possible by the new peace and security of eighteenth-century France, since they often involved replacing town walls and ramparts with public parks and promenades.

The Place Royale was echoed in other countries, notably the Amalienborg of 1750 at Copenhagen, with its corner palaces inspired by the Place Vendôme. In Brussels, a Place Royale was begun in 1766 by the Hapsburg governor of the Netherlands, Charles de Lorraine, in imitation of the squares in French towns such as Bordeaux, Reims and Rouen.

Christopher Wren's plan for London

The chief town plan of Baroque England was that for the City of London by Christoper Wren which we have already briefly noted. Presented to Charles II following the Great Fire of 1666, this radical plan drew elements from papal Rome which Wren knew from engravings

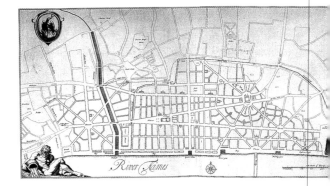

534 Wren's plan for London (1666)

and from le Nôtre's axial garden designs at Vaux-le-Vicomte and Versailles which he had seen on his visit to France in 1665–6. Once again, as at Berlin and Versailles, we see the confluence of garden design and town planning in this period. Wren also incorporated quays along the Thames, inspired by those in Paris. One of the first attempts to combine a rectangular street network with wide diagonal avenues, including hexagonal or star shaped squares, it was a subtle yet complex design which was a precursor of much later planning, including that of Washington. Though greatly admired, it had no chance of being executed in London without the centralized planning control that England was far from possessing.

Building regulations: the role of conformity

Amsterdam, the richest city in the newly established Dutch Republic by the start of the sixteenth century, became the most important trading market in the world in the next century. Living only for commerce, it lacked the usual defining emblems of a great city such as cathedral, castle, university and monastery. Nonetheless, to protect its houses and warehouses from the sea, Amsterdam, rather like Venice, was obliged to adopt strict control over building and planning. The project for extending the city with three impressive concentric canals with wide quays, the famous Herrengracht, Keizersgracht and Prinsengracht, was approved in 1607

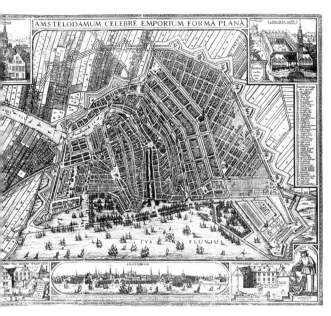

535 Plan of Amsterdam (1623)

536 Grande Place, Brussels (rebuilt from 1697), with the Town Hall (1402–63)

and completed in the 1620s, with a second phase of development added in the 1660s. Precise building ordinances regulated house construction and zoning, while the whole scheme was unusual as an initiative from the town itself with no superior authority involved.

The development of the town of Versailles from the 1670s until the first decade of the eighteenth century, though the product of a totally different political system from that at Amsterdam, was similarly governed by building regulations more complete than any that had operated in the medieval towns we saw in Chapter 5. Strict ordinances controlled the height, width, number of floors, building materials and even colours of houses, while owners were to keep their pavements clean and well lit with lamps.

The history of regulations concerned purely with aesthetic appearance is one that needs further exploration, but it is clear that a feeling for the *genius loci* meant that new buildings were sometimes required

to be in conformity with existing historical prototypes. The Flemish town of Arras, French from 1659 and rich from its manufacture of cloth and tapestry, is memorable for its two squares, the Petite Place (now Place des Heros), which had been the market place from the Middle Ages, and the Grande Place, surrounded by tall arcaded and gabled houses of the late seventeenth century in a Flemish brick and stone style. The uniformity in the two squares is not an accident, for an ordinance of 1692 required new owners in both to match their façades to those of the recently erected, but now destroyed, Maison de l'Ecu d'Or. A further ordinance in 1718 continued to insist that all façades should be identical. History repeated itself when, following the destruction in the First World War of much of the two squares, they were completely rebuilt by Pierre Paquet in the 1930s. They have now mellowed down so much that few visitors to this historic town realize how new the buildings are.

Similarly, after the destruction of the Grande Place in Brussels in the French bombardment of 1695, a decree of 1697 granted permits to rebuild only if new work were carried out in conformity with the Italo-Flemish Baroque style that had been developed through the seventeenth century for the gabled Guild Houses. As a result, the Grande Place is a largely eighteenth-century recreation of an earlier square. The Plaza Mayor in Madrid, built in the early seventeenth century on the basis of mid-sixteenth-century designs, was faithfully rebuilt in the same style after two fires in the seventeenth century and, most remarkably, by the neo-classical architect Juan de Villanueva (1739–1811) after a final fire in 1790.

8 Eighteenth-century Classicism

The impact of Rome

The leading themes in this chapter, the classical architecture of the French Enlightenment and the Picturesque gardens and garden buildings of England, were potent influences throughout Europe and beyond. The language of international neo-classicism was established in the 1740s at the French Academy in Rome by French *pensionnaires* (scholars) who had been awarded the Grand Prix as students of the Academy in Paris. Beginning with projects for festival decorations in the form of temples and triumphal arches, they soon turned to the design of public buildings on a megalomaniac scale with endless colonnades, stone domes and complex plans inspired by the baths of ancient Rome. They rejected the spirited movement and rich ornament of Baroque architecture as incompatible with the stylistic purity and structural honesty which they came to regard as the essence of antique architecture. The catalyst in this process was Giovanni Battista Piranesi (1720–78), so it is with an investigation of him and his context that this chapter will begin.

Piranesi

Italy during this period was still a collection of widely differing and often opposed states, many of them controlled by outside powers, so that, as in Germany, there was no single cultural centre nor any architectural coherence. Nonetheless, Rome became in the first half of the eighteenth century a compelling centre of interest for architects throughout Europe, partly because of the combined impact of Piranesi and of the presence of the young Grand Prix winners at the French Academy.

Piranesi's powerful influence over all the architects of the neo-classical movement from Peyre to Soane was the result of his wonderfully evocative representations of the monuments of ancient and modern Rome, and of his actual designs for furniture and interior decoration. Yet his artistic roots were Baroque, for he had been trained in Venice, where the art of Baroque stage design and the tradition of topographical painting had united to produce the type of fanciful topographical view known as the *capriccio*, typified in the work of the painter Marco Ricci (1676–1730).

Piranesi moved to Rome in 1740 and there came under the influence of Giovanni Paolo Pannini who, having worked for Juvarra in the 1720s on stage design, was now Professor of Perspective at the French Academy. It was here that Pannini developed the *veduta ideata* (imaginary view), a type of painting in which accurately rendered monuments of ancient Rome were assembled in imaginary compositions. In 1743 Piranesi produced his first book of engravings, *Prima Parte di Architetture e Prospettive* ('First part of architecture and perspective'), containing imaginative ruin scenes inspired by Marco Ricci and Giuseppe Bibiena, of which the most memorable is the 'Ancient Mausoleum'. This combines echoes from the mausolea of imperial Rome (p. 77), from Borromini's S. Ivo (p. 289) and from Fischer von Erlach (p. 323) in a creative vision of the essential unity of the classical language of architecture in whatever period. An equally potent image was the plan of a college which he published in 1750 in his *Opere Varie* ('Various works'). Resembling the baths of ancient Rome, this vast and complex plan for an intellectually improving public building coloured the visionary

projects of countless French students competing for the Grand Prix of the French Academy.

After Venice and Rome, the chief influence on Piranesi was Naples, which he almost certainly visited in c.1743–4. The fluent and colouristic work of the painter Luca Giordano (1632–1705) influenced his technique, though the excavations at Herculaneum, begun in 1738, made an even more decisive impact. He is said to have worked in the studio of Giovanni Battista Tiepolo in Venice in 1744 but by the end of the year he had established himself as a print-dealer in Rome, opposite the French Academy. It was now, in c.1745, that he produced his astonishing *Carceri* plates, disturbing images of prison interiors which show the influence of Juvarra, Francesco Guardi and Tiepolo. In different mood was his *Le Antichità Romane* ('Roman antiquities', 1756), intended as a substantial record of ancient Rome with plans, sections and, above all, emphasis on construction, features which make it a turning-point in the history of Roman archaeology. The principal intention of the *Antichità* was the application of archaeology to contemporary design, and in their personal contact with Piranesi in Rome architects such as Chambers, Adam and Mylne (pp. 377, 382) were all affected by this ambition.

Between c.1748 and his death thirty years later Piranesi published his *Vedute di Roma* ('Views of Rome'), a set of 137 plates which represented the buildings of Rome in an increasingly romantic and dramatic way. His emotional involvement was heightened as he became increasingly conscious of the destruction of ancient Rome, and as his 'Roman' stand was threatened by the pro-Greek party from the mid-eighteenth century onwards, represented by scholars, archaeologists and architects such as Johann Joachim Winckelmann, Marc-Antoine Laugier, the Comte de Caylus, Julien-David Leroy, James Stuart and Nicholas Revett. In opposition to the arguments of this group Piranesi published his

Della Magnificenza ed Architettura de' Romani ('On the magnificence and architecture of the Romans', 1761) in which he wrongly argued that the Etruscans were the sole founders of Roman civilization, that they were an older race than the Greeks and had perfected painting, sculpture and the technical arts before the Greeks. The splendid plates in this book stressed the variety and richness of Roman architectural ornament rather than the supposed sparseness of Etruscan construction.

Following an attack on the book by the French collector and publisher Pierre-Jean Mariette, Piranesi published the *Parere su l'Architettura* ('Thoughts on architecture', 1765) with additional plates after 1767 which were a bizarre combination of Egyptian, Greek, Etruscan and Roman motifs. This heady eclecticism was his way of confounding the pedantry of the Graeco-Roman debate. He justified it by quoting from Ovid that 'Nature renews herself constantly – to create the new out of the old is, therefore, also proper to man', and by publishing *Diverse Maniere d'adornare i Cammini* ('Different ways of decorating chimneypieces', 1769). These imaginatively eclectic designs for chimney pieces and accompanying wall decoration, published with 'An Apologetical Essay in Defence of the Egyptian and Tuscan Architecture', were influential throughout Europe, especially on Adam, Dance and the Empire Style.

As a practising architect Piranesi was less successful and influential. In the early 1760s he reconstructed for Cardinal Rezzonico the priory church and headquarters of the Order of Malta on the Aventine hill in Rome. His strange entrance piazza, with commemorative pillars bearing decorative reliefs and flanked by obelisks, ball finials and urns, has a hallucinatory neo-Mannerist quality. The chapel itself resembles one of Piranesi's own etchings, with its crisply detailed surfaces covered with ornament rich in Maltese and Rezzonico symbolism: military and antique, staccato and slightly wooden, *appliqué* like the braid on a soldier's uniform, the decorative treatment is anticipatory of the Empire Style.

Piranesi was well aware of his fertile eclecticism, his creative fantasy and his love of ceaseless experiment. 'I

537 *Opposite* Piranesi: Engraving of an 'Ancient Mausoleum', from *Prima Parte di Architetture e Prospettive* (1743)

538 The Tempietto Diruto, Villa Albani, Rome (1751–67), by Winckelmann and Marchionni

539 Entrance front of S. Maria del Priorato, Aventine Hill, Rome (1764), by Piranesi

need', he wrote, 'to produce great ideas and I believe that were I given the planning of a new universe, I would be mad enough to undertake it.' This Enlightenment belief that a new and ideal world could be created by a return to first principles also coloured the romantic outlook of the German scholar Johann Joachim Winckelmann (1717–68). Among the many drawn to Rome during the course of the eighteenth century, few were more influential than Winckelmann, who settled there in 1755. Books such as his *History of Ancient Art* (1764) were important for creating a seductive and idealized image of Greek culture, though this was partly fired by his homosexual instincts. Curiously, he had seen very little Greek art or architecture at first hand, so that what he propagated was effectively a myth in which he read back into Greek art the calmness and smoothness he admired in High Renaissance artists such as Raphael.

As curator and librarian from 1758 to the great collector Cardinal Alessandro Albani, Winckelmann seems to have acted as adviser in the design of the Villa Albani built in 1751–67 by the architect Carlo Marchionni (1702–86). In general disposition the Villa Albani is late Baroque but it is encrusted internally and externally with antique and neo-classical reliefs and carvings, creating an effect rather like Piranesi's priory church of the Order of Malta. This is particularly true of the two 'Greek temples', which consist of porticoes attached to the wings of the villa and combine antique columns and sculpture in an eclectic neo-antique design. The hand of Winckelmann can be detected here, as in the remarkable Tempietto Diruto, an artificial ruin composed largely of antique fragments picturesquely sited on one side of the garden.

The origins of the Picturesque

The garden buildings at the Villa Albani, which are like a three-dimensional realization of a *capriccio* painting, had already been anticipated in England. Indeed, in 1770 the influential connoisseur Horace Walpole claimed that the new art of landscape gardening had turned England into a country where 'every journey is made through a succession of pictures'. This preoccupation with pictorial values in the design of both buildings and gardens is the basis of the eighteenth-century artistic movement we know today as the Picturesque. It was the invention of a prosperous, leisured and educated society which was concerned with the pursuit of aesthetic experience through the appreciation of nature and art and especially through travelling. These travels began with the Grand Tour of the continent and ended with the search for picturesque scenery in England, Scotland and Wales.

The exploration undertaken by the eighteenth-century man of taste was intellectual as well as physical. It encouraged him to think sympathetically about cultures other than his own and to investigate them in the spirit of detached irony characteristic of the age of the Enlightenment. The eighteenth century saw the birth of archaeology and, by beginning the systematic exploration of Greek antiquity, undermined the superiority which had been accorded since the Renaissance to Roman architecture. The attempt to give visual expression to these reflections accounts for much of the strangeness and the poetry of the landscape gardens of eighteenth-century England such as Shugborough, Kew and Stourhead.

We have already seen how this new eclectic approach to the past coloured Fischer von Erlach's *Entwurff einer historischen Architektur* of 1721 (p. 324), which appeared in an English edition in 1730. The historical buildings are shown in animated perspective views in their natural or landscaped settings and include figures in appropriate costumes. The use of such pictorial techniques helps set the buildings in historical context. Indeed, perhaps the most striking architectural impact of the Picturesque is the wholly new emphasis which it placed on architecture as part of an environment. We can interpret the word 'environment' so as to mean not only the physical setting, whether rural or urban, but also the historical setting. As a result of this approach, architecture came to be valued for its narrative or evocative capabilities.

One of the clearest ways in which this new approach to architecture was expressed was in the appreciation of ruins and in the creation of new or instant ruins. Admiration for a ruin is a clear indication of a belief that there are other things more important about a building than either its fulfilment of the function for which it was designed, or the visual effect intended by its architect. Thus architects like Sir William Chambers, Robert Adam and Sir John Soane, perhaps at once excited and frustrated by this shift in their role, began to imagine in drawings and watercolours what their own buildings would look like when change and decay had reduced them to ruins. Once again, we are brought back to Piranesi, the artist who was most preoccupied with the ability of ruins to stimulate the imagination and the intellect.

Lord Burlington and William Kent

We should recall that the desire to penetrate the secrets of antique design and construction had been a leading ambition of Italian architects from Alberti to Borromini. To understand why such ambitions failed to make much impact in England it is necessary to glance for a moment at English history. The arrival of Renaissance culture at the court of Henry VIII in the early sixteenth century had been prematurely arrested by the breach of that monarch with the papacy. The ensuing Reformation led to the isolation of England from much of the continent, and especially from Rome. The fact that the break with Rome was cultural as well as religious meant that, as late as the early eighteenth century, England still had much ground to make up in terms of the assimilation of the classical ideals of Renaissance Italy. One way of interpreting the so-called neo-classical movement in England during the eighteenth century is as an attempt to catch up with those ideals.

This view helps to explain the career of someone like William Kent (c.1685–1748), which seems impossibly varied until one considers that what made him so desirable to his English patrons was his uniquely authentic knowledge of Italian culture. He had spent ten years in Italy from 1709, where he had studied painting in Rome. Here he met the Earl of Burlington (1694–1753), the wealthy patron and connoisseur who was to make his career and in whose household he was to live at Burlington House, Piccadilly, from 1719 until his death. Anxious to bring about a Renaissance of the arts in England, Burlington brought Kent back from Italy as a history painter, trained in the Italian pictorial tradition. He also brought the Italian sculptor Giovanni Battista Guelfi to live at Burlington House and played an important part in establishing Italian opera in England, the musical equivalent of the grand manner in painting.

In potential conflict with this Romanizing programme was the contemporary ambition to establish a national style of moderate classicism, free from Baroque exaggeration. This style was seen by Burlington and his circle as the accompaniment to the definitive establishment of a constitutional monarchy and of Protestantism as the national orthodoxy. In this new political disposition the country was run by the great landowning families of the Whig party who had deprived the monarch of many of his powers when, in the Revolution of 1688, they had invited William of Orange to accept the throne. The moral and aesthetic philosophy of the 3rd Earl of Shaftesbury (1671–1713) envisaged the emergence of a national style of architecture as the inevitable consequence of this newfound English 'liberty' in politics, religion and social organization. In his *Letter Concerning the Art or Science of Design* (1712) he argued: 'The taste of one kind brings necessarily that of the others along with it. When the free spirit of a nation

turns itself this way . . . the public eye and ear improve: a right taste prevails and in a manner forces its way.'

Shaftesbury never specified the style he expected would prevail and it was left to Lord Burlington to promote, somewhat unimaginatively, neo-Palladianism as the expression of the spirit of the nation. The claim for Palladianism as a national style rested on the fact that it had already been introduced into England a century earlier by Inigo Jones (p. 277). The neo-Palladians now assumed that Jonesian classicism would have become more fully acclimatized had the national taste not been corrupted in the meantime by the extravagance of Baroque designers. The enduring monument of neo-Palladianism was the three volumes, each containing 100 plates, of *Vitruvius Britannicus* (1715–25), edited by the architect Colen Campbell (1676–1729). Intended as a record of the modern buildings of Britain, both public and private, and especially of the country houses of the ruling families, this also stressed the superiority of 'Antique Simplicity' over the 'affected and licentious' forms of the Baroque.

The varied work of William Kent reflects these and other conflicting tendencies. Though a naturally exuberant artist trained in late-Baroque Rome, he was expected to comply with the chaster stylistic ambitions of Burlington. The range of possibilities is well exemplified in Kent's work for George II at Kensington Palace in the 1720s, where he decorated three interiors in contrasting styles: the staircase with murals in an illusionistic Venetian Baroque manner; the Cupola Room in a neo-antique style anticipating later eighteenth-century effects with its coffered ceiling, giant pilasters, statues in niches and bas-relief over the chimneypiece; and the Presence Chamber, where the painted ceiling is a remarkable revival of the arabesque style devised by artists like Raphael, Giovanni da Udine and Vasari in imitation of the decoratively frescoed interiors of the ancient Romans.

Lord Burlington had been fortunate enough to purchase a large quantity of drawings by Palladio, including his studies of the baths of ancient Rome.

Published by Burlington in 1730 with the Italian title *Fabbriche Antiche disegnate da Andrea Palladio* ('Ancient buildings drawn by Palladio'), these drawings of the baths, with their spatially varied interiors containing apses and screens of columns, had a marked influence on eighteenth-century planning, for example on Burlington's Assembly Rooms at York (1731–2) and Kent's unexecuted designs of the 1730s for new Houses of Parliament. Kent's finest building is Holkham Hall, Norfolk, designed in the early 1730s in collaboration with its owner, the Earl of Leicester, and Lord Burlington. It was a pure work of art, conceived as a

shrine for paintings and sculpture specifically bought for it in Italy by Lord Leicester. Its plan with four outlying pavilions was inspired by Palladio's unexecuted Villa Mocenigo, but its most spectacular interior, the combined entrance and staircase hall, united features from the colonnaded basilicas of ancient Rome, Vitruvius's so-called Egyptian Hall, and Palladio's curved screen of columns in the church of Il Redentore in Venice (p. 250). There is a similar contrast between a restrained Palladian façade and a dramatic interior at one of Kent's last buildings, 44 Berkeley Square, London, the house he built in 1742–4 for Lady Isabella Finch. It contains one of the most dynamic Baroque staircases in the country, as well as a saloon with a coffered painted ceiling vying in richness with those by Giulio Romano at

540 The Cupola Room, Kensington Palace, London, decorated by William Kent (1720s)

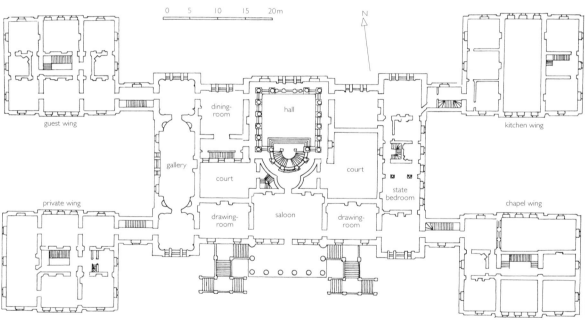

541, 542 *Top and above* Kent: Garden front and plan of Holkham Hall, Norfolk (begun 1734)

the Palazzo del Tè (p. 230). The house thus encapsulates the history of Italian design from Mannerism through Palladianism to Baroque.

The Elysian Fields at Stowe, Buckinghamshire, and the garden at Rousham, Oxfordshire, both of the 1730s,

survive with their numerous classical garden buildings as precious and evocative examples of Kent's pioneering genius in the development of the Picturesque garden and of landscape architecture. The intentions of Kent and his patrons in creating these nostalgic dream worlds, with their echoes of antique buildings, are many and varied. They could draw for guidance on a number of visual traditions. First there were the heroic landscape

543 *Above* Kent: The Temple of Ancient Virtue, in the Elysian Fields, Stowe, Buckinghamshire (c.1732)

paintings of Claude Lorrain (1600–82) and Nicolas Poussin (1594–1665) with their evocations of classical temples and ruins in pastoral settings. Then there were Italian Renaissance gardens, some of which Kent seems to have regarded as authentic recreations of antique originals: for example, the hemi-cycle of busts of Roman emperors at the Villa Brenzone on Lake Garda is one of the models for his Temple of British Worthies at Stowe. Finally there were the letters in which the younger Pliny described his remarkable villas at Laurentinum and in Tuscany (p. 71). In his *Villas of the Ancients Illustrated*, published in 1728 with a dedication to Lord Burlington, Robert Castell reconstructed Pliny's Tuscan villa so as to suggest a model for the combination of a formal symmetrical house set in informal gardens looking towards the open country beyond. Pliny had described the life he led in his villas where, relaxing from the cares of state, he hunted, collected books and works of art, and improved agricultural methods and the welfare of his workers. This, too, provided a model emulated by landowners in eighteenth-century England.

Robert Adam

One of the most successful applications of this complex aesthetic to the creation of a great house and landscape is at Kedleston, Derbyshire. Here a house linked by quadrant colonnades to four pavilions, as at Palladio's Villa Mocenigo, was planned in c.1758 by Matthew Brettingham (1699–1769) for Sir Nathaniel Curzon,

544 Staircase at 44 Berkeley Square, London (1742–4), by Kent

later 1st Viscount Scarsdale. Brettingham, who had supervised the construction of Holkham from 1734, was dropped in 1759 in favour of James Paine (1717–89) who, in turn, was superseded in c.1760 by Robert Adam (1728–92). This constant changing of architects for others believed more fashionable was characteristic both of the lordly ways of the great Whig landowners and of the importance they attached to keeping abreast of fashion. Indeed in 1758 Curzon consulted a fourth architect, James 'Athenian' Stuart (1713–88), who at that moment seemed, wrongly as it turned out, to be a serious rival to Robert Adam on the architectural scene.

545 *Above* The Marble Hall at Kedleston, Derbyshire (1760s), by Adam

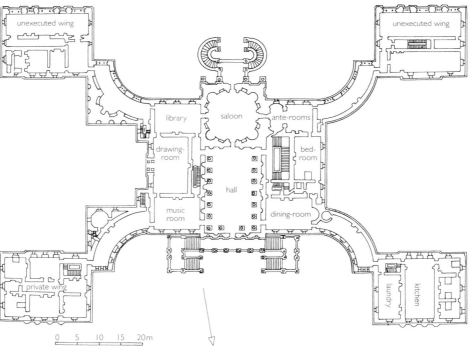

unexecuted wing

unexecuted wing

library

saloon

ante-rooms

drawing-room

bedroom

hall

music room

dining-room

private wing

laundry

kitchen

0 5 10 15 20m

N

546 *Left* Plan of Kedleston, by Adam

Kedleston was completed during the 1760s, though only two of its four pavilions were executed. One of these, as at Holkham, consists of the private family quarters, for the state apartments in such houses were never intended for daily use. Adam's chief external alteration was the south front which took the form of a romantic evocation of the Arch of Constantine in Rome. One can describe such a theatrical gesture as Picturesque in that it is an architectural parallel to *capriccio* paintings like Claude's *Landscape with the Arch of Constantine* (1651), where the urban monument has been transferred to a pastoral setting. This imperial theme, regardless of its ideological appropriateness in the home of a Derbyshire landowner, was echoed in the interior of this grandiose mansion where the front door within the giant Corinthian portico leads directly into the great hall, intensely cold during much of the year. Here the walls are flanked by Corinthian columns, as in Palladio's reconstruction of Vitruvius's Egyptian Hall, and adorned with niches containing casts of antique sculpture and with grisaille panels of Homeric subjects as in Palladio's illustration of the Temple of Mars in Rome. The spatial contrast is exhilarating as one passes from this room to the rotunda or saloon, a noble domed space inspired by the Pantheon: at 62 feet (19m) high it is 22 feet (6.5m) higher than the hall. The general form of the hall and rotunda is derived from Paine's reworking of Brettingham's designs for the house, but where Paine had separated them by the main staircase, Adam placed them next to each other in the relationship of the Roman domestic atrium and vestibulum, a disposition he described in *Ruins of the Palace of the Emperor Diocletian at Spalatro* (sic). Here he claimed that Roman interiors provided models of 'diversity of form, as well as of dimensions', where modern architects often merely produced 'a dull succession of similar apartments'.

Adam's recreation of antique Roman splendour for modern domestic purposes was an achievement unequalled since the days of Raphael and certainly unique in Europe at that moment. How had he acquired this ability at the age of scarcely more than thirty? After an admirable architectural training in Scotland by his gifted father William Adam, he set off for Italy in 1754, where he made friends with two of the most influential image-makers in the architectural scene in Europe, Piranesi and the French artist, Charles-Louis Clérisseau (1721–1820). The numerous views of ancient ruins painted by Clérisseau, who taught both Adam and Chambers, were an important influence on the development of the Picturesque tradition, since they suggested that buildings were at their most attractive when in decay and when seen through the medium of watercolour paintings.

During Adam's four-year stay in Italy he inspected buildings and interior design of all periods, evidently making a special study of the re-creation of the painted and stuccoed interiors of ancient Rome by Renaissance artists such as Raphael and Vasari. In some ways the climax of his Grand Tour was his journey with Clérisseau in 1757 to Split in Dalmatia to make measured drawings of the ruins of Diocletian's palace, which he published in sumptuous form in 1764. He was wise to study antique domestic rather than sacred or public building, since it was a subject little studied by archaeologists and one of much interest to modern architects. As we have noted, it enabled him to speak with authority about the kind of planning he had adopted at Kedleston. His expedition to Split (Spalato) was doubtless undertaken in deliberate rivalry with that of James Stuart and Nicholas Revett, who spent four years in Athens from 1751 measuring for the first time the buildings of classical Greece. The publication in 1762 of the first of their long-awaited volumes on *The Antiquities of Athens* turned Stuart temporarily into a formidable rival to Adam and placed him on a level with Winckelmann as one of the leading European authorities on Greek antiquity. The intensely ambitious Adam did everything he could to blacken Stuart's name, ensuring, for example, that he was dismissed from Curzon's service at Kedleston.

Adam's finest early interiors are at Syon House, a medieval and Jacobean building near London which he remodelled in 1762–9 for Sir Hugh Smithson

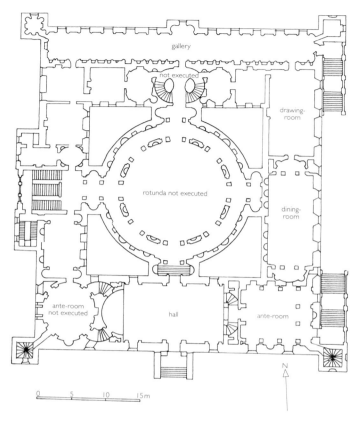

547 Adam: Plan of Syon House, Middlesex (remodelled 1762–9)

(1715–86), created Duke of Northumberland in 1766. Smithson resolved, according to Adam, 'that the whole might be executed entirely in the antique style'. However, while realizing this ambition Adam at the same time looked to contemporary France as a guide in the planning and disposition of his interiors. He argued that 'A proper arrangement and relief of apartments are branches of art in which the French have excelled all other nations', adding, in a memorable sentence, 'To understand thoroughly the art of living, it is necessary, perhaps, to have passed some time amongst the French.' At the same time he indicated his sympathy with English Picturesque ideals by emphasizing rather than concealing the awkward shift in ground level at the south end of the

entrance hall. Here he claimed that his introduction of curved steps behind a screen of columns 'gives an additional pictoresque to the scene', emphasizing that 'The inequality of levels has been managed in such a manner as to increase the scenery and add to the movement, so that an apparent defect has been converted into a real beauty.' Adam's approach to design is so much coloured by Picturesque rather than by theoretical architectural ideals about correctness of proportion or of ancient detail that he here writes about interior space exactly as though he were a landscape designer such as Capability Brown (p. 383).

The same concern for pictorial effect coloured the design of the adjacent ante-room (fig. 554). Here 12 free-standing columns of blue marble 'serve', in Adam's words, 'to form the room and heighten the scenery'. Moreover the columns conformed to the patron's wish for antique authenticity, since they are ancient Roman ones excavated from the bed of the River Tiber. Adam designed new white and gold capitals for them in a Greek Ionic order inspired by, though not copied from, those of the Erechtheion in Athens. He also capped them with elegant gilded statues of male figures, a combination found in ancient Roman public architecture such as triumphal arches but not in domestic interiors. The entrance to the anteroom is flanked by two magnificent bas-reliefs of martial trophies in gilded stucco. These were carved by Joseph Rose in imitation of the trophies of the emperor Augustus on the Campidoglio in Rome, which had already been imitated by Giovanni da Udine at Raphael's Villa Madama in Rome and engraved by Piranesi in 1753.

The ante-room has a neo-antique opulence recalling the work of Pirro Ligorio, whose sumptuous Casino of Pius IV in the Vatican Gardens was a special favourite of Adam. It is remarkable that the glistening polychromy of Adam's eclectic interior, one of the finest of its date in Europe, should have been conceived purely as a setting for 'servants out of livery . . . and tradesmen', in contrast to the hall, which was for servants in livery. The development of the bell-pull was soon to dispense with the need for public waiting-rooms for servants at the heart of the house, and also caused the gradual disappearance of male liveried servants as pure elements of display in noble houses. The ante-room was immediately followed by the dining-room where, for once, Adam ignored the precedent of the French in whose plans dining-rooms did not receive special emphasis. Adam felt that the dining-room and its decorative treatment should be given particular attention in England where, thanks to the different political situation, each man could feel he had a stake in the government and was thus accustomed to sit after dinner discussing politics and public affairs long after the ladies had retired to the adjacent drawing-room.

Adam produced a series of interiors of astounding loveliness all over England and Scotland, at Bowood, Osterley, Nostell, Kenwood and Saltram during the 1760s, and, during the next decade, at Mellerstain, Alnwick, Headfort and Newby where his sculpture gallery prefigures later eighteenth- and early nineteenth-century museums. Much of Adam's work at this time consisted of transformations or enlargements of existing country houses, prompted by the contemporary concern to keep up to date with changing visual and social fashions. However, in London in the 1770s he had the opportunity of designing several new town houses, including 20 St James's Square and the now demolished

548 Second Drawing Room of 20 St James's Square, London (1771–4), by Adam

549 Adam: Portico on the south front at Stowe House (now School), Buckinghamshire (1771), executed by T. Pitt (1772–4)

Derby House. The ingenious plans of these provided rooms of contrasting shapes, often apsed or oval with screens of freestanding columns, on the long narrow sites typical of London houses. At Derby House in Grosvenor Square the succession of three drawing-rooms and an ante-room opening into each other on the first floor in order to ease circulation at parties was, according to Adam, 'an attempt to arrange the apartments in the French style, which . . . is best calculated for the convenience and elegance of life'. He regretted, however, that lack of space had forced him to place the separate suites of Lord and Lady Derby on the ground and first floors respectively, and not on the same floor as they would have been in Paris.

Although his delicately painted and stuccoed neo-antique interiors, disposed so as to create effects of Picturesque movement, are his greatest achievement, Adam could also produce monumental exterior architecture, as in his south front at Stowe House (1771), the Old Quad of Edinburgh University (1789–93) and Gosford House, Lothian (c.1790–1800).

Chambers and Wyatt

After the imagination and sparkle of Adam his principal rivals, Chambers and Wyatt, can seem respectively staid and showy by comparison. The early years and architectural training of Sir William Chambers (1723–96) gave him an international perspective which set him apart from his contemporaries in Britain. From the ages of about 17 to 26 he was in the service of the Swedish East India Company which enabled him to visit India and China. He followed this by studying at J.-F. Blondel's Ecole des Arts in Paris in 1749–50, and there was in touch with Peyre and de Wailly (pp. 393ff), who were to follow him to Rome and become life-long friends. During Chambers's stay in Italy from 1750–55 he was influenced, like Adam, by Piranesi and Clérisseau. In Rome, he prepared a design in 1751 for a mausoleum in the gardens at Kew for Frederick, Prince of Wales. This solemn domed rotunda was inspired by the recreations of antique Roman mausolea produced by architects at the French Academy in Rome in the 1740s such as Challe and Le Lorrain. However, under the influence of Clérisseau, he showed it in one drawing as a ruin, thus demonstrating how Picturesque sensibility tended to dethrone architecture (fig. 559).

Though the mausoleum was not executed, Chambers laid out the Picturesque gardens at Kew for the Prince's widow in 1757–63 with a range of classical and oriental buildings including the Temple of Peace, Palladian bridge, Alhambra, mosque, pagoda and ruined arch, of which the last two survive today. This exotic realization of the plates in Fischer von Erlach's *Entwurff einer historischen Architektur* was recorded by Chambers in his *Plans . . . of the Gardens and Buildings at Kew* (1763). Together with his *Plans of Chinese Buildings, Furniture, Dresses . . . Temples, Houses, Gardens etc.* (1757) and *Dissertation on Oriental Gardening* (1772), this established him as a master of the so-called 'jardin anglo-chinois' or Anglo-Chinese garden which was widely imitated on the continent. However, in England his views on landscape gardening seemed an increasingly old-fashioned product of Rococo sensibility in contrast to the work of Lancelot 'Capability' Brown (1716–83), who surrounded many of the greatest country houses in England with broad undulating parkland, lacking in human or architectural interest yet producing an atmosphere of beneficent calm.

Two of Chambers's most interesting early works are on the outskirts of Dublin and Edinburgh respectively: the Casino at Marino House (1758–76) and Duddingston House (1763–8). The Casino is a French *pavillon*, a miniature house in a classical style close to the fanciful engravings of the French architect Jean-Laurent Le Geay, with whom Chambers was personally acquainted. Duddingston was an important landmark in the development of the country house, for Chambers here abolished the *piano nobile*. Placing the principal interiors on the ground floor enabled the portico to be brought to ground level, save for a simple stylobate, as in Greek temples rather than raised up on steps as in the characteristic Roman temple. With the main rooms at ground level the way was opened for direct access from them to the garden, a disposition which became popular in the Regency period (c.1790–c.1820) with its Picturesque mingling of house and garden.

In 1761 King George III, whose architectural tutor Chambers had been, created the new royal office of

550 Chambers: The pagoda at Kew Gardens, Surrey (1761–2)

551 The Casino at Marino House, near Dublin (1758–76), by Chambers

552 *Left* Part of the river front of Somerset House, London (1776–96), by Chambers

553 *Below left* Gandon: The Four Courts, Dublin, from across the Liffey (begun 1786)

554 *Opposite* Adam: the ante-room at Syon House, Middlesex (c.1761–5), incorporating antique columns

Architect of Works, appointing Chambers and his great rival Adam to share the post. With his sympathies for French architecture, Chambers responded enthusiastically to a post which seemed to resemble that of First Architect to the King in France. He wanted to establish a public architectural style of dignity and decorum comparable to that promoted in France by dynasties of architects like the Gabriels and the Mansarts. He was also instrumental in founding the Royal Academy of Arts in 1768 as a parallel to the French Academy, and published in 1759 the first part of a projected *Treatise on Civil Architecture*, which was intended to refine and stabilize English taste. Though there were few significant royal commissions in England his greatest achievement was a public building, Somerset House (1776–96), built in London as government offices, the first of their kind on such a scale in Europe. The building as a whole paid tribute to Palladio and Inigo Jones but with the addition of elegant and superbly crafted detail in the Louis XVI style. Drama is provided in the design of the spatially adventurous oval and semi-circular staircases and the open screens of columns above rusticated arches, which impart a Piranesian air to the river front. Despite its large size, Somerset House is handled with such refined understatement that its overall effect is not as monumental as it ought to be but remains an accumulation of details.

Chambers's pupil James Gandon (1743–1823) showed that he was more capable than his master of producing monumental public architecture. In his County Hall, Nottingham (1770–2), and in various buildings begun in the 1780s at Dublin including the Custom House, Rotunda Assembly Rooms, Parliament

555 Engraving of the interior of the Pantheon, Oxford Street, London, by Wyatt (1769–72)

556 Wyatt: The Cupola Room at Heaton Hall, Manchester (c.1772)

House (now Bank of Ireland) and Four Courts, he successfully synthesized the Franco-Palladian tradition adopted by Chambers with an indigenous monumentality derived from Wren.

In marked contrast to the sober Gandon was the far more prolific and stylistically varied architect James Wyatt (1746–1813). After an architectural training in Venice and Rome during the 1760s he returned to a Britain dominated by the work of the Adam brothers whose style he was quick to imitate and whose principal plasterer, Joseph Rose, he frequently employed. He made his name with his first work, the Pantheon in Oxford Street, London (1769–72), the most spectacular assembly rooms in the country. Though the clearly defined internal space of the Roman Pantheon, enclosed by solid walls, had appealed to Renaissance architects as an image of clarity and order, Wyatt, in search of new pictorial experiences, looked to the Byzantine Hagia Sophia in Constantinople as a source. Thus, despite its name, Wyatt's great domed space was surrounded by two-storeyed colonnades and apses which owed more to Hagia Sophia than to the Pantheon. He followed this with Heaton Hall near Manchester (c.1772), a neoclassical simplification of Paine's still partly Palladian design for Kedleston. At Heaton the colourful Cupola Room, painted by Biagio Rebecca, is an early example of the so-called 'Etruscan' style. Wyatt's first essay in this style, preceding any by Adam, can be seen in his temple on an island in the river Thames in the gardens of Fawley Court, Buckinghamshire (1771). With its figured medallions and tablets painted in black and terracotta on a pale green ground, the decoration of the temple was inspired by the coloured plates in Sir William Hamilton's *Collections of Engravings of Ancient Vases* (4 vols., 1766–70).

In the 1780s he provided similarly exquisite interiors, and in the next decade he built two fine classical country houses, Castle Coole, Co. Fermanagh, Ireland, and Dodington Park, Avon. Castle Coole is a formal symmetrical essay of Palladian origin but Dodington (1798–1813) marks a new departure towards the kind of relaxed asymmetry which was to be a feature of Regency architecture. A colossal Corinthian *porte-cochère* of Roman scale dominates the entrance front but is balanced by a quadrant conservatory leading somewhat surprisingly to a centrally-planned domed chapel. It is astonishing to consider that at the same time as building Dodington Wyatt was at work on one of the most flamboyant country houses of the eighteenth century, the Gothic Fonthill Abbey, Wiltshire, built in 1796–1812 for the eccentric aesthete, William Beckford. Here was asymmetry on an unparalleled scale, with an irregular cruciform plan converging on a central octagonal tower of such staggering height and flimsy construction that it crashed to the ground in 1825. The wilful originality of Fonthill (fig. 560) shattered for ever the balance and harmony of 18th-century architecture.

Dance and Soane

Another architect who tended, in a very different and more cerebral way, to undermine eighteenth-century certainties was George Dance (1741–1825). He enjoyed nearly six years of architectural training in Rome from

557 Entrance front to Wyatt's Dodington Park, Avon (1798–1813), with the conservatory on the left

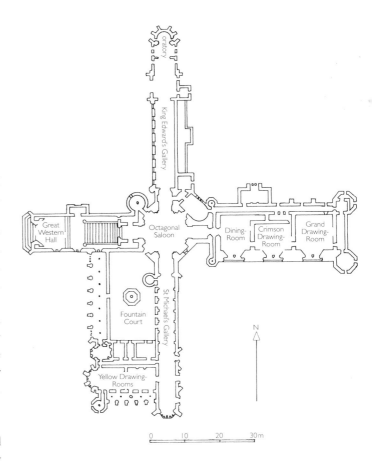

558 Wyatt: Plan of Fonthill Abbey, Wiltshire (1796–1812)

1759, during which time he became a competent practitioner of the new Franco-Italian classicism deriving from the French Academy in Rome. This is evident from the design for a public gallery with which he won a gold medal in the Academy at Parma in 1763. Its undemonstrative horizontal skyline and bleak but powerfully rusticated walls recur in his executed designs for Newgate Prison, London (1768–80; dem. 1902), where the festoons of chains over the entrance doorways caused the same shudders of horror as did the imaginary prisons engraved by Piranesi, whom he had met in Rome. As a forbidding symbol of justice and retribution, Newgate can be seen as an expression of Burke's concept of the Sublime, the aesthetic category which he added to the Beautiful in his influential book of 1757, *A Philosophical Enquiry into our Ideas of the Sublime and the Beautiful*. The sublime was a term used to describe reactions such as awe and terror to natural phenomena, but in eighteenth-century England and France it was transferred to the visual arts, especially to buildings and works of art expressing superhuman grandeur. Dance's

559 *Above* Design by Chambers for the mausoleum of the Prince of Wales, as a ruin (1751–2)

560 *Opposite* Engraving (1823) of the south end of St Michael's Gallery, Fonthill Abbey, by James Wyatt (1796–1812)

561 *Below* Dance: Newgate Gaol, London (1768–80; now demolished) with the Governor's house in the centre

Newgate Gaol was also a realization of the 'speaking architecture' of contemporary France, where the French classical tradition had been interrupted by Nicolas Le Camus de Mézières's call for an architecture of mood and sensation (p. 406).

Dance and his more distinguished disciple Sir John Soane (1752–1837) were concerned to create what the latter called 'the poetry of architecture', a term which, like 'mysterious light', also used by Soane, derives from Le Camus de Mézières. Dance's Common Council Chamber at the Guildhall in London (1777–8; dem.

1908) dissolved the traditional domed space into an interior resembling a parachute or tent by making the dome and pendentives part of the same sphere. Soane developed this theme as the basis of a new interior architecture of haunting poetry. A pupil of Dance from 1768, he worked in the office of Henry Holland (1745–1806) from 1772–8 and then spent two years in Italy absorbing the language of international neoclassicism and admiring the 'awful grandeur' of the Greek temples. In 1788 he was fortunate enough to be appointed architect to the Bank of England, and by the

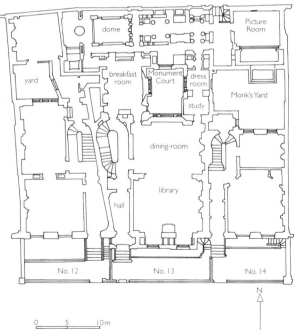

1790s his practice was exceeded in importance only by that of James Wyatt, following whose death in 1813 he was appointed one of the three attached architects to the Board of Works with Sir Robert Smirke and John Nash.

It was in the design of the Stock Office at the Bank of England in 1792, a process in which he was assisted by Dance, that Soane realized Dance's aim of an 'architecture unshackled' in which the trappings of the classical language were reduced to a system of incised lines and grooves defining vaulted top-lit spaces of strangely poetic effect. He continued this theme at the Bank, in interiors such as the Consols Office (1798–9) and the Colonial and Dividend Offices (1818–23). The Law Courts which he provided in 1822–5 within the medieval Palace of Westminster, and his Privy Council Chamber in his new Board of Trade and Privy Council Offices (1824–6), represented the climax of his uniquely personal and romantic blend of classic and Gothic, characterized by mysterious lighting effects and hanging vaults.

All the buildings by Soane which have been mentioned so far have been demolished, so to experience the Soanean aesthetic at first hand we must turn to the remarkable house-cum-museum which he created for himself between 1792 and 1824 in Lincoln's Inn Fields, London. This survives intact with a series of evocative interiors, crowded with Soane's collection of antique and modern works of art, and forming the ultimate phase in the treatment of interior space as akin to varied natural scenery which Adam had first developed in the 1760s. Indeed, Soane's play with changes of level, top-lighting, mirrors and scenic complexity, together with the constant antique allusions, make the building the climax of the Picturesque

562 *Above left* Soane: The Consols Office, the Bank of England, London (1798–9; now demolished)

563 *Left* Plan of the ground floors at 12, 13 and 14 Lincoln's Inn Fields (Sir John Soane's Museum), London (1792–1824), by Soane

movement in neo-classical Britain. Soane wrote of the Breakfast Room (fig. 565), with its shallow pendentive dome detached from the walls at either end so as to resemble a canopy:

> The views from this room into the Monument Court and into the Museum, the mirrors in the ceiling, and the looking glasses, combined with the variety of outline and general arrangement in the design and realization of this limited space, present a succession of those fanciful effects which constitute the poetry of architecture.

The rise of neo-classicism in France

In the eighteenth century, reaction set in to the rich elaboration of Baroque and Rococo architectural ornament as well as to the equally elaborate ritual associated with life in the ceremonial rooms of parade in seventeenth- and early-eighteenth-century palaces. The Petit Trianon at Versailles, built for Louis XV by Ange-Jacques Gabriel (1698–1782) in 1761–4, is the perfect expression of this twin reaction. In the façades of the main body of the house there is not a curved line to be seen. This beautifully proportioned stone prism, with its reticent skyline of unbroken horizontals, relies for effect not on Baroque fireworks but on subtlety and restraint. In function, too, it represents a shift away from the Baroque etiquette of court life at the château of Versailles and the Grand Trianon, since it was commissioned by the king as a place where he and his mistress, Madame de Pompadour, could be alone together and could enjoy watching the pastoral life of the nearby farm.

The Petit Trianon is designed with sensitivity to its setting, which it complements rather than dominates. The axes of the entrance front and the garden are at right angles to each other, since the garden, which was on the west side and at a higher level than the entrance front,

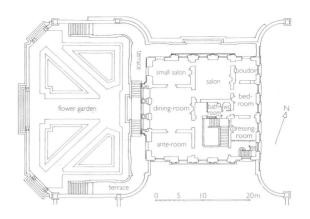

564 Plan of the principal floor of the Petit Trianon, Versailles (1761–4), by Gabriel

had already been established. All four façades are thus subtly different and command quite different outlooks: the south entrance front and the north front are articulated simply with pilasters; the east front, looking on to the botanical garden, is not articulated with the orders; while the west or principal front, facing the king's garden, has appropriately richer freestanding Corinthian columns. External staircases on the west and north fronts allow for direct access to the gardens. Inside, the provision of three storeys, unusual in a comparatively modest building, gave Gabriel the freedom to provide services at the most convenient points so that the whole house could run as smoothly as possible. Indeed, Gabriel's original plans for the dining-room and adjacent buffet or servery show two mechanical or flying tables which, having been laid by servants in the basement, would rise into the rooms above, enabling the meal to be eaten with the minimum of servants present. The absence of conventional dining-tables would also allow an uninterrupted vista along the west front, thus explaining the otherwise unusual placing of dining-rooms along the main garden front.

In fact the flying tables were never constructed. Madame de Pompadour died in 1764, when only the walls of her Trianon were completed. Work on the interior continued until 1769 when the king dined in it for the first time. On his death five years later a new phase in the history of the Petit Trianon opened, when Marie-Antoinette, wife of Louis XVI, began to

565 *Opposite* The Breakfast Room (1812) of Sir John Soane's Museum, London, by Soane

566 *Above* The Hameau at Versailles (c.1774–c.1783), by the architect Richard Mique, the gardener Antoine Richard and the painter Hubert Robert

567 Gabriel: West front of the Petit Trianon, Versailles (1761–4)

transform the park into an English-style garden with the help of her gardener, Antoine Richard, and her architect, Richard Mique. Formality was replaced by irregular lakes, rockwork grottoes and undulating lawns, culminating in the celebrated Hameau, or Normandy village, complete with its rustic farm and dairy. It could be claimed that the English garden and the Hameau, though visually very different from Gabriel's Trianon of roughly twenty years before, are intellectually a consequence of a similar demand for apparent naturalness and simplicity (fig. 566).

This demand had been made from the beginning of the century by a succession of architectural theorists – Michel de Frémin in 1702, Jean-Louis de Cordemoy in 1706, Marc-Antoine Laugier in 1753 and 1765 – calling for a return to a primitive classical lucidity in which all unnecessary ornament would be eliminated by making the orders functional and not decorative. Nature and

antiquity were supposed to be the twin models for this ideal building type. Indeed, following hints in Vitruvius, Laugier postulated the primitive hut, fashioned from living trees and branches, as the origin of the classical temple, and even as a model which modern architects ought to keep before them at all times. This combination of reason and romance, of sophistication and rusticity, lies at the heart of eighteenth-century classicism. It found characteristic expression in the ambiguous attitude towards the newly discovered baseless Doric column of the ancient Greeks. Eyes accustomed to the decorative sophistication of the orders as used from Roman times onwards were shocked by the more starkly modelled columns of the Greeks, which archaeologists were excavating and publishing from the mid-eighteenth

568 Gabriel: Place de la Concorde, Paris (1753–75): the north side, with La Madeleine (see p. 442) in the background

century. Greek Doric was invested with an aura of primeval simplicity in tune with the workings of nature herself, a theme poetically expressed in the juxtaposition of Greek Doric columns with artificial rockwork, as, for example, at Claude-Nicolas Ledoux's gateway to the salt works at Arc-et-Senans (1775), and at François-Joseph Bélanger's grotto in the grounds of the villa known as the Folie de St-James, Paris (c.1780).

Apart from the Petit Trianon, Gabriel produced a number of other smaller buildings in the 1750s and 1760s which set an example to his contemporaries of how to combine elegance with severity: these include Madame de Pompadour's Pavillon Français in the grounds of the Petit Trianon and her Ermitage at Fontainebleau, and a group of hunting lodges or pavilions in the forests near Versailles. These are untypical of his commissions for, having succeeded his father as First Architect in 1742, he was extensively employed on vast royal commissions at Versailles, Compiègne and Fontainebleau; and, in Paris, on the Place Louis XV, now Place de la Concorde (1753–75), and the Ecole Militaire (1751–88). The sober monumental style he adopted on these occasions consciously echoed that established in the seventeenth century during the reign of his royal patron's grandfather, Louis XIV, this stylistic continuity thus suggesting continuing political stability.

Soufflot and Ste-Geneviève

The complex variety of Nancy, with its combination of Baroque and Rococo elements in a setting of formality and surprise, did not accord with the ideals of the most thoughtful and influential architects of the mid-

569 *Opposite* The interior of the Panthéon, Paris (Ste-Geneviève), begun 1757 by Soufflot

570 *Above* La Solitude, Stuttgart (1763–7), by P.-L.-P. de la Guêpière

eighteenth century. The most distinguished of those who were giving serious thought to the creation of a new architecture, classical, rational and reformed, was Jacques-Germain Soufflot (1713–80). The fourteenth child of a provincial lawyer, he refused to adopt his father's profession and in 1731 went to study architecture in Rome. Returning after seven years, he

was commissioned to build the Hôtel-Dieu (Hospital) at Lyons in 1740. His austerely monumental design helped bring him to the attention of Madame de Pompadour, who was establishing her ascendancy at Louis XV's court in the later 1740s. Anxious to secure the royal appointment of Superintendent of Buildings for her eighteen-year-old brother, the future Marquis de Marigny, she arranged for Soufflot to accompany him on a tour of Italy in 1749 to complete his architectural education. On this tour Soufflot revisited the French Academy in Rome where, during the 1740s, the young designers who influenced English style of the time had been creating a heady neo-antique style marked by a fantastic profusion of columns, stone domes, obelisks and bas-reliefs.

A group including Soufflot travelled south from Rome in 1750 to visit Paestum, Naples and doubtless also the excavations at Herculaneum. The first measured drawings ever published of the Greek temples at Paestum (p. 29), which must at that time have seemed provocatively primitive, were Dumont's engravings of 1764, based on drawings made by Soufflot fourteen years earlier.

In 1755, on the recommendation of Marigny, the king appointed Soufflot architect of a great new church dedicated to the patron saint of Paris, Ste-Geneviève. It was intended to rival in magnificence St Peter's in Rome and St Paul's in London. Soufflot rose to the occasion with a revolutionary new church, which owed little to those erected in Paris during the previous century but instead gave splendid and lucid expression to the varied intellectual and visual ideals of theorists like Perrault, Cordemoy and Laugier, and of designers trained at the French Academy in Rome like Le Lorrain and Petitot. Its effect depends principally on a combination of immense freestanding columns and long horizontal lintels uninterrupted by the piers or pilasters of

571 Exterior of the Panthéon, Paris (begun 1757), by Soufflot

Renaissance and Baroque churches. Modified in execution from 1757, the church as originally proposed was approached by a massive temple portico consisting of 24 columns taller than those of the Panthéon in Rome. Below was a vast stone-vaulted crypt supported on Greek Doric columns, again simplified a little in execution. The nave walls were to be pierced with numerous windows like those in a Gothic cathedral, allowing light to flood into the nave through the colonnades, while the dome is supported by the slenderest of piers, each wrapped around with three engaged columns (fig. 569).

This lightness of construction and of appearance was a reflection of the appreciation of Gothic architecture which Soufflot shared with the influential theorist Laugier, and which at the time was revolutionary. Contemporaries were quick to applaud Soufflot for his daring and beautiful combination of Greek and Gothic, antique and modern, reason and the picturesque. The architect Brébion explained that Soufflot's aim was 'to reunite in one of the most beautiful forms, the lightness of construction of Gothic buildings with the purity and magnificence of Greek architecture'. It is true, however, that the church as we have it fails fully to translate Soufflot's beautiful idea into permanent structural reality: cracks in the masonry soon appeared, so that the crossing piers were made more massive in 1806, while the side windows had been blocked in on the advice of the influential scholar and author, A.-C. Quatremère de Quincy, in 1791.

In the same year the building was secularized by the Revolutionary government and turned into the Panthéon – a monument in which national heroes are buried – which it remains to this day. This process was undoubtedly aided by its templar form: indeed, in its bold originality, its comprehensive scale, and its overthrow of traditional ecclesiastical forms in favour of those of the antique temple, it can be seen as a parallel to the contemporary *Encyclopédie, ou Dictionnaire raisonné des sciences, des arts et des métiers* (1751–77) by J. Diderot and J. d'Alembert. This, the first encyclopedia, was an

572 Trouard: Interior of St Symphorien, Versailles (1767–70)

attempt to summarize the knowledge of the day in the light of a rational explanation of the universe and a sceptical attitude to religion.

Whereas in eighteenth-century England the country house was the building type in which new ideas were worked out, in France church design still remained a natural focus of experiment. In the decade following the construction of Ste-Geneviève three new churches brought together on a smaller scale many of the rationalist ideals of Perrault, Laugier and Soufflot. Designed by architects who had been trained at the French Academy in Rome, they are St Louis at St Germain-en-Laye (designed 1764, built 1766–87 and 1823–4) by N.-M. Potain (1713–96); St Symphorien at Versailles (1767–70) by L.-F. Trouard (1729–94); and St Philippe du Roule, Paris (designed 1768, built

573 Massachusetts State House, Boston (1795–8), by Bulfinch

1772–84) by J.-F.-T. Chalgrin (1739–1811). These basilican churches are roofed with coffered barrel-vaults resting on the unbroken entablatures of rows of freestanding columns which, at St Symphorien, have a distinctly Greek Doric flavour. Their appeal is more intellectual than visual, for they strike the visitor primarily as grave demonstrations in stone of an architecture of load-bearing parts from which surface charm has been ruthlessly eliminated.

Peyre and de Wailly

After Soufflot, Marie-Joseph Peyre (1730–85) was one of the architects who exercised most influence on the course of eighteenth-century classicism. In 1753–6 he studied at the French Academy in Rome, where he made surveys of the most important archaeological sites such as the Baths of Diocletian and Caracalla and Hadrian's Villa at Tivoli. His aim of promoting a new monumental architecture inspired by these antique prototypes was demonstrated in his *Oeuvres d'architecture* ('Works of architecture', 1765) which contained his designs for academies, palaces and cathedrals with vast symmetrical colonnades, domes and porticoes. These were characterized by a megalomaniac scale and a stony impracticality which exercised a somewhat baleful influence on later projects by Boullée, Ledoux and Durand. Though this was the first time such projects had been published, the style had been established in the opening years of the century at the Accademia di San Luca in Rome in the competition entries of architects such as Filippo Juvarra, Carlo Marchionni, and Carlo Stefano Fontana, nephew of Carlo Fontana.

Apart from the Théâtre de l'Odéon, Paris (1767–82), with its forbidding façade, Peyre built little of consequence. However, his remarkable unexecuted design of 1763 for a palace for the Prince de Condé, a cousin of Louis XV, inspired the Hôtel de Salm, built in the early 1780s by Pierre Rousseau (1751–1810) for Prince Frederik of Salm-Kyrberg. Frederik was one of the many German princes who loved French style and culture and who, unusually in his case, chose to live in Paris rather than to import French architects to his own country. He paid doubly for his enthusiasm, since he was not only ruined financially by the extravagance of the Hôtel de Salm, but was also eventually guillotined.

The scant evidence available to Peyre about the domestic architecture of the ancient Romans led him to incorporate in his Condé palace features proper to both the public and sacred architecture of the antique world. The same problem had confronted James Paine and Robert Adam a year or so before at Kedleston, where they furnished a modern house with a hall inspired by the Temple of Mars, a saloon by the Pantheon and a garden front by the Arch of Constantine. Peyre thus invested the traditional Parisian hôtel or town house, grouped round a courtyard, with the dignity and splendour of ancient Roman public architecture. The courtyard was separated from the street by an open colonnade punctuated in the centre by a triumphal arch, while the entrance portico of the house itself led directly into a solemn circular hall, reminiscent of a temple but enriched with a ring of freestanding columns screening the staircase.

In incorporating some of these features into the Hôtel de Salm Rousseau could look for inspiration to another building indebted to Peyre, the School of Surgery in Paris (1769–75), by Jacques Gondoin (1737–1818). Hailed as a masterpiece of classicism by many contemporaries, this striking building was described by Peyre as a 'monument [which] announced

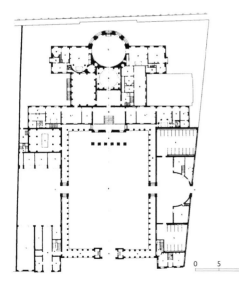

574 *Above* Entrance arch and colonnade of the Hôtel de Salm, Paris (1783), by Rousseau

575 *Left* Plan of the Hôtel de Salm, by Rousseau

COUPE *prise sur les deux Sens du principal Corps de Logis*

ÉLÉVATION

PLAN D'UN BÂTIMENT QUI CONTIENDROIT LES ACADÉMIES,
ET TOUT CE QUI EST NÉCESSAIRE À L'ÉDUCATION
de la Jeuneße.

576, 577 *Top and above* Section, elevation and plan of academies
from Peyre's *Oeuvres d'architecture* (1765)

a temple more than any of our churches'. Certainly it lent eloquent support to the growing demand of surgeons for recognition as an independent professional body. The imposing Ionic colonnade along its street façade has a no-nonsense look with its unbroken horizontal entablature and its daring omission of conventional mouldings from the frieze. The celebrated anatomy theatre which lies directly behind the main portico combines the semi-circular plan of the antique theatre with the coffered top-lit dome of the Pantheon. This arresting stroke of architectural imagination produced an interior which was widely imitated in the design of parliamentary debating chambers in the nineteenth century.

Another building as admired as the School of Surgery was the theatre built in 1772–80 by Victor Louis (1731–c. 1807) in the rich and expanding town of Bordeaux. This was only the second freestanding theatre built in France, for theatres on this scale were an eighteenth-century innovation, the first being Soufflot's at Lyons of 1754 (since rebuilt). Louis's templar exterior, with its magnificent colonnade of twelve Corinthian columns extending the whole length of the entrance front, prepares the visitor for the splendour of the staircase hall within. Constructed of stone, always regarded as the noblest building material, this great square hall with its open colonnaded first floor and its masonry umbrella vault is a neo-classical variation on

578 *Above* Engraving of the anatomy theatre in the School of Surgery, Paris (1769–75), by Gondoin. The opening in the dome is today filled in.

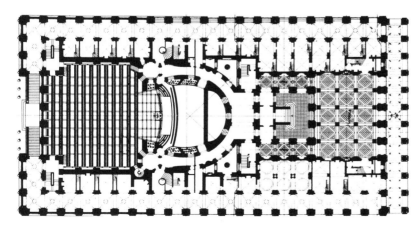

579 Plan of the Grand Theatre, Bordeaux

the tradition of Renaissance and Baroque stone staircases in sixteenth- and seventeenth-century France. What was new in theatre design was Louis's striking emphasis on the staircase and circulation spaces so as to create a dramatic spectacle even before the auditorium was reached. Here the prosperous citizens of Bordeaux could promenade in the kind of magnificent setting previously associated with the courts of kings and princes. Louis's achievement influenced such rich nineteenth-century staircases as that by George Basevi, Charles Robert Cockerell and Edward Middleton Barry at the Fitzwilliam Museum, Cambridge (1834–75), and by Charles Garnier at the Paris Opera (1861–75).

Marie-Joseph Peyre and Charles de Wailly (1730–1798) had expressed similar ideas to Louis's in the staircase and colonnaded foyer of their Théâtre Français (later de l'Odéon, and now de France), designed in 1767–70, built in 1779–82 and since partly remodelled. De Wailly introduced a more poetic note than was present in the sterner prose of architects like his partner Peyre or like Gondoin. Interested in the fruits of recent archaeological research, as can be seen in his Greek Revival columns at the Hôtel de Voyer (c.1760), he was yet alive to Baroque drama, as in his sumptuous saloon at the Palazzo Spinola (now Campanella), Genoa (1772–3), with its Piranesian assembly of columns, vaulted arches and mirrors. The two elements come together in his château at Montmusard near Dijon, built in 1764–72 for the Marquis de la Marche, traveller, man of letters and First President of the Burgundy Parlement.

Montmusard was one of the most picturesquely classical buildings in France, for projecting from its entrance front was an open semicircular colonnade for which it is hard to think of any direct precedent. In fact this stunning colonnade was simply the completion of a circular open court within the château proper. De Wailly described this Doric court as a 'Temple of Apollo' and the circular room to which it led as the 'Saloon of the Muses', with the result that the building has been claimed as the first secular building in eighteenth-

580 Louis: The staircase of the theatre at Bordeaux (1772–80)

century France to be dedicated as a temple. Even Soufflot's great Parisian church was known as the 'Temple de Ste-Geneviève' while Gondoin's School of Surgery had also been likened to a temple.

The kind of intricacy and surprise characteristic of Montmusard was echoed in the group of five houses planned by de Wailly in the rue de la Pépinière (now de Boétie), Paris, in 1776–9. Only two of these were completed, one for himself and one for the sculptor Augustin Pajou, and both are now demolished. It is a measure of the widening of eighteenth-century patronage that an architect could have amassed a sufficient fortune to build himself a town palace on a scale previously associated with noblemen and financiers. Visitors to de Wailly's house entered by

581 *Above* Exterior of de Wailly's Château at Montmusard, near Dijon (1764–72; now partly demolished), from a painting by J. B. Lallemand

582 *Below* Section of de Wailly's own house in the Rue de la Pépinière (now de Boétie), Paris (1776–9)

Plan général des trois maisons. N°1.

Échelle à

Une partie de la face de la Maison du côté du jardin. N°2

carriage into a circular vestibule with a fountain and a ring of Greek Doric columns, from which a top-lit circular staircase led to the principal apartments strung out on the first floor between a terrace and a winter garden. Another stair led up to a belvedere perched at the very top of the house, commanding views over Paris and the surrounding countryside. Thus by c.1770 the traditional Parisian house had been revolutionized, and de Wailly with his essentially pictorial imagination was able to breathe new life into the repertoire of motifs derived from the baths and villas of ancient Rome. The closest parallel to his house is the Hôtel de Thélusson of 1778–83 by Ledoux, a dramatic pile approached through an apparently half-submerged Roman arch.

Ledoux and the Picturesque

The ingenuity, surprise and near-asymmetry which characterize de Wailly's house and the Hôtel de Thélusson were also some of the leading qualities of the Picturesque movement, especially as expressed in garden design. Though this was essentially an English movement, the way had been prepared for it in France by the influential writings of the philosopher Jean-Jacques Rousseau (1712–78), for example his two volumes of *Discours* published in 1750 and 1754. Arguing that man was originally free, virtuous and happy but had been corrupted by society and city life, Rousseau made a lyrical and sentimental plea for man to return to a simple life in harmony with nature. One of the first visual expressions of this attitude was the celebrated garden at Ermenonville, near Paris. With its numerous Picturesque garden buildings, this was laid out from the 1760s by the Marquis de Girardin, a friend of Rousseau who lived at Ermenonville and was buried on an island in the lake. Girardin was assisted by J.-M. Morel and the painter Hubert Robert, who specialized in depicting the romantic aspect of ruined buildings. In 1777 Girardin published *De la composition des paysages* ('On the composition of landscapes') in which, inspired by Rousseau, he emphasized the power of landscape to appeal to the senses and the soul. The implications of this

583 Ledoux: Hôtel de Thélusson, Paris (1778–83)

new approach to the associational mingling of architecture and landscape were enshrined in a book published by Nicolas Le Camus de Mézières in 1780 under the title *Le génie de l'architecture; ou, l'analogie de cet art avec nos sensations* ('The spirit of architecture or the analogy of that art with our feelings').

Le Camus's adoption of expressive forms so as to evoke sentiments appropriate to the particular character of a building was echoed in the visionary schemes of Etienne-Louis Boullée (1728–99) in the 1780s and 1790s. The megalomaniac scale of his libraries, museums, tombs, pyramids and gate towers, bathed in strange lights and shadows, celebrated a romantic belief in the power of elementary geometrical shapes – cube, cylinder, pyramid and, especially, sphere – to move the soul. The architect had now become a visionary who could create a new world, a priest who could change men's hearts. It was a dangerous role for an architect to adopt; indeed, Boullée never attempted it in practice. The only eighteenth-century architect who did was the more practical and more ambitious Claude-Nicolas Ledoux (1735–1806).

The leading French architect in the years immediately before the Revolution of 1789, Ledoux operated on a larger canvas than any of the architects we

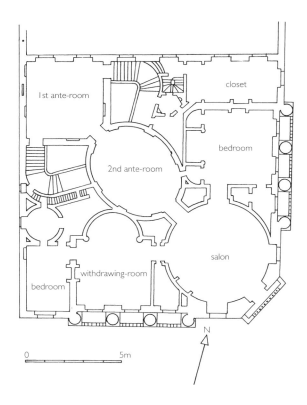

584 Ledoux: Plan of the first floor of the Hôtel de Montmorency, Paris (1769)

585 Boullée: Design for a monument to Newton (c.1784)

have so far investigated in this chapter. Apart from designing numerous town houses of the utmost elegance and a small number of châteaux, he was responsible for a celebrated theatre at Besançon, the saltworks at Arc-et-Senans, the prison at Aix, the town gates or toll houses of Paris, and a visionary project for an ideal town at Chaux. Ledoux differed from most of his architect contemporaries in three important respects: he was not born in Paris; he did not receive his professional training at the French Academy in Rome, though he did compete unsuccessfully for the Prix de Rome; and he never travelled to Rome or Italy. It is tempting to relate these facts to his architectural originality, to his dependence on the evocations of ancient Rome in Piranesi's engravings, and to his sensitivity to nature.

One of the earliest of Ledoux's comparatively few surviving buildings is the Hôtel d'Hallwyl, Paris (1766–7), with Tuscan colonnades in the garden forming a space like a Roman atrium. By a Picturesque trick this colonnade was to have been continued in a mural painted on a wall in the street behind the hôtel. Ledoux's Hôtel de Montmorency (1769), now demolished, was a brilliant treatment of a corner site with planning of Rococo complexity and ingenuity behind sober neo-classical façades. With their engaged Ionic columns the two main façades are identical, apparently in recognition of the equal claims to Montmorency lineage of the Prince and Princesse de Montmorency, whose separate suites of rooms are thus given architectural expression.

Nearby Ledoux built an enchanting one-storeyed house in 1773–6 for the celebrated dancer Marie-Madeleine Guimard. It was paid for by two of her lovers. The block on the street contained a small theatre, but the main body of the house across the courtyard was known as the Temple of Terpsichore, the Muse of Dancing. Its emphatically neo-antique entrance front boasted a row of Ionic columns screening an apsed and coffered niche: a combination of elements from the Roman baths and from the Temple of Venus and Rome, which had been exploited by William Kent in his Temple of Venus at Stowe as early as 1731. Ledoux is known to have travelled in England, where he may have visited Stowe or seen similar screens of columns in interiors by

586 Engraving of entrance front of the Hôtel Guimard, Paris (1773–6), by Ledoux

Robert Adam. In a more solemn mood Ledoux built the theatre at Besançon (1775–84). In its strikingly original interior he abandoned the conventional tiers of boxes in favour of an arrangement of semicircular banks of seats recalling the classical amphitheatre. Above these the auditorium was encircled by a colonnade of unfluted Greek Doric columns, probably the most extensive use of that order in any French building.

Not far from Besançon Ledoux built the saltworks of Arc-et-Senans in 1775–9 on a D-shaped plan, with a Doric gateway sheltering a primitive grotto in the centre

of the curved range, and the fantastically rusticated house of the director in the centre of the straight side. The power and strength of these buildings, which recall the Mannerist style of Giulio Romano, may seem excessive for their function. However, at a time when the death penalty was the reward for illicit distillation of salt, and the evasion of the salt tax was leading to extensive smuggling and robbery, the apparently defensible quality of Ledoux's buildings may have had some poetic justification.

The same aggressive mood marks the fifty *barrières* or customs buildings erected from his designs in 1784–7 as part of a new wall encircling the whole of Paris, including the new areas which had grown up during the eighteenth century. The commission came from the Ferme Générale, the customs service, as a means of suppressing the widespread smuggling by which customs duties were being avoided. The erection of these *barrières* naturally caused tremendous alarm amongst the Parisian population. Indeed, they were physically attacked during the Revolution as a symbol of the *ancien régime*, even though their powerfully original style has been described in the twentieth century as 'Revolutionary'. It is tragic

587 Director's house at the saltworks of Arc-et-Senans, near Besançon (1775–9), by Ledoux

588 Ledoux: The Barrière de la Villette, Paris (1784–7)

589 Engraving of a perspective view of Ledoux's town of Chaux (designed from c.1780; published 1804)

that only four of these sculptural masterpieces survive today – the barrières de la Villette, d'Orléans, du Trône and de Monceau – but to visit any one of them is to be immediately aware of the daunting grandeur of Ledoux's architectural imagination. The apparent lack of superfluous ornament and the exaggerated scale of all the parts have made observers aware of the transience of their own opinions. In 1784 the colourful English author and collector, William Beckford, drew attention to these 'custom-house palaces . . . which from their massive, sepulchral character look more like the entrances of a necropolis, a city of the dead, than of a [living] city. While they found few imitators in France, their rhetorical severity inspired such German architects

as Gilly and Weinbrenner to create a new phase in German architecture (pp. 415, 482).

The last project of Ledoux which it remains for us to investigate is his ideal town of Chaux. Stylistically a development from the abstract geometry of his *barrières*, the scheme was physically a visionary extension of his saltworks at Arc-et-Senans. He duplicated the semicircular plan of the saltworks so as to form a circular centre surrounded by a tree-lined boulevard, beyond which was an extraordinary series of public buildings extending far into the wooded countryside. These buildings, which did not include a hospital, theatre, market house or museum, are as unprecedented in function as they are original in form. They include the Pacifère, a kind of idealized law court in which quarrels would be settled amicably; the Oikéma or Temple of Love, a house of sexual instruction with a plan resembling an erect phallus; the Cenobium or Asylum of Happiness, a commune for sixteen families; the House of Education; the Panarethéon or Temple of Virtue; the Temple of Memory; the church, a vast windowless structure apparently destined for rites more secretive than those of Christianity; and the cemetery, an awe-inspiring catacomb in the form of an immense sphere. More modest structures were treated in a similarly symbolical way: the house of the charcoal burners was a dome resting on tree-trunks; the house of those who made hoops for barrels was a cube inscribed with concentric circles; while the even more bizarre house for the water authority was an open cylinder like a gigantic water-pipe, through the centre of which the river Loue rushed in a waterfall.

Plainly Ledoux can never have expected architecture of this kind to be built. It is essentially an allegory, presenting in compelling visual form some of the social, philosophical and moral reflections which, inspired by the writings of Rousseau, had been current in France from the mid-century. Ledoux's designs, and the sentimentally rhetorical text with which he accompanied them, constitute a poetical vision in which architecture is seen as an instrument of egalitarian social reform: a novel role for architecture which it was scarcely capable of sustaining.

Despite his Rousseauesque language, Ledoux himself was not a political revolutionary. Indeed, he was imprisoned as a royalist in 1793–4 on the slender grounds of his employment by the aristocracy, his ownership of real estate, and his *barrières*, which were detested by the people. It was during his period of imprisonment that he completed his Utopian scheme for Chaux which he presented to the world in 1804, two years before his death, in a sumptuous publication, called *L'Architecture considérée sous le rapport de l'art, des moeurs et de la législation* ('Architecture considered in respect of art, morals and law'). This he dedicated not to some visionary thinker but to Tsar Alexander I, autocrat and architectural patron, then still in alliance with Napoleon.

The classical tradition elsewhere in Europe

Italy

The presence of Piranesi and Winckelmann in Rome had, as we have seen, helped to make the city once more a focus for architectural and intellectual activity. Thereafter its importance declined, though we should note that Winckelmann's successor as Keeper of Antiquities at the Vatican, the archaeologist Giovanni Battista Visconti, initiated the transformation of a large part of the Vatican into the celebrated institution known as the Museo Pio-Clementino. The architects Michelangelo Simonetti (1724–81) and Pietro Camporese (1726–81) provided the Pantheon-like Sala Rotonda, the Sala delle Muse, the Sala a Croce Greca and a magnificent tunnel-vaulted coffered staircase. Their style was continued further by Raffaello Stern (1774–1820), who added the imposing top-lit gallery known as the Braccio Nuovo in 1817–22. Not surprisingly, these prestigious interiors were destined to exercise wide influence throughout Europe and beyond.

Outside Rome in other Italian centres enthusiasm for all things French resulted in Ennemond-Alexandre Petitot (1727–1801), a pupil of Soufflot and a former *pensionnaire* at the French Academy in Rome, being called as architect to the grand-ducal court at Parma in 1753. This was on the recommendation of the Comte de Caylus, the influential antiquarian, collector, and author of *Recueil d'antiquités égyptiennes, étrusques et romaines* ('Collection of Egyptian, Etruscan and Roman Antiquities', 7 vols., 1752–67). Petitot's executed works are less extensive than his influence on the architectural development of Lombardy through his publications and through the Academy he founded in 1757. In Sicily a similar influence was exerted by Léon Dufourny (1754–1818), a pupil of Le Roy and Peyre, who finally brought Sicilian Baroque to an end during his six-year stay in the island from 1787.

Eighteenth-century Venice saw the development of a different architectural tradition, largely centred on an unadventurous Palladian revival. An early monument in this tradition is SS. Simeone e Giuda (1718–38) by Giovanni Scalfarotto (c.1690–1764), a Pantheon-inspired church which was followed by a more 'correct' version of the antique source in the form of S. Maria Maddalena, a church designed in 1748 and built in the 1760s by Scalfarotto's nephew and pupil, Tommaso Temanza (1705–81). Temanza was a friend of Françesco Milizia (1725–98), who was important as an early architectural historian, publishing in 1768 his *Le Vite de'piu celebri architetti d'ogni nazione e d'ogni tempo* ('Lives of the most celebrated architects of all nations and periods'). Milizia's rationalist and neo-classical bias was derived from the revolutionary Venetian theorist Carlo Lodoli (1690–1761), whose views were recorded by his two followers, Count Algarotti (1712–64) and Andrea Memmo (1729–93). Inspired by hints in the writings of Perrault and Cordemoy, Lodoli developed a grimly functional approach to architecture which implicitly rejected the classical vocabulary as largely ornamental. This idea was taken up by Laugier in the 1750s, and more destructively by Durand around 1800.

The architectural scene in Milan, under Austrian rule, was controlled by Giuseppe Piermarini (1734–1808), who had worked for Vanvitelli at Rome and Caserta in 1750–68. He worked extensively in a somewhat arid neo-Palladian style, as in his Palazzo Reale (1769–78) and Scala Theatre (1776–78). Piermarini's work was criticized by Milizia, who may have found more to his taste the Palazzo Serbelloni in Milan, designed in 1775 and built in 1779–94 by Simone

590 Simonetti and Camporese: The Sala delle Muse, the Museo Pio-Clementino, Vatican (1773–80)

591 Entrance to the Palazzo Serbelloni, Milan (1775–94), by Cantoni

Cantoni (1739–1818). The unusual central three bays of this palace boast freestanding Ionic columns behind which runs a continuous figured frieze, striking a Greek note in a composition inspired by the Parisian town houses of Bélanger. Piermarini's pupils, Luigi Canonica (1764–1844) and Leopoldo Pollack (1751–1806), worked in a livelier style mingling elements from Piermarini's Palladianism and contemporary French architecture. Pollack surrounded his principal work, the Villa Reale-Belgioioso (1790–3) in Milan, with an elaborate Picturesque garden. This was one of the first of its kind in Italy, though it had been preceded by the remodelling of the Baroque gardens of the Villa Borghese in Rome for Prince Marcantonio Borghese. Here in

1782–1802 Antonio Asprucci (1723–1808) and his son Mario (1764–1804), with the help of a Scottish landscape painter, Jacob More, added temples, pools and ruins.

Germany

Until 1806 Germany consisted of over 300 territories or principalities, all of which owed nominal allegiance to the Holy Roman Emperor: since the fourteenth century this had been the Habsburg ruler of the Austrian Duchies as well as King of Bohemia and of Hungary. The lack of a single cultural or political centre such as London or Paris means that the story of German architecture in this period lacks coherence. Instead there are wholly unconnected buildings dependent on individual patrons, often designed by imported French architects, and exercising virtually no influence.

Central and southern Germany until the mid-eighteenth century and later was dominated by the Asam brothers, Neumann, Fischer and Zimmermann, who produced a magnificent late efflorescence of the Baroque style long after it had been abandoned in other parts of Europe. Classical ideals arrived in northern Germany at

592 Knobelsdorff: German State Opera House (1741–3) and St Hedwig's church (1747–73) in the Opernplatz (originally Forum Fridericianum), Berlin

593 Erdmannsdorff: Interior of the Villa Hamilton at Schloss Wörlitz, near Dessau (c.1790)

Berlin and Potsdam towards the mid-century as a result of the outward-looking policies as well as of the admiration for France and England of Frederick the Great, King of Prussia (1712–86). In 1740 Frederick gave his friend, the architect Georg von Knobelsdorff (1699–1753), the commission for designing the Berlin opera-house, intended to form one side of a new Forum Fridericianum, a kind of cultural *place royale*. Knobelsdorff's neo-Palladian opera-house was inspired by buildings like Colen Campbell's Wanstead (c.1714–20), illustrated in *Vitruvius Britannicus*, a copy of which Frederick owned. As a result of Frederick's interest in English design, his friend, the Italian theorist Count Francesco Algarotti (1712–62), wrote a letter to Lord Burlington in 1751 in which, having described him as 'the restorer of true architecture in this century', he asked him to send drawings of his buildings to Frederick.

In 1747–8 Knobelsdorff designed the Catholic church of St Hedwig in Berlin, a miniature version of the Pantheon. Similarly neo-antique designs for the church were also made at this time by the gifted French architect Jean-Laurent Le Geay (c.1710–c.1786), who

had been a *pensionnaire* at the French Academy in Rome in 1737–42. In 1756 Frederick appointed him as royal architect, in which capacity he designed the Communs at Potsdam in 1763. The Communs is a vast service wing in front of the Neues Palais in the form of a semicircular colonnade flanked by a pair of domed and porticoed pavilions. It is an astonishing realization of the ideals of the Franco-Italian classicism of the 1740s, which had already arrived in Germany in Knobelsdorff's colonnade in front of Schloss Sans Souci at Potsdam of 1745.

Frederick the Great's French and English enthusiasms were shared by Prince Franz von Anhalt-Dessau (1740–1817), whose interest in the ideals of the French Enlightenment led him to lay out an English landscaped park at Wörlitz near Dessau of the kind admired in France as an expression of 'liberty'. Indeed, in 1782 the park was provided with a re-creation of the poplar-planted island containing the tomb of Rousseau in the landscaped garden of Ermenonville, near Paris. The lake-landscape at Wörlitz has at its heart the neo-Palladian country house designed in 1769 by Friedrich Wilhelm von Erdmannsdorff (1736–1800) in a style recalling Chambers's Duddingston (p. 383). In 1765–66 Prince Franz and his architect travelled together in Italy where they met Clérisseau, Winckelmann and Sir William Hamilton, then forming his influential collection of Greek painted vases. Erdmannsdorff subsequently built at Wörlitz an extraordinary re-creation of the Villa Hamilton near Naples, with exquisite painted and stuccoed interiors and neo-Greek furniture. Nearby was a miniature Vesuvius, a man-made cone of rocks about 80 feet (24m) high which could be made to belch forth smoke. Thus the park at Wörlitz became a series of souvenirs of the Grand Tour, rather as Hadrian's Villa at Tivoli (p. 73) contained stylistic echoes of a wide range of buildings which Hadrian had admired in different parts of Greece, Italy and Egypt.

One of the loveliest gardens in Germany after Wörlitz is Schwetzingen, near Mannheim, where a Baroque layout was enhanced with neo-classical garden buildings in 1761–95 by Nicolas de Pigage (1723–96) for Karl Theodor, Elector Palatine from 1742 and Elector of Bavaria 1778–99. Pigage, born in Lunéville, Lorraine, and trained by J.-F. Blondel in Paris, built the Bath House at Schwetzingen, a dazzlingly elegant Louis XVI *pavillon* from which a trellis-work passageway leads enticingly to a circular aviary surrounded by fountains. The gardens also contain a very large mosque designed by Pigage. Like Chambers's at Kew, which inspired it, it is an ornamental and evocative feature, not intended for use as a real mosque.

In the 1760s Philippe de la Guêpière (c.1715–73), another French pupil of Blondel, provided two handsome *pavillons* for the Duke of Württemberg: Solitude (fig. 570), on a hill near Stuttgart, and Monrepos, near Schloss Ludwigsburg. The French architect Pierre-Michel d'Ixnard (1723–95) was responsible for introducing French neo-classical ideals into south-west Germany. His masterpiece is the Benedictine monastery of St Blasien (1768–83) in the Black Forest, dominated by the domed abbey church which is inspired distantly by the Pantheon. Ixnard was also responsible for the electoral palace at Koblenz, designed in 1777 for the Elector of Trier as virtually the last of the German princely palaces on this scale. Executed in modified form in 1780–92 by A.-F. Peyre, brother of the more famous M.-J. Peyre, its uneventful 39-bay-long façade is a daunting reminder of the emptiness and megalomania which often underlie the visionary schemes of French neo-classical architects.

After Erdmannsdorff's Schloss Wörlitz and Ixnard's St Blasien, one of the boldest statements of neo-classical ideals in eighteenth-century Germany was the Museum Fridericianum at Kassel, built by Simon-Louis du Ry (1726–99) in 1769–79. The du Ry family, who had left France as Huguenot refugees, were court architects to the Landgraves of Hesse-Kassel from 1685 to 1799. Simon-Louis, trained by Blondel in Paris, designed the Museum Fridericianum for Landgrave Friedrich II to form one side of a new square, the Friedrichsplatz. Often regarded as the first independent museum building, it is another neo-Palladian exercise inspired by

594 Mosque in the gardens at Schwetzingen, near Mannheim (1778–95), by Pigage

Campbell's Wanstead. In search of something more architecturally exciting, the Landgrave commissioned designs from Ledoux in 1775 for a town palace at Kassel and from Charles de Wailly a decade later for a new palace at Wilhelmshöhe, about six miles from Kassel. Neither was executed and the large chilly palace built at Wilhelmshöhe in 1786–92 from designs by du Ry and his pupil Heinrich Jussow (1754–1825) followed English Palladian precedent. What is especially memorable at Wilhelmshöhe is the Baroque park with its numerous buildings culminating in the Hercules tower (1701–18), designed by the Italian architect Giovanni Guerniero on a hill-top site above a giant cascade. Just as exciting is the extensive mock Gothic castle known as Löwenburg (Lion Fort), designed in 1790 by Jussow and executed in 1793–1802 as a realization of Robert Adam's castle designs, which Jussow may have seen on his visit to England in the 1780s. Löwenburg was the extravagant child of Landgrave Wilhelm IX's absorption with medieval chivalry.

A move to reject the French taste we have seen so far in this chapter was made by Frederick the Great's

595 *Above* Jussow: The mock Gothic castle of Löwenburg at Schloss Wilhelmshöhe, near Kassel (designed 1790; built 1793–1802)

596 *Right* The Brandenburg Gate, Berlin (1789–94), by Langhans

successor as King of Prussia, Friedrich Wilhelm II, who reigned from 1787 to 1797. In 1788 he summoned to work for him in Berlin three German-born architects, Erdmannsdorff from Dessau, Langhans from Breslau (now Wrocław) and David Gilly from Stettin (now Szczecin). The first product of this attempt to make Berlin a German cultural centre was the Brandenburg Gate, built by Carl Gotthard Langhans (1732–1808) in 1789–94 at the western entrance to the city. A pioneering monument of the Greek Revival inspired by the Propylaea on the Athenian Acropolis, the Brandenburg Gate was widely admired at the time as a tangible expression in the modern world of the ennobling moral force of ancient Greek culture as eulogized by Winckelmann. This attitude to the Doric style was encouraged by Le Camus de Mézières' *Le génie de l'architecture*, translated into German in 1789, with its claim that both function and sentiment can be expressed through a proper choice of form.

Beliefs such as these, combined with a strong dose of incipient Prussian nationalism, found expression in

1796 in the most important of the several competitions for a monument to Frederick the Great. Of the designs submitted by the six architects who entered the competition of 1796, Langhans, Erdmannsdorff, Hirt, Haun, Gentz and Friedrich Gilly (1772–1800), those by Gilly were incomparably the finest. His image of a solemn Greek Doric temple set on a high podium in a sacred precinct, approached through a gateway recalling one of Ledoux's *barrières*, fired the imagination of a generation of young architects, including the leaders of German architecture in the first half of the nineteenth century, Karl Friedrich Schinkel and Leo von Klenze.

Captivatingly presented in a watercolour perspective inspired by English Picturesque precedent, the monument was also a stern symbol of Prussian order designed in a severe stripped style similar to some of the effects aimed at by Dance and Soane.

One of the key monuments in this Franco-Prussian style was the Berlin Mint (1798–1800; dem. 1886), designed by Gilly's brother-in-law, Heinrich Gentz (1766–1811). Its uncompromising cubic forms, enlivened by a neo-Greek figured frieze designed by Gilly, are the perfect expression of Hirt's belief in the elevated tone and constructional completeness of Greek Doric as expressed in his *Die Baukunst den Grundsätzen der Alten* ('Architecture according to the principles of the ancients', Berlin 1809).

Heinrich Gentz was one of a group of architects brought to the grand-ducal capital of Weimar by Johann Wolfgang von Goethe (1749–1832), who was helping to make the town one of the most remarkable cultural centres of its day in Germany. Having first championed Gothic as a Germanic style akin to the forces of nature in his *Von deutscher Baukunst* ('On German Architecture', 1773), Goethe later sang the praises of Greek Doric following his visit to Sicily and Paestum in 1787. Goethe called for a return to first sources in art, and had a poetic vision of the German soul as expressed spiritually in the twin poles of Greek and Gothic. The Schloss or palace at Weimar was remodelled under Goethe's guidance from 1789 onwards as a statement of neo-classical ideals by Gentz, Nicolaus Friedrich von Thouret (1767–1845) and Johann August Arens (1757–1806). Thouret and Arens were both trained in Paris, the latter by de Wailly. The most striking interior in the Schloss is Gentz's superb Greek Doric staircase (1800–3), while in the park Arens had built the so-called Roman House in 1791–7 as a place of retirement for the Grand Duke Karl August of Saxe-Weimar (1757–1828). Despite its name this was an original exercise in a Greek Doric style, containing a basement entrance or crypto-porticus with stumpy Paestum Doric columns supporting a shallow segmental arch. Derived from Ledoux, this powerful primitivism was an importance influence on Friedrich Gilly, who sketched it on a visit to Weimar in 1798.

Poland

Stanisław August Poniatowski (reigned 1764–95), the last king of Poland before its partition in 1795, summoned numerous French and Italian painters and sculptors to his court and was responsible for bringing the architecture of the French Enlightenment to his country. It was he who commissioned the celebrated views of Warsaw by Bellotto and he who, on a visit to Paris in 1754, met the brilliant young architect Victor Louis and brought him back to Warsaw as architect in 1765. Louis made a set of magnificent designs for remodelling the royal castle in Warsaw in a style dependent on Piranesi and Peyre which anticipated that of his masterpiece, the theatre at Bordeaux (p. 404). Though unexecuted, they influenced a generation of architects in Poland, including the Italian-born Dominik Merlini (1731–97), court architect from 1773, and Jan Chrystian Kamsetzer (1753–95), who together provided the royal castle in Warsaw with a series of superb Louis-Seize-style interiors in 1776–85. The lower part of the extensive park of the royal castle at Ujazdów in the suburbs of Warsaw was formerly a zoo but was remodelled as a Picturesque garden from 1774 with numerous garden buildings and pavilions. Among these are Merlini's Myślewicki Palace (1775–7) and his more successful Łazienki Palace (1775–93), the king's lakeside summer palace. A seventeenth-century bath-house in origin, the Łazienki Palace was enlarged for Stanisław August in several stages from 1775 to 1793. Extended in 1788 by Kamsetzer, who provided the magnificent two-storeyed ballroom, it is a festive building with open colonnades which owes something to Gabriel and Adam. Elsewhere in the Łazienki Park Kamsetzer provided a semi-circular neo-antique theatre in 1790–1. More Palladian than the Łazienki Palace is Merlini's Królikarnia (1782–6), Warsaw, a house dominated by an Ionic portico and a domed rotunda. The architect Stanisław Zawadzki (1743–1806) produced a similar centrally-planned composition in his neo-Palladian house at Lubostrón (1795–1800), while his house at Śmiełów (1797) has a central block with pavilions linked by quadrants.

599 Merlini: South façade of Łazienki Palace, Ujazdów, near Warsaw (1775–93)

The adoption of neo-classical ideals in church design began with the Lutheran church at Warsaw (1777–81) by Szymon Bogumil Zug (1735–1807), who was born in Dresden and arrived in Warsaw in 1762. Like the Catholic church of St Hedwig in Berlin, the Lutheran church in Warsaw is distantly inspired by the Pantheon, though the columns of its emphatic tetrastyle portico are in a version of Greek Doric. Even more impressive is the cathedral at Wilno (Vilnius, now the capital of Lithuania), remodelled in 1777–1801 from designs by Wawrzyniec Gucewicz (1753–98), who had been trained in Rome and Paris. With its hexastyle Doric portico on the west front, its colonnaded side façades, and its reredos behind the high altar treated like an antique temple front, it is a perfect example of neo-classical stylophily. In the 1780s Gucewicz remodelled the town hall at Wilno and Bishop Massalski's palace, both in a similarly uncompromising neo-antique manner.

Poland took enthusiastically to the *jardin anglais*, which arrived around 1770 as a result of the influence of Sir William Chambers and of visits to England by Polish patrons. The first garden was probably that at Powazki, laid out just north of Warsaw for Princess

Izabella Czartoryska (1746–1835), who visited England three times, in 1768, 1772–4 and 1789–91. Powazki was the work of S. B. Zug and the French painter Jean Pierre Norblin – the princess's husband had brought the latter to Poland, where he stayed for thirty years. Zug contributed a chapter describing Polish gardens to Hirschfeld's influential *Theorie der Gartenkunst* ('Theory of the art of gardening', vol. V, 1785), while Princess Izabella published a popular handbook called *Reflections on the Planting of Gardens* (1st ed., 1805). Powazki is now a cemetery in a modern suburb and nothing of its eighteenth-century flavour survives. However, at Natolin, south of Warsaw, an enchanting *pavillon* survives from the designs of Zug.

Built in 1780–2 for Izabella Lubomirska, sister-in-law of Izabella Czartoryska, Natolin resembles an elaborate garden building, for its principal oval interior is open to the garden through a curved screen of Ionic columns, a device echoing de Wailly's Montmusard of 1764. Its interiors were beautifully painted by Vincenzo Brenna with architectural and landscape subjects as well as arabesques. In 1799 it became a property of the Potocki family through the marriage of Izabella Lubomirska's daughter Alexandra. Further decoration

in the Empire Style was now introduced and the entrance front was remodelled with a Greek Doric order.

Zug was also involved in the design of the finest Polish Picturesque garden, called, appropriately, Arkadia. It was laid out in 1777–98 on the Radziwiłł family estate of Nieborow for Princess Helena Radziwiłł (1745–1821), a close friend and regular correspondent of Izabella Czartoryska. About two miles from the main palace at Nieborow, the garden of Arkadia could thus be used for parties without the need for a substantial house on the site. It is a lake-landscape crowded with fanciful buildings and ruins, including an aqueduct, Arch of Boulders, House of the High Priest, Gothic chapel and Rousseau island inspired by that at Ermenonville. The best of them is the Ionic Temple of Diana (1783) at the head of the lake with a complex plan of curved and circular interiors. The total effect of Arkadia, like that of all 'English' parks in Poland, is somewhat cramped and resembles a series of stage sets. This is doubtless because French gardens were so often the channel of transmission of knowledge about English parks.

The romantic garden laid out in the 1770s at Puławy, the principal seat of the Czartoryska family, was greatly extended in the 1790s for Princess Izabella Czartoryska with the help of her English head gardener, James Savage, and an Irish gardener, Denis McClear. In 1790–4, Christian Piotr Aigner (1756–1841) added the Marynki Palace at Puławy, a substantial villa inspired by Neufforge, and in 1798 began to erect a chain of Picturesque buildings including a Gothic House, Chinese Pavilion and an elaborate Temple of the Sibyl inspired by the celebrated Temple of Vesta or Sibyl at Tivoli.

Eighteenth-century gardens continued to be enriched with elaborately historical buildings well into the nineteenth century, as shown, for example, by the Greek Doric temple of 1834–8 at Natolin by the Italian Henrico Marconi (1792–1863), and the Ionic and Egyptian temples in the Garden of the Belvedere, Warsaw, designed by Jakub Kubicki (1758–1833).

600 Exterior of the pavilion at Natolin, near Warsaw (1780–2), by Zug

601 The Amalienborg Palace, Copenhagen (1750–4), by Eigtved

Scandinavia

Sweden and Denmark were quick to adopt the new style of mid-eighteenth-century France. In 1754, on the recommendation of the Comte de Caylus, Louis-Joseph Le Lorrain (1715–59), who had been an influential student at the French academy in Rome from 1740 to 1748, designed a dining-room for Count Carl Gustav Tessin, a former ambassador to France, at his country house at Åkerö, some sixty miles from Stockholm. Le Lorrain's illusionistic wall decorations, painted on canvas after 1754 by a local Swedish decorator, were articulated with a row of Ionic columns separated by niches containing statues and fountains. This is one of the earliest neo-classical interiors anywhere, though it is close in mood to William Kent's Cupola room at Kensington Palace of 1722 (p. 375). In the same year, 1754, King Frederick V of Denmark (reigned 1746-66) invited Nicolas-Henri Jardin (1720–99) to Copenhagen

to solve the problem of the design of the royal church, the Frederikskirke. A friend of Le Lorrain, Jardin had won the Grand Prix in 1741 and had spent the years 1744–7 at the French Academy in Rome, where he was much influenced by Piranesi.

Niels Eigtved, an architect of late Baroque sympathies, had produced designs for the Frederikskirke in 1752 which Jardin attempted to bring up to date with French and Roman detailing. Jardin's designs were not executed but the domed church with its Corinthian portico, executed later with assistance from Harsdorff, is a dominant accent in the palace square of Amalienborg, an octagonal *place royale* designed in a Baroque style by Eigtved in 1750–4. One of the four identical buildings forming this square, today the Amalienborg Palace, was originally the town house of Count A. G. Moltke. In 1755 he commissioned Jardin to design the dining-room, which was executed in 1757 in white and gold with Ionic pilasters, gilded trophies and urns. Like Le Lorrain's at Åkerö, it is a milestone in neo-classical interior design.

602 Ehrensvärd: Model for a dockyard gate at Karlskrona (1785)

603 The Chinese House, Drottningholm (1763–9), replacing that of 1753

Jardin was first professor at the Royal Academy of Fine Arts in Copenhagen, established in 1754 in imitation of the French Academy; his most gifted pupil was Caspar Frederik Harsdorff (1735–99), who subsequently studied under J.-F. Blondel in Paris. Harsdorff's principal work was the royal mortuary chapel of Frederick V in Roskilde cathedral, designed in 1763 and executed in 1774–9. With octagonal coffering derived from the Basilica of Maxentius in Rome, its chaste interior, completed in 1825 from Harsdorff's designs by his pupil C. F. Hansen, was as 'advanced' in neo-classical terms as anything of its date in Europe. However, a more arrestingly neo-Greek mood was introduced by Carl August Ehrensvärd (1745–1800), a remarkable figure who was a colonel in the Swedish navy, a student of military architecture, an artist and amateur architect. He broke his naval career to travel in Italy in 1780–2, where he was profoundly impressed by the power and vigour of the Greek Doric temples at Paestum. On his return he designed in 1782 a monument in the Gustav Adolf Square in Stockholm which combined an Egyptian pyramid with a Doric temple. Indeed, his atmospheric watercolour sketches of Doric architecture in Nordic landscapes contain

columns so stunted as to have an Egyptian or proto-Doric character. This is also true of his powerful design for a dockyard gate at Karlskrona which survives in the form of a model of 1785.

Another architect of French 'Revolutionary' sympathies was Louis-Jean Desprez (1743–1804), a pupil of Blondel and a Grand Prix winner in 1776, who lived in Sweden from 1784 until his death. Court stage-designer to King Gustav III of Sweden (reigned 1771–92), Desprez produced many fantastic stage designs for the theatres at Gripsholm and Drottningholm in a manner derived from Piranesi. Gustav III also gave employment to Fredrik Magnus Piper (1746–1824), who was important for introducing the English landscaped garden to Sweden. The founding of the Swedish East India Company in 1731 opened up the Far East and so led to an appreciation of Chinese gardens. In the 1750s Carl Ekeberg published *An Account of Chinese Husbandry* and a rococo Chinese House was built at Drottningholm for Queen Ulrica. Having studied at the Royal Academy of Arts at Stockholm, Piper was given a scholarship to study landscape gardening in England, Italy and France. He travelled in England, probably with a letter of introduction to Sir William Chambers, in 1772–6 and 1778–80, making sketches which still survive of gardens such as Kew, Stowe, Stourhead and Painshill. In 1780 he was appointed surveyor of the royal household to Gustav III, for whom he laid out a picturesque lake-landscape at Haga from 1781, an estate just north of Stockholm which the future king had bought ten years earlier as a rural retreat. His less ambitious garden at the royal residence of Drottningholm, to the west of Stockholm, was begun in 1780.

Russia

St Petersburg had been founded by Peter the Great in 1703 as a port of entry for western influence into Russia. Here Italian, French, British, German and Russian architects worked during the next century and a half to create a city which is one of the most enthralling statements in the world of the ideals of international classicism. During the reign of the Empress Elizabeth (1741–62) the fashion was for florid Rococo, in which style the Italian architect Count Bartolommeo Rastrelli (1700–71) built the palace of Tsarskoe Selo (1749–56), about 15 miles (24km) from St Petersburg, and the vast Winter Palace (1754–62) in St Petersburg itself. The reaction of Elizabeth's niece Catherine the Great (reigned 1762–96) against this style had been anticipated by the influential Count Ivan Shuvalov, a friend of Voltaire; as early as 1759 he had summoned Jean-Baptiste-Michel Vallin de la Mothe (1729–1800) to St Petersburg to supervise the construction of the Academy of Fine Arts to a design which he had commissioned

from J.-F. Blondel. A pupil of Blondel, who was his cousin, Vallin de la Mothe introduced a style based on Palladio, Gabriel and Blondel in the Academy of Fine Arts (1765), which he considerably varied from Blondel's design, and in the first or Old Hermitage (1764–7), commissioned by Catherine as a retreat from the Winter Palace. Vallin de la Mothe also built the Gostinny Dvor (markets) on the Nevski Prospect in St Petersburg in 1761–82, and the superb Doric entrance gateway (1765) to the New Holland Canal in the grand French academic manner.

The impact of Vallin de la Mothe led to two young Russian architects, Vasili Ivanovich Bazhenov (1737–99) and Ivan Yegorovich Starov (1743–1808), being sent to Paris in the early 1760s for training under de Wailly. They had previously been trained in the St Petersburg Academy but the additional French instruction resulted, for example, in Bazhenov's New Arsenal (1769) in St Petersburg and, on a grander scale, in his unexecuted plans for the reconstruction in c.1772 of the Kremlin as a vast triangular classical palace. Another major uncompleted project commissioned from Bazhenov by Catherine was the palace of Tsaritsyno (c.1787) near Moscow. Bazhenov designed this in a neo-Gothic style which anticipated the nineteenth-century revivals of national styles for political and patriotic purposes. More fortunate was Starov, who built at Nikolskoe in 1774–6 a country house for Prince Gagarin

604 J.-F. Blondel and J.-B.-M. Vallin de la Mothe: River front of the Academy of Fine Arts, St Petersburg (1765), from across the Neva

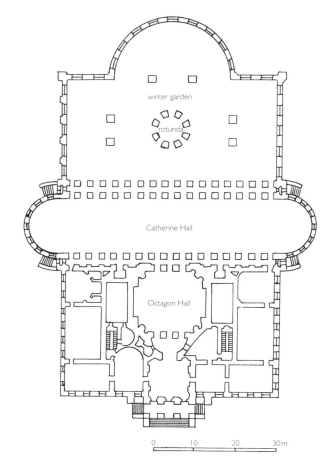

winter garden

rotunda

Catherine Hall

Octagon Hall

0   10   20   30m

605 Plan of the Tauride Palace, St Petersburg (1783–8), by Starov

606 The Catherine Hall, Tauride Palace, St Petersburg

and a church dominated by a huge freestanding circular belfry, a colonnaded exercise in neo-classical geometry. In St Petersburg Starov built the dignified cathedral of the Trinity, Alexander Nevski Lavra (1776) and his masterpiece, the Tauride Palace (1783–8), commissioned by Catherine for her lover, Gregory Potemkin, whom she made Prince of Tauris after his conquest of the Crimea. The austere 13-bay front of the Tauride Palace, with a Tuscan portico and a shallow dome, leads through a square vestibule to a Pantheon hall and thence to the immensely long 'Catherine Hall', flanked on each side by 18 pairs of unfluted Greek Ionic columns. This in turns leads to an enclosed winter garden containing a small centrally-placed tholos or circular colonnade. Here was an antique poetry surpassing the effects achieved by Paine and Adam at Kedleston (p. 378) to which the Tauride Palace was a Russian parallel.

English neo-Palladianism was in fact introduced to Russia by the Italian architect Giacomo Quarenghi (1744–1817), trained as a painter in Bergamo and in Rome. He was summoned to Russia by Catherine in 1779, where his numerous works included in the 1780s the monumental neo-Palladian English Palace in the English Park at Peterhof and, in St Petersburg, the Hermitage Theatre, State Bank and Academy of Sciences. In the next decade he built in a similar style the palace at Ostankino near Moscow for Count Sheremetev. The Sheremetev Palace has a new Picturesque liveliness, with the chiaroscuro of its colonnaded interiors, including its richly ornamented theatre and, in the park, its Italian and so-called Egyptian pavilions. The execution of the Sheremetev Palace was supervised by Matvei Feodorovich Kazakow (1733–1812), who provided Moscow with many public buildings, churches and private palaces in a monumental classical style. One of the most important is his huge triangular Senate Building, erected in the Kremlin in 1771–85 in partial fulfilment of Bazhenov's project.

The most sophisticated architect brought from Europe to Russia was the Scottish-born Charles Cameron (c.1743–1812), who was active in Rome in

607 Exterior of the Sheremetev Palace, Ostankino, near Moscow (1790s), by Quarenghi

the 1760s preparing his impressive book on *The Baths of the Romans explained and illustrated, with the Restorations of Palladio corrected and improved*, which he published in 1772 with texts in English and French. It was probably this book which brought him to the notice of Catherine

the Great. He entered her service in 1779, remaining as a court architect for the rest of his life. In 1773 Catherine had invited Clérisseau to submit designs for a house in the antique style to be built in the grounds at Tsarskoe Selo, but she was annoyed with his grandiose palatial proposals. The more realistic Cameron, by

608 Cameron: Exterior of the Cameron Gallery, Tsarskoe Seloe (1782–5)

contrast, added a series of dazzling apartments to Rastrelli's Tsarskoe Selo from 1779. Together with the adjacent Cold Baths, Agate Pavilion and Cameron Gallery, added in 1782–5, these were unsurpassed in Europe for their inventive neo-classical brilliance. These fanciful stuccoed and painted interiors have a liveliness of invention which recalls but exceeds the work of Adam, while the polychromatic use of exotic materials, such as agate, bronze, malachite, ceramics and moulded glass, shows a response to a Russian enthusiasm for glitter which was to emerge later on in the jewellery of Peter Carl Fabergé. The long open colonnades on the south front of the Cameron Gallery seem inspired by those at West Wycombe Park, Buckinghamshire, of the 1760s, while the curved staircases leading down to the lake at the south end are a brilliant response to the problems presented by the sloping site.

English precedent is again recalled in the palace at Pavlovsk, built by Cameron for Catherine's son, Grand Duke Paul, in 1781–5 with a colonnaded hall and rotunda evidently inspired by those at Kedleston. The picturesque park at Pavlovsk, with a model town at its gates, was dotted with at least 60 garden buildings, of which the most impressive is Cameron's Temple of Friendship (1779–80). This domed tholos surrounded by 16 Doric columns was the first monument of the Greek Revival in Russia.

The rise of classicism in the USA

American architecture begins to develop into something of international interest around 1700, with the erection after 1699 of the public buildings of Williamsburg, newly established as the capital of Virginia. The Capitol, Governor's House and William and Mary College are, however, extremely modest in comparison with the buildings by Wren and his associates to which they are ultimately indebted. The red-brick house known as Westover, Charles City County, Virginia (1730–5), is still in the Williamsburg tradition but the impact of Anglo-Palladianism on domestic architecture is first felt

609 *Opposite* Interior of King's Chapel, Boston (1749–54), by Harrison

610 *Left and below* Exterior and plan of Drayton Hall, Charleston, S.C. (1738–42), probably designed by its owner, John Drayton

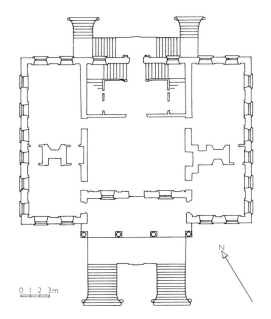

0 1 2 3m

at Drayton Hall, Charleston, South Carolina (1738–42), designed, probably by its owner, John Drayton, in imitation of Palladio's Villa Pisani at Montagnana. The combination of this kind of Palladianism with the potent influence of James Gibbs is typified in Mount Airy, Richmond County (1758–62), a villa with quadrant ranges leading to two flanking wings. It is based on two designs published in Gibbs's *Book of Architecture* (1728).

By this time America at last possessed an architect, albeit one born in England, who could work in a Gibbsian-Palladian manner independently of English models. This was Peter Harrison (1716–75), who was born in York of Puritan parents and emigrated to America in 1740. He finally settled near Newport, Rhode Island, in c.1748, where he and his brother traded in luxury goods with England, South Carolina and the West Indies. His first building, the Redwood Library, Newport (1748–50), is of wood cleverly disguised to resemble chamfered stone rustication. With its Doric portico, the building has a convincing temple-like air which is unusual for its date in America. It is a piece of Burlingtonian classicism, a reminder that as a young man Harrison must have seen Burlington's Assembly Rooms rising in York (p. 375). Harrison's King's Chapel, Boston, Massachusetts (1749–54), his next building and the only one for which he accepted a professional fee, has an interior distantly inspired by Gibbs's St Martin-in-the-Fields, and a west front with a tower and an unpedimented balustraded portico combining references to Gibbs and Inigo Jones. Lacking professional architectural training, he put to good use the excellent library which he had built up of architectural books. His remaining public buildings, all in a similarly inventive Palladian-Gibbsian mode, were the Touro Synagogue (1759–63), the first public synagogue in colonial America, and the Brick Market (1760–72), both in Newport, and Christ Church, Cambridge (1760–1). So much did Gibbs's designs for the Church of England become the model for all colonial churches, regardless of their religious denomination, that the First Baptist Meeting House, Providence, Rhode Island, designed in 1774–5 by Joseph Brown, boasted a timber spire inspired by one of the variants for St Martin-in-the-Fields published in Gibbs's *Book of Architecture*.

Thomas Jefferson

American architecture assumes an unquestioned international significance for the first time with Thomas Jefferson (1743–1826), who was influenced by French neo-classicism in his search for an architecture which would symbolize the values of the newly established republic. Once again France was of central importance, as it was for eighteenth-century developments in Italy, Germany, Poland and Scandinavia. Statesman, politician, lawyer, author, educator and architect, Jefferson may have been the first American to have thought objectively about architecture in terms of a return to first principles. This was not only appropriate for the man who was to draft the Declaration of Independence, but was entirely in harmony with the ideals of the neo-classical theorists and architects of contemporary Europe. On the conclusion of the War of Independence against Britain in 1784, Jefferson was appointed American Ambassador in Paris where he rented as his embassy the exceptionally elegant Hôtel de Langeac (c.1780) by J.-F.-T. Chalgrin. He remained in Europe for four years, during which time he travelled in Italy and Holland and visited England in 1786 to study the art of landscape gardening.

In Paris he met that elder statesman of neo-classicism, Clérisseau, whose book *Antiquités du Midi de la France* ('Antiquities of the South of France', 1778) he acquired. As a result he visited the so-called Maison Carrée at Nîmes, the superbly preserved early Imperial Roman temple, for which he conceived a passionate admiration. Indeed, in 1785 he took it as his model when designing with Clérisseau's assistance the State Capitol at Richmond, the town to which the capital of Virginia had, at his suggestion, been transferred from Williamsburg so as to eliminate the last vestiges of

611 *Opposite* Exterior of the First Baptist Meeting House, Providence, Rhode Island (1774–5), by Brown

612 *Above* Jefferson: Garden front of Monticello, near Charlottesville (begun 1771; remodelled 1793–1809)

613 *Right* Plan of Monticello by Jefferson

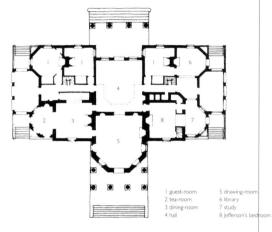

1 guest-room	5 drawing-room
2 tea-room	6 library
3 dining-room	7 study
4 hall	8 Jefferson's bedroom

British rule. As the first public building of templar form anywhere since ancient times, the Capitol was a rejection of English architectural precedent and a programmatic statement of high reforming ideals.

Jefferson's own house, Monticello, near Charlottesville, Virginia, was begun in 1771 on a plan based on one in Robert Morris's *Select Architecture* (1755) and adapted to a façade in Palladio's *Quattro Libri*; it was conceived as a modest version of a French *pavillon*. However, in 1793–1809 he extended and remodelled it into a complex villa with an octagonal domed centre and low wings on both fronts. It is subtly linked to its setting by means of elegant service buildings which form a large U, not in front of the house as in Palladian precedent, but flanking the garden at the rear. Terminating in pavilions containing Jefferson's law office and estate office, the long low service wings are set into the side of the hill so as not to interfere with the view. They are connected to the house with semi-subterranean passages recalling the crypto-porticus of Roman buildings such as Hadrian's Villa at Tivoli and Pliny's Laurentine Villa.

The remodelling of Monticello, completed during Jefferson's term as third President of the United States from 1801 to 1809, gave it the effect of a one-storeyed building like the villas of ancient Rome or modern neo-antique houses such as Rousseau's Hôtel de Salm in Paris (1783), with which Jefferson, in his own words, 'was violently smitten'. The intricate planning, with its clear separation between public and private rooms, derived from contemporary Paris, is asymmetrical and provided Jefferson with a remarkable L-shaped suite of bedroom, cabinet and bookroom, forming what is virtually one continuous space. The unprecedented novelty, at least in American terms, of the interior distribution is paralleled in the numerous gadgets which have always attracted the attention of visitors: double doors contrived so that when one is opened the other opens

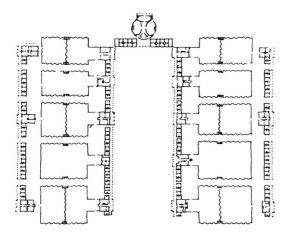

614 *Above* Plan of University of Virginia, Charlottesville (1817–26) by Jefferson

615 *Right* Jefferson Library of the University of Virginia, Charlottesville (1817–26)

automatically; Venetian blinds round the bed; the entrance porch with a weather-vane on the ceiling and, on the wall below, a clock which has a second face in the hall; and the dumb waiter concealed in the side of the dining-room chimneypiece designed for bringing wine from the cellar. These remind one of the eccentricity of an experimental scientist like the young Christopher Wren, determined to think things out for himself.

What especially remains in the mind about Monticello is the astonishing poetry of its natural setting on a high sunlit plateau in the mountains, a choice which surprised Jefferson's contemporaries. Monticello, which was the centre of a working farm and estate, recalls the life of ancient Roman farms or villas as evoked in the writings of Virgil, Cicero, Horace, Varro or Pliny the Younger. Jefferson evidently conceived Monticello as a symbol of order, harmony and industry, an institution at once poetic and functional, classical and modern, Roman and American. It was, nonetheless, a private creation. He had seen all along that public education would be necessary to fulfil his vision of a new American society. His promotion as early as 1779 of a 'Bill for the More General Diffusion of Knowledge' flowered in the passing by the Virginia Legislature in 1816 of a bill establishing a Central College. This, the University of

Virginia at Charlottesville, was built from Jefferson's own designs in 1817–26.

The architectural form of the university was rooted in ideas for an 'academical village' which Jefferson had been developing in 1804–10. As built, this comprised two lines of five pavilions linked by colonnades and containing lecture rooms and accommodation for ten professors, which faced each other across a vast lawn. Following a suggestion by the architect Benjamin Henry Latrobe, the head of the composition was marked by a great circular library modelled on the Pantheon and built from Jefferson's designs in 1823–7. No previous university had been planned in this way, though the pavilion layout may have been suggested by the unusual disposition of Louis XIV's château of Marly, which Jefferson had visited while in Paris. This quintessentially absolutist monument of pre-Revolutionary France was an ironical model for the libertarian Jefferson! The pavilions themselves, all differently designed, are elegant and witty versions of Palladian sources with correct antique detailing. One of them, Pavilion IX, with its screen of columns passing in front of a round-headed exedra, seems inspired by Ledoux's Hôtel Guimard in Paris of 1770. Behind the linking colonnades, which act as sheltered passageways, are rooms or dormitories for the students. Behind these are gardens, separated by serpentine walls, in which the professors might grow vegetables. Thus Jefferson created an ideal academic community with the special blend of contemplation and industry, of empirical yet profoundly classical architecture, and with the perfect spatial relationship between buildings and gardens, which had characterized his private paradise at Monticello.

Bulfinch and Latrobe

Jefferson's desire for monumental public buildings as symbols of the high moral purpose of the infant republic led him to announce a competition in 1792 for the United States Capitol and President's House in the new federal capital of Washington.

The building of the new Capitol was not completed till 1827 and the first legislative buildings erected after Jefferson's Capitol at Richmond were the State Houses at Hartford, Connecticut (1792–6) and at Boston, Massachusetts (1795–8). Both were designed by Charles Bulfinch (1763–1844), a self-taught gentleman architect who, unlike Jefferson, was content to offer post-colonial Americans what their pre-revolutionary predecessors had wanted, reminiscences of English taste in the 1770s and 1780s. Bulfinch visited England during his European tour in 1785–7 and the influence of Chambers, Adam, Wyatt and Mylne is evident in all his works, including the Massachusetts State House. This monumental building (fig. 573) is partly inspired by Chambers's Somerset House and contains a fine House of Representatives Chamber which echoes Wyatt's Pantheon. Bulfinch provided Boston with a theatre, several churches and many of its most attractive row or terraced houses, including the elegantly Adamesque Tontine Crescent (1793–4), the first of its kind in America, paralleled in Bath though not in London at that moment. His New South Church, Boston (1814), is an eclectic combination of a neo-classical octagonal nave preceded by a portico of faintly Greek Doric flavour surmounted by a steeple which, at the request of the building committee, follows a Gibbsian model. Happier is his Lancaster Meeting House, Lancaster, Massachusetts

(1816–17), a clean, unadorned and elegantly geometrical composition with a chaste Ionic cupola logically surmounting the vertical rectangular mass of the entrance lobby. This is preceded by an unusual Doric portico with stuccoed pilasters separating three tall arches of thin unmoulded brick.

It was Bulfinch who brought the Capitol in Washington to its initial completion in 1827. In Jefferson's competition of 1792 for a Capitol and a President's House, the commission for the latter (the future White House) had been won with an old-fashioned design by the Irish architect James Hoban (c.1762–1831) inspired by one in James Gibbs's *Book of Architecture*. The somewhat incoherent design of the Capitol was the outcome of a problematical alliance between William Thornton (1758–1828), the Frenchman Etienne (Stephen) Hallet (c.1760–1825), George Hadfield (1763–1826), Benjamin Latrobe (1764–1820) and Bulfinch. Its most memorable external features today, the huge dome and colonnaded wide wings approached up vast flights of steps, were added by Thomas U. Walter in 1851–65 during the Presidency of Abraham Lincoln. The finest features of the building are the interiors created after the fire of 1814 from designs by Latrobe, to whose career we should now turn.

A designer of great brilliance and the first fully professional architect to work in America, Latrobe was the most influential architect of his generation. He was born near Leeds in Yorkshire, and his father was the leading minister of the Moravian congregation in England, a civilized man who was a friend of Samuel Johnson and Charles Burney. His mother, perhaps even more significantly for his future career, was a Pennsylvanian who left him land in America on her death in 1794. Thanks to the Moravian school system, Latrobe received in England and in German Silesia an excellent general education in classics, modern languages, history, theology, biology and geology. He was an able watercolourist and, like his father, a musician. In the 1780s he studied engineering and from c.1789–92 was a pupil of the architect S. P. Cockerell. In Sussex he built

616 *Above* Thornton, Hallet, Hadfield, Latrobe and Bulfinch: Exterior of the Capitol, Washington (initial building: 1792–1827; dome and wings: 1851–65)

617 *Below* Plan of the Capitol, Washington

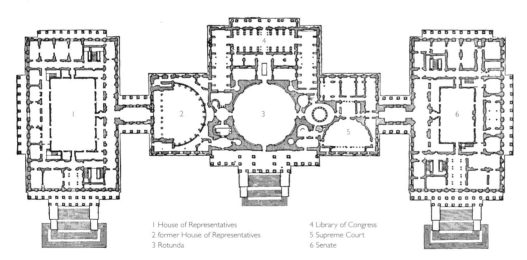

1 House of Representatives
2 former House of Representatives
3 Rotunda
4 Library of Congress
5 Supreme Court
6 Senate

two houses in the early 1790s, Hammerwood Lodge and Ashdown House, in an uncompromisingly geometrical style influenced by Soane and Ledoux. His first wife died in childbirth in 1793 and, failing to find significant architectural commissions in England during the Napoleonic Wars, he set off in November 1795 on the 15-week journey to North America. Here in 1797–8 he built his first American building, the State Penitentiary,

Richmond, Virginia, a vast semi-circle approached through an awesome unmoulded archway recalling the designs of Gilly or Soane. The first modern prison in America, its design was in sympathy with Jefferson's long-expressed views on penal reform.

Becoming increasingly bored with the narrow life of Richmond, he withdrew from it in 1798 and bought an 80-acre island in the Falls of James river, writing to a friend of 'shutting myself up in my island to devote my hours to literature, agriculture, friendship, and the education of my children'. At this time, 1798–9, he prepared 'An Essay on Landscape explained in tinted drawings' to instruct a young woman called Susan Spotswood in the art of watercolour painting. His approach and technique are reminiscent of Humphry Repton's and he completely accepted the Picturesque tradition as defined by Uvedale Price and Payne Knight, whose poem *The Landscape* (1794) he described as 'elegant but ill-natured'. He was also working in these years on the Bank of Pennsylvania (1798–1800) in Philadelphia, the national capital from 1790 to 1800 and the largest city in America. The Bank recalls Jefferson's radical approach in its rational empiricism: with a Greek Ionic portico at each end it resembles a temple, yet has no order of any kind along the side walls. Marble-built, it is stone-vaulted throughout for the first time in America and is logically dominated by the square domed

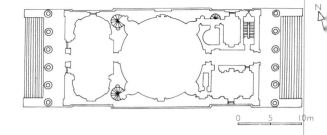

618 Plan of the Bank of Pennsylvania, Philadelphia (1798–1800), by Latrobe

banking-hall at the centre. The Bank was followed in 1799–1801 by the Pump House of the Philadelphia Waterworks, of which Latrobe was the engineer. This was a rectangular Greek Doric building surmounted by a bare rotunda, perhaps inspired by Ledoux's Barrière de la Villette. Latrobe's finest surviving building, St Mary's Roman Catholic cathedral at Baltimore,

619 Interior of St Mary's Roman Catholic cathedral, Baltimore (designed 1804–8; built 1809–18), by Latrobe

620 Latrobe: The Supreme Court Chamber, the Capitol, Washington (1815–17)

Maryland, was designed in 1804–8 and executed in 1809–18. The cross-shaped plan, huge entrance portico and plain wall surfaces may have been suggested by Soufflot's Ste-Geneviève but the floating interior space with its segmental dome hovering on segmental arches is close in mood to Soane's halls at the Bank of England, which Latrobe must have known. The onion-shaped tops of the belfry towers were added in 1832, not to Latrobe's designs, but the lengthening of the choir in 1890 conformed to Latrobe's original intentions.

Soane is again recalled in Latrobe's work at the Capitol in Washington carried out in his capacity as Surveyor of Public Buildings, a post given him by Jefferson in 1803. By this date the north wing of Thornton's design containing the Senate Chamber had been built; the balancing south wing, destined for the House of Representatives, had been begun; while the great rotunda between them, eventually built by Bulfinch, had not yet even been started. Latrobe now built the House of Representatives, completed in 1811 as an elliptical chamber flanked by twenty-four Corinthian columns with capitals modelled on those of the Choragic Monument of Lysicrates (p. 43). In 1809 he built the Supreme Court Chamber below the Senate Chamber in the north wing, based on plans he had made in 1806–7. It was damaged by fire in 1814, rebuilt by Latrobe and fully restored in 1975. With its three arches supported on stunted Greek Doric columns of sandstone and its strangely lobed umbrella-like half-dome, this magical interior can only be paralleled in the work of Dance, Ledoux, Soane, Gilly and in the crypto-porticus of the Roman House at Weimar by Arens. In the adjacent lower staircase-vestibule Latrobe provided columns with an American order of maize-leaf capitals, described by the congressmen as 'corn-cob capitals'. The nationalist flavour of these capitals and of the tobacco-leaf capitals used elsewhere in the building was prefigured by Laugier who called, in his *Observations sur l'architecture* (1765), for a new order of classical architecture.

621 Latrobe: The staircase vestibule with maize-leaf capitals in the Capitol, Washington (1815–17)

Much of Latrobe's work was damaged by the British fleet in August 1814 when they set fire to the Capitol and President's House. Latrobe, whose job as surveyor had ceased in 1812, was recalled in 1815 to rebuild the Capitol. He now remodelled the House of Representatives in the south wing in the form of a semicircular theatre, which had been his preferred solution as early as 1803. In the north wing he formed a two-storeyed domed circular vestibule, which is a close parallel to interiors by Soane such as his virtually contemporary National Debt Redemption Office. In 1816 Latrobe wrote to Jefferson of this wonderful space:

> The columns of the rotunda, 16 in number, must be more slender than the Ionic order will admit, and ought not to be of the Corinthian because the chamber itself is of the Ionic order. I have therefore composed a capital of leaves and flowers of the tobacco plant which has an intermediate effect approaching the Corinthian order and retaining the simplicity of the Clepsydra or Temple of the Winds.

Finally, we may quote from a letter to Latrobe of 1812 in which Jefferson sums up the significance of the Capitol and the miraculous identity between him and his architect by describing the building as 'the first temple dedicated to the sovereignty of the people, embellishing with Athenian taste the course of a nation looking far beyond the range of Athenian destinies'.

Town planning

The contribution of the French Enlightenment
Comprehensive town planning emerges in the mid century as the product of Enlightenment thinking in the age of improvement. This was produced in reaction to the dominant role previously played in such matters by princes and prelates. Among the most important urban developments of the eighteenth century are those in Bath, Edinburgh, Lisbon and St Petersburg, the only one of this group to be founded as a capital city. What we have seen so far has been mainly the insertion of planned elements into existing towns. Transitional between Baroque planning and the total planning of the Enlightenment is Nancy, the capital of Lorraine, where Emmanuel Héré de Corny, as we have already noted, created a series of three linked squares of contrasting shapes in 1752–5 which connected the old town with the new.

Meanwhile, Voltaire published a far-sighted and influential essay, 'The Embellishments of Paris', in 1749 in which he proposed making the city more healthy, convenient and efficiently functioning. His ideas were taken up by the architect Pierre Patte (1723–1814), whose book *Monuments érigés en France à la gloire de Louis XV* (Paris 1765) included plans for the improvement of Paris by several architects. Superimposed on a single map of the city, these suggested total replanning on a breathtaking scale. To these schemes he added a discussion of various problems of urban hygiene, a topic he developed further in his *Mémoires sur les objets les plus importans de l'architecture* (Paris 1769). Here were proposals for law courts, prisons, town hall, markets, an improved street network with tree-lined avenues, market places, the separation of the sick and the dead, and even free university courses. He called, in effect, for a master plan in one of the first uses of this term in the modern sense.

Theory and practice in London

In eighteenth-century England the power of the church and the monarchy was far more limited than on the continent of Europe so London could boast few of the great monuments, royal palaces, churches, private mansions, public fountains and formal planning schemes that featured in the Baroque city. Instead, from around 1700, London increasingly specialized in the residential square, a tradition in which Inigo Jones had been a pioneer at Covent Garden Piazza of 1631–3.

This urban housing was often a speculative development by great landowning families or by major institutions. Leasehold properties on long leases, they rarely followed an imposing uniform design like the French Place Royale. A partial exception was provided by Grosvenor Square, Mayfair, an early and very large development commissioned from 1725 by Sir Richard Grosvenor. The design of the houses on the north and east sides, simplified from an elaborate proposal by Colen Campbell, suggested a single palatial building with a pedimented centrepiece, but the remaining two sides were developed on a more irregular basis. None of these houses survives today, but Bedford Square, Bloomsbury, which was completed by Thomas Leverton (1743–1824) in 1782 to a unified design, is still intact.

Meanwhile, John Gwynn (1713–86) had made extensive proposals, scarcely realized before the nineteenth century, which went far beyond domestic architecture. With Paris as his avowed model, Gwynn took the existing street pattern of London and transformed it with new squares, palaces and public buildings. Many of these projects, published in his book *London and Westminster Improved. Illustrated by Plans. To which is prefixed a Discourse on Publick Magnificence* (London 1766), were eventually taken up, culminating in the work of John Nash from 1811–25.

622 Leverton: Bedford Square, London (1782)

Bath, Dublin, Edinburgh

If the country house is the best known British contribution to eighteenth-century architecture, Georgian town houses and town planning are scarcely less significant. The centre of innovation was the city of Bath, which rose in popularity throughout the century as a spa to which London society would retreat in the summer months. John Wood (1704–54) built Queen Square in 1729–36, in which the unified palatial façades on the north side boast a central pediment over attached columns and a rusticated basement. This incorporation of individual houses in a monumental scheme was something of a novelty in England, though it was being attempted at about the same time in London at Grosvenor Square, and probably derives from Mansart's Place Vendôme, Paris (begun 1698). Determined to recreate a Roman atmosphere in a city which had been an important one in Roman Britain, Wood proposed a series of linked visual centres to which he gave the romantic names 'Royal Forum', 'Grand Circus' and 'Imperial Gymnasium'. North of Queen Square he laid out from 1754 what he called the Circus, an outrageously inventive version of the Colosseum turned inside out, consisting of 33 houses with façades treated monumentally like those in Queen Square. Again, it should be remembered that Mansart had built the circular Place des Victoires in Paris in 1685. Wood's Circus is entered by three streets but since they are not placed opposite each other they do not seriously break the circular effect, which recalls the kind of *rond point* seen in gardens by Le Nôtre. Wood, indeed, had been involved in the 1720s in laying out the formal gardens

623 Aerial view of Lansdowne Crescent, Bath (1789–93), by Palmer

at Bramham Park, Yorkshire, which have often been attributed to Le Nôtre himself.

Wood's son John (1728–81) completed his father's grandiose scheme for Bath by adding the Assembly Rooms (1769–71) and Royal Crescent (1767–75), a curved row of 30 houses commanding views of the open country. Its unique semi-elliptical form, a kind of demi-Colosseum, is the first example in British architecture of the crescent, a type that was to be widely imitated into the nineteenth century at Bath, Buxton, London, Hastings, Brighton and, above all, Edinburgh, which contains what is arguably an even more extensive realization than Bath of late-Georgian urban ideals. At Bath the architect John Palmer (c.1738–1817) added Lansdowne Crescent (1789–93), higher up the hill from the Royal Crescent whose Picturesque qualities it takes even further. It follows a convex-concave-convex plan which seems a natural response to the gentle undulations of its hillside site. In blending classical and Picturesque ideals it summarizes perfectly the dominant themes of

eighteenth-century English architecture.

In Edinburgh, the medieval Old Town was confined within walls on a mountain ridge below the Castle. When it was decided to create a New Town on the adjacent ridge across the valley, the marsh was drained and the two ridges linked by a bridge. The competition of 1766 for the New Town was won by the local architect James Craig (1744–95) with a grid plan in which two squares were linked by a central street. Though not an inventive plan, this was bordered by streets left unbuilt on their outer sides so as to open up fine views of the Old Town on one side and of open country on the other, an idea possibly inspired by the younger Wood's work at Bath.

The tradition of public buildings that had begun in Dublin after the restoration of the monarchy in 1660 was strikingly advanced by Sir Edward Lovett Pearce (c.1699–1733) in works such as his Parliament House of 1729. This new urban vitality also found expression in developments from the late 1740s such as Sackville (now O'Connell) Street, which was followed by the establishment in 1757 of the Wide Street Commissioners, an unusual and influential product of

Enlightenment idealism. Exercising strict control over new buildings, which incorporated ground-floor shops with residential accommodation over, the Commissioners widened existing streets to 98 feet (30m) or more as well as creating new ones. James Gandon (1742–1823) further transformed the city with a series of public buildings, including the Four Courts (1786–1802), which were important for the sensitivity with which he related them to the river.

St Petersburg and Lisbon

St Petersburg was founded in 1703 by Peter the Great as an attempt to bring Russia politically, economically and culturally closer to western Europe. The three radiating streets were inspired, as we have seen, by those at Versailles, while the city was also crossed by tree-bordered canals echoing those which Peter the Great had seen in Amsterdam. The unfortified city of St Petersburg on its vast site took decades to take shape, indeed it was almost abandoned on Peter the Great's death in 1725, much being added in the reign of Catherine the Great (1762–96). Nonetheless, it was found so impressive as a modernizing vision that leading figures of the Enlightenment hailed it as a triumph of the age of improvement, Voltaire praising what he called 'Russia's march towards civilization' in his *Essai sur les mœurs* (1750).

The destruction in 1755 of the centre of Lisbon by an earthquake shook the traditional belief of many in Divine Providence, a mood capitalized on by Voltaire in his *Poème sur le désastre de Lisbonne* (1756) and in his *Candide* (1759). However, the disaster led to a massive redevelopment of the city in which the urban planning ideals of the Enlightenment were realized. The king's chief minister, later ennobled as the Marques de Pombal, assisted by the military engineer Eugénio dos Santos de Carvalho (1711–60) and the Hungarian Carlos Mardel, laid out 20 hectares (50 acres) of the city as a model of rationalism in economics, city planning and architecture, with due attention paid to safety, economy, water and sanitation, as well as to anti-seismic construction.

624 View of St. Petersburg

625 The Praça do Comércio, Lisbon (after 1755)

At the core was the vast arcaded Praça de Comércio, not a royal square but a grand, if functional, space, approached from the river Tagus to which it was open on the south side. It was flanked by buildings housing the port authorities, government services and facilities for commercial associations. On the north side a triumphal arch led to a grid of streets, in which nearly uniform apartment blocks of three storeys with mansards contained business premises on the ground floor.

North America

The British founded colonial cities on the grid plan in America, though many of the towns in New England grew on modest, organic lines. An exception was New Haven, Connecticut, 1638, laid out on a core of nine absolutely equal square blocks, with a central village green. Probably owing something to Vitruvian precedent, it was the first planned town of its kind in

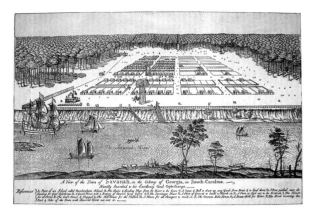

626 *Top left* View of
Savannah, Georgia

627 *Top right* Plan of
Williamsburg (from
1699)

628 *Above left and left*
View and plan of
Washington

New England. Philadelphia, William Penn's new
settlement in Pennsylvania, followed in 1681–3 with a
vast grid plan. By contrast, Annapolis, Maryland, was
laid out by Governor Francis Nicholson in 1694 with
the full panoply of Baroque effects, *rond points* and
radiating avenues, though on an incongruously miniature
scale. Another pattern was adopted in 1733 at Savannah,
Georgia, where the huge chess board plan had no set

boundary and no central square. Instead, it consisted of
an expandable grid of small wards, each with its own
small square.

One of the most novel and attractive towns is
Williamsburg, capital of Virginia from 1699, where a
new emphasis was laid on the relation of major buildings
to the main boulevard. The terminations of the main
vista were no longer the palace and church of European
cities but collegiate and legislative buildings.

The climax of the eighteenth-century planned town
in America was reached with the choice by George
Washington in 1790 of a site on the banks of the
Potomac for the capital of the newly independent states
of America. The task of laying out the new town of
Washington was given to a Frenchman, Major Pierre
L'Enfant (1754–1825), who sought the advice of
Jefferson. L'Enfant's avenues radiating from the Federal
House (later Capitol) and the President's (later White)
House echoed those of absolutist Versailles, however
ironically in this home of democracy. In a novel response
to the site the Capitol and President's House
commanded views of the Potomac.

9 The Nineteenth Century

THE FRENCH REVOLUTION OF 1789 HAD BOTH SHOCKED and inspired onlookers throughout Europe and North America. Nothing in political life could ever be taken for granted again, an instability that was reflected in France in the rapidly changing systems of government in the eighty years which followed the revolutionary violence. These included a dictatorship, two empires, legitimist and elective monarchies, and three republics. In the countries which had united against Napoleon in a long war which did not end till 1815, initial reaction took the form of a return to conservative monarchical government, though there were revolutions in many countries in 1830 and especially in 1848.

These revolutions were led by members of the middle classes who wanted a say in government, for the industrial revolution, begun in England in the 1780s, had produced a newly prosperous and confident middle class as well as a newly poor urban working class. Though the philosopher and political activist Karl Marx (1818–83) was wrong in predicting the imminent triumph of the proletariat as a result of the dialectical process of history in his *Communist Manifesto* (London 1848), the nineteenth century was nonetheless marked by vigorous debate about topics such as the living conditions of the working classes and the relation of Christianity to traditional social order. Similarly far-reaching questions were asked about the role of traditional styles in the practice of architecture in the modern industrial world.

France

The rational tradition from Percier and Fontaine to Viollet-le-Duc

In France public architectural education provided one element of cultural stability which remained remarkably intact in a period of rapid political change. French architecture in the nineteenth century was coloured by the intellectual and visual ideals of a single academic institution, the Ecole des Beaux-Arts (School of Fine Arts), in a way which had no parallel in any other European country. The Ecole des Beaux-Arts had been established in 1819 as the successor to the celebrated architectural school conducted by the Académie Royale d'Architecture, founded by Colbert in 1671 but dissolved by the Revolutionary Convention in 1793. Its teaching programme, conceived essentially as a preparation for the design of monumental public buildings, culminated in the competition for the Grand Prix de Rome which was held, with few breaks, from 1720 to 1968. The programme for this was determined and the entries judged by the Académie des Beaux-Arts, which had been founded under Napoleon in 1803 as one of the four academies comprising the Institut de France. The prestige, continuity and high seriousness of a system of architectural education which was unique in Europe made France the natural centre for intellectual debate about architecture during the eighteenth and nineteenth centuries.

The impact of Napoleon on architecture was less than on the development of French political and cultural institutions in general. It was in fact Napoleon's first wife Josephine who discovered the talents of Charles Percier

629 Percier and Fontaine: The Rue de Rivoli, Paris (from 1802)

(1764–1838) and Pierre-François-Léonard Fontaine (1762–1853), who were to become her husband's official architects in 1801. Both pupils of A.-F. Peyre, they studied together in the late 1780s at the French Academy in Rome, where they made a pact of eternal friendship, swearing never to marry. They remained faithful to each other and were buried in the same tomb in the Père-Lachaise cemetery.

In 1799, the year in which Napoleon became First Consul, Josephine engaged them to rebuild her newly acquired house at Malmaison, which they extensively redecorated in 1800–2. The style they adopted became known as the Empire Style, though in fact it was a more emphatic and brightly coloured version of the neo-antique decorative style established on the eve of the Revolution by architects such as Bélanger and P.-A. Pâris, for whom Percier had once worked. The tent bedroom designed in 1777 by François-Joseph Bélanger

for the Comte d'Artois at the Bagatelle in Paris now became the model for numerous interiors decorated with real or simulated drapery, for example Josephine's flamboyant bedroom at Malmaison (fig. 709). The technique was made newly fashionable during the Empire period by its associations with military campaign tents. The mark of Percier and Fontaine's Empire Style, as instantly recognizable as the decorative style of Robert Adam, was stamped on the interiors of the Louvre and the Tuileries as well as on the royal châteaux of Compiègne, St-Cloud and Fontainebleau. Napoleon and his relatives also carried it like some military trophy right across Europe to Germany, Italy, Spain, Holland and Scandinavia, while the publication by Percier and Fontaine of their *Recueil de décorations intérieures* (1801) drew their work to the attention of a wide professional audience.

In Paris Percier and Fontaine built less extensively than Nash did in London, though in terms of urban organization they did much to realize Napoleon's schemes for new roads, markets and fountains and for

630 Percier and Fontaine: The Arc du Carrousel, Paris (1806–8)

removing abattoirs and cemeteries to the outskirts. In 1811 they planned the gigantic palace of Chaillot, larger than Versailles, for Napoleon's infant son, the King of Rome. This would have faced across the Seine an equally megalomaniac complex of academic buildings including an Ecole des Beaux-Arts, university and archives. The awesome scale of this unexecuted scheme, recalling the visionary projects of Ledoux and Durand, reminds us that Percier and Fontaine had been the Grand Prix winners in 1785 and 1786 with projects for a 'Sepulchral monument for the sovereigns of a great empire' and for a 'Building uniting the three academies'. Their proposals

for linking the Louvre and the Tuileries palace resulted in the building of the arcaded rue de Rivoli and associated rue des Pyramides from 1802. The first of the great urban transformations of nineteenth-century Paris, these achieve their effect not through richness of detail but through extreme length and sparse ornament. These streets thus contrast effectively with the Arc du Carrousel, built by Percier and Fontaine in 1806–8 as the gateway to the now demolished Tuileries palace, which was Napoleon's chief Parisian residence. Modelled on the Arch of Septimius Severus in Rome, it is a polychromatic and richly carved object which is very much the product of its architects' skill as designers of furniture and interior decoration.

The Arc du Carrousel was just one of the souvenirs of imperial Roman public buildings which the Emperor Napoleon commissioned as monuments to his reign and military achievements in 1806 when, following the battle of Austerlitz, he was at the height of his powers. They include the Arc de Triomphe by A.-F.-T. Chalgrin (1739–1811); the giant Corinthian portico, twelve columns wide, of the Chambre des Deputés by Bernard Poyet (1742–1824); and the completion by A.-P. Vignon (1763–1828) of the church of the Madeleine as a secular Temple of Glory. Vignon's imposing if somewhat lifeless exterior is that of a Roman Corinthian temple, while the opulent interior, designed and executed by J.-J.-M. Huvé (1783–1852) in 1825–45, is modelled on the Roman baths.

These bold if stylistically unadventurous echoes of the antique past were accompanied by a doctrine which represented the climax of rational French architectural thought in the eighteenth century. The principal books in which this doctrine was now enshrined were the *Traité théoretique et pratique de l'art de bâtir* ('Theoretical and practical treatise on the art of building', 1802–3) by Jean-Baptiste Rondelet (1734–1829), and the *Précis des leçons d'architecture données à l'Ecole royale polytechnique* ('Summary of architecture lessons given to the Royal Polytechnic School', 1802–5) by Jean-Nicolas-Louis Durand (1760–1834). Rondelet, a pupil of Soufflot, was Professor of Stereotomy at the Ecole Spéciale d'Architecture and later at the Ecole des Beaux-Arts from 1806–29; Durand, Boullée's favourite pupil, taught at the Ecole Polytechnique from its inception in 1795 till 1830. In their enormously influential teachings, the two men reduced architecture to two of its elements, structure and formal geometry, Rondelet arguing that it was no more than a mechanical solution to specific practical problems. This bluntly materialist and mechanistic approach recurred in the writings of Auguste Choisy (1841–1909), for example in the three volumes of his *L'Art de bâtir chez les Romains* (1873), *chez les Byzantins* (1883), and *chez les Egyptiens* ('The Art of building among the Romans, Byzantines, and Egyptians',

631 Church of the Madeleine, Paris: interior by Huvé (1825–45) (see fig. 568 for exterior)

1904), and in his *Histoire de l'architecture* ('History of architecture', 2 vols., 1899). A distinguished engineer at the Ecole des Ponts et Chaussées (School of Road Engineering), Choisy was particularly admired by Viollet-le-Duc.

With the active support of A.-C. Quatremère de Quincy, Perpetual Secretary of the Académie des Beaux-Arts from 1816 to 1839, followers of Durand and Rondelet such as E.-H. Godde, L.-P. Baltard, L.-H. Lebas, and A.-H. de Gisors established a formula with which they provided the expanding towns of post-Napoleonic France with countless public buildings. They built churches, town halls, hospitals, law courts, schools, barracks, prisons and asylums in a lean classical style eloquent of public probity and social order.

Impressive though this achievement was, the un-adventurous nature of its aesthetic and intellectual content was bound to be challenged before long. A new emphasis, unexpectedly centred in a debate about polychromy, was provided by Jacques-Ignace Hittorff (1792–1867), who was born in Cologne but trained in Paris under Perçier at the Ecole des Beaux-Arts from 1811 and then worked with F.-J. Bélanger. In 1822 he travelled to Italy, and there met the English architect Thomas Leverton Donaldson (1795–1885), who first fired him with the notion that ancient Greek architecture had been coloured. In search of proof, Hittorff visited Sicily where his discovery of traces of painted stucco on the limestone temples at Selinus led to researches eventually published as *Restitution du temple d'Empédocle à Sélinonte; ou, l'architecture polychrôme chez les grecs* ('Restoration of the Temple of Empedocles at Selinontus; or polychrome architecture among the Greeks', 1851). In 1827 he published with Karl von Zanth his *Architecture antique de la sicile* ('Ancient architecture of Sicily') and in 1829–30 delivered lectures and exhibited drawings in Paris in which he claimed that Greek temples had originally been painted yellow with patterns, mouldings and sculptural details in bright red, blue, green and gold.

Hittorff's overthrow of Winckelmann's conception of Greek art as pure and colourless (p. 372) naturally caused tremendous controversy, even though several German and English scholars and architects, including Cockerell, William Kinnaird, Klenze and Otto Magnus von Stackelberg, had been aware of polychromy and in some cases had published their researches. Hittorff's earliest attempts to revitalize the classical tradition with colour were made in the Champs-Elysées in Paris, where he added bright paint to the porticoes of two of his centrally-planned buildings of iron and glass. These were the Rotonde des Panoramas (1838–9; dem. 1857) which contained a painting of the Battle of Moscow in the Napoleonic Wars, and the Cirque Nationale (1840), a centre of public entertainment which can seat 6,000 spectators.

His major opportunity came with the decoration of the Parisian church of St Vincent de Paul, built from his

632 Hittorff: Polychromatic façade of the Cirque Nationale, Paris (1840)

designs in 1830–46 on a commanding site approached by a great flight of curving steps high above the Place Lafayette (now Place Franz Liszt). Behind its forceful façade, dominated by square twin towers reminiscent of those at Cockerell's Hanover Chapel, lies a rich basilican interior with double aisles flanked by two-storeyed colonnades supporting an open timber-trussed roof. In 1849–53 the nave and apse were frescoed by Ingres's followers, Flandrin and Picot, with a procession like that on the Parthenon frieze, while stained glass, mainly in red and yellow, was designed by Hittorff and executed in 1842–4 by Maréchal and Gugnon. The columns were of yellow scagliola marble and the entablatures and

633 Hittorff: West front of St Vincent de Paul, Paris (1830–46)

mouldings were gilded, while the roof trusses and ceiling coffers were painted brilliant blue and red, flecked with gold in imitation of twelfth-century decoration at Monreale and elsewhere in Sicily, which Hittorff liked to imagine was a latter-day expression of ancient Greek polychromy. This lustrous interior was to be rivalled in richness by the extraordinary treatment Hittorff proposed for the façade in 1844. The wall of the portico was to be covered with 13 large painted enamel panels by Antoine-Jean Gros's pupil, Pierre-Jules Jollivet. Several of these were put up but were removed on the orders of the clergy, who were shocked at the nudity of Adam and Eve. His last major work was, significantly for the mid-nineteenth century, a railway station, the Gare du Nord in Paris (1861–5). Here he achieved the movement and vigour he desired in classical architecture, not by polychromy but by emphatic sculptural handling of the architectural members.

Hittorff seemed important to a group of slightly younger architects – Gilbert, Duban, Labrouste, Duc and Vaudoyer – as someone whose vision of ancient polychromy had challenged the received classical orthodoxy and had therefore opened the way to a new architecture. These romantic radicals, later and somewhat inaccurately called *Néo-Grecs* ('New Greeks'), were influenced by the Utopian socialist ideals expressed in the writings of the social reformers C.-H. de R. Saint-Simon (1760–1825) and Charles Fourier (1772–1837). They were thus concerned to enhance the life-giving qualities of architecture by making moral and social ideals shape its form and character. The career of Emile-Jacques Gilbert (1793–1874), a pupil of Durand, was devoted to hospitals, prisons and asylums, for example the lunatic asylum at Charenton (1838–45), near Paris, which has as its focus a Greek Doric chapel sporting a brightly coloured interior. Félix-Jacques Duban (1797–1870), a pupil of Percier, designed the Ecole des Beaux-Arts itself. Built off the rue Bonaparte in 1832–58, its arcuated façade contains restrained references to the antique and Renaissance buildings of Rome, including triumphal arches, the Colosseum and the Cancelleria. The courtyard in front incorporated an even more eclectic mixture of medieval and Renaissance details of buildings rescued from different parts of France by Alexandre Lenoir from 1795 for his Musée des Monuments Français.

The most distinguished of this group of 'romantic radical' architects was Pierre-François-Henri Labrouste (1801–75). He shocked the Academy, of which he was then a *pensionnaire*, by sending it from Rome in 1828 a restoration study of the three Doric temples at Paestum in which he claimed that one of them, the Temple of Hera I, was not a temple but a civil assembly hall. He showed it in use adorned with large paintings, trophies,

634 *Opposite top* Hittorff: Exterior of the Gare du Nord (1861–5)

635 *Opposite bottom* Duban: Elevation of the courtyard front at the Ecole des Beaux-Arts, Paris (1832–58)

inscriptions and graffiti, explaining that 'the walls of the portico, I imagine, would also be covered with painted notices, serving as a book'. He also provided the building with a hipped roof and, of course, with polychromatic ornament. What the Academy found shocking was the representation of the building not as an ideal monument but actually in use in accordance with Labrouste's belief that architecture reflected social aspirations. Another unacceptable implication of Labrouste's restoration was his argument that the 'basilica' at Paestum, the most primitive architecturally of these three Greek buildings in colonial Italy, was not, as had been supposed, the earliest but the most recent, the reason for its primitive or imperfect Doric language being that the building was the furthest removed in time from the temples of Greece of which it was a colonial descendant. This alarmed the Academicians because it struck at the foundations of the classical language, by implying that architectural forms are so deeply rooted in a particular time, place and way of life that they cannot be transported to other periods or countries.

As a result of what they took to be an onslaught on their ideals the Academy ensured that Labrouste received no major commission for nearly a decade. Moreover, none of his students was ever awarded the Grand Prix, though they venerated him in the *atelier* which he ran from 1830 to 1856. His great chance came in 1838 when he was appointed architect for the new Bibliothèque Ste-Geneviève near the Panthéon. The library which he designed in 1838–9 and built in 1843–50 has always been regarded as one of the greatest masterpieces of nineteenth-century architecture, extravagant tribute being paid to it, for example, by the American architects McKim, Mead and White, who took it as the model for their Boston Public Library (1887–95). Labrouste's library is of an uncompromising and radical novelty. A simple unrelieved rectangle with an almost utilitarian flavour, it is not dressed up with columns, porticoes or pediments. Relief is provided by the extraordinary device, decided on in 1848, of inscribing the façade with the carved names of 810

authors arranged chronologically from Moses to the Swedish chemist Berzelius (died 1848), so as to encapsulate the history of the world from Judaism to modern science. The programme was inspired by the writings of Auguste Comte (1798–1857), founder of the Positivist system of philosophy which depended exclusively on positive facts and observable phenomena. It was a parallel to the architectural doctrine propounded by Durand at the Ecole Polytechnique, where Comte had been both a pupil and teacher. With its 7,000 letters in rigid columns or panels, the façade has sometimes been compared to a sheet of newsprint, while even the chaste ornamental carving seems printed on the surface: indeed, the cast-iron paterae supporting the swags in the ground-floor frieze are impressed with the library's monogram and book-stamp, an interlaced SG for Ste Geneviève, the patron saint of Paris.

This unusual demonstration of function on the façade of the library is obviously related to Labrouste's belief that a building is a framework for human activity rather than a demonstration of the ideal beauty of the classical orders, a belief he had expressed in his treatment of the walls of the basilica at Paestum with their 'painted notices, serving as a book'. It is also possible to see the library as a reflection of the architectural ideals expressed in the second edition (1832) of *Notre-Dame de Paris* by Victor Hugo, with whom Labrouste was in close touch. Hugo argued that architecture had originally evolved as a form of writing, a means of communication like literature. This it remained in its greatest periods, Greek and Gothic.

The arcuated façades of the Bibliothèque Ste-Geneviève, though austere, yet recall a range of great buildings from the early Renaissance onwards, such as Alberti's Tempio Malatestiana at Rimini, Sansovino's library in Venice, and two libraries in Cambridge, one by Wren and one by Cockerell. Inside, the entire upper portion of the building is devoted to a single vast reading-room composed of two barrel-vaulted aisles divided by a central row of columns. This unusual central spine recalls medieval refectories such as that at the

636 Entrance front of the Bibliothèque Ste-Geneviève, Paris (designed 1838–9; built 1843–50), by Labrouste

637 Interior of the main reading-room at the Bibliothèque Ste-Geneviève, Paris

former Abbaye de St Martin des Champs, Paris, which Vaudoyer was shortly to turn into a library for the Conservatoire des Arts et Métiers. What is especially remarkable about this reading-room is that the slender columns and the gracefully decorated arches which they support form an independent system of cast-iron, one of the earliest applications of this material in a monumental public building. Labrouste thus relates his building to the industrialized society of his day in a manner at once rationalist and poetic.

Labrouste was influenced by the egalitarian social philosophy known as *Saint-Simonisme* after its founder, C.-H. de R. Saint-Simon, which proposed that scientists and industrialists should replace the landed, military and priestly interests in government. In their pamphlet, *Aux artistes: du passé et de l'avenir des beaux-arts* ('To artists: on the past and future of the fine arts', 1830), the *Saint-*

638 *Opposite* Labrouste: The main reading-room, the Bibliothèque Nationale, Paris (1859–68)

639 *Above* Duc: The Salle de Harlay in the Palais de Justice, Paris (1857–68)

Simonistes, like Hugo, recognized two previous ideal or 'organic' phases of architecture, pre-Periclean Greek and medieval Gothic. Labrouste hoped that his Bibliothèque St-Geneviève would generate a third of these ideal phases, which were believed to be 'organic' because they were expressive of a coherent body of social ideals and religious belief. It was further felt that it was precisely the lack of any such unitary outlook which accounted for the inadequacy of nineteenth-century architecture. Hence the attempt to regenerate architecture through programmes of Utopian socialism, religion or, as in Labrouste's case, the religion of humanity which Comte developed from 1842.

Labrouste went on to design the *salle des imprimés* or main reading-room (1859–68) at another great Parisian library, the Bibliothèque Nationale. In this magical space the slenderest iron columns, crowned with lively foliage capitals, support a cluster of nine domes of glass and porcelain. It is surrounded by an outer arcade richly decorated in the Pompeiian style and containing lunettes painted to resemble the gardens of the Luxembourg, a favourite reading spot for students. The building lacks an ambitious exterior, so the greatest classical rival to the Bibliothèque Ste-Geneviève in mid-nineteenth-century Paris is the Palais de Justice by Louis-Joseph Duc (1802–79), especially the imposing entrance range of 1857–68 containing the entrance hall, the Salle de Harlay. We know that Duc, a pupil of Percier and a fellow *pensionnaire* of Labrouste at the French Academy in Rome, designed this as both a tribute and a corrective to the Bibliothèque Ste-Geneviève. The powerfully sculptural high-shouldered façade along the rue de

640 Vaudoyer: West front of Marseilles cathedral (1845–93)

nineteenth-century French architect, Viollet-le-Duc, as a building where 'everything holds together, everything is connected by a clear thought', it also gained for Duc a prize of 100,000 francs from Napoleon III in 1869 as the best work of art produced during the Second Empire.

The last example that we can mention here of the romantic eclecticism devised by the circle round Labrouste in the 1830s is Marseilles cathedral (1845–93) by Léon Vaudoyer (1803–72). This strident and somewhat ungainly domed edifice is an astonishing polychromatic medley of Byzantine, Florentine and Cairene forms on a plan with a French Romanesque east end. Built of local materials, this combination of Mediterranean and north European features symbolizes the role of Marseilles as the seaport link between these cultures, so that it was seen at the time not as meaningless eclecticism but as a thought-provoking summary of its time and place.

In the meantime Labrouste's radical reassessment of the aims and meaning of classical architecture had been paralleled by a similar investigation into the Gothic. The rationalist interpretation of Gothic structure by neo-classical theorists in the eighteenth century was succeeded by the romantic nationalism exemplified in the title of A.-L. Millin's *Antiquités nationales; ou, recueil de monumens pour servir à l'histoire générale et particulière de l'empire français* ('National antiquities; or, collection of monuments for use in the general and detailed history of the French Empire', 6 vols., 1790–6). This interest in French medieval history flowered in the strange Musée des Monuments Français which the scholar and antiquary Alexandre Lenoir began to establish in 1795 in the former Convent of the Petits Augustins, now a part of the Ecole des Beaux-Arts. Here he assembled in a picturesquely evocative medley medieval architectural fragments, sculpture and glass which had been rescued from buildings ravaged during the Revolution. Its elegiac mood influenced François-René de Châteaubriand, whose essay *Le Génie du Christianisme* ('Spirit of Christianity', 1802), identified the Catholic faith with

Harlay is divided into bays which are glazed in their upper parts and display inscriptions below, as at the Bibliothèque Ste-Geneviève. But Duc separated his bays with a massive applied order of Doric columns which are manifestly sculptural and not load-bearing. The result of Duc's wish to separate the expressive from the functional constituents of architecture, they are a poetic statement of the Doric order as the highest form of architectural expression. By contrast, the over-structured stone vaulting of the great entrance hall within stresses the working parts of a building in an extraordinarily dramatic way. Admired by the leading

the Gothic style in a way soon to be emphasized more strongly by Pugin in England.

We can trace Lenoir's impact on Victor Hugo's *Notre-Dame de Paris* (1st ed. 1831); he also lies behind Hugo's outrage at the vandalizing of ancient buildings which had continued since the Revolution. The awareness of the need to restore medieval architecture led to the establishment in 1830 of the office of Inspecteur-Général des Monuments Historiques by the historian and statesman François Guizot (1787–1874), on his appointment as prime minister by King Louis-Philippe. This was followed in 1837 by the creation of the Commission (later Service) des Monuments Historiques, with the task of classifying historic buildings as well as supervising and funding their restoration. It became the model for similar institutions throughout Europe.

In 1834 the romantic novelist, archaeologist and historian Prosper Mérimée (1803–70) was appointed Inspecteur-Général des Monuments Historiques. He became responsible for introducing the brilliant young architect and theorist Eugène-Emmanuel Viollet-le-Duc (1814–79) into the world of historical restoration. In 1840, at Mérimée's request, Viollet began work on the restoration of the Romanesque church at Vézelay, and joined J.-B.-A. Lassus (1807–57) on that of the Sainte-Chapelle in Paris. In 1844, again with Lassus, he began the restoration of Notre-Dame itself and on the provision of a new chapter-house. The rich polychromy of their work, for example in the restored Sainte-Chapelle which was much admired by Pugin on a visit in 1844, was a parallel to that of Hittorff and his circle. However, Viollet effected a far greater break with conventional academic taste than did Romantic classicists like Labrouste. He refused to enroll at the Ecole des Beaux-Arts and was throughout his life an enemy of the Ecole and the Académie and everything he thought they stood for. Increasingly socialist and atheist in outlook, he was determined to present his beloved Gothic as the functional solution of material problems and not as a manifestation of Catholicism. This he did in the most famous of his many books, *Dictionnaire raisonné*

SALLE VOÛTÉE
FER ET MAÇONNERIE.

641 Viollet-le-Duc: Design for a concert hall (c.1866), from *Entretiens sur l'architecture*, 1858–72

de l'architecture française du XIe au XVIe siècle ('Rational dictionary of French architecture from the 11th to the 16th centuries', 10 vols., 1854–68), where he also explained Greek and Byzantine architecture in similar terms. The book is unalluringly presented and is thus a parallel to his almost deliberately ungainly buildings, for example his churches of the 1860s at Saint-Denis and Aillant-sur-Tholon, which are the result of an aggressive no-nonsense approach.

Viollet believed that adherence to rational systems of structure and organization, together with adoption of new materials such as iron, would result in a new architectural language exclusive to the nineteenth century. In his book *Entretiens sur l'architecture* ('Discussions on architecture'), published between 1858 and 1872, he went so far as to sketch what this new architecture might look like. He shows us a polyhedral concert-hall designed in c.1866 with a ceiling vaulted in iron and brick which is supported on graceless iron struts like canted stovepipes. Similar awkwardness informs another unexecuted design for a market hall with a ceiling supported by V-poles. In fact Louis-Auguste Boileau (1812–96) had built a wholly Gothic church in Paris, St-Eugène (1854–5), in which the columns, tracery and ribs were of iron while even the vaults were covered with metal sheets.

An architect of predominantly classical sympathies whose hard rationalist approach united him intellectually with Viollet-le-Duc was the prolific Joseph-Auguste-Emile Vaudremer (1829–1914). For two Parisian churches, St-Pierre de Montrouge (1864–72) and Notre-Dame d'Auteuil (1876–80), he chose a stern Romanesque manner which undoubtedly influenced the American architect H. H. Richardson. Perhaps his most characteristic achievements are his schools, in particular the Lycée Buffon, a vast building erected in the Boulevard de Vaugirard in 1887–9. Here he combined symmetrical Beaux-Arts planning round three courtyards with façades in a kind of functional Renaissance style constructed of light yellow brick and limestone, patterned with pink brick and green tiles. The courtyards are treated like cloisters with open first-floor galleries in which stone columns with concrete capitals support iron roofs. This astringent architecture, with its 'rational' use of materials and its structural polychromy, is neither Gothic nor classic. Contriving to combine many of the ideals of the Ecole des Beaux-Arts with those of Viollet-le-Duc, it influenced the design of countless institutional buildings throughout the cities and towns of France, the history of which has yet to be written.

From the Second Empire to the Paris Exposition of 1900

Vaudremer has taken us beyond the 1850s and 1860s where we left Viollet-le-Duc. We should return to those decades to witness the birth of a scheme for altering the face of Paris along lines remote from Viollet's sympathies. The organizing genius of this far-reaching plan was that of Baron Georges-Eugène Haussmann (1809–91), born in Paris into a Protestant bourgeois family with firm Bonapartist loyalties. After the Revolution of 1848, Haussmann supported the cause of Louis-Napoleon who, as Emperor Napoleon III, appointed him Prefect of the Seine Department in June 1853. In the same month he summoned Haussmann to St-Cloud and showed him a map of Paris on which he had marked the building projects he had in mind, all in different coloured crayons so as to indicate the order of precedence. The emperor's ambitions in modernizing the historic city were complex, but included a wish to make it into a magnificent imperial capital with appropriate public monuments, yet at the same time capable of housing a growing population and of exploiting new developments in trade, industry and transport. He was also motivated by a genuine desire to improve the living conditions of his subjects by demolishing slums. It did not, of course, escape his attention that these very slums had been the breeding-ground since the 1780s of revolutionary groups who could easily erect impromptu barricades across the narrow entrances.

Haussmann retained his post until 1870, during which time he remodelled the entire city along monumental lines based on traditional French urban planning derived from Baroque precedent. Grand streets and boulevards lined with regular classical façades led up to ronds-points (traffic circles) where major public buildings and churches were erected to close the vistas. All this was accompanied by a modern drainage system with underground sewers which discharged into new conduits rather than the Seine, new water supplies, gas street-lighting and public fountains. New bridges were constructed over the Seine; new parks were laid out, such as the Bois de Boulogne, Bois de Vincennes, Parc Monceau and Parc des Buttes-Chaumont; new theatres were built, as well as new markets, including the celebrated Halles Centrales.

The architects employed to carry out this vast building programme included J.-C.-A. Alphand (1817–91), Victor Baltard (1805–74), H.-M. Lefuel (1810–80), G.-J.-A. Davioud (1823–81) and, the most gifted, Jean-Louis-Charles Garnier (1825–98). Alphand and Davioud were responsible for the new parks of which that of Buttes-Chaumont (1864–7) is the liveliest. It is a picturesque composition with a temple perched on a high rock like an eighteenth-century garden but it was not, like them, conceived as an escapist paradise. Rather, it was a part of the social life of the industrialized city, of which it commands impressive views.

Baltard, who constructed the Halles Centrales in 1854–70, had won the Grand Prix de Rome at the Ecole des Beaux-Arts in 1833 and was a protégé of the painter J.-A.-D. Ingres (1780–1867), for whom he painted the polychromatic background for his *Antiochus and Stratonice*. Baltard's tastes were for stone-built markets but, influenced by the engineer, Hector Horeau,

642 Aerial view of the Opéra, Paris, by Garnier, showing the boulevards laid out by Haussmann (1854–70)

643 Alphand and Davioud: The Parc des Buttes-Chaumont, Paris (1864–7), created on the site of a quarry

644 Exterior of St-Augustin, Paris (1860–71), by Baltard

Haussmann forced him to switch to iron and glass for the 14 pavilions connected by roofed streets which formed his Halles Centrales. These were demolished by misguided planners in 1973. Baltard's church of St-Augustin (1860–71) well encapsulates the mood of the Second Empire with its bustling and somewhat indigestible extravagance, and its confident eclecticism of style combined with cast-iron columns. Indeed, the swelling forms of St-Augustin, encrusted with ostentatious ornament, seem the very expression in stone of the women's fashions of the day.

Lefuel's sumptuous extensions finally linking the Louvre with the Tuileries were begun in 1854 with high pavilion roofs which set an influential pattern in France and the United States. Four years later Davioud designed the first of his four elaborately architectural fountains,

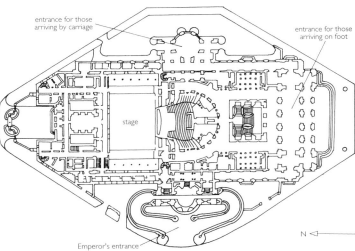

entrance for those
arriving by carriage

entrance for those
arriving on foot

stage

Emperor's entrance

N

645 *Left* Davioud: Fontaine St-Michel, Paris (1858)

646 *Above* Plan of the ground floor of the Opéra, Paris (1862–75), by Garnier

the Fontaine St-Michel, a Baroque monument marking the beginning of Haussmann's Boulevard St-Michel.

Rarely can a great city have been transformed with such feverish activity in so short a time with such mountains of carved stone and ornamental stucco. It exerted tremendous influence, throughout Europe and beyond, on the development of major cities such as Rome, Vienna, Brussels, Lyons and Toulouse It must be confessed, however, that in Paris only one of the individual buildings is unquestionably a masterpiece of the first rank. This is the Opéra, built in 1862–75 from designs by Garnier which were of such imperial magnificence that the architect himself summed up their style to the Empress Eugénie as the 'style Napoléon III'. In books published in 1871, 1878 and 1881, Garnier made it clear that his aim was to produce an opera house where every part of the building contributed to the experience of visitors, representing in their diversity the whole of Second Empire society. He arranged the circulation of the building for the convenience and

delight of those arriving, whom he placed in four categories: the carriage-borne and the pedestrian, with tickets and without. They have separate entrances and vestibules of varying degrees of splendour, while the emperor had a separate carriage ramp encircling a rotunda on the side elevation. In fact Napoleon fell from power in 1870 and his pavilion, no longer required, remains uncompleted to this day.

Garnier saw opera as a ceremonial embodiment of man's most primitive instincts, a ritual coming together to share dreams and imaginings. The spectators were there to be seen as well as to see. They, too, were actors. Thus the drama of an evening at the opera was to begin not in the auditorium but in the main foyer, where there were mirrors set in the columns to allow women to adjust their finery before ascending the grandiose staircase (fig. 701). In one of the most original architectural descriptions of all time, Garnier tells us how the marbles, chandeliers and arched colonnades of the staircase, which was inspired by Victor Louis's at the

Bordeaux theatre (1773–80) (p. 403) were intended to create a mood of radiant content, to which the sumptuously dressed spectators would respond in their facial expressions and their animated greetings to their acquaintances. The lobbies, corridors and foyers surrounding the staircase, many of them open to it, were rich in sculpture, gilding and colouring and were larger than those in any previous theatre. They catered for a wide variety of activities, including, for example, smoking-rooms for men and ice-cream parlours for women.

Polychromatic ornament was also a feature of the exterior, which was enriched with gold mosaic and gilded ornamental details. The monumentality and near-sobriety of the entrance front, which deliberately eschews Baroque excess, reminds us that Garnier had received the classic French architectural education as a pupil of Lebas at the Ecole des Beaux-Arts, where he won the Grand Prix in 1848. In Rome he made studies of Trajan's Column and the Temple of Vesta, then travelled to Sicily and, in 1852, to Greece. As he subsequently explained, it was in Greece that he 'understood for the first time the magical power of art and the majesty of antique architecture'. His, of course, was no longer the vision of Greece which Winckelmann would have understood, since it was essentially the product of post-Hittorffian polychromatic ideals. The restoration study he made in 1852 of the Temple of Jupiter Panhellenius on the island of Aegina, dependent on the researches of C. R. Cockerell and F. C. Penrose, was as vibrantly coloured as that eventually published by Cockerell in 1860 (p. 463).

The Paris Exposition of 1889 demonstrated a wholly different side of French dynamism in architecture and design. Two permanent structures associated with it attracted the admiration of visitors from all over Europe: the Three-Hundred-Meter Tower, designed by the engineer Gustave Eiffel (1832–1923), and the Palace of Machines (1886–9; dem. 1910), designed by the architect Ferdinand Dutert (1845–1906) and constructed with the assistance of the engineers Contamin, Pierron and Charton. Both buildings depended on techniques in metal construction originally developed in connection with railway bridges and stations. Dutert, a product of the Ecole des Beaux-Arts, won the Grand Prix in 1869. The great rectangular hall of his Palace of Machines was roofed in a single span with the aid of 20 transverse three-hinged arches of iron. Photographs of the buildings in modern architectural books always show the austerely functional iron and glass structure just before completion, so that it lacks the coloured glass, paintings, mosaic and ceramic bricks with which it was clothed, and which were expected by contemporaries. Gustave Eiffel, architect of the celebrated tower which came to bear his name, was born in Dijon and studied at the Ecole Centrale des Arts et Manufactures in Paris where he specialized in metal construction. He built numerous iron railway-bridges in France, Europe and South America, for example the imposing Garabit Viaduct (1885–8), not far from that masterpiece of ancient Roman engineering, the Pont du Gard. The Eiffel Tower was a brilliantly imaginative assembly of many small parts, strong, lightweight and wind-resistant, into a monumental whole of unforgettable profile. Its design is governed by aesthetic, not technical considerations: for example, the huge sweeping arches which connect the feet of the tower and appear to help carry its weight are the reverse of load-bearing, for they are decorative features suspended from the superstructure.

It should not be thought that, despite these technical innovations, the classical tradition of which Garnier's Opéra was so dazzlingly opulent an expression petered out in the later nineteenth century. It must be stated, however, that the Opéra has not been equalled as a work of art by any single building erected in France from that day to this. The numerous architects who, deliberately avoiding the Baroque extravagance of many of Garnier's imitators, carried Beaux-Arts ideals into the early twentieth century, included E.-G. Cocquart (1831–1902), P.-G.-H. Daumet (1826–1911), H.-A.-A. Deglane (1855–1931), P.-R.-L. Ginain (1825–1908),

647 *Left* Eiffel: The Eiffel Tower, Paris (1889)

648 *Above* Laloux: Exterior of the Gare du Quai d'Orsay, Paris (designed c.1896–7; built 1898–1900)

Germain, is a subtle Hellenistic Greek essay which owes much to Duc. Pascal was a tremendously influential educator of Beaux-Arts students, including no less than 48 Americans. In his Faculté de Médecine et de Pharmacie (1880–8) at Bordeaux, Pascal deployed the same impeccable classicism as Ginain. His pupil, Nénot, designed one of the largest public buildings of his day in Paris, the Nouvelle Sorbonne (1885–1901). A magnificent if somewhat ostentatious product of the planning ideals of the Ecole des Beaux-Arts, the Sorbonne was influential in America where, for example, the architects McKim, Mead and White hung a framed drawing of it in their office.

As we approach 1900 a greater exuberance is noticeable, especially in the work of Laloux, Deglane and Girault. Laloux is memorable for his two railway stations, that at Tours (1895–8) and the Gare du Quai d'Orsay, Paris (designed c.1896–7; built 1898–1900). The florid façade of the Parisian terminus of the Orléans–Paris line, with its seven great arches below a frothily decorated skyline, fronts a superb multi-domed vestibule which deploys on a larger scale some of the themes of Labrouste's Bibliothèque Nationale (p. 449). This magnificent entry into the heart of Paris was one of the three permanent structures built in connection

C.-L. Girault (1851–1932), V.-A.-F. Laloux (1850–1937), P.-H. Nénot (1853–1934) and J.-L. Pascal (1837–1920). There has been a conspiracy of silence in twentieth-century critical literature about the skill, knowledge and influence of these classical architects.

Cocquart and Daumet both designed sumptuous interiors at Duc's Palais de Justice, while the latter rebuilt the château of Chantilly (1875–82), adding a masterly staircase of great visual drama. Ginain, a pupil of L.-H. Lebas, won the Grand Prix in 1852 and made a restoration study of the Greek theatre at Taormina while in Italy. His most distinguished building, the Ecole de Médecine (1878–1900) in the Boulevard St-

649 *Above* Staircase at the Nouvelle Sorbonne, Paris (1885–1901), by Nénot

650 *Below* Deglane, Louvet and Thomas: Exterior of the Grand Palais, Paris (1895–1900)

with the Paris Exposition of 1900. The others, which more or less face it across the Seine, are the Grand and Petit Palais, built in 1895–1900 as tributes to the style of Garnier. They have exuberantly classical exteriors of stone and extremely complicated plans which were hailed at the time as proof of the vitality of Beaux-Arts ideals. Girault's Petit Palais has a trapezoidal plan enclosing a semicircular garden court surrounded by a colonnade. The Grand Palais, designed by Deglane, A. Louvet and A.-E.-T. Thomas, boasts a colonnaded stone exterior containing a remarkable iron and glass interior capped by a swelling dome. It has been described as a Palace of Machines inside a conventional museum, and thus enshrines many of the architectural and theoretical ideals of nineteenth-century France, a period which was one of the most intellectually challenging in the history of western architecture.

Britain

Regency and Early Victorian

Flushed with national pride following its hard-won victory over Napoleon, increasingly enriched by the rapid growth of the industrial revolution, and ruled by a monarch – the Prince Regent, from 1820 George IV – who was obsessed with image-making in general and with interior design in particular, Britain was ideally poised for a period of building expansion after 1815. An important initiative for the improvement of central London had come in 1811 with the reversion to the Crown, after a long lease, of Marylebone Park. This was an area of over 500 acres right on the northern edge of central London, ripe for redevelopment. The architect John Nash (1752–1835) provided a remarkable plan for building individual villas and terraces (row houses) in and around a picturesquely landscaped park which would preserve something of the existing rural character. He further proposed to link this with the West End, and with the Prince Regent's palace of Carlton

651 Cumberland Terrace, Regent's Park, London (1825), by Nash

652 View of Park Village West (1824–8), by Nash

653 Plan of Luscombe Castle, Devon, by Nash

0   3

1 hall
2 inner hall
3 morning-room
4 serving-room
5 veranda
6 drawing-room
7 library

House in Pall Mall, by creating a new street, known as Regent Street, running north to south. The Prince Regent was delighted with the scheme, declaring that 'it will quite eclipse Napoleon' when it was outlined to him in 1811. Largely built in the ten years following 1815, it represented a triumph of Picturesque ideals brought, for the first time on such a scale, to an urban setting. Nash described how the villas in the park were to be carefully sited in relation to each other and to groves of trees in such a way 'that no villa should see any other, but each should appear to possess the whole of the Park'. He also justified the deliberately irregular grouping of the buildings in the new street by claiming that such 'Individuality and variety of design . . . may produce the same effect to the eye as the High Street of Oxford so generally admired'.

Nash had developed this scenic approach to architectural design in association with his former partner Humphry Repton (1752–1818), who had succeeded Capability Brown as the principal landscape gardener in the country. Together they designed a number of country houses and villas which blended nature and architecture into an asymmetrical whole of astonishing freedom. Nash was a pupil of one of the pioneers of villa design, Sir Robert Taylor (1714–88), in whose office he would have been familiar with the demand for houses which, rather than being the centres of large landed estates, were escapist rural retreats for rich merchants and bankers whose real source of wealth was not in the land but in the city.

Perhaps the loveliest small house of this type by Nash and Repton is Luscombe Castle, Devon (1800–4), for the banker Charles Hoare. Set in a remote and lushly wooded valley, it has a roughly cruciform plan which seems to explode outwards from the circular lobby at its heart. A characteristic feature is the large verandah which opens off the octagonal drawing-room and is open to the garden in the summer but closed with glass doors in the winter. This blurs the distinction between interior and exterior with a spatial freedom which anticipates that of Frank Lloyd Wright (see pp. 565–77). As a miniature castle Luscombe is also important for reducing, to a small scale suitable for middle-class residences, the formula established in the first of the asymmetrical castellated country houses of the eighteenth century, Downton Castle, Herefordshire (1772–8). This was a landmark in the development of an irregular architecture to blend with an irregular landscape. Nash knew both this pioneering building and its owner and designer, the influential Picturesque theorist, Richard Payne Knight (1750–1824). In two small streets, the so-called Park Villages, which he built in 1824–8 on the north-eastern edge of Regent's Park, Nash repeated the Luscombe theme on a yet smaller scale in a series of modest houses. Here he provided a seductive model for suburban

654 *Above* Nash: Luscombe Castle, Devon (1800–4) (with Sir Gilbert Scott's chapel of 1862 in the foreground)

655 *Right* Windsor Castle from the south as remodelled by Wyatville (1824–40)

development which was followed well into the twentieth century.

It is appropriate in an architect who was above all a master of illusion that two of Nash's principal commissions, both from the Prince Regent, should have been for the complete transformation of existing buildings, Brighton Pavilion (1815–21) and Buckingham Palace (1825–30). By a spectacular conjuring trick he transformed Brighton Pavilion, built for the Prince in a chaste classical style by Henry Holland in the 1780s, into a neo-oriental extravaganza without parallel in Europe (fig. 577). His remodelling of Buckingham House, originally built in 1702–5, into a metropolitan palace was less successful, perhaps because he lacked the training to organize the classical language coherently on so vast a scale, and in his mid-seventies was too old to acquire it. The architect Sir Jeffry Wyatville (1766–1840) provided George IV with a more stirring visual symbol of the British monarchy in his enlarging and remodelling of Windsor Castle from 1824–40 in a massive medievalizing style. Finding the skyline provided by the squat twelfth-century Round Tower inadequately commanding now that he had heightened other parts of the castle, Wyatville raised its height by some 30 feet (9m) by adding a false top in the form of a collar, an audacious but scenically masterful stroke entirely in accordance with Picturesque doctrine.

In London Sir John Soane (1753–1837) was busy in the 1820s creating appropriate settings, all now destroyed, for the ceremonies of public life at Westminster and Whitehall. His work here, in the individual style he had established in the 1790s (see p. 389), was carried out in his capacity as one of the three 'Attached Architects' to the Office of Works, a crown appointment which he had secured in 1813 in conjunction with Nash and Smirke.

Sir Robert Smirke (1780–1867), a generation younger than Soane and Nash, introduced a new element into the story of English architecture, though one we have already explored in nineteenth-century France. Temples or churches, palaces and major civic buildings predominated in our chapters from the ancient world to the end of the eighteenth century. New building types

now arose, as a result of demands created by the industrial revolution, and by the growth of the democratic institutions which accompanied the transference of power to a newly prosperous bourgeoisie. The extensive career of Smirke reflects this wide range of opportunities: apart from building numerous churches and country houses in Greek and Gothic styles, he was responsible in London between 1808 and 1836 for the British Museum, the General Post Office, the completion of the Royal Mint and of the Milbank Penitentiary, the rebuilding of the Custom House, Covent Garden Theatre, the Royal College of Physicians, King's College, Whitmore's Bank, the Equitable Assurance Company's office, the United Service Club, the Union Club and the Oxford and Cambridge Club, and extensive premises for barristers in the Inner Temple. This amounts to a recipe for a recognizably modern city. It was to be repeated throughout Europe after 1815 as towns and cities

renewed themselves with administrative buildings in the centre and institutions such as abattoirs and cemeteries on the outskirts.

Smirke's own activities as a public architect were by no means confined to London. He provided county courts or shire halls at various towns throughout Britain as well as gaols, hospitals, markets and bridges. The range of building types seems almost more important than their actual architectural expression. Indeed, it must be admitted that, with the exception of the British Museum (1823–46), which is memorable for the seemingly endless parade of Greek Ionic columns comprising its façade, Smirke's architectural language is singularly unimaginative for someone who had been a pupil of both Soane and Dance. His serviceable style with its minimum ornamental detail and its air of Greek restraint was widely imitated, for it was noted that his buildings were not prohibitively expensive, nor did they decay, leak or fall down. He was also a pioneer in the use

656 *Opposite* Smirke: Entrance front of the British Museum, London (1823–46)

657 *Above* Exterior of the Royal College of Physicians, Edinburgh (1844–6), by Hamilton

of load-bearing foundations of lime concrete and in the introduction of cast-iron beams in public and domestic architecture. Cast iron had been a feature of industrial buildings such as Marshall, Benyon and Bage's flour mill at Ditherington, Shropshire (1796–7), North Mill at Belper, Derbyshire (1804), and the Cloth Mill at Kings Stanley, Gloucestershire (1812–13). These revolutionary fireproof buildings of brick and iron, avoiding the use of timber, were well on the way to full iron-frame construction.

In Scotland the Greek Revival was adopted for public buildings with such panache that the city of Edinburgh, helped by the drama of its natural setting, became justly known as the Athens of the North. The bold essays in the Greek Revival by Thomas Hamilton (1784–1858) included the Royal High School (1825–9) and the more eclectic Royal College of Physicians (1844–6), while William Henry Playfair (1790–1857) provided the scarcely less imposing Royal Institution (1822–6) and

adjacent National Gallery of Scotland (1850–7). Perhaps the finest British monument to commemorate the continuing impact of Greece and Rome in the first half of the nineteenth century is St George's Hall, Liverpool. This magnificent product of the civic pride of an expanding industrial city contains two law courts, a vast barrel-vaulted assembly hall and a concert hall. It was designed in 1839–40 by the young Harvey Lonsdale Elmes (1814–47), who had not then travelled abroad, though in 1842 he visited Germany and saw monumental classical buildings by Schinkel and Klenze which, through illustrations, may already have impressed him. The construction of St George's Hall was completed after Elmes's death in 1847 by the engineer Robert Rawlinson and finally by C. R. Cockerell, who in 1851–4 designed the interior of the beautiful elliptical concert hall, surrounded by an undulating balcony supported by caryatids.

Charles Robert Cockerell (1788–1863) was the most gifted and knowledgeable architect of his day in Britain. His talents would doubtless have found fuller expression in France, where it is not difficult to imagine him teaching at the Ecole des Beaux-Arts while engaged on the design of a monumental public building in Paris. In the course of an unusually extended Grand Tour from 1810 to 1817 he had been the first to notice and measure the entasis of the columns of the Parthenon, while his spectacular discoveries of Greek architecture and sculpture at Bassae and Aegina also made him particularly sensitive to what he saw as the sculptural basis of Greek design. A fastidious and self-critical architect, he has left us diaries of 1821–32 in which we can trace the hesitant progress of his attempts to apply his unique knowledge to modern design so as to create an architecture uniting, to quote a phrase from his diary in 1822, 'the richness of Rococo and the breadth and merit of Greek'.

Disapproving of his master, Robert Smirke, and his rival William Wilkins (1778–1839), for their too rigid adherence in some buildings to exclusively Greek models, Cockerell was open to influence from classical buildings of all periods. He saw himself as the inheritor of the whole classical language of architecture, not just of a small or privileged part of it. Buildings such as his Ashmolean Museum and Taylorian Institution (1839–45) in Oxford and the Cambridge University Library (today Squire Law Library, 1837–40) contain daring conjunctions of Grecian columns with Roman arches. They have a boldness of scale, a refinement of line and a range of eclectic though never indigestible stylistic references in which Cockerell combines the springing lines of the Greeks, the rich surface textures of Italian

Mannerism, and the massive drama of English Baroque architects such as Vanbrugh and Hawksmoor. The result is a unique English equivalent to the work of Hittorff, Duc and Labrouste. His achievement was recognized in France, where he became one of the eight foreign associates of the Académie des Beaux-Arts.

Cockerell's marked tendency to draw for inspiration on Italian sixteenth-century architecture was paralleled in a rather more obvious way by Sir Charles Barry (1795–1860), who was responsible for bringing the Italian Renaissance palazzo to the streets of London in the form of the Travellers' Club (1829–32) and, more completely, in the Reform Club (1837–41), next door in Pall Mall. The Italianate theme was appropriate for the Travellers' Club, an institution which was in some ways the culmination of the eighteenth-century Grand Tour, since one of its functions was to provide a place in

658, 659 *Left and below* Plan and exterior of St George's Hall, Liverpool (designed 1839–40), by Elmes. The sculpture in the pediment has been removed.

660 Cockerell: Façade of the Taylorian Institution at the Ashmolean Museum, Oxford (1839–45)

which English gentlemen might return hospitality to foreigners who had received them abroad. The choice of the Palazzo Farnese as a model for the Reform Club was symbolically less appropriate. The Reform Club had been founded by members of the Radical and Whig factions in the wake of the Reform Bill of 1832 which extended the franchise to the new industrial rich. Architecturally Barry's building was a triumph, with a noble interior organized round a great central court surrounded by galleries and, in deference to the English climate, covered with a glazed roof. Combining this coherent and lucid spatial articulation with the most advanced mechanical services in the field of heating, lighting and ventilation, the club was one of the few contemporary English buildings admired by leaders of French architectural thought such as Daly and Hittorff.

Barry provided a series of spectacular country houses for patrons whom the industrial revolution had transformed into millionaires. These included the 2nd Duke of Sutherland, for whom he remodelled Trentham, Staffordshire (1833–49) and Cliveden, Buckinghamshire (1850–1), the latter with proud façades recalling sixteenth-century Italian models such as Vignola's Palazzo Farnese at Caprarola. For the Duke of Sutherland's brother, the 1st Earl of Ellesmere, Barry built the palatial Bridgewater House, London (1846–51), but his principal work in London is, of course, the Palace of Westminster and Houses of Parliament. He won this prestigious commission in a competition in 1836 and it was built from his designs in 1840–70, its construction during the last decade being supervised by his son, E. M. Barry. The terms of the competition stipulated that the new building should be 'Gothic or Elizabethan', a romantic gesture intended to emphasize the historic continuity of the British parliamentary system. Barry would have preferred a Renaissance Italian model, and his river front is thus completely symmetrical. Its mass and pattern recall Inigo Jones's unexecuted projects for the Palace of Whitehall, even though its detailing, designed by Pugin, was based on authentic Gothic models.

465

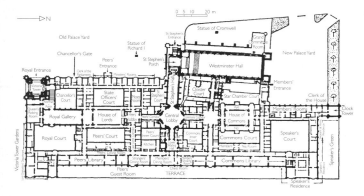

661 *Above* Plan of the Palace of Westminster, London (1840–70) by Barry

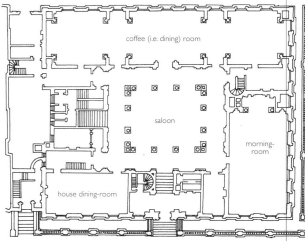

663, 664 *Above and opposite* Ground-floor plan and Main Saloon of the Reform Club, London (1837–41), by Barry

662 Aerial view of the Palace of Westminster and Houses of Parliament, with Westminster Abbey in the foreground and St Stephen's Hall in the centre (see Chapter 5)

Gothic Revival

Augustus Welby Northmore Pugin (1812–52), Barry's reluctant partner, was a fanatical enthusiast of Gothic. His passionate belief in the superiority of medieval over all other architectural periods was to have a profound impact on nineteenth-century architecture in England and beyond. In a series of polemical illustrated books, beginning with the uncompromisingly titled *Contrasts; or, a Parallel between the Noble Edifices of the 14th and 15th centuries, and similar buildings of the Present Day; Shewing the Present Decay of Taste* (Salisbury 1836), he wrote of Gothic architecture and design as though they possessed the unchallengeable authority and permanence of the doctrines of the Roman Catholic church, to which he was converted in 1834. His image of a whole moral order enshrined in the culture of a particular age was curiously close to the Grecian myth propagated by Winckelmann (p. 372), and may have been coloured by the romantic approach to Gothic in the early nineteenth-century writings of Friedrich Schlegel in Germany and François-René de Châteaubriand in France. This approach quickly led to the belief that only men of good moral character could design good works of art, a view which John Ruskin was soon to espouse in such aphorisms as: 'A foolish person builds foolishly, and a wise one sensibly; a virtuous one, beautifully; and a vicious one, basely' (*Queen of the Air*, 1869).

Pugin's defence of his chosen style, on the grounds that it was 'not a style but a principle', involved the claim that Gothic was 'true' because it was the result of an honest use of materials in which structure was exposed and function thereby demonstrated. Architectural thinking of this kind was wholly new in England, though in France, as we have seen, it had been since the eighteenth century the standard method of interpretation of both classic and Gothic architecture. Taken to its extreme, as in the writings of Laugier, it abolished the classical language of architecture by removing everything except load-bearing members. Just as Laugier's fanaticism was condemned by Sir William Chambers, so was Pugin's by Cockerell, who was understandably alarmed at the narrowing of the range of architectural possibilities which Pugin's doctrines implied. He doubtless realized, for example, that Pugin's analysis was false even when applied to the interpretation of medieval buildings: the fourteenth-century octagon at Ely Cathedral achieves its poetic effects, as we saw in Chapter 5 (p. 177), by reliance on sham vaults and concealed load-bearing supports.

Pugin was a prolific architect of Catholic churches but in a Protestant country where full Catholic emancipation had only been granted as recently as 1829, his practice was inevitably hampered by lack of wealthy patrons. The principal exception was the 16th Earl of Shrewsbury, who paid for Pugin's neo-fourteenthcentury Catholic church of St Giles, Cheadle, Staffordshire

665 Scott: The Albert Memorial, Kensington Gardens, London (1863–72)

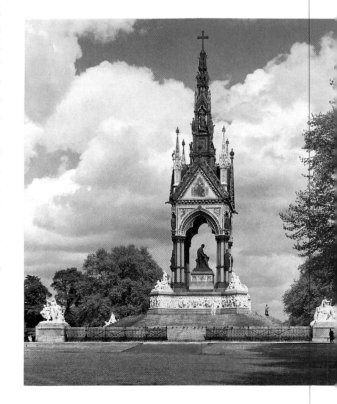

(1840–6), with its gorgeously polychromatic painted interior (fig. 706), and who commissioned the Hospital of St John at Alton, Staffordshire. Built in c. 1840–4 as a combined alms-house with chapel, school and village hall, this well demonstrates the social gospel which underlay the Christian revival and the accompanying Gothic Revival in Victorian England. However, as a group it is overshadowed by the adjacent Alton Castle, built for Lord Shrewsbury by Pugin in 1847–51. This towering neo-medieval pile was simply a seigneurial gesture serving no practical purpose, since the pious earl lived in nearby Alton Towers.

The Church of England underwent a spiritual revival in the early nineteenth century in which a return to Gothic was regarded, as it was by Pugin, as evidence of a return to Christian orthodoxy. Anglicans, more numerous and more prosperous than Catholics, were better able to put Pugin's principles into practice. Pugin's contemporary Sir George Gilbert Scott (1811–78) provided countless Gothic churches, beginning with St Giles, Camberwell, London (1842–4), but was also a specialist in secular buildings, publishing *Remarks on Secular and Domestic Architecture, Past and Present* (1857), to prove that Gothic was perfectly appropriate for this purpose. A wholly ecclesiastical flavour predominates in his Albert Memorial, Kensington Gardens, London (1863–72), the national memorial to Queen Victoria's consort over whose seated statue rises a sumptuous shrine or baldacchino of astonishing height. Albert, as a kind of secular saint, was appropriately enshrined within this frankly religious monument inspired by Gothic tabernacles such as that by Orcagna of the mid-fourteenth century in the church of Or San Michele, Florence. Scott's spired and pinnacled Midland Grand Hotel, St Pancras, London (1868–74), a design which the architect himself considered possibly '*too good* for its purpose' as a station hotel, is in some sense a compensation for his disappointment at the Foreign Office. His Gothic designs for the Foreign Office were found too High Church and High Tory in tone by the old-fashioned Whig prime minister, Lord Palmerston, who

forced him to redesign them in an Italian Renaissance style. Nevertheless, with its asymmetrically placed corner tower overlooking the Picturesquely landscaped St James's Park like a country house by Barry, Scott's Foreign Office (1862–73) is, thanks to Palmerston, one of his happiest buildings.

Scott was a self-made professional man with a highly successful career, in which he worked on over a thousand buildings and accumulated a substantial fortune. A sterner sense of artistic dedication coloured the careers of Butterfield and Street whose work, with that of Edward Buckton Lamb, Samuel Sanders Teulon, William Burges and James Brooks, dominated what is known as the High Victorian movement, lasting from 1850 to 1870. An early monument of this aggressive phase of the Gothic Revival, marked by strident polychromy and assertive muscularity of outline and detail, is All Saints, Margaret Street, London (1849–59). This was built by William Butterfield (1814–1900) as the model church of the influential Ecclesiological Society, founded in 1839 as the Cambridge Camden Society to promote the revival of correct, i.e. medieval, church building and liturgy. Butterfield developed his polychromatic brick Gothic in a series of masterly churches such as St Alban, Holborn (1859–62) and All Saints, Babbacombe, Devon (1865–74), and deployed it as consistently in educational buildings such as Keble College, Oxford (1867–83), and Rugby School, Warwickshire (1858–74; chapel 1870–2).

It was also around 1850 that John Ruskin (1819–1900) began to support the Gothic Revival in books such as *The Seven Lamps of Architecture* (1849) and *The Stones of Venice* (3 vols., 1851–3). His seven lamps included Sacrifice, which is necessary because architecture involves artistic effort and is not just a mechanical solution of a material problem; Truth, which calls for the avoidance of 'false' materials, hidden supports, and machine production; Power, signified by the control of mass and shade; Memory, or the need to build for the future because buildings only become great through the passing of time and the acquisition of historical association; and Obedience, the faithfulness to past forms instead of the feverish search for new ones. Ruskin was influential firstly because the moral emphasis in his writing responded to a particular chord in the Victorian outlook; secondly because he wrote convincingly about architecture as something that passionately mattered; and finally because of the grandeur and poetry of his prose, an example of which we have already quoted in our account of St Mark's, Venice (p. 103). It may not be too much of an exaggeration to say that he is the most captivating writer on architecture of all time. Thus his lyrical account of the cultural and artistic significance of the city in *The Stones of Venice* encouraged, not always to his satisfaction,

the progress of a Venetian Gothic revival in English architecture. The same book contains a chapter, 'On the Nature of Gothic', in which the claim that the beauty of medieval art was a result of the pleasure the workman had taken in creating it was used by William Morris (1834–96) to justify the ideals of the Arts and Crafts movement and of the emergent theories of socialism.

Among those in sympathy with Ruskin was George Edmund Street (1824–81), a deeply religious man who believed that good buildings could only be produced by

666 Exterior of the chapel, Keble College, Oxford (1867–83), by Butterfield

architects and patrons sharing Christian intentions. In his *Brick and Marble in the Middle Ages: Notes of a Tour in the North of Italy* (1855) he argued that in the modern search for an architecture of truth and purity Italian Gothic provided valuable inspiration, since it was a way of building in which the principal materials, brick and marble, were employed in both decoration and construction. Street built numerous churches with this tough and scarcely very Gothic use of materials, but his largest building was the Law Courts in London, built in 1874–82 as the last national monument in the Gothic Revival style. The long entrance front to the Strand is architecture of undeniable power and conviction, its lively pinnacled silhouette and vigorous asymmetry forming an object lesson in how to place a monumental building successfully in a narrow street. However, the internal planning was inept, and sacrificed convenience to a vast vaulted hall of markedly ecclesiastical appearance but with little symbolical and no practical function.

Perhaps the most captivating entry in the Law Courts competition, which took place in 1866, was that by William Burges (1827–81), who produced a dream-like vision of the medieval city with 18 cloud-capped towers, flying paths and bridges, and a crenellated Tuscan campanile, 335 feet (102m) high. Its exuberant fantasy encouraged many younger architects to move away from the sterner mood and simpler massing of the mid-century. Burges himself found in the 3rd Marquess of Bute (1847–1900), Catholic convert, heir to an industrial fortune and reputedly the richest man in the world, a patron who had some eccentricities in common with the 'mad' king Ludwig II of Bavaria, Wagner's admirer. Burges completely rebuilt for the marquess both Cardiff Castle (1868–81) and, not far away, Castell Coch (1875–81), each with opulent interiors rich in symbolism and narrative art recalling the work of the pre-Raphaelite painters (fig. 712). The exteriors of these Wagnerian dream-castles, which combine massive unadorned walls with machicolated towers capped by slender spires, are indebted to the reconstructions of

667 Street: The Law Courts, the Strand, London (1874–82)

French medieval castles in Viollet-le-Duc's *Dictionnaire de l'architecture française du XIe au XVIe siècle* (1854–68). 'We all crib from Viollet-le-Duc', he openly admitted, 'although probably not one buyer in ten reads the text.' However, Burges was disappointed when in 1873 he visited Viollet's gargantuan reconstruction for Napoleon III of the château of Pierrefonds (1858–70); though Viollet's skyline is impressive from a distance, the courtyard elevations are confused and the interiors lifeless. Burges himself influenced the development of later-nineteenth-century architecture in America, by introducing his massive forms into the multi-towered buildings he designed but only partly executed for the American Episcopalians at Trinity College, Hartford, Connecticut (1873–82).

Burges and his contemporaries were, like their patrons, in revolt against the materialism and the squalor which the unchecked tide of the industrial revolution was bringing in its wake. Ruskin was perhaps the most influential of those who condemned the inhumane consequences of the new technology. Like Pugin, he included among these the Crystal Palace, built in Hyde

668 Lithograph of Crystal Palace, Hyde Park, London(1851), by Paxton

Park to house the Great Exhibition of 1851 from designs by Sir Joseph Paxton (1801–65). This astonishing structure of cast iron, wrought iron and glass, rising in three stepped tiers bisected by a higher barrel-vaulted transept, has sometimes been hailed as a revolutionary step on the way to modern architecture. In fact, it would be more appropriate to regard it as the climax of a tradition of greenhouse and railway-shed design established in the 1830s and 1840s. Iron and glass were not, and never have been, appropriate materials for anything more than a very narrow range of building types. Paxton himself knew this, and for the costly châteaux he built in the 1850s and 1860s for members of the Rothschild family – Mentmore, Buckinghamshire, Ferrières near Paris, and Pregny outside Geneva – he selected neo-Elizabethan or neo-Renaissance modes. He felt that these, suitably combined with integral systems of heating and artificial ventilation, were as appropriate for their function as the Crystal Palace was for its.

It would also be wrong to regard the Crystal Palace as merely a technological solution of a practical problem: it was aesthetically memorable for the poetry of its curved-roofed transept, for the application of decorative timberwork both inside and out, and for the carefully thought-out polychromy of its interior. Devised by Owen Jones (1809–74), this consisted of bold stripes of red, yellow and blue separated by white. Fired by recent discoveries concerning the polychrome decoration of Greek temples, and believing that only primary colours were used in the greatest periods of art, Jones's aim was to heighten the impression of vastness and light by creating a kind of architectural landscape. Influenced, like Labrouste, by the Utilitarian Positivism of Comte (p. 446), he believed in the scientific laws and predictable effects of colour. He expounded these views in his magisterial book, *Grammar of Ornament* (1856).

Shaw and the Late Victorians

Meanwhile reaction was setting in to the solemnity, the moralizing and the heavy ecclesiastical tone of the High Victorian era. The leading figure was Richard Norman Shaw (1831–1912), who, significantly, is known as an architect of houses rather than churches. He devised an architectural language known as the 'Old English' style which incorporated rural vernacular techniques such as tile-hung or half-timbered walls, tall chimneys, steep roofs, and mullioned windows with leaded lights. This was intended to be relaxed, unpretentious and comfortable, in contrast to the showy or churchy effects of earlier nineteenth-century mansions in Gothic, baronial or Italianate styles. From the mid-century the accumulators of commercial fortunes could begin to escape by train from their city offices to rural retreats where they could preserve the image of a pre-industrial life.

One of the first examples of the Old English style was Leyswood, Sussex, designed and built by Norman Shaw in 1866–9 for his cousin William Temple, the prosperous director of the Shaw Savill shipping line. Adapting his design to a steeply sloping site with consummate Picturesque skill, Shaw provided an irregular house loosely strung out round three sides of a courtyard, recalling a manorial garth, and approached through a high tower like those on the gateways of German medieval towns. In 1870–2 he built a similar house called Grims Dyke at Harrow Weald, near London, for the genre painter Frederick Goodall. This is a split-level house united by a meandering staircase, from the half-landing of which access is gained to a subsidiary wing containing the artist's studio, placed at a canted angle to the rest of the house. Viollet-le-Duc praised the house in his *Habitations Modernes* (1875) for its additive plan suggestive of growth down the centuries. This admiration of the effects of growth and change in architecture was fundamental both to Picturesque theory and to Ruskin's understanding of architecture as living history. Shaw took the theme to extreme lengths in the house he built as an 'essay in the Sublime' at Cragside, Northumberland, for Sir William (later 1st Lord) Armstrong, a millionaire armaments manufacturer, scientist and inventor. Cragside extended over the hillside between 1869 and 1884 in a way not originally envisaged by its patron, sprouting endless gables, Gothic archways, soaring chimneys and unexpected areas of half-timbering.

For urban situations, where this explosive ebullient architecture seemed less suitable, Shaw devised a style which became known as 'Queen Anne'. Though that monarch had reigned from 1702 to 1714, the new so-called 'Queen Anne' style drew as much on seventeenth- as on early-eighteenth-century sources. With its carved red brick and shaped gables set off by sparkling white woodwork, decorative verandahs, balustrades and balconies, the 'Queen Anne' style proved instantly

669 Engraving of the exterior of Leyswood, Sussex (1866–9), by Shaw

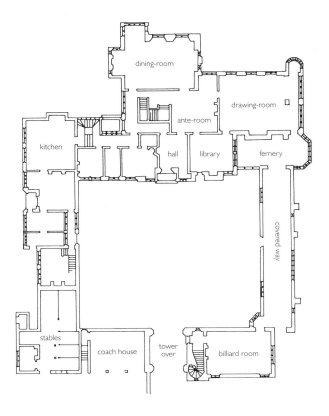

670 Plan of the ground floor of Leyswood

671 *Above* Champneys: Exterior of Newnham College, Cambridge (1874–1910)

672 *Right* The house and garden at Cragside, Northumberland (1869–84), by Shaw

popular and was taken up by architects such as William Eden Nesfield (who, as Shaw's partner in 1866–8, had had a hand in inventing it), Bodley, Stevenson, Ernest George, G. G. Scott junior, Godwin and Champneys. Shaw used it in New Zealand Chambers (1871–3), the offices in the City of London for the Shaw Savill shipping line; in his own house at 6 Ellerdale Road, Hampstead, London (1874–6 and 1885–6); in Lowther Lodge, Kensington (now the Royal Geographical Society, 1875–7); and in Swan House (1875–7), Chelsea Embankment. At Bedford Park, London, he built in 1877–80 a whole village in this style, complete with an inn, shops and an exceptionally unecclesiastical-looking church. Artistically-minded members of the educated middle classes flocked to live in what can claim to be the first garden suburb ever built. The young ladies of Bedford Park might be lucky enough to be educated at Newnham College, Cambridge, surely the happiest of all monuments in the 'Queen Anne' style. This gracious rambling building was erected from 1874 to 1910 as the second ladies' college in Cambridge, from designs by Basil Champneys (1842–1935).

Shaw's changeful artistic temperament made him dissatisfied with his vernacular and 'Queen Anne' make-believe world. For example, in a letter to the Arts and Crafts architect J. D. Sedding in 1882, he suspected '1st that old work is *real* and 2nd that ours is not real, but only like real'. He thus turned to the classical tradition for reality, believing that his neo-vernacular architecture was a fake, and certainly the half-timbering at Cragside was scarcely a technique indigenous to Northumberland. This adoption of classicism was further encouraged, first by his increasing role as an architect of town houses in London, and secondly by the commissions he received in the 1880s for the sympathetic remodelling of eighteenth-century country houses such as Moor Place, Hertfordshire. This culminated in the immense Bryanston, Dorset (1889–94), a sumptuous and eclectic neo-Wren palace in geranium-red brick with lavish Portland stone dressings concealing a complex web of iron and steel girders and central-heating pipes. The patron, who can have had no idea that the way of life envisaged by such a building was to come to an end exactly twenty years after its completion, was the 2nd Viscount Portman.

A happier example of Shaw's domestic classicism was his rebuilding in 1890–4 of the house known as Chesters, Northumberland, with a bold quadrant colonnade making a lordly neo-antique gesture as the centre of the west front. The style also appeared in commercial buildings like the Alliance Assurance Offices (1901), St James's Street, London, with a ground floor composed of three giant rusticated arches. Finally, in old age, he made designs for the replacement of Nash's Regent Street in 1904–11 in an imperial Baroque. Here his characteristic showmanship created the Edwardian grand manner at a stroke.

In attempting to summarize the influential genius of Richard Norman Shaw we should remember that he once declared it his aim to unite 'the contradictory geniuses of Cockerell and Pugin'. This seemingly impossible ambition was perhaps realized in New Scotland Yard, the Metropolitan Police Offices which rose from his designs in 1886–90 on the Embankment in London. This massive four-square building follows a

673 Shaw: Exterior of New Scotland Yard, the Embankment, London (1886–90)

674 Garden front of Standen, Sussex (1892–4), by Webb

675 Campanile and façade of Westminster cathedral (1894–1903), by Bentley

Netherlandish Renaissance model, with circular corner towers and high gables combined with Baroque details. Difficult to classify stylistically, it does not look like a piece of period revival but relies for effect on its overall mass and its emphatic use of materials: granite for the lower storeys and red brick streaked with Portland stone bands for the upper. The building is so unusual that it gives the impression of having been designed by an architect working from first principles.

New Scotland Yard is the building in which Shaw came closest to the work of Philip Webb (1831–1915),

one of the founder members of the firm of Morris and Company, established by the artist and social reformer William Morris with the hope of improving Victorian design. Webb sought a way out of the stylistic battles of the nineteenth century in his practical if astringent houses, in which he combined medieval features such as pointed arches and gables with convenient eighteenth-century features like wooden sash windows. By the 1890s he had largely given up period ornamental detail and in a house such as Standen, Sussex (1892–4), sought to prove that true architecture grew naturally out of function and materials. Derived from the vernacular traditions of local country buildings between the sixteenth and eighteenth centuries, houses like Standen were greatly admired by Webb's contemporaries and followers as models of integrity. However, his personal hand is often to be recognized in his compositional technique which, as a result of his determination to avoid easy Picturesque charm, can be awkward and disjointed.

One major public building of these years was enthusiastically received by those seeking 'real' architecture. This was Westminster cathedral (1894–1903), the masterpiece of John Francis Bentley (1839–1902). The choice of an 'Italo-Byzantine' style for the new Catholic cathedral at Westminster, which was partly due to a wish not to compete with Westminster Abbey, harmonized with the taste for Byzantine architecture, craftsmanship and symbolism, already a feature of the Arts and Crafts designers who had grown up under the influence of William Morris. It was, of course, a natural development from Ruskin's obsession with Venice, a city dominated by the great Byzantine church of St Mark's. W. R. Lethaby (1857–1931), an idiosyncratic pupil of Shaw, now published *The Church of Sancta Sophia, Constantinople, a Study of Byzantine Building* (London and New York, 1894), in which he concluded that 'A conviction of the necessity for finding the root of architecture once again in sound common-sense building and pleasurable craftsmanship remains as the final result of our study of S. Sophia'. In its poetry and its high seriousness, its religious meaning and its emphasis on the almost moral value of craftsmanship, Westminster cathedral expresses many of the deepest concerns of Victorian England. Following the precepts of nineteenth-century theorists like Pugin, Viollet-le-Duc and Choisy, it is 'truthful' building of load-bearing parts not dependent on concealed iron or steel reinforcements. The busy exterior of Bentley's cathedral, of red brick striped with bands of stone, owes much to Shaw and Webb, particularly to the former's similarly coloured New Scotland Yard, but the most moving part is the dark interior, sparkling with mosaic and marble, where bare brick piers rise to support the three shallow concrete domes hovering high above the nave. As Lethaby said, 'inside, the instant impression is that of reality, reason and power, serenity and peace; almost a sense of nature – the natural law of structure'.

Germany, Austria and Italy

Schinkel and Klenze

The high level of intellectual and even moral debate which was generated in architectural circles in nineteenth-century France and England was reflected in Germany by figures as various as Karl Friedrich Schinkel, Heinrich Hübsch and Gottfried Semper. The impetus came from Prussia, where a heightened sense of national identity had been provoked by Napoleon's occupation of Berlin in 1806–8. Wilhelm von Humboldt, the political writer and statesman who established Berlin University in 1809, reformed the entire educational system of Prussia along the neo-humanist ideals of the eighteenth-century Enlightenment as expressed in the works of philosophers like Jean-Jacques Rousseau, scholars like Johann Joachim Winckelmann, and educational reformers like Johann Friedrich Pestalozzi. The state became the whole authority for education, which was available to all classes. Drawing parallels between Greek culture and German history, the programme concentrated on

Greek, Latin, German and mathematics, with little emphasis on religion. The Prussian crown prince, Friedrich Wilhelm (1795–1861; reigned 1840–58), was a would-be architect and an influential architectural patron throughout his career. His ambition was to fuse Greek, Gothic and Teutonic elements in a vision of a united Germany, which he spelled 'Teutschland', following the patriotic fashion which had become popular during the Wars of Liberation against Napoleon, 1813–15. The architect who gave expression to the philosophical idealism of the Prussian state was the crown prince's architectural tutor and friend, Karl Friedrich Schinkel (1781–1841). His appointment by Wilhelm von Humboldt in 1810 as an architect in the Department of Public Works began a career as a civil servant in which he was to dominate architectural development in Prussia and beyond for 30 years.

Taught at the Berlin Architectural Academy, where he was profoundly influenced by Friedrich Gilly (p. 415), in particular by his entry in the competition of 1796 for a monument to Frederick the Great, Schinkel's first building of significance was a mausoleum in 1810 for Queen Luise who had been especially identified with the Prussian struggle against Napoleon. The mausoleum, in the garden of Schloss Charlottenburg near Berlin, is a severe Greek Doric temple. This style was chosen by the king, yet in the same year Schinkel exhibited at the Berlin Academy a more romantic tribute to the late queen's memory in the form of drawings for an elaborate Gothic mausoleum with an explanatory commentary. Just as Gilly had envisaged his Greek Doric monument to Frederick the Great as a symbol of Prussian order, so Schinkel upheld Gothic as an embodiment of the national spirit. Deriving from A. W. von Schlegel the idea of Greek and Gothic as twin poles, he conceived the ambition of synthesizing both in a new style where each would be improved by the other. He demonstrated this in his designs of 1815 for a national cathedral on the site in Berlin proposed by Gilly for his Frederick the Great monument. Intended to commemorate the Wars of Liberation, this was a project close to the heart of the crown prince. Though Schinkel's cathedral is Gothic in style, its choir is crowned with a dome, a synthesis of forms prefigured in the thirteenth-century Gothic dome of the Romanesque baptistery at Pisa (see p. 147) which he had drawn on his visit to Pisa in 1804. In 1811 he had made a similar building the focus of his painting *Abend* (Evening).

Schinkel's enthusiasm for Gothic at the start of his career was not only an expression of high ideals but was also part of his sympathy for French neo-classical theory, in which Greek and Gothic were admired, in contrast to Roman architecture, for their structural honesty. One of his most important early buildings, the Berlin Schauspielhaus (theatre, 1818–21), is conceived as a kind of trabeated classical grid with continuous bands of windows separated only by virtually unmoulded piers. This light framework has an almost Gothic openwork flavour. Together with the Neue Wache (guard-house, 1816–18), Altes Museum (1823–33) and remodelling of the cathedral (1820–1), the Schauspielhaus was one of a group of public buildings in Berlin with which Schinkel gave expression to the new cultural and political ambitions of Prussia. All have a pronounced Grecian character.

The revolutionary idea of a public museum on the scale of the Altes Museum, with contents arranged chronologically and didactically, had emerged for the first time around 1800 in Berlin in proposals by the philosopher Alois Hirt who taught Schinkel at the Bauakademie. It harmonized well with Schinkel's belief that architecture should educate and improve the public by awakening them to a sense of their own identity. For the Altes Museum he chose a plan inspired by one in Durand's *Précis* with a central Pantheon rotunda and a long entrance colonnade. The building does not seek to impress with ambitious architectural display or showy pediments but is a sober statement of civic order resembling a Hellenistic stoa. The daunting row of eighteen Greek Ionic columns which constitutes the entire façade appears at first sight to insulate the building from the outer world; yet, as the visitor approaches, he

discovers that entry is invited by means of a remarkable open staircase contained within the depth of the colonnade. This dissolution of the barrier between internal and external space is beautifully emphasized by Schinkel in a drawing of the staircase, which shows the landing peopled with visitors using it as a semi-open-air viewing platform for the city of Berlin. They are enjoying a perspective view, intriguingly framed by the Ionic capitals of the colonnade, towards the royal Schloss at the far end of the Lustgarten, a public square given new dignity by Schinkel when he placed the museum on reclaimed marshy ground at its northern end.

Schinkel's careful siting of the museum, taking account of the views from it as well as towards it, is characteristic of his constant concern to relate his buildings to their setting, whether urban or rural. Thus, in the engravings of his work which he published as *Sammlung architektonische Entwürfe* ('Collection of architectural designs' 1819–40), for example the illustration of the staircase at the Altes Museum, he made a point of including perspective views so as to emphasize the contribution of his buildings to the whole environment.

In this environmental concern he is closer to the ideals of John Nash than to those of contemporary French architects. Just as Nash had brought to town planning in London a Picturesque ability to blend architecture and nature, so Schinkel had acquired an understanding of the scenic element in architectural composition during the years from 1806 when, as there were few architectural commissions in occupied Berlin, he became a designer of scenery for panoramas, dioramas and, later, for the stage. He also produced many oil paintings, especially of buildings in romantic landscapes, which rival the work of C. D. Friedrich in brilliance of technique and atmospheric effect.

Schinkel's skill as a Picturesque planner is best appreciated in the three surviving country houses he built for three of the king's sons: Schloss Glienicke (1824–6) at Klein Glienicke, Berlin, for Prince Karl; Schloss Charlottenhof (1826–7) at Sanssouci, Potsdam,

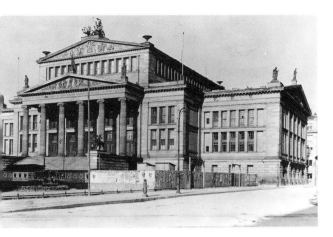

676 *Above* Schinkel: East façade of the Schauspielhaus, Berlin (1818–21)

677 *Top right* Schinkel: Staircase behind the colonnade in the Altes Museum, Berlin (1823–33)

678 *Bottom right* Plan of the Altes Museum

679 *Below* Colonnade on the entrance front of the Altes Museum

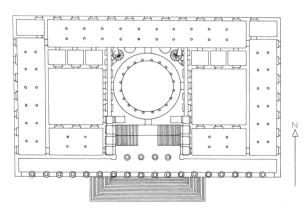

680 Schinkel: Schloss Charlottenhof, Sanssouci, Potsdam (1826–7)

for the Crown Prince; and Schloss Babelsberg (1833–5), built near Potsdam for Prince Wilhelm in a style directly inspired by the neo-Gothic country houses of Nash and Wyatville. As a brilliant transformation of a modest existing house into a stylish and asymmetrical neo-classical composition, Glienicke is the kind of conjuring trick at which Nash was particularly adept. The stable wing is capped by an Italianate tower which forms a pivot for the whole loosely grouped composition. At Charlottenhof, on a sloping site with a terraced garden flanked by a canal, a long pergola links the Greek Doric portico of the main house with a semicircular arbour ending the axis at the far end of the garden. The general disposition was suggested by the Crown Prince, but its crisply inventive realization was entirely by Schinkel who prepared several panoramic views showing the intimate interconnection of the house, garden and park. This theme was stated with even greater subtlety in the complex of garden buildings erected in 1829–40 in the grounds of Schloss Charlottenhof. This asymmetrical group of Court Gardener's house, tea pavilion and Roman bath-house in a range of classical and Italianate vernacular styles interpenetrates with loggias, passages, steps, vine-covered trellises, canals and an asymmetrical sheet of water, in eloquent demonstration of Schinkel's belief that 'architecture is the continuation of nature in her constructive activity'.

The Court Gardener's house with its Italianate tower may be inspired by the plate depicting a 'Villa, designed as the residence of an artist, in J. B. Papworth's *Rural Residences* (1818). However, when Schinkel paid a lengthy visit to Britain in 1826, ostensibly to collect information about modern museum design and display techniques, he was not impressed by the classical or Picturesque work of contemporary architects such as Nash, Soane or Smirke. What struck him most forcibly was the architectural impact of the industrial revolution: the design of factories, warehouses, dock buildings and bridges. He developed a love-hate relationship with the giant red-brick mills and factories with their iron beams, columns and staircases forming a fireproof internal framework. He was determined to take this form of construction back to Berlin and to civilize it by the addition of the aesthetic or poetic content which to him was an essential part of architecture. His Feilner House (1828–9; dem. c.1945), built for a manufacturer of terracotta ornament, bricks and stoves, was an original essay in constructional polychromy of the kind in which Hittorff and his circle were to indulge in the 1830s and 1840s. Its façade incorporated unpainted beige terracotta and bricks of two colours, red and violet, frankly exposed in a city which was then accustomed to stuccoed façades scored to imitate masonry joints. An even more daring exposure of an industrial material in a domestic setting occurred in his remodelling of a mansion off the Wilhelmstrasse in Berlin (1830–2; dem. 1946) as a palace for Prince Albrecht, a younger brother of the Crown Prince. The principal staircase there was an extensive and elaborate structure of cast iron, echoing those Schinkel had seen in English mills but elegantly ornamented with neo-Pompeiian frills.

The themes Schinkel introduced in the Feilner House were exploited more fully in the building which was to be his favourite, the new Bauakademie (1831–6; dem. 1961). This was the headquarters both of the celebrated Berlin school of architecture and of the Public Works Department of which Schinkel had been Chief Architect since 1815. His post involved examination of all state building schemes throughout Prussia, thus establishing a consistent style for public buildings in northern Germany in the early nineteenth century. His dedication to the cause of architecture and of the new Prussia was underlined by his decision in 1836 to live in the Bauakademie, where he remained until his death five years later. The building was a freestanding cube like some Italian Renaissance palazzo, four storeys high with four façades each eight bays long. The bays were separated by piers corresponding roughly to the internal vertical divisions which, as in English mills, were segmental brick arches carrying brick cap vaults and linked by horizontal iron beams. The façades were red and violet brick with decorative trim in beige terracotta and glazed violet tiles, and incorporated panels of carved terracotta depicting the history of architecture from antiquity to the Renaissance. Thus Schinkel sought to civilize a functional building in some ways representing the fusion of Greek and Gothic which had preoccupied him at the start of his career.

We should consider at the same time as the Bauakademie the many notes which Schinkel left towards a comprehensive Architectural Textbook, not published till 1979. Here he emphasized his belief that the functionalism of Durand and Rondelet was not enough: 'the principle of Greek architecture is to render construction beautiful, and this must remain the principle in its continuation'. Architecture is the expression of high ideals and consideration must always be given to the demands of history, poetry and beauty.

These considerations coloured two unexecuted designs for visionary palaces produced towards the end of his life, one of 1834 on the Acropolis in Athens for the newly elected King of Greece, the former Prince Otto von Wittelsbach, and one of four years later at Orianda in the Crimea for the Empress of Russia, the former Princess Charlotte of Prussia. The Empress's brother, the Prussian Crown Prince, persuaded Schinkel to make both these designs, and their lush decorative treatment may be partly attributable to his influence. The Acropolis palace, in which the Parthenon itself is almost reduced

681 Schinkel: Exterior of the Bauakademie, Berlin (1831–6)

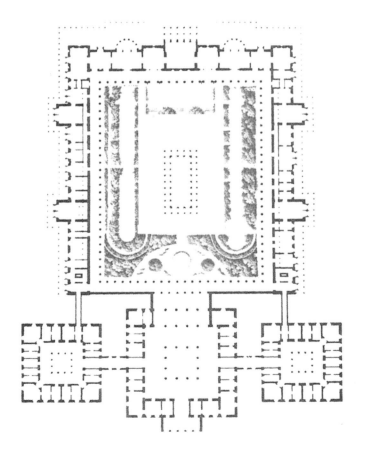

682 Plan of the palace at Orianda, Crimea (1838), by Schinkel

683 Design for the Garden Court of the palace at Orianda, by Schinkel

to the status of a garden ornament, seems to be the climax of a tradition which began with Athenian Stuart's (p. 377) Greek Doric temple at Hagley in 1758. The central hall of the palace is an extraordinary combination of Greek, Roman, medieval and modern industrial themes, open to an exotic garden court and enriched with lavish polychromatic ornament. The palace at Orianda is a yet more extravagant statement of similar ideals. Its long horizontal lines, hugging a cliff-top site above the Black Sea, are broken only by a white temple, a late offspring of Gilly's Frederick the Great monument, which seems to hover miraculously above the palace. The sectional drawings show how this temple was raised on a high podium containing a sculpture museum, which stood in the centre of the inner garden court.

The extent and variety of Schinkel's work, coupled with his sense of mission, helped ensure his wide influence for a generation after his death, especially in Berlin. His followers included Friedrich August Stühler (1800–65) and Johann Heinrich Strack (1805–80). Stühler built the Neues Museum (1843–50) in a style sympathetic to Schinkel's adjacent Altes Museum and, in cooperation with Strack, added the nearby National Galerie (1865–9) following a sketch by King Friedrich Wilhelm IV who, as Crown Prince, had been so closely associated with Schinkel. Raised above an imposing flight of steps, the National Galerie is a Corinthian temple which is yet another tribute to Gilly's monument to Frederick the Great.

Schinkel's impact was also felt strongly in towns under Prussian rule such as Bonn, Aachen, Elberfeld, Cologne and Dusseldorf; though architects like Georg Laves in Hanover, Clemens Wenzel Coudray in Weimar, and Carl Ludwig Wimmel, Franz Forsmann and Alexis de Châteauneuf in Hamburg, were also strongly influenced by him. In southern Germany neo-classicism was brought to Karlsruhe by Weinbrenner, to Darmstadt by Georg Moller, to Stuttgart by Nicolaus Friedrich von Thouret and the Italian émigré Giovanni Salucci, and to Munich by Fischer and Klenze. Friedrich Weinbrenner (1766–1826) was important from 1800 to 1826 for transforming the Baroque court-town of Karlsruhe into a bourgeois town of the nineteenth century with a full range of post-Napoleonic civic buildings. In the early 1790s he met David Gilly in Berlin and then studied in Rome where he produced

684 Stühler and Strack: Exterior of the National Galerie, Berlin (1865–9)

numerous designs in a visionary Franco-Prussian style inspired by Ledoux and close to the revolutionary abstractions of Friedrich Gilly. Back in Karlsruhe, he was forced to adopt a more conventional Durandesque style, though the buildings in his Market Place and Schloss-strasse (today Karl-Friedrichstrasse) are grouped in an episodic asymmetrical manner which is closer to Nash than to French precedent. In the Market Place the portico of the Protestant church (1806–20), flanked by the grammar school, faces but does not repeat exactly that of the town hall (1807–14) opposite. The Schloss-strasse leads south from the Market Place to the octagonal Rondell Platz with the V-planned Margrave's Palace (1803–13). The vista was terminated by the now demolished Ettling Gate (1803), a Greek Doric propylon inspired by Langhans's at Berlin. Next to this was Weinbrenner's own house (1801; dem. 1873), an ambitious building in which he ran his celebrated school of architecture, training leading architects of the next generation such as Hübsch, Moller and Châteauneuf. Nash followed his example of living and working in a prominent position in a new street of his own design, while Schinkel similarly chose to live in a school of architecture. Elsewhere in Karlsruhe Weinbrenner designed the court theatre, museum, chancellery, synagogue, assembly rooms, shops and the Catholic church of St Stephen (1808–14), a Pantheon-inspired building which is a product of the religious toleration of the Napoleonic Duchy of Baden. He also designed model dwellings for all classes, some of which were executed as modest terrace (row) housing. Like Schinkel and Klenze, he extended his influence by publishing his own designs in a series of illustrated volumes.

The transformation of Munich from a Baroque court town into a modern capital city was carried out by Leo von Klenze (1784–1864), the greatest German architect of the nineteenth century after Schinkel, whose career ran closely parallel. It was seeing Gilly's designs for a monument to Frederick the Great which fired Klenze, as it did Schinkel, with the ambition of becoming an architect and of creating monuments which reflect and stimulate a mood of high idealism. In Crown Prince Ludwig (1786–1868, king of Bavaria 1825–48), Klenze found a patron as architecturally ambitious as Schinkel's Crown Prince of Prussia and with more funds and more power. Following the alliance of Bavaria with Napoleon, it was made a kingdom in 1806. Plans were now drawn up for the enlargement of Munich into a royal capital which were partly executed by the architect Karl von Fischer (1782–1821), whose Prince Karl Palace (1803–6) and Theatre (1811–18), modelled on the Odéon in Paris, were the first neo-classical buildings in Munich. The announcement in 1814 by the Munich Academy of a competition for a military hospital, a German national monument (Walhalla), and a museum for antique sculpture (Glyptothek), reflected the cultural ambitions of Crown Prince Ludwig, who had sought designs for the sculpture gallery as early as 1811 from the Italian architect Giacomo Quarenghi and from the German archaeologist Carl Haller von Hallerstein (1774–1817). In 1815 Ludwig encouraged Klenze to submit alternative schemes to those of Fischer, official court architect since 1809. Klenze's designs were selected in 1816, when Ludwig appointed him court architect and sent him to Paris to acquire further sculpture for the Glyptothek.

After his initial training under the Gillys at Berlin, Klenze had been a pupil in Paris of Durand and of Percier, and it was from Durand's *Précis* that he borrowed the general form of his Glyptothek with its one-storeyed, vaulted galleries lit from above and from high side windows. Built in 1816–30 as the earliest public sculpture museum in the world, the Glyptothek has an aloof marble exterior contrasting with the rich polychromatic decoration of the interiors with their coloured scagliola work, white and gold stucco, carvings by Ludwig Michael Schwanthaler, and frescoes by Peter Cornelius and his pupils of scenes from Greek mythology and history. When the building was restored in the 1960s following wartime bomb damage the interior decoration was not reinstated, so that the building no longer enters into that lively dialogue with its contents which was so vital a part of the neo-classical concept of the function of architecture and ornament. The most famous work of art housed in the Glyptothek is the pedimental sculpture from the temple at Aegina, discovered in 1811 by a team of international archaeologists and scholars which included Cockerell and Hallerstein. On the wall behind the sculpture Klenze painted a coloured representation of the temple in which he anticipated the revolutionary investigations of Hittorff and Zanth into the polychromatic architecture of the ancient Greeks.

At Klenze's Munich Pinakothek (designed 1822; executed 1826–30), a picture gallery largely housing Italian paintings, the façade treatment is inspired by the Cancelleria and the Belvedere courtyard at the Vatican, while the novel and influential plan provides seven large

685 The Feldherrnhalle, Munich (1840), by Gärtner

top-lit galleries flanked on one side by intimate rooms for the smaller pictures, opening into each other and into the main galleries. This shift to a Renaissance style was echoed with less appropriateness in the neo-*quattrocento* domestic buildings in the Ludwigstrasse, the long broad street leading north from the Residenz outside the old city walls, which Klenze laid out from 1817. As a completely new street added to an historic city centre, it is bolder than anything Schinkel created in Berlin or Percier and Fontaine in Paris, and can be paralleled only by Nash's Regent Street in London. It became over the years an extraordinary sequence of historical souvenirs, or a kind of frozen Grand Tour like a recreation of the plates in Durand's *Recueil et parallèle des édifices de tout genre anciens et modernes* (Paris 1800). Thus it was eventually closed with a building at each end, designed in 1840 by Friedrich von Gärtner: at the south the Feldherrnhalle (Hall of the Field-Marshals), an imitation of the fourteenth-century Loggia dei Lanzi in Florence, and at the north the Siegestor (Gate of Victory), modelled on the Arch of Constantine and rivalling the arches erected in Paris, London and Milan.

A similar programme inspired Klenze's Max Josephs Platz where in 1826–35 he built for Ludwig on the north side the Königsbau of the Residenz, inspired by the Palazzo Pitti and the Palazzo Rucellai in Florence, and on the south side the Main Post Office (1836), modelled on Brunelleschi's Foundling Hospital and incorporating polychromatic decoration. For the king, who had succeeded as Ludwig I of Bavaria in 1825, he also provided the equally eclectic court chapel of All Saints at the Residenz in 1826–37. This was modelled at the king's request on the twelfth-century Palatine chapel at Palermo, which he had visited with Klenze in 1823. Klenze replaced the Muslim honeycomb roof of the original Sicilian model with a series of shallow domes inspired by S. Marco in Venice, which he and Ludwig had visited in 1817. The exterior was in a North Italian Romanesque style, while frescoes and mosaics on a gold ground contributed a richer Byzantine note to the interior of this sumptuous shrine. As an eclectic essay in the *Rundbogenstil*, the chapel was a demonstration of Klenze's curious belief that the principles of Greek architecture lived on in the round-arched style. In spite of this belief, Klenze was in his published writings a far more dedicated upholder than Schinkel of the eternal values of Greek architectural language and of its application to present-day needs.

Klenze was fortunate enough to be given the opportunity of expressing his faith in antiquity in the design of four monumental public buildings, all commissioned by Ludwig, the Walhalla near Regensburg; the Befreiungshalle (Hall of Liberation) near Kelheim; and the Ruhmeshalle (Hall of Fame) and Propylaea, both in Munich. These four monuments lack a practical function but are expressive of an idea. They thus represent the flowering of the belief that architecture should shape the moral conscience of a nation. Hinted at by Winckelmann, this was given powerful expression in Prussia from the 1790s. Indeed, it was during a visit to occupied Berlin in 1807 that Crown Prince Ludwig of Bavaria first conceived the idea of a great German national monument as a symbol of pan-German unity, 'Walhalla' being the hall of heroes in Teutonic mythology. In 1809–10 Karl von Fischer submitted two sets of designs for this Pantheon of Germans, combining features from the Parthenon and Pantheon. A public competition announced in 1814 was entered by over fifty architects including Klenze, Schinkel, Gärtner, and Ohlmüller, who proposed an elaborate Gothic monument despite the fact that a Greek temple had been stipulated. In 1819 Ludwig approached Klenze for new designs which, finalized in 1821, were executed in 1830–42 on a superb hillside site 300 feet (90m) above the Danube. Externally it is a brooding mass of unpolished grey marble; the interior is sumptuously polychromatic, lined with rich marbling and studded with portrait busts of great Germans and a figured frieze, carved by Martin von Wagner in 1837, depicting the early and mythical history of Germany up to Christianization. The moral purpose of this national shrine was made explicit by King Ludwig who claimed:

686 *Top left* Klenze: The Walhalla, near Regensburg, from across the Danube (designed 1821; built 1830–42)

687 *Centre left* Klenze: The Befreiungshalle, near Kelheim (1842–63)

688 *Bottom left* Klenze: The Propylaea, marking the entrance to the Königsplatz, Munich (1846–60)

'The Walhalla was erected so that the German might depart from it more German and better than when he had arrived.'

Like the Walhalla, the Propylaea and Ruhmeshalle are large-scale exercises in the Greek Doric style, but the Befreiungshalle is a more original conception. It was executed in 1842–63 as the most ambitious German monument to the Wars of Liberation against Napoleon. Originally designed by Gärtner in a fussy *Rundbogenstil* manner, it was completely altered by Klenze, who took over after Gärtner's death in 1847. Its cylindrical mass, like a disturbing inflated version of the Mausoleum of Theodoric at Ravenna, is a severe piece of abstract geometry, windowless but enlivened with a ring of 18 female figures, 20 feet (6.5m) high, carved by Johann Halbig to represent the German provinces. The richly polychromatic interior is encircled by 34 angels or winged victories carved in Carrara marble by Schwanthaler, standing between circular bronze shields and adopting alarmingly life-like postures.

Gärtner and Semper in Munich and Vienna

Klenze's main rival, Friedrich von Gärtner (1782–1847), a pupil successively of Fischer, Weinbrenner, Durand and Percier, worked extensively in Munich in the *Rundbogenstil* manner, for example in his Ludwigskirche (1829–44) and State Library (1832–43), next door to each other in the Ludwigstrasse. Another influential *Rundbogenstil* propagandist was Heinrich Hübsch (1795–1863), successor as architect at Karlsruhe to his teacher Weinbrenner. Hübsch's famous essay of 1828, *In welchem Stil sollen wir bauen?* ('In what style shall we build?'), posed the question which architects throughout Europe were to agonize over for the remainder of the century. Rejecting the Doric idealism of Weinbrenner, Hirt and Klenze, he argued, like Labrouste in France, that Greek architecture was too deeply rooted in the social and economic conditions of its time to serve as a model in the nineteenth century. He wanted to develop a new arched and vaulted architecture of brick or small stones which would incorporate in a rational and empirical way features from Byzantine, Romanesque, Lombardic and early Italian Renaissance buildings. He demonstrated his theories in the Trinkhalle (pump room, 1837–40) at the spa of Baden Baden, an impressive and original building, though in lesser hands the *Rundbogenstil* quickly became a narrowly historical revival.

This can be seen in the neo-*cinquecento* and neo-Baroque work of Klenze's pupil, Gottfried Semper (1803–79), the most important architectural theorist of nineteenth-century Germany. He closely resembles Viollet-le-Duc, not only as a brilliant and influential writer about architecture who was anxious to return to first principles, but as an architect whose own buildings were of somewhat lacklustre quality. At Dresden his principal buildings, all in an Italian Renaissance style, are the Opera House (1837–41), the Oppenheim Palace (1845), for a banker, and the Picture Gallery (1847–54), which completed the fourth open side of the Baroque Zwinger. In 1871–8, after a fire, he rebuilt the Opera House in a Baroque manner which he also adopted for his final buildings in Vienna: two identical museums of 1872–81 for Art History and Natural History, and the Hofburg Theatre (1874–88).

Semper's principal publications were *Die vier Elemente der Baukunst* ('The four elements of architecture', Brunswick 1851), and *Der Stil in den technischen und tektonischen Künsten, oder praktische Aesthetik* ('Style in the industrial and practical arts, or practical aesthetics', 2 vols., 1860–3). Here he reduced everything of significance in the origins of architecture art and crafts to four fundamental processes of making and their

689 Semper: The Opera House, Dresden (1871–8)

associated materials: weaving, moulding, building in timber and building in stone. These comprised the four elements of a house: 'the first and most important, the moral element of architecture' was 'the hearth as the centre'; then came 'the earthen platform surrounded by the pilework as terrace, the roof on columns (pillars), and finally the wall which is a woven bamboo mat (fence) serving as a space divider or wall'. The specific model he had in mind was the Caribbean bamboo hut from a village near the Port of Spain, Trinidad, displayed at the Great Exhibition in the Crystal Palace, London, where Semper had helped arrange some of the exhibits. His complex and not always very lucid arguments implied that pattern-making preceded structural technique so that it was legitimate to regard ornament as in some sense more fundamental than structure. Ornament, however, was in itself symbolic of high ideals, a point he emphasized by prefacing *Der Stil* with an illustration of a funeral wreath which, he argued, was man's earliest ornamental and constructive creation. He went on to show how in later periods religious and political ideals could also shape architecture, claiming, like Pugin, that 'Monuments of architecture are in fact nothing but the aesthetic expression of social, political and religious institutions.'

The idea of architecture as a continuous process over a long period, built up from a few basic types, had been suggested to Semper by Baron Cuvier's classification of prehistoric animals in the Jardin des Plantes in Paris on the basis of the functioning of their parts, not according to their visual resemblances. Semper thus appeared to be offering a method of interpretation which was a parallel to Darwin's in *The Origin of Species* (1859). This was one of the aspects of Semper's thinking which made his work so fascinating to architects such as Hendrik Petrus Berlage in the Netherlands, Otto Wagner in Vienna, and Louis Sullivan and Frank Lloyd Wright in Chicago. However, it would be wrong to believe that he was proposing an evolutionary Darwinian approach, since he realized that while a return to the pterodactyl was unthinkable, a revival of an earlier architectural style

was always feasible. Thus, though he personally disapproved of Gothic and Baroque, he made designs in both styles, believing Baroque to be symbolically appropriate for public museums, that is 'palaces of the people', in the heart of imperial Vienna.

Semper's striking contributions to Vienna were commissioned by the Emperor Franz Joseph (reigned 1848–1916) as the heart of his programme for transforming the old-fashioned capital of his vast empire along the lines of Napoleon III's Paris. The fortifications surrounding the old city were demolished in 1857 and in the following year Ludwig Förster (1797–1863) won the competition for the Ringstrasse, a monumental boulevard with freely grouped public buildings, which was to take their place. The layout was more green and open, and the style of the monuments more varied, than in Haussmann's Paris. Indeed, it was Munich, the first city to be laid out as a museum of styles, which provided a model for this eclectic assembly of grandiose public buildings.

The leading architect in Vienna was the Danish Theophilus Hansen (1813–91) who provided the Army Museum (1849–56), in collaboration with his father-in-law, Förster, in a polychromatic Byzantine style, and the vast Parliament House (1873–83) which is a late monument in the international Greek Revival manner. Between the Parliament House and the University stands the Rathaus (town hall, 1872–83), designed by Friedrich von Schmidt (1825–91) in yet a third style, a gawky symmetrical Gothic akin to that of contemporary works by Scott and Waterhouse in England. A long tradition of stylistic interpretation in the nineteenth century lay behind this extreme eclecticism: the Byzantine style, as a variant of the *Rundbogenstil*, was seen as a serviceable modern style suitable for military purposes; the international Greek Revival was an appropriate expression of the impartial wisdom of sound government; while Gothic town halls were familiar symbols of the civic pride of the historic cities of Europe.

In Berlin the restraining influence of Schinkel meant that exuberant imperial display of this kind was delayed

690 Aerial view of Vienna showing the Ringstrasse (from 1858). The two museums (*centre right*) and the New Hofburg (*centre left*) were begun in the 1870s by Semper and Hasenauer. (Photo Luftreportagen Hausmann, Vienna)

until later in the century. Characteristically ponderous examples of this neo-*cinquecento* and neo-Baroque manner are the Reichstag Building (1884–94) by Paul Wallot (1841–1912), the cathedral (1888–1905) by Julius Raschdorf (1823–1914), and the Kaiser Friedrich (later Bode) Museum (1896–1904) by Ernest von Ihne (1848–1917). Far livelier work was commissioned in Bavaria by the eccentric King Ludwig II (1845–86), who fully inherited the Wittelsbach building-mania of his grandfather, Ludwig I. Rich enough to make his private fantasies become realities, he commissioned Georg von Dollmann (1830–95) to design Schloss Linderhof (1870–86), a neo-Rococo paradise inspired by Garnier, and Schloss Herrenchiemsee, an imitation of Versailles begun in 1878 but never completed. In very different

691 Exterior of the Parliament House, Vienna (1873–83), by Hansen

mood was the Wagnerian Schloss Neuschwanstein, begun for him in 1869 from designs by Eduard Riedel (1813–85). The eclectic interiors of this towering medieval dream-castle (fig. 713), though more successful than those at Viollet-le-Duc's Pierrefonds, lack the brilliance and coherence of Burges's at Cardiff and Castell Coch.

Italy

The sense of cultural and artistic unity which had existed in Italy since the Middle Ages and the Renaissance was accompanied in the early nineteenth century by a passion for political independence and unity, partly inspired by the ideals of the French Revolution and of the Napoleonic period. At this time Italy was still a collection of independent states of which some, like Venice, Istria and Dalmatia, were under Austrian rule. The movement for freedom, known as *risorgimento*, came above all from Sardinia whose monarch, Victor Emmanuel II, became king of Italy in 1861, following a long military struggle between Austria and Sardinia. Gaining Venetia in 1866, Victor Emmanuel completed the process of unification in 1870 by annexing Rome which now became the capital of the new Italian state.

There was no architect or architectural thinker in nineteenth-century Italy of the status of those whom we have investigated in France, England and Germany. However, there is much late neo-classical architecture of high quality, often with a stern Greek Revival flavour. A great temple-mausoleum for the sculptor Antonio Canova was built in 1819–33, largely from his own designs, in a mountainous setting above Possagno. Uniting themes from the Parthenon and the Pantheon, this echoes some of the unexecuted projects for the Walhalla near Regensburg. Among the architects whom Canova consulted over its design was Antonio Selva (1751–1819), whose pupil Giuseppe Jappelli (1783–1852) was an eclectic and romantic architect of a type more familiar in England. He was indeed an anglophile, as is clear in the bizarre work with which he rose to fame, the Caffè Pedrocchi, Padua, where he built a striking Greek Doric wing in 1826–31, juxtaposed with a Venetian Gothic wing, the Pedrocchino, added in

692 Canova and Selva: The Canova Mausoleum, near Possagno (1819–33)

693 Exterior of the Caffé Pedrocchi, Padua (Greek Doric wing 1826–31; Venetian Gothic wing 1837–42), by Jappelli

1837–42 following his visit to England in 1836. The colourful interiors in contrasting Egyptian, Moorish, Gothic and French Empire styles may be influenced in part by the study he made of the work of Thomas Hope.

In Naples Pietro Bianchi (1787–1849) was commissioned to redesign the church of S. Francesco di Paola opposite the Royal Palace in 1817. This church had been begun in 1808 for Joachim Murat during the French occupation, from designs by Leopoldo Laperuta and Antonio de Simone, with flanking quadrant arcades inspired by Bernini's in the Piazza S. Pietro. Bianchi made it an echo of the Pantheon with the high windowless drum reminiscent of the visionary projects of eighteenth-century French Grand Prix contestants. Echoes of Ledoux can be sensed in the daunting rustication and seemingly endless Ionic colonnade of the façade of the Teatro S. Carlo, Naples (1810–11), by Antonio Niccolini (1772–1850).

A megalomaniac colonnaded and domed fantasy, the Villa d'Adda Cagnola at Inverigo, was begun in 1813 as his own residence by the Marchese Luigi Cagnola (1762–1833), the architect largely responsible for the transformation of Milan during the Napoleonic occupation. He was one of a number of architects who provided Milan, then under the control of Eugène de Beauharnais, with a series of imposing classical gates echoing in boldness of impact, though not in stylistic invention, Ledoux's *barrières* in Paris. The grandest is Cagnola's Arco del Sempione (or della Pace, 1806–38), based on the Arch of Septimius Severus in Rome. His churches included S. Lorenzo, known as La Rotonda (1822–3), at Ghisalba, an imposing echo of the Pantheon, while he added an extraordinary campanile to the church at Urgnano in 1824–9. This five-storeyed circular tower is surmounted by a ring of caryatids carrying the dome, as in some imaginative fantasy by Joseph Michael Gandy. The imposing church of S. Carlo al Corso in Milan (1836–47) was the principal work of Carlo Amati (1776–1852). One of the happiest and latest of the many echoes of the Pantheon, it contrives to continue the Corinthian portico in the form of colonnades on the flanking buildings, thus creating a scenic forecourt like the colonnaded urban settings of the temples of ancient Rome.

Alessandro Antonelli (1799–1888), Professor of Architecture at Turin from 1836–57, was a prolific late classical architect who made many contributions to the cities of Turin and Novara in Piedmont. His gargantuan and obsessively columnar architecture is well demonstrated by his remodelling of the cathedral (1854–69) and the church of San Gaudenzio (1858–78), both in Novara, but his most remarkable building is the so-called Mole Antonelliana, Turin, 536 feet (163.35m) high. Begun in 1863 as a synagogue, this was found so striking that it was purchased by the City of Turin while under construction for use as a civic museum, and was only completed in 1900 by Antonelli's son, Costanzo. With their towering domes and spires, S. Gaudenzio and the Mole Antonelliana have become accepted as key symbols of their respective cities.

Rome is not rich in neo-classical buildings in the nineteenth century. The best work is probably the Braccio Nuovo (1817–22) in the Vatican, a sculpture museum commissioned by Pope Pius VII and designed by Raffaello Stern (1774–1820). This was really a continuation of themes established in the Museo Pio Clementino in the 1770s, discussed in Chapter 8. The same pope, finally re-established in power in 1816 after the downfall of Napoleon, also continued with the plans by Valadier for improving the Piazza del Popolo and the adjacent Pincio hill which had been approved in 1811 under the Napoleonic administration as part of a programme for relieving unemployment. The Piazza del Popolo was the principal entrance to Rome from the north before the coming of the railway. In 1816–24 Giuseppe Valadier (1762–1839) provided it with two great hemi-cycles and created a terraced garden on the Pincio with ramps and carriageways ascending the hill. At the summit he built the remarkable Casino Valadier (1816–17), a coffee-house of aggressively original design with different elevations on the entrance front, terrace front and sides. It is both functional and Picturesque, with Greek Doric loggias surmounted by wholly ornamental freestanding Ionic columns, and a curved entrance portico in which Ionic columns are combined, irregularly, with a Doric triglyph frieze. The richly decorated interiors are similarly complex with vaults and domes and neo-antique frescoes.

Valadier was also responsible for the restoration of the Arch of Titus and the Colosseum in 1819–20 and for the design of numerous villas, of which the most ambitious is the Villa Torlonia, transformed from the former Casino Torlonia. With its high porticoes and encircling Greek Doric colonnades, the Villa Torlonia was again altered in c.1840–2 by the minor Roman architect and painter, Giovanni Battista Caretti (1803–78), and by Jappelli who probably provided the exotic garden buildings and ruins with which its Picturesque park is dotted.

The rising nationalism which resulted in the political unification of Italy in 1861 and the choice of Rome as the capital nine years later encouraged on the one hand a neo-Renaissance Revival, inspired by Haussmann's work in Paris, and on the other a new enthusiasm for Italy's own Gothic past. Among the most original and successful products of a combination of this neo-Renaissance taste with the use of new materials such as iron and glass are the great galleries or shopping arcades of which the first was the Galleria Vittorio Emanuele II in Milan, designed in 1861 by Giuseppe Mengoni (1829–77) and executed in 1865–7. This cruciform gallery with its barrel-vaulted glazed roof and elaborate stucco decoration in a Milanese Renaissance taste was promoted by English entrepreneurs, and incorporated metal and glass imported from England. It was widely imitated in Italy, at Naples, Genoa and Turin.

The redevelopment of Rome after 1870 was almost as striking as that of Paris or Vienna. In novels such as *Don Orsino* (1892), the Italian-born American author Francis Marion Crawford (1854–1909) well conveyed the turbulent activity of these years, the conflicts and interactions between old families and new wealth, princes and property developers, supporters of the historic papacy and of the upstart monarchy. One of the principal beneficiaries of the real-estate boom in this period was the retiring but prolific architect of domestic and commercial buildings, Gaetano Koch (1849–1910). Typical of his sober sensitive work in a neo-*cinquecento* style which blends perfectly into the Roman scene are the following buildings, all of the 1880s: the Palazzo Pacelli which, like the nearby Palazzo Massimi by Peruzzi, follows the delicate curve of the street; the Piazza dell'Esedra with quadrant façades which nobly confront Michelangelo's Sta Maria degli Angeli, formed out of the Baths of Diocletian; and the enormous Palazzo Boncampagni (later Palazzo Margherita and today the American Embassy), modelled on the Palazzo Farnese. Another sensitive architect who tends to be omitted from accounts of western architecture because he was

694 *Opposite* Mengoni: The Galleria Vittorio Emanuele II, Milan (designed 1861; built 1865–7)

not stylistically innovative is Pio Piacentini (1846–1928). He built widely in Rome in local materials – travertine, pink brick and stucco – beginning with the Palazzo delle Esposizione (1878–82), an exhibition building with a triumphal arch as the climax of its façade.

Guglielmo Calderini (1837–1916) brought a much richer ornamental treatment to this neo-Renaissance language, which became known as the 'Stile Umberto' after the second king of Italy, Umberto I (reigned 1878–1900). His first major work in this style was a new façade for the early-seventeenth-century cathedral at Savona. Built in 1880–6, this is a robust development from Vignola's Gesù. His chief monument was the vast Palazzo di Giustizia (1888–1910) on the banks of the Tiber in Rome. This combines Beaux-Arts planning with

695 *Left* Calderini: Exterior of the Palazzo di Giustizia, Rome (1888–1910), from across the Tiber

696 *Below* The monument to Victor Emmanuel II, Rome (designed by Sacconi 1884)

697 *Opposite* Emilio de Fabris: The west front of Florence cathedral (1867–87)

a sumptuous surface texture which still derives from *cinquecento*, not Baroque sources.

The most notorious product of the *Stile Umberto* is the gargantuan Monument of 1885–1911 to Victor Emmanuel II, a high Corinthian colonnade crowning innumerable flights of steps, which dominates Rome from its artificial hill in the enlarged Piazza Venezia at the foot of the Capitoline Hill. The first competition for a monument to the king under whom Italian unity had been established stipulated a design 'which would resume the history of the country and at the same time be a symbol of the new age'. Announced in 1880, it was won by the Frenchman Paul-Henri Nénot, but since an Italian architect seemed desirable for so nationalist a monument a second competition was held in 1882 and finally a third, which was won in 1884 by Count Giuseppe Sacconi (1854–1905). His design placed an equestrian monument in front of a vast architectural backdrop, inspired by the Hellenistic Acropolis at Pergamon with its monumental altar of Zeus, and by Luigi Canina's restoration of the Roman Republican Temple of Fortuna at Praeneste with its terraces, ramps and colonnades ascending the hillside. Henry-Russell Hitchcock has complained that Sacconi's audacious monument 'illustrates the total decadence of inherited standards of Classicism in Europe towards the end of the century'. However, the building is surely a masterly exercise in the expressive handling of the orders, and what is in questionable taste is its assertiveness in such an historic setting. The choice of white Brescian marble instead of the mellower Roman travertine was not made by Sacconi, while the design was considerably altered after his death by the executant architects, Koch, Manfredi and Piacentini.

The kind of intellectual approach which we have seen in England, France and Germany to the problems posed by the range of historical styles available to the nineteenth-century architect made a late arrival in Italian architectural circles. The key figures are Pietro Estense Selvatico (1803–80), a pupil of Jappelli, and his disciple, Camillo Boito (1836–1914). Selvatico, who absorbed ideas from the Comte de Montalembert, Pugin and Viollet-le-Duc, published *Sulla architettura e scultura in Venezia, dal Medio Evo sino ai nostri giorni* ('On architecture and sculpture in Venice from the Middle Ages to the present', Venice 1847), which made him something of an Italian parallel to Ruskin. Much of the energy of Gothic Revivalists in Italy went into the task of completing the unfinished façades of medieval churches. Selvatico was a prominent figure in the committee which eventually selected a design by Emilio de Fabris (1808–83) for the west front of Florence cathedral. Erected in 1867–87, this luxuriantly polychromatic marble composition harmonized with Giotto's adjacent campanile.

The selection committee also included Viollet-le-Duc and his disciple Boito, who taught for nearly half a century at the Brera Academy in Milan and published a book much influenced by Viollet, *Architettura del Medio Evo in Italia, con una introduzione 'Sullo stile futuro dell'Architettura italiano'* ('Architecture of the Middle Ages in Italy, with an introduction "On the future style of Italian architecture"', 1880). Boito's Hospital of 1871 at Gallarate in the north of Milan is an aggressive essay in Viollet-le-Duc's most rationalist manner, but at Padua, in his Palazzo delle Debite (1872) and Municipal Museum (1879), he adopted a rich North Italian or Venetian Romanesque which came to be known as the *Stile Boito*, and can be regarded as a parallel to English High Victorian Gothic. His best known work in the *Stile Boita* came at the end of his career, the Casa Verdi in Milan (1899–1913) which contains the polychromatic tomb-chamber of the composer Giuseppe Verdi's librettist, Arrigo Boito, the architect's brother. The building has a whiff of the *Stile Floreale*, the Italian version of Art Nouveau which we will investigate in the next chapter.

Scandinavia, Russia and Greece

Scandinavia and Finland

The Scandinavian countries are important in the story of late neo-classicism for their superb urban architecture and town planning, though, like other European countries, they subsequently adopted a range of *Rundbogenstil* and Gothic idioms, sometimes inspired by what is known as national romanticism. The leading architects who remodelled the capital cities of Scandinavia in the international Greek Revival style are Christian Frederik Hansen (1756–1845) and Michael Gottlieb Birkner Bindesbøll (1800–56) in Denmark; Christian Heinrich Grosch (1801–65) in Norway; and the German-born Carl Ludwig Engel (1778–1840) in Finland. Hansen turned Copenhagen from a medieval and Baroque town into a neo-classical one. His group of town hall, courthouse and prison (1803–16), linked by two bold archways across a side street, is a memorable essay in the Franco-Prussian style which Gilly had developed out of Ledoux. Hansen also rebuilt the cathedral of Our Lady at Copenhagen, the Vor Frue Kirke, in 1811–29. Designed in 1808–10, this has a

698 Hansen: Copenhagen town hall, courthouse and prison linked by archways (1803–16)

699 Bindesbøll: The courtyard of the Thorvaldsen Museum, Copenhagen (1840–44)

noble barrel-vaulted interior recalling Boullée's projected Bibliothèque Nationale.

Hansen's pupil, Bindesbøll, produced one of the most remarkable buildings of its day in Europe, the Thorvaldsen Museum in Copenhagen. A remodelling of an existing structure, this was executed in 1840–4 though Bindesbøll had made designs as early as 1834. It was built to house the sculpture and collections of the neo-classical sculptor Bertel Thorvaldsen (1768–1844), who presented them to his native country, though he had lived and worked in Rome for 41 years from 1798. His chill neo-antique sculpture rivals Canova's as an expression of Winckelmann's ideals, but the museum is a startling monument to the discovery of polychromy which brought to an end Winckelmann's image of Greece. Built round a courtyard with classical façades in an austere Schinkelesque taste, though with splayed Egyptian door frames, the museum boasts animated murals in plaster intarsia on its exterior walls. Resembling a frieze dropped to ground level, these depict the transport of the sculpture from Rome to Copenhagen. They thus help make the building a symbolic framework for human activity, an ambition which was shared at this moment by Labrouste.

700 *Above* Trinity Church, Boston (1872–7), by Richardson

701 *Opposite* The grand staircase of the Paris Opéra (1862–75), by Garnier

Bindesbøll had visited Paris in 1822 where he studied under Franz Christian Gau, one of those who favoured polychromy. The Thorvaldsen Museum is richly decorated with coloured ornament and in the courtyard, which contains the sculptor's tomb, the walls are apparently dissolved by murals depicting oaks, palms and bay trees. Just so did painted nature invade architecture in Labrouste's Bibliothèque Nationale and the vestibule of his Bibliothèque Ste-Geneviève.

At the end of his life Bindesbøll prepared designs for the University Library at Copenhagen as a series of glass-roofed pavilions round a dome. However, the commission went to his follower Johan David Herholdt (1818–1902), whose brick *Rundbogenstil* library was erected in 1855–61 as an important landmark in the development of a national romantic tradition in late-nineteenth-century Danish architecture.

In Norway, which separated from Denmark in 1814, the foundation of a new capital at Christiania (Oslo) enabled Hansen's pupil, Heinrich Grosch, to design

three handsome Greek Revival buildings: the Exchange (1826–52), Norwegian Bank (1828) and University (1841–52). Three years after the incorporation of Finland into Russia as a Grand Duchy in 1809 the capital of Finland was established at Helsinki, where Johan Albrecht Ehrenström (1762–1847) provided the city plan and Carl Engel designed the major public buildings as well as many private houses. The Senate Square is one of the great set-pieces of European neo-classicism, dominated by the high, domed, Lutheran cathedral, raised on a mighty flight of steps. Designed from 1818

and built in 1830–51, the cathedral is flanked by the Senate (1818–22) and the University (1828–32), both containing magnificent Greek Doric staircases. Engel's adjacent University Library (1833–45) has an octagonally-coffered dome and fine colonnaded reading-rooms.

Poland and Russia

After the Congress of Vienna in 1815, the Emperor of Russia became King of Poland, a country which had already lost its independence in 1795. The development of Warsaw after 1815 as a neo-classical capital resembling St Petersburg began with the remodelling in 1818–22 by Merlini's pupil, Jakub Kubicki, of the Belvedere Palace, but the leading architect was the

702 The Senate Square, Helsinki (from 1818): the University and Library (*centre*), Senate (*foreground*), cathedral (right), all by Engel

Florentine-born Antonio Corazzi (1792–1877). He provided the Staszic Palace (1820–3, today Association of the Friends of Science); the Schinkelesque Wielki Theatre (1826–33); and the astonishing group of colonnaded and porticoed palaces of 1823–30 in the Dzierzyński Square which are today the Ministry of Finance and the Bank of Poland, the latter turning the corner in a vast curve comprising two storeys of round-arched openings.

The Russian Emperors Alexander I (reigned 1801–25) and his brother Nicholas I (reigned 1825–55) were determined to follow the example of Catherine the Great by the definitive establishment of St Petersburg as a capital without parallel for the splendour of its public buildings. In the opening years of the nineteenth century a range of classical styles was adopted in St Petersburg in an attempt to catch up with developments in European architecture. These included buildings in the international classicism of the mid-eighteenth century, in a neo-Greek style inspired by Ledoux, and in a grandiose Palladianism. Andrei Nikiforovich Voronikhin (1760–1814), who began as a serf sent abroad by his master to study architecture, was a pupil of de Wailly in Paris. His cathedral of the Virgin of Kazan at St Petersburg (1801–11), with its domed centre flanked by quadrant colonnades, was like a realization of the visionary project for a cathedral published in 1765 by de Wailly's partner, Peyre. However, Voronikhin soon switched to the more fashionable Greek Revival for his Academy of Mines (1806–11), which is dominated by an imposing decastyle portico of Paestum Doric columns.

The French architect Thomas de Thomon (1754–1813), who may have been a pupil of Ledoux, designed the Grand (Bolshoi) Theatre (1802–5; destroyed 1813) after the model of the Théâtre-Français in Paris by Peyre and de Wailly. Like Voronikhin, he turned Greek for his next major building, the Exchange (1805–16, today the Naval Museum). This building, his masterpiece, is a peripteral Greek Doric temple enclosing a barrel-vaulted hall lit by semicircular windows above the

703 Voronikhin: Cathedral of the Virgin of Kazan (1801–11), St Petersburg

colonnade. With its sturdy Doric order inspired by the temples of Paestum, which de Thomon knew at first hand, this brilliant adaptation of a temple to commercial purposes is superior both to Latrobe's Bank of Pennsylvania, Philadelphia (1798–1800), and to Chalgrin's Paris Bourse (1808–15). The Russian-born Adrian Dmitrievich Zakharov (1761–1811), also trained in Paris where he was a pupil of Chalgrin in 1782–6, was responsible for the New Admiralty (1806–23) which, a quarter of a mile long, may be the largest neo-classical building in the world. A remodelling of an existing structure, its most arresting feature is the central pavilion facing the river Neva where a massive triumphal arch, perhaps inspired by Rousseau's entrance to the Hôtel de Salm in Paris, is crowned by a square Ionic colonnade and then by the tall gilded spire of the

704 Exterior of the Exchange, St Petersburg (now the Naval Museum) (1805–16), by de Thomon

705 *Opposite* The Royal Pavilion, Brighton, remodelled by Nash (1815–21): exterior of the saloon

706 *Above* Polychromatic decoration in a chapel at St Giles, Cheadle, Staffordshire (1840–6), by Pugin

707 Zakharov: The New Admiralty, St Petersburg (1806–23), showing the spire preserved from the earlier building

previous building on the site. The stucco façades are painted bright yellow and encrusted with white stucco ornament, following a local tradition devised to achieve maximum brilliance in this snowbound northern capital.

The prolific Karl Ivanovich Rossi (1775–1849) effected a shift away from the Greek Revival to a more adaptable but no less megalomaniac Palladianism in buildings like his New Michael Palace (1819–25, today the Russian Museum), commissioned by Alexander I as a home for his youngest brother. Equally grandiose were his Army General Staff buildings and adjacent arches

(1819–29), which form a vast hemi-cycle in Palace Square in front of the Winter Palace, designed by Rastrelli in the Baroque style in the 1750s. In the middle of this square the French architect Auguste Ricard de Montferrand (1786–1858), trained by Percier, built the Alexander Column in 1829, a Doric column which has been claimed as the largest granite monolith in the world. He also built the enormous St Isaac's cathedral (1817–57) on a Greek-cross plan with a dome and four Corinthian porticoes two of which are flanked by a pair of smaller cupolas relating uneasily to the monumental central dome. The interior shows a shift away from neo-classical ideals, for it is lavishly enriched with paintings, mosaic and sculpture, including polychromatic marbles, porphyry, malachite and lapis lazuli. The great gilded dome, inspired by that at Soufflot's Ste-Genevieve, is supported on a cast-iron framework which was the earliest use in Russia of this material on such a scale.

Vasili Petrovich Stasov (1769–1848), who had worked extensively in Moscow from 1808, completed the Picturesque Chinese Village at Tsarskoe Seloe, near St Petersburg, in 1817–22 and built the Moscow Gate (1834–8) on the outskirts of St Petersburg to commemorate the military campaigns of Nicholas I in 1826–31. Constructed, surprisingly, of cast iron, this massive Greek Doric propylon cogently united the ancient world with the present day. Italian and French influence in St Petersburg eventually gave way to German, a shift probably encouraged by the fact that many of the nineteenth-century emperors had German wives. Following a fire at the Winter Palace in December 1837, Leo von Klenze was summoned from Munich by Nicholas I to design the New Hermitage Museum on the banks of the Neva between the Palace and the Hermitage Theatre. Erected of grey marble round three courtyards in 1842–51, with trabeated façades of Schinkelesque inspiration, this monumental museum is remarkable for the asymmetrical planning of its various wings and floors, each planned around its specific contents, paintings, sculpture, books, prints and drawings, coins and medals, armour, vases and applied arts.

Meanwhile in Moscow, stricter and less cosmopolitan in flavour than St Petersburg, the principal early-nineteenth-century architects were the Italian-born Domenico Gilardi (1788–1845), Afanasy Grigoryev (1782–1868), and Osip Beauvais (1784–1834). They were responsible for public buildings and private houses in Moscow and the surrounding countryside in an emphatic Greek Revival manner, of which the Widows' House (1809–18) and the Guardianship Council Building (1823) by Gilardi and his father, Giacomo, are characteristic examples. Beauvais, who directed the rebuilding of Moscow after the disastrous fire of 1812, formed two squares round his new Bolshoi Theatre (1821–4) which rival in splendour those being created in St Petersburg, Helsinki, Munich and Berlin.

The German-Russian architect Konstantin Andreevich Thon (1794–1881) built the Great Kremlin Palace (1838–49) in a confused late-classical style, but his church of the Redeemer (1839–93), also in Moscow, has a Russo-Byzantine flavour which makes it the first significant monument of the nationalist Slav Revival of later-nineteenth-century Russian architecture. From the 1840s several scholars began to investigate early Russian architecture and, as in other European countries, their publications were accompanied by new buildings in these historical styles. This movement was part of the ever-growing strength of nationalism throughout Europe during the nineteenth century. The accompanying turn away from the architecture of international neo-classicism to what is often known as national romanticism was especially marked in Finland and the Scandinavian countries in the years around 1900. One of the most important early monuments in the Slav-Russo-Byzantine Revival was the Historical Museum in Moscow (1874–83). This is a fanciful and rather overloaded assembly of Russian sixteenth-century motifs designed by an architect of English descent, Vladimir Ossipovich Sherwood (1832–97). The cathedral of St Vladimir at Kiev was initiated in 1862 to mark the thousandth anniversary of the Russian nation. Built in 1876–82 from designs by Alexander Vikentievich Beretti, it is a more historically accurate version of the Russo-Byzantine style and has a full programme of appropriate interior decoration. The Church of the Resurrection (1883–1907) by A. A. Parland, commemorating the spot where Alexander II had been assassinated, brought this exuberant Slav style to St Petersburg. Here, in a wholly neo-classical city, it was less appropriate than in Moscow with its rich medieval past.

Greece

To Germans, nurtured from the time of Winckelmann on the belief that the ideals of ancient Greece were being reborn on German soil, it seemed too good to be true that in 1833 a German prince, Otto von Wittelsbach, should be offered the throne of the newly established kingdom of Greece, recently liberated from Turkish domination. As a result, Athens, then a modest town of

708 Exterior of the Historical Museum, Moscow (1874–83), by Sherwood

709 *Overleaf* The Empress Josephine's bedroom (1812) at the Château of Malmaison, by Percier and Fontaine

710 Hansen brothers: (*l. to r.*) the National Library (1885–1921), the University (1839–50), the Academy of Science (1859–87), Athens

under 10,000 inhabitants, was transformed into a model neo-classical town with historically appropriate buildings, just as Munich had been by King Otto's father, Ludwig I of Bavaria. Ambitious schemes for palaces and public buildings by Klenze and Schinkel were rejected in favour of designs for a new town plan and royal palace by Klenze's rival, Friedrich von Gärtner. His work was of lower quality than that of the two Danes, Hans Christian Hansen (1803–83), appointed Royal Greek Architect in 1834, and his brother Theophilus Eduard Hansen (1813–91), who arrived in Athens in 1838. Their severe Greek Revival style, characterized by crystalline clarity of detail, is best experienced in the noble group of three public buildings in Gärtner's axial main street, the University (H. C. Hansen, 1839–50), Academy of Science (T. E. Hansen, 1859–87), and National Library (T. E. Hansen, 1885–1921). H. C. Hansen was also an archaeologist and was involved in excavations on the Acropolis, where he restored the Temple of Nike Apteros. With the French architect F.-L.-F. Boulanger, T. E. Hansen built the Zappeion

(1874–88), an exhibition hall with a stylish circular court surrounded by an Ionic colonnade. Another prolific architect was Hansen's pupil Ernst Ziller (1837–1923), who in 1890 designed a house for the celebrated archaeologist Heinrich Schliemann (today the Supreme Court). By this time the Greek Revival of the early nineteenth century seemed old-fashioned and irrelevant. Schliemann did not seek the reproduction of any Mycenaean or even Greek effects, so that Ziller provided him with a comfortable modern house in an Italianate Renaissance manner with open arcaded loggias.

In the meantime both Hansen brothers had left Athens, Theophilus for Vienna in 1846 and Hans for Copenhagen about four years later. Their experiences in Greece, where they had studied Greek Byzantine architecture, enabled them to develop a richly polychromatic Byzantine style which, with its sensible round-headed window openings, seemed more adaptable to modern requirements than their columnar Greek Revival manner. T. F. Hansen, as we have already seen, used this for his Army Museum at Vienna (1849–56), while Hans Hansen did the same at his Hospital at Copenhagen (1856–63).

711 Poelaert: The Palais de Justice, Brussels (1862–83)

Belgium and Holland

The Netherlands in the nineteenth century followed the familiar pattern of transition from late neo-classical and Greek Revival styles to Romanesque, Gothic and Renaissance Revivals. There is little of outstanding quality, though in Belgium one building literally towers above all others. This is the Palais de Justice in Brussels (1862–83) by Joseph Poelaert (1817–79), a gargantuan neo-Baroque building which rivals Garnier's Paris Opéra as one of the most memorable classical buildings of nineteenth-century Europe. Trained in Paris under J.-N. Huyot and L. Visconti, in 1856 Poelaert was appointed city architect for Brussels, where six years later he was given the commission for the Palais de Justice after an international competition had failed to produce an acceptable design. Poelaert's Palais de Justice, like that by Duc in Paris which he had doubtless studied carefully, has just a hint of ancient Indian architecture in its massive but sculptural handling of the orders. Piranesi, too, is recalled in its spatial complexity and especially in its sensational expression of the majesty of the law. Indeed, as a masterly statement of the aesthetic of the Sublime, it is without parallel in European architecture.

In Holland, the leading architect in the second half of the nineteenth century is Petrus Josephus Hubertus Cuypers (1827–1921). His admiration for Viollet-le-Duc, to whom he is a Dutch parallel, led him to visit Paris as early as 1849. His numerous buildings of honestly exposed brickwork have the same unlovable character as Viollet's, while in his restorations of medieval churches he was concerned, like Viollet, with restoring them back to a supposedly pure primitive state by removing all subsequent accretions. In Amsterdam he worked in a high-gabled Dutch Renaissance style in his Rijksmuseum (1876–85) and Central Station (1881–9), but his output consisted mainly of sober Catholic churches, for example at Eindhoven, Amsterdam, Leeuwarden and Hilversum. For these he chose a Gothic Revival style in contrast to the neo-Renaissance of his secular buildings. This burst of Catholic building activity in a Calvinist country was the consequence of the restoration of the Catholic hierarchy in 1853. In the previous year Cuypers, a devout Roman Catholic, had founded the studio of Cuypers and Stoltenberg for the production of ecclesiastical furnishings and sculpture, as Morris was shortly to found his own firm, and George Gilbert Scott junior the firm of Watts & Co. Cuypers's emphasis on the crafts and on 'honest' use of materials made him both a close parallel to Pugin and Morris in England, and also an important forerunner of H. P. Berlage, whose work we shall investigate in a separate chapter devoted to Art Nouveau (Chapter 10).

712 *Overleaf left* Chimney-piece in the Chaucer Room (c.1877–90) at Cardiff Castle, by Burges

713 *Overleaf right* The Singers' Hall, Schloss Neuschwanstein, Bavaria, by Riedl (begun 1869)

USA

Greek and Gothic to the mid-century

America followed the pattern we have seen in towns as different as Milan and Helsinki, Karlsruhe and Edinburgh, which were given a new appearance of dignity and authority in the early nineteenth century by programmes of public works in an international late-neo-classical style. Athenian democracy of the fifth century represented an ideal of civic order and severity with which Americans were quick to identify, with the result that the dominance of the Greek Revival was more complete in America than in any European country. It was Benjamin Latrobe (1764–1820), as we have seen (p. 430), who was largely responsible for giving an accepted professional status to the practice of architecture as well as for creating a rational and classical language for the public buildings of the new democracy. His pupils Robert Mills (1781–1855) and William Strickland (1788–1854) dominated the architectural scene until the mid-century, though they lacked Latrobe's brilliant imagination.

Mills, conscious of being the first architect born and trained in America, resembled Smirke in England in his practical and ready response to the problems posed by a wide range of new building types, commercial, industrial and governmental. Behind a façade inspired by Ledoux's Hôtel Guimard, his Washington Hall, Philadelphia (1809–16) provided an undivided space capable of holding nearly 6,000 people. His other auditoria, mainly ecclesiastical in function, included the Monumental Church, Richmond, Virginia (1812), an octagonal building in a stark Greek Revival manner recalling that of Gentz in Berlin. In 1822–7 he built in the same style the County Records Office (today South Carolina Historical Society) in his native Charleston, South Carolina. With its unfluted Greek Doric columns and simplified entablature, this is known as the 'Fireproof Building' because it was the first American building to be conceived from the start in terms of fireproof

714 Exterior of the Treasury Building, Washington (1836–42), by Mills

materials: brick for the walls, partitions and groin vaults; iron for the window frames and shutters; stone for the staircases. In 1830 Mills moved to Washington, where six years later he won the competition for the Washington Monument which he had designed in 1833. Not completed till 1888, this is a gigantic obelisk 555 feet (170m) high. In 1836, he was put in charge of public buildings in the federal capital and as a result was responsible for the Treasury Building (1836–42), Patent Office (1836–40, now National Portrait Gallery) and Old Post Office (1839–42, now International Trade Commission). The impressive scale of these porticoed and colonnaded buildings immediately gave Washington the unmistakeable stamp of a great capital city. In his interiors, too, Mills showed himself a respectable successor to Latrobe, whose Supreme Court Chamber in the Capitol is recalled in the entrance lobby of the Patent Office. Here squat columns of the Delian Doric order support a groined vault around which rise the twin curved arms of the cantilevered staircase.

William Strickland's first major work was the Second Bank of the United States, Philadelphia (1818–24), a rectangular building with a Greek Doric portico, modelled on the Parthenon, occupying the whole of each of the shorter ends. The long sides, by contrast, are wholly astylar. The colonnaded barrel-vaulted banking-hall is given minimal exterior expression so as not to compromise the temple-like effect of the whole building. In Washington, his United States Naval Asylum (1826–33) and United States Mint (1829–33) anticipated Mills's grandiose use of columns, but his Merchants' Exchange at Philadelphia (1832–4) is a more imaginative composition. Here the apex of the triangular site is filled with a handsome hemi-cycle of Corinthian columns crowned by a tall circular lantern, modelled on the Choragic Monument of Lysicrates in Athens (p. 43). As so often in Strickland's buildings, the details are taken directly from Stuart and Revett's *Antiquities of Athens*. In 1838 he travelled in Europe where he visited London, Liverpool, Paris and Rome. On his return he designed his most ambitious building, the State Capitol at his native town of Nashville, Tennessee (1845–59), with an immense Ionic portico at each end and a central Lysicratean lantern. Nashville also boasts Strickland's First Presbyterian Church (1848–51), a major monument in a heavy neo-Egyptian style which was more widely adopted in America in 1830–50 than in Europe. To American patrons it had the appeal at once of novelty and immutability, and of a wisdom more profound than that of modern Europe. Thus, though not generally considered suitable for churches and houses, it was frequently used for cemetery entrances, jails and court-houses, with their hints of the permanent enclosure and immortality of Egyptian culture. Its connotations of secrecy led to its adoption for the temples of Freemasons and Mormons, while the hydraulic concerns of the Nile-based civilization of the Egyptians made the style seem appropriate for reservoirs and bridges.

A new building type with which America was to become especially associated was the grand hotel. In America, as in Europe, these were welcomed by a newly prosperous and mobile middle class which lacked access to grand private houses while travelling. Moreover, in a new democratic country such as America it was a building type which provided something of a substitute for the glamour of the royal palaces of Europe. The first

715 Entrance front of the Merchants' Exchange, Philadelphia (1832–4), by Strickland

important example was Tremont House, Boston (1828–9; dem. 1894), by the prolific architect Isaiah Rogers (1800–69). Its chill Doric exterior conceals a novel plan, functional but elegant, in which a lateral corridor centres on a circular domed entrance lobby with the reception office opening off it. With its baths, water-closets and gas-lit public rooms it set new standards for mechanical services, a field in which grand hotels were to lead the way during the nineteenth century. Rogers went on to build the Merchants' Exchanges in New York (1836–42) and Boston (1841–2), the former perhaps inspired by Schinkel's Berlin Schauspielhaus. Another noble Schinkelesque work is the Ohio State Capitol at Columbus (1838–61),

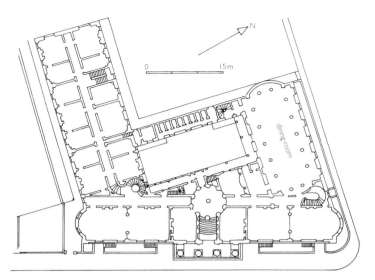

716 *Above* Rogers: Plan of Tremont House, Boston (1828–9)

717 *Below* Exterior of the Ohio State Capitol, Columbus (1838–61), by Walter, Cole and Rogers

718 *Below* Façade of Girard College for Orphans, Philadelphia (1833–48), by Walter

where a circular drum surrounded by pilasters and lacking a dome towers above a long colonnade of unfluted Greek Doric columns. Worthy of Ledoux, this monumental building was the result of a competition won by Henry Walter of Cincinnati, though the final design owed much to contributions by Thomas Cole (1801–48) and Isaiah Rogers.

Strickland's two pupils Alexander Jackson Davis (1803–92) and Ithiel Town (1784–1844), who worked in partnership from 1829 to 1835, continued his style in numerous public buildings such as the Connecticut State House at Hartford (1827–31) and the United States Custom House, New York City (1833–42), both inspired by the Parthenon. Another pupil of Strickland, Thomas Ustick Walter (1804–87), designed one of the most beautiful late neo-classical monuments in America, Girard College for Orphans, Philadelphia (1833–48). The principal building, Founder's Hall, is a peripteral Corinthian temple ingeniously disguising a functional three-storeyed interior which contains 12 classrooms with fireproof vaulting in brick. Reinforced with iron, the whole building is clad in marble In 1850 Walter responded with great aplomb to the task of adding wings and a new dome to the far-from-Greek United States Capitol at Washington. Constructed in 1855–6 on a great web of cast iron, this monumental echo of Wren's dome at St Paul's and of Montferrand's at St Isaac's cathedral, St Petersburg (completed 1857), is one of the most memorable of all architectural tributes from the new world to the old.

Like many American architects of his generation Walter was a man of immensely practical gifts who could turn his hand to major engineering projects, for example the harbour works he constructed in Venezuela in 1843–5. He was also a domestic architect who added in 1835–6 a great Greek Doric portico on to the country house known as Andalusia, fifteen miles north of Philadelphia. This was the estate of Nicholas Biddle, statesman, writer and banker, who, unusually for Americans of his generation, had studied Greek architecture at first hand. An influential figure in the

719 Upjohn: Tower and spire of Trinity Church, New York City (1841–6)

him a Gothic ruin, considered one of the first of its kind in America.

The Greek Revival in America, inspired by English buildings and English archaeological publications, has always been admired as a successful transplantation from Europe to the new world. The style became totally acclimatized in both public and domestic architecture as a colourful and convincing expression of national consciousness. The 1840s and 1850s saw the rise of a Gothic Revival no less influenced by England but far less successful than the Greek. The Picturesque cult of styles, Greek Gothic, Tudor, Italianate, Egyptian, had raged in America as in England in the early nineteenth century, but the building which, more than any other, set a new standard of accuracy in the Gothic Revival was Trinity Church, New York City (1841–6). This was designed by Richard Upjohn (1802–78), who had emigrated to America from England in 1829 and was a devoted member of the Protestant Episcopal Church, the American cousin of the Church of England which had recently espoused the Gothic Revival. Trinity Church is an elaborate essay in English Perpendicular Gothic, apparently inspired by the perspective of the ideal church published by Pugin in his *True Principles of Pointed or Christian Architecture* (1841). It was the start of a career in which Upjohn designed nearly forty churches, by no means all Gothic, for, like many of his contemporaries in Germany, but unlike Pugin, he adopted the *Rundbogenstil.* Studying this first of all in books such as Moller's *Memorials of German Gothic Architecture* and Hope's *Historical Essay on Architecture* (1835), and second on a visit to Europe in 1850, he subsequently built St Paul's church, Baltimore, Maryland (1854–6), as an essay in Lombardic Romanesque. The choice of style was not arbitrary for in 1859 Upjohn was prepared to admit, as Pugin had never been, that, despite his devotion to Gothic, he 'could not but acknowledge that many of the most impressive Christian monuments were not Gothic'. He emphasized that 'the Lombard and other Romanesque styles' and even the Pantheon in Rome had deeply impressed him as examples of religious architecture.

Greek Revival in America, he was largely responsible for the form of Walter's Girard College. Of Quaker ancestry, Biddle had a motto that 'There are but two truths in the world – the Bible and Greek architecture.' Despite this devotion to truth, the portico at Andalusia, though exactly copied from the Theseion in Athens, is entirely constructed of wood, while in the Picturesque park which he laid out round the house, Walter built for

720 *Above* Renwick: The Smithsonian Institution, Washington (1847–55)

721 *Below* Gilman and Bryant: The City Hall, Boston (1862–5)

Upjohn was a respected public figure, associated with the rise of the architectural profession and with the increasing wealth and influence of the Protestant Episcopal Church. He became first president of the American Institute of Architects which was founded in 1857, after an abortive attempt by T. U. Walter in 1836, two years after the founding of the Institute of British Architects.

New theories and new directions from Hunt to Richardson

Upjohn's principal rival as a Gothic church architect was James Renwick (1818–95), who was responsible in New York City for the Anglican Grace Church (1843–6) and the Roman Catholic St Patrick's cathedral (1858–79). Like Upjohn he turned to the *Rundbogenstil*, for example at the Smithsonian Institution, Washington (1847–55), built of brownstone in the form of a picturesquely disposed Romanesque monastery with numerous delicately detailed towers. Later in his career, following a visit to the Paris Exposition of 1855 with the banker and art-collector William Corcoran, he ushered in a wholly new phase in American architecture with two buildings in the French Second Empire Style, the Corcoran (now Renwick) Gallery of Art, Washington (1859–71), and Vassar College, Poughkeepsie, New York (1861–5). Vassar was built for the philanthropist Matthew Vassar who stipulated the sixteenth-century Tuileries Palace in Paris as a model.

A more sophisticated and more influential Second Empire monument is Boston City Hall of 1862–5 by Arthur Gilman (1821–82) and Gridley Bryant (1816–99). Gilman was consultant with Alfred B. Mullet (1834–90) on the design of one of the largest of these Parisian-inspired public buildings, the State, War and Navy Building (1871–85; now Old Executive Office Buildings) at Washington. The neo-Renaissance idiom of Second-Empire Paris had already made an impact on Richard Morris Hunt (1827–95), the first American to be trained at the Ecole des Beaux-Arts in Paris. He entered the Ecole in 1846 and joined the atelier of

722 Hunt: Saloon in The Breakers, Newport, Rhode Island (1892–5)

Hector Lefuel (1810–80), under whom he worked on the extension of the Louvre in 1854–5. One of Hunt's most impressive works, the Lenox Library, New York City (1870–5; dem. 1912), was in an arcuated style derived from Durand and Labrouste. Later he adopted the French late-medieval manorial style of the Jacques Coeur house at Bourges (p. 165), in châteaux and town houses for the commercial aristocracy of America, for example the W. K. Vanderbilt House, New York City (1878–82; dem. c.1920), and the colossal Biltmore House, Asheville, North Carolina (1888–95), for George W. Vanderbilt. At the once modest summer colony of Newport, Rhode Island, he provided four palatial retreats, the most celebrated being The Breakers (1892–5), for Cornelius Vanderbilt II, a sumptuously decorated Genoese *cinquecento* palazzo centring on a two-storeyed hall. In the 1890s he returned to the Beaux-Arts classicism in which he had been trained for the design of the domed Administration Building at the World's Fair, Chicago (1891–3), of which more later, and the entrance range of the Metropolitan Museum of Art in New York (1894–5). Enormously prolific, he was

723 Potter: Nott Memorial Library (now Alumni Hall), Union College, Schenectady, New York (1858–9 and 1872–8)

greatly respected in his lifetime as a founder member and president of the American Institute of Architects and as an architect who gave systematic professional training to pupils in his own atelier. Unlike many of his contemporaries in America and Europe, he did not invest architecture with moral attributes or see it as a vehicle for social reform. This, together with his stylistic diversity, made him temporarily unfashionable during much of the twentieth century.

Returning to the development of the Gothic Revival, we can see that by the 1860s it had moved into a phase comparable with, and indeed inspired by, High Victorian Gothic in England. The tremendous popularity of the writings of Ruskin in America helps account for buildings such as the National Academy of Design, New York City (1863–5), by Peter B. Wight (1838–1925), modelled on the Doge's Palace in Venice, and the equally striking Nott Memorial Library (now Alumni Hall), Union College, Schenectady, New York (1858–9 and 1872–8), by Edward Potter (1831–1904). Though it is inspired by the Baptistery at Pisa, the Nott Library has an exposed iron skeleton behind its polychromatic arcaded skin. As a compelling expression of a passionately held belief that ideals of truth and frankness were enshrined in medieval architecture and in modern materials, the building invites comparison with a contemporary English work, the University Museum at Oxford. Designed in 1853 by Sir Thomas Deane, Son and Woodward, and executed in 1855–60 with support from John Ruskin, the University Museum contains an iron and glass interior within a stone exterior of Italian Gothic inspiration. Terracotta imported from England was used in the ambitious Museum of Fine Arts, Boston, Massachusetts (1870–6; dem.), by John

724 *Above* Entrance to the Pennsylvania Academy of Fine Arts, Philadelphia (1871–6), by Furness

725 *Left* Furness: The Provident Life and Trust Company, Philadelphia (1876–9; now demolished)

Sturgis (1834–88) and Charles Brigham (1841–1925). The first public art museum in America, this combined references to the University Museum at Oxford and to the South Kensington (now Victoria and Albert) Museum in London, begun in 1859 by Captain Francis Fowke as a Germanic *Rundbogenstil* essay characterized by extensive use of buff terracotta ornament in a North Italian Renaissance vein.

A church with strident polychromy and a campanile like that at Street's St James-the-Less, Westminster, is Holy Trinity, New York City (1870 and 75; dem.), at Madison Avenue and 42nd Street. Despite its Ruskinian exterior, it had an elliptical interior arranged like an auditorium. This was to suit the extremely evangelical tastes of the pastor who, although this was an Episcopal church, wanted attention concentrated on the pulpit, not the altar. The architect was Leopold Eidlitz (1823–1908), who was born in Prague, emigrated to New York in 1843, and designed many churches in a range of medieval styles, often of continental rather than of English origin. A building as aggressive as any by Eidlitz, and in an emphatically High Victorian Gothic style, is the Memorial Hall at Harvard University, Cambridge, Massachusetts

(1865–78), by William Ware (1832–1915) and Henry Van Brunt (1832–1903). It looks like a cathedral but in fact consists of a theatre forming an apse, a dining-hall forming a nave, and the common circulation area forming the transepts. Van Brunt, a prolific architectural writer, translated the first volume of Viollet's *Entretiens* in 1875, but was nonetheless sympathetic to the turn to Beaux-Arts classicism in American architecture from the 1880s.

A more original response to Ruskin's plea for an expressive and truthful Gothic architecture came from Frank Furness (1839–1912), who was also much influenced by the theoretical writings of Leopold Eidlitz. An early work in Furness's mature style is his Pennsylvania Academy of the Fine Arts in Philadelphia (1871–6), which provided long top-lit galleries behind a symmetrical façade rich with carving and contrasting textures, but chunky and forceful in its handling. Eidlitz's conception of architectural language as a simulation of physical gesture, demonstrated in his book *The Nature and Function of Art* (1881), was given explosive expression in Furness's most celebrated building, the now demolished Provident Life and Trust Company (1876–9) in Philadelphia. Its massive façade of huge granite blocks was dominated by over-structured supports seemingly assembled as a deliberately exaggerated demonstration of the claim that load-bearing in architecture is akin to animal strength in nature. The building thus fulfilled Eidlitz's wish for an architecture that could 'perform acts . . . of muscular and nerve function'. Its aggressive tone has much in common with Viollet-le-Duc's proposals in his *Entretiens sur l'architecture* for a new rationalist architecture while in the interior new materials were exposed in a way which would also have appealed to Viollet. The walls of the main hall were lined with patterned tiles in green and white, while the roof had skylights supported by polychromatic iron girders.

The influence respectively of Ruskin and Viollet-le-Duc can be seen in the twin ideals of 'organicism' and 'reality' proposed in the influential writings of the architectural journalist Montgomery Schuyler (1843–1914). He found the ideal expression of these qualities

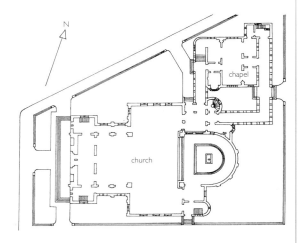

726 Richardson: Plan of Trinity Church, Boston (1872–7)

in the work of Henry Hobson Richardson (1838–86), who opened up a new phase in the history of American architecture. It was no longer England but France, and especially the Ecole des Beaux-Arts, to which American architects looked for inspiration. Richardson was the first American architect to create an individual style which subsequently became national, and the first to influence European architects. His creative eclecticism produced an integrated but variable style dependent on the adaptable round-arched style of Romanesque Europe.

Trained at the Ecole des Beaux-Arts in 1859–62, Richardson subsequently worked in the offices of Labrouste and Hittorff before returning to America in 1865. His early works echo contemporary Gothic Revival work in England; in the next decade, however, he adopted a rock-faced Romanesque which, though of French origin, was indebted not to Labrouste but to Viollet-le-Duc's rationalist disciple, Vaudremer. This style surfaced in Boston in his Trinity Church (1872–7; fig. 700). The massive sculpturally modelled forms of this church recall the Romanesque buildings of Spain and France as well as the Byzantine buildings of Constantinople and Venice, but the vigorous handling and especially the strong earthy materials – rough-surfaced pink granite with brownstone trim – make the whole building a cogent unity, not a mere assembly of eclectic detail. Inside, the Greek-cross plan rises to a timber roof of double-curved profile inspired by the work of Burges in England. The walls and roof are painted with

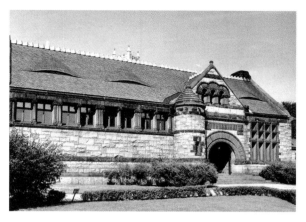

727 *Above* Richardson: Crane Memorial Library, Quincy (1880–2)

728 *Right* Richardson: Ames Gate Lodge, North Easton, Massachusetts (1880–1)

decoration as polychromatic as Burges himself would have wanted. This is the work of John La Farge, who was also responsible for the pre-Raphaelite-style stained glass, except for that of 1880 and 1883 by Morris and Burne-Jones in the north transept and south chapel.

At his Sever Hall, Harvard University (1878–80), Richardson exchanged his customary granite and brownstone for the more genial red brick of the adjacent eighteenth-century ranges in Harvard Yard. The result is an equivalent to, though far from an imitation of, Vaudremer's *lycée* style. However, in his Austin Hall (then the Law School) of 1880–4 at Harvard he returned to the powerful style of Trinity Church. He also adopted a version of this for his Crane Memorial Library, Quincy, Massachusetts (1880–2). This sturdy building is the most original of a group of five small public libraries which he designed in the 1870s and 80s. These are stylistically related to his Ames Gate Lodge, North Easton, Massachusetts (1880–1), perhaps the most striking example of his use of boulders for wall construction so as to create an organic effect. This unusual commission, for a substantial entrance lodge to the Ames family estate, called for a dwelling for the gatekeeper as well as a Bachelor Hall where the young men of the family might entertain their friends. Richardson provided a rugged building which seems to grow out of the earth like Frank Lloyd Wright's later Prairie Style (see p. 567).

Richardson's two favourite buildings, the Allegheny County Court House and Jail in Pittsburgh, Pennsylvania (1883–8), and the Marshall Field Wholesale Store in Chicago, Illinois (1885–7; dem. 1930), are both arcuated compositions executed in quarry-faced granite. However, they eschew the Picturesque effects of his earlier work in favour of a symmetry which reflects his training at the Ecole des Beaux-Arts. The plan of the Allegheny Court House is a characteristic Beaux-Arts layout with a magnificent staircase in which the vaults are carried on arches. Though cast-iron columns were incorporated in the construction of the building, the masonry walls were still load-bearing. By the time it was finished new techniques were being developed in Chicago which enabled the weight of the external walls to be carried on the internal metal frame.

Turning to domestic architecture, we find the same reaction against the consequences of the industrial revolution and the same return to a pre-industrial vernacular tradition which occurred in England in the 1870s in the work of Norman Shaw and his circle. The first monument in the American version of the 'Old English' manner of Shaw and Nesfield was the Watts Sherman house in Newport, Rhode Island (1874–5), nominally designed by H. H. Richardson but doubtless owing much to his assistant Stanford White. Influenced in its design by the perspectives and plans published in

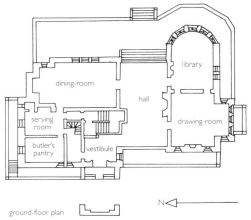

ground-floor plan

729, 730 *Above and left* Exterior and ground floor plan of Watts Sherman House, Newport, Rhode Island (1874–5), by Richardson

the *English Building News* and *Builder* of Shaw's manorial houses and of his New Zealand Chambers in the City of London, the Watts Sherman house is an irregularly disposed composition sporting half-timbering, sweeping gables, tall chimneys, long bands of casement windows, oriels, and carved sunflowers. In place of English tile-hanging on the roof and walls, it introduces American wooden shingles: hence the modern name, 'Shingle Style', for this new type of domestic architecture. The Watts Sherman house has a living hall open to the staircase and extending the full depth of the plan, a feature which was to be developed in the Shingle Style as part of a tendency towards an open-plan house. Designed for a climate with very hot summers and very cold winters,

Shingle Style houses needed fewer internal doors than their English counterparts because they had central heating in the winter, while in the summer it was desirable to encourage breezes. The presence of a Japanese pavilion at the 1876 Centennial Exposition in Philadelphia encouraged the taste for spatially fluid houses with strong horizontal lines, broad eaves, latticework, emphasis on construction and craftsmanship, and intimate relation to their setting. One of the fruits of this new enthusiasm was Edward Morse's illustrated book, *Japanese Houses and their Surroundings* (Boston 1886), while open internal planning later became the hallmark of the houses of Frank Lloyd Wright.

In the meantime the firm of McKim, Mead and White had designed some of the finest of all Shingle Style houses in the 1880s, for example their H. Victor Newcomb house of 1880–1 in Elberon, New Jersey, with superb open-plan interiors divided by grilles, lattices or sliding doors; their Isaac Bell house, Newport, Rhode Island (1883); and their William G. Low house, Bristol, Rhode Island (1886–7; dem. c.1955), where the whole building is contained under a single broad gable, nearly 140 feet (43m) long, epitomizing Ruskin's belief in the moral expressiveness of the all-sheltering roof.

Sullivan and the origin of the skyscraper

The career of McKim, Mead and White developed along a very different path from the Shingle Style, but before continuing with our investigation of it we should return to Chicago where, following the devastating fire of 1871, the need to rebuild rapidly in fireproof materials encouraged the architect-engineer William Le Baron Jenney (1832–1907) to take the first step towards the development of what has become known as skyscraper construction. 1871 also saw the completion in New York of the first office building planned with an integral passenger elevator. It was, of course, the development of the technology of the elevator in New York in the 1850s and 1860s which made possible the subsequent development of skyscraper construction in Chicago. After taking the first steps in this direction in his first Leiter Building (1879), Jenney produced his best-known work, the ten-storeyed Home Insurance Building (1884–5; dem. 1931), which incorporated a skeleton of cast-iron and steel beams and wrought iron girders on to which were bolted cast-iron shelves. These carried most of the weight of the external masonry cladding, which was aesthetically of somewhat clumsy design. Jenney's unvisual approach may have been influenced by his training in the Ecole Centrale des Arts et Manufactures in Paris in 1853–6, where the utilitarian doctrine of Durand still held sway. William Holabird (1854–1923) and Martin Roche (1853–1927), who had both worked in Jenney's office, were responsible for the Tacoma Building (1887–9; dem. 1939), also in Chicago. Here they made more consistent use of the techniques pioneered in the Home Insurance Building and introduced a novel foundation consisting of reinforced concrete rafts which were valuable as stabilizing elements in sandy soil or in the muddy soil of Chicago. The Tacoma Building was also clothed in a more harmonious façade than the Home Insurance Building. Consisting largely of multiple bay windows, it influenced the Reliance Building in Chicago (1890–5) by Daniel Burnham (1846–1912) and John Root (1850–91).

Louis Henry Sullivan (1856–1924) was yet another architectural giant who moved to Chicago in the 1870s, when the city was the burgeoning metropolis of the middle west. A pupil of Jenney and then of Vaudremer in Paris, he and his partner Dankmar Adler (1844–1900) designed the massive Chicago Auditorium Theater and Hotel Building (1887–9), one of the largest and most complex buildings in the whole of America, incorporating an office block in addition to the theatre and hotel. Sullivan's first proposals envisaged façades sprouting fancifully with oriels, turrets, spires and dormers, but he eventually selected a sturdy rock-faced composition inspired by the arcuated treatment of Richardson's Marshall Field Wholesale Store. Whereas Sullivan's façades are of load-bearing brickwork faced with granite and limestone, the floor, vault and roof loads of the theatre are carried on a remarkable framework of cast and wrought iron. Though seating over 4,000 spectators, the theatre has perfect sightlines and acoustics. For its interiors and for those of the hotel, especially the lobbies, bar and dining-room, Sullivan devised a lush and fluid ornament in the form of gilded plaster relief inspired by plant forms.

In such celebrated office buildings as the Wainwright Building in St Louis, Missouri (1890–1), and Guaranty Building, Buffalo, New York (1894–6), Sullivan and Adler rejected the duality of the Chicago Auditorium constructional system with its load-bearing masonry walls and internal iron frame. Instead, they adopted full steel-skeleton construction which, for the first time, was clothed in an aesthetically convincing manner. Aware of the need to create an expressive language out of the vocabulary of skyscraper construction, Sullivan wrote in 'The Tall Office Building Artistically Considered' (1896): 'It must be every inch a proud and soaring thing, rising in sheer exultation that from bottom to top it is a unit without a single dissenting line.' At the Wainwright Building he gave poetic expression to this image of verticality by introducing false, i.e. non-loadbearing, brick piers in between the structural piers on the façade which are of steel clad in brick. The façade thus appears

731 Sullivan and Adler: The Wainright Building, St Louis, Missouri (1890–1)

732 *Above* Sullivan and Adler: The Guaranty Building, Buffalo, New York (1894–6)

as a grid of identical brick piers or mullions, but only half of these correspond to the structural reality. Their presence is required to create the vertical emphasis characterizing the 'soaring thing' of which Sullivan wrote in 1896. In the Guaranty Building, another vertically emphatic design, the piers are connected at the top by arches and there is a far less emphatic cornice, so that the eye is scarcely interrupted on its upward course. However, the building is more richly ornamented than the Wainwright Building, the surface cladding consisting of terracotta carved in low relief

with delicate geometrical ornament. The effect produced by the façades is curiously close to the 'poetic industrial' style devised by Schinkel for his Bauakademie and especially for his unexecuted Berlin Library of 1835.

Sullivan gave his Carson Pirie and Scott Department Store, Chicago (1899–1901 and 1903–4), a markedly horizontal rhythm to emphasize the flat selling floors in contrast to the vertically piled up offices of the Wainwright and Guaranty Buildings. With their bands of windows set in white terracotta, the upper storeys contrast with the elaborately ornamental treatment of the two lowest floors. There the shop-windows serve as picture frames, composed of ductile cast-iron ornament in dynamic curvilinear patterns which are a parallel to those of contemporary Art Nouveau designers in Europe. Despite his love of vivacious and exotic ornament of this kind, Sullivan called for a temporary ban on architectural decoration in his book *Kindergarten Chats* (1901), believing that the nineteenth century had suffered from a surfeit of repetitive historically-inspired ornament. His outlook was governed by the energetic search for a new style which would harmonize with the American democratic experiment. His belief in inevitable development and progress amounted to a cultural parallel to Charles Darwin's theories on the evolution of species.

McKim, Mead and White and the return to classicism

In 1893 Sullivan designed the Transportation Building for the World's Columbian Exposition at Chicago, an international exhibition which commemorated the 400th anniversary of the discovery of the New World by Columbus. This was the fifteenth world fair (the second in America), the first having been the Great Exhibition in London in 1851. At the Chicago Exposition, the largest up to that date, Sullivan's building, painted in bold colours, was dominated by a huge entrance arch

733 The Court of Honor, World's Fair, Chicago (1893), planned by Burnham with buildings by McKim, Mead & White, Hunt and Atwood

with rich abstract ornament. It stood out from the general run of buildings which, to Sullivan's annoyance, were in a grandiose Beaux-Arts classicism. Historians sometimes claim that while Chicago and the west had been experimenting with new types of architecture, New York and the east had returned to a classicism which was displayed with such panache at the World's Fair that it helped bring the Chicago School to an end and so changed the course of American architecture. In fact the story is more complicated, because the Chief of Construction for the Fair, Daniel Burnham, was himself a leader of the Chicago School. We have already noted his steel-framed Reliance Building of the early 1890s, but for the Fair he planned a vast Court of Honor around a lagoon flanked with monumental buildings. These were in the profusely classical Beaux-Arts style of France in the 1870s and 1880s. In reality they were temporary exhibition halls of iron and glass fronted with pilastered façades painted white. Electrically lit at night, this

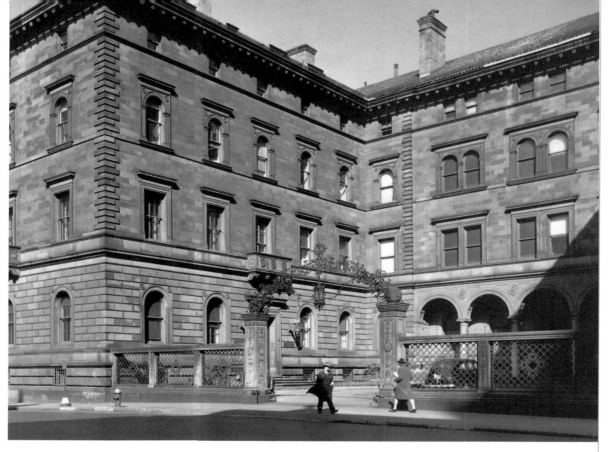

734, 735 *Above and below* McKim, Mead and White: Exterior and plan of the Villard Houses, New York City (1882–5)

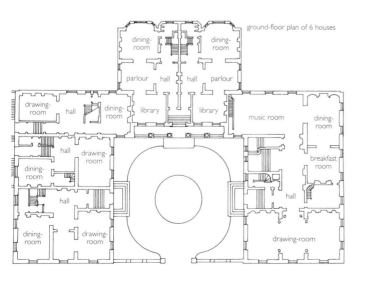

assembly of domes, triumphal arches and colonnades made a stunning impact. The architects included MeKim, Mead and White, Hunt, and Charles Atwood (1849–95), who designed the only permanent structure associated with the Fair, the Palace of Fine Arts. The plan of the whole exhibition was also conceived along axial Beaux-Arts lines and exercised a wide influence on American town-planning in the early twentieth century.

The most important architects who contributed to the World's Fair were McKim, Mead and White who, receiving nearly 1,000 commissions between 1870 and 1920, enjoyed the largest architectural practice in the world. Charles Follen McKim (1847–1909) was influenced as a young man by the high architectural ideals of Ruskin, yet he also studied at the Ecole des Beaux-Arts in Paris in 1867–70 where he joined the atelier of P.-G.-H. Daumet. After working in the office of H. H. Richardson until about 1873, he formed a partnership with William Rutherford Mead (1846–1928) and then in 1879 with Stanford White (1853–1906), who had also

736 McKim, Mead and White: The Boston Public Library (1887–95)

worked with Richardson. After their early open-plan Shingle Style houses they turned to public buildings, a field in which they provided an image of civic order more extensive than anything which had been achieved anywhere in the world since the days of ancient Rome.

This was a surprising development in a country noted for maintaining a romantic tradition of Jeffersonian agrarianism, expressed in the concept of the 'wicked city' and upheld by McKim, Mead and White's younger contemporary, Frank Lloyd Wright. McKim, Mead and White responded to the opportunities provided by the need for new public and commercial buildings and on the whole rejected the skyscraper, which they rightly regarded as productive of inharmonious urban spaces. Whereas Sullivan built individual monuments of startling originality, McKim, Mead and White sought to create an urban environment out of the common language of classicism which had been used to express ideals of grandeur, stability and joy in most civilizations from the Greeks onwards. Thus, though they were not interested in theory, unlike Sullivan and Wright, there can be little doubt that their architectural idealism owed something to the values enshrined in Ruskin's *Seven Lamps of Architecture*. Respecting local traditions and materials, they tended to adopt different classical sources for different categories of building: for public buildings they looked to the monuments of ancient Rome or of the High Renaissance in Italy; for buildings with less sober functions, like their Madison Square Garden, New York City (1887–91; dem. 1925), they looked to the exuberant Renaissance styles of Spain or northern Italy; and for educational and domestic buildings, to the Georgian tradition of colonial America as, for example, in their house for A. A. Pope at Farmington, Connecticut (1898–1901), inspired by George Washington's home at Mount Vernon.

Their first major works came in 1882. Both in New York City, like so many of their subsequent buildings, they are the Villard Houses and the premises of the American Safe Deposit Company and Columbia Bank. The latter is a Sullivanesque composition with the two lowest floors in rusticated sandstone; there are terra-cotta panels between the windows of the brick upper storeys, and an attic storey with colonnaded loggias. The Villard Houses (1882–5), commissioned by the railway and shipping magnate Henry Villard, provided six residences in a five-storeyed U-shaped block round an open courtyard facing the back of St Patrick's cathedral in Madison Avenue. Resembling a single monumental palazzo, these form a street composition of dignity, modelled on the Bramantesque language of buildings such as the Cancelleria in Rome (p. 224).

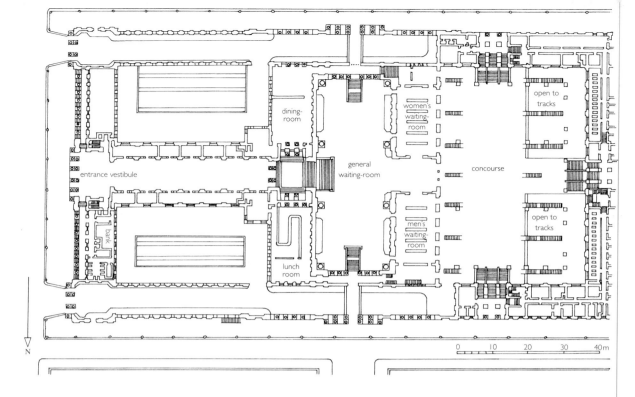

Within the plan, the following labels appear:

dining-room

women's waiting-room

open to tracks

entrance vestibule

general waiting-room

concourse

bank

men's waiting-room

open to tracks

lunch room

N

0   10   20   30   40m

737 McKim, Mead and White: Plan of Pennsylvania Station, New York City (1902–11)

The building which was at once taken as a symbol of the new American classicism was their Boston Public Library (1887–95). This imposing monument of plain white granite established Boston as a centre of western culture, with its 700,000 volumes and its calm dignity confronting the florid vigour of Richardson's Trinity Church on the opposite side of Copley Square. Before selecting Labrouste's Bibliothèque Ste-Geneviève as his model, McKim had considered the Palazzo Farnese, the Louvre pavilions, and Duban's Ecole des Beaux-Arts in Paris. Unlike the Parisian model, the Boston library is disposed round four sides of a courtyard treated as a charming cloister like those at the Cancelleria or the Palazzo Venezia. The rooms housing the varied functions of the library are distributed round these ranges empirically and functionally, not according to axial Beaux-Arts principles. The building is of traditional construction with load-bearing walls, though to carry the weight of the books the floors are carried on vaults of flat tiles resembling modern thin concrete shells. The interiors of the library were richly embellished with murals by John Singer Sargent, Edwin Austin Abbey and Pierre Puvis de Chavannes, and sculpture by Augustus Saint-Gaudens. This cooperation between architects, painters and sculptors was new in American architecture, but was extensively imitated, most notably at the Library of Congress at Washington, designed in 1873 by John Smithmeyer (1832–1908) and Paul Pelz (1841–1918), but not built and decorated till 1886–97.

Rhode Island State Capitol (1891–1903) was a monument in which McKim, Mead and White symbolized ordered and humane government. Crowned by a dome owing much to Wren and Soufflot, and with severely classical interiors inspired by Latrobe, this Georgian-Federalist souvenir set a pattern which was widely followed in new State Capitols, beginning with that by Cass Gilbert (1858–1934) at Minnesota (1895–1905), and continuing with those in Virginia, Florida, Alabama, South Dakota, Pennsylvania, Idaho and Utah. McKim, Mead and White made a similar dramatic impact in the field of academic buildings. Their New York University (1892–1903) and Columbia University (1894–8) create an extended cultural

738 *Above* Colonnaded exterior of Pennsylvania Station, by McKim, Mead and White

739 *Below* McKim, Mead and White: Concourse inside Pennsylvania Station

environment, centred in each case on a great domed library recalling the layout of Jefferson's University of Virginia and of the Court of Honor at the World's Fair. The centrally-planned saucer-domed library at New York University stands on a steeply sloping site which is ringed by an encircling colonnade on a high podium. In this memorable and dynamic composition the open colonnade, which serves as a Hall of Fame, leads to the Hall of Languages on one side of the library, and to the never-executed Hall of Philosophy on the other.

At the United States Military Academy, West Point, New York, White designed the Cullum Memorial Hall (1893–8) as one of the most austere buildings the partnership ever produced. This compelling expression of military strength has minimal fenestration and is adorned solely by a row of engaged but load-bearing Ionic columns. In the softer atmosphere of Harvard University, by contrast, McKim chose a red-brick Federalist Georgian style for the Harvard Union (1899–1901), while in the urban setting of Fifth Avenue, New York, his University Club (1896–1900) is a huge Florentine palazzo. In conformity with the humanist ideals of McKim, Mead and White, the most important interior of the club is the long, groin-vaulted library, so sumptuously decorated that it seems to have strayed from the Vatican Palace. Indeed, its decorative treatment was modelled on Pintoricchio's Borgia Apartments in the Vatican and incorporates canvas panels painted in Rome by H. Siddons Mowbray.

Also in Fifth Avenue were two buildings by White of 1903, both now demolished, the Gorham Company Building, a Sullivanesque palazzo, and Tiffany's where, to express the sparkle of the best-known jeweller in America, he selected Sanmicheli's Palazzo Grimani in Venice as his model. In the same year rose McKim's superb Morgan Library in 36th Street off Madison Avenue, New York, for the neo-Medicean banker and collector, J. Pierpont Morgan. Inspired by Ammanati's Nymphaeum at the Villa Giulia in Rome, it was constructed of marble so finely cut as to dispense with mortar joints, as in the buildings of fifth-century Athens.

Intended to be 'permanently available for the instruction and pleasure of the American people', the building and its contents are the epitome of patrician classical scholarship in a modern democracy.

With their Pennsylvania Station, New York (1902–11), the firm reached the zenith of its achievement, uniting the splendours of the ancient world with the conveniences of modern transport and of modern constructional techniques. Thus the general waiting-room was modelled on the tepidarium of the Baths of Caracalla, with all the dimensions increased by 20 per cent. It was clad in Roman travertine, quarried near Tivoli, and concealed a steel frame from which the plaster vaults were hung. Equally breathtaking was the adjacent concourse which, by contrast, was entirely of steel and glass but divided, like the waiting-room, into three high groin vaults. The circulation routes throughout the vast building, covering a site of nearly eight acres, were handled in a visually impressive way, though they involved much more walking than the more compact Grand Central Station, New York (1903–13), also boasting a noble Beaux-Arts concourse, by Reed and Stem, and Warren and Wetmore. Pennsylvania Station has probably never been equalled as a triumph of engineering and organization in which the classical language was used to ennoble a mundane activity. Its shameful demolition in 1963–5 marked the nadir in American architectural life.

Town planning
The eighteenth-century legacy
Seventeenth- and eighteenth-century town planning provided powerful images for nineteenth-century cities. Napoleon, who saw himself as the dynamic creator of towns as well as empires, drew on the Baroque convention of closing vistas with dominant porticoes in his remodelling of Paris. The vista across Gabriel's Place Louis-XV, now renamed de la Concorde, was terminated to the south by a giant portico added to the Palais Bourbon and to the north by that of the new church of the Madeleine of 1807 by Pierre Vignon, whose design was personally selected by Napoleon.

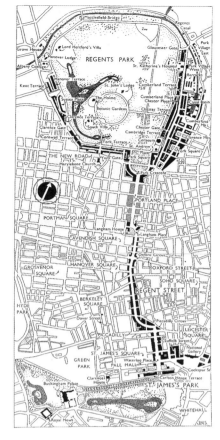

740 *Above* Plan of London (1812–33) by Nash

741 *Above right* Randolph Crescent, Ainslie Place and Moray Place, Edinburgh (c.1822–30)

Edinburgh's expansion was influenced by Bath and by Nash's London when the rigid grid plan of Craig's New Town of 1768 was extended with crescents and terraces. These reached a climax in the estate of the Earl of Moray laid out in c.1822 to c.1830 from designs by James Gillespie Graham (1776–1855). In this example of spectacularly Picturesque town planning, Randolph Crescent led through the oval Ainslie Place which itself opened into the dodecagonal Moray Place.

In Germany the ideals of the Enlightenment which stressed public buildings as the expression of civic virtue found fruit in the planning of Karlsruhe by Friedrich Weinbrenner from c.1800 to 1826, and of Berlin and Munich from 1816 to the 1840s by Karl Friedrich Schinkel and Leo von Klenze respectively. This royal idealism, which went back in Germany to Frederick the Great (1712–86), produced a humane urban fabric incorporating museums, schools, theatres, churches and palaces. John Nash's Regency London of 1812–33 was an essentially English contribution to this tradition, influenced by eighteenth-century Picturesque theory.

On the continent, town planning in places as far apart as Athens and Paris continued to follow Baroque practice. Leo von Klenze's partially executed radiating plan of 1834 for the new city of Athens, though not aligned on the new royal palace and leaving sites free for an archaeological zone, was clearly dependent on Versailles. Baron Haussmann's massive contribution to Paris from 1853–70, with features such as the Etoile of avenues radiating from Napoleon's Arc de Triomphe, added nothing in terms of planning, except increased scale, to the established traditions of papal Rome.

Model industrial towns

The developments just described were threatened in the course of the nineteenth century by a huge expansion in population, and especially its concentration in unplanned cities where slum conditions often prevailed. This massive urban growth posed new problems on an equally massive scale, making existing arrangements for commerce, administration and industry, largely craft-based, seem inadequate in a world increasingly dominated by industrial manufacturing. This threat to the life and forms of the traditional European city is one which continues to the present day and the history of town planning in the nineteenth and twentieth centuries is in large part the history of a reaction to it.

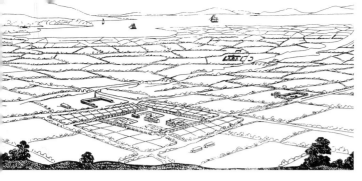

742 *Above* Owen: Design for a 'village of co-operation' (after 1800)

743 *Above* Godin: Familistère, Guise, France (1859–70)

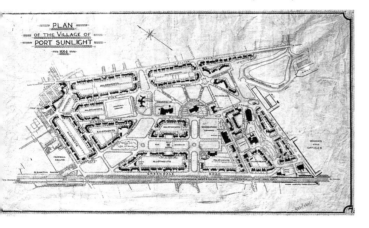

744 *Above* Plan of Port Sunlight (from 1889)

As early as 1800 Robert Owen (1771–1856), a social reformer, founded New Lanark in Scotland as a community centred on his cotton mill, with school, hospital, community centre, co-operative shop and living accommodation. It attracted so much attention as a society created not primarily for profit but to provide good conditions for workers, so that in 1825 Owen was able to propose a second model industrial town for 1200 people in New Harmony, Indiana. This was to be a large rectangular enclosure surrounded by terraced houses commanding views outwards of the surrounding countryside and farmland, forming what would later be called a green belt.

C.-N. Ledoux in his far more ambitious plans of 1804 for the Ideal Town of Chaux was one of the first architects to suggest a vast, planned industrial town, though Chaux was also, significantly, a garden city. Ledoux influenced Charles Fourier (1782–1827), a philosopher and social critic, not an architect, who proposed in 1822 an ideal community which he called a *phalanstère*. A self-supporting organization on a large scale, this was a social collective requiring an enormous building which seemed to be a blend of palace and hospital.

Inspired by this, J.-B. Godin built the *familistère* at Guise, France, in 1859–70, centred on his iron foundry. Intended for 400 families who would share the fruits of their labour, it was built for the manufacture of stoves and survived as such for about a century. The paternalist tradition of industrial communities found even more complete expression in the English model town of Saltaire, near Shipley, Yorkshire, developed from 1854 to 1872 by Sir Titus Salt, a Bradford wool manufacturer who decided to move his mills out of Bradford to a new site in open country. Laid out on a gridiron plan by the architects Lockwood and Mawson, Saltaire consists of a vast new mill and associated estate for the workers, with good houses, separate from the factory buildings. In addition, there was a school, Congregational and Methodist churches, hospital, laundries and Institute, but no public houses or pawnbrokers' shops. Intended to be morally and socially improving, it demonstrated that industrial development need not be haphazard and left to chance but could be planned. Moreover, this could be achieved without revolutionizing the existing social, political and economic structure as French theorists had assumed.

The company town was adopted elsewhere in Europe where, to avoid housing workers in slums and also to control them more easily, Alfred Krupp founded

Kronenberg near Essen, Germany, in 1873. More ambitious was the model industrial town of Port Sunlight, Cheshire, created by William Lever, 1st Viscount Leverhulme (1851–1925), and built by the architects William and Segar Owen, and others, from 1889 to 1922. Initially following an informal village plan, it was overlaid with an axial Beaux-Arts layout in which the Lever soap factory at one end was balanced by the art gallery at the other, suggesting that soap and art both 'do you good'. The socially improving aim of Port Sunlight was further stressed by the provision among the neo-Tudor houses of a library, school, social centre, non-denominational church and temperance hotel.

United States of America

The new plan of 1811 for Manhattan, closely based on that of 1796 by Casimir Goerck, the city surveyor, was one of the most memorable of the nineteenth century. The whole peninsula, 11 miles (18km) long, was covered with a grid plan incorporating twelve principal avenues crossed by one hundred and fifty narrower streets. The small individual lots allowed as many inhabitants as possible to have access to the river bank, for shipping was initially a vital part of the cityscape. The streets were not completed for 60 years, while the skyscrapers, which give New York City its most characteristic form, did not arrive until 1890. No less central to the image of the city is Central Park, though it was delayed by political battles and debate as to its use.

Public parks had first been proposed in the eighteenth-century Enlightenment by French and German garden theorists such as Claude-Henri Watelet and Christian Hirschfeld who wished to extend to the people the landscaped parks which had previously been the preserve of kings and princes. They quickly became popular in nineteenth-century cities as a way of counterbalancing the over-crowded, smoke-polluted slums, as in Birkenhead Park, Cheshire, of 1843–7 by Sir Joseph Paxton. The competition for Central Park, on an altogether more magnificent scale, was won in 1858

745 *Above* Plan of Manhattan (1811), by Goerck

746 *Above* Perspective view of Central Park, New York (1858), by Olmsted and Vaux

747 *Above* Plan of Llewellyn Park, New Jersey (1853–7), by Davis

533

by Frederick Law Olmsted (1822–1903) and the English-born architect and landscape architect Calvert Vaux (1824–95), who had both admired the work of Paxton. On its 840 acre (350 hectare) site, Central Park was laid out from 1863 to c.1880 with artificial hills, lakes, woodland and a novel separation of routes for commercial and recreational vehicles, as well as for pedestrians and horse-riders, by means of bridges, tunnels and viaducts. The vast areas of water at the centre were the Croton Aqueduct reservoirs that supplied the city with water. Central Park remains, with the skyscrapers that sprung up round it, the most memorable feature of Manhattan. It was the first of many parks in American cities of which the Golden Gate Park, San Francisco (1871–6), by William Hammond Hall (1846–1934) is one of the most popular.

In 1853–7, Alexander Jackson Davis (1803–92) planned the pioneering layout of Llewellyn Park, West Orange, New Jersey, as a Picturesque suburb. A hilly site of 350 acres (140 hectares) became a residential community of 60 villas on large sites linked by winding roads. Though novel for America, it had been anticipated by Birkenhead Park as a combination of residential suburb and public open space. It was followed by Olmsted and Vaux who designed the suburb of Riverside, seven miles south-west of Chicago, in 1868. Chicago itself had grown by 1880 to a city of a million inhabitants on a seemingly unending grid plan. Here in the 1880s and 1890s rose the first steel-frame skyscrapers, those aggressive high-rise symbols of modernity which were to transform the urban grain of New York and other great American cities. They nonetheless underlined the dichotomy at the heart of nineteenth-century American planning between the grid on the one hand, and the park or Picturesque suburb on the other, which was created in deliberate opposition to the grid. Indeed, Olmsted had himself claimed that the park was 'a directly remedial way to enable men to better resist the harmful influences of ordinary town life and to recover what they lose from them'.

Further moves to ameliorate conditions in towns and cities led to the founding as early as the 1850s of civic improvement societies in New England. These eventually flowered in the American cities of the early twentieth century that were influenced by the World's Columbian Exposition at Chicago in 1893 and the publication in 1903 of *Modern Civic Art, or the City Made Beautiful* by Charles Mulford Robinson (1869–1917).

748 General plan of Riverside, Chicago (1869), by Olmsted and Vaux

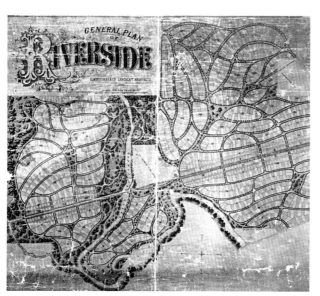

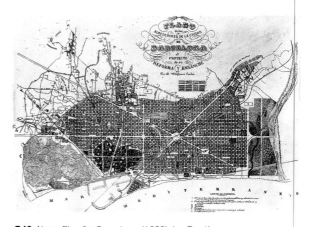

749 *Above* Plan for Barcelona (1859), by Cerdà

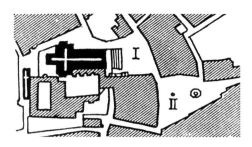

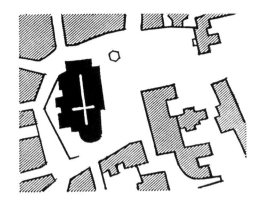

750 Group of four plans of town squares from Camillo Sitte, *City Planning According to Artistic Principles*

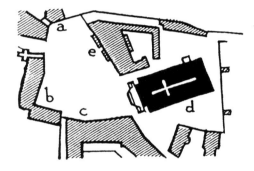

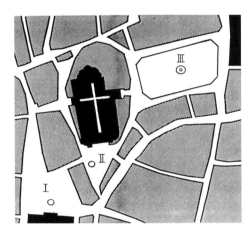

Developments in Europe

In nineteenth-century Paris we have seen Haussmann's work as an inspired legacy of Baroque planning and have touched on his influence in cities such as Vienna and Rome. New thinking was represented in Spain by the Spanish Catalan architect and engineer Ildefonso Cerdà (1815–76), who was the first to try to apply what were thought of as scientific principles to urban as well as to rural planning. In his influential book *Teoría general de la urbanización* (1867) he popularized the word 'urbanization', while as early as 1859 he had planned a gigantic expansion of Barcelona on a gridiron plan, intersected by two diagonal avenues. The ultimate chessboard plan, egalitarian and utilitarian, it ignored the historic fabric of the city. It was intended to have a central green space but this was subsequently built over.

The ideas of Cerdà were followed in other Spanish cities such as Madrid and Bilbao and were developed by Arturo Soria y Mata (1844–1920) in the 'linear city' which ruralized the city and urbanized the countryside. He put this into practice from 1894 in the Ciudad Lineal, Madrid, while his periodical, *La Ciudad Lineal* (1897–1932), the first to be devoted to urban design, was an influence on Frank Lloyd Wright.

In Germany, parallel theories of urban design to those of Cerdà were promoted by Richard Baumeister (1833–97) and by Joseph Stübben (1845–1936), author of *Der Stadtbau* (1890) and designer of developments in many German cities, notably Cologne and Düsseldorf.

The supposedly scientific basis and geometric uniformity of this planning was opposed by the Austro-Hungarian architect Camillo Sitte (1843–1903) in his widely influential book of 1889, translated as *City Planning According to Artistic Principles* and often reprinted in the twentieth century. In a series of telling diagrams of historic towns, emphasizing the role of open spaces and of irregularity, he encouraged the replacement of the grid plan by more flexible and adaptable forms inspired by what became known as 'townscape'.

10 Art Nouveau

MANY OF THE DOMINANT VISUAL AND INTELLECTUAL preoccupations in architectural circles throughout Europe in the nineteenth century were given expression around 1900 in a colourful architectural language which was known as Art Nouveau in France, Belgium, Britain and the USA; as *Jugendstil* in Germany, Austria and Scandinavia; and as *stile Floreale* in Italy. Art Nouveau architects realized some of the leading ambitions of the nineteenth century. Chief among these was the search for a new style as a way out of the stylistic impasse, a concern we have seen expressed in the writings of Hübsch in Germany as early as 1828. The form of Art Nouveau buildings was also frequently influenced by the nineteenth-century emphasis on the use of 'new' materials such as iron and glass which had helped shape the Crystal Palace in London and the Palace of Machines in Paris. The calls for structural honesty by Viollet-le-Duc and for organic design by Sullivan were also given expression by Art Nouveau architects who, in addition, shared the belief of men like Ruskin and Cuypers in the necessity of reviving craftsmanship.

Perhaps the most important single influence on continental, though not on British, Art Nouveau, was Viollet-le-Duc's demand, in the second volume of his *Entretiens* (1872), for a 'sinewy' architecture incorporating iron so as to achieve a lighter structure. This was prefigured in a novel building which Viollet admired, the Menier Chocolate Works at Noisiel-sur-Marne, near Paris, built in 1871–2 by Jules Saulnier (1828–1900) with a metal frame encased in polychrome brick and tile. More important, since they made more extensive use of iron and glass, were two influential department stores in Paris, the Bon Marché (1869–79) by L.-C. Boileau and Eiffel, and Au Printemps (1881–3) by Paul Sédille (1836–1900). While their outer walls were still of masonry construction, though with very large windows, their interiors were iron cages with conventional partitions largely replaced by slender iron mullions so as to obstruct the sales areas as little as possible.

Belgium and France

The keen sense of novelty which characterized Art Nouveau designers and their patrons was part of the rapidly changing mood of cities such as Brussels, Barcelona, Turin and Milan, which were transformed in the 1880s and 1890s by modern industrial techniques. The new captains of industry and professional men included a number of aesthetic sensitivity who sought to express their dynamic creativity and their separateness from the old aristocracies by acquiring houses and works of art in a style which had all the shock of the new. This new style emerged in the Maison Tassel of 1892–3 in the rue Paul-Emile Janson, Brussels, by the architect Victor Horta (1861–1947). The house was built for Professor Tassel who taught mathematics at Brussels University and was professionally associated with the Solvay family of industrial chemists, who also became important patrons of Horta. Having studied in Paris for 18 months from 1878, Horta was profoundly impressed by the monumental classical urbanity of the city and its new buildings of iron and glass, such as the Bon Marché store. He was determined to bring the best of these Parisian traditions to Brussels. The gently curved façade of the Maison Tassel is a unique juxtaposition of stone, glass

751 Staircase of the Van Eetvelde House, Brussels (1895–8), by Horta

and iron with a broad central bank of bow windows which, widening as they rise, are separated by slender iron mullions and surmounted by exposed cast-iron beams. Inside, the principal reception zone is a flowing T-shaped space; the living-area can be screened off from the dining-area, which ends in a bay window projecting into the garden. Interest concentrates on the exceptionally fluid staircase (fig. 769). This lyrical composition of exposed ironwork resembling plants under water incorporates much floral ornament, which spreads on to the surrounding walls in the form of painted decoration.

Horta's most ambitious staircase is that at the house of Edmond van Eetvelde in avenue Palmerstone, Brussels (1895–8), an octagonal space ringed with a circle of frail iron columns. These seem to sprout at the top into tendril-like forms, which are in fact patterns in coloured glass forming part of the glazed dome above the staircase. Even the glass shades of the electric lamps in this naturalistic interior are fashioned in the form of flower petals. His finest private house in Brussels is the Hôtel Solvay, built in 1894–1900 in the avenue Louise for a member of the Solvay family. Behind the curved façade of stone, iron and glass is a succession of reception rooms flowing into each other and separated by glass screens, some of which are removable. These ceremonial spaces are approached from an imperial-plan staircase as in an eighteenth-century *hôtel particulier* in Paris. The Hôtel Solvay is, indeed, a sumptuous house incorporating sumptuous materials – onyx, marble, ormolu, inlaid parquet floors, brocades – in which every detail, from the curving door handles and hinges to the light-fittings, is the result of a controlling aesthetic imagination.

Horta's patrons – capitalists, engineers and entrepreneurs – were rich enough to be able to experiment with progressive political views. In particular they supported the Belgian Workers' Party, founded in 1885, for whom Horta designed the Maison du Peuple, Brussels (1895–1900; dem. 1964), a commission gained through his Solvay connections. This building followed the plan of its curious wedge-shaped site in the circular place Emile Vandervelde. Its very large curved façades combined brick, stone, metal and glass with an almost deliberate clumsiness, which recalls Viollet-le-Duc's attempts at structural honesty in his *Entretiens*. The design of the balconied auditorium, flanked by sloping metal supports, was more harmonious on account of its symmetry, but its acoustics were poor and its position at the top of the building was inconvenient. Horta's innovative period was short-lived and he soon returned to the Beaux-Arts classicism in which he had been trained in Paris and at the Brussels

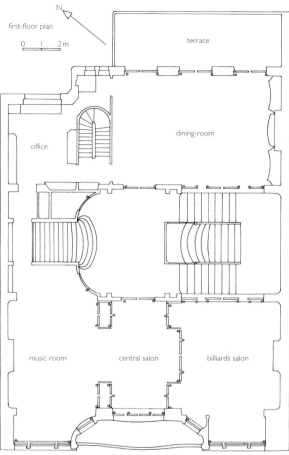

752, 753 Horta: Plan and entrance front of the Hôtel Solvay, Brussels (1894–1900)

Academy. He felt that this was more adaptable for twentieth-century purposes than the costly fantasies in which the Solvay, Eetvelde and Tassel families were prepared to indulge.

Though Horta was the leading Belgian Art Nouveau architect he was not the only one. We should note Paul Hankar (1850–1901), whose own house of 1893 in the rue Defacqz, Brussels, was in an Art Nouveau style characterized by windows sporting wooden tracery of Japanese inspiration. In Holland, we find that the dynamic curves of Horta or Hankar are replaced by straight lines. Nonetheless, we can still sense the presence of Art Nouveau ideals in the romantic seeking

after fundamentals and in the emphasis on craft in the work of the leading Dutch architect, Henrik Petrus Berlage (1856–1934).

We have seen in the last chapter how the architect Petrus Cuypers, friend and admirer of Viollet-le-Duc, helped bring about the renewal of Dutch architecture. Cuypers's follower Berlage studied architecture in 1875–8 at the Zurich Polytechnic School where the influence of Semper, a teacher there from 1855–71, was still strong. Responding to the intellectual climate of Holland in the 1880s and 1890s with its movements for social reform and its intense religious debate, Berlage developed a new architectural language of great power

754, 755 *Above and below* Horta: Exterior and plan of the Maison du Peuple, Brussels (1895–1900; now demolished)

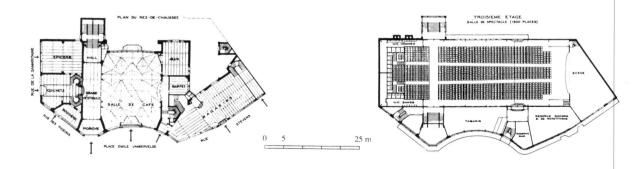

and sobriety which owed much to his study of Semper and Viollet-le-Duc. The key buildings were the Diamond Workers Union, Amsterdam (1898–1900), with its chunky primitivist staircase surrounded by white and yellow glazed brickwork, and the Amsterdam Exchange (1898–1903), for which his earlier designs of 1884–5 and 1896 had been in more conventional historical modes. As redesigned in 1897–8, this large public

building with its rugged, largely unadorned brickwork, its bold clock tower and mullioned windows seemed to have found a way out of the language of historical revivalism towards a strong and timeless vernacular appropriate to the new century. It was also appropriate, so Berlage thought, to an age of socialism in which the use of period styles would be condemned as an expression of bourgeois individualism: rich men might collect styles as they might collect pictures, but in the age of the common man a common style ought to prevail. Berlage's Exchange was to be widely influential on continental architecture into the 1920s. Inside, its three exchange halls were a lesson in rational construction in brick, iron and glass which would have pleased Viollet-le-Duc, though the composition is more harmonious than he could have made it.

In France the dominant Art Nouveau architect was Hector Guimard (1867–1942), trained at the Ecole des Arts Décoratifs and then from 1885 at the Ecole des Beaux-Arts, which he left in 1889 without a diploma in order to work for a construction company. His Ecole du Sacré Coeur, Paris (1895), is directly inspired by the work of Vaudremer and De Baudot by whom he was taught at the Ecole des Beaux-Arts. Its upper floors are supported on iron V-shaped stilts derived from the illustrations in Viollet-le-Duc's *Entretiens*. However, he was profoundly influenced by seeing Horta's work on a visit to Brussels in 1895 and immediately changed his designs for a luxurious apartment block in the rue La Fontaine, Paris, known as Castel Béranger (1894–9). It emerged with a striking staircase hall designed as a metal cage of iron, glass bricks and faience, approached through a memorable entrance gate of wrought iron and

copper forming a vivacious composition which somehow united Gothic, Rococo and Japanese effects. The façade contains particoloured brick, rubble, millstone, sandstone and glazed ceramic tiles in a rather frenetic advertisement for 'handcrafted' materials. This vernacular romanticism was highly popular in France around these years, the façade of the Castel Béranger being awarded a prize by the City of Paris in 1898. In the same year Guimard published an album of 65 plates illustrating the building, and he even moved his own studio to it.

The Paris Exposition of 1900 coincided with the erection of entrances to the newly completed underground railway in Paris, the Métropolitain. Though Guimard did not enter the competition of 1898, he was given the commission for the entrances through the

756 *Right* Exterior of Castel Béranger, Paris (1894–9), by Guimard

757 *Below* Berlage: The Exchange, Amsterdam (1898–1903): detail of exterior

758 Guimard: Entrance to a Métro station, Paris (c.1900)

patronage of a friend who was president of the Municipal Council of Paris. His strange iron Métro stations with their protective glass canopies like dragonfly wings, and their green-painted stalks like antennae, settled on the city in 1900–13 like a cloud of locusts. The passing of time has made them seem an essential part of the traditional Parisian scene, but they were designed as a deliberate affront to the Beaux-Arts classicism of the day. Of three basic types, they were constructed out of interchangeable prefabricated parts of metal and glass. In 1907 Guimard issued a catalogue of castings for architectural details for a wide variety of functions, including cartouches for balconies, bell pushes and street numbers. He was not really interested in the Arts and Crafts doctrine of 'truth to materials' and his fluid designs could be executed in any material.

Guimard's shortlived Salle Humbert de Romans, Paris (1897–1901; dem. 1907), provided behind a somewhat gawky stone façade a remarkable concert-hall with eight metal supports, sheathed in mahogany, leaning inwards like jungle trees to support the yellow-glass cupola. This strange grotto-like room, part Gothic and part Art Nouveau, with an organ superintended by Saint-Saens, was designed as the focus of a 'school of divine art'. This was the brainchild of a Dominican priest who opened it without the permission of his ecclesiastical superiors and was shortly banished from the country. A building with a more successful façade was Guimard's Maison Coilliot (1898–1900), a house and shop at Lille for a ceramics merchant. Faced with green enamelled lava blocks, the façade recedes in its upper storeys behind curvilinear membranes of timber and ceramic to produce an almost shocking effect like photographs of open-heart surgery. One of the most successful and popular of all Art Nouveau architects, Guimard designed numerous apartment blocks and villas. With their curved windows, flamboyant brackets, random rubblework and overhanging eaves, they proved all too easy to imitate.

759 Façade of Maison Coilliot, Lille (1898–1900), by Guimard

The famous Samaritaine Department Store (1904–7), by Jourdain, is clearly derived from Sedille's Printemps Store (1882–3), with its iron-frame interior.

The principal Art Nouveau centre in France apart from Paris was Nancy, appropriately since it had been a home in the eighteenth century of Rococo, an asymmetrical style at once fluttering and fluid, having much in common with Art Nouveau. Nancy had benefited commercially by the German annexation of Metz in 1871 as the capital of German Lorraine, and was undergoing considerable urban expansion. However, the leading figures in the so-called School of Nancy which flourished from 1894 to 1914 were not architects but glass-makers and furniture-makers like Emile Gallé (1846–1904) and Louis Majorelle (1859–1926). The architects, less successful, included Emile André (1871–1933), Eugène Vallin (1856–1922), and Lucien Weissenburger (1860–1929), who was responsible for no. 24 rue Lionnois (1903–4), and nos. 60–62 quai Claude-le Lorrain (1902).

Scotland and England

In England there is little Art Nouveau architecture of significance, although many of its decorative forms and leading ideas had been developed by English designers and writers from the 1880s, especially in the field of book design and textiles. In Scotland, by contrast, the architect Charles Rennie Mackintosh (1868–1928) won an international reputation, especially for interior design and furnishing. Glasgow, his native city, was a prosperous industrial centre with a flourishing tradition of classical architecture, led by Sir John James Burnet who had been trained at the Ecole des Beaux-Arts in Paris, and a no less interesting Scottish neo-vernacular style, especially associated with the architect James MacLaren (1843–90). Mackintosh rejected the classical language but was deeply influenced by the Scottish castle and manor-house style known as the Baronial tradition, by the writings of Pugin and Ruskin, and by W. R. Lethaby's

Guimard's numerous rivals in Paris included Charles Plumet (1861–1928), Jules Lavirotte (1864–1924), Frantz Jourdain (1847–1935), Georges Chedanne (1861–1940), and Xavier Schoellkopf. At their best they worked in a more sophisticated style than Guimard, skilfully blending their powerful stone-built façades with organic detailing into the site plans and street lines of the nineteenth-century Parisian boulevards. A happy example is Schoellkopf's apartment block at no. 29 boulevard de Courcelles (1902), with its circular freestanding lodge for the concierge, wrapped round with a semicircular passage into which the staircase opens. Plumet was responsible for many similar apartment blocks and *hôtels particuliers* in the 16th *arrondissement* (district), while Lavirotte adopted a more exuberant style with sculpted glazed bricks for his apartment block at no. 29 avenue Rapp (1900–1), and his Céramic Hôtel, no. 34 avenue de Wagram (1904).

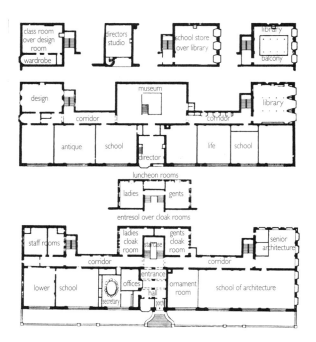

760 *Above* Plan of the Glasgow School of Art (1906–10) by Mackintosh

761 *Right* Mackintosh: Interior of the library, Glasgow School of Art

762 *Opposite* Mackintosh: West or library façade of Glasgow School of Art

preoccupation with craft and symbolism in his book *Architecture, Mysticism and Myth* (1891). With his friend Herbert McNair and two sisters, Frances and Margaret Macdonald, Mackintosh was making graphic designs, posters, decorative panels and repoussé metalwork from 1893 in an Art Nouveau style which had much in common with the work of continental Symbolist artists like Jan Toorop in Belgium and Edvard Munch in Norway, and of Aubrey Beardsley and James McNeill Whistler in England.

In 1896 the firm of Honeyman and Keppie, at which Mackintosh had been an assistant since 1889, won the competition for a new Glasgow School of Art with a remarkable design which was entirely by Mackintosh. The main entrance wing of granite was built in 1897–9. Its huge north-facing studio windows suggest an uncompromising functionalism which is in fact relieved by the poetic asymmetry and sculptural modelling of

the entrance bay, and by the wrought-iron brackets and railings which sprout into abstract yet plant-like finials. The plastic quality of the entrance bay seems inspired by two remarkable buildings in London, MacLaren's nos. 10 & 12 Palace Court, Bayswater (1889–90), and the Whitechapel Art Gallery by Charles Harrison Townsend (1850–1928), designed in 1895, published in *The Studio* in that year, and executed in 1897–9. Mackintosh's building is on a dramatically sloping site, which he exploited in the short east elevation towering up like some Scottish medieval castle, an effect heightened by the sparse asymmetrical fenestration and the use of small-scale random ashlar. In 1906 the authorities were ready to complete the school by building the west end containing the library. Mackintosh now remodelled his designs of 1896 to provide a soaring west façade which was far more stylized and abstract than the east. This hauntingly original design, executed

in 1906–10, is dominated by the three 25 feet (7.5m) high oriel windows lighting the library. The strange half-cylinders of stone flanking these windows were originally intended to be carved with figure sculpture, though in their bare state they add to the mannered geometry of the composition. The library within is a poetic demonstration of the realities of timber construction in imaginative fulfilment of the ideals of Pugin, though combined with a hint of Japanese lattice-work. The timber ceiling is supported by timber columns from which horizontal joists run back to carry the gallery surrounding the room. The theme of support extended through space is further emphasized by the functionless chamfered or scalloped balusters which stand on top of these joists. This spatial complexity recurs in the Willow Tea Rooms (1903–4), the best of the numerous tea-rooms which he designed for Miss Catherine Cranston in Glasgow.

Outside Glasgow he built two houses, Windyhill, Kilmacolm (1899–1901), and the more ambitious Hill House, Helensburgh (1902–3), in a simplified Scottish vernacular tradition, with sandstone walls covered in the traditional rough-cast or harling to keep them weatherproof. Inside, by contrast, there were white, light rooms of great freshness with delicate stencilled patterns in mauve and green, white enamelled woodwork and mannered elongated furniture. These interiors were influential in Germany and Austria, Windy hill being illustrated in the Darmstadt journal, *Dekorative Kunst*, in March 1902, and Hill House and the Willow Tea Rooms in *Deutsche Kunst und Dekoration* in March and April 1905. In the meantime Mackintosh and his associates, 'The Four', had been invited to decorate and furnish a room at the Secessionist Exhibition in Vienna in 1901. In 1901 he won the second prize in the competition for a 'House for an Art Lover', promoted by the *Zeitschrift für Innendekoration* in Darmstadt. He sent in a startling design close to his Glasgow houses, and far more original than the design by the English architect Hugh Mackay Baillie Scott (1865–1945) which was awarded the first prize.

Germany, Austria and Italy

Baillie Scott was a prolific and influential designer of bold, broad-eaved neo-vernacular houses like those of C. F. A. Voysey (1857–1941), but often incorporating experimental open plans similar to those of Frank Lloyd Wright. The houses of both Baillie Scott and Voysey became internationally known, thanks partly to their publication in *The Studio*. Germany, already determined to rival England as a naval and industrial power, was particularly conscious that English architects such as Shaw and Webb and their numerous followers had developed an enviably relaxed style of domestic architecture. This led to the curious attachment to the German Embassy in London from 1896 to 1903 of the architect Hermann Muthesius (1861–1927) in order to study recent developments in English architecture and housing. As a result he published several books on English architecture of which the most important was the three-volumed study, *Das englische Haus* ('The English house', Berlin 1904–5).

Even before the publication of this book Baillie Scott and C. R. Ashbee had been summoned to Darmstadt in 1897 by Ernst Ludwig, Grand Duke of Hesse, to design a new drawing-room and dining-room in the neo-Baroque grand-ducal palace. More importantly, Ernst Ludwig founded an artists' colony on the Mathildenhöhe, a hill outside Darmstadt, in 1899 and called to it in that year the Viennese architect Joseph Maria Olbrich (1867–1908). A pupil at the Vienna Academy of Fine Arts of Carl von Hasenauer, a principal architect of the Ringstrasse, Olbrich was buoyant and colourful as a designer and a personality. On the Mathildenhöhe he built the Ernst Ludwig Haus (1899–1901), a communal studio-building to house the exhibition of the artists' colony in 1901. Staged under the title 'A Document of German Art', it was the first of the many exhibitions held throughout Europe in the early twentieth century of artists with a self-consciously reforming mission. The Ernst Ludwig Haus is approached through a portentous arched recess rich

763 *Above* Main entrance of Ernst Ludwig Haus, Darmstadt Artists' Colony (1899–1901), by Olbrich

764 *Right* Wagner: The Imperial and Royal Post Office Savings Bank, Vienna (1904–6 and 1910–12)

with symbolical ornament and flanked by two huge figures of Man and Woman, representing the role of the building as a 'Temple of Work'. Olbrich built a number of the artists' houses in the colony, including his own of 1899, a playful Art Nouveau jewel. In 1907 he added the strange Hochzeitturm, or Wedding Tower, crowned with five rounded protuberances like organ pipes. Though these recall the stepped gables of late-medieval brick buildings in North Germany, the building undoubtedly achieves something of the abstract character which marks Mackintosh's contemporary west wing at the Glasgow School of Art.

Olbrich was not prepared to apply this kind of novelty to more mundane buildings in urban settings, designing the functionalist neo-Gothic Tietz department store in Düsseldorf (1906–9), and the elegantly neo-classical Joseph Feinhals villa in Cologne (1908–9), with its Greek Doric colonnade. The building for which he was best known at the time of his summons to Darmstadt was the Secession building in Vienna (1897–8), the exhibition hall and club-house of a newly-founded group of architects, sculptors and painters who were reacting against the official taste of the Academy. With its cubic composition and carved floral ornament, the building seems to be indebted to Harrison

Townsend's Whitechapel Art Gallery, though it is crowned by a highly original and romantic openwork dome of gilt wrought-iron laurel leaves (fig. 773). This symbolizes the role of the building as a temple of art from which issued the *Ver Sacrum* ('Sacred Spring'), the title of the Secessionist journal. It is approached through bronze doors by the Austrian Post-Impressionist artist, Gustav Klimt, below the portentous inscription: 'To the Age its Art; to Art its Freedom'.

Olbrich was a pupil of the leading Viennese architect, Otto Wagner (1841–1918), who had built extensively in free-Renaissance styles in the Ringstrasse from 1870. However, on his appointment as professor at the Vienna Academy of Fine Art in 1894 he chose to deliver an address calling for the abandonment of the historical styles, a position which he elaborated in his book, *Moderne Architektur* (1895). He put his beliefs into practice in his iron and glass underground railway-stations for the Vienna Stadtbahn (1894–1901), and in his lyrical Majolikahaus, an apartment block of 1898 faced in ceramic tiles decorated with coloured plant forms which flow vivaciously across the façade (fig. 774). More sober is his enormous Imperial and Royal Post Office Savings Bank, won in competition in 1903 and built in two phases in 1904–6 and 1910–12. Its four upper storeys are sheathed in white marble plaques fastened to the façade with exposed aluminium bolts. The entrance front is crowned by two stylized angels, also of aluminium, by the sculptor Othmar Schimkowitz. This fresh yet understated façade is in keeping with Wagner's published views on the modern city which, with its rapid vehicular movement, should no longer be dominated by the emphatically individual and plastic façades of the Ringstrasse. The central banking-hall, with its glazed roof supported on a light, riveted-steel framework and its glass block floor, has always been admired as a logical and harmonious use of new materials.

In the design of his contemporary St Leopold's church (1905–7), which serves as the chapel of the Steinhof Asylum near Vienna, Wagner returned to the more fanciful style of his pupil Olbrich's Secession building. Wagner's domed cruciform church has something of the festive air of an exhibition building, punctuated with angels, wreaths and acroteria by Schimkowitz, and saints by Richard Luksch, all in gilded copper like the cupola and ribs of the dome. As with the Post Office Savings Bank, the exterior gains lightness by being sheathed in marble fastened with metal rivets. The dome is entirely for external effect and plays no part in the interior, which is predominantly white in colouring but adorned with mosaics by Rudolf Jettmar and stained glass by Kolo Moser (1868–1918). The overall effect of clean and sparkling craftsmanship is a perfect expression of the ideals of the Wiener Werkstätte, a craft studio founded in 1903 by Josef Hoffmann (1870–1956) and by Kolo Moser, who had also been a founder of the Secession in 1897. The financial director and backer of the Werkstätte was the Viennese industrialist Fritz Wärndorfer, for whom Mackintosh had created a fancifully Art Nouveau music room in Vienna in 1902.

Trained at the Vienna Academy of Fine Art by Hasenauer and by Wagner, Josef Hoffmann became an admirer of English ideals of architecture combined with craftsmanship, as expressed in the writings of Ruskin, the designs of Morris, and the Guild of Handicraft

765 *Above* High altar of St Leopold's Church, Steinhof Asylum, near Vienna (1905–7), by Wagner

766 *Opposite* Hoffmann: South side of the Stoclet House, Brussels (1905–11), with the fountain

founded by C. R. Ashbee in 1888. In preparation for founding the Wiener Werkstätte Hoffmann visited England in 1902 where he met Hermann Muthesius. Hoffmann's masterpiece, the Stoclet House, Brussels (1905–11), is one of the most refined and luxurious private houses of the twentieth century. Built for a wealthy banker and art collector, Adolphe Stoclet, it is evidently inspired by Mackintosh's entry in the competition of 1901 for a House for an Art Lover, yet its

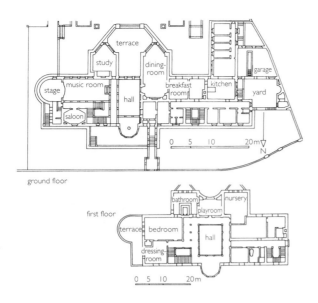

ground floor

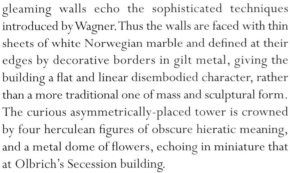

first floor

767 *Left* Plan of the ground and first floors of the Stoclet House (1905–11), by Hoffmann

768 *Above* Dining-room of the Stoclet House

gleaming walls echo the sophisticated techniques introduced by Wagner. Thus the walls are faced with thin sheets of white Norwegian marble and defined at their edges by decorative borders in gilt metal, giving the building a flat and linear disembodied character, rather than a more traditional one of mass and sculptural form. The curious asymmetrically-placed tower is crowned by four herculean figures of obscure hieratic meaning, and a metal dome of flowers, echoing in miniature that at Olbrich's Secession building.

The interiors of the Stoclet House, resplendent with glittering marbles, mosaics, onyx, gold, glass, teak and leather, set off to perfection the esoteric Stoclet collection of antique, oriental and modern works of art; they also provided a stylish background for many brilliant house-parties which included figures prominent in the Russian ballet such as Stravinsky and Diaghilev, as well as Cocteau, Paderewsky, Anatole France and Sacha Guitry, who recorded their names in a silver-covered guest book. They would dine beneath Gustav Klimt's shimmering mosaic of swirling stylized tree-forms and would sit in the two-storeyed galleried great hall, a parallel in glistening marble to Mackintosh's more homespun library in the Glasgow School of Art. All the furniture, glass, china and cutlery were designed by Hoffmann and made by the Wiener Werkstätte. Indeed, as one visitor observed, 'The flowers, always of a single

tone, on the table, and Mr Stoclet's tie were in perfect harmony with his wife's dress.' The house then, was less a pioneer of the modern movement than the culmination of the aesthetic movement of the 1880s and 1890s as typified in fictional heroes such as Joris-Karl Huysmans' Des Esseintes and Oscar Wilde's Dorian Gray. Hoffmann was not a doctrinaire modernist and was not interested in new technological developments. His kinship with the aesthetic movement was not diminished by the fact that he designed in a rectilinear style rather than in the curves customarily associated with Art Nouveau. Like many of his generation he reverted to a quieter, more classical language after about 1905 and was willing to work for the German government as organizer of Austrian arts and crafts after the incorporation of Austria into the Third Reich in 1938.

Germany was important as a centre for Art Nouveau design in textiles, jewellery and furniture but less so in architecture. The Swiss-born Hermann Obrist (1863–1927) moved to Munich in 1894, where he helped found the Munich Vereinigten Werkstätten für Kunst im Handwerk in 1897. The ultimate inspiration of craft workshops of this kind was the firm which had

769 *Opposite* The staircase of the Tassel House, Brussels (1892–3), by Horta

770 Endell: Façade of the Elvira Photographic Studio, Munich (remodelled 1896–7; now demolished)

been founded in 1861 by the English artist and social reformer William Morris (1834–96). Obrist's embroidery designs, often incorporating the so-called 'whiplash' curve, influenced August Endell (1871–1924) who remodelled the now destroyed façade of the Elvira Photographic Studio in Munich in 1896–7, providing it with an astonishingly dynamic semi-abstract relief in plaster resembling a giant sea-horse coloured red and turquoise. This gripping design was an expression of Endell's belief in the artistic significance of empathy, that is the spectator's identification with the particular quality of *life* conveyed in an individual work of art. This belief, which he shared with Obrist, was derived from the influential teachings in the psychology of aesthetics of Theodor Lipps (1851–1914) under whom he had studied philosophy and aesthetics at Munich from 1892. Endell returned to his native city of Berlin in 1901 and

published *Die Schönheit der grossen Stadt* ('The beauty of the large town') seven years later.

Art Nouveau arrived at Dresden in 1897 with the showing of a room designed by Henry van de Velde (1863–1957) for the Dresden Exhibition. Van de Velde was essentially an international figure, like the Rococo designer Peter Anton von Verschaffelt (1710–93) in the courts of eighteenth-century Europe. Born in Antwerp, he was trained as a painter there and under Carolus Duran in Paris, where he moved in Symbolist and Post-Impressionist circles. However, under the influence of Morris and Voysey he turned to architecture and the decorative arts, especially typography and book decoration, after 1893. In 1895–6 he built the Villa Bloemenwerf for himself and his young family at Uccle, near Brussels, on a roughly hexagonal plan with elevations which are half English Arts and Crafts, half Flemish vernacular. He designed all the furniture, fittings, carpets, silver and cutlery, including his wife's clothes: flowing kimonos adorned with serpentine motifs. He even selected the colour compositions of the food she served. The house was visited and admired by Toulouse-Lautrec and by Siegfried Bing, a Hamburg art dealer. Bing invited van de Velde to design interiors in 1896 for his shop in Paris, the Maison de l'Art Nouveau, which gave its name to the whole movement. In 1898 van de Velde moved to Berlin, where he designed five lavish interiors including shops for the Havana Cigar Company (1899–1900) and, in 1901, for the imperial barber, Haby. Next he moved to Weimar, where in 1906 he designed the grand-ducal Saxon School of Arts and Crafts with large fenestration recalling Mackintosh's Glasgow School of Art. He became director of the Weimar School two years later and devoted much of his energy to establishing fruitful contacts between craft unions and business enterprises. At a meeting in 1914 of the Deutscher Werkbund, which had been founded

771 D'Aronco: Central rotunda at the International Exhibition of Decorative Arts, Turin (1902)

772 Façade of Palazzo Castiglioni, Milan (1901–3), by Sommaruga

DER·ZEIT·IHRE·KVNST·
DER·KVNST·IHRE·FREIHEIT·

in Munich in 1907 to improve the quality of industrial design in accordance with the ideals of Muthesius, van de Velde and Endell spoke up for individualism in design, in opposition to Muthesius's call for increased standardization.

In the fashion-conscious world of international exhibitions Art Nouveau spread like wildfire. Indeed, some of Mackintosh's interiors and furniture, made of

773 *Above* The Secession building, Vienna (1897–8), by Olbrich: Detail of the entrance with its metal tracery dome

774 *Opposite* The Majolikahaus, Vienna, by Wagner: The street façade (1898)

cheap wood nailed together, have a poor-quality, insubstantial air as though they were designed to be sent in packing-cases from one capital to another. One of the

554

most influential expositions was the International Exhibition of Decorative Arts held at Turin in 1902 where interiors by Horta and Mackintosh were displayed. The exhibition romanticized new industrial techniques, which it was optimistically hoped would improve the life of the poor. The architect was Raimondo D'Aronco (1857–1932), at that moment working under the Ottoman rulers in Constantinople where he was involved in a Turkish vernacular revival. His central rotunda at Turin, which he claimed was inspired by Hagia Sophia, was a fluid ebullient design, dripping with figure sculpture and symbolical ornament, and doubtless owing much to Olbrich's work at Darmstadt. Few Italian Art Nouveau buildings carried plasticity to such extreme lengths. D'Aronco himself completely dropped it for his Palazzo Comunale at Udine (1908–32) where, in an historic setting, he wisely adopted a neo-Renaissance manner.

Giuseppe Sommaruga (1867–1917), much influenced by Otto Wagner, worked in a monumental style which is well demonstrated in his Palazzo Castiglioni in Milan (1901–3). Built for a prosperous engineer, this grandiose monument is of Austrian Baroque inspiration but encrusted with heavy sculptural ornament handled in an Art Nouveau manner. It proved highly influential. His last major work, the Hotel Tre Croce at Campo dei Fiori near Varese (1907–12), has an unusual V-shaped plan and a deeply-projecting, arcuated, Piranesian porch.

Spain

Art Nouveau in Spain was inextricably involved with the cultural and political revival which took place from the 1880s in Catalonia, an area which had lost its independence to the Castilians four centuries earlier. This many-faceted movement for renewal and for Catalan separatism was centred in Barcelona and known as 'Rebirth'. It involved the revival of the Catalan language and the study of local history and of indigenous

arts and crafts. Before attempting to predict what kind of architecture such a movement would be likely to promote, it should be remembered that Catalan Nationalists were extremely heterogeneous, including Catholics as well as Marxists, and both the right and the left in politics. As in other countries the writings of Ruskin and Viollet-le-Duc acted as a powerful stimulus to the creation of the new architecture. We know, for example, that Antoni Gaudí i Cornet (1852–1926), the leading Spanish Art Nouveau architect, had annotated the second volume of Viollet-le-Duc's *Entretiens* as a student and had read Ruskin in translation.

Antoni Gaudí began as a Gothic Revivalist but in his characteristically exuberant Casa Vicens for Don Manuel

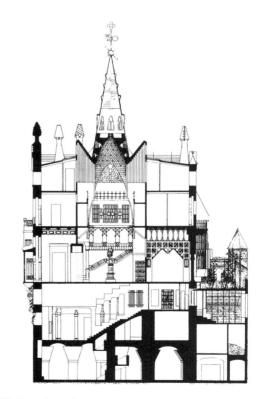

775 *Above* Gaudí: Section of the Palace Güell, Barcelona (1885–9)

776 *Opposite* Gaudí: Exterior of the Casa Vicens, Barcelona (1883–5)

777 *Opposite* The cathedral of the Sagrada Familia, Barcelona, by Gaudí: Detail of the Nativity transept (1903–30)

778 *Above* The Assembly building at Chandigarh, India (1951–65), by Le Corbusier

779 *Above* Gaudí: The central domed hall at Palau Güell, Barcelona (1885–9)

780 *Left* Exterior of Gaudí's Casa Batlló, Barcelona (1904–6)

781 *Opposite* Gaudí: The Greek Theatre at Park Güell, Barcelona (1900–14)

Vicens in Barcelona (1883–5), a part neo-Gothic, part neo-Moorish villa, the railings and gates have an early Art Nouveau flavour. His Palau Güell, Barcelona (1885–9), a house for the textile magnate Don Eusebio Güell, is entered through a pair of parabolic arched gateways containing grilles of exuberantly Art Nouveau metalwork. Gaudí's father had been a coppersmith and had trained his son in the art of metalwork. The use of

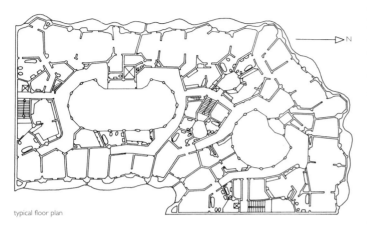

typical floor plan

782 Gaudí: Plan of the Casa Milá, Barcelona (1906–10)

parabolic, as opposed to pointed or semicircular arches, was also to be characteristic of Gaudí, who chose them for their static quality, not just because of their novel profile. The roofscape of the Palau Güell, forming an abstract sculptural composition with chimneypots and ventilators faced in coloured glass, tiles and mosaic, also set a precedent which Gaudí was often to follow. The spatial variety and complexity of the interior, rivalling Sir John Soane's Museum in Picturesque effect, culminates in the central domed hall which rises to the top of the building and is lit by a cupola lined with hexagonal tiles and punctuated with numerous small apertures like stars. The magical effect of this interior recalls the creations of Baroque architects like Guarini, with more than a hint of the Alhambra.

On the edge of Barcelona Gaudí laid out an estate, Park Güell, in 1900–14, intended to recall an English garden suburb. The houses were never built and what survives is a weird collection of grottoes and porticoes echoing the garden buildings of some fantastic eighteenth-century landscaped park. The principal building is the Greek Theatre, with tilted Greek Doric columns surmounted by an undulating entablature which, decorated with moulded ceramics, also serves

as a bench terminating the roof terrace. The columns, hollow for drainage purposes, support flat vaults faced with glass mosaic and glazed tile fragments. The use of brightly coloured ceramic tiles is a longstanding tradition in the Iberian peninsula, where it was originally introduced by the Arabs.

In the city of Barcelona Gaudí was responsible for two apartment houses with curvilinear façades and fluid organic planning which strain belief. That these apartments, boasting interiors with completely curved walls, could actually find purchasers is a mark of the astonishing faith in the new Catalan architecture on the part of the prosperous middle classes of Barcelona. The first apartment house, which was a remodelling of an existing building, is the Casa Batlló (1904–6). Its façade, faced with iridescent pieces of broken ceramic predominantly pale blue in colour, is crowned by a hump-backed roof which, with its lozenge-shaped tiles and its crested profile, resembles a dragon. This bizarre feature may allude to the legend of St George and the Dragon which was an important part of the mythology of Catalan nationalism. At one side rises a turret capped with a cross and the initials in gold of the Holy Family. The *piano nobile* is framed by a sculptured web, closely resembling bones, made of concrete.

Gaudí had a freer hand in the much larger and more unified Casa Milá (1906–10), which he built round two nearly circular courtyards in the same street as the Casa Batlló, the fashionable Paseo de Gracia. Here the entire undulating building seems like molten lava or like a rock formation eroded by the impact of wind or water. Indeed, it is popularly known as 'La Pedrera' (the quarry), and its cliff-like character may allude to Montserrat (serrated cliffs), the Catalonian mountain range with its much-visited monastery of Our Lady of Montserrat. The stone façade of the Casa Milá is enlivened with balconies of wrought iron tortured so as to resemble glistening bunches of seething seaweed, perhaps the most vivacious Art Nouveau metalwork anywhere. The fantastic skyline develops themes he had initiated at the Casa Vicens.

783 Street façades of the Casa Milá, Barcelona

Gaudí's best-known work in Barcelona, the Expiatory Temple of the Holy Family (the Sagrada Familia), has a complicated building history. Having been a dandy as a young man, Gaudí became a deeply pious Catholic later in life and the Sagrada Familia is a uniquely personal record of his religious faith, his belief in the spiritual rejuvenation of his native Catalonia, and his love of symbolism, poetry and mystery in architecture. His reading of Goethe and Ruskin encouraged in him the desire to reproduce natural forms exactly. He surrounded himself with photographs of natural and animal forms, skeletons and living people, yet his powerful imagination led him to devise ornamental schemes of bizarre and sometimes nightmarish characters. The Sagrada Familia was begun in 1882 from designs by Francesc de Paula del Villar i Carmona as a conventional cruciform Gothic church. Gaudí took over in the following year and by 1887 had completed the crypt, largely to Villar's designs. In 1891–3 he built the outer walls of the chevet in a freer Gothic than Villar's, but the great change came with his design for the east (liturgical south) transept façade, built in 1893–1903 and dedicated to the Nativity (fig. 777). In 1903–30 the Nativity transept, with its gables resembling stalactites, was completed with the addition of towers and openwork cone-shaped spires of astonishing height, crowned with tentacle-like finials of coloured broken tiling. The balancing west transept, dedicated to the Passion, was built from 1954 according to Gaudí's designs of 1917. Work still continues slowly on the nave, structurally the most original part of the whole church, on the basis of the experimental designs made by Gaudí between 1898 and his death in a tram-car accident outside the church, in 1926. He treated the piers as tree-trunks, tilting them inwards so as to counteract the thrust of the vault without recourse to any props or flying buttresses, which he dismissed as 'crutches'.

Though Gaudí towered above his contemporaries, he was not isolated as an architectural innovator in Catalonia at the turn of the century. We should recall his lifelong friend and collaborator Francesc Berenguer y Mestres (1866–1914) and, more especially, Luis Domènech y Montaner (1850–1923), who became first president of the separatist political movement, Unio Catalana, in 1892. Domènech's masterpieces, grandiose in scale and exotic in detail, are the Hospital of S. Pau, Barcelona (1902–10), and the Palau de la Música Catalana (1905–8), the former with an extended layout like an English garden city.

Art Nouveau architecture was essentially a European phenomenon, but in our account of it we have referred in passing to the work in America of both Sullivan and Frank Lloyd Wright. It is also worth mentioning that in the field of interior decoration and glassware America could boast the brilliant designer Louis Comfort Tiffany (1848–1933). Sullivan's surface ornament, which we noted in the last chapter, was clearly analogous to Art Nouveau, while Wright's buildings also constituted an independent parallel to contemporary work in Europe. To his individual achievement we should at last turn our attention.

11 The Twentieth Century

USA up to 1939

It was in the twentieth century that America overtook Great Britain as the major political and industrial power in the world. However, during this period there has been only one American architect, Frank Lloyd Wright, who is placed by universal agreement in the first rank. Otherwise, the story up to the Second World War is largely one of European influence, first that of the Ecole des Beaux-Arts in Paris, where so many American architects were trained, and secondly that of émigré architects from Austria and Germany such as Schindler, Neutra, Gropius and Mies van der Rohe. In fact one of the most potent of all images of modernity had been created as early as 1913 in New York in skyscrapers such as the Woolworth Building with its soaring Gothic poetry. However, in the 1920s architects in Europe, in particular Gropius and Le Corbusier, replaced this vision with a set of bleak models for high-rise buildings which exerted an unhappy influence on both American and European cities.

Frank Lloyd Wright

The World's Fair of 1893 in Chicago consolidated Beaux-Arts classicism as the mainstream in American architecture. This tradition survived until the 1940s, although no classical architects were as consistently brilliant as McKim, Mead and White, whose best work had been done by 1910. While architects such as Horace Trumbauer, Paul Philippe Cret and John Russell Pope produced monumental public buildings in the classical style, and Cram, Goodhue and Rogers churches and colleges in the Gothic style, domestic architecture was brought to a new pitch of high if idiosyncratic refinement by Frank Lloyd Wright (1867–1959). The most individual architect and one of the most flamboyant personalities of modern America, Wright enjoyed a career of such length and an output so varied and productive that he seems less like one man than a series of movements. In Wright's own opinion, his diverse achievement was united by his belief, constantly repeated for fifty years from 1908, that he was creating an 'organic' architecture.

The son of a peripatetic Baptist minister and a Welsh émigrée mother, Wright spent much of his boyhood on his uncles' farms in Madison, Wisconsin. He received comparatively little formal education but read widely, for example Ruskin and in particular Emerson, whose emphasis on self-reliance, individualism and optimism influenced him greatly. In 1887 he left for Chicago and joined the office of the architect Joseph Lyman Silsbee (1848–1913), who had brought the Shingle Style from the East to the Midwest. Wright soon left to become an assistant of Sullivan and Adler, then at work on their Chicago Auditorium Building. Wright, who was to be profoundly coloured by Sullivan's search for a new architecture with an 'organic' basis, owed much in his early work to both Silsbee and Sullivan. The house he built for himself in Oak Park, Chicago, on his marriage in 1889 is a modest essay in the Shingle Style with Japanese overtones. By contrast, his Charnley House, Chicago (1891–2), and Winslow House, River Forest, Illinois (1893), are handsome symmetrical boxes of Roman brick with terracotta trim in a Sullivanesque manner. Their formal geometry makes them look classical though they lack any classical detailing.

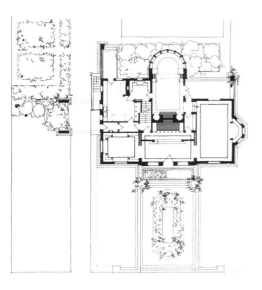

784, 785 *Above and right* Plan and view of the Winslow House, River Forest, Illinois (1893), by Wright

786 *Below* Warren Hickox House, Kankakee, Illinois (1900), by Wright

In 1893 Wright was dismissed by Sullivan for working on private 'bootlegged' commissions, and by the end of the decade he had developed a personal language of memorable sophistication. In effect this was the Shingle Style with the Picturesque clutter replaced by Wright's intense feeling for geometry, clarity and consistency, resulting in a linear play of intersecting walls and masses. His fondness for this method of composition went back to the maple blocks with which he had played as a child as part of the Froebel educational methods. Though he took the open plan of the Shingle Style with internal walls treated as independent screens, he avoided dormer windows and tall chimneys, cellars and attics, and relied for effect on long horizontal lines interrupted as little as possible by doors and small windows. This personal language appears in his River Forest Golf Club, River Forest, Illinois (1898), and Warren Hickox House, Kankakee, Illinois (1900). It was known as the Prairie Style after a design Wright published in 1901 in the *Ladies' Home Journal* entitled 'A Home in a Prairie Town'. A house in this style by Wright could have a plan in the form of an 'X', 'T' or 'L', sometimes with a split-level or double-height living area, but usually with the dining-room, living-room and study in line with and open to each other, and also anchored to a fireplace on the inside wall with service areas behind it.

Wright wrote in endless self-praise of his achievement in these houses, which he summarized as 'breaking the box'. In fact this process had been anticipated in the Picturesque houses of Nash in England and in the Shingle Style in America. Among the finest examples of Wright's numerous Prairie houses are the Ward Willits House, Highland Park, Illinois (1901), the Darwin D. Martin House, Buffalo, New York (1904), the Avery Coonley House, Riverside, Illinois (1908), and the Frederick C. Robie House, Oak Park, Chicago (1909). The use of the term 'Prairie Style' is, of course, romantic nostalgia, for these are suburban villas built for the beneficiaries or accumulators of new industrial wealth. The prominent hearths in these houses were also symbolical rather than functional, in view of the emphasis Wright put on central heating. Situated in a densely built-up suburb, the Robie House was built for Frederick Robie, a bicycle and automobile manufacturer. Ford's first car was made in 1896, the Ford Motor Company was established in 1903, and the provision of a three-car garage at the Robie House makes it something of a pioneer. At the same time it is an eloquent restatement of Ruskin's belief in the moral value of the all-sheltering roof, though in order to achieve his hovering cantilevered roofs with a projection of 20 feet (6m) Wright incorporated the most up-to-date steel joists. The materials used throughout the Robie House were expensive, not only the steel but also the specially made thin Roman bricks, nearly a foot long (0.3m), with their vertical joints cleverly concealed so as to emphasize the horizontal lines of the whole composition.

A colourful parallel to Wright's Prairie Style was worked out in the brilliantly sunny climate of California, where the brothers Charles Sumner Greene (1868–1957) and Henry Mather Greene (1870–1954) produced a series of luxurious 'bungalows' of timber construction in the first decade of the century. Perhaps the finest of these West Coast houses is the David B. Gamble House at Pasadena, built in 1908–9 for a member of the Gamble family who had made a fortune in manufacturing. With its dramatically emphasized rafters and eaves, this is assembled like a giant piece of cabinet work and contains Tiffany glass as well as specially designed furniture by Greene and Greene. A similar emphasis on construction informs much of the work of Bernard Maybeck (1862–1957) who had been trained at the Ecole des Beaux-Arts in Paris. Here he had been much influenced by the theories of Viollet-le-Duc, as is clear not only from his medieval sympathies but also from his interest in exposed structure, new materials and technologies. However, he was more adventurous stylistically than Viollet, as can be appreciated in his masterpiece, the First Church of Christ Scientist, Berkeley, California (1910). External features such as the Japanese-style pavilion roofs and the

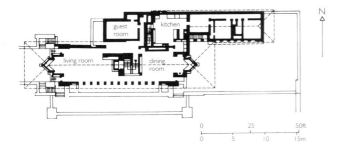

787, 788 *Above and below* Wright: Plan and exterior of Robie House, Oak Park, Chicago (1909)

classical piers do not conflict with the Gothic tracery inside because the dominant visual element is everywhere provided by the emphatically exposed structural elements, which consist of reinforced concrete and of massive timber beams.

Two novel non-domestic works by Wright of about this time are the Larkin Administration Building, Buffalo, New York (1904; dem. 1949–50), designed for a mail order business, and the Unity Temple (1906), a Unitarian church at Oak Park, Chicago. In both the office block and the church a solid sculptural exterior, largely unrelieved by windows, leads to a monumental interior, top-lit from

789 *Above* Exterior of the David B. Gamble House, Pasadena
(1908–9), by the Greene brothers

790 *Below* Wright: Unity Temple, Oak Park, Chicago (1906)

a glass ceiling and surrounded by galleries approached from staircases concealed in pylons at the corners of the building. The interiors of both buildings, especially the Larkin Building which included an air-conditioning system, were like shrines insulated from the outer world. While the Larkin Building is of reinforced concrete faced in brick, the walls of the Unity Temple are of massive poured concrete with the slab-like roofs and internal galleries of reinforced concrete. The exterior of the Temple recalls pre-Columbian Mayan architecture, though the interior has the rectangularity of outline and ornament which is paralleled in contemporary designs by the Wiener Werkstätte. The similarity is particularly close in the main auditorium with its re-entrant corners, its two tiers of galleries, and its emphatically geometrical light-fittings, all of which unite to form an interlocking linear web of space and line.

The Austrian analogy reminds us that Wright was approached in 1909 by the German publisher Ernst Wasmuth with a proposal which resulted in the publication in Berlin of two books illustrating his work, *Ausgeführte Bauten und Entwürfe von Frank Lloyd Wright* ('Completed buildings and projects of Wright', 1910), and *Frank Lloyd Wright: Ausgeführte Bauten* (1911). The second of these had a preface by the English Arts and Crafts designer C. R. Ashbee and, though less sumptuous than the first, exercised a wider influence, especially on Dutch and German architects, including Berlage and Gropius.

In 1909, a year of crisis in Wright's life, he gave up his successful practice in Chicago and eloped to Europe with Mamah Borthwick Cheney, the wife of one of his former clients. On his return he retreated to Taliesin, a farm near Spring Green, Wisconsin, and in 1911 began a house for his mother which he soon extended for himself and Mrs Cheney. Taliesin, Welsh for 'shining brow', was a rambling asymmetrical composition hugging the hilly landscape and 'organically' constructed of the local fieldstone. With its broad eaves, secluded courtyards, walled gardens, pools and trees, this low spreading group of buildings was the first of the agrarian craft settlements which Wright founded as part of his growing lack of sympathy with the modern industrial city. It was half destroyed in 1914, in a fire started by Wright's cook, who axed to death Mrs Cheney and five other people as they tried to escape. As rebuilt, first in 1914–15, secondly following another major fire in 1925, and finally in the 1930s for the Taliesin Fellowship which Wright established in 1932, the place has grown extensively, yet still follows the same principles of design settled in 1911. It is not only a house but also combines a drawing-office, farm buildings and dwelling quarters for the disciples of the Taliesin Fellowship. It became known as Taliesin East when in 1938 Wright began Taliesin West in the desert near Phoenix, Arizona, as a winter retreat for himself and the Fellowship. Laid out on a scattered triangular plan developed from that of Taliesin East, its low canted walls of purple and tan volcanic stone and its timber roofs with louvres and canvas screens created a potent image of a mythical proto-Indian architecture. After Wright's death air-conditioning was introduced and the canvas replaced by fibreglass.

By 1932 Wright had become at Taliesin East what he remained for the rest of his life, a garrulous guru of unparalleled egotism, a semi-educated philosopher-architect with endless neo-Emersonian nostrums for setting America to rights, culturally, politically, morally and economically. The students were given little formal architectural instruction but were expected to imbibe the atmosphere of genius and organic wholeness radiating from Wright's colourfully dressed person as he sat before them in the evenings, literally on a platform. His third wife Olgivanna Milanoff, a Montenegrin divorcée whom he had married in 1928, did much to encourage the millenarian semi-mystical atmosphere of Taliesin, for in the early 1920s she had been a student at a similar establishment at Fontainebleau, the Institute for the Harmonious Development of Man. This was run by George Ivanovich Gurdjieff (1874–1949), the Russian hypnotist, drug healer and instructor in the occult.

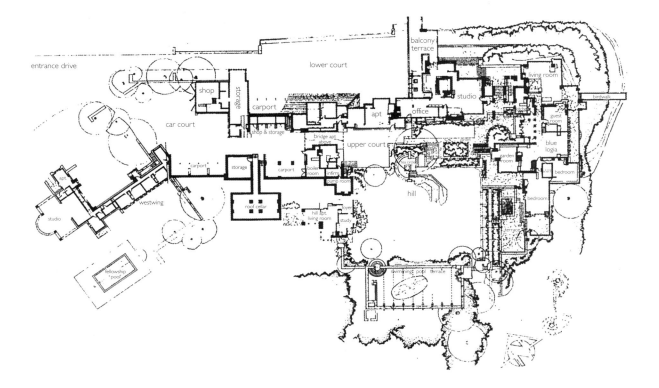

791 Wright: Plan of Taliesin East, near Spring Green, Wisconsin (begun 1911; rebuilt 1930s)

The self-adulatory mood of Wright's later years at Taliesin should not distract us from the real merits of his 'organic' architecture, especially in its immediate post-Prairie House phase. This is demonstrated in two remarkable buildings designed near the start of the First World War, Midway Gardens, Chicago (1913–14; dem. 1929), and the Imperial Hotel, Tokyo (1915–22; dem. 1967). Midway Gardens consisted of a restaurant and a vast courtyard containing an open-air café with an orchestra shell and dance floor. It was built of brick and patterned concrete blocks on a symmetrical plan, though the fanciful corner towers were crowned with abstract linear constructions intended to echo the tendency to abstraction in contemporary European painting. Wright gave the flamboyance and grandeur of Midway Gardens even freer expression in his Imperial Hotel, commissioned by the Japanese imperial household for the reception of western visitors and dignitaries. Like Midway Gardens, the hotel was laid out on an axial Beaux-Arts plan, forming a rough 'H' which

enclosed a pool and two garden courts with a 1,000-seat theatre at the rear. Constructed of brick with heavy, abstract, decorative detail in a tough greenish-yellow lava, it recalled the massive effects of sixteenth-century Japanese military architecture. Its foundation was a floating raft cantilevered from concrete piles, designed with the assistance of the engineer Paul Muller. This enabled the building to withstand the great earthquake which devastated large sections of Tokyo in 1923, though it should be pointed out that it was on the periphery of the shock zone. The most unexpected feature was the jazzy and aggressive internal decoration of pre-Columbian character, incongruously carved out of the local ponderous lava.

Abstract sculptural ornament in concrete, not in lava, recurs in a group of five brilliantly inventive houses in southern California which Wright designed around 1920. Built of pre-cast concrete blocks, imprinted with perforated geometrical patterns and bound together with steel rods, their massing and ornament have a distinctly pre-Columbian Mayan flavour. The most extravagant of them, Hollyhock House, was built on Olive Hill, Los Angeles, in 1919–20 for the artistic

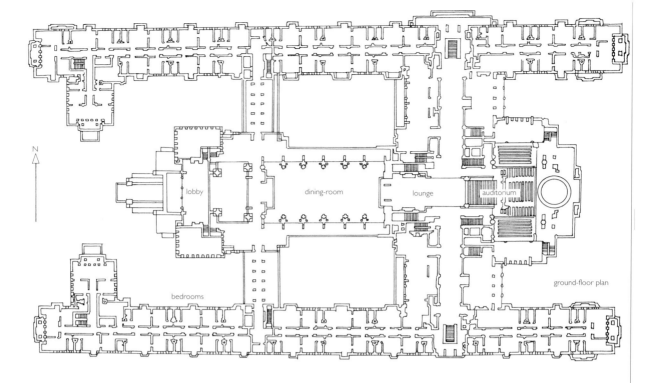

N↑

lobby

dining-room

lounge

auditorium

bedrooms

ground-floor plan

792 Plan of the Imperial Hotel, Tokyo (1915–22), by Wright

patron and social reformer Aline Barnsdall. Its magical blend of low battered walls, strange oriental pinnacles, garden court, roof terraces, pools, fountain, loggia and patio, give it a dream quality recalling something between a Minoan palace and a Mayan stronghold. In its spatial complexity, its masterly relation to its landscape setting, and its escapist or visionary character, it is a parallel to a contemporary house like Castle Drogo by Wright's opposite number in England, Edwin Lutyens. However, houses such as Hollyhock House and La Miniatura, Pasadena (1923), built as an artistic retreat for another middle-aged lady, Alice Millard, could scarcely be regarded as solutions to the wider problems of the modern house with which Wright was ostensibly so concerned. Indeed, he appeared increasingly isolated from the contemporary scene from the mid-1920s to the mid-30s when he indulged in attacks on leading modern architects in Europe, especially on what he regarded as the sterile factory aesthetic of Le Corbusier.

Wright's own career was widely assumed to have ended at this time but in 1936, in his seventieth year, he designed two buildings which once more put him in the forefront of modern design, the Administration Building for the S. C. Johnson Wax Factory at Racine, Wisconsin, and Fallingwater, Bear Run, Pennsylvania, a luxurious weekend house for Edgar Kaufmann, owner of Kaufmann's Department Store in Pittsburgh.

Fallingwater can be interpreted as a spectacular affront to the International Modern style, whose characteristic white concrete slabs Wright handled in his own 'organic' manner by romantically cantilevering them over a waterfall and anchoring them to the living rock with walls of rustic stonework. As a further rebuff to the clinical whiteness of International Modernism he fought, unsuccessfully, to have the exterior concrete surfaces covered with gold leaf, but in the end he had to accept a waterproof cement paint in a light ochre colour. By this time he had come to regard the expressive potentialities of reinforced concrete used in cantilevered constructions as the essence of the organic architecture which he had been advocating for so long. He never used the material more daringly than in Fallingwater, his first house of reinforced concrete, though technical imperfections made it necessary for repairs to be made as early as 1953–5 and again in 1976.

793, 794 *Above and left* View and plan of Fallingwater, Bear Run, Pennsylvania (1936), by Wright

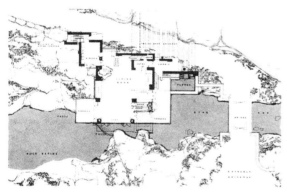

Lovell Beach House, Newport Beach, California (1922–6), and Neutra's steel-framed Lovell 'Health House', Hollywood Hills, Los Angeles (1927–9). Influenced by Wright's modernism as well as by De Stijl, they prepared the way for the reception of Gropius and Mies van der Rohe, whose impact was not widely felt until after the war.

Reinforced concrete used in a manner which Wright described as 'organic' is the hallmark of his other masterpiece of 1936, the Johnson Administration Building. This is celebrated for the poetic interior of the central office hall, dominated by 60 tapered mushroom-like columns 30 feet (9m) high, spreading at the top into reinforced concrete discs like lily pads. The spaces between these pads are filled with tubes of pyrex glass casting a diffused light, so that the visitor imagines himself in a pool looking up at the underneath of the lily pads. Though

Wright did not exercise much influence in America before the Second World War, but we ought to mention here two exceptions, the Viennese architects Rudolph Schindler (1887–1953) and Richard Neutra (1892–1970). They emigrated to America in 1913 and 1923 respectively and spent several years at Taliesin East before settling in Los Angeles. They specialized in houses in the whitened concrete style of the International Modern Movement such as Schindler's concrete-framed

these slender concrete columns are hollow to carry away storm water from the roof, they are structurally unnecessary, supporting nothing but their own lily-pad tops. Like the underfloor heating, air-conditioning, auditorium or theatre, and squash court, they are there to help provide a pleasing environment for modern factory workers. Like many of Wright's works from the Unity Temple onwards, the Administration Building turns its back on the city in which it stands and creates an inward-looking hermetic atmosphere intended to foster a sense of community.

Commissioned by a company run in an old-fashioned and extremely paternalistic way, the building realized some of the ideals proposed by Wright in 1935 in his Broadacre City. This was part of his programme for urban decentralization, first announced in his book of 1932, *The Disappearing City*. His name for this new reformed or alternative American society, which he spent the last 25 years of his life attempting to promote, was Usonia. Broadacre City, which might extend to 100 square miles (260 sq.km), would consist of homesteads of one acre for each family, intermingled with public buildings and small industrial areas. Lacking in the kind of recognizable

795 Interior of the Administration Building at the S. C. Johnson Wax Factory, Racine, Wisconsin (1936), by Wright

urban centre which many would regard as providing architects with opportunities for exercising their art at its highest level, Broadacre City did little more than institutionalize the existing drift towards faceless suburbia. Wright applied the term Usonian to a series of mainly small moderately-priced houses which, beginning with the first Herbert Jacobs House, Madison, Wisconsin (1936), he continued to build for the rest of his career. Generally one-storeyed, these informal houses, designed for servantless families, relied on timber and brick construction, eschewing plastering and wallpaper and also replacing the dining-room with a kitchen-dining area. Wright relied on a simple module or grid of two feet by four (0.6 × 1.2m) to shape the plan.

Buildings in traditional styles

Wright's numerous public buildings of the 1940s and 1950s, which became ever more plastic and expressionist, will be mentioned in passing later in this chapter. For the moment we should return to the mainstream of American architecture up to the Second World War, which in general remained faithful to the traditional styles.

The City Beautiful movement now flowered into what has been called the American Renaissance: this, in effect, was the consequence of the custom of sending American architects to the Ecole des Beaux-Arts in Paris for their training. The classical language established by McKim, Mead and White, and by Carrère and Hastings in their New York Public Library (1897–1911), was continued by architects such as Horace Trumbauer (1868–1938) in his Widener Memorial Library, Harvard University (1914) and Philadelphia Museum of Art (1931–8), and by the architects responsible for rebuilding San Francisco after the earthquake of 1906. Here an imposing civic centre was laid out with five major buildings on cross axes. Including the Civic Auditorium (1913–15) by John Galen Howard (1864–1931), and the Public Library (1915–17) by George W. Kelham (1871–1936), they were dominated by the City Hall (1912–13) by John Bakewell

(1872–1963) and Arthur Brown (1874–1957), with a dome inspired by that of St Peter's in Rome.

Howard, Bakewell and Brown had all been trained at the Ecole des Beaux-Arts. So, too, had Paul Philippe Cret (1876–1945). A Frenchman born in Lyons who emigrated to America in 1903, he became a professor of architecture at the University of Pennsylvania, a post he held until 1937. His Pan American Union, Washington (1907), Indianapolis Public Library (1914) and Detroit Institute of Art (1922) are typical of his lucid planning combined with sober Beaux-Arts façades with neo-Greek and Renaissance Italianate detailing. His Hartford County Building, Hartford, Connecticut (1926), has a façade articulated with square piers in the stripped classical manner popular in the 1920s and 1930s in Scandinavia, France, Italy and especially Germany. Cret gave this idiom memorable expression in his American Battle Monument Memorial at Château Thierry, France (1928), and in his Folger Shakespeare Library, Washington (1929), though this contains sumptuous neo-Jacobean interiors to recall Shakespeare's time.

Henry Bacon (1866–1924), who had worked as an assistant of McKim, Mead and White, was responsible for the Lincoln Memorial, Washington (1911–22), a white marble Doric temple above a pool. This luminous vision is on axis with a westwards extension of the Mall, which had originally been laid out in the 1790s by the French engineer Pierre-Charles L'Enfant (1754–1825). L'Enfant's proposals were developed from 1901 by McKim and Burnham, whose extension of the Mall to the south was eventually terminated by the Jefferson Memorial (1934–43), the masterpiece of John Russell Pope (1874–1937). Pope took the Pantheon as his model but replaced its robust Corinthian order with a chaste Ionic which he wrapped around the exterior of the rotunda in the form of a colonnade. The result is the perfect if belated realization of the visionary Grand Prix projects of eighteenth-century French architects. Pope, who had been trained at the American Academy in Rome and at the Ecole des Beaux-Arts in Paris in 1897–9,

produced a large number of academic classical buildings in New York City, New York State and Washington. The ablest disciple of McKim, his refined work in Washington includes Constitution Hall (1929), the National Archives Building (1933–5) and the National Gallery of Art (1937–41).

Of course not all architectural production in these years consisted of colonnaded public buildings in tree-lined, axially laid-out boulevards. It could be claimed that American architects now brought the one-family house for prosperous middle-class clients to a level of comfort, convenience and elegance which have never been surpassed. From 1918 to 1933 Addison Izner (1872–1933) built a model town and surrounding villas at Palm Beach, Florida, a brilliant urban conception insufficiently appreciated by architectural historians. More extravagant is the Villa Vizcaya, Miami, Florida (1914–16), built as a winter home for the industrialist James Deering by F. Burrall Hoffmann (1884–1980) and Paul Chalfin (1874–1959). This is a lavish Italianate palazzo of stuccoed reinforced concrete, set in terraced water-gardens which were completed in 1923 from

designs by Diego Suarez (1888–1974) and Paul Chalfin. There were countless architects, craftsmen and garden-designers able to provide more realistic homes in a range of styles from English Tudor and Georgian to American Colonial. Typical are John F. Staub (b.1892) and Philip Trammell Shutze (b.1890), whose practices were based respectively in Houston, Texas, and Atlanta, Georgia. Shutze's finest work is probably Swan House, Atlanta (1926–8), an eclectic symphony on the theme of an English neo-Palladian mansion, set in an Italian Baroque garden. In the city of Atlanta Shutze provided stylish neo-classical public buildings such as the Temple of the Hebrew Benevolent Congregation (1931–2) and the Academy of Medicine (1940).

Gothic was popular for ecclesiastical and collegiate commissions and also, surprisingly, for skyscrapers. The leading ecclesiologist and medieval scholar was the Boston architect Ralph Adams Cram (1863–1942), a pious Puginian Anglo-Catholic who was in partnership with Goodhue from 1892 to 1914 and with Ferguson from 1899. Cram visited England in the 1880s, where he admired the refined Perpendicular Gothic of Bodley

796 *Opposite* Aerial view of the Jefferson Memorial, Washington (1934–43), by Pope

797 *Above* Aerial view of the Villa Vizcaya, Miami (1914–16), by Hoffmann, Chalfin and Suarez

798 *Below* Shutze: Temple of Hebrew Benevolent Congregation, Atlanta (1931–2)

and Sedding. He echoed their qualities of strength and freedom in his powerful early church of All Saints, Ashmont, Boston (1891), and in his St Thomas's church, Fifth Avenue, New York (1905–13), with its rich detailing by Goodhue. Cram's principal building, the cathedral of St John the Divine, New York (1911–42), is a towering essay in French Gothic. Cram and Ferguson designed the University Chapel and Graduate College at Princeton University, New Jersey (1911–37), in a weighty Perpendicular Gothic. This style reappeared at Yale University, New Haven, Connecticut, where James Gamble Rogers (1867–1947) worked extensively, beginning with his Memorial Quadrangle and Harkness Tower (1916–19).

More interesting than Rogers was Cram's partner Bertram Grosvenor Goodhue (1869–1924), who was responsible for the high angular forms of the Cadet Chapel (1903–10) at the United States Military

Academy at West Point, New York City. Goodhue's Catholic church of St Vincent Ferrer, New York (1914–18), reflects the influence of Giles Gilbert Scott's Liverpool Cathedral (p. 641), which he had seen in progress on his visit to England in 1913. The high vaults of St Vincent's were of light Guastavino tiles which enabled Goodhue to dispense with flying buttresses and to minimize the bulk of the supporting piers. Boldness and height are also features of his Rockefeller Chapel at the University of Chicago (1918–28), while his St Bartholomew's church, New York (1914–19), is inspired by Bentley's combination of Byzantine and Italian Romanesque forms at Westminster cathedral, London. Goodhue's masterpiece was in some ways more original than his churches. This is the Nebraska State Capitol in Lincoln, designed in 1916 and executed in 1920–32. It is raised on a cruciform Beaux-Arts plan organized round four courtyards at the heart of which stands not a dome, as had been customary in state capitols since

799 Nave of the cathedral of St John the Divine, New York City: work by Cram from 1911

800 Goodhue: The Nebraska State Capitol, Lincoln (designed 1916; built 1920–32)

that by Bulfinch at Boston, but a tower. This monument of great power and delicacy, which it is not possible to classify as Gothic or classical, has something of the elemental quality of the tower of Eliel Saarinen's Helsinki Railway Station (1904–14), which Goodhue admired.

The skyscraper

The architect famous for bringing poetry to the skyscraper by giving the office building something of the quality of a cathedral was Cass Gilbert (1859–1934), whose Woolworth Building, New York (1910–13), at 760 feet (232m) high was for 20 years the tallest office building in the world. Dominated by a central tower which owed something to the profile of Barry's Victoria Tower at the Houses of Parliament in London, the Woolworth Building was clad in lightweight, fireproof terracotta, rich in Decorated Gothic detail. The vertical thrust of the Gothic style made Gilbert's sensitive application of this detail seem appropriate even to a building of this scale and function.

In Chicago, always anxious to rival New York, a competition for the 'world's most beautiful office building' was announced in 1922 by the Chicago Tribune. Over 260 designs were submitted in this prestigious competition; 100 of them were from architects in Europe, where the skyscraper represented a deeply romantic challenge, since none had so far been built. Eliel Saarinen's 'organic' Gothic design for the Chicago Tribune Tower, awarded second prize, was widely admired, especially by the ageing Sullivan. The entries by the German Max Taut and by Gropius and Meyer were articulated in the chill square way which, endlessly imitated throughout the world in the next 70 years, gave rise to the deserved condemnation of many modern office blocks as 'packing cases'. The winning design, inspired by the Gothic style of the Woolworth Building in New York, was by Raymond Hood (1881–1934) and John Mead Howells (1868–1959). Hood had been a draughtsman in the office of Cram, Goodhue and Ferguson before entering the Ecole des Beaux-Arts in

801 Gilbert: The Woolworth Building, New York City (1910–13): an early photo

Paris in 1905. The success of his Chicago Tribune Tower led to his American Radiator Building, New York (1924), where the steel frame was cased in black brick, with simplified Gothic ornamental features towards the top, carved in gilded stone. The building was dramatically floodlit so it became at night an advertisement billboard, glowing appropriately as a symbol of the heating appliances sold by its owners. Hood's McGraw Building, New York (1930–2), paved the way for the transition to the International Style in skyscraper design.

Architects and patrons were seeking an architectural language appropriate to the post-First-World-War

802 The American Radiator Building, New York City (1924), by Hood

commercial boom in America which lasted until the Stock Market crash in 1929. There was no European parallel in these years to this affluence, and the triumph of capitalism and democracy in America seemed as unconnected with the avant-garde modernism of advanced circles in western Europe as with the traditional historical styles. The solution adopted was to bring to the design of the skyscraper, appropriately an American invention, the streamlined style of which one variant appeared in the work of German Expressionist architects such as Poelzig and Höger, and another in the

Art Deco style popularized at the Paris Exposition of 1925. An important part in the growth of the Art Deco skyscraper was played by Ralph Thomas Walker (1889–1973) who, late in his partnership with Andrew C. Mackenzie (1861–1926), Stephen F. Voorhees (1878–1965) and Paul Gmelin (1859–1937), designed the New York Telephone (Barclay-Vesey) Building (1923–6) in New York City. This had the characteristic pyramidal profile in consequence of the New York City zoning law of 1916, which required set-backs from the lot line above certain heights to allow more light into the streets. Ely Jacques Kahn (1884–1972) was responsible for a large number of Art Deco skyscrapers in the 1920s and 1930s. The best known is the Empire State Building (1930–2) by Raymond Shreve (1877–1946), Lamb & Harmon, but the liveliest is the Chrysler Building (1928–30), New York City, by William Van Alen (1883–1954). This is surmounted by a telescoping aluminium top like a diminishing series of melon slices, as original in form as it is memorable as an advertising symbol.

The streamlined or Art Deco style was essentially an urban style of instant communication for commercial offices, banks, stores, hotels, apartment blocks and the headquarters of the media. It ran parallel with buildings in quite different styles, sometimes designed by the same architect. Thus, in a typically American combination of industrial dynamism and social conservatism, a business tycoon of these years might live in a neo-Tudor suburban mansion, work in an Art Deco skyscraper, visit a neo-Georgian country club at the weekends, and educate his sons at a neo-Gothic college, all built in the 1920s. One of the most hydra-headed of this period's architects was Albert Kahn (1869–1942), whose own career as a self-made entrepreneur, eventually employing a staff of over 600 in his office, was characteristic of this expansive period. Typical of his domestic work is the Edsel B. Ford House, Grosse Pointe, Michigan (1926–7), designed in a Cotswold neo-Tudor style for a leading automobile manufacturer. In an academic setting he chose a restrained classicism, as in his William L. Clements

803 Howe and Lescase: Philadelphia Savings Fund Society, Philadelphia (1929–32)

The building which made the International Modern style of contemporary Europe acceptable for skyscraper office blocks in America was the Philadelphia Savings Fund Society, Philadelphia, Pennsylvania (1929–32), by George Howe (1886–1955) and William Lescase (1896–1969). Howe brought to its design a sense of the logical distribution of functions which he had acquired as a pupil at the Ecole des Beaux-Arts in Paris, while Lescase, a Swiss architect, was familiar with recent International Style buildings in Europe. A third influence came from the patron who wanted the façades of this costly and prestigious 32-storey tower to be designed with an eye-catching vertical emphasis. He did not get his way entirely because Howe and Lescase condemned visual effects of this kind as reminiscent of the Gothic flavour of skyscraper design in the previous decades. Such verticality was inconsistent with the structural configuration of the building, in which the tiers of horizontal office floors were cantilevered from a steel core. Though some might find the building as executed visually unlovely, it is a complex and intellectually stimulating work in which the different parts – ground-floor shops, first-floor bank, office floors and tower containing services and elevators – are clearly expressed, clad in different materials and given different fenestration patterns. The second fully air-conditioned office block in America, and thus in the world, it was also the first to stand on a podium of shops and public banking halls.

Raymond Hood now dropped his earlier and more decorative style, and in skyscrapers in New York City such as the Daily News Building (1929–30) and Rockefeller Center (1930–40) adopted the featureless slab-like format inspired by German architects such as Gropius and Meyer. Rockefeller Center had been initiated in 1928 as part of the desire of the New York Metropolitan Opera Company for a new auditorium. Following their withdrawal as a result of the financial crash of 1929, their place was taken by a very different patron, the Radio Corporation of America. The architects Reinhard and Hofmeister, with Harvey Corbett and Raymond Hood as design consultants, now

Library, University of Michigan, Ann Arbor (1920–1), with its Brunelleschian loggia. However, in his numerous factories, for example the Ford Glass Plant, Dearborn, Michigan (1922), he developed a wholly functional language. Abolishing the traditional multi-storey factory, he applied this language to one-storey buildings of wide span, lit through roofs with a serrated profile. Though he was responsible for countless such factories, including over 500 in the USSR between 1929 and 1932, he insisted that this industrial style was inappropriate for domestic and institutional purposes.

804 Radio City Music Hall, New York, interior (1932)

produced a complex of towers dominated by the tallest and thinnest, for the Radio Corporation, with a rather mean plaza at its foot. To assist in the design of the 6,200-seat Radio City Music Hall, intended for vaudeville as well as film, they engaged the impresario and radio personality Roxy (Samuel L. Rothafel). Opened in 1932, this was one of the most dazzling of the many romantic or 'atmospheric' motion-picture theatres which were such a feature of American life in the 1930s. From the 140-foot (43m) long grand lobby, enriched with black glass, mirrors, polished metals and lights beneath a golden ceiling, visitors pass to the auditorium where the stage is set within huge telescoped arches, patterned like the sun and capable, with the help of subtle lighting, of simulating a range of naturalistic effects.

Europe up to 1939

Early twentieth-century Berlin: Messel and Behrens

Twentieth-century German architecture up to the Second World War had something of the extreme variety of the three dramatically different political systems which succeeded each other during these years; first,

the German Empire of the Hohenzollern dynasty which collapsed in 1918, bringing down its constituent kingdoms, princedoms and grand duchies; then the Weimar Republic; and finally the National Socialism established in 1933. Independently of the search for an 'Art Nouveau' conducted by so many European architects in the 1890s, Germany was preoccupied at this time by its own attempts to find a style appropriate to the still young German Empire. It seemed important that this style should be of recognizably northern European rather than Mediterranean character. Thus, in the first decade of the century, architects such as Ludwig Hoffmann (1851–1932), Alfred Messel (1853–1909), Theodor Fischer (1862–1938) and Fritz Schumacher (1869–1947) developed a sensitive and original classical language which, avoiding the Baroque extravagance of the Wilhelmine style of the later nineteenth-century, revived German Renaissance and neo-classical modes, often echoing the vernacular tradition of southern Germany.

One of the most creative of these architects was Messel, whose influential Wertheim Department Store in Berlin was built in three stages, beginning with the façade in the Leipzigerstrasse in 1896–7, then that in the Voss-strasse in 1901, and finally the strikingly independent façade of 1904 in the Leipziger Platz. All of these, especially the last, were characterized by grids of giant mullions, largely unmoulded though sometimes combined with Art Nouveau or Gothic details. The main hall had an iron frame, iron stairs and galleries, and internal glass walls. The arresting exterior articulation was echoed by Olbrich in his Tietz Department Store, Düsseldorf (1907–9). Messel's National Bank of Germany in the Behrensstrasse, Berlin (1906–7), had a Greek Doric entrance porch and striking Greek Doric interiors in the style of Gentz, while its façade was marked by a chunky and aggressive handling of classical elements which was to be a characteristic of German classicism up to 1940. Among the architects who adopted this modernized Teutonic neo-classicism was German Bestelmeyer (1874–1942), for example in his

805 *Above* Leipziger Platz façade of the Wertheim Department Store, Berlin (1904), by Messel

806 *Left* Messel: Exterior of the National Bank of Germany, Behrensstrasse, Berlin (1906–7)

807 *Below* Bonatz: Stuttgart Railway Station (designed 1911–13; built 1913–28)

Ludwig-Max University extension (1906–10), insurance company headquarters (1916) and Technical High School (1922), all in Munich. The same powerfully direct language was adopted by Paul Bonatz (1877–1951), whose masterpiece is the Stuttgart Railway Station, designed in 1911–13 and executed in 1913–28.

The most important of the architects influenced by Messel was Peter Behrens (1868–1949), who wrote an appreciative obituary of him in 1909. Behrens enjoyed a career with even more stylistic contrasts than that of Frank Lloyd Wright, an architect whom he at some points resembled. Working happily under the Empire, the Weimar Republic and the Nazis, he produced buildings in a remarkable variety of modes: Art Nouveau, Tuscan proto-Renaissance Revival, monumental industrial, stripped classical, Expressionist, International Modern and Third Reich classical. He had been deeply influenced by the aesthetic theories of Riegl and Worringer which centred on concepts such as *Kunstwollen* (will to form), stressing the primacy of artistic will over material conditions, and *Zeitgeist* (the spirit of the age). Behrens's understanding of architecture as the cultural essence of the changing spirit of successive ages helped make him particularly ready to work for clients and régimes with differing cultural and political aims.

He was trained as a painter, and his career began in the romantic world of the Darmstadt Artists' Colony with its almost mystical faith in the regenerative role of the Arts and Crafts. In 1899 he became one of the original seven artists of the Colony, where in the following year he built himself an intensely aesthetic little house with a strong Art Nouveau flavour and a partially open plan which has been compared to that of Frank Lloyd Wright's own house of 1889 at Oak Park. In 1902 he designed the Hamburg Vestibule for the International Exhibition of Decorative Art at Turin, a poetic grotto-like interior recalling the work of Guimard.

In the following year he left the Artists' Colony at Darmstadt and became director of the Kunstgewerbeschule (Arts and Crafts School) at Düsseldorf, where he came into contact with industrialists, receiving his first commission from the AEG (German Electricity Company) in 1907. Following his move to Düsseldorf he designed a group of buildings in 1905–6 in complete contrast to his earlier manner. Breathing a fresh neo-antique spirit with distinct resemblances to the Tuscan proto-Renaissance of the eleventh and twelfth centuries, these include the crematorium of 1906–7 at Delstern near Hagen. The most significant of the group, this is inspired by S. Miniato al Monte, Florence (p. 147). It is pervaded with an atmosphere of mystic geometry which Behrens considered appropriate to its function as the first, and therefore controversial, crematorium in Prussia.

In 1907 Behrens was appointed artistic consultant to the powerful and expanding German Electricity Company, for which Messel had worked from 1902 to 1906. Behrens's best-known work for the AEG is his Turbine Factory of 1909 at Berlin-Moabit. He wanted to turn what is essentially an iron and glass hangar into an expressive statement about the poetry of modern power in the Germany of the Empire. He thus provided

808 Behrens: The AEG Turbine Factory, Berlin-Moabit (1909)

the short ends of the rectangular building with functionally unneccessary concrete façades which rise from the ground at a sloping angle like the battered pylons of Egyptian or Mycenaean architecture, as recaptured by Gilly in his project of c.1800 for a city gate. A further echo of neo-classical Berlin is provided in the side wing of the Turbine Factory, which echoes the trabeated articulation of Schinkel's Schauspielhaus. Behrens, with no formal training as an architect, still less as an engineer, was forced to rely for the structural design of the Turbine Factory on the engineer Karl Bernhard. It was, however, Bernhard who was obliged to adapt the design of the three-hinged metal arches in the interior to the weighty gable-end which had already been chosen by Behrens on purely visual and expressive grounds. The Turbine Factory was followed by another temple of power in Berlin, the AEG Small Motors Factory (1909–13), where the Schinkelesque façade on the Voltastrasse, 642 feet (196m) long, resembles an ancient stoa with its daunting row of engaged brick columns, 65 feet (20m) high. Contemporaries found its show of elemental strength reminiscent of Paestum or Stonehenge.

The Small Motors Factory was one of three huge factories which Behrens created for the AEG in the enormous Humboldthain complex in Berlin-Wedding. These include the High Tension Materials Factory of 1908 with its pitched tiled roof, corner towers and brick façades hung over a concealed steel frame. It helps to create the impression that the whole area is a modern industrial parallel to a medieval agricultural settlement, with giant barns of glass and iron. In its patronage of Behrens the AEG was indirectly supporting the Deutscher Werkbund, which had been founded by Hermann Muthesius in 1907 as an association of manufacturers, architects, designers and writers. Their aim was to create national standards in industrial product design and to promote sales of high-quality German products in the international market. Behrens created a unified graphic style for the publications and exhibitions of the AEG, characterized by the use of

809 Voltastrasse façade of the AEG Small Motors Factory (1909–13), by Behrens

emphatic neo-Carolingian type-faces. He was perhaps the first to create a corporate image in connection with the marketing of industrial products. In these ambitions he was supported by Walter Rathenau, later the German Foreign Minister, one of the directors of the AEG and a son of its founder. Deliberately striving to emulate Friedrich Gilly, Walter Rathenau maintained a belief in spiritual values and was determined not to be dominated by technology.

Behrens's concern to find an appropriate and expressive solution to every architectural task made him an ideal architect for Dr Theodor Wiegand, an archaeologist who had excavated at Priene, Miletus and Samos. Appointed Director of the Antiquities of the Royal Prussian Museums in 1910, Wiegand commissioned a superb neo-antique private house from Behrens which was built in Berlin-Dahlem in 1911–12. Constructed of finely laid ashlar with a peristyle of

810 Façade of Haus Wiegand, Berlin-Dahlem (1911–12), by Behrens

unfluted Doric columns, this is a strikingly Schinkelesque variant of the Hellenistic houses of Priene, Delos and Pompeii which Behrens had visited in 1904. Not unjustly, Behrens came to see himself as the Schinkel of the twentieth century. Indeed, just as Schinkel was the climax of a vision of antiquity which went back to Winckelmann, so Behrens was the embodiment of a fresh understanding of classical culture which had been made possible from the later nineteenth century by the discoveries of German archaeologists like Schliemann, Wiegand and Furtwängler, and by the researches of Riegl and Strzygowski into the architecture and crafts of late antiquity.

The strongly archaeological flavour of the Haus Wiegand, which was untypical of Behrens's work as a whole, was probably due to Dr Wiegand, who had made restorations of the domestic buildings of Priene. A more characteristic work was Behrens's prestigious German Embassy at St Petersburg (1911–12). Just as he had sanctified labour in his AEG factories so in his Embassy he sanctified the state. He claimed that 'German art and technology will thus work towards the one end: the power of the German nation'. He took the stripped classicism of his AEG Small Motors Factory and developed it in a way appropriate to the imposing setting of the Germany Embassy next to St Isaac's cathedral. Its monumental scale pays tribute to that of the neo-classical buildings of St Petersburg, while its colonnaded front,

formerly crowned by an equestrian group, recalls Schinkel's Altes Museum and Langhans's Brandenburg Gate. Its harsh and somehow authoritarian vocabulary, echoing that of Messel's AEG Office Building on the Friedrich-Karl-Ufer, Berlin (1905–6), was to be widely influential, especially on the buildings of the Third Reich. Inside, the entrance hall, with its coffered ceiling and its colonnade of fluted Greek Doric columns of black porphyry, leading through glass doors into an inner garden court, is obviously inspired by the similar disposition in Schinkel's proposed Schloss Orianda (p. 481).

The rise of Expressionism and the work of Poelzig

The search for an expressive style, of which we have found evidence in Behrens's work, was paralleled in the contemporary obsession with the erection of national monuments commemorating the path to German unity from 1813 to 1871. As a result of this nationalist mythology, inherited by the last Kaiser (reigned 1888–1918) from monarchs such as Ludwig I of Bavaria, the architect Wilhelm Kreis (1873–1953) had produced by 1914 over 40 national monuments, many of them to Bismarck. His elemental and militantly monumental style had great expressive power, which is also well displayed in his Provincial Museum of Pre-History at Halle (1911–16), with its cyclopean stonework and its corner towers recalling the late Roman Porta Nigra at Trier. Scarcely less prolific was the architect Bruno Schmitz (1858–1916), from whom Kreis derived much of his increasingly abstract language. Schmitz's imperial monuments to Kaiser Wilhelm I (reigned 1871–88) include those of 1896–7 on the Kyffhauser near the Porta Westfalica and at the Deutsches Eck near Koblenz, but the climax of his glorification of German history was the Völkerschlacht Memorial in Leipzig, commemorating the Battle of the Nations of October 1813. He won the competition for this in 1896 but it was built slowly from 1900 to 1913, of reinforced concrete faced with porphyry granite. Brooding

menacingly on an artificial hill at the end of an extended axial vista, this gigantic tower with its chunky primeval detailing is terrifying in its evocation of brute force. Containing high domed chambers, it combines the qualities of tower and cave which were to have a special appeal to Expressionist designers.

One of the first to use the term 'expressionism' was the art-historian Wilhelm Worringer in 1911 in the context of paintings by Matisse and Van Gogh. Worringer developed Riegl's *Kunstwollen* ('will to form') as an eternal force expressive of the psychology of Northern Germanic man. Another powerful influence on German artistic thinking at this moment came from the philosopher Friedrich Nietzsche (1844–1910). In his

811 *Left* Schmitz: The Völkerschlacht Memorial, Leipzig (1900–13)

812 *Below* Skylight in the entrance hall at the head offices of the I. G.-Farben Dye Factory, Höchst, Frankfurt-am-Main (1920–1), by Behrens

813 Interior of the Centennial Hall, Breslau (1911–13), by Berg

writings, which provided a dark and irrational note, he finally overthrew the Apollonian or balanced image of Greek culture, as eulogized by Winckelmann and Goethe, in favour of a Dionysian image of intoxicating dynamism. The Expressionist movement was also coloured by Nietzsche's concept of the Superman in a state of perpetual emotional excitement who would fight to establish his will over the naturalism and neo-romanticism of modern art and drama. The leading Expressionist artists in Germany were the Russian painter Vassily Kandinsky (1866–1944) and Franz Marc (1880–1916). Their explosive expressions of symbolic abstraction are among the earliest examples of non-representational or non-objective art.

This style is paralleled architecturally in the work of Hans Poelzig, Eric Mendelsohn, Fritz Höger, Dominikus Böhm, Bruno Taut, and even in a few post-war works by Behrens himself, for example, the Head Offices of the I. G.-Farben Dye Factory at Höchst, Frankfurt-am-Main (1920–1), and the Dombauhütte (Cathedral Masons' Lodge) at the Exhibition of Applied Art in Munich in 1922. The exteriors of the Höchst building, perhaps influenced by the Amsterdam School of Kramer and de Klerk, represent a return to a north German medieval brick tradition with massive arches, a bridge, and a giant clock tower with Gothic numerals on one of its faces. However, the four-storeyed entrance hall has multi-faceted and corbelled brickwork with something of the forcefulness of Wright's interiors at the Imperial Hotel, Tokyo. The jagged brickwork echoes as it rises the colours of the spectrum and at the top, where it meets the crystalline skylight, it turns to bright yellow, the colour of joy according to Goethe in his *Theory of Colours*. This electric and transcendent interior, resembling a

814 *Above* Auditorium of the Grosses Schauspielhaus, Berlin (1918–19), by Poelzig

cosmic crystal, could be interpreted as a reaction to the cataclysmic horror of the First World War, for the view straight ahead was terminated by the names of 600 employees who had been killed in the war.

The principal Expressionist architect was Hans Poelzig (1869–1936) who, after a training at the celebrated Technical High School at Berlin-Charlottenburg, was appointed Director of the Royal Arts and Crafts Academy in Breslau (Wrocław) in 1903, remaining there until 1916. His appointment, along with that of Behrens in Düsseldorf, Bruno Paul and Hermann Muthesius in Berlin, and van de Velde in Weimar, was a consequence of Muthesius's policy of placing leading artists at the head of the most influential schools of applied arts. Poelzig's most important early work is the water tower and exhibition hall at Posen, Silesia (Poznań, Poland), which he built for the Posen Exhibition of 1911. It can be interpreted as an inventive and dynamic

expression of Riegl's 'will to form' in which an emphatic Germanic monumentality is bestowed on an industrial building type. Its heptagonal steel frame, filled with panels of brickwork in herringbone and diaper patterns, is enriched with three tiers of lean-to roofs, giving the building an unforgettable profile. It should be compared with the Centennial Hall built at Breslau in 1911–13 from designs by Max Berg (1870–1947) as another of the many commemorations of the defeat of Napoleon at Leipzig in 1813. The giant reinforced concrete dome of the Centennial Hall has a span of 225 feet (67m), which made it then the largest dome in the world. In the interior, 32 flying ribs descend to a circular ring-beam which is supported on four great arches, while four apses help resist the lateral thrust. This dynamically exposed structure is concealed on the exterior by the stepped tiers of clerestorey fenestration. These are treated in a classical manner, which was part of Poelzig's desire to create an *architecture parlante* expressive of the period commemorated in the centennial exhibition.

Poelzig adopted an entirely different Expressionist language in his Grosses Schauspielhaus in Berlin (1918–19) for the brilliant impresario Max Reinhardt. Converted out of a market hall which had already been adapted to serve as a circus, this 'Theatre of the Five Thousand' was a fruit of the 'People's Theatre' movement of the later nineteenth century. The aim of this populist rhetoric was to provide 'total theatre' for everyone as part of a popular culture in which there would be no distinction between stage and auditorium, no boxes or even differently priced seats. Poelzig designed the interior as a kind of magic cave or image of the cosmos, defined by a dome hung astonishingly with continuous rings of stalactites or icicles. Perhaps suggested initially by Islamic stalactite vaulting, these were romantically silhouetted with concealed artificial lighting. In this ecstatic interior Poelzig seems to have come under the influence of Bruno Taut (1880–1938).

Other Expressionist architects in Germany and Holland

A highly influential communicator of ideas and creator of fantastical Expressionist designs, Taut established a 'mythology' of glass: he saw it as promoting in modern man a new self-awareness and freshness of approach which would eventually help diminish evil in the world. The simplified frieze or string-course of the Glass Pavilion, which Taut built for the glass industry at the Deutscher Werkbund Exhibition at Cologne in 1914, was inscribed with aphorisms such as 'coloured glass destroys hatred'. These were composed by the anarcho-socialist poet and novelist Paul Scheerbart (1863–1915), who, in turn, dedicated his book *Glasarchitektur* ('Glass architecture') of 1914 to Taut. The Glass Pavilion was a pineapple-shaped multi-faceted glass dome of rhomboid prisms, rising from a 14-sided base of glass bricks. The prisms were faced with coloured glass on the inside where there was an ambitious cascade of water animated by a play of coloured lights from a kaleidoscope. Far more exaggerated fantasy informed the illustrations in Taut's books, *Alpine Architecture* (Hagen 1919), *The City*

815 Taut: The Glass Pavilion, Deutscher Werkbund Exhibition, Cologne (1914)

Crown (Jena 1919), and *The Dissolution of Cities* (Hagen 1920). Here he envisaged a network of crystal domes and caves symbolizing the aspirations of a society, which he spelled out in the windy self-contradictory language of Utopian socialism.

On at least one occasion, fantasies akin to Taut's became reality. This was in the Einstein Tower at Berlin-Neubabelsberg (1919–24), designed by Eric Mendelsohn (1887–1953) as one of the most visionary and sculpturally abstract architectural monuments of the Expressionist movement. After an initial training in Berlin, Mendelsohn became a pupil of Theodor Fischer at the Technical High School in Munich in 1910. The Nietzschean dynamism of the Expressionists in that city was immediately reflected in Mendelsohn's numerous small sketches, many of them made while he was fighting on the German front in the First World War, for plastically conceived buildings with 'futuristic' or emphatically non-historical overtones.

The Einstein Tower, in which he realized these ambitions, was paid for by the German government as an observatory and astrophysical laboratory for Einstein. It has a memorable shape, half abstract yet half suggestive of a crouching high-necked beast with front paws extended. Mendelsohn hoped to execute these curvilinear forms, expressive of the poetry and mystery of the unexplored universe, in reinforced concrete.

816 Façade of the Schocken Department Store, Stuttgart (1926), by Mendelsohn

817 Exterior of the Scheepvarthuis, Amsterdam (1912–16), by Mey, Kramer and de Klerk

However, owing to difficulties in the supply of materials, much of it is in brick coated with cement. His hat factory of reinforced concrete and brickwork at Luckenwalde (1921–3) is Expressionist in the jagged angularity of its profiles, which recall the contemporary sketches and woodcuts of Lyonel Feininger. Even after he had helped create the calmer horizontal lines of the International Modern Movement from the mid-1920s, Mendelsohn injected a streamlined plastic energy into key buildings in this new style such as the Schocken Department Stores at Stuttgart (1926) and Chemnitz (1928–9).

In Holland an indigenous Expressionism, which has become known as the 'Amsterdam School', flourished between about 1915 and 1930. This grew out of the emphasis on brick of Berlage and his followers which led to an attempt to revive the medieval brick vernacular

architecture of northern Europe. An important early monument of the Amsterdam School is the Scheepvarthuis (1912–16), erected as offices by a group of shipping companies. Its reinforced concrete frame is clothed in a spectacular brick façade of aggressively jagged verticality from the designs of Johan van der Mey (1878–1949), with assistance from Piet Kramer (1881–1961) and Michel de Klerk (1884–1923). Kramer and de Klerk, who became the leading Dutch Expressionist architects, combined the use of brick with a plastic fantasy which sometimes rivalled the moulded forms of Mendelsohn's Einstein Tower. Amsterdam was stirred at this time by political and social reform, expressed primarily in the numerous socialist and communist groups founded to improve the level of workers' housing, which had declined during the rapid industrialization of the city in the later nineteenth century. The best works of de Klerk and Kramer were workers' housing estates carried out between 1913 and 1922 for two socialist housing societies, De Dageraad (The Dawn) and Eigen Haard (Our Hearth). These massive blocks of patterned polychromatic brickwork with whimsical gables, turrets and oriel windows brought a new level of liveliness, variety and craftsmanship to workers' housing.

Something of the flavour of the Amsterdam School is found in one of the most arresting Expressionist buildings in Germany, the Chilehaus, Hamburg (1923–4), by Fritz Höger (1877–1949), an office block of brick, the traditional Hamburg material. Its stabbing angularity in plan and profile culminates in its acute-angled corner which, soaring up like the prow of a ship, represents the function of the building as shipping offices. The field of church architecture offered obvious scope for the exciting forms and the high-flown visionary ideals of Expressionism. The leading figures were the

818 *Above right* Mendelsohn: The Einstein Tower, Berlin-Neubabelsberg (1919–24)

819 *Right* Höger: The Chilehaus, Hamburg (1923–4)

Protestant Otto Bartning (1883–1959) and the Catholic Dominikus Böhm (1880–1955), who reinterpreted the poetry of Gothic construction with the benefit of modern structural techniques. Bartning's project of 1921 for a Sternkirche (star church) is a crystalline structure in the style of Taut, with parabolic arches of the kind devised by Gaudí for his chapel at the Colonia Güell (1898–c.1915). This unexecuted vision was realized by Böhm in dramatic concrete churches such as that of St Engelbert, Cologne-Riehl (1930–2), which is a circular building roofed with great parabolic lobes, making a bizarre impression on the exterior. Böhm was fired by the ideals of the liturgical movement which aimed at heightening the visible and audible participation of the congregation in the Mass.

Two of the most interesting complexes of public buildings in Germany in the 1920s, both with much in common, are Adolf Abel's Press Exhibition buildings and Stadium at Cologne, and Wilhelm Kreis's exhibition buildings and art museum, built along the edge of the Rhine at Düsseldorf in 1925–6 for the Gesolai Exhibition. At the head of the vista Kreis placed the circular Rheinhalle, a planetarium which serves today as a concert hall. It is an Expressionist extravaganza with an

821 Kreis: The Rheinhalle, Düsseldorf (1925–6)

external arcade of jagged V-shaped arches and brickwork in lozenge-shaped patterns, and a giant domed interior articulated with stalactite vaulting which recalls that in Poelzig's Grosses Schauspielhaus in Berlin. By contrast, the open corner pavilions in the garden court are in a stripped classical style which was to influence P. L. Troost and Albert Speer, Hitler's principal architects.

Gropius and the Bauhaus

Among those architects who, like Kreis, passed through an Expressionist phase, none has become better known than Walter Gropius (1883–1969). Like Behrens, with whom he worked from 1907 to 1910, he did not begin as an Expressionist. Trained at the Technical High School at Berlin-Charlottenburg, he was the son of an architect, Walther Gropius, and great-nephew of a more famous architect, Martin Gropius, from whom he inherited a veneration for the Prussian classicism of Schinkel. His early industrial buildings, the Fagus shoe-last factory at Alfeld-an-der-Leine, near Hildesheim (1911–12), and the model factory and office building at the Werkbund Exhibition of 1914 at Cologne, were designed with his partner, the theosophist architect Adolf Meyer (1881–1929). They are carefully controlled essays on themes inspired by Behrens and Frank Lloyd Wright. Their flat roofs, glass curtain-walling, and glazed corner

820 Gropius: The Fagus Factory, Alfeld-an-der-Leine, near Hildesheim (1911–12)

staircases, both rectangular and semi-circular, were to be widely influential on the post-war International Modern Style as transparent images of movement.

In the midst of the turbulent political and intellectual life of Germany following the disastrous end of the First World War and the fall of the German Empire in 1918, Gropius became inspired by the radical visionary Utopianism of Taut. He joined left-wing artistic groups such as the *Arbeitsrat für Kunst* (Working Council for Art), *Novembergruppe* and *Die gläserne Kette* (The Glass Chain), a network for the exchange of letters organized by Taut. The *Arbeitsrat* was interested in the recreation of the medieval building-lodges and Gropius was soon busy designing Tautian *Wohnberger* (mountains for living). The climax came with Gropius's proclamation of 1919, in which he published his proposal to turn the Academy of Fine Art and the School of Arts and Crafts at Weimar, of which he had been appointed director that year, into a Bauhaus (house of building). The Bauhaus manifesto was illustrated with an Expressionist woodcut by Lyonel Feininger of the 'cathedral of the future', depicted as the cathedral of socialism. Gropius wrote of 'the new structures of the future . . . which will one day rise toward heaven from the hands of a million workers like the crystal symbol of a new faith'. Structures of this kind, the modern equivalent to the medieval cathedral, were also envisaged by Taut in his *The City Crown* as crystal temples dedicated to the socialist brotherhood of man. Taut is also partly responsible for the note of guild socialism in the Bauhaus manifesto, which saw the new house of building as a craft workshop like the old cathedral. Thus, though the manifesto included as one of the aims of the Bauhaus the 'corporate planning of comprehensive Utopian designs – communal and cultic buildings – with long-range goals', the emphasis for the first few years of the school's existence was not on architectural education but on craftsmanship and painting. The first staff appointments were painters and sculptors, including Gerhard Marcks and Lyonel Feininger in 1919 and Johannes Itten, Kandinsky and Klee in 1922. It was

822 *Above* Feininger: Frontispiece woodcut of the 'cathedral of the future', from the Bauhaus manifesto (1919)

823 *Below* Gropius and Meyer: Entrance front of the Sommerfeld House, Berlin-Dahlem (1920–1)

824 Ground-floor plan of the Bauhaus, Dessau (1925–6), by Gropius

not until 1927 that an architect, the Marxist Hannes Meyer, was appointed head of the newly established department of building.

The most influential figure in the Bauhaus teaching programme up to 1922 was Itten, who was responsible for the compulsory *Vorkurs* (preliminary course). In accordance with the naive faith of the Bauhaus that modern man must destroy the past before building the perfect earthly society, Itten's *Vorkurs* rejected all the traditional goals and techniques common to western European culture. Instead, he provided a series of exercises intended to promote the self-discovery of the student by removing his existing intellectual and emotional impediments.

The first opportunity for the realization of the Bauhaus ideal of uniting the arts and crafts under architecture came with the commission of a house for Adolf Sommerfeld, a sawmill owner and building contractor. The Sommerfeld House at Berlin-Dahlem (1920–1) was designed by Gropius and Meyer as an Expressionist variant on the theme of the peasant log-house with the angular and crystalline forms fashionable in Expressionist circles. Some of its jazzy ornamental detail, especially the notched beam ends, is similar in mood to Wright's in the Imperial Hotel, Tokyo.

The arrival in Weimar in 1921 of the abstract painter Theo van Doesburg (1883–1931) brought Gropius into contact with the Calvinistic simplicity and rectangularity of the Dutch movement *De Stijl* (the style). This had been founded in Amsterdam in 1917 by the painter Piet Mondrian, the architect Jacobus Johannes Pieter Oud, and van Doesburg, who is supposed to have claimed that 'the square is to us as the cross was to the early Christians'. The Expressionist emphasis on the crafts had doubtless been encouraged by the loss of faith in technology which had been brought about in some quarters by the mechanized mass slaughter of the First World War. However, the return of confidence in technology, coupled with the geometrical aesthetic of *De Stijl,* enabled Gropius to move to a position in 1923 of abandoning Itten's 'witches' kitchen' and of appointing the anti-Expressionist Hungarian artist László Moholy-Nagy (1895–1946) to run the *Vorkurs*. In contrast to Itten, Moholy-Nagy chose to dress in a kind of boiler-suit so that he looked like an industrial worker. In support of this new image, Gropius delivered an important lecture in 1923 with the title 'Art and Technology – a New Unity'. Architecturally this meant a return to the factory aesthetic which he had pioneered in his Fagus Factory of 1911.

This shift of stylistic emphasis was reflected in the physical removal of the Bauhaus to Dessau from Weimar. At Dessau in 1925–6 Gropius and Meyer put up a new home for the Bauhaus of reinforced concrete and glass curtain-walling, with a plan and elevations assembled

825 The Bauhaus, Dessau: bridge and workshop wing

with a studied asymmetry which was doubtless inspired by Dutch abstract or Neo-Plasticist painters such as Mondrian and van Doesburg. Resembling a factory, though there was no real justification for its doing so, it exercised a chilling influence during the next half-century on the design of a range of building types such as schools, houses and flats, which were also made to look like factories. This radical minimalist architecture was the result of an attempt to reject everything 'bourgeois' or 'impure', including pitched roofs, columns, ornament, mouldings, symmetry, generosity and warmth.

From Adolf Loos to the International Modern Style

The path to Gropius's pseudo-industrial minimalism had been cleared by architects such as Loos in Austria, Oud and Rietveld in Holland, and Le Corbusier in France. The aesthetic of Adolf Loos (1870–1933) is stated in his polemical essay *Ornament and Crime* (1908), an attack on

ornament sparked off by his disapproval of the Viennese Secessionists and doubtless owing much to Sullivan's essay *Ornament in Architecture* (1892), which he seems to have read on his visit to America in 1893. Loos expressed his theories in white, flat-roofed houses such as the Steiner House, Vienna (1910), with its stark, box-like garden front. Despite the external severity of his houses, their interiors are elegantly enriched with expensive materials, for he never overcame the dichotomy between his love of the costly products of traditional craftsmanship and his belief that vernacular and classical models were inappropriate for modern bourgeois man. The Steiner House was followed by a series of houses in which he developed his concept of the *Raumplan* or 'plan of volumes'. Featuring in the mass housing he designed in his capacity as architect to the Housing Department of Vienna in 1920–2, this reached a climax in complex split-level houses such as the Moller House, Vienna (1928), which were close in spirit to the villas of Le Corbusier.

Loos's mass housing schemes were not executed, but in Holland J. J. P. Oud (1890–1963), appointed housing

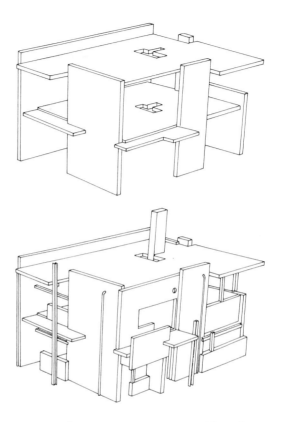

826 *Above* Dudok: the Town Hall, Hilversum (1924–31)

827 *Right* Schröder House, Utrecht, by Rietveld: Elements of construction (1924)

architect to the city of Rotterdam in 1918, reacted against the mannerist elements of the School of Amsterdam and erected workers' housing of white cubist simplicity at Hoek van Holland (1924–7) and at the Kiefhoek Estate, Rotterdam (1925). The geometrical severity current in Holland in the 1920s was partly the result of enthusiasm for the early work of Frank Lloyd Wright, which had been greater in Dutch architectural circles than anywhere else in Europe. Thus buildings by Willem Marinus Dudok (1884–1974) in Hilversum such as his Town Hall (1924–31), which is an abstract brick composition of bare overlapping planes and volumes, are not only Wrightian but are also close to the compositional methods of the leading *De Stijl* or Neo-Plasticist painters. In promoting their new style, these painters had aimed at juxtaposing two-dimensional elements so as to provide inter-relationships which would be characterized by a 'new plasticity'. 'We demand', wrote van Doesburg, 'the building up of our environment according to creative laws, deriving from a set principle. These laws, linked to those of economics, mathematics, engineering, hygiene, etc. lead to a new plastic unity.' Though the language is empty and pretentious, like that of many other early-twentieth-

century manifestos, it was accompanied by a dynamic three-dimensional expression which is especially associated with the work of Gerrit Rietveld (1888–1964).

A cabinet-maker by training, Rietveld designed the celebrated Red and Blue chair in 1918 and the Schröder House at Utrecht in 1924, both of which seem assembled from sliding or moveable parts with planes overlapping at their intersections. The Schröder House, with its flexibly-planned principal floor which could either be used as an almost unbroken single space or divided with sliding panels into four rooms, is a realization of propostion 11 in van Doesburg's *16 Points of a Plastic Architecture* (1924):

The new architecture is anti-cubic, that is to say, it does not try to freeze the different functional space cells in one closed cube. Rather, it throws the

828 Exterior of the Schröder House, Utrecht

functional space cells (as well as the overhanging planes, balcony volumes, etc.) centrifugally from the core of the cube. And through this means, height, width, depth, and time (i.e. an imaginary four-dimensional entity) approaches a totally new plastic expression in open spaces. In this way architecture acquires a more or less floating aspect that, so to speak, works against the gravitational forces of nature.

Though in realizing these essentially twentieth-century ambitions the Schröder House can claim to be the first monument of the International Modern movement, it was constructed of wholly traditional materials, timber, brick and plaster. Thus the modern style was not conceived as an expression of reinforced concrete construction, but was an image of modernity imposed regardless of practical considerations. What is also noticeable at the Schröder House is the simple will to shock, for it is a small semi-detached villa added whimsically on to the end of a modest row of nineteenth-century houses. The colours, yellow, blue and red, in which some of its external features are picked out, are those selected as the primary colours for *De Stijl* by the mystical mathematician, Dr Schoenmaekers, who was a powerful influence on Mondrian. Schoenmaekers invented the term 'Neo-Plasticism' as part of his mystical cosmology, and argued that yellow, red and blue 'are the

only colours existing', since yellow symbolizes the vertical movement of the sun's rays; blue, the horizontal line of power which is the course of the earth round the sun; and red, the mating of both.

The International Modern style was given appropriately international expression at the Weissenhofsiedlung (white house estate) laid out at Stuttgart by the Deutscher Werkbund as part of a workers' housing exhibition in 1927. This consists of terraced (row) and detached houses and apartments in the new flat-roofed minimalist style which are somewhat clumsily related to each other and to the site, though the original scheme of 1925 was for an Expressionist hill-village with a unified and organic distribution of buildings. The architects in 1927 included Gropius, Poelzig, Behrens, Bruno and Max Taut, Corbusier, Oud, and Ludwig Mies van der Rohe (1886–1969) as artistic director. In 1908–11 Mies had worked in Behrens's office in Neubabelsberg where he had absorbed the current Schinkel Revival, as can be seen in his neo-classical Perls house, Berlin-Zehlendorf (1911), Urbig house, Berlin-Neubabelsberg (1914), and project of 1912 for the Bismarck Monument at Bingen.

After the war Mies was caught up in the Expressionist enthusiasm for glass of Taut and his circle. In 1920–1 he made a crystalline design for a visionary glass skyscraper on a plan as curvaceous as any by Hugo Haring or Gaudí. His entry in the competition of 1928 for remodelling the Alexander Platz in Berlin, which he proposed surrounding with soulless slab blocks was an ominous foretaste of the barbarous treatment of historic city centres by modern planners. His monument of 1926 in Berlin to the Communists Karl Liebknecht and Rosa Luxemburg was an abstract rectilinear composition of twisted clinker brick, enlivened with a hammer and sickle inscribed within a large star. Though Expressionist in its aggressive stridency, it is inspired as a composition by the paintings of the *De Stijl* movement with a strong dose of influence from Frank Lloyd Wright. The same combination of Dutch and Wrightian influence informs the low horizontal lines and free plans of buildings such

829 Mies van der Rohe: Design for a glass skyscraper (1920–1)

830 Mies van der Rohe: Interior of the German Pavilion, the International Exhibition, Barcelona (1929)

Pavilion with the 'Barcelona chair'. Of leather and stainless steel with an X-frame of faintly neo-Greek or Schinkelesque character, this became one of the hallmarks of avant-garde domestic interiors in Europe and North America. Mies became director of the Bauhaus in 1930 but he closed it down three years later in face of opposition from the National Socialist regime. After a brief but influential visit to England in 1934 he settled in America, there starting a new career which we shall investigate in due course.

The classical tradition in inter-war Germany, Czechoslovakia and Slovenia

It should be stressed that the International Modern style represented only one aspect of architecture in Germany between the wars. Leading architects such as Wilhelm Kreis, Emil Fahrenkamp, Hermann Giesler and German Bestelmeyer, worked in the 1920s and 1930s in the powerful adaptable language that had been established by the time of the First World War. Office blocks in Düsseldorf such as Kreis's Wilhelm-Marx House (1922–4) austerely echo the brick style and vertical emphasis of Messel and Höger, as do the buildings of 1924–7 for the Rhine Steel Works at Düsseldorf and Nuremberg by Kreis's pupil and successor as professor of architecture at Düsseldorf, Emil Fahrenkamp (1885–1966).

The architectural approach encouraged by the National Socialist party was essentially pluralist in that it supported the use of the modern style of steel and glass for factories; the classical style for major public buildings; and a range of regional vernacular styles for country buildings. Renewed emphasis was now put on the search for a classic national style which had pre-occupied architects such as Heinrich Tessenow (1876–1950) before the First World War. The stripped Doric style of Tessenow's Festival House at Hellerau near Dresden (1910–12), and of Josef Hoffmann's Austrian Pavilion at the Werkbund Exhibition at Cologne (1914), was a particular source of inspiration in the 1920s and

as his German Pavilion at the International Exhibition at Barcelona (1929), with its open internal spaces divided by asymmetrically placed screens of glass or polished marble. The cantilevered tubular steel chair which, based on suggestions by Marcel Breuer and Mart Stam, he had designed for the Weissenhof exhibition houses, was replaced in the more luxurious Barcelona

831 Tessenow: The Festival House, Hellerau, near Dresden (1910–12)

30s for architects such as Kreis in his Art Museum at Düsseldorf (1925–6), and for Paul Ludwig Troost (1878–1934) in his Temples of Honour in Munich (1934–5; dem. 1947). Commemorating National Socialists who had fallen in the *putsch* of 1923, these open classical mausolea of moderate scale were visually appropriate punctuation marks in the monumental setting of Klenze's Königsplatz. Another successful and stylish classical building of this period is the theatre at Saarbrücken, with its sweeping hemi-cycle of columns in the simple Tuscan Doric order. This was erected in 1938 from designs by Paul Baumgarten to mark the return of the Saar to Germany.

A number of Bavarian government offices and public buildings were built in Munich by Bestelmeyer and Troost, including the latter's heavy Schinkelesque House of German Art (1933–7). These generally harmonized well with the city's late neo-classical atmosphere, but in Berlin Albert Speer (1905–81), a pupil of Tessenow, was responsible for a megalomaniac master plan from 1937 which envisaged inflated and unreal public buildings along vast avenues with a triumphal arch and a gigantic 'people's hall' beneath the biggest dome in the world. Both the impossible scale of the architecture and the accompanying populist rhetoric about the morally improving role of 'community experience' repeat exactly the architectural effusions of Boullée and Ledoux in late-eighteenth-century France. Speer's major executed work, the now demolished New Chancellery, Berlin (1938–9), was a more realistic essay in stripped

832 Entrance courtyard of the New Chancellery, Berlin (1938–9), by Speer

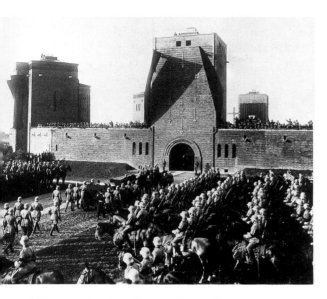

833 Kruger: Tannenberg Monument (1924–7)

classicism with a complex plan cleverly adapted to the long and awkward site. The buildings of the Berlin Olympic Stadium (1934–6), with its Gate, Square and May Field, by Werner March and Albert Speer, have often been admired as a fresh and brilliant modern adaptation of a classically inspired language.

The deep-rooted monument mania of Germany reached a climax in the 1930s and 1940s. Once again the 1920s had suggested the appropriate architectural language, in the form of the Tannenberg Monument, East Prussia (1924–7; dem. 1945), designed by the brothers Walter and Johannes Kruger. This grim circle of eight rectangular granite towers, in which Hindenburg was buried in 1935, was built in commemoration of the Battle of Tannenberg in August 1914 in which Russian forces had been defeated by German. In form and function it was a source of inspiration to Wilhelm Kreis, who after 1941 adopted a similarly Boullée-esque language for the giant abstract monuments in celebration of 'German sacrifice and victory' which he was ordered to execute across Europe. A stylistically related building type was the *Ordensburg*, or

citadel of order, of which a number were erected in 1935 on remote hilltop sites as training and community centres. The rock-faced semi-Romanesque style of Bestelmeyer was adopted by Hermann Giesler for the *Ordensburg* at Sonthofen, Bavaria, which blends well with its romantic setting, as does another surviving *Ordensburg* at Vogelsang, south of Cologne. Under the general direction of Fritz Todt, the roads and bridges forming the new *Autobahn*, some of them designed by Paul Bonatz, also harmonized well with the sweeping scale of the landscapes through which they passed.

The Slovenian Jože Plečnik (1872–1957) built extensively in Prague, including the church of the Sacred Heart (1928) and additions to the Castle (1920–30), as well as in Ljubljiana. He is increasingly hailed as the most inventive of all twentieth-century classicists.

Early twentieth-century France and the Louis Seize Revival

French twentieth-century architecture up to the Second World War was in general less interesting than in Germany, despite the presence of two contrasting geniuses, Auguste Perret and Le Corbusier. We have already touched on the vigorous Art Nouveau strain. We should now take account of the opposition in French architecture to Art Nouveau. One of the forms this took was a Louis Seize Revival which, though it has been neglected by architectural historians, was led by architects of considerable finesse such as Charles-Frédéric Mewès, René Sergent, Walter Destailleur, and the Grandpierre brothers. These scholarly and refined architects followed on from Laloux, Girault and Nénot, whom we admired in Chapter 9, to provide an ideal setting for the opulent cosmopolitan world of high society in the last years before the Great War, a world recorded so imaginatively in the novels of Proust.

Charles-Frédéric Mewès (1858–1914) formed a partnership in 1900 with the English architect Arthur Davis (1878–1951) who, like him, had been trained at the Ecole des Beaux-Arts and in the same atelier. The architectural practice of Mewès and Davis, which

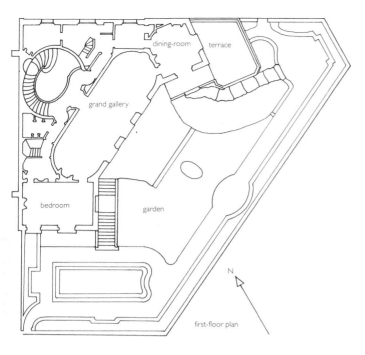

dining-room   terrace

grand gallery

bedroom   garden

N

first-floor plan

834 Plan of the first floor at 18, Avenue Elysiée-Reclus, Paris (1908–9), by Mewès

continued long after the former's death, was a kind of multinational company which was much rarer then than it would be today. Apart from Davis in England, Mewès had representatives in Germany, France, Spain and South America. His best independent works are his own house in a mannered Giulio Romano-like style at no. 36 boulevard des Invalides, Paris (c.1888), and the brilliantly planned *pavillon* for the actor Lucien Guitry at no. 18 avenue Elisée-Reclus, Paris (1908–9; dem. c.1960). For the diamond merchant and banker Jules Porgès he built an enormous chateau in 1899–1904 at Rochefort-en-Yvelines, in the Rambouillet area, distantly inspired by Rousseau's Hôtel de Salm in Paris. In partnership with Davis, Mewès was responsible for a number of major buildings in central London, including the Ritz Hotel (1904–6) and the Morning Post Offices (1906–7). Introducing not only a suave Louis Seize classicism into the capital, but also the most up-to-date steel-frame construction, imported from Chicago, these can be seen as a parallel to the contribution to American architecture of McKim, Mead and White.

835 *Opposite top* West entrance front of the Château of Voisins, Rochefort-en-Yvelines (1903–6), by Sergent

836 *Opposite bottom* Sergent: Grand salon of the Musée Nissim de Camondo, 63 rue de Monceau, Paris (1910–13)

The career of René Sergent (1865–1927) was similar to that of Mewès. Between 1901 and 1915 he erected numerous sumptuous private houses in Paris, châteaux in the neighbouring countryside, and the Trianon Palace Hôtel in Versailles. His château of Voisins not far from Mewès's at Rochefort-en-Yvelines, was built for the Comte de Fels in 1903–6 as an impeccable paraphrase of the style of A.-J. Gabriel (1698–1782), on whom Fels was to publish a scholarly monograph in 1912. The climax of this atavistic recreation of eighteenth-century perfection came with the mansion Sergent built in Paris in 1910–13 at 63 rue de Monceau for Comte Moïse de Camondo, a member of the fabulously wealthy banking family. Now known as the Musée Nissim de Camondo, it was built round Moïse's superb collection of eighteenth-century French furniture, decorative arts, boiseries and paintings. Though its entrance façade is modelled on Gabriel's Petit Trianon, the building is by no means a dead reproduction: for example, its complex L-shaped plan is essentially a post-eighteenth-century conception.

Perret, Garnier and Sauvage

In the meantime the infinite adaptability of the classical tradition was being demonstrated in the very different architecture of Auguste Perret (1874–1954), whose achievement it was to draw reinforced concrete construction into the orbit of the French rationalist tradition. The son of a builder, he was trained from 1891 under Guadet, a pupil of Labrouste, at the Ecole des Beaux-Arts, where he was joined two years later by his brother, Gustave. They left without taking diplomas in order to be free to practise as building contractors in the family firm established by their father. Auguste Perret believed that the demand for structural integrity, as called for by theorists such as Viollet-le-Duc, Choisy and

837, 838 Façade detail and plan of 25 bis, rue Franklin, Paris (1903–4), by Perret

1 kitchen
2 dining-room
3 drawing-room
4 bedroom
5 smoking-room
6 boudoir

Guadet, could be realized by adopting the recently invented technique of reinforced concrete. Though accepting Viollet's belief in Greek and Gothic architecture as the expression of rational construction and ostensibly disapproving of the Renaissance, he was inescapably influenced by the French classical tradition from François Mansart onwards. This was characterized by framed and panelled façades forming a crisply trabeated architecture which seemed an echo of timber construction. These solid stone façades were articulated with non-load-bearing pilasters and engaged columns which were aesthetic expressions of functional support. However, in reinforced concrete construction the wall was a functional framework with an infilling of non-load-bearing materials and corresponded throughout to constructional reality.

Reinforced or ferro-concrete construction, in which the concrete is threaded with steel rods and mesh so as to give it tensile strength, had been pioneered by François Coignet in the 1850s. It was developed slowly by him and then by Francois Hennebique (1842–1921),

who took out two important patents in 1892. Hennebique used the technique mainly in industrial buildings, but the first multistorey apartment building of ferro-concrete is Perret's no. 25 bis rue Franklin, Paris (1903–4). The reinforced concrete frame is clearly expressed on the exterior, though it is sheathed in strips of ceramic tiling, while the same material is used to form attractive petal patterns in the non-load-bearing panels between. To have as many rooms as possible in the front, each with a window, he eliminated the customary courtyard and instead canted the front façade inwards, creating a kind of vestigial courtyard at the front of the building. His novel use of glass bricks for the stair and bathroom towers at the rear enabled him to build to the extremity of the site – since, had he adopted conventional window openings, the rear wall would have had to be brought forward so as not to infringe the neighbours' easement rights. In fact the building was deeply rooted in the French rational tradition, for the plan, including the division of each apartment into a ladies' and a gentlemen's side, was inspired by one by Viollet-le-Duc. Perret avoided all internal load-bearing walls, replacing them with thin and sometimes moveable screens between slender point-supports or piers, a technique which was to be adopted by Corbusier.

At the Théâtre des Champs-Elysées, Paris (1911–12), Perret provided a more harmonious and classical façade based on a design for the building by Henri van de Velde. The reinforced concrete frame is masked on the front elevation and the adjacent rounded corner by a skin of grey marble. This incorporates large panels of figure sculpture by Antoine Bourdelle set in emphatic frames so that the reliefs resemble the carved metopes in a Doric frieze. A stripped Doric austerity reigns in the bare interiors, also of grey marble, for example the foyer and staircase, though in the coved dome of the main auditorium he allowed colour in the form of Symbolist paintings by Maurice Denis and K.-X. Roussel.

Other architects who chose to enrich concrete with materials such as glazed earthenware, ceramics and mosaics included Paul Guadet, as in his own house at no. 95 boulevard Murat (1912), and André Arfvidson (1870–1935) in his artists' studios in the rue Campagne-Première (1915–20). Perret's war memorial church of Notre-Dame du Raincy (1922–3) at Le Raincy north east of Paris, is the first major aesthetically satisfactory use of exposed ferro-concrete, not covered with decorative cladding. In this glass and concrete cage, like a modern version of King's College chapel, Cambridge, the non-load-bearing outer walls consist simply of a reticulated screen of open panels in pre-cast concrete, filled with coloured glass. This is arranged in the sequence of the spectrum, from yellow at the entrance to purple at the high altar. Internally, a continuous segmental shell vault over the nave and transverse barrel-vaults over the narrow aisles are supported by four rows of free-standing columns, 37 feet (11m) high.

839 Perret: Théâtre des Champs-Elysées (1911–12)

Perret not only gave the columns a version of Greek entasis and diminution, with a diameter of 17 inches (43cm) at the foot rising to 14 (35.5cm) at the summit, but also a version of Gothic fluting, since they were modelled in the casting with fillets and projections like Gothic compound piers. The strange western tower similarly combines an effect of soaring Gothic verticality with the use of piled-up cylinders like classical columns. Indeed, the church in its entirety can be seen as a late product of the call by French architectural theorists from the time of Perrault for a rational Graeco-Gothic synthesis, as illustrated by Soufflot in his church of Ste-Geneviève (the Panthéon).

Though Notre Dame du Raincy is aesthetically satisfactory, it has turned out to be a failure from a

constructional point of view. By 1985 the rusting metal reinforcements were exposed beneath the crumbling concrete surfaces in large areas of the church, both outside and inside. The sad fate of the building, presenting restorers with a near-insoluble problem, seems to contradict the generally held view that Perret, by acting as contractor as well as architect, was in an unusually strong position to ensure the highest standards of execution. The lesson of the building is that concrete, as the ancient Romans and as some of Perret's contemporary critics knew, should ideally be clad in an attractive and durable facing material.

840 *Opposite* Perret: Interior of Notre-Dame du Raincy, Le Raincy, near Paris (1922–3), looking west

841 *Below* Tony Garnier: Design for residential quarter from *Une Cité Industrielle*, 1917

In his apartment block at no. 51–5 rue Raynouard, Paris (1929), which, like his 25 bis rue Franklin, contained a flat for himself as well as his drawing office, he took the theme of the rue Franklin block and expressed it in the exposed ferro-concrete he had used at Le Raincy. The trabeated façades are symmetrically ordered, while the triangular site enabled Perret in planning his own apartment to indulge in the elegant geometrical games which Ledoux had enjoyed in the Hôtel Montmorency (1770). Perret also designed two government buildings in Paris with rather unusual functions, the Mobilier National (1934–5), a storehouse for antique furniture belonging to the French state, and the Musée des Travaux Publics (1936), designed to house engineering models but now the home of the Economic and Social Council. In contrast to most contemporary and subsequent buildings of reinforced concrete, Perret's

are notable for their refinement of detail, the careful proportioning of their structural beams and piers, their finely modelled cornices and mouldings, and their slender columns with entasis, delicate capitals and faceted surfaces like Greek fluting. With their harmonious and largely symmetrical distribution of blocks round axial courtyards, and their grave hypostyle halls, the Mobilier National and Musée des Travaux Publics constitute a classic example of French logic and order in architecture. Unfortunately, they suffer from the drawback of being essentially cerebral and not visual. Thus it is more attractive to read about their logic in architectural history books than to see its visual consequences at first hand in the buildings themselves, which are deprived of life by their grey and unprepossessing concrete surfaces.

Two experimental architects who shared something of Perret's vision should be mentioned here, Tony Garnier and Henri Sauvage. The designs of Tony Garnier (1869–1948) for a modern urban Utopia, prepared in 1901–4 and exhibited at the Ecole des Beaux-Arts in 1904, were published in two volumes as *Une Cité Industrielle* ('An industrial city') in 1917. The planning of this neo-Arcadian city, with its parks and trees and its cubic classical buildings of white reinforced concrete, was a combination of the formal axiality and grid patterns of Haussmann and the Beaux-Arts tradition with the more irregular street layouts analysed by Camillo Sitte in his influential book, *Der Städte-Bau nach seinen künstlerischen Grundsätzen* ('City building according to artistic principles', Vienna 1889), which was translated into French in 1902. Reacting against the unplanned nineteenth-century growth of industrial cities like his native Lyons, Garnier gave great consideration to the separation of functions in his ideal city, so that buildings for governmental, cultural, residential, industrial and agricultural purposes occupy separate zones, clearly linked by roads of appropriately varying size. This zoning set an unhappy precedent for the planners of twentieth-century cities since it creates dead administrative and shopping centres, in marked contrast to the vibrant life of the historic cities of Europe which is created precisely by the intermingling of domestic and public buildings. Garnier's naive Utopianism led him to plan his city without churches, law courts, police station, barracks or prison, on the grounds that these would no longer be necessary in the ideal socialist city, an idea he could well have borrowed from Ledoux's *Ville idéale des salines de Chaux* of 1804. He was appointed city architect of Lyons in 1905 but failed to produce any buildings of real distinction.

A better architect than Garnier, though of puzzlingly ambiguous outlook, was Henri Sauvage (1873–1932). He began as a strikingly vivacious Art Nouveau designer and ended by proposing stepped concrete ziggurats which rival the Futurist projects of Sant'Elia. He was trained at the Ecole des Beaux-Arts where he met the brother of Louis Majorelle, the Art Nouveau furniture manufacturer at Nancy. As a result Sauvage gained the commission for the Villa Majorelle at Nancy, which he built in 1898–1901 in a striking half-medieval, half-Art Nouveau style as a centre for the Majorelle family and firm. A contrasting interest in low-cost bourgeois housing resulted in an apartment block at 26 rue Vavin, Paris (1912), which Sauvage designed with his partner Charles Sarazin. With its reinforced concrete frame cheerfully faced in white and blue faience tiles, this exploits the stepped-back form, which was a way of achieving height within the existing building regulations. Sauvage gave this theme even bolder expression in his large apartment block in the rue des Amiraux, Paris (1923–4), built for a socialist housing cooperative and containing at its core a top-lit indoor swimming-pool. His preoccupation with stepped buildings culminated in 1927–31 in the design of a series of unexecuted hotels and apartment houses in Paris in the form of towering neo-Babylonian pyramids.

Le Corbusier

One of the most significant cultural events of the 1920s was the Exposition Internationale des Arts Décoratifs et Industriels Modernes, held in Paris in 1925 as the first

international exhibition of decorative arts since the Great War. In the periphery of this exhibition was an architectural time-bomb, ignored or despised by many: the Pavillon de l'Esprit Nouveau, designed by Le Corbusier and his partner and cousin, Pierre Jeanneret. This stark white box with a tree growing through the middle of it had an annexe containing a model of Le Corbusier's Plan Voisin for Paris, which proposed ripping out much of the historic centre of the city and replacing it with a group of 18 gigantic skyscrapers. Both the Pavillon and the Plan Voisin were the product of Le Corbusier's thinking over a period of several years. Born in 1887 at La Chaux-de-Fonds, Switzerland, as Charles-Edouard Jeanneret, Le Corbusier (as he called himself

842 *Left* Exterior of 25 rue Vavin, Paris (1912), by Sauvage

843 *Below* Model of Le Corbusier's Plan Voisin for Paris (1925). The Louvre is at lower left.

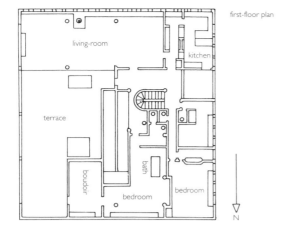

first-floor plan

living-room

kitchen

terrace

boudoir

bath

bedroom

bedroom

N

844, 845 *Above* Plan and exterior of the Villa Savoye, Poissy (1929–31), by Le Corbusier

846 *Left* Section of the Villa Savoye

847 *Below* Le Corbusier: Ville Contemporaine (1922)

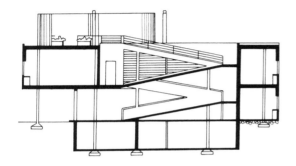

from 1920) studied art and architecture in 1900–5 under the painter Charles L'Eplattenier at the Ecole d'Art at La Chaux-de-Fonds, the local school of applied arts. Under the influence of Ruskin, Nietzsche, Sitte and the social ideals of the Arts and Crafts movement, to which L'Eplattenier had introduced him, Le Corbusier prepared

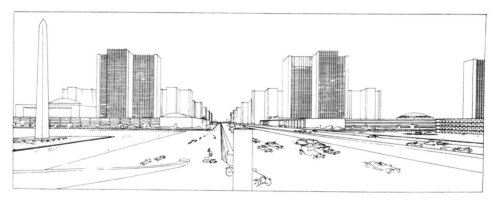

an uncompleted and unpublished book in 1910 called *La Construction des Villes* ('The building of cities'). This was a sensitive study of town planning based on Sitte's analyses of historic towns, an approach which Le Corbusier was totally to repudiate in his subsequent career and in such books as *Urbanisme* (1925).

Also influential on the young Le Corbusier was the period during which he worked in Perret's office in Paris in 1908–9 and in Behrens's in Berlin-Neubabelsberg in 1910–11. Their classicizing influence, and perhaps that of Frank Lloyd Wright, can be seen in early works at La Chaux-de-Fonds such as the villa he built for his parents in 1911–12 and the villa for Anatole Schwob (1916–17). His project of 1914–15 for simple low-cost houses of reinforced concrete, which he called Domino, was inspired by Garnier's Cité Industrielle and by the minimalist style of Adolf Loos. The name Domino was coined from 'Domus' (house) plus 'innovation'.

He developed this theme in his successive projects for 'Citrohan' houses in 1919–22 which he published in his journal *L'Esprit Nouveau* ('The new spirit') and in his book *Vers une architecture* ('Towards an architecture', 1923). The name Citrohan was a deliberate variant of that of the motor manufacturer Citroën so as to suggest that the houses were as efficient and up-to-date as motor cars. In keeping with his ambition of abolishing conventional walls and rooms these houses were raised off the ground so as to float above stilts or pilotis, and incorporated roof patios and split-level planning. This Citrohan type was finally realized in houses of 1922–3 at Vaucresson, Seine-et-Oise, and for the Purist painter Amédée Ozenfant at 53 avenue Reille, Paris, and also in the Pavillon de l'Esprit Nouveau at the Paris Exposition of 1925. This pavilion, essentially a dwelling unit of the Citrohan type, was presented in the form of a flat from one of the apartment blocks in his proposed Ville Contemporaine of 1922. The most ambitious examples of these uncomfortable show-piece houses are the villa at Garches (1927) and the Villa Savoye at Poissy (1929–31), but the type had been demonstrated in miniature in the workers' housing estate at Pessac, near

Bordeaux, which Le Corbusier had designed for the industrialist Henri Frugès in 1925. These white concrete houses were, however, found unacceptable by their occupants, who attempted to make them more habitable and recognizably domestic by filling in the useless empty spaces beneath the pilotis, replacing the roof terraces with pitched roofs, and shortening the long strips of windows to more conventional forms.

The thinking which lay behind Pessac was part of the belief current in avant-garde circles in the 1920s and 1930s that architecture ought to do you good and should serve as an instrument of moral and social reform. This rhetoric can be detected in Le Corbusier's *Vers une architecture*, an influential collection of slogans proclaiming the virtues of a machine aesthetic, some of them echoing the oft-repeated tenets of the rationalist tradition in French architectural thinking, others justifying his chosen architectural language in moral and hygienic terms. One of the most extreme expressions of Le Corbusier's approach was his Plan Voisin for the arrogant destruction of much of the centre of Paris between Montmartre and the river Seine. This was named after Gabriel Voisin, proprietor of one of the motor firms, including Peugeot and Citroën, who subsidized the Pavillon de l'Esprit Nouveau. In its utter disregard for the site and for local customs, it can in some ways be regarded as the *reductio ad absurdum* of Beaux-Arts planning, though similar failures were to recur in his city of Chandigarh in the 1950s. With their axially placed skyscrapers linked with giant highways for high-speed traffic, the Ville Contemporaine and the Plan Voisin provided a seductive visual imagery which was to be adopted throughout the world with unhappy effect after the Second World War, though central Paris has so far largely escaped this treatment. The historical sensitivity which Le Corbusier had learned from Camillo Sitte had been replaced by a worship of the poetry of speed and machinery: 'The city that has speed', he claimed, 'has success.'

In the early 1930s Le Corbusier was able to realize on a comparatively modest scale, in Paris, some of the

848 Le Corbusier: Exterior of the Swiss Pavilion, the University City, near Paris (1930–2)

proposals for a Utopian city which he made in 1933 in his book *La Ville Radieuse* ('The radiant city'). These hugely influential buildings, the progenitors of numerous slab blocks the world over, include the Swiss Pavilion (1930–2) in the University City in the south of Paris, and the Salvation Army Hostel (1929–33), known as the Cité de Refuge. The Swiss Pavilion is a four-storey rectangular slab block of steel-frame construction raised on large pilotis of reinforced concrete and containing student dormitories. This is linked to a high stair tower and a one-storeyed refectory or lounge, both of which sport one elevation that is concave in plan. These curves were intended to offset the uncompromising rectangularity which reigns elsewhere in the building.

Moreover, the curved exterior wall of the refectory is coated with rubble stonework, to contrast with the unadorned panels of reconstructed stone on the blank end walls of the main dormitory block. To protect inhabitants from the sunlight streaming through the continuous bands of fenestration on the main south-facing façade, the windows were subsequently fitted with aluminium blinds, 'thus', as one architectural historian complained, 'interrupting the purity of the original form'.

Similar problems bedevilled the Salvation Army Hostel, which also had a great curtain wall of glass, again facing south, with hermetically sealed windows. These were to have been double-glazed with hot and cold air circulating between the two skins, but this system was not adopted; the greenhouse effect was eventually tempered by improved air-conditioning and the construction of a concrete *brise-soleil* in front of the entire façade. Though this was the work of another architect, it followed hints made by Le Corbusier in 1933 for the treatment of tall buildings in Algiers. Modern architecture has often been described and defended as though it were the inevitable response to new materials and techniques. In fact it was the result of an iconoclastic image of modernity for the creation of which the technology often did not exist and in some cases never has. For example, the preoccupation with glass, which had its origins in the fantasies of Taut, has produced a chain of functionally problematical buildings from the 1930s up to I. M. Pei's Hancock Building, Boston, Massachusetts (1972).

For the Universal Exposition held in Paris in 1937 Le Corbusier designed the Pavillon des Temps Nouveaux with vertical supports of steel latticework, tensile steel cables and a tented canvas roof suspended in a catenary curve. This curious image, derived from the reconstruction of the Hebraic tabernacle in the wilderness which Le Corbusier had proposed as a model in *Vers une architecture*, was combined with references to contemporary aeronautical construction. The political iconography of the Pavillon was made clear in the inscription over its pulpit-like rostrum, 'a new era has begun, an era of solidarity'. This was a slogan of the Popular Front, the union of Communist, Socialist and Radical parties, founded in 1935, which ran France in 1936–7 with Léon Blum as prime minister. The building did, indeed, resemble a shrine of the new modernist faith, as outlined in Corbusier's *Ville Radieuse*, with its pulpit and, mounted on its axis like the Commandments above an altar, the Athens Charter which had been proclaimed in 1933 by CIAM, the International Congresses of Modern Architecture. CIAM had been founded in 1928 with Le Corbusier and the engineer and art-historian Sigfried Giedion as dominant members. The most extreme and dogmatic of its documents was the Athens Charter, which insisted on the importance in city planning of functional zoning and of high-rise, widely-spaced apartment blocks.

Though Le Corbusier was the leading architect in the new style, his outlook was shared by architects such as Robert Mallet-Stevens (1886–1945), André Lurçat (1894–1970), and Pierre Chareau. Mallet-Stevens's houses in the rue Mallet-Stevens, Paris (1926–7), are cubist concrete boxes, while Lurçat's school at Villejuif, Seine (1931), is a striking essay in the International Style. The house by Chareau for Dr Dalsace in the rue Saint-Guillaume, Paris, designed in collaboration with B. Bijvouet, has an exposed iron and glass façade which earned the building the Corbusier-inspired name of 'machine à habiter'. Some of Le Corbusier's ideals for city planning emerged in Villeurbanne, an industrial quarter of Lyons where M.-L. Leroux provided a group of skyscrapers in 1932–5 surrounding M.-R. Giroux's contemporary but stripped classical Hôtel de Ville.

French architecture in traditional styles between the wars

The most characteristic product of what one might describe as the establishment in the French architectural scene in the 1930s was the Palais de Chaillot, built in Paris in 1935–7 from designs by Jacques Carlu, Louis-Hippolyte Boileau and Léon Azéma. This was conceived

849 The 1937 International Exposition, Paris, with the Palais de Chaillot by Carlu, Boileau and Azéma

850 Barge: Ste-Odile, Paris (1936)

as a monumental group of permanent structures, built for the International Exposition or Paris World's Fair of 1937 to house exhibition and concert halls. The group terminates the magnificent axial vista leading from Gabriel's Ecole Militaire to the Eiffel Tower. Another ambitious building erected for this Exposition was the Pontifical Pavilion by Paul Tournon (1881–1964), with its angular jazzy interiors in the so-called 'Art Deco' style which had been established at the international exposition in Paris of 1925. Tournon, a professor from 1925 at the Ecole Nationale Supérieur des Beaux-Arts, of which he became director in 1942, was the leading ecclesiastical architect in France between the two world wars.

The great burst of church building from the 1920s was partly occasioned in northern France by the devastations of the First World War, and was also stimulated in the Paris area by the body known as the 'Chantiers du Cardinal'. As often before, neo-Byzantine styles were popular: they seemed to lack the specific historical associations of classical or Gothic buildings and thus could be used to express a kind of neutral modernity. An imposing example is J. Barge's Ste-Odile, avenue Stéphane Mallarmé, Paris (1936).

The best architect associated with the Exposition of 1937 was Roger-Henri Expert (1882–1955), who was responsible for the layout of the fountains between the Palais de Chaillot and the Seine, and also for the dramatic floodlighting. It was for exhibitions, with their inherent need to capture the attention of the public, that the architectural use of lighting was first exploited. It featured in the World's Fair at Chicago in 1893 but was given its most imaginative expression by Albert Speer in the 1930s. In the 'cathedrals of light' which he created as a backdrop for party rallies he realized the 'architecture of shadows' hinted at in the late eighteenth century by Boullée.

Expert's Pavillon du Tourisme at the Exposition in Grenoble in 1925 was a vigorous Art Deco composition. However, in a group of villas of 1924–7 at Arcachon in the south-west of France, notably the Villa Téthys and Villa Kypris, he combined Art Deco hints with a stripped classical vocabulary. These elegant houses offer a curious foretaste of American post-modernism of the 1980s, though Expert was more fastidious as a designer than Graves or Moore. His French Legation at Belgrade (1928–33) continues the Arcachon theme but in a weightier, more classical way, while his interiors for the steamboat 'Le Normandie' (1931–5) are Art Deco at its most fashionable and most streamlined. The many architects whose work has the traditional yet modern flavour of Expert include Albert Laprade (1883–1978), designer of the Musée des Colonies at Vincennes.

The diversity of the pavilions at the 1937 Exposition paralleled the extreme political divisions in Europe during the tragic build-up to the Second World War. However, the German pavilion, designed by Albert Speer and containing as a principal exhibit his designs for the Party Rally site at Nuremberg, was in a similarly stripped classical style to the Russian Pavilion designed by Boris Iofan (see p. 647). The two buildings faced each other in a dramatic confrontation which was to be realized on the battlefield all too soon.

851 Ostberg: Stockholm Town Hall (designed 1908, executed 1911–23)

852 Klint: Façade of Grundtvig Church, Copenhagen (1913, 1921–6), with adjacent housing

Scandinavia and Finland

Scandinavian and Finnish architecture brought to a climax in the early twentieth century the National Romanticism which had emerged in the cultural and political climate of the 1880s and 1890s. This implied a reaction from the arbitrary reproduction of a range of European historical styles, characteristic of mid- and later-nineteenth-century architecture, towards a more sophisticated reinterpretation of indigenous styles. One of the first and finest examples is the Town Hall at Copenhagen (1892–1902) by Martin Nyrop (1849–1923), though the Municipal Council was initially worried that the design did not conform to one or other of the accepted traditional styles. With its crenellated Gothic skyline combined with Dutch or Northern Renaissance fenestration, its use of local materials such as dark red brick, Staevns limestone and Bornholm granite, and its fine craftsmanship, it set a precedent which reached a climax in Stockholm Town Hall, romantically set on the water's edge. Designed by Ragnar Östberg (1866–1945) in 1908 and executed

with modifications in 1911–23, this elegant evocation of a mythical national past blended references to the Doges' Palace at Venice with Swedish Romanesque and Renaissance overtones. Its mannered refinement of detail, combined with clean lines which looked recognizably 'modern', enabled it to exercise a wide influence on European architects between the wars who were reluctant to accept the International Modern style.

The Engelbrekt parish church in Stockholm (1906–14) by Lars Israel Wahlman (1870–1952), with a fussy exterior but an imposing interior with parabolic brick arches, is another early monument of National Romanticism, while in Copenhagen the Grundtvig church (1913, 1921–6) by Peder Vilhelm Jensen-Klint (1853–1930) is a more startling recreation of Baltic Gothic in Expressionist terms. Its stepped façade of colossal height with a configuration like organ pipes reaches a high pitch of emotional tension. At the same time it is well related to the surrounding houses, which were completed by his son Kaare Klint (1888–1954) in 1940. An earthier and more organic style with some Art Nouveau overtones was adopted by Sigfrid Ericson (1879–1958) for his Masthuggs church, Göteborg (1910–14). Hugging the barren rock by the harbour, this has a warm interior with a high timber roof like a log cabin. Like many of his contemporaries, Ericson subsequently adopted a refined classicism.

Nowhere was National Romanticism given more organic and powerful expression than in Finland. Here it is especially associated with Lars Sonck (1870–1956) and Eliel Saarinen (1873–1950), whose work combines references to Scandinavian medieval architecture, continental Art Nouveau, and Richardsonian Romanesque. Sonck's most characteristic works in Finnish granite are the neo-medieval church, now cathedral, of St John at Tampere (1902–7), with its strong primitivist flavour; the Telephone Company building in Helsinki (1905), in a rock-faced neo-Richardsonian Romanesque; and the church in the Kallio district of Helsinki (1908–12), with a high Arts and Crafts tower containing bells for which Sibelius wrote

853 Sonck: Detail of entrance front of the Telephone Company Building, Helsinki (1905)

854 Saarinen, Gesellius and Lindgren: Villa Hvitträsk, Kirkkonummi, near Helsinki (begun 1902)

855 Aerial view of Helsinki railway station, Helsinki (1904–14), by Saarinen, Gesellius and Lindgren

a carillon. For Sibelius, whose patriotic romanticism is the musical parallel to the work of Sonck and Saarinen, Sonck had built in 1904 a country villa in an indigenous log-cabin tradition called 'Ainola' at Järvenapää. This was the style which Saarinen adopted for the Finnish pavilion at the Paris Exposition of 1900, designed with Herman Gesellius (1874–1916) and Armas Lindgren (1874–1929) with whom he was in partnership from 1896. In 1902 the three men began work on a remarkable complex of three houses, to serve as their joint homes and studios, on a steep hillside above Hvitträsk near Kirkkonummi. With their steep roofs and inglenooks in an Arts and Crafts style owing much to Norman Shaw, these form perhaps the most impressive domestic examples of National Romanticism.

The first major public work of the partnership, won in competition in 1901 and built in 1905–12, is the National Museum in Helsinki, which echoes the robust if quirky style of Sonck with the irregularly surfaced Finnish granite laid in stones of deliberately contrasting sizes. Saarinen, Gesellius and Lindgren went on to win

the competition for Helsinki railway station in 1904 which they built to a simplified design in 1906–14. Its round entrance arch flanked by giant figure sculpture, its austere vertical lines and sculpturally moulded tower, are indebted to Olbrich and to Viennese Secessionism as exemplified in Hoffmann's Palais Stoclet. It is a monument of European significance and should be compared to contemporary stations in slightly more classical styles such as that at Stuttgart by Bonatz, at Karlsruhe by August Stürzenacker, and at Basel by Robert Curjel and Karl Moser. Saarinen's elegant Town Hall at Lahti (1911–12) also has a Secessionist flavour which recurs, combined with Gothic romance, in his powerful design of 1922 for the Tribune Tower at Chicago, already noted. He subsequently emigrated to America, where his carefully designed and derivative buildings include the Dudok-inspired Crow Island School, Winnetka, Illinois (1939–40).

Shortly before the Great War there was a decisive shift in Scandinavian and Finnish architecture away from National Romanticism to a revival of the Romantic Classicism of the years around 1800. This corresponded to and was influenced by the contemporary return to neo-classicism in Germany and Austria of architects such as Behrens, Tessenow and Hoffmann. The search for a

856 Courtyard of the Police Headquarters, Copenhagen (1919–24), by Kampmann

Bindesbøll's Doric sensibility, and for the vibrant use of colour in Greek architecture and in Far Eastern arts and crafts, flowered in his Faaborg Museum for Fynsk Malerkunst (1912–15). This adoption of neo-classicism had been prefigured in the addition to the New Carlsberg Glyptothek of 1901–6 by the eclectic architect Hack Kampmann (1856–1920), who had studied at the Ecole des Beaux-Arts in Paris in 1882. His masterpiece is the new Police Headquarters in Copenhagen (1919–24), an austere neo-classical building organized round a circular colonnaded courtyard with a diameter close to that of the Pantheon. This courtyard was suggested by the brilliant young architect Aage Rafn (1890–1953), whom Kampmann employed on the project.

Rivalling the Police Headquarters in classical sobriety is the Oregaard Grammar School (1922–4), north of Copenhagen, by Edvard Thomsen (1884–1980) and G. B. Hagen (1873–1941). This has a lucid articulation which clearly indicates Thomsen's known enthusiasm for Perret and Behrens, and contains furniture designed by Thomsen in imitation of that by Bindesbøll at the Thorvaldsen Museum. With Frits Schlegel Thomsen built the Søndermark Crematorium (1927–30) in Copenhagen, a bare classical box, its entrance front enlivened with an Expressionist sculpture of an angel by Utzon Frank. A similar classicism, largely stripped of ornamental detail, was also used for low-cost urban housing as in the huge blocks in the Borups allé, Copenhagen, by Povl Baumann (1878–1963), a pupil of Messel, in 1916, and by Kay Fisker (1893–1965) in 1922–3.

In Sweden the prolific Östberg was now joined by two brilliant architects, Ivar Tengbom (1878–1968) and Gunnar Asplund (1885–1940). Tengbom's magnificent Stockholm Concert House (1920–6) is perhaps the finest monument of twentieth-century Nordic classicism. The simplicity of its cubic mass is scarcely compromised by the row of ten Corinthian columns rising the full height of the entrance front, because they are not only extremely attenuated but are also set close

national style with a purity of line which would be a refreshing contrast after the curvilinear elaboration of Art Nouveau and the heavy textures of National Romanticism, led in Germany to a revival of interest in the Prussian architect Schinkel, and in the Nordic countries to a new enthusiasm for neo-classical architects like Harsdorff and especially Hansen and Bindesbøll. Carl Petersen (1874–1924) was profoundly influenced by seeing Bindesbøll's drawings for the Thorvaldsen Museum at an exhibition in the new Town Hall at Copenhagen in 1901. His enthusiasm for

857 *Above* Entrance lobby of the Stockholm Concert House (1920–6), by Tengbom

858 *Below* The Woodland Crematorium, Stockholm (1935–40), by Asplund

859 *Above* Asplund: Entrance façade of the Stockholm City Library
(1920–8)

860 *Below* Plan and section of of Asplund's Stockholm City Library

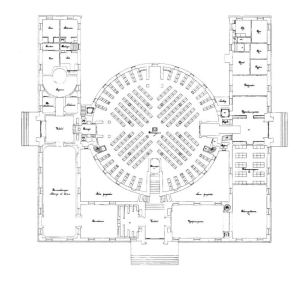

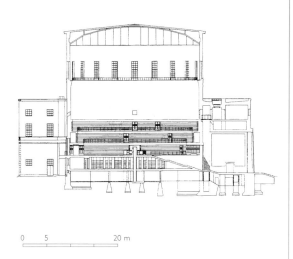

0   5   20 m

to the wall behind. The main concert hall resembles an open classical courtyard, since it has no visible roof but an atmospheric ceiling resembling the sky. At the far end a high portico in false perspective incorporates an organ grille. The same attenuated elegance is evident throughout his work as, for example, in his delicately neo-classical School of Economics (1926) and Swedish Match Company building (1928), both in Stockholm. In a similar style Erik Lallerstedt (1864–1955) provided the Law and Humanities Faculties at Stockholm University (designed 1918; executed 1925–7), while the Uppsala architect Gunnar Leche (1891–1954) designed Vaksala School, Uppsala (1925–7), in the style of Ledoux and of Louis-Jean Desprez (1743–1804), who had worked for King Gustav III of Sweden in the 1780s.

The strength of these buildings lies in the fact that though they belong firmly to the classical tradition, they can be seen as a successful twentieth-century fulfilment of the incipient modernism which characterized the search for simplicity of many neo-classical architects in late-eighteenth-century Europe. A fine example is Gunnar Asplund's Woodland Chapel of 1915 in the

Woodland Cemetery in southern Stockholm. The romantic primitivism of this building, a combination of a temple and a forest cabin, was inspired by the Thatched Palace, a cottage *orné* with a colonnade of simple timber columns built in 1793 at Liselund on the island of Møn in south-east Denmark. Asplund's major work is Stockholm City Library (1920–28) which, again looking back to the 1790s, recalls the work of Ledoux and Boullée. The abstract geometry of its great bare cylinder rising above an uncompromising cube reflects the feeling for poetic minimalism which led Asplund to look with some sympathy on the work of Le Corbusier. Indeed, as

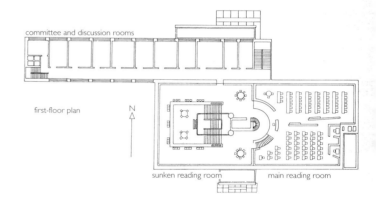

861, 862 *Right and below* Plan and lecture room of the City Library, Viipuri (1933–5), by Aalto

863 *Above* Exterior of the Villa Mairea, Noormarkku (1937–8), by Aalto

864 *Opposite* Aalto: Interior of the Finnish Pavilion, the World's fair, New York City (1939)

chief designer from 1928 of the Stockholm Exhibition of 1930, Asplund encouraged the arrival of the International Modern style in Sweden. However, he remained personally ambivalent about it, as can be seen in his best-known work, the Crematorium of 1935–40 at the Woodland Cemetery. Its open loggia of square unmoulded piers is the closest realization in western architecture of Gilly's dream of a timeless trabeated architecture in his project for a mausoleum of c.1800. Poetically related to its landscape setting at the end of a long driveway, and flanked by a large cross, Asplund's severe building takes the art of reduction to extreme lengths in one of the most eloquent and poignant of all syntheses of the pagan, Christian and modern worlds.

The most interesting Scandinavian architects between the two world wars were those who, despite mild flirtations with the International Modern style, continued to work in the style sometimes known as Nordic Classicism which lasted from 1910 to 1930.

However, in Finland one architect, Alvar Aalto (1898–1976), made an original contribution to the Modern Movement, though his major work dates from after 1945. Starting in a low-key classicism in his Workers' Club at Jyväskylä (1923–4) and church at Muurame (1926–9), he adopted the language of Mendelsohn and Mies van der Rohe for his building of 1928–9 at Turku for the newspaper *Turun Sanomat*. His Tuberculosis Sanatorium of 1929–33 at Paimio is a reinforced concrete structure which, rivalling the Bauhaus in size, was inspired by Johannes Duiker's Zonnestraal Tuberculosis Sanatorium at Hilversum (1928), a daring essay in the constructivist aesthetic which he had doubtless seen on his visit to the city in 1928.

One of Aalto's most important early works is his City Library at Viipuri, executed in 1933–5 from a design gradually developed from 1927 to 1933. Incorporating such Gropius-inspired features as a glazed staircase wall, it was significant in Aalto's career for its introduction of a quintessentially Finnish material, wood. This appears in the ceiling of the lecture room, which has a continuously undulating profile composed of battening applied in a series of curves. Though partly introduced for aesthetic reasons, this also helped solve an acoustic problem which, it should be admitted, was of Aalto's own

623

making, since the room was manifestly too long and narrow to be appropriate for its function as a setting for lectures and discussions. The complex play of changing floor levels in the library, while adding to the overall aesthetic interest of the building, was similarly a practical inconvenience so far as the librarians were concerned. It was at this time that Aalto's interest in humanizing the machine-based aesthetic of the Modern Movement led him to develop what he called 'the world's first soft wooden chair', of bent plywood made from laminated beechwood. The numerous chairs which he designed in this mode made him internationally famous as a furniture designer.

Though he attended the CIAM meetings in 1929, 1930, and, the most famous of them, in 1933 in Athens, he continued to develop a softer and more vernacular modernism than that favoured by the Congress's vice-presidents, Gropius and Le Corbusier. This process can be traced in Aalto's own house and studio at Munkkiniemi, Helsinki (1936), in the Villa Mairea at Noormarkku (1937–8), in the stepped workers' housing

at Kauttua (1938), and in the Finnish Pavilions for the World's Fairs at Paris in 1937 and at New York two years later. Recurrent features were informal courtyard plans owing something to Scandinavian vernacular traditions, irregular massing, and the use of natural timber, especially in the form of external woodstrip cladding. The use of timber reached its climax in the Finnish Pavilion at New York with its giant serpentine wall which, in a spirit of Borrominesque fantasy, actually tilted inwards as it rose so that the large photographs displayed on it could be clearly seen from below.

Futurism, classicism and Rationalism in Italy

Italian architecture between the wars is an object lesson in the need for caution before supposing that architectural style is an expression of politics. Though we do not condemn Greek temples on architectural

865 Entrance façade of the Central Station, Milan (1913–30), by Stacchini

866 Sant'Elia: Design for a 'casa a gradinata' from *Città Nuova* (1914)

grounds because we disapprove of the bloody sacrifice of animals for which they were designed, we have been encouraged to believe that buildings erected by modern political régimes of which we disapprove must consequently be architecturally objectionable. This view seemed justified by the architectural situation in Germany in the 1930s, since the classicism frequently favoured by the National Socialists happened to be a style considered unacceptable and out of date by most modern architectural writers. In Italy, however, not only

867 *Overleaf left* The Seagram building, New York City, by Mies van der Rohe (1954–8)

868 *Overleaf top right* Garden front of Deanery Garden, Sonning, Berkshire, by Lutyens (1899–1902)

869 *Overleaf bottom right* The Portland Public Service Building, Oregon, by Michael Graves (1979–82)

625

were some of the leading Modern Movement architects passionate Fascists, but arguably the best single building in the International Modern style in Italy is Terragni's Casa del Fascio (house of fascism) at Como of 1932–6.

Architecture in twentieth-century Italy, as in other European countries, began on the one hand with Art Nouveau, which we have touched on in Chapter 10, and on the other with a monumental classical style which in Italy is typified in the work of Cesare Bazzani (1873–1939). His heavy neo-Renaissance Biblioteca Nazionale Centrale (1906–35), Galleria Nazionale d'Arte Moderna (1911), and Ministerio dell'Educazione Nazionale (1913–28), all in Rome, continued the aggrandizement of the capital which had been begun at the time of Unification. More interesting is Milan central station (1913–30) by Ulisse Stacchini, a gargantuan structure which almost rivals in bombastic splendour Poelaert's Palais de Justice in Brussels. Stylistically it owes much to the blocky classicism combined with Stile Floreale detailing of Calderini's Palazzo di Giustizia in Rome of 1888–1910. As Milan station was largely built during the 1920s it has been regarded as a typical expression of Mussolini's overweening ambition, but in fact it was designed before he came to power in 1922.

It is remarkable that some of the most forceful of all images of modernity in the twentieth century were contemporary with the design of Milan station. These were by the architect Antonio Sant'Elia (1888–1916), who was killed in the First World War before he could begin to execute his visionary sketches of the cities of the future. In dynamic drawings which seem close to those of Olbrich and Mendelsohn he conjured up an aggressive urban world of stepped-back apartment blocks with illuminated skyline advertising, and skyscrapers enmeshed with aircraft strips and highways on different levels. Prepared in 1912–14, these were exhibited in Milan in May 1914 under the title *Città Nuova* ('New City') or *Milano 2000* together with an accompanying *Messagio* on modern architecture which was reprinted in July as the Manifesto of Futurist Architecture. The Futurist movement, more widely adopted in painting than in architecture, was initiated by the poet and dramatist Filippo Tomaso Marinetti (1876–1944), an enthusiastic supporter of Mussolini, in his Foundation Manifesto of 1909. This declaration of total war on the past was coloured by Marinetti's romantic reaction to the rapid technological transformation of the industrial cities of north Italy in the period from 1900 to 1912. 'We declare', he claimed, 'that the splendour of the world has been enriched by a new beauty – the beauty of speed. A racing car with its bonnet draped with exhaust pipes like fire-breathing serpents – a roaring racing car, rattling along like a machine-gun, is more beautiful than the winged victory of Samothrace.' Marinetti's imagery and Sant'Elia's expression of it were soon to be echoed in the work of Le Corbusier.

In Italy the desire of the Futurists for violence and danger was more than fulfilled in the course of the First World War, and the country returned, like Scandinavia, to a fresh neo-classical style. This was enthusiastically supported by Mussolini, Fascist dictator of Italy from 1922 to 1943, as an expression of his imperial ideals. He was able to draw on able architects such as Piacentini, Petrucci, Morpurgo and Frezzotti, much of whose best work was in the field of urban development and town planning. Despite the new Roman-Italian empire established by Mussolini, these architects did not adopt a sumptuous imperial Roman manner but rather a spare unadorned style of primary geometric forms which was influenced by current excavations, particularly in Ostia, Portus and Rome.

Marcello Piacentini (1881–1961), son of the architect Pio Piacentini whose sympathetic contributions to late-nineteenth-century Rome we have already admired, was one of the most dominant figures in Italian architecture before the Second World War. Beginning with the magnificent neo-classical Palace of Justice at Messina (1912–28), he went on to redevelop the town centres of Bergamo (1917) and Brescia (1927–32), before playing a decisive role in the commissions which produced a master plan for Rome (1931), for Rome

870, 871 General view, with the Church of the Annunciation in the background, and plan of the new town of Sabaudia (1933)

University (1932–3) and, from 1937, for the Universal Exposition planned for Rome in 1941–2. In addition to promoting these largely neo-classical schemes, he was professor of architecture in Rome from 1920 and founded the leading architectural journal, *Architettura ed Arti Decorative*, with Gustavo Giovannoni in 1921. Though far from hostile to the International Modern style, he played an important role in questioning its general suitability to Italy in view of the climate and the rich indigenous architectural traditions.

The Fascist government was responsible for the creation of five new towns in 1932–9 south of Rome in the province of Lazio. These were made possible by the draining of the Pontine marshes, a project planned by Julius Caesar and revived by Mussolini who regarded himself as his heir. The towns are organized, like thousands of Italian towns before them, round a square dominated by a church and town hall for which

Piacentini's handsome square at Brescia provided an obvious precedent. The largest of them, Littoria (now Latina), by O. Frezzotti, contains apartment blocks north of the main square which are clearly based on those excavated at Ostia, while the square itself is approached dramatically through porticoes of those unmoulded square piers which appealed so much to contemporary architects in Germany. The towns of Sabaudia (1933), largely by Luigi Piccinato, and Pontinia were in a rather more modern flat-roofed idiom, while Aprilia and Pomezia (1938–40) were more elegantly traditional. Aprilia, laid out in 1936–8 by Petrucci and Tufaroli, was centred on an attractive arcaded square dominated by the church of St. Michele, with its campanile and its west front framing a high apsed niche. Clearly inspired by the apse in the ancient temple of Venus and Rome, which had been cleared of later buildings in the early 1930s, this façade proclaimed the

Catholic church as an essential part of the unity between ancient Rome and the Rome of Mussolini.

In Rome Vittorio Ballio Morpurgo was responsible for the unhappy Piazza Augusto Imperiale in 1936–41. Involving the demolition of a vast area of housing, this provided a monumental open setting for the ancient Roman Mausoleum of Augustus which, now cleared of its later accretions, emerged as a bald and dull building. Dull, too, were the stripped classical buildings with which Morpurgo surrounded the square. The destruction of the Spina del Borgo quarter of Rome near St Peter's in the 1930s was another consequence of Mussolini's wish to create what he conceived of as imperial Roman vistas in place of the contrasts and surprises of Baroque Rome, which he was unable to appreciate. Here Piacentini created the bland and monumental Via della Conziliazione which leads in a straight line from the Tiber to the Piazza S. Pietro.

Though Mussolini was intimately involved with major building enterprises for a range of political,

economic and cultural reasons, he was not emotionally involved with contemporary classical architecture in a way that Hitler, the architect *manqué*, was. Leading architects such as Terragni, Mazzoni, Pagano and Michelucci were free to practise in the International Modern style, or Rationalism as it was known in Italy. Perhaps the most striking example of Fascist patronage of the Modern Movement was the Casa del Fascio at Como (1932–6) by Giuseppe Terragni (1904–43). He had already erected in Como one of the first monuments in Italy in the reinforced concrete manner of Gropius and Mendelsohn, the Novocumum apartment block (1927–8), but the Casa del Fascio was an altogether more original and sophisticated statement in this style. Rich with marble revetments, it is laid out on a perfectly square plan, in axis with the east end of the Duomo on the opposite side of the Piazza del Impero. Its open grid-like elevation leads to a trabeated glass-roofed atrium surrounded by four floors of galleries and offices. A row of 16 glass doors, electrically operated so as to open simultaneously, allowed the fascist militia to flood dramatically into the political arena of the piazza: a perfect expression of the convergence of Futurist and Fascist mentality. This building is Terragni's masterpiece, but he went on to design numerous others in a similar manner, notably the Sant'Elia Nursery School (1936–7) and the Giuliani–Frigeno apartment block (1939–40), both in Como.

There was serious debate throughout the 1930s about the merits of the Modern Movement in architecture, for example in connection with the design of Florence railway station, which was in an historically sensitive spot opposite the apse of Alberti's church of S. Maria Novella. Mazzoni, at heart a modernist, prepared a design in 1931 in a simple classical style, but in the end the commission went to a group of architects led by Giovanni Michelucci whose glass and concrete station, erected in 1934–6, is in stark contrast to its setting. In Rome, by contrast, Mazzoni designed the stylistically more appropriate Stazione Termini with side wings sporting superimposed arcades echoing those of the

872 Exterior of the Casa del Fascio, Como (1932–6), by Terragni

873 Mazzoni: Colonia Marina del Calambrone, Livorno (1925–6)

nearby Aqua Claudia. Work was halted during the war and the station was completed to a different design in 1951 by Eugenio Montuori. A leading Fascist architect who refused to design in the traditional classical language of Italy was Giuseppe Pagano (1896–1945). Grimly insistent on seeing architecture as an instrument of social reform, he produced a design in 1931 for replacing an historic area of Turin along the Via Roma with large blocks in the International Modern style. The approval by the régime of this controversial scheme marked the peak of Mussolini's acceptance of the Modern Movement. Pagano's major executed works, such as the Istituto Fisico (1932–5) at Rome University are singularly charmless.

Angiolo Mazzoni (1894–1970), by contrast, was one of the freshest and most individual architects at work in Italy between the wars. Prepared to design in the classical style where appropriate, he was at the same time a director of the Futurist newspaper *Sant'Elia* in 1934–5. His early designs are in an imaginative style inspired by Olbrich, but with his Villa Rosa Maltoni-Mussolini (1925–6), better known as the Colonia Marina del Calambrone, a seaside school near Livorno for the children of post-office workers and railwaymen, he established his personal style: this might be described as Futurism with a human face. Features such as the bare

874 The exterior of the History Faculty building, Cambridge, by James Stirling (1964) (see p. 652)

cylindrical water-tower wrapped round with a spiral staircase, and the strange circular towers flanking the entrance front, ringed with close-set unmoulded shafts of marble, have a Surrealist quality which is closely paralleled in the dream-world paintings of Giorgio de Chirico (1888–1978), with their depopulated Renaissance buildings, strange towers and courtyards. The same half-mechanistic, half-lyrical style recurs in his Centrale Termica (1932–4) at Florence station which, with its audacious iron spiral staircase leading to a high catwalk, is like a recreation of Sant'Elia's sketches. Mazzoni designed numerous post and telegraph offices and railway stations for the state postal and railway system, whose service he entered in 1921. These are always characterized by a dynamic play of contrasting horizontal and vertical volumes, though they range stylistically from the post office at Grosseto (1932) with its high rusticated tower to that at Agrigento (1931–4) which is a pure cylinder.

Giovanni Muzio (1893–1982) was also a prolific architect of buildings which can be related to the metaphysical world of Giorgio de Chirico. His key work in this vein is his apartment house (1919–20) in Milan, nicknamed *Ca'brutta* by the Milanese for its stark use of classical features. Muzio, who taught at the Milan Polytechnic Institute from 1935–1963, later developed a timeless Lombardic classicism which can be seen in his Catholic University of Milan (1921–49) and in his church of S. Antonio at Cremona (1936–9).

Lutyens, the conservative genius

In England up till 1939 Sir Edwin Lutyens (1869–1944) towered above all other architects of his generation, just as his contemporary, Frank Lloyd Wright, did in America. Throughout his long and prolific career which included every kind of commission from cottages to town planning, he was a master of spatial play, whether in his freely-planned organic houses hugging the soil, or in his public, commercial and ecclesiastical buildings. As a brilliant handler of space he resembled Wright, who spoke enthusiastically of his work to students at Taliesin

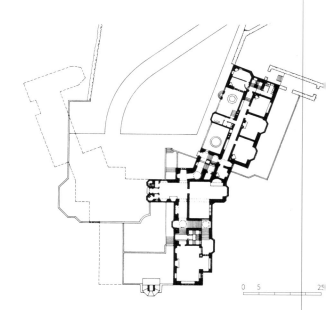

875, 876 *Above and right* Plan and entrance façade of Castle Drogo, near Drewsteignton, Devon (1910–32) by Lutyens

West. Like Wright, Lutyens was hostile to the International Style. Lutyen's hostility extended to the Modern Movement as a whole, while Wright, by contrast, was equally dismissive of the entire classical language of architecture. Like Ledoux, but unusually for an English architect, Lutyens was gifted with a feeling of mass and geometry. This is evident even in his smallest buildings, as it is in those of Ledoux.

Lutyens received little formal training, though the period he spent in 1887–9 in the office of Ernest George, a talented pupil of Norman Shaw, enabled him to begin his career by designing rambling houses in a picturesque vernacular style derived from Shaw. These include Munstead Wood, Surrey (1896–7), for Gertrude Jekyll, the brilliant gardener who did much to promote his career. They reflect the increasing nostalgia for a lost rural world which also resulted in the foundation of the National Trust for Places of Historic Interest or Natural Beauty in 1895, and of the influential magazine *Country Life* two years later. However, Lutyens's early houses also increasingly revealed his mastery of mass and volume which resulted in such masterpieces as Deanery Garden,

Berkshire (1899–1902; fig. 868), built for Edward Hudson, founder and proprietor of *Country Life*. At Deanery Garden Lutyens characteristically preserved an existing garden wall along the road, piercing it with an unobtrusive entrance arch leading into a passage which runs along the edge of the cloistered entrance court. This passage then burrows into the house, where it gives access to the staircase and then forms part of the double-height living hall. Finally it emerges on the south front, whence it continues as an off-axis garden path.

The subtle spatial flow of Deanery Garden with its numerous cross-axes is as characteristic of the mature work of Lutyens as it is of Wright in his Prairie Style houses, though Wright often chose a tauter cruciform plan, as in the Ward Willitts house. The theme recurs in Lutyens's Little Thakeham, Sussex (1902), where the two-storeyed living hall merges into the staircase and its balconied landing. Space also flows into the room from

877 Finsbury Circus façade of Britannic (now Lutyens) House, London (1920–3), by Lutyens

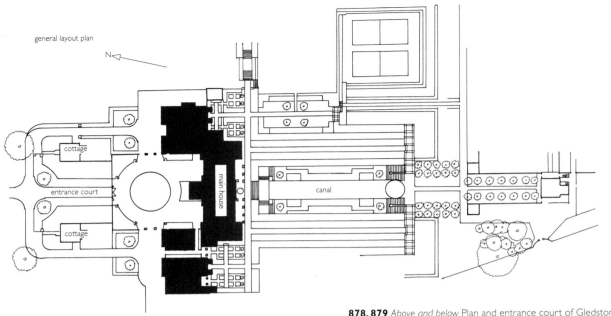

general layout plan

N

cottage

entrance court

cottage

main house

canal

878, 879 *Above and below* Plan and entrance court of Gledstone Hall, Yorkshire (1922–6), by Lutyens

880 Above Shchuko and Gelfreich: Lenin State Library, Moscow
(1928–41)

the first-floor corridor, which opens into the hall through a balcony over the chimneypiece. This spatial ingenuity reached a climax in Castle Drogo, Devon (1910–32), with its complex web of Piranesian vaulted staircases, its shifting floor levels, and internal windows. Built of local granite so that it resembles a natural outcrop on its remote and romantic hillside, Castle Drogo is as organically related to its setting as Wright's Fallingwater. This never-completed neo-feudal fantasy, built for the head of one of Britain's largest grocery chains, is one of the most astonishing houses of the twentieth century, though its construction has caused far-reaching problems of water-penetration.

In the meantime Lutyens's sense of order had led him, as it had led Shaw before him, to discover the classical language of architecture and its capacity for creating harmony, strength and repose. His work now became a dynamic combination of classical and Picturesque values. The first fruits of his rediscovery of the Mediterranean classical tradition was the startling villa called Heathcote, built in 1906 in a suburban setting at Ilkley, Yorkshire, for a local businessman. Its bold

effects recurred on a huger scale at his Britannic (now Lutyens) House, London (1920–3), for the Anglo-Iranian Oil Company. With a concave façade to Finsbury Circus and a straight front along Moorgate incorporating a bank and an underground (subway) station, this monumental steel-frame office building is clad in a Portland stone skin of Genoese Baroque vivacity. Its vigorous rustication is taken up with unusual effect in Lutyens's Midland Bank, Poultry, London (1924–37), a building which contracts as it rises thanks to a uniquely subtle proportional system. Each course of stone is an eighth of an inch (3.2mm) less in height than the one below it, while the rustication is discontinued at various levels, each time involving a recession of one inch (25.4mm) in the vertical plane. Even in a country house such as Gledstone Hall, Yorkshire (1922–6), delicate adjustments of this kind are used to give the building a living sensitivity: for example, the height of each successive course of the cream-coloured local limestone is diminished. Moreover, as in many of Lutyens's

881, 882 *Opposite and below* Plan and entrance front of Viceroy's House, New Delhi (1912–31), by Lutyens

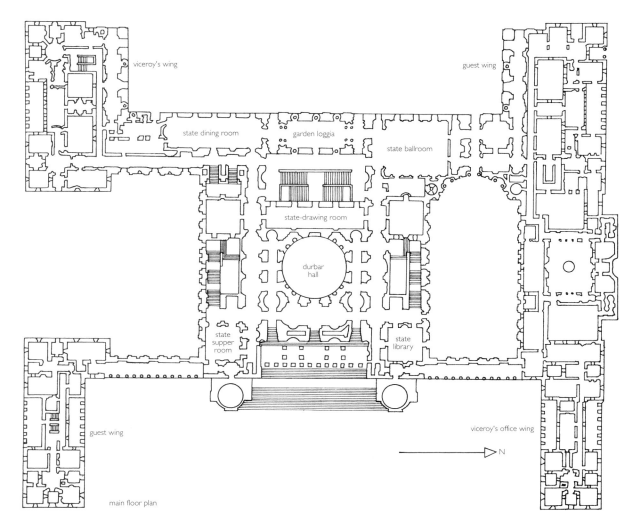

viceroy's wing

guest wing

state dining room

garden loggia

state ballroom

state-drawing room

durbar hall

state supper room

state library

guest wing

viceroy's office wing

N

main floor plan

buildings, the walls are slightly inclined or battered inwards, creating a sensation of growth and life akin to that produced by the optical refinements of the ancient Greeks. The formal grouping of the house and its forecourt with twin lodges and cottages is as masterly as the way in which the house is integrated with its terraced architectural garden, where the central axis is continued by a long canal leading the eye towards the distant countryside. This whole carefully controlled play of contrasting levels and axes is as brilliant as François Mansart's at Balleroy. It is a classic example of Lutyens's ability to relate a house organically to its setting.

This skill, which he shared with a long line of English architects in the Picturesque and, later, the Arts and Crafts traditions, was of inestimable value to him in carrying out the greatest commission of his career,

Viceroy's House (1912—31) and the associated town-planning scheme at New Delhi. It is an irony that a virtually untrained English architect should have been responsible for one of the most monumental classical complexes in modern architecture — exactly the kind of scheme for which generations of French and American architects had been trained at the Ecole des Beaux-Arts in Paris. By a further irony, British rule in India came to an end only 15 years after the completion of Viceroy's House. Nevertheless, the building, now Rashtrapati Bhavan, has adjusted well as the official residence of the President and is accepted as a convincing symbol of order and stability in the largest democracy in the world.

Surmounted by a titanic dome, the cliff-like walls of Viceroy's House with their pronounced inward inclination are constructed of pink and cream Dholpur sandstone. The design has an abstract quality which achieves its effect through mass and geometry rather than through rich classical detail or ornament. This is sometimes known as Lutyens's 'elemental' language, in which the classical vocabulary of Rome and the Renaissance seems reduced to a pure essence after a process of distillation. It is the tangible expression of what he had already written about the orders: 'They have to be so well digested that there is nothing but essence left . . . the perfection of the Order is far nearer nature than anything produced on impulse and accident-wise. Every line and curve the result of force against impulse through the centuries.' Though he resisted the pressures to adopt traditional Indian styles, Lutyens brilliantly incorporated certain Moghul features such as the *chattris* or roof pavilions, and the *chujjas* or broadly projecting cornices which create welcome shadows. The lower part of the dome has a banded rectangular patterning of Buddhist origin, derived from such monuments as the circular palisade of the Great Stupa at Sanchi in India. This was not chosen for arbitrary eclectic reasons but because its grid-like form is in profound harmony with the whole geometrical basis of Lutyens's design.

Another blend of different traditions is the great Moghul Garden at Viceroy's House, where Lutyens applied his skill as a designer of English gardens and his innate sense of abstract geometry to an animated recreation of the water-gardens of India. Lutyens's plan of the city of New Delhi, inspired by that of Washington, DC, and based on a triangle of 60 degrees, is the boldest of essays in Beaux-Arts axial layout. Centred on the great avenue leading past the Secretariats, designed by Herbert Baker, to Viceroy's House, the monumentality is tempered by the low density and the lavish planting, which derive from the English garden city. Lutyens had already tried his hand at town planning in the central square he designed for Parker and Unwin's Hampstead Garden Suburb in London. Here in 1908–10 he provided a group composed of two contrasting churches with their parsonages, as well as the social and educational Institute building and a number of houses. His formal but not

883 Lutyens: Hampstead Garden Suburb, with St Jude's church (1908)

884 Lutyens: Memorial to the Missing of the Somme, Thiepval, near Arras (1927–32)

885 Rogers and Piano: The Pompidou Centre, Paris (1971–7) (see p. 657)

strictly symmetrical layout contrasted with the informal vernacular freedom of the rest of the suburb.

The timeless abstract grandeur of Delhi recurred in two masterpieces designed by Lutyens in the 1920s, the Memorial to the Missing of the Somme at Thiepval, near Arras, France (1927–32), and the Roman Catholic cathedral of Christ the King at Liverpool (1929–41), of which only the imposing crypt was ever built. The most solemn and powerful of the many monuments to those who gave their lives so pointlessly in the Great War, the Thiepval Arch can be read as a series of intersecting triumphal arches of increasing height. These provide a series of blank surfaces on which are inscribed the names of over 70,000 missing men. The result is one of the most moving buildings of the twentieth century: a piece of sublime geometry in which slender arches, rising from constantly changing floor levels, frame views of a pastoral and now peaceful scenery. He again used the triumphal arch theme at Liverpool cathedral, where it

886 Choir of the Anglican cathedral, Liverpool (1904–80), by Scott

formed the basis of the south entrance front, a design which we can appreciate in the magnificent model made in 1934. The narrowness of the nave (52 feet; 16m), in comparison with its great height (138 feet; 42m), gave it a Gothic proportion despite its classical articulation. There would have been a dramatic spatial release as one passed from the nave into the vast circular space beneath the dome, the largest in Christendom. This stupendous monument of pinkish buff brick interwoven with bands of silver-grey granite not only united classic forms and Gothic proportions but welded together two building types which had preoccupied the imagination of architects since the days of ancient Rome, the dome and the triumphal arch.

Traditionalism and modernism in Britain

The cathedral which stands today on top of Lutyens's immense vaulted crypt is a tawdry concrete octagon erected in 1962–7 from designs by Frederick Gibberd (1908–80) as a typical expression of the space-age aesthetic of its day. Another cathedral planned for Liverpool was happily completed to designs by its original architect: the Anglican cathedral, won in competition in 1903 by Giles Gilbert Scott (1880–1960). Work on this red sandstone building began in 1904 to Scott's comparatively conventional Gothic designs, but he transformed these in 1909–10 and 1924 to produce a building of the power and drama associated with the aesthetic category of the Sublime. Its monumental massing is contrasted with areas of concentrated decoration evoking the richness and delicacy of Spanish late Gothic. Though predominantly a church architect until the end of the 1920s, Scott was subsequently involved with a large number of essentially twentieth-century commissions ranging from telephone kiosks to power stations. However, like Lutyens he had received little that would be taken seriously as professional training by his contemporaries in countries such as France or America. He had had no formal academic education in a school of architecture, nor any technical training other than in the office of the sensitive church architect Temple Moore (1856–1920).

One of Scott's most characteristic churches, built of specially made thin pink bricks, is St Andrew's, Luton, Bedfordshire (1931–2). Its low-slung streamlined nave, suggestive of power, is appropriate to Luton as a car-manufacturing centre, while the emphatic sloping buttresses and massive western tower have an almost Expressionist force. It recalls the use of brick by German architects such as Wilhelm Kreis. Scott was also sympathetic to contemporary American architecture and was a friend of Bertram Goodhue. On receiving the commission for Cambridge University Library in 1923, he was invited to inspect the major academic libraries in the United States of America, since the Rockefeller Foundation was making a substantial contribution towards the cost of the new building. Scott's library is a not wholly successful compromise between the need to provide on the one hand an aesthetically satisfactory building with a traditional flavour, and on the other, purely functional book-stacks with vertical grid-like fenestration. The long horizontal lines of Scott's original design were happier than those of the building as executed, which is dominated by a bulky central tower required by the Rockefeller Foundation. This tower, a steel frame clad in slim two-inch (5cm) bricks, has a vertical detailing reminiscent of Goodhue's Nebraska State Capitol.

At the same time as designing this powerhouse of learning in Cambridge, Scott was at work on Battersea Power Station (1930–4), a controversial building near the centre of London which became for the British public the archetypal symbol of modernity. The general form of the building had been settled and construction begun by the time Scott was called in to provide an acceptable exterior treatment. His remarkable achievement was to civilize the brutality of industry by the use of beautiful brickwork carefully laid with straw-coloured mortar, by giving the chimneys a hint of timeless classicism with the addition of fluting, and by the aspiring verticality of all his lines and details. Scott was interested in being a 'modern' architect in a way in which Lutyens was not. He was more sympathetic to modern techniques and materials such as reinforced concrete but was extremely reluctant to expose concrete, which he regarded as a visually crude material inevitably marred by graceless weathering. With their respect for materials and for tradition, both Lutyens and Scott rejected the International Style as pure showmanship. They recognized, for example, the

887 *Above* Lanchester and Rickards: Exterior of the Wesleyan Central Hall, Westminster, London (1905–11)

888 *Opposite* Scott: Side elevation of St Andrew's Church, Luton (1931–2)

889 Scott: Battersea Power Station, London (1930–4), from the Thames

impracticality of its white plastered walls and flat roofs, which would require constant maintenance and repair. Before glancing at those who were persuaded of the suitability of the International Style, we should note some of the architects who, though less in stature than Lutyens and Scott, made some original contributions to the development of the classical tradition.

The combination of exuberantly classical façades and Beaux-Arts planning, unfamiliar in British public buildings, had been demonstrated at the start of the century at Cardiff City Hall and Law Courts (1897–1906) by H. V. Lanchester (1863–1953) and Edwin Rickards (1872–1920). This set a pattern which was widely imitated in public buildings up to the First World War, though Baroque exuberance was sometimes replaced by a restrained French Beaux-Arts manner, as

in the Edward VII Galleries at the British Museum. These were built in 1904–14 by the Scottish architect Sir John Burnet (1857–1938), who had been trained at the Ecole des Beaux-Arts. Lanchester and Rickards's domed Wesleyan Central Hall (1905–11) brought the confidently swaggering language of Cardiff to a prominent site in London, opposite the west front of Westminster Abbey. French influence of a different kind coloured the work of Mewès and Davis whose Parisian-looking Ritz Hotel (1904–6) in London we have already noted (p. 602) in our account of early-twentieth-century French architecture. With its façades and interiors designed by an Anglo-French architectural partnership, and its steel frame manufactured in Germany and designed by a Swedish engineer who had worked in Chicago, the Ritz is very much part of the political *entente cordiale* established in 1904 between England and France, and of the markedly cosmopolitan high society

891 *Above* Coates: Lawn Road Flats, Hampstead, London (1932–4)

890 *Above* Exterior of Zimbabwe House (formerly the British Medical Association building), Strand, London (1907–8), by Holden

892 *Below* Mendelsohn and Chermayeff: De la Warr Pavilion, Bexhill (1933–6)

which flourished during the reign of Edward VII (1901–10).

A more individual voice was provided by Charles Holden (1875–1960), who seems to have been concerned by the possible structural irrelevance of the stone cladding which it was customary to add to the new steel-frame structures. His reaction to this problem was to produce stone façades in which classical elements were deployed in an anti-rational or Mannerist way. This began in his library wing for the Law Society in Chancery Lane, London (1903–4), but was more evident in his British Medical Association Building (now Zimbabwe House), Strand, London (1907–8). This stands on the site of C. R. Cockerell's Westminster Life and British Fire Office (1831), from which it may derive its combination of figure sculpture and round-arched openings. The rectilinear treatment of the façade and the subtle interweaving of different planes have a Michelangelesque feel. This bony mannered treatment, which seems to reflect expressively the tough steel skeleton within, is paralleled in a number of London buildings by the partnership of John Belcher (1841–1913) and John James Joass (1868–1952), notably Mappin House, Oxford Street (1906–8), and the Royal Insurance Building, Piccadilly (1907–8). During the 1920s the leading classical architects included Curtis Green (1875–1960) and Vincent Harris (1879–1971), who both provided a bold classical synthesis of English and French classical traditions. Green was responsible for two striking buildings which almost face each other in Piccadilly, the Wolseley Motor Showroom (1922, now China House), and the Westminster Bank (1926), while Harris designed a number of major public buildings in the 1920s, the execution of which was completed during the 1930s. These included Sheffield City Hall, Leeds Civic Hall and, his finest work, the circular Central Library at Manchester and the adjacent Town Hall extension, with its high gabled end providing a note of abstract poetry.

The arrival of the International Style around 1930 was attended by much controversy. The stark flat-roofed buildings seemed little adapted to the English climate or countryside, while their spatial freedom and open planning, though novel in Germany or France, had long been anticipated in England in the domestic tradition which reached back from Lutyens via Shaw to Nash. To a great extent the International Style was imported by architects who arrived in England during the 1930s from other countries, notably the refugees from Nazi Germany, including Gropius, Mendelsohn and Marcel Breuer. They were especially associated with the design of private houses for members of the professional classes. One of the earliest buildings in this style was Lawn Road Flats, Hampstead (1932–4), a stark four-storey block of flats of exposed cream-painted concrete, designed by Wells Wintemute Coates (1895–1958) who had been trained in Toronto. Gropius, who was in partnership with Maxwell Fry (1899–1987) in 1934–6, designed a house in Old Church Street, Chelsea (1935–6), for the playwright Benn Levy. This is of steel-frame construction clad in plastered brickwork, but it has since been weather-proofed in hanging tiles. Next door is the contemporary Cohen House, designed by Mendelsohn in partnership with the Russian-born Serge Chermayeff (1900–96). They were also responsible for the De la Warr Pavilion at Bexhill, Sussex (1933–6), a seaside leisure centre with great metal windows which have not weathered well, contrasting dynamically with sculpturally composed ranges of plain white stucco.

Modernism and traditionalism in the USSR

The National Romanticism of late-nineteenth-century Russia, and the Neo-classical Revival which succeeded it around 1900, continued to colour architectural production until the Revolution in 1917. Both were thenceforward seen as symbols of the Czarist régime by Communist and avant-garde architects. Vladimir Tatlin (1885–1953), painter and stage-designer, provided a cogent image of the new post-revolutionary world in his design of 1919–20 for an iron and glass monument to the Third International Communist Congress, the

893 Tatlin: Model of the monument to the Third International Communist Congress, Moscow (1921)

Komintern, held in Moscow in 1921. This wholly unrealistic spiralling monument, 1,310 feet (400m) high, would have been taller than the Eiffel Tower. It is known to us from a model of its supporting framework, 16 feet (5m) high, which Tatlin made in wood and netting. This consists of two intertwined spirals set on a skew, within which were to be suspended three or possibly four glass rooms or volumes, each of which would rotate around its axis: the lowest at the rate of one revolution per year, the central one at one revolution per month, and the uppermost at one per day. The lowest, which would take the form of a cube,

would house legislative assemblies; the central one, pyramidal in shape, would house the International's executive committees; and the uppermost, a cylinder, would serve as an information office for the international proletariat. Intended for the distribution of manifestos and propaganda, this would be surmounted by radio masts. Since this scheme has been taken seriously by many architectural writers on the subject of Russian Constructivism, it has become an essential part of modernist mythology. Certainly, were this kind of kinetic architecture capable of construction in the 1920s, it would have been a commanding expression of a revolutionary society perpetually on the move.

Something of the flavour of Tatlin's monument is found in the Pravda Newspaper Building, Moscow (1924), by the Vesnin brothers, Aleksandr (1883–1959) and Viktor (1882–1950), with its searchlight, loudspeaker and digital clock. This had in turn been preceded by the Lenin Tribune project of 1920, a steel rostrum resembling a crane. This was designed by El (Eleazar Markevich) Lissitzky (1890–1941), architect, painter and graphic designer, who had been a pupil of Olbrich in Darmstadt in 1909–11. Appointed professor of architecture at Vitebsk in 1919, he proclaimed a doctrine which he called PROUN, from Pro-Unovis, 'For the School of New Art'. This was a new state of art 'between painting and architecture', and can be seen as a parallel to the work of Rietveld. Indeed, Lissitzky exercised considerable influence on van Doesburg and on De Stijl when he joined that movement in 1922 during his stay in Holland.

One of the most successful architects was Konstantin Melnikov (1890–1974), whose early buildings and projects of 1916–17 were in the revived Romantic Classical style of Ledoux. He soon turned to a kinetic Constructivism akin to that of Tatlin, as in his unexecuted design for the Pravda building of 1924 with each floor motorized so as to be able to rotate independently around the central core. More realistic was the USSR Pavilion which Melnikov provided for the Exposition des Arts Décoratifs at Paris in 1925. This

894 Iofan: Model of the Palace of the Soviets, Moscow (from 1933)

corner, containing the staircase, which recalls the work of Gropius and Terragni.

The protracted competition of 1931–3 for the Palace of the Soviets in Moscow, intended to be the Soviet answer to the capitalist League of Nations building of 1927 in Geneva, was the occasion for a great debate about the architectural style appropriate for the revolutionary socialist state. The establishment under Stalin from 1932 of Social Realism in the figurative arts was accompanied by the suppression of the various architectural factions which had supported Functionalism and Constructivism, in favour of a single Union of Soviet Architects which would follow the party line. Constructivism was now seen as esoteric, elitist and international, and instead architects were expected to adopt a nationalist language which would appeal to the proletariat. Melnikov was accused of 'formalism' by the Union in 1937 and was silenced as an architect. Rejecting entries by Le Corbusier, Mendelsohn, Gropius, Perret and Poelzig in the competition for the Palace of the Soviets, the jury selected a partially classical design by Boris Mikhailovich Iofan (b.1891). This was deeply ironical in view of the fact that the same sequence of events had occurred at Geneva, where designs for the League of Nations building by architects such as Le Corbusier had been rejected in favour of Nénot's classicizing scheme. Iofan elaborated his design after 1933, in collaboration with Vladimir Alekssevich Shchuko (1878–1939) and Vladimir Gelfreich (1885–1967), into a colossal wedding-cake in which circular colonnaded tiers were surmounted by a statue of Lenin offering his hand to the world.

Iofan practised in Italy from 1917 to 1924; he joined the Italian Communist Party in 1921 and two years later built the Soviet Embassy in Rome in a stripped classical style. The Soviet Pavilion he provided for the Paris Exposition of 1937 was similar in style to that of Albert Speer's German Pavilion, which it confronted axially. His colleague Shchuko designed the neo-classical propylaea (1923) at Quarenghi's elegant Smolnyi Institute in St Petersburg (1806–8), and the Lenin State Library in Moscow (1928–41) in a style close to the

dynamic structure was an essay in geometrical progression, in which a rectangular plan was divided by a diagonal staircase penetrating the open timber framework and creating two triangular areas on the ground floor.

Melnikov was responsible for another arresting geometrical essay in the form of the house he built for himself in 1927 at no. 10 Krivoarbatskii Pereulok, Moscow, composed of two interlocking cylinders. In 1927–9 he built six workers' clubs in a starkly geometrical style in Moscow, intended to act as 'social condensers'. One of the most striking is the Rusakov Club for the transport workers' union, with a tripartite fan-shaped plan containing three high-level cantilevered lecture halls. These are dramatically expressed on the grim, largely windowless exteriors of reinforced concrete. Ilya Golosov (1883–1945) designed the Zuyev Workers' Club (1926–8) with a dynamic circular glazed

stripped classicism of contemporary Germany. The modern movement was now equated with western decadence, so that neo-classicism remained the officially favoured mode of design in Russia up to the late 1950s. In the United States of America a parallel tradition survived in Washington DC, where federal buildings were erected into the 1950s in neo-classical styles symbolizing stability and continuity in the public realm.

Modernism after 1945

For thirty years after the Second World War the various images of modernity established in the 1920s and 1930s held undisputed sway, though in many cases they were now developed and extended by the same architects, including Wright, Corbusier, Mies van der Rohe and Aalto. However, from the 1970s there was mounting disquiet, on the part of both the general public and of architects, with the aggressive new world that had been created. Alarm was also caused by the structural failures of previously prized modern buildings, especially in England where the climate plays havoc with glass walls

and flat roofs, while the damage done by wilfully insensitive rebuilding in the historic towns and cities of Europe brought unprecedented popularity to the preservation movement.

The most influential form-givers in the years immediately after the war were Corbusier and Mies van der Rohe, and it is a measure of the variety of which the Modern Movement was capable that their outlooks should have been so opposed. Mies continued with his chill minimalism in steel and glass, while Corbusier developed a more sensational sculptural style, though generally expressed in the visually unalluring medium of concrete. Frank Lloyd Wright continued to be as prolific as ever, but his work was increasingly coloured by an aesthetic which can only be described as science-fiction kitsch, as in his spiralling Guggenheim Museum in New York (designed 1942–3; built 1957–60), or his mile-high skyscraper proposed for Chicago in 1957.

Mies van der Rohe was responsible for half a dozen buildings during the 1940s at the new campus of the

895 Wright: Exterior of the Guggenheim Museum, New York City (designed 1942–3; built 1957–60)

896 *Above* The Alumni Memorial Hall, Illinois Institute of Technology (1945–6), by Mies van der Rohe

897 *Right* The Farnsworth House, Plano, Illinois (1945–50), by Mies van der Rohe

Armour Institute (later the Illinois Institute of Technology), Chicago, where he had been appointed professor of architecture in 1938. His work here celebrated an industrial vocabulary of steel-frame construction with glass and beige brick infill, in which the standard American I-beam, as opposed to the cruciform columns he had used in the 1930s, played an important visual and structural role. The Alumni Memorial Hall at IIT (1945–6) set a pattern he was to follow in his numerous multi-storey office and apartment blocks of the 1950s and 1960s, in which a curtain of I-beam mullions framing the windows combines on the same plane with the structural steel columns to create a kind of woven surface pattern. The most celebrated of these are his two identical and adjacent apartment blocks, 26 storeys high, at Lake Shore Drive, Chicago (1948–51), and the Seagram Building, New York City (1954–8), designed in collaboration with Philip Johnson, clad in bronze and brown-tinted glass (fig. 867). There is nothing about the Lake Shore Drive blocks to suggest that they contain apartments rather than offices: indeed, they had been preceded by a building which pioneered the glass curtain

wall for tall office blocks, the United Nations Secretariat, New York City (1947–53), designed by a group of architects led by Wallace K. Harrison (1895–1981) in consultation with Le Corbusier. Such high-rise blocks have been enormously influential, for example on Skidmore, Owings and Merrill's Lever House, Park Avenue (1952), and Chase Manhattan Bank (1961), both in New York City, as well as on many less happily-sited office blocks in European cities. In his Farnsworth House, Plano, Illinois (1945–50), Mies applied his industrial aesthetic to an elegant but costly weekend retreat with all-glass external walls which needed to be hung with curtains. Further concessions to its domestic function included spraying the exposed structural steelwork white and facing the podium, steps and floor with travertine. Its patron, Dr Edith Farnsworth, found it too expensive to live in and made an unsuccessful attempt to sue the architect. The architect Charles Eames (1907–78) built Eames House, Santa Monica (1945–9), as an early example of the influence of Mies van der Rohe who, at the end of his career, designed the National Gallery, Berlin (1963–8), still in the language he had introduced at MIT.

The only other post-war architect of comparable influence to Mies van der Rohe was Le Corbusier, whose Unité d'Habitation at Marseilles (1946–52) was seen as a turning-point in modern domestic design. It is an immense 18-storey block containing over three hundred apartments, partly inspired by the socialist ideals of theorists like Fourier, and providing communal facilities such as a kindergarten, gymnasium, indoor shopping street and rooftop children's pool. Originally conceived in terms of steel construction, it was rethought as a reinforced concrete structure following difficulties in the supply of materials. In this process Le Corbusier finally abandoned the smooth machine-wrought surfaces admired between the wars, in place of a deliberately rough finish displaying the impress of the timber planking in which the concrete had been cast. This

898 Le Corbusier: The Unité d'Habitation block, Marseilles (1946–52)

899 Plan and section of the Unité d'Habitation, Marseilles, by Le Corbusier

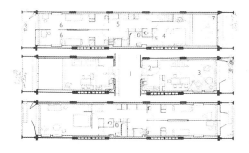
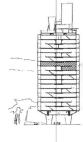

1 internal street
2 entrance
3 living-room and kitchen
4 parents' bedroom
5 wardrobe and shower
6 childrens' room

chunkiness of detail was echoed in the form of the massive *brise soleil* at the Unité; this followed the type adopted by Oscar Niemeyer (born 1907) in the Ministry of Education and Public Health headquarters in Rio de Janeiro, Brazil (1936–45), on which Le Corbusier had acted as consultant. With Lucio Costa (1902–98), Niemeyer was responsible for Brasilia (1957–70), the monumental new capital of Brazil, where curvaceous buildings contrast with slab blocks. Imitation of Le Corbusier's *béton brut* (raw or unfaced concrete) was the keynote of an architectural style, appropriately known as New Brutalism, which prevailed in Britain during the 1960s and was also known in Europe and the United States of America.

Béton brut also gave a brutal character to Le Corbusier's most striking later works: the chapel of Notre-Dame-du-Haut at Ronchamp, near Belfort (1950–5); the governmental buildings at Chandigarh, India (1951–65); the Dominican monastery of La Tourette at Eveux-sur-Arbresle, near Lyons (1953–60); and the Carpenter Center for the Visual Arts, Harvard University (1960–3), his only work in America. At Chandigarh, founded in 1951 as the administrative capital of the Punjab, Le Corbusier provided a group of public buildings which form the capitol complex: the Secretariat, the High Court and the Palace of the Assembly (parliament) (fig. 770). They are a memorably inventive attempt to create monumentality without recourse to traditional classical vocabulary. The massiveness and near-megalomaniac scale of these buildings with their distinctive profiles, especially the shell or parasol roofs of the Assembly, make them effective as sculptural symbols of civic order. It must be confessed, however, that they are functionally disastrous, while their isolation from the rest of the city means that the residential quarters are even less interesting than their uniform low-rise buildings already make them. Thus, as a leading authority on Le Corbusier's work at Chandigarh was forced to conclude, 'Almost any older Indian town, with its narrow streets and inward-orientated courtyard houses, demonstrates a more satisfactory method of coming to terms with a predominantly pedestrian environment, a tropical climate, and a high population density than is evidenced in Chandigarh.' But this aspect of the new city was not only a deliberate consequence of Le Corbusier's passion for novelty; it also reflected the ambitions of Prime Minister Nehru who, flushed with pride following the ending of British rule in India in 1947, said of Chandigarh, 'Let this be a new town, symbolic of the freedom of India, unfettered by the traditions of the past . . . an expression of the nation's faith in the future.'

Architecture 'unfettered by the traditions of the past' was achieved in more dramatic and successful fashion at the pilgrimage chapel at Ronchamp, with a reinforced concrete form concealed behind billowing neo-Expressionist forms. The strange poetry of this unique sculptural building exercised little direct influence, but the design of the Maisons Jaoul (1952–6), a pair of houses for the Jaoul family in Neuilly, Paris, had widespread repercussions, especially in Britain. Walls of coarsely-laid brickwork are divided by broad horizontal beams of plank-shuttered concrete, while the use of exposed brickwork for the interior walls shows the same deliberate disregard for sophistication. The consciously primitive or vernacular techniques shocked the British architect James Stirling, who wrote of the Maisons Jaoul in 1955 that it is 'disturbing to find little reference to the rational principles which are the basis of the modern movement'. However, the flats which he designed at Ham Common, London (1957), in collaboration with James Gowan (b.1923), echoed the Maisons Jaoul closely, as did certain features of major buildings by Sir Basil Spence (1907–76), for example the combination of segmental concrete arches and red brick at his controversial Household Cavalry Barracks, London (1970).

The moral earnestness behind the exposure of raw materials, the will to avoid polish and elegance, and the puritanical dislike of comfort, were displayed at their most devastating in the work of Peter Smithson (b.1923), in partnership with his wife Alison from 1950.

900, 901 *Above and below* Exterior and isometric of Notre-Dame-du-Haut, Ronchamp, near Belfort (1950–5), by Le Corbusier

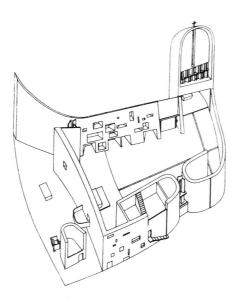

Their Secondary Modern School at Hunstanton, Norfolk (1949–51), was the first monument of New Brutalism in England. It is inspired by the welded steel frame and brick-panel architecture of Mies van der Rohe at the Illinois Institute of Technology, with the addition of an English Arts and Crafts emphasis on the 'honest' use of materials. Thus the structural materials, steel, precast

concrete slabs and bricks, are visibly exposed, without plaster and often without paint, while the plumbing and electrical conduits are also visible. The result will attract or repel according to one's aesthetic tastes, but what is irrefutable is that the building was virtually unworkable from the start. Equal if not greater problems have been caused by Stirling's History Faculty Building, Cambridge (1964; fig. 874). Of hard red brick and industrial glazing, this neo-Constructivist essay in pseudo-functionalism has suffered from extensive water-penetration, acoustical problems, and tiles falling dangerously from the exterior. Although, it developed so many faults, it still has many admirers who are fascinated by its unconventional dynamics.

The heavy concrete buildings of Sir Denys Lasdun (b.1914) are also Brutalist in intention, though they have an unusual consistency, deriving from his belief in architecture as urban landscape. His buildings, layered like geological strata and frequently incorporating exposed walkways, swept by wind and rain, include a 14-storey cluster block of apartments at Bethnal Green in the east end of London (1955), the University of East Anglia (1962–8), and the National Theatre, London (1967). The extensive work of Sir Leslie Martin (b.1908) began with the Royal Festival Hall, London (1948–51), designed with Robert Matthew, Peter Moro and Edwin Williams, as the first major public building in Britain in the International Modern Style. Leslie Martin's increasing use of brick rather than concrete suggested an affinity to Alvar Aalto, as in his several university and college buildings at Oxford and Cambridge.

A stark brutalism was also a feature of American architecture in these years, for example in two celebrated and contrasting buildings at Yale University, the Art and Architecture Building (1958–63) by Paul Rudolph (b.1918), and the Art Gallery (1953) by Louis Kahn (1901–74). The Art Gallery, a Miesian essay akin to the Smithsons' school at Hunstanton, is noticeable for the juxtaposition of its featureless façade of yellow brick with the richly plastic Italianate façade of the adjacent Gallery as built from designs by Egerton Swartwout in

902 *Above* Interior of one of the Maisons Jaoul, Neuilly, Paris (1952–6), by Le Corbusier

903 *Right* Exterior of the Secondary Modern School, Hunstanton, Norfolk (1945–51), by A. and P. Smithson

904 *Below* Lasdun: The National Theatre, London (1967), and the South Bank arts complex

905 Interior of the Trans World Airways Terminal, Kennedy Airport, New York City (1956–62), by Saarinen

1928. Rudolph's Art and Architecture Building is a dynamic configuration of colliding forms in abrasive concrete which is similar to the work of Lasdun in England. Its monolithic tower-like elements consisting of hollow piers for services create a vertical thrust which reappears in the Richards Medical Research Building, University of Pennsylvania (1958–61), by Kahn, with its heavily emphasized brick towers, mostly for staircases, air-conditioning and other services. Paul Rudolph's Earl Brydges Memorial Library, Niagara Falls, New York (1970–5), shared some of the defects of Stirling's History Faculty Building. Rudolph's strident cantilevered forms produced such complicated intersections of roof, window and wall, that they proved

too difficult to be made successfully watertight. One of Kahn's most admired buildings was his Kimbell Art Museum, Fort Worth, Texas (1967–72).

Similar work to Kahn's was provided at Yale University in the form of the Samuel Morse and Ezra Stiles Colleges (1958–62), designed by Eero Saarinen (1910–61), who had earlier shown that he could design with a lighter touch. After his Miesian General Motors Technological Center, Warren, Michigan (1945–56), he turned to a livelier, more curvilinear style, especially in his neo-Expressionist Dulles Airport, Chantilly, Virginia (1958–62), and Trans World Airways Terminal, Kennedy Airport, New York (1956–62). In these two airport buildings he gave more tangible expression to the poetry of flight than any other modern architect. The only comparable building, and one which may have influenced him since he was a judge in the competition for it, is the

Opera House at Sydney, Australia (1956–73), by the Danish architect Jørn Utzon (b.1918). Having worked under Asplund in 1942–5, Aalto in 1946, and Wright in 1949, Utzon became obsessed by the search for an organic architecture, that is, one which would resemble natural forms. He achieved this in Sydney Opera House, where the concert halls, on a series of terraces recalling the platforms of Mayan or Aztec architecture, are roofed with two sets of reinforced concrete shells in the form of elliptical paraboloids. Rising from the water, these recall for some the billowing sails of a galleon, and for others the wings of a bird in flight.

The German architect Hans Scharoun (1893–1972) was responsible for Philharmonie, the hall for the Berlin Philharmonic Orchestra, Berlin (1956–63), a late example of Expressionist or 'organic' architecture. For the Tokyo Olympic Games, the Japanese architect Kenzo Tange (b. 1913) designed the National Gymnasium (1961–4), seating 15,000 below its twin tensile catenary roofs. Further dynamic and poetic expressions of the possibilities of reinforced concrete came from the Italian Luigi Nervi (1891–1979), beginning with his Municipal Stadium, Florence (1929–32), seating 35,000 people beneath a cantilevered roof. After the war he developed a technique known as *ferrocemento* in which a series of steel meshes within the concrete make it more tensile than ordinary reinforced concrete. His masterpieces in this idiom, both in Rome, are the Palazzetto (1956–7) and Palazzo dello Sport (1958–9), the latter with a dome 328 feet (100m) in diameter.

The Danish architect Arne Jacobsen (1902–71) responded to the industrialized image of the International Modern Movement in curtain-walled buildings such as his Rodovre Town Hall, Copenhagen (1955). The Italian Carlo Scarpa (1906–78) specialized in the design of galleries and museums, one of his most striking being the remodelling of the Museo Castelvecchio, Verona (1956–64). Mario Botta (b. 1943) was a key member of the Ticino, or Ticinese School, returning to a Rationalist form, ultimately inspired by the stripped classicism of the years around 1900. Typical

906 Exterior of the Baker Dormitory, the Massachusetts Institute of Technology, Cambridge (1946–7), by Aalto

is Botta's drum-like house of brick-faced concrete, the Casa Rotonda, Stabio, Ticino (1980–2).

In Finland Alvar Aalto, whom some have praised for trying to give modern architecture a human face, entered in the 1940s into the most productive phase of his career. This began in 1946 when, following his appointment as a visiting professor at the Massachusetts Institute of Technology, Cambridge, he designed a residential building for senior students at the Institute, the Baker Dormitory (1946–7). Built of red brick like many of the older buildings in Boston, Cambridge, Yale and Princeton, this has an unusual serpentine front facing the Charles River, on to which most of the student bedrooms look. This was Aalto's first use of red brick in a major urban building. It was to be an expressive feature of much of his work in the 1950s and 1960s and may have been influenced by the tradition of brickwork in the Baltic or in New England. His National Pensions Institute, Helsinki (1948, executed 1952–6), is an asymmetrical group of monumental administrative buildings grouped round an internal courtyard and podium, creating the kind of urban landscape which was to appeal to Lasdun. Aalto developed this on a more intimate scale in his village centre at Säynätsalo

907 Nave of Vuoksenniska Church, Imatra, Finland (1956–9), by Aalto

(1949–52), and on a large scale in the Technical University at Otaniemi (1955–64). Aalto's centre at Säynätsalo, a small but economically important forest village, consists of a modest U-shaped administration block, containing the council chamber, library and offices, with a timber pergola on two sides, and a freestanding library enclosing the courtyard on the fourth side. All this is raised above the level of the surrounding ground and is approached from two open staircases, one of which is of massed earth set in planks. The secret little court or piazza has a vernacular or farmyard-like quality, with its architectural elements, which have not weathered well, distributed in a seemingly casual way.

Both the planning and the sparse angular forms of the brick buildings at Säynätsalo reflect the overriding search for novelty which has been one of the keynotes of the modern movement. Some architects, including Aalto and Eero Saarinen, seemed to find it necessary to approach the task of designing each building as though

908 *Opposite top* Aalto: Administrative centre of Säynätsalo village, Finland (1949–52)

909 *Opposite below* Aalto: Harbour front of the head office of the Enso-Gutzeit Company, Helsinki (1959–62)

no building of that particular function had ever been designed before. This is true of Aalto's head office for the Enso-Gutzeit Company (1959–62), which stands out awkwardly in the otherwise picturesque and traditional setting of Helsinki harbour. In less historically sensitive settings Aalto's search for novelty could be more appropriate. One of his most plastic or neo-Expressionist compositions is the church at Vuoksenniska, Imatra, eastern Finland (1956–9), set in the middle of a forest, which was subsequently destroyed in a hurricane. The plan of the nave comprises three asymmetrical shell forms which, in order to accommodate three different sizes of congregation, can be separated by sliding curved walls. The ceiling also takes the form of shells while the walls, of double shell construction, bend menacingly inwards.

In the 1960s and 1970s the modern movement entered a Mannerist phase characterized by the playful use of elements previously taken with deadly seriousness. One of the most celebrated examples of late modernism is the Pompidou Centre, Paris (1971–7), by Renzo Piano (b.1937) and Richard Rogers (b.1933). The ideology of modernism, with its emphasis on the truthful approach to structure, which went back to Viollet-Le-Duc and beyond, was here made into a huge public joke: thus the services and working parts of the building, all brightly coloured, are exposed as exterior ornament (fig. 885).

Recognizably late modern in a different way are the buildings in England of Norman Foster (b.1935), for example the Willis-Faber and Dumas head office, Ipswich, Suffolk (1972–5). This has a huge undulating façade entirely of bronze-tinted glass, which reflects the surrounding buildings by day but is transparent when its interiors are illuminated at dusk. It thus seems a lively variant on the early modernist obsession with glass and with slick technical efficiency. Ieoh Ming Pei, who was born in China in 1917 and emigrated to America in 1935, has produced vast and bombastic public buildings, for example the East Building of the National Gallery of Art, Washington DC (1974–8), and the John F Kennedy

910 Pei: The John F. Kennedy Library Complex, Boston (1979)

911 Rogers: Lloyds Building, London (1978–86)

Library complex, Boston (1979), which carry to an extreme the modernist preoccupation with bare geometrical mass. Eamonn Roche (b.1922) and John Dinkeloo (1918–81), who worked with Eero Saarinen in the 1950s, designed the Ford Foundation Headquarters, New York (1963–8), with an enormously influential atrium.

Richard Rogers' partner from 1970–7, the Italian architect Renzo Piano, has continued the High Tech tradition in the Beyeler Museum, Rieden, Basel (1995–7), and the Debis Building, Berlin (1998). The British architect Nicholas Grimshaw (b. 1939) designed the Stock Exchange and Communications Centre, Berlin (1991–5), as an example of what he called 'democratic openness and transparency'. Avoiding a tower block, Grimshaw's building recalls a metallic vertebrate with its back of nine steel arches.

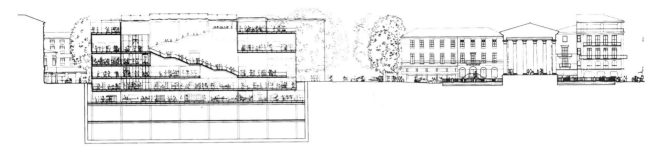

912 *Above* Foster: Cross section of the Carré d'Art (Médiathèque), Nîmes (1984–93)

913 Foster: Carré d'Art, Nîmes

Foster, Richards and Grimshaw are key figures in what is often known as High Tech architecture, Rogers claiming that his buildings point to a future in which 'architecture will no longer be a question of mass and volume but of lightweight structures whose super-imposed transparent layers will create form so that architecture will be dematerialized'. Examples of his work are the Hong Kong and Shanghai Bank, Hong Kong (1979–86), and his costly Lloyd's Building, London (1978–86), with mechanistic façades featuring stainless steel tubes concealing service pipes.

At Nîmes, France, Foster built the Carré d'Art (1984–93), a public library and an art museum known as the Médiathèque, in one of the most historically sensitive sites in Europe. In the centre of a square at the heart of this ancient Roman city stands the Maison Carrée (fig. 68), the most perfectly preserved Roman temple after the Pantheon. On one side of the square stood an opera house of 1803 with an elegant and appropriate neo-classical colonnade which was demolished to make way for the Médiathèque, even though the Roman character of Nîmes had been respected by all previous architects in the city from the eighteenth century onwards. With its thin concrete supports and glass walls, silk-screened white, and its deliberate avoidance of the mouldings that are part of the grammar, indeed, the good manners, of traditional architecture, the Médiathèque seems to turn its back on the heritage of this ancient town. Intriguingly, that was not the intention of its architect who, like his many admirers, believes that its grid façade suggests a trabeated structure and so conducts a civilized dialogue with the ancient temple that it confronts.

Post-Modernism

The attempt of the modern movement to change man through architectural revolution and the destruction of memory threatened to do violence to his dignity and identity. An early text questioning modernism was by the architect Robert Venturi, *Complexity and Contradiction in Architecture* (1966), in which he recommended a revival of the 'presence of the past' in architectural design. His aim was to show how architecture, before the modern movement, was capable of embodying many levels of meaning simultaneously. He sought to include in his own buildings qualities that he described, obscurely, as 'inclusion, inconsistency, compromise, accommodation, adaptation, superadjacency, equivalence, multiple focus, juxtaposition, or good *and* bad space.' More importantly, by demolishing a puritanical hatred of ornament, he opened up a new pluralistic, permissive architecture, a contextualism of outlook and a concern for the environment. One of his first works was his Vanna Venturi House, Chestnut Hill, Pennsylvania (1961–5), an abstracted version of a Shingle Style house.

Another popular expression of this change of mood was an exhibition, significantly called 'The Presence of the Past', held in Venice in 1980 as the first international exhibition organized by the Venice Biennale and subsequently shown in Paris and San Francisco. One of the principal exhibits was the Strada Nuovissima, a street in which 20 façades were designed by a variety of architects including Robert Venturi, Charles Moore, Ricardo Bofill, Hans Hollein and Léon Krier, most of whom used the orders in a dramatic, mannered or playful way. The element of exaggeration in Post-Modern classicism reminds one that the style is a development from modernism which, as we have noted, had itself entered a mannerist phase.

It has been argued that Post-Modernism includes the straight traditionalism of Alan Greenberg and Quinlan Terry, the neo-modernism of Richard Meier and Aldo Rossi and the exuberant, near-Baroque flavour of the

914 Johnson: AT & T Building, New York (1978–84)

recent commercial buildings of Skidmore, Owings and Merrill, and Terry Farrell. The playful element that frequently occurs in it was brought to the centre of Manhattan by Philip Johnson (b. 1906) in his skyscraper office building of 1978–84 for the American Telephone and Telegraph Company. In this building, sheathed in granite over a reinforced steel skeleton, he returned to the pre-First World War New York tradition of making sense out of skyscrapers by treating them classically with a base and crowning cornice; the base is conceived as a Serlian arch, while the broken pediment seems halfway between Chippendale and Ledoux. The AT & T building,

915 Johnson: College of Architecture, University of Houston (1983–5)

however surprising, should not be regarded as a maverick in Johnson's career. He had long since rejected the Miesian language of his Glass House, New Canaan, Connecticut (1940), despite having produced a seminal book with H.-R. Hitchcock called *The International Style: Architecture since 1922* (New York 1932) and a monograph on Mies van der Rohe in 1947. His arcaded water-pavilion of 1962 in the grounds of the Glass House had a Schinkelesque flavour, which recurred on a large scale in his elegant Amon Carter Museum of Western Art, Fort Worth, Texas (1961), the Sheldon Memorial Art Gallery for the University of Nebraska at Lincoln (1963), and the New York State Theater at the Lincoln Center (1964).

However, Johnson's stark East and Garden Wing additions to the Museum of Modern Art, New York City (1964), marked a puzzling return to a faceless modernism. Livelier is the Investors' Diversified Services Building, a giant, lozenge-shaped office block that he and his partner, John Burgee, built in 1968–73 at Minneapolis, Minnesota. Nestling against its lower storeys is a skylit indoor concourse of a crystalline, multi-faceted character reminiscent of the Expressionist 'city crowns' proposed by Bruno Taut in 1919. A more appropriate associationism was reached in the College of Architecture, University of Houston, Texas (1983–5), where Johnson and Burgee produced a rare echo of Ledoux's House of Education in his Ideal Town of Chaux of c.1780 (pp. 409).

The populist, theatrical quality of Post-Modern classicism, which has been variously described as 'camp' and 'kitsch', strongly colours the Piazza d'Italia, New Orleans, Louisiana (1975–80), designed by Charles Moore (b. 1925) as a social focus for the Italian community in the city. His deployment of highly coloured classical features in a fairground manner is similar to the technique of Michael Graves (b. 1934) in his controversial Portland Public Service Building at Portland, Oregon (1979–82; fig. 869). With associations ranging from Egyptian to Art Deco, this mighty tower of painted concrete, which originally was to have been decorated with immense glass-fibre garlands, is the most emphatic expression of the pluralism that is at the heart of American Post-Modernism. On a smaller and happier scale are two spirited variants on Palladian villa themes, both by Charles Moore, of 1978–81: Rudolph House, Massachusetts, and Sammis Hall which is part of the Banbury Conference complex at Cold Spring Harbour, New York.

916 *Above* Moore: Piazza d'Italia, New Orleans (1975–80)

917 *Below* Bofill: The Palace of Abraxas, an apartment block at Marne-la-Vallée (1978–83)

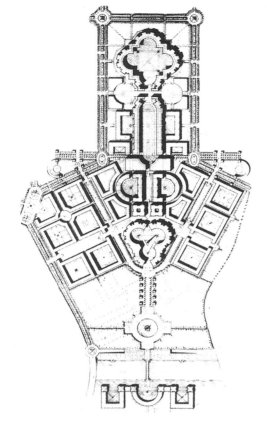

918 *Above* Plan of Bofill's housing scheme for Montpellier (1985–8)

919 *Below* Langdon & Wilson and Genter: Main peristyle and garden façade of the J. Paul Getty Museum, Malibu (1970–5)

The new awareness of the 'Presence of the Past' was impressive for being a European, not just an Anglo-American phenomenon. Thus, some of its most striking achievements were by a Spanish architect, Ricardo Bofill (b. 1939), working in France: these include two housing projects of titanic scale near Paris, known as Les Arcades du Lac, Saint-Quentin-en-Yvelines (1975–81) and the Palace of Abraxas, Marne-la-Vallée (1978–83). A similarly grand project at Montpellier (1985–8), has a more logical and appropriate physical connection with the main square of the ancient city. Here Bofill's buildings represented a successful attempt to provide an urban development as part of the existing city centre, rather than in anonymous and far-flung suburbs.

Another building designed with even closer historical resonances was the J. Paul Getty Museum, Malibu, California (1970–5). Ultimately inspired by the ancient Roman Villa of the Papyri at Herculaneum, this was designed by the Los Angeles partnership of Langdon and Wilson with Edward Genter as the project architect and archaeological advice from Dr Norman Neuerberg. With its sumptuous interiors, peristyle and formal

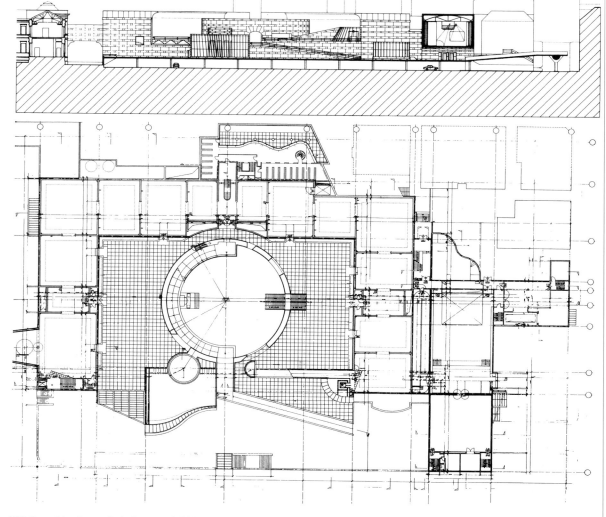

920 Plan of the Staatsgalerie, Stuttgart (1980–3) by Stirling

gardens, this impeccable recreation of ancient Roman luxury realizes the ambitions of numerous architects and patrons in the neo-classical period, of whom Schinkel and the Prussian Crown Prince Friedrich-Wilhelm (p. 477) were among the most significant. Successful, too, is the Clos Pegase Vinery, Napa Valley, California (1987), by Michael Graves, though some critics question why such a building should recall the layout of some ancient sanctuary.

America, richer than European countries, was freer than the latter during the 1970s and 1980s to indulge in Post-Modern experiments. Indeed, the English architect James Stirling found more popularity abroad than at home. His School of Architecture at Rice University, Houston, Texas (1980), an L-shaped building in a round-arched, semi-Romanesque style, is a good example of how to incorporate new buildings into an existing complex, in this case a campus built gradually from 1909 to 1941 from designs by Cram, Goodhue and Ferguson. Stirling's New Building and Chamber Theatre at the Staatsgalerie, Stuttgart (1980–3), is an aggressive assembly of technological or Constructivist imagery combined with fine craftsmanship, polished sandstone surfaces and unusual polchromy. Echoes of many ages of architecture are here evoked from antiquity through Klenze and Gärtner to the present day.

At Embankment Place, a robust building by Terry Farrell (b. 1938) overlooking the river Thames at

921 *Above* Stirling: New Building, Staatsgalerie, Stuttgart

922 *Below* Venturi: Sainsbury Wing, National Gallery, London
(1987–91)

923 *Above* Pei: Pyramid, Musée du Louvre, Paris (1983–9)

Charing Cross Station, London (1987–90), trains run into the lower part, so the elevation of the office accommodation that surmounts it is a high, glazed curve, locating the building within the tradition of the nineteenth-century train shed.

Venturi's Sainsbury Wing at the National Gallery, London (1987–91), was also intended as an ironic commentary on the fragmentation of the classical tradition in modern architecture. In the initial competition for the National Gallery extension in 1982–3, which included entries from Richard Rogers, Arup, and Skidmore, Owings and Merrill, the winning design, by Ahrends, Burton and Koralek, was memorably described by the Prince of Wales as 'a monstrous carbuncle on the face of an elegant and much loved friend'. Striking a chord in the heart of the general public, this criticism led to the appointment of a private committee which chose in 1986 the American partnership, Venturi, Rauch and Scott Brown, to design a building to be paid for by a benefaction from the Sainsbury family. Venturi approached the task almost as a stage designer, saying, 'I like the oblique view of Wilkins looking towards Gibbs' St Martin in the Fields, and I feel a syncopation in the build up of columns. The power of classicism is that it can be modified and still hold its power.' Its fragmented classicism, as well as the deliberately contrasting side elevation in functionalist brick, are intended as commentaries on modern uncertainty about the classical language.

924 Nouvel: Institut du Monde Arabe, Paris (1981–7)

Similarly, the Louvre in Paris was provided with a major addition which made ironic play with historical references. This was the 71 feet (22m) high Pyramid (1983–9), with which Ieoh Ming Pei (b. 1917) marked his new underground entrance to a reorganized Louvre. Though less transparent during the daytime than Pei had intended, this monument of glass and steel deliberately denies the essential characteristics of the pyramid which are solidity and immutability. Requiring constant costly

925 *Left* Rossi: Palazzo Hotel, Fukuoka (1987–9)

926 *Below* Plan of the Getty Centre, Los Angeles (1985–97), by Meier

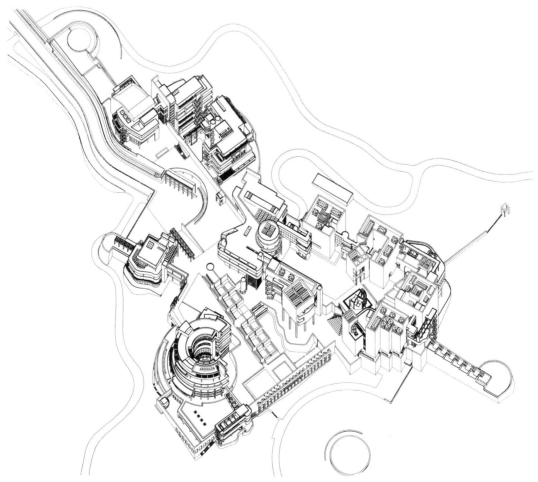

cleaning and difficult to cool internally, its maintenance is a problem. The grand axial vista leading from the pyramid to the Arc de Triomphe terminates on the far side of the Arc de Triomphe with the Grande Arche de la Défense (1981–9). By the Danish architect Johann Otto von Spreckelsen (1929–87), this is less an arch than a gigantic, hollowed-out cube. Also in Paris is the Institut du Monde Arabe (1981–7) by Jean Nouvel (b. 1945). Its south front is memorably hung with gilt filigree panels recalling Islamic traditions, while its giant transparent staircase is no less spectacular.

Pei and Nouvel are Late Modern rather than Post-Modern architects. The same is true of architects such as the Dutch Structuralist Herman Hertzberger (b. 1932), Aldo Rossi (1931–97) and Richard Meier (b. 1934). With its honeycomb of public and private spaces, Hertzberger's Centraal Beher Insurance Offices, Appeldoorn, Holland (1970–2), was intended to provide a friendlier space than the customary open-plan office. Rossi used stripped classical forms inspired by Italian Fascist architecture of the 1930s, as in his San Cataldo Cemetery, Modena (1971–85), and Palazzo Hotel, Fukuoka, Japan (1987–9). Meier, similarly, restores the white purity of the International Modern style. For him, 'White is the ephemeral emblem of perpetual movement': hence the white-panelled, enamelled metal syntax of buildings such as his Getty Center for the History of Art and the Humanities, Los Angeles, California (1985–97), and his City Hall and Central Library, The Hague (1986–95).

Town planning

The Garden City

The Garden City Movement could be seen as an attempt to resolve the dichotomy between the park and the grid which we noted in nineteenth-century America. The principal proponent of the Garden City, Sir Ebenezer Howard (1850–1928), had indeed spent five years in America in the 1870s where he was influenced by Walt Whitman, Ralph Waldo Emerson and theories of the roots of beauty in nature. The proposals in Howard's To-

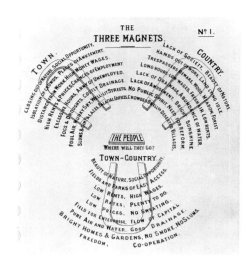

927 *Above* Diagram of the three magnets (town, country and town and country) from Ebenezer Howard, *Garden Cities of Tomorrow* (1902)

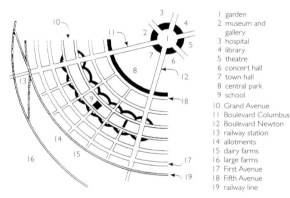

1 garden
2 museum and gallery
3 hospital
4 library
5 theatre
6 concert hall
7 town hall
8 central park
9 school
10 Grand Avenue
11 Boulevard Columbus
12 Boulevard Newton
13 railway station
14 allotments
15 dairy farms
16 large farms
17 First Avenue
18 Fifth Avenue
19 railway line

928 *Above* Ebenezer Howard: Garden City Ward and Centre (1898)

morrow: *A Peaceful Path to Real Reform* (1898), republished as *Garden Cities of Tomorrow* (1902), led to the creation of the first British Garden City at Letchworth, Hertfordshire, designed by the architect Sir Raymond Unwin (1863–1940) in 1904.

Howard envisaged economically self-supporting satellite towns of about 30,000 inhabitants, without major roads encircling them or railways running through them. Containing green areas, they would also be surrounded by agricultural land, but the centre of Letchworth lacks significant public buildings, the largest building still being the Spirella Corset Factory of 1912 near the railway station. Letchworth was followed by Welwyn Garden City and, from 1906, by Hampstead Garden Suburb, the title of the latter recognizing its role as a dormitory suburb. But because of the involvement from 1908 of Sir Edwin Lutyens who created a formal centre at Hampstead, flanked by churches and an institute, it is of more architectural distinction than Letchworth.

The low densities and the zoning that separated housing from industries created a pattern which was influential throughout Europe, the first Garden City in Germany being that of Hellerau, at Dresden, built in 1909–14 by Richard Riemerschmid. There are further examples in Belgium in the 1920s at Brussels and Kappelveld. In England some of these ideals were taken up in the New Towns policy after 1945, which created towns such as Harlow, Crawley and Stevenage to take the strain off London. The essentially anti-urban character of these New Towns was partly a consequence of the policy of moving people out of the bomb-damaged parts of London instead of rebuilding the old streets.

Clarence Stein (1882–1975), landscape architect, urban designer and founder of the Regional Planning Association, applied the Garden City theories to two urban developments featuring communal gardens and the separation of traffic from pedestrians: Sunnyside Gardens, Queens, New York, from 1924, and Radburn, New Jersey, from 1929. Stein was associated with the polemical writer on urbanism, Lewis Mumford (1895–1990), author of books such as *The Story of Utopias* (1922) and *The Culture of Cities* (1938), and a disciple of Ebenezer Howard and Patrick Geddes. In his attempt to reinstate spiritual values and the relation of the town to the natural environment, Mumford was critical of the modern dependence on technology, but his message was confused by his belief in large-scale centralized intervention.

The City Beautiful
The City Beautiful Movement in America had a fuller understanding of the importance of urbanism, partly out of sympathy for the French Beaux-Arts tradition. After the first expression of City Beautiful ideals at the World's

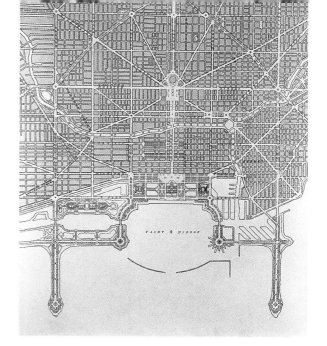

929 Plan for Chicago (1907), by Burnham and Bennett

Columbian Exhibition of 1893 in Chicago, the coordinator, Daniel Burnham (1846–1912), went on to design the McMilland plan for Washington, in collaboration with C. F. McKim and F. L. Olmsted, in an attempt to compensate for the erosion of L'Enfant's plan. He followed this with his most ambitious work, the extension plan for Chicago of 1906–9, with Edward Bennett (1874–1954), but he also worked in other cities including Cleveland and San Francisco.

Functionalism and after
The dominance of the Garden City was challenged by the pioneers of International Modernism in the international housing exhibition that opened at Stuttgart in 1927, and included the famous Weissenhofsiedlung (p. 600). This featured contributions by Gropius and Le Corbusier who was a key figure at CIAM (International Congress of Modern Architecture), the meeting of the leading modern architects which Sigfried Giedion organized in 1928. Other architects present included Berlage, Lissitsky, Rietveld and Stam. The dogmas of International Modernism that they promoted, functionalization,

930 Weissenhofsiedlung, Stuttgart (1927)

931 Modern Berlin, with office blocks (1993-96), by Beringer & Wawrik

standardization and rationalism, were formulated in the Athens Charter of 1933. Traditional cities would be replaced by functional zoning with high-rise blocks and huge traffic arteries. Cornelis van Eesteren (1897–1988), a Dutch architect influenced by the Bauhaus, produced the General Extension Plan for Amsterdam in 1936, while CIAM principles were still being upheld 20 years later in the design for Brasilia by Lucio Costa (1902–98). Similarly, Le Corbusier's post-war Unité d'Habitation, sometimes known as the Cité Radieuse, at Marseilles (p. 651) was indebted to social housing projects such as the *phalanstère* of Fourier.

The endless post-war schemes proposed throughout the developed world, from those of Archigram in Britain to those of Metabolism in Japan, seemed novel at the time, yet were united in their reliance on High Tech components and their rejection of traditional urbanism. All were unable able to solve satisfactorily the problems of modern urban life and transport. The failure to achieve a convincing urban language was notably demonstrated in Berlin which, rebuilt in the closing years of the twentieth century as the capital of the newly reunited country, was little more than a set of unrelated monuments in conflicting styles by fashionable prima donna architects.

The weaknesses of the urban planning practices associated with Ebenezer Howard, Le Corbusier, CIAM and the Athens Charter had been memorably exposed as early as 1961 by Jane Jacobs (b.1916) in her book *The Death and Life of Great American Cities*. She demonstrated that zoning, the dominance of the motor car and the reliance on statistics produced a numbing uniformity that was killing the variety and complexity of traditional cities, which it should be the aim of modern architects to recreate. Her challenge has been taken up in the theory and increasingly extensive practice of Léon Krier and of the partnership, founded in Florida in 1980, of Andres Duany and Elizabeth Plater-Zyberk, who specialize in traditionally designed urban communities.

Architecture for the Millennium

At the start of a new millennium it is natural for us to reflect on what the new era should look like. The principal architectural choices seem to be a muted post-modernism which continues to flourish with its flashy, jokey ornament added as commercial packaging; High Tech architecture, with the science fiction flavour of its constant exposure of technology; Deconstructivism, a typical end-of-century phenomenon characterized by a will to shock in which dislocation and fragmentation are highly valued; and finally, the return of a traditional architecture, with roots in a timeless language, both vernacular and classical. All four types, which sometimes overlap, have many adherents.

The Spanish engineer-architect Santiago Calatrava has created a breathtaking TGV Railway station at Lyon-Satolas, France (1990–4), known as 'the bird'. With vast, functionless wings stretching high up into the air above the concourse, this High Tech fantasy is indebted to a chain of abstract sculptural buildings such as Saarinen's Kennedy Airport (fig. 905), though Calatrava has also

932, 933 *Above and below* Calatrava: Exterior and interior of the TGV Railway Station, Lyon-Satolas (1990–4)

934 *Opposite* Outram: Interior of the Judge Institute of Management Studies, Cambridge (1992–5)

935 *Above left* Kurokawa: Aerial view of the Hiroshima City Museum of Contemporary Art, Hiroshima (1988)

936 *Above* Isozaki: Tsukuba Centre Building, Ibaraki (1979–83)

claimed that it was inspired by Salvador Dali's painting of melting watches. An individual Post-Modernist voice is that of John Outram (b. 1934) who, in the course of his career, has abandoned High Tech forms for an architecture of rich colour and exotic symbolical ornament, well exemplified in his striking rebuilding of Old Addenbrooke's Hospital, Cambridge, as the Judge Institute of Management Studies (1992–5). He believes in working out iconographic programmes, as recommended by Charles Jencks in *Towards a Symbolic Architecture* (1985).

Numerous powerful attempts have been made in Japan to synthesize western modernism with traditional Japanese aesthetics and religion. Kisho Kurokawa (b. 1934) designed the Hiroshima City Museum of Contemporary Art, Hiroshima (1988), as an essay in what he called the philosophy of symbiosis. Sixty per cent of the floor space is below ground, above which rises a series of linked gable roofs recalling the earthen

Edo storehouses of the seventeenth century, though the materials range from natural stone to aluminium. Arata Isozaki (b. 1931) designed the Tsukuba Centre Building, Ibaraki (1979–83), a vast assembly of buildings including a concert hall, community centre, hotel, shopping mall and open air theatre. It is a kind of vast, futuristic synthesis of classical, medieval, neo-classical, Egyptian, Japanese and Indian elements, in which, so Isozaki believes, uniformity is attained through diversity. Tadeo Ando (b. 1941) has tried to link his buildings to the landscape and the elements, including earth and water, placing part of them underground. With its hidden courtyards, his Kidosaki House, Tokyo (1982–6), has an

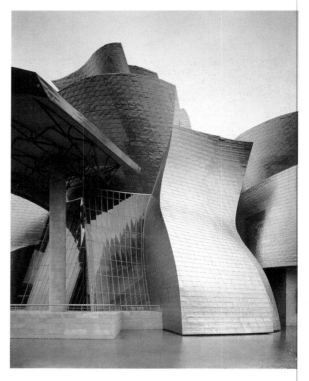

937 Ando: Church of Light, Osaka (1987–9)

938 Gehry: Guggenheim Museum, Bilbao (1991–7)

austere mystery, while his Church of Light, Osaka (1987–9), relies for its effect on the play of sunlight on raw concrete.

The leading architects of the populist yet aggressive architecture of Deconstructivism are Eisenman, Gehry, Libeskind, Koolhaas and the latter's pupil, the Iraqi-born Zaha Hadid (b. 1950), whose work includes the Vitra Fire Station, Weil-am-Rhein (1991–3), with its expressive jagged forms. Frank Gehry (b. 1929), a prolific, Canadian-born American architect, began with the Gehry House, Santa Monica (1978–88), an assembly of tilted cubes incorporating low-cost, corrugated metal panels. His Energie-Forum-Innovation, Bad Oeynhausen, Germany (1995), an electricity supply centre and exhibition hall incorporating zinc, stucco and glass, is a bewildering variety of intersecting buildings which contain advanced ecological technologies including solar and wind energy, and water recycling. Gehry's spectacularly fragmented Guggenheim Museum, Bilbao, Spain (1991–7), incorporates Spanish limestone

but the predominant effect is provided by the grey titanium panels based on a technique in the aerospace industry.

Coop Himmelbau, an Austrian group formed in 1968, are well known for their conversion of the rooftop of 6, Falkenstrasse, Vienna (1983–8), for a firm of lawyers. The seemingly unstable addition recalls a glass and steel bird perched on the roof, referring to the 'falcon' in the name of the street below. Their Systems Research Department at Seibersdorf, near Vienna (1995), is a disturbing composition of fragmented, shifting planes, suggesting the process of change and exploration to which the building is dedicated. The Austrian architect Hans Hollein (b. 1934) made his name with elegant Viennese shops incorporating fractured elements in their façades, but has since moved on to more monumental works such as his Städtisches Museum, Münchengladbach (1972–82).

Rem Koolhaas (b. 1944), the Dutch architect who formed OMA (Office for Metropolitan Architecture) in

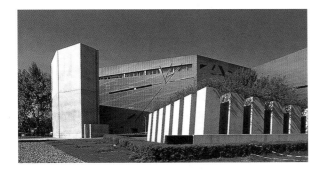

939 Libeskind: Jewish Museum, Berlin (1989–99)

940 Eisenman: Wexner Center for Visual Arts, Columbus, Ohio
(1985–9)

London in 1975, designed the Museum of Art, Rotterdam (1987–92), and specializes in a kind of creative anarchism. This same is true of Daniel Libeskind (b. 1946), a Polish-born American architect, whose grey, zinc-clad Jewish Museum, Berlin (1989–99), has a jagged Star of David plan and internal spaces that are intentionally disturbing. The kind of positive nihilism, conceived in order to recognize and come to terms with the fragmentation and alienation so characteristic of the modern world, is also boldly expressed in the Wexner Center for the Visual Arts, Columbus, Ohio (1985–9). By Peter Eisenman (b. 1932), it features a shattered tower and truncated arch.

The growing concern at the end of the twentieth century with the environmental implications of man-made 'global warming' was part of a wide variety of cultural, social and political movements, including the search for an environmentally sustainable architecture. The inventor and environmentalist Stewart Brand, author of *The Whole Earth Catalog*, published a devastating study in 1994 called *How Buildings Learn: What Happens After They're Built*, in which he pointed out the structural disadvantages of supposedly functional buildings by architects such as Stirling, Piano and Rogers. He showed that more money is now spent on changing existing buildings than on building new ones. The quest for a more humane architecture has developed in reaction to those aspects of twentieth-century life and art that have resulted in disorientation and alienation, in destruction of both the street and the countryside, in the lack of a sense of community, in the speedy obsolescence of buildings, and in the obsession with technological gadgetry. Architecturally, the reaction against this has produced a great variety of designs, ranging from public libraries to new towns, which are marked by a sense of permanence and a sensitivity to locality, which totally reject the iconoclasm of the modern movement and of High Tech.

One extremely sympathetic response to its site is the National Museum of Roman Art, Mérida, Spain (1980–6), built from designs by Rafael Moneo (b. 1937). It is situated in an ancient Roman city from which it derives its powerful interior of brick arches. Another Spanish museum, the Galician Centre for Contemporary Art, Santiago de Compostela (1988–95), by the

941 Moneo: National Museum of Roman Art, Merida (1980–6)

942 *Above* Greenberg: Staircase hall, News Building, Athens, Georgia (1988–92)

943 *Opposite above* Terry: Richmond Riverside, Richmond, Surrey (1984–9)

944 *Opposite below* Krier: Atlantis, a new town in Tenerife (1988)

Portuguese architect Alvaro Siza (b. 1933), features modern construction beneath granite cladding.

Allan Greenberg (b. 1938), the leading traditional architect in the United States, provided handsome new public rooms at the heart of Washington DC, during the 1980s. A sequence of lobbies, ante-chamber and reception rooms culminates in the elliptical Treaty Room which is used for signing treaties. Its Corinthian order, based on that used by John Russell Pope at the National Archives Building, Washington (1936), incorporates the Great Seal of the Secretary of State. His expressive and instructive architecture is also seen in the offices of the Secretary and Deputy Secretary of State, with their views of the Mall and Lincoln Memorial.

Greenberg's News Building in Athens, Georgia (1988–92), for the production of three newspapers and two magazines, boasts an austere Doric portico of unfluted baseless columns. This is a reference to Greek Revival architecture of the Southern states which has been ignored in new buildings in Athens and the nearby University of Georgia. The building reveals unexpected variety as we move through it, beginning with the curved wall behind the portico, largely glazed yet fully articulated with mouldings. Within is a great stair hall where the Doric and Ionic orders are vibrant with polychromy. There is a steep slope to the rear of the site where two lower floors, serving industrial functions, are given Schinkelesque trabeated forms.

Another architect who has refused to indulge in Post-Modern games is Quinlan Terry (b. 1937), who has built Brentwood cathedral, Essex (1990–1), a basilican addition to a Gothic Revival church, and a massive Greek Doric Library for Downing College, Cambridge (1991–3). He was also responsible for a large urban development known as Richmond Riverside (1984–9), which showed that commercial development can take place in the centre of a historic town without ruining it.

With its delectable courts, terraces and archways, Richmond Riverside is an important contribution to the process of urban reconstruction and the creation of new towns and villages, which featured strongly from the late twentieth century. Pioneering figures in this movement are the Krier brothers, Robert and Léon, who consistently emphasized the primacy of the task of

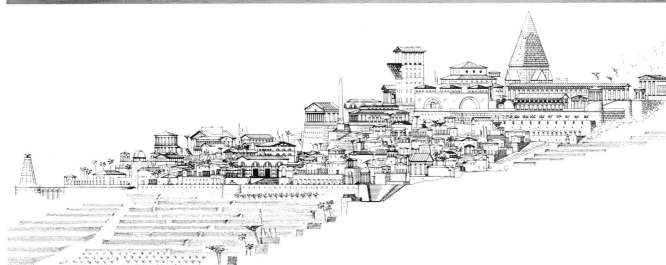

recreating urban order through reviving the traditional hierarchies of streets, squares, public buildings and monuments, which modern architects, planners and developers had everywhere destroyed. Both brothers were born in Luxemburg, Robert in 1938, Léon in 1946. Robert was associated with the revival by Aldo Rossi of Italian rationalism of the 1920s, particularly of Terragni. Thus Robert Krier's white housing in the Ritterstrasse, Berlin (1978–80), has the ghostly monumentality of the painter de Chirico, whom we noted in discussing the work of Angiolo Mazzoni (p. 631). Two German architects, Oswald Ungers (b. 1926) and Josef Kleihues (b. 1933), both with neo-Rationalist

945 *Left* O'Connor, Tagliaventi and others: Rue de Laeken, Brussels (1989–94)

946 *Below* Krier: Initial proposal for the New Town at Poundbury, Dorset (built from 1988)

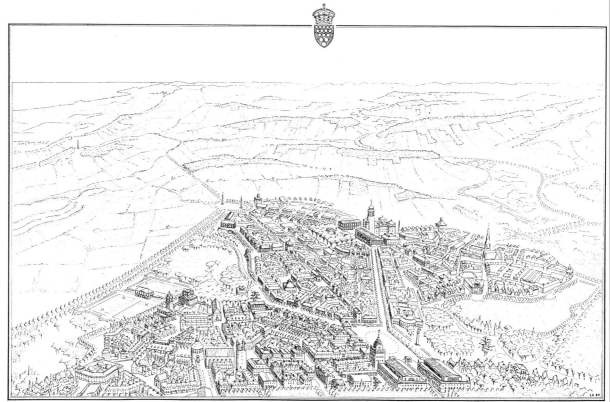

and minimalist tendencies, have designed, respectively, the German Embassy, Washington DC (1988–94), and Haus Sommer at the Brandenburg Gate, Berlin (1994–7), the latter paying respectful attention to its classical neighbour.

Léon Krier, who has been a particular opponent of stylistic pluralism and Post-Modernism, condemning it as unserious kitsch, has devoted much time to largely unexecuted schemes for ordered and harmonious ideal developments. These include projects in Paris for the La Villette quarter (1976) and for Les Halles (1979), and in Berlin for the city centre (1977) and for Tegel (1980). His recreation in 1985 of Pliny's villa, as an image of an ideal city, and his stunningly evocative project for the city of Atlantis, Tenerife, Spain (1988), were echoed in miniature in his projected school for 500 pupils at Saint-Quentin-en-Yvelines, France (1977–9), with its timeless, beautifully disposed courts like a realization in spartan Doricist terms of the ninth-century project for the ideal monastery of St Gall (p. 112). Traditional ideals of communal order are here given a new relevance in an educational institution intended for a modern bourgeois and working-class suburb.

The Rue de Laeken, Brussels, a historic street in the heart of Brussels which had been destroyed in an unsympathetic programme of comprehensive modern development, was completely rebuilt in 1989–94 by a group of young architects from different European countries who were inspired by Léon Krier. These included Liam O'Connor, Gabriele Tagliaventi, Javier Cenicacelaya and Inigo Salona, Jean-Philippe Garlic and Valerie Negre. Their work included the demolition of the 'Tour Bleue', a hostile tower block of the 1950s of aluminium and glass panels.

Ramon Fortet has designed a master plan for reurbanizing the periphery of the town of Olot, Spain (1985–9), where he has built a vast crescent like those of Wood in England. Jean-Pierre Errath has worked from 1978–92 on reconstructing the historic French city of Bordeaux, where eighteenth-century urban architecture had been degraded by modern additions. Léon Krier has

947 Duany and Plater-Zyberk: New town of Seaside, Florida (1987)

948 Porphyrios: Office Building, Brindley Place, Birmingham (1997–8)

949 Simpson: Envisaged perspective of the masterplan for Paternoster Square, London (1992)

designed a new town of modest houses at Poundbury, Dorset (1988–96), on the Duchy of Cornwall estate of the Prince of Wales. In the United States Jaquelin Robertson is responsible for many such schemes including the master plan and Clubhouse for New Albany, Ohio, where he has contrived to preserve a rural character. Better known are urban developments by Andres Duany (b. 1950) and Elizabeth Plater-Zyberk (b. 1950), including the new town of Seaside (1987) and the new village of Windsor (1989–96), both in Florida, and New Town, Gaithersburg, Maryland (1988–96). With houses of load-bearing construction, rafters and columns, these conform to a programme that Duany and Plater-Zyberk call the Traditional Neighborhood Development Ordinance, intended to serve as a model for towns free from traffic.

Another individual talent is Demetri Porphyrios (b. 1948) whose individual design philosophy, rooted in building craft, is poetically demonstrated at Belvedere Village, Ascot (1989), in vernacular forms, and in Grove Buildings Quadrangle, Magdalen College, Oxford (1995–9). His vernacular residential ranges at Magdalen College merge into a neo-classical theatre where the scale is large and the classical detailing crisp and frugal in a truly Hellenic spirit. Porphyrios' office building at Brindley Place, Birmingham (1997–8), by contrast, helps establish a new urban landscape. It is dominated by a somewhat Italianate classical clock tower which was provided in response to the client's request for a landmark sign. Behind its self-supporting outer masonry skin is a steel frame which is exposed in a light, glazed atrium with detailing recalling Schinkel, Klenze, Lewerentz and Asplund.

The works of John Simpson (b. 1954) include additions to Buckingham Palace where his extensive new Queen's Gallery (1999–2001) develops themes from the work of John Nash, the architect of the palace in the 1820s. The search for meaning in architecture, partly provoked by the manifest nonsense of much Post-Modern ornament, is accompanied by developments in art-historical scholarship such as *Architecture and Meaning on the Athenian Acropolis* by Robin Rhodes (1995), *Bearers*

950 Bofill: National Theatre, Barcelona, Spain (1992–5)

of Meaning: The Classical Orders in Antiquity, the Middle Ages, and the Renaissance by John Onians (1988), and *The Lost Meaning of Classical Architecture: Speculations on Ornament from Vitruvius to Venturi* by George Hersey (1988). Onians claims that the orders are not a solution to structural problems, but bearers of meaning in which people formulate their relation to each other and to the gods. Hersey discusses certain terms and passages from Vitruvius and other ancient texts so as to extract a fuller range of the meanings, associations and images that lurk inside the words. He believes that classical ornament once evoked semantic resonances which he identifies as *tropes*, i.e. puns, and describes the origins of decoration in the rituals of hunting and sacrifice of the Greeks, mentioning in particular the erection of trophies of the arms of defeated enemies. He sees the process of reassembling the remains of the sacrificial victims as analogous to the construction of temples, and notes the many architectural terms that also refer to parts of the body.

A templar building which neatly contrives to combine aspects of both High Tech and traditional architecture is the National Theatre of Catalonia, Barcelona (1992–5), by Ricardo Bofill. In one of the most commanding buildings of the 1990s, Bofill brilliantly adapted the temple form to new materials and new functions, combining symmetry, harmony and order with an overriding concern for aesthetic effect. Moreover, its monumental dimensions, 315 by 184 feet (96 × 56m), make it larger than any temple in the ancient world. The robust Doric colonnades along the side walls are the ideal foil to the walls of clear glass with minimal supports or frames. The colonnades are not continued on the entrance front, which seems open like the great mouth of a nineteenth-century train shed such as Hittorff's Gare du Nord in Paris.

One of the cleverest visual elements is Bofill's solution of the age-old problem of opera houses, which is how to deal with the high fly-tower. At Glyndebourne Opera House, Sussex (1989–94), the widely admired architect Michael Hopkins (b. 1935) chose to expose the bulky tower as a frankly industrial unit in sharp contrast to the main building with its load-bearing walls of mellow brick. Bofill, by contrast, treats the fly-tower as a miniature temple astride the crown of the roof, rather as an architect such as James Gibbs, at St Martin-in-the-Fields (fig. 517), had solved the problem of how to combine the tower necessary for bell-ringing with the pediment required by a classical church. The theatre is a modular building designed on a 26 by 26 foot (8 × 8m) grid in which every floor and wall measurement is a multiple or fraction of this. The great semicircular amphitheatre, described as 'a bull-ring inside a temple' by the project architect Jean-Pierre Carniaux drops dramatically down from the entrance foyer. Unusually,

681

951 Beeby: Harold Washington Library Center, Chicago (1990–2)

the foyer is on a level with the top of the auditorium, at the centre. It contains three separate theatres, a television studio, theatre school and scenery workshop, all at modest cost.

The quest for an architecture in harmony with nature and tradition was expressed by the American architectural educator Norman Crowe in his book, *Nature and the Idea of a Man-Made World: An Investigation into the Evolutionary Roots of Form and Order in the Built Environment* (1995). Studying the connections between the natural and the man-made in traditional towns and cities, farms and gardens, buildings and works of civil engineering, he seeks to learn the lessons lost by the modern movement, which sees the built world through the abstractions of post-Enlightenment science. He aims to re-establish nature as the paradigm for creation as well as the ancient idea that we are responsible for maintaining a harmony between nature and what we

make ourselves. He sees the city as 'the culminating expression of all these characteristic responses to nature', stressing particularly Aristotle's understanding of the city as the place for 'the good life'.

The need to restore the city is one of the greatest concerns of the millennium. A monumental building in Chicago commissioned as part of that urban renewal is the Harold Washington Library Center, built in 1990–2 by Thomas Beeby (b. 1941) of Hammond, Beeby and Babka. The central public library for Chicago, it occupies a whole block at the decaying south end of the Chicago loop. An inspiring example of a modern public building, it yet has a traditional nobility of scale and material: of magnificent materials, including red granite on a rusticated base, it is also rich in symbolic ornament which terminates in the spectacularly flowing aluminium acroteria on the pediments. Designed like a huge flowering column, it places library services at the base, the main bulk of the collection on the six central floors, and the administrative offices and winter garden at the

952 Erick van Egeraat: ING Bank, Budapest (1995)

953 Alsop & Störmer: Le Grand Bleu, Marseilles (1994)

954 Bruder: Phoenix Public Library, Phoenix (1995)

top of the building. The winter garden is a beautiful, glazed re-creation of an urban courtyard for public receptions, but sadly it is not approached by a monumental staircase but by a confusing network of escalators. Nonetheless, this building is a masterpiece in the heroic tradition of Sullivan and the city of Chicago, though it would be unthinkable without the vast range of modern technological services that it incorporates. Thus, firmly rooted in the past, it yet points forward to the future.

Attention should be paid to the transformation of architecture through the use of fabric membranes inflated by air pumps, stretched over tent poles or hung from external scaffolding. The first use of this technique for a large-span structure, incorporating Teflon-coated fibreglass as an architectural membrane, was the Hajj Terminal at the King Abdulaziz International Airport at Jeddah (1981), by Horst Berger and the firm of Skidmore, Owings and Merrill. Designed to accommodate 100,000 pilgrims in a series of high tents, it was echoed by Berger in the Cynthia Woods Mitchell Centre for the Performing Arts in the Woodlands, Texas (1990).

The global economy that developed from the 1990s, and the collapse of the former Eastern European bloc, led to buildings in Hungary such as the ING Bank, Budapest (1995), by the Dutch architect Erick van Egeraat. On top of a listed nineteenth-century neo-classical building, he provided a daring addition in the form of a 'whale' made of wood, aluminium and glass. The Neue Messe, Leipzig, Germany (1996), by the Hamburg architects Meinhard von Gerkan (born 1935), Marg and Partner, in association with the British architect Ian Ritchie, similarly symbolizes economic growth in the post-Communist world. It is a great international trade fair, exhibition and conference complex, incorporating a vast glass barrel-vaulted hall, 820 feet (250m) long, 98 feet (30m) high and 262 feet

955 Pei, Cob Freed and Partners: Main Public Library, San Francisco (1996)

(80m) wide. Rivalling the breathtaking span of nineteenth-century railway stations, it is dominated by glass panels seemingly without means of support. Another product of an international partnership is the Hôtel du Département des Bouches-du-Rhône, Marseilles (1994), by the Anglo-German team of William Alsop (born 1947) and Jan Störmer, with interior design by Andrée Putman. Nicknamed 'Le Grand Bleu', from its predominant colouring which was chosen to complement the Côte d'Azur, it features a cigar-shaped wing sheltered by mobile sun-shades.

The current expansion of the global electronic network, including computer and television technology, and the virtual image as a medium for electronic information, may have a destabilizing effect on conventional patterns of activity as well as on architecture. However, as a language of communication, architecture has survived many other intellectual revolutions, just as the printed book seems to have survived the threat from computer technology.

That this may be the case is suggested by two great American libraries in contrasting styles. The Phoenix Public Library, Phoenix, Arizona (1995), by the local architect William Bruder is a High Tech machine with fully glazed north and south façades protected from the fierce sunlight by mechanically controlled metal blinds and prehensile fabric sails. By contrast, the Main Public Library, San Francisco, California (1996), by James Ingo Freed of Pei Cob Freed and Partners, is a monumental building in a simplified Beaux-Arts style with Art Deco touches, designed to harmonize with the Beaux-Arts classicism of the early-twentieth-century Civic Center. However, it contains the most advanced technology conceivable, with High Tech electronic equipment including 300 work stations. The divergent architectural expression of these two utterly modern buildings in Phoenix and San Francisco suggests that the architecture of the twenty-first century will not be lacking in diversity.

Glossary

abacus the flat slab on top of a capital supporting the entablature

absidiole a small chapel projecting from the apse of a church or cathedral

abutment solid stone- or brickwork built against an arch or vault and counteracting its lateral thrust

acroterion (pl. **-ia**) the plinth at the feet or apex of a pediment which holds statues or ornaments; the entire ornamental element at these angles

adytum the inner sanctuary of a Greek temple, entered only by the priest

ambulatory the aisle running round an apse

anta (pl. **-ae**) structural strengthening of a wall termination, resembling a pilaster, generally placed at the ends of the projecting walls of a portico

antefix (pl. **-ae**) decorative blocks placed on the lateral edges of a roof to conceal the ends of the tiles

apse a semi-circular or polygonal structure, especially the termination of a chancel or chapel, which is seen as a recess inside a building and as a projection outside

architrave the lowest of the 3 parts of an entablature, resting directly on the columns; also applied to moulded door or window surrounds

axial layout planned longitudinally (as opposed to centrally) along an axis

atrium 1. the inner court of a Roman house, open to the sky; 2. an open court in front of an Early Christian church

ashlar regularly dressed masonry

arcuated a term descriptive of a building dependent on the use of the arch, not of the post and lintel (trabeated)

barrel vault simple vault, generally of semi-circular section

belvedere a small look-uut tower, sometimes on the roof of a house

boiserie French word for panelling, especially carved, of the 17th and 18th centuries

brise-soleil a sun-break, often of concrete, applied to overfenestrated façades

buttress pier of brick or stone giving additional strength to the wall to which it is attached

buttress, flying an arched support carrying the thrust of a vault to an outer buttress

campanile (pl. **-i**) Italian word for bell-tower, usually detached from the main building

catenary curve the curve formed by a chain or rope hanging from two points not in the same vertical line

cavetto concave moulding about a quarter-circle in section

cella principal interior of a temple, housing the cult image

chamfered a corner truncated at an angle of about 45°

chancel the east end of a church containing the main altar, often used to describe the continuation of the nave east of the crossing

cheek-walls low walls protecting the flanks of a flight of steps

chevet French word for the east end of a church including apse and ambulatory

clerestorey the upper part of the side walls of a building, especially a church, rising above the aisle roofs and pierced by windows

coffering sunken square or polygonal panels in ceilings, vaults and in the soffits of arches

corbel a bracket or projecting block, usually of stone, serving as a support for another member

cornice the crowning projecting moulding of an entablature

corona projecting upper member of a cornice

cottage orné a rustic cottage, often thatched, orignating in the Picturesque movement of the 18th century

cruciform cross-shaped in plan

curvilinear making play with curves

cusp projection carved on the underside of an arch, especially in Gothic architecture; two cusps form a trefoil, three a quatrefoil, and so on

dentil small square block resembling a tooth, used in horizontal rows in cornices

dormer window with its own roof set vertically in a sloping roof

dosseret a block placed on top of a capital, especially in Byzantine and Romanesque architecture, to help carry the voussoirs of the surmounting arcade

echelon, echelon apse apse flanked by chapels placed in a stepped or ladder-wise manner

echinus the convex or ovolo moulding like a cushion below the abacus of a Doric capital

egg-and-tongue an ovolo moulding ornamented with egg-shapes alternating with arrow-heads

engaged order columns attached to or sunk into a wall or pier

entablature the upper part of an order consisting of architrave, frieze and cornice

entasis slight convex curve given to the profile of columns

exedra an apse or niche

fascia a plain horizontal band in an architrave which may incorporate two or three such bands

fenestration the arrangement of windows in a façade

frieze the central part of an entablature between the architrave and cornice, sometimes decorated with figure sculpture

garth closed garden, especially the space enclosed by a cloister

giant order columns or pilasters rising from the ground floor through more than one storey

groin vault a vault caused by the intersection at right angles of two barrel vaults

guttae small peg-like projections carved beneath the mutules and triglyphs of a Doric entablature

herm a pier ending in a head or bust

hexastyle term descriptive of a six-columned portico

in antis term descriptive of a portico with columns which do not project from but range with the flanking walls

Isabelline style florid Gothic style in Spain under Isabel I (1479–1504)

lancet a narrow pointed window, much used in 13th-century Gothic

lierne vault a ribbed vault incorporating liernes, i.e. decorative tertiary ribs not springing from the principal boss or springers

liturgical east end the altar end in a church that is not geographically orientated east/west

loggia an open gallery or verandah, often incorporating an arcade

lunette a semi-circular opening

majolica a type of coloured glazed earthenware

Manueline style the rich Late Gothic style found in Portugal and named after King Manuel I (1495– 1521)

megaron a square or rectangular room of Mycenean origin preceded by a porch and containing a central hearth and four columns supporting the roof

metope the square panel between two triglyphs in a Doric frieze

minaret a tall slender tower with balconies, usually related to a mosque

modillion a bracket or console used in the Corinthian or Composite cornice

Mozarabic style of Islamic inspiration developed by Christians in Spain in the 9th–11th centuries

Mudéjar Spanish Christian architecture in a Muslim style and largely the work of Muslim architects

mutule flat slab-like member carved on the underface of the Doric cornice, one above each metope and each triglyph

narthex large vestibule at the western end of a church

nave the main arm of a church, west of the crossing and generally flanked by aisles

neo-plasticism name given to the style of the Dutch artistic movement *De Stijl*, 1917–31

nymphacum grotto or garden building dedicated to the nymphs

ogee a double-curved line incorporating concave and convex parts

opisthodomus space or open porch at the back of a Greek temple, sometimes used as a treasury

organic (esp. with ref. to F. L. Wright) descriptive of buildings with curved shapes, supposedly close to natural forms

pastas south-facing loggia in a Greek house

pavillon a small villa or pleasure pavilion

pediment triangular vertical gable above a portico, door or window

pendentive the spherical triangle or concave spandrel connecting the corners of a square or polygonal interior with a circular dome

peripteral descriptive of a building surrounded by a single row of columns

peristyle a row of columns surrounding a temple or court

piano nobile the principal storey of a building, of greater height than the other storeys and raised above a basement or ground floor

pier a mass of masonry serving as a vertical support

pilaster a shallow decorative pier resembling a flattened column, projecting very slightly from the wall surface

pilotis stilts or pillars carrying the weight of a building in such a way as to raise it off the ground

plasticity sculptural modelling

polychrome many-coloured

portal doorway

porte-cochère a portico through which wheeled traffic can pass

post and lintel a term descriptive of trabeated construction i.e. vertical supports carrying horizontal beams

prodigy house name given to a group of extravagant country houses built in England around 1600

pronaos vestibule of a temple behind the front row of columns

propylon classical freestanding gateway

prostyle with a row of columns one deep

pteron an external colonnade, especially round a temple

putto (pl. -i) small boy or cherub, painted or carved

pylon rectangular tower, especially a tapered one

quadriga sculptural group of a chariot drawn by four horses

quadripartite vault vault in which each bay contains four cells

quattrocento, cinquecento 15th-century, 16th-century

re-entrant corners corners with angles pointing inwards

retable (retablo) painted or carved screen behind an altar

reredos screen wall, usually decorated, behind an altar

revetment 1. wall supporting a mass of earth or water; 2. facing, especially of marble, to a wall built of another material

rotunda circular building or room, usually domed

rustication masonry (or masonry simulated in stucco) in which the blocks are separated by deeply-cut joints

sala terrena a ground-floor room giving access to the garden, often decorated naturalistically or like a grotto

Salomonic term descriptive of a column twisted like barley-sugar in the Temple of Solomon in Jerusalem

sedilia seats for clergy carved in stone on the south wall of a chancel

sgraffito incised decoration of different colours on plaster

socle base or pedestal

squinch a small arch set diagonally across the internal angle of a square building to smoothe the transition to a circular or polygonal superstructure

stoa covered colonnade

strapwork 16th-century decoration in France, the Netherlands and England consisting of interlaced bands resembling cut leather

stylobate the platform on which a colonnade stands

tholos a circular building

tierceron rib secondary rib leading from one of the main springers in a vault to a place on the ridge-rib

torus semi-circular convex moulding, especially on the base of an Ionic column

trabeated descriptive of architecture based on the post-and-lintel system of the Greeks in contrast to the arcuated system of the Romans

travertine an Italian cream-coloured limestone which polishes well

tribune 1. apse of a basilica; 2. gallery in a church

trifurium an arcaded passage in the wall of a church above the arcade and below the clerestorey

triglyph vertically-grooved block separating the metopes in a Doric frieze

trompe l'oeil illusionistic painting

tympanum 1. triangular or segmental vertical surface enclosed by the mouldings of a pediment; 2. area between the lintel of a doorway and the surmounting arch

vault an arched ceiling

volute the spiral scroll on the corners of Ionic and Corinthian capitals

voussoir a wedge-shaped stone or brick in an arch

westwork the two-storeyed and towered west end of a Carolingian or Romanesque church with an upper room open to the nave

ziggurat a temple-tower, e.g. the Tower of Babylon, with stepped storeys linked by ramps

For Further Reading

This list is restricted to books published in English; the date of first publication is given in brackets

Chapter 1

D. Arnold, *Building in Egypt: Pharaonic Stone Masonry*, New York & Oxford 1991

A. Badawy, *A History of Egyptian Architecture*, 3 vols, Cairo, Berkeley & Los Angeles 1954–68

H. Crawford, *The Architecture of Iraq in the 3rd Millennium*, Copenhagen 1977

H. Crawford, *Sumer and the Sumerians*, Cambridge 1991

S. Downey, *Mesopotamian Religious Architecture: Alexander through the Parthians*, Princeton 1988

H. Frankfort, *The Art and Architecture of the Ancient Orient* (1954), New Haven and London 1996

B. Kemp, *Ancient Egypt: The Anatomy of a Civilisation*, London 1989

S. Lloyd, *Ancient Architecture*, London 1986

S. Lloyd, *The Archaeology of Mesopotamia* (1978), London 1984

J. Postgate, *Early Mesopotamia*, London 1992

W. S. Smith, *The Art and Architecture of Ancient Egypt* (1958), New Haven & London 1998

D. Wildung, *Egypt: From Prehistory to the Romans*, Cologne 1999

Chapter 2

T. Ashby, *The Aqueducts of Ancient Rome*, Oxford 1935

B. Ashmole, *Architect and Sculpture in Classical Greece*, London 1972

R. Bianchi Bandinelli, *Rome the Late Empire*, London 1971

R. Bianchi Bandinelli, *Rome the Centre of Power, Roman Art to AD 200*, London 1970

M. Bieber, *The History of the Greek and Roman Theatre*, Princeton 1961

J. Boardman, *The Greeks Overseas*, Harmondsworth 1964

J. Boardman, *Pre-Classical: From Crete to Archaic Greece*, London 1967

M. T. Boatwright, *Hadrian and the City of Rome*, Princeton 1987

J. S. Boersma, *Athenian Building Policy from 561/0 to 405/4 BC*, Groningen 1970

A. Boëthius, *The Golden House of Nero*, Ann Arbor 1960

A. Boëthius, *Etruscan and Early Roman Architecture* (1970), Harmondsworth 1978

M. Blake, *Ancient Roman Construction in Italy from the Prehistoric Period to Augustus*, Washington 1947

M. Blake *Roman Construction in Italy from Tiberius through the Flavians*, Washington 1959

M. Blake & D. Taylor-Bishop, *Roman Construction in Italy from Nerva through the Antonines*, Philadelphia 1973

R. Brilliant, *Roman Art from the Republic to Constantine*, London 1974

F. E. Brown, *Roman Architecture*, New York 1961

R. Carpenter, *Greek Art*, Philadelphia 1962

R. Carpenter, *The Architects of the Parthenon*, Harmondsworth 1972

J. R. Clarke, *The Houses of Roman Italy, 100 BC–AD 250: Ritual, Space, and Decoration*, Berkeley and Los Angeles 1991

R. M. Cook, *Greek Art*, London 1972

J. J. Coulton, *The Architectural Development of the Greek Stoa*, Oxford 1976

J. J. Coulton, *Greek Architects at Work*, London 1977

G. Cozzo, *The Colosseum, the Flavian Amphitheatre*, Rome 1971

W. B. Dinsmoor, *The Architecture of Ancient Greece*, London and New York 1950

M. I. Finley, ed., *The Legacy of Greece: A New Appraisal*, Oxford 1981

T. Fyfe, *Hellenistic Architecture*, Cambridge 1936

M. Grant, *Cities of Vesuvius*, London 1974

M. Henig, *Architects and Architectural Sculpture in the Roman Empire*, Oxford 1990

J. H. Humphrey, *Roman Circuses: Arenas for Chariot Racing*, London 1986

R. Jenkins, ed., *The Legacy of Rome: A New Appraisal*, Oxford 1992

T. Kraus, *Pompeii and Herculaneum*, New York 1975

A. W. Lawrence, *Greek Architecture* (1957), Harmondsworth 1983

M. Lyttelton, *Baroque Architecture in Classical Antiquity*, London 1974

W. L. MacDonald, *The Political Meeting Places of the Greeks*, Baltimore 1943

W. L. MacDonald, *The Architecture of the Roman Empire*, New Haven 1965

W. L. MacDonald, *The Pantheon*, London 1976

W. MacDonald & J. Pinto, *Hadrian's Villa and its Legacy*, New Haven and London 1995

A. D. Mackay, *Houses, Villas and Palaces in the Roman World*, London 1975

N. Marinatos and R. Hägg, eds., *Greek Sanctuaries: New Approaches*, London and New York 1993

R. D. Martienssen, *The Idea of Space in Greek Architecture*, Johannesburg 1956

R. Meiggs, *Roman Ostia* (1960), Oxford 1973

S. G. Miller, *The Prytaneion*, University of California 1978

E. J. Nash, *Pictorial Dictionary of Ancient Rome*, 2 vols., London 1961–2

J. Onians, *Art and Thought in the Hellenstic Age*, London 1979

J. Percival, *The Roman Villa*, London 1976

W. H. Plomme, *Ancient and Classical Architecture*, London 1956

J. J. Pollitt, *The Ancient View of Greek Art: Criticism, History and Terminology*, New Haven & London 1964

J. J. Pollitt, *The Art of Greece 1400–31 BC. Sources and Documents*, Englewood Cliffs, New Jersey 1965

J. J. Pollitt, *The Art of Greece c. 753 BC–AD 337: Sources and Documents*, Englewood Cliffs, New Jersey 1966

R. F. Rhodes, *Architecture and Meaning on the Athenian Acropolis*, Cambridge 1995

D. S. Robertson, *A Handbook of Greek and Roman Architecture* (1929), Cambridge 1964

M. Robertson, *A History of Greek Art*, 2 vols., Cambridge 1975

F. Sear, *Roman Architecture*, London 1982

J. Steele, *Hellenistic Architecture in Asia Minor*, London 1992

P. Tourniktiotis, ed., *The Parthenon and its Impact in Modern Times*, Athens 1994

J. Travlos, *Pictorial Dictionary of Ancient Athens*, London 1971

V. T. Vermeule, *Greece in the Bronze Age*, Chicago 1972

Vitruvius, *de Architectura*, ed. F. Granger, 2 vols., Harvard University Press 1945 and 1970

A. Wallace-Hadrill, *Houses and Society in Pompeii and Herculaneum*, New Jersey 1994

J. B. Ward-Perkins, *Cities of Ancient Greece and Italy, Planning in Classical Antiquity*, New York 1974

J. B. Ward-Perkins, *Roman Imperial Architecture* (1970), Yale 1994

R. E. Wycherley, *How the Greeks Built Cities* (1949), London and New York 1962

Chapter 3

J. Beckwith, *The Art of Constantinople*, New York 1961

J. Davies, *The Origin and Development of Early Christian Church Art*, London 1952

O. Demus, *The Church of San Marco in Venice*, Cambridge, Mass. 1960

O. Demus, *The Church of Haghia Sophia at Trebizond*, Edinburgh 1968

H. Faesen & V. Ivanov, *Early Russian Architecture*, London 1972

J. A. Hamilton, *Byzantine Architecture and Decoration*, London 1933

R. Krautheimer, *The Early Christian Basilicas of Rome*, 5 vols., Vatican City 1937–77

R. Krautheimer, *Early Christian and Byzantine Architecture* (1965), Harmondsworth 1975

R. Krautheimer, *Rome, Profile of a City, 312–1308* (1980), Princeton 1983

W. MacDonald, *Early Christian and Byzantine Architecture*, New York 1962

G. Mathew, *Byzantine Aesthetics*, London 1963

T. F. Mathews, *The Byzantine Churches of Istanbul*, Pennsylvania State University Press 1976

D. Talbot Rice, *The Art of Byzantium*, London 1959

D. Talbot Rice, ed., *The Great Palace of the Byzantine Emperors*, Edinburgh 1958

S. Runciman, *Byzantine Style and Civilization*, Harmondsworth 1975

C. Stewart, *Early Christian, Byzantine and Romanesque Architecture*, London 1954

E. H. Swift, *Hagia Sophia*, New York 1940

P. A. Underwood, ed., *The Kariye Djami*, 4 vols., New York & London 1966–75

Chapter 4

J. Beckwith, *Early Medieval Art*, London 1964

P. Binski, *Westminster Abbey and the Plantagenets: Kingship and the Representation of Power 1200–1400*, New Haven and London 1995

T. S. R. Boase, *English Art 1100–1216* (1953), Oxford 1968

T. S. R. Boase, *Castles and Churches of the Crusading Kingdom*, London, New York, Toronto 1967

D. Bullough, *The Age of Charlemagne*, New York & London 1966

H. Busch & B. Lohse, eds., *Romanesque Europe*, London 1969

A. W. Clapham, *English Romanesque Architecture before the Conquest*, Oxford 1930

A. W. Clapham, *English Romanesque Architecture after the Conquest*, Oxford 1934

A. W. Clapham, *English Romanesque Architecture in Western Europe*, Oxford 1936

K. J. Conant, *Carolingian and Romanesque Architecture 800–1200* (1959), new ed., New Haven & London 1993

J. Evans, *Cluniac Art of the Romanesque Period*, Cambridge 1950

J. Evans, *Monastic Life at Cluny, 910–1157*, London 1931

J. Evans, *The Romanesque Architecture of the Order of Cluny* (1938), Farnborough 1972

E. Fernie, *The Architecture of the Anglo-Saxons*, London 1983

E. A. Fisher, *The Greater Anglo-Saxon Churches*, London 1962

H. Focillon, *The Art of the West*, vol. 1, *Romanesque Art*, London 1963

C. H. Haskins, *The Renaissance of the Twelfth Century*, Cambridge, Mass. 1927

G. Henderson, *Early Medieval*, Harmondsworth 1972

W. Horn and E. Born, *The Plan of St. Gall*, 3 vols., University of California Press 1979

J. Hubert, J. Porcher & W. F. Volbach, *Europe in the Dark Ages* (1967), London 1969, and *Carolingian Art* (1968), London 1970

P. Lasko, *Ars Sacra 800–1200*, Harmondsworth 1971

H. J. Leask, *Irish Churches and Monastic Buildings: 1. The First Phase and the Romanesque*, Dundalk 1955

A. K. Porter, *Lombard Architecture*, 4 vols., New Haven 1915–17

R. Stalley, *Early Medieval Architecture*, Oxford 1999

D. Talbot Rice, *English Art 871–1100*, Oxford 1952

C. Ricci, *Romanesque Architecture in Italy*, London & New York 1925

G. T. Rivoira, *Lombardic Architecture: Its Origin, Development and Derivatives*, 2 vols. (1910), New York 1975

H. M. and J. Taylor, *Anglo-Saxon Architecture*, 3 vols., Cambridge 1965–78

R. Tolman, *Romanesque: Architecture, Sculpture, Painting*, Cologne 1997

W. M. Whitehill, *Spanish Romanesque Architecture of the Eleventh Century*, London 1941

G. Zarnecki, *Romanesque Art*, London 1971

Chapter 5

E. Arslan, *Gothic Architecture in Venice* (1970), New York 1971

E. Baldwin Smith, *The Architectural Symbolism of Imperial Rome and the Middle Ages*, Princeton 1956

J. Baum, *German Cathedrals*, London 1956

J. Bony, *The English Decorated Style*, Oxford 1979

J. Bony, *The French Gothic Architecture of the 12th and 13th Centuries*, University of California Press 1983

R. Branner, *Burgundian Gothic Architecture*, London 1960

R. Branner, *St Louis and the Court Style in Gothic Architecture*, London 1964

R. Branner, *Chartres Cathedral*, New York 1969

P. Brieger, *English Art 1216–1307*, Oxford 1957

D. R. Buxton, *Russian Mediaeval Architecture*, Cambridge 1934

J.-F. Leroux-Dhuys, *Cistercian Abbeys: History and Architecture*, Cologne 1998

J. Evans, *Art in Medieval France*, Oxford 1948

J. Evans, *English Art 1307–1461*, Oxford 1949

J. Evans, ed., *The Flowering of the Middle Ages*, New York, Toronto & London 1966

P. Fergusson, *Architecture of Solitude, Cistercian Abbeys in Twelfth Century England*, Princeton 1984

J. F. Fitchen, *The Construction of Gothic Cathedrals* (1961), London 1981

H. Focillon, *The Art of the West in the Middle Ages* (1938), London 1963

P. Frankl, *The Gothic, Literary Sources and Interpretations during Eight Centuries*, Princeton 1960

P. Frankl, *Gothic Architecture*, Harmondsworth 1962

T. G. Frisch, *Gothic Art 1140–1450: Sources and Documents*, Englewood Cliffs, New Jersey 1971

L. Grodecki, *Gothic Architecture* (1976), New York 1977

J. H. Harvey, *The Gothic World 1100–1600*, London 1950

J. H. Harvey, *The Mediaeval Architect*, London 1972

J. H. Harvey, *The Perpendicular Style*, London 1978

G. Henderson, *Gothic*, Harmondsworth 1967

G. Henderson, *Chartres*, Harmondsworth 1968

W. C. Leedy, *Fan Vaulting*, London 1980

E. Mâle, *Religious Art in France: The Twelfth Century* (1922), Princeton 1978

E. Mâle, *Religious Art in France: The Thirteenth Century* (1898), New York 1973

E. Panofsky, *Gothic Architecture and Scholasticism*, Latrobe 1951

E. Panofsky, *Abbot Suger on the Abbey Church of St-Denis* (1946), Princeton 1979

O. von Simson, *The Gothic Cathedral*, New York 1956

W. Swaan, *The Gothic Cathedral*, London 1981

W. Swaan, *The Late Middle Ages: Art and Architecture from 1350 to the Advent of the Renaissance*, London 1977

R. Tolman, *Gothic: Architecture, Sculpture, Painting*, Cologne 1998

M. Trachtenberg, *The Campanile of Florence Cathedral*, New York 1971

A. L. J. van de Walle, *Gothic Art in Belgium*, Brussels n.d.

G. Webb, *Architecture in Britain: The Middle Ages* (1956), Harmondsworth 1965

J. White, *Art and Architecture in Italy, 1250–1400*, Harmondsworth 1966

R. Willis, *Architectural History of Some English Cathedrals* (1842–63), Chicheley 1972–3

C. Wilson, *The Gothic Cathedral*, London 1990

Chapter 6

J. Ackerman, *Palladio*, Harmondsworth 1960

J. Ackerman, *The Architecture of Michelangelo* (1961), Harmondsworth 1970

J. Ackerman, *Distance Points: Essays in Theory and Renaissance Art and Architecture*, Cambridge, Mass. 1991

L. B. Alberti, *On the Art of Building in Ten Books* (1484), transl. by J. Rykwert, N. Leach & R. Tavernor, Cambridge, Mass., and London 1988

G. C. Argan and B. Contardi, *Michelangelo Architect*, London 1993

G. G. Argan, *The Renaissance City*, New York 1969

H. Ballon, *The Paris of Henri IV: Architecture and Urbanism*, Cambridge, Mass., and London 1991

L. Benevolo, *The Architecture of the Renaissance*, 2 vols. (1968) London 1970

J. Bialostocki, *The Art of the Renaissance in Eastern Europe*, Oxford 1976

A. Blunt, *Artistic Theory in Italy 1450–1600*, Oxford 1935

A. Blunt, *Philibert de l'Orme*, London 1958

B. Boucher, *Andrea Palladio: The Architect in his Time*, New York, London and Paris 1994

A. Braham and P. Smith, *François Mansart*, 2 vols., London 1973

A. Bruschi, *Bramante* (1973), London 1977

J. C. Burckhardt, *The Civilization of the Renaissance in Italy* (1860), London 1950

A. Chastel, *The Age of Humanism, Europe 1430–1530*, New York 1964

D. R. Coffin, *The Villa in the Life of Renaissance Rome*, Princeton 1979

R. Coope, *Salomon de Brosse and the Development of the Classical Style in French Architecture from 1565–1630*, London 1972

J. Evans, *Monastic Architecture in France from the Renaissance to the Revolution*, Cambridge 1964

Filarete, *Treatise on Architecture* (c.1460), New Haven and London 1965

R. A. Goldthwaite, *The Building of Renaissance Florence*, Baltimore and London 1980

V. Hart and P. Hicks, transl., *Sebastiano Serlio on Architecture*, New Haven and London 1996

F. Hartt, *Giulio Romano*, 2 vols., Yale 1958

L. Heydenreich, *Architecture in Italy 1400–1500* (1974), New Haven and London 1996

H.-R. Hitchcock, *German Renaissance Architecture*, Princeton 1981

E. J. Johnson, *S. Andrea in Mantua*, Pennsylvania University Press 1975

R. Klein & H. Zerner, *Italian Art 1500–1600: Sources and Documents*, Englewood Cliffs, New Jersey 1966

For Further Reading

H. & S. Kozakiewiczowie, *The Renaissance in Poland*, Warsaw 1976

G. Kubler, *Building the Escorial*, Princeton 1982

M. Levey, *Early Renaissance*, Harmondsworth 1967

M. Levey, *High Renaissance*, Harmondsworth 1975

H. Lotz, *Architecture in Italy 1500–1600*, New Haven and London 1995

W. Lotz, *Studies in Italian Renaissance Architecture*, Cambridge, Mass. 1977

T. Magnuson, *Studies in Roman Quattrocento Architecture*, Stockholm 1958

G. Masson, *Italian Villas and Palaces*, London 1959

G. Mazzotti, *Palladian and other Venetian Villas*, Rome 1966

H. Millon, ed., *The Renaissance from Brunelleschi to Michelangelo: The Representation of Architecture*, London 1994

P. Murray, *The Architecture of the Italian Renaissance* (1963), London 1969

P. Murray, *Renaissance Architecture*, New York 1971

Palladio, *The Four Books of Architecture* (1570), Cambridge, Mass 1997

Andrea Palladio 1508–1580, Arts Council of Great Britain 1975

Corpus Palladianum, Pennsylvania State University Press, 1968 – in progress

A. Payne, *The Architectural Treatise in the Italian Renaissance*, Cambridge 1999

P. Portoghesi, *Rome of the Renaissance*, London 1972

M. N. Rosenfeld, *Sebastiano Serlio: On Domestic Architecture*, New York and Cambridge 1978

E. E. Rosenthal, *The Cathedral of Granada*, Princeton 1961

E. E. Rosenthal, *The Palace of Charles V in Granada*, Princeton 1985

P. Rotondi, *The Ducal Palace of Urbino*, London 1969

I. Rowland, *The Culture of the High Renaissance: Ancients and Moderns in 16th-century Rome*, Cambridge 1998

H. Saalman, *Filippo Brunelleschi. The Cupola of Santa Maria del Fiore*, London 1980

H. Saalman, *Filippo Brunelleschi: The Buildings*, London 1993

J. Shearman, *Mannerism*, Harmondsworth 1967

G. Smith, *The Casino of Pius IV*, Princeton 1977

W. Stechow, *Northern Renaissance Art 1400–1600: Sources and Documents*, Englewood Cliffs, New Jersey 1966

R. Tavernor, *Alberti and the Art of Building*, New Haven and London 1998

D. Thomson, *Renaissance Paris: Architecture and Growth 1475–1600*, London 1984

G. Vasari, *The Lives of the Painters, Sculptors and Architects* (1550), London, 4 vols., 1927

G. B. da Vignola, *The Regular Architect: or the General Rule of the Five Orders of Architecture* (1562), London 1669

R. Wittkower, *Architectural Principles in the Age of Humanism* (1949), New York 1971

C. W. Zerner, *Juan de Herrera: Architect to Philip II of Spain*, New Haven and London 1993

Chapter 7

J. van Ackere, *Baroque and Classical Art in Belgium 1600–1789*, Brussels n.d.

R. W. Berger, *A Royal Passion: Louis XIV as Patron of Architecture*, Cambridge 1994

A. Blunt, *Sicilian Baroque*, London 1968

A. Blunt, *Art and Architecture in France 1500–1700* (1953), New Haven and London 1973

A. Blunt, *Baroque and Rococo Architecture in Naples*, London 1975

A. Blunt, ed., *Baroque and Rococo Architecture and Decoration*, London 1978

A. Blunt, *A Guide to Baroque Rome*, London 1982

J. Bourke, *Baroque Churches of Central Europe* (1958), London 1962

J. Connors, *Borromini and the Roman Oratory*, Cambridge, Mass., 1980

K. Downes, *English Baroque Architecture*, London 1966

K. Fremantle, *The Baroque Town Hall of Amsterdam*, Utrecht 1959

K. Harries, *The Bavarian Rococo Church*, New Haven & London 1983

E. Hempel, *Baroque Art and Architecture in Central Europe*, Harmondsworth 1965

H. Hibbard, *Carlo Maderno and Roman Architecture 1580–1630*, London 1971

H.-R. Hitchcock, *German Rococo: The Zimmerman Brothers*, London 1968

H.-R. Hitchcock, *Rococo Architecture in Southern Germany*, London 1968

J. Hook, *The Baroque Age in England*, London 1976

F. Kimball, *The Creation of the Rococo* (1943), New York 1964

R. Krautheimer, *The Rome of Alexander VII, 1655–1667*, Princeton 1985

G. A. Kubler & M. Soria, *Art and Architecture in Spain and Portugal and their American Dominions 1500–1800*, Harmondsworth 1959

W. Kuyper, *Dutch Classicist Architecture*, Delft University Press 1980

J. Lees-Milne, *English Country Houses; Baroque*, London 1970

D. Lewis, *The Late Baroque Churches of Venice* (1967), New York & London 1979

T. Marder, *Bernini, the Art of Architecture*, Abbeville Press, New York, London, Paris 1998

T. Marder, *Bernini's Scala Regia at the Vatican Palace*, Cambridge 1997

A. H. Mayor, *The Bibiena Family*, New York 1945

H. A. Meek, *Guarino Guarini and his Architecture*, New Haven and London 1988

H. Millon, ed., *The Triumph of the Baroque: Architecture in Europe 1600–1750*, London 1999

C. Norberg-Schulz, *Baroque Architecture*, New York 1971

C. Norberg-Schulz, *Late Baroque and Rococo Architecture*, New York 1971

C. F. Otto, *Space into Light, the Churches of Balthasar Neumann*, Cambridge, Mass. 1979

J.-M. Pérouse de Montclos, *Versailles*, New York, London & Paris 1991

R. Pommer, *Eighteenth-century Architecture in Piedmont*, New York & London 1976

P. Portoghesi, *Rome Barocca: The History of an Architectonic Culture* (1966), Cambridge, Mass. 1970

N. Powell, *From Baroque to Rococo*, London and New York 1959

J. Rosenberg, S. Slive & E. H. ter Kuile, *Dutch Art and Architecture 1600–1800* (1966), Harmondsworth 1972

E. F. Sekler, *Wren and his Place in European Architecture*, London 1956

R. Smith, *The Art of Portugal 1500–1800*, London 1968

L. Soo, *Wren's 'Tracts' on Architecture and Other Writings*, Cambridge 1998

V. L. Tapié, *The Age of Grandeur. Baroque and Classicism in Europe* (1957), London 1960

P. Thornton, *Seventeenth-century Interior Decoration in France and England*, New Haven and London 1978

R. Tolman, ed., *Baroque: Architecture, Sculpture, Painting*, Cologne 1998

P. Waddy, *Seventeenth-Century Roman Palaces: Use and the Art of the Plan*, Cambridge, Mass., & London 1990

M. Whinney and O. Millar, *English Art 1625–1714*, Oxford 1957

R. Wittkower, *Art and Architecture in Italy 1600–1750* (1958), 3 vols, New Haven and London 1999

R. Whittkower, *Studies in the Italian Baroque*, London 1975

Chapter 8

The Age of Neo-Classicism, Council of Europe Exhibition Catalogue, London 1972

A. Braham, *The Architecture of the French Enlightenment*, London 1980

J. Burke, *English Art 1714–1800*, Oxford 1976

C. W. Condit, *American Buildings: Materials and Techniques from the Beginning of the Colonial Settlements to the Present*, Chicago 1964

J. M. Crook, *The Greek Revival* (1972), rev. ed. London 1995

I. A. Egorov, *The Architectural Planning of St Petersburg*, Athens, Ohio 1968

L. Eitner, *Neoclassicism and Romanticism 1750–1850: Sources and Documents*, vol. I, Englewood Cliffs, New Jersey 1970

S. Eriksen, *Early Neo-Classicism in France*, London 1974

J. Eyres, *Building the Georgian City*, New Haven and London 1998

J. Fowler and J. Cornforth, *English Decoration in the 18th Century* (1974), London 1978

M. Gallet, *Paris Domestic Architecture of the 18th Century*, London 1972

H. Groth, *Neoclassicism in the North: Swedish Furniture and Interiors 1770–1850*, London 1990

G. H. Hamilton, *The Art and Architecture of Russia* (1954), Harmondsworth 1983

T. Hamlin, *Greek Revival Architecture in America*, Oxford 1944

W. Herrmann, *Laugier and Eighteenth Century French Theory*, London 1962

W. J. Hipple, *The Beautiful, the Sublime, and the Picturesque in Eighteenth-Century British Aesthetic Theory*, Carbondale 1957

H. Honour, *Neo-Classicism*, Harmondsworth 1969

M. Ilyin, *Moscow Monuments of Architecture: Eighteenth – the First Third of the Nineteenth Century*, 2 vols., Moscow 1975

W. G. Kalnein, *Architecture in Eighteenth-century France*, New Haven & London 1995

E. Kaufmann, *Architecture in the Age of Reason*, Harvard 1955

R. Kennedy, *Greek Revival in America*, New York 1989

V. & A. Kennett, *The Palaces of Leningrad*, London 1973

A. Kuchamov, *Pavlosk, Palace and Park*, Leningrad 1975

C. Meeks, *Italian Architecture 1750–1914*, New Haven 1966

R. Middleton and D. Watkin, *Neo-Classical and 19th century Architecture* (1977), New York 1980

J. Morley, *Regency Design 1790–1840*, London 1993

N. Pevsner, ed., *The Picturesque Garden and its Influence outside the British Isles*, Washington DC 1974

A. Picon, *French Architects and Engineers in the Age of Enlightenment*, Cambridge 1992

W. H. Pierson, *American Buildings and their Architects: The Colonial and Neo-Classical Styles*, New York 1970

R. Rosenblum, *Transformations in Late 18th century Art*, Princeton 1967

L. M. Roth, *A Concise History of American Architecture* (1979), New York 1980

J. Rykwert, *The First Moderns, the Architects of the 18th century*, Cambridge, Mass. 1980

J. Rykwert, *On Adam's House in Paradise*, New York 1972

C. Saumarez Smith, *Eighteenth-century Decoration: Design and Domestic Interiors in England*, London 1993

K. Scott, *The Rococo Interior: Decoration and Space in Early 18th-century Paris*, New Haven and London 1995

D. Shvidkovsky, *The Empress and the Architect: British Architecture and Gardens at the Court of Catherine the Great*, New Haven and London 1996

O. Siren, *China and the Gardens of Europe of the 18th century* (1950), Dumbarton Oaks 1990

D. Stillman, *English Neo-classical Architecture*, 2 vols., London 1988

J. Summerson, *Architecture in Britain 1530–1850* (1953), 9th ed., Yale 1993

C. Tadgell, *Ange-Jacques Gabriel*, London 1978

P. Verlet, *French Furniture and Interior Design in the 18th century*, London 1967

A. Vidler, *The Writing of the Walls: Architectural Theory in the Late Enlightenment*, Princeton 1987

A. Vidler, *Claude-Nicolas Ledoux: Architecture and Social Reform at the End of the Ancien Régime*, Cambridge, Mass. 1990

D. Watkin, *Sir John Soane: Enlightenment Thought and the Royal Academy Lectures*, Cambridge 1996

D. Watkin & T. Mellinghoff, *German Architecture and the Classical Ideal, 1740–1840*, London 1987

M. Whiffen & F. Koeper, *American Architecture 1607–1976*, London & Henley 1981

D. Wiebenson, *Sources of Greek Revival Architecture*, London 1969

D. Wiebenson, *The Picturesque Garden in France*, Princeton 1978

J. Wilton-Ely, *Piranesi as Architect and Designer*, New Haven & London 1993

R. Wittkower, *Palladio and English Palladianism*, London 1974

G. Worsley, *Classical Architecture in Britain: The Heroic Age*, New Haven and London 1995

Chapter 9

T. Aidala, *The Great Houses of San Francisco*, London 1974

M. Aldrich, *Gothic Revival*, London 1994

B. Bergdoll, *Karl Friedrich Schinkel: An Architecture for Prussia*, New York 1994

C. Brooks, *Gothic Revival*, London 1999

D. B. Brownlee, *The Law Courts, the Architecture of G. E. Street*, Cambridge, Mass. 1984

D. F. Burg, *Chicago's White City of 1893*, University Press of Kentucky 1976

G. Butikov, *St Isaac's Cathedral, Leningrad* (1974), London 1980

F. Choay, *The Modern City, Planning in the 19th century*, New York 1969

P. Collins, *Changing Ideals in Modern Architecture 1750–1950*, London 1965

C. W. Condit, *American Building Art, The Nineteenth Century*, New York 1960

L. Craig, *The Federal Presence, Architecture, Politics and National Design* (1978), Cambridge, Mass. 1984

R. Dixon and S. Muthesius, *Victorian Architecture*, London 1978

A. Drexler, ed., *The Architecture of the Ecole des Beaux-Arts*, London 1977

H. J. Dyos and M. Wolff, eds., *The Victorian City, Image and Reality*, 2 vols., London 1973

C. L. Eastlake, *A History of the Gothic Revival in England* (1872), Leicester 1970

R. A. Etlin, *The Architecture of Death*, Cambridge, Mass. 1984

N. Evenson, *Paris, a Century of Change 1878–1978*, New Haven and London 1979

C. Fox, ed., *London – World City 1800–1840*, New Haven and London 1992

G. German, *Gothic Revival in Europe and Britain*, London 1972

S. Giedion, *Space, Time and Architecture* (1941), Cambridge, Mass. 1967

S. Giedion, *Mechanization Takes Command* (1948), New York 1955

M. Girouard, *The Victorian Country House* (1971), New Haven and London 1979

M. Girouard, *Sweetness and Light, the 'Queen Anne' Movement, 1860–1900*, Oxford 1977

H. S. Goodhart-Rendel, *English Architecture since the Regency*, London 1953

T. Hall, *Planning Europe's Capital Cities: Aspects of 19th-century Urban Development*, London 1997

S. P. Handlin, *The American Home: Architecture and Society 1815–1915*, Boston 1979

G. Hersey, *High Victorian Gothic, a Study in Associationism*, Baltimore 1972

H.-R. Hitchcock, *Early Victorian Architecture in Britain*, 2 vols., New Haven & London 1954

H.-R. Hitchcock, *Architecture, 19th and 20th centuries* (1958), Harmondsworth 1987

S. Jervis, *High Victorian Design*, Ottawa 1974

J. R. Kellett, *The Impact of Railways on Victorian Cities*, London 1969

R. G. Kennedy, *Greek Revival America*, New York 1989

E. Kirichenko, *Moscow Architectural Monuments of the 1830s–1910s*, Moscow 1977

R. Longstreth, *On the Edge of the World, Four Architects in San Francisco at the Turn of the Century*, Cambridge, Mass. 1983

F. Loyer, *Architecture of the Industrial Age, 1789–1914*, New York 1982

C. C. Mead, *Charles Garnier's Paris Opera: Architectural Empathy and the Renaissance of French Classicism*, Cambridge, Mass., and London 1991

C. Meeks, *The Railroad Station*, New Haven 1956

R. Middleton, ed., *The Beaux-Arts and Nineteenth-century French Architecture*, London 1982

S. Muthesius, *The High Victorian Movement in Architecture*, London 1971

J. K. Ochsner, *H. H. Richardson, Complete Architectural Works*, Cambridge, Mass. 1982

D. J. Olsen, *The Growth of Victorian London*, London 1976

N. Pevsner, *Some Architectural Writers of the Nineteenth Century*, Oxford 1972

N. Pevsner, *Pioneers of Modern Design* (1936), Harmondsworth 1964

W. H. Pierson, *American Buildings and their Architects, Technology and the Picturesque. The Corporate and Early Gothic Styles*, New York 1978

M. H. Port, ed., *The Houses of Parliament*, New Haven and London 1976

M. Port, *Imperial London: Civil Government Building in London 1851–1915*, New Haven and London 1995

H. G. Pundt, *Schinkel's Berlin*, Cambridge, Mass. 1972

J. W. Reps, *Monumental Washington, the Planning and Development of the Capital Center*, Princeton 1967

J. M. Richards, *The Functional Tradition*, London 1958

W. D. Robson-Scott, *The Literary Background of the Gothic Revival in Germany*, Oxford 1965

L. M. Roth, *McKim, Mead and White, Architects*, London 1984

P. B. Stanton, *The Gothic Revival and American Church Architecture*, Baltimore 1968

A. Sutcliffe, *Towards the Planned City: Germany, Britain, the United States and France 1780–1914*, New York 1981

D. Van Zanten, *Architectural Polychromy of the 1830s* (1970), New York & London 1977

D. Van Zanten, *Designing Paris: The Architecture of Duban, Labrouste, Duc and Vaudoyer*, Cambridge, Mass. 1987

D. Van Zanten, *Building Paris: Architectural Institutions and the Transformation of the French Capital, 1830–1870*, Cambridge 1994

A. Zador, *Revival Architecture in Hungary: Classicism and Romaticism*, Budapest 1985

Chapter 10

F. Borsi and E. Godoli, *Paris 1900*, London 1978

Y. Brunhammer and G. Naylor, *Hector Guimard*, London 1978

E. Casanelles, *Antonio Gaudí: A Reappraisal*, New York 1967

G. Collins, *Antonio Gaudí*, London 1960

R. Descharnes and C. Prévost, *Gaudí, the Visionary*, New York 1971

H. Geretsegger, M. Peintner & W. Pichler, *Otto Wagner 1841–1918*, New York and London 1970

T. Howarth, *C. R. Mackintosh and the Modern Movement* (1952), London 1977

R. Macleod, *C. R. Mackintosh*, London 1968

S. T. Madsen, *Art Nouveau*, London 1967

N. Pevsner and J. M. Richards, eds., *The Anti-Rationalists*, London 1973

N. Powell, *The Sacred Spring, the Arts in Vienna 1898–1918*, New York 1974

R. Russell, ed., *Art Nouveau Architecture*, New York 1979

R. Schmutzler, *Art Nouveau*, New York and London 1962

E. Sekler, *Josef Hoffmann, the Architectural Work* (1982), Princeton 1985

A. Service, *London 1900*, London & New York 1979

P. Singelenberg, *H. P. Berlage: Idea and Style*, Utrecht 1972

P. Vergo, *Art in Vienna 1898–1918* (1975), Oxford 1981

Chapter 11

H. Allen Brooks, *The Prairie School*, Toronto 1972

U. Apollonio, *Futurist Manifestos*, London 1973

R. Banham, *Theory and Design in the First Machine Age*, London 1960

R. Banham, *Megastructures, Urban Futures of the Recent Past*, London 1976

R. Banham, *The New Brutalism, Ethic or Aesthetic?*, London 1966

R. Banham, *The Architecture of the Well-tempered Environment* (1969), London 1984

P. Bayer, *Art Deco Architecture*, London 1992

L. Benevolo, *History of Modern Architecture*, 2 vols. (1960), London 1971

R. H. Bletter & C. Robinson, *Skyscraper Style – Art Deco New York*, New York 1975

T. Budensieg, *Industrielkultur. Peter Behrens and the AEG, 1907–14* (1979), Cambridge, Mass. 1984

L. Burckhardt, ed., *The Werkbund. History and Ideology 1907–33* (1977), New York 1980

J. Campbell, *The German Werkbund – the Politics of Reform in the Applied Arts*, Princeton 1968

P. Collins, *Concrete, the Vision of a New Architecture*, London 1959

C. W. Condit, *American Building Art: The 20th Century*, New York 1961

C. W. Condit, *Chicago 1910–29, Building, Planning and Urban Technology*, Chicago 1973

A. Drexler, *Transformations in Modern Architecture*, New York 1979

L. K. Eaton, *American Architecture Comes of Age: European Reaction to H. H. Richardson and Louis Sullivan*, Cambridge, Mass. and London 1972

R. Economakis, ed., *Building Classical: A Vision of Europe and America*, London 1993

B. Farmer & H. Louw, ed., *Companion to Contemporary Architectural Thought*, London 1993

R. Fishman, *Urban Utopias in the Twentieth Century*, New York 1977

K. Frampton, *Modern Architecture 1851–1945*, New York 1983

K. Frampton, *Modern Architecture, a Critical History* (1980), London 1985

M. Franciscono, *Walter Gropius and the Creation of the Bauhaus in Weimar*, Chicago and London 1971

M. Friedman, ed., *De Stijl: 1917–1931, Visions of Utopia*, Oxford 1982

B. Gill, *Many Masks: A Life of Frank Lloyd Wright* (1987), London 1988

B. Gravagnulo, *Adolf Loos, Theory and Works*, New York 1982

A. Stuart Gray, *Edwardian Architecture: A Biographical Dictionary* (1985), London 1988

H.-R. Hitchcock and P. Johnson, *The International Style: Architecture since 1922*, New York 1932

H.-R. Hitchcock, *In the Nature of Materials 1887–1941, the Buildings of Frank Lloyd Wright*, New York 1942

C. Hussey and A. S. G. Butler, *Lutyens Memorial Volumes*, 3 vols., 1951

R. G. Irving, *Indian Summer. Lutyens, Baker and Imperial Delhi*, New Haven and London 1981

J. Jacobs, *The Death and Life of Great American Cities*, Harmondsworth 1961

C. Jencks, *Modern Movements in Architecture*, Harmondsworth and New York 1973

C. Jencks, *The Language of Post-Modern Architecture* (1977), London 1984

C. Jencks, *Post-Modernism: The New Classicism in Art and Architecture*, London 1987

W. H. Jordy, *American Buildings and their Architects. The Impact of European Modernism in the Mid-Twentieth Century*, New York 1972

A. Kopp, *Town and Revolution, Soviet Architecture and City Planning 1917–1935*, New York and London 1970

S. Kostof, *The Third Rome 1870–1950: Traffic and Glory*, Berkeley 1973

R. Krier, *Urban Space*, London and New York 1979

L. Krier, *Albert Speer, Architecture 1932–1942*, Brussels 1985

L. Krier, *Architecture Choice or Fate*, London 1998

Le Corbusier, *Towards a New Architecture*, London 1927

C. Lodder, *Russian Constructivism*, New Haven 1983

R. Miller, ed., *Four Great Makers of Modern Architecture: Gropius, Le Corbusier, Mies van der Rohe, Wright*, New York 1963

B. Miller Lane, *Architecture and Politics in Germany 1918–1945*, Cambridge, Mass. 1968

J. Milner, *Tatlin and the Russian Avant-Garde*, New Haven 1983

J. Pallasmaa, H. O. Anderson *et al.*, *Nordic Classicism 1910–1930*, Helsinki 1982

A. Papadakis and H. Watson, ed., *New Classicism: Omnibus Volume*, London 1990

W. Pehnt, *Expressionist Architecture*, London 1973

L. M. Peisch, *The Chicago School of Architecture*, London 1964

R. J. van Pelt & C. W. Westfall, *Architectural Principles in the Age of Historicism*, New Haven and London 1991

D. Porphyrios, *Sources of Modern Eclecticism: Studies on Alvar Aalto*, London 1982

P. Portoghesi, *The Presence of the Past*, Venice Biennale 1980

C. Rowe, *The Mathematics of the Ideal Villa and other Essays*, Cambridge, Mass. 1977

A. Scobie, *Hitler's State Architecture: The Impact of Classical Antiquity*, Pennsylvania State UP 1990

V. Scully, *The Shingle Style*, New Haven 1955

J. Sergeant, *Frank Lloyd Wright's Usonian Houses*, New York 1976

A. Service, *Edwardian Architecture and its Origins*, London 1975

D. Sharp, *Modern Architecture and Expressionism*, London and New York 1966

B. A. Spencer, ed., *The Prairie School Tradition*, New York 1979

F. Starr, *Konstantin Melnikov. Solo Architect in a Mass Society*, Princeton 1978

R. A. M. Stern, *Modern Classicism*, London 1988

M. Tafuri, *Architecture and Utopia: Design and Capitalist Development*, London 1976

A. Tarkhanov & S. Kavtaradze, *Stalinist Architecture*, London 1992

R. R. Taylor, *The Word in Stone, the Role of Architecture in National Socialist Ideology*, Berkeley 1974

N. J. Troy, *The De Stijl Environment*, Cambridge, Mass. 1983

R. Venturi, *Complexity and Contradiction in Architecture*, New York 1966

R. Venturi, D. Scott-Brown and S. Izenour, *Learning from Las Vegas*, Cambridge, Mass. 1972

R. Walden, ed., *The Open Hand: Essays on Le Corbusier*, Cambridge, Mass. 1977

D. Wiebenson, *Tony Garnier, the Cité Industrielle*, New York 1969

J. Willett, *The New Society 1917–1933: Art and Politics in the Weimar Period*, London 1978

H. Wingler, *The Bauhaus: Weimar, Dessau, Berlin and Chicago*, Cambridge, Mass. 1969

W. de Wit, ed., *The Amsterdam School. Dutch Expressionist Architecture, 1915–1930*, Cambridge, Mass. 1983

S. Wrede, *The Architecture of Erik Gunnar Asplund*, Cambridge, Mass. 1979

F. L. Wright, *An Autobiography*, New York 1932

General

E. Baldwin Smith, *The Dome, a study in the History of Ideas*, Princeton 1971

Encyclopedia of World Art, 15 vols., New York, Toronto, London 1959–69

J. Fleming, H. Honour & N. Pevsner, *The Penguin Dictionary of Architecture* (1966), London 1991

H. M. Colvin, *Architecture and the After-Life*, New Haven and London 1991

J. S. Curl, *The Art and Architecture of Freemasonry*, London 1991

J. S. Curl, *Dictionary of Architecture*, Oxford 1999

E. A. Gutkind, *International History of City Development*, 8 vols., London 1964–72

G. Hersey, *The Lost Meaning of Classical Architecture: Speculations on Ornament from Vitruvius to Venturi*, Cambridge, Mass. 1988

H.-W. Kruft, *A History of Architectural Theory from Vitruvius to the Present*, London & New York 1994

The Grove Dictionary of Art, 34 vols, London 1996

Macmillan Encyclopedia of Architects, 4 vols., London & New York 1982

J. Onians, *Bearers of Meaning: The Classical Orders in Antiquity, the Middle Ages, and the Renaissance*, Princeton 1988

N. Pevsner, *An Outline of European Architecture* (1943), Harmondsworth 1963

D. Porphyrios, *Classical Architecture*, London 1991

M. Praz, *An Illustrated History of Interior Decoration*, London 1964

P. de la Ruffinière du Prey, *Pliny's Villa from Antiquity to Posterity*, Chicago and London 1994

J. Rykwert, *The Dancing Column: On Order in Architecture*, Cambridge, 1996

G. Scott, *The Architecture of Humanism* (1914), London 1980

R. Scruton, *The Aesthetics of Architecture*, London 1979

V. Scully, *American Architecture and Urbanism*, London 1969

J. Summerson, *The Classical Language of Architecture* (1963), London 1980

P. Thornton, *Authentic Décor, the Domestic Interior 1620–1920*, London 1984

A. Tzonis and L. Lefaivre, *Classical Architecture: The Poetics of Order*, Cambridge, Mass. 1986

Acknowledgements

A. C. L. Brussels: 711, 753; AKG, London: 298, 596, 833, 931; Aerofilms Ltd, Boreham Wood: 301, 408, 623, 642; Archives of The Temple (Hebrew Benevolent Congregation), Atlanta: 798; Archivi Alinari, Florence: 65, 82, 145, 304, 307, 312, 334, 336, 338, 358, 419, 421, 430, 436, 438, 449, 590, 591, 772; Anderson: 329, 347, 434, 453; Broghi: 314, 351, 694; Wayne Andrews, Chicago: 587, 609, 612, 643, 714, 715, 717, 718, 719, 720, 721, 722, 723, 724, 725, 728, 729, 731, 734, 736, 738, 785, 786, 788, 789, 790, 795, 800, 848, 896, 898; Arcaid, Kingston upon Thames (Richard Bryant): 930, 939: (Colin Dixon): 361: (Martin Jones): 625: (Lucinda Lambton): 706, 868: (Ezra Stoller/Esto): 804; Archipress, Paris: (Pascal Lemaitre) 532, (Franck Eustache) 703, (Manez & Favret) 839; The Architectural Association, London: 816; F. R. Yerbury: 801, 802, 818, 852, 857, 859; The Architectural Press, London: 820, 845, 881, 903; Martin Charles: 890; Archivo Fotográfico Oronoz, Madrid: 293, 299; Archivo Iconografico SA, Barcelona: 247, 383, 777; Arxiu MAS, Barcelona: 292; James Austin, Cambridge: 188, 232, 313, 318, 319, 332, 335, 348, 378, 410, 574, 588, 631, 633, 634, 635, 637, 638, 639, 644, 645, 758; BPK, Berlin: Back cover, 2, 8; Bauhaus Archiv, Berlin: 822, 823, 824; Tim Benton, London: 460, 751, 756, 763, 776, 812, 817, 837, 842; John Bethell, St Albans: 712; Bibliotheca Hertziana, Rome: 124, 311, 528; Bibliothèque Nationale, Paris: 585; Bildarchiv Foto Marburg: 12, 60, 155, 224, 270, 271, 272, 382, 386, 391, 393, 396, 411, 475, 492, 530, 531, 593, 594, 595, 596, 597, 598, 599, 676, 677, 680, 681, 684, 687, 689, 754, 764, 765, 766, 768, 770, 805, 806, 807, 808, 809, 810, 811, 813, 814, 815, 819, 825, 826, 831, 832; Ricardo Bofill, Paris/Deidi von Schawen: 917; Boudot-Lamotte, Paris: 7; The British Architectural Library, RIBA, London: 841; (F. R. Yerbury): 856; Judith Bromley Photography, Chicago: 951; Courtesy of bruderDWLarchitects: (photo by Bill Timmerman) 954; Jim Buchman: 942; Bulloz, Paris: 636, 650; Santiago Calatrava: 932, 933; Camera Press Ltd, London: 700; Martin Charles, Middlesex: 664, 769, 911; Jean-Loup

Charmet, Paris: 583, 743; Chicago Architectural Photographing Company: 733; Commonwealth War Graves Commission, Maidenhead: 884; Conway Library, Courtauld Institute, London: 220, 227, 231, 233, 248, 249, 250, 255, 256, 258, 259, 282, 287, 294, 302, 303, 323, 326, 344, 349, 369, 381, 409, 416, 424, 425, 496, 516, 539, 572, 872; Peter Cook: 934; Country Life, London: 654, 879; Roderick Coyne: 106 Crown copyright. Reproduced with the permission of the Controller of Her Majesty's Stationery Office: 182; Sylvie Desauw: 945; The Design Council, London/Jack Pritchard: 891; John Donat, London: 37, 651, 874; Andres Duany and Elizabeth Plater-Zyberk: 947; The Dunlap Society, Essex NY/Richard Cheek: 620, 621; Edifice, London: (Darley) 883, 924; Esto Photographics Inc. Mamaroneck, NY (Wayne Andrews) 727, 803: (Peter Aaron): 869, (Jeff Goldberg: 940; Foundation Le Corbusier, Paris/DACS 1986: 843; ©Fotografica Foglia, Naples: 67; Fototeca Unione, Rome: 29, 50, 52, 68, 69, 70, 72, 73, 75, 88, 91, 99, 105, 108, 113, 115; French Government Tourist Office, London: 629. The J. Paul Getty Museum, Malibu/Julius Shulman: 919; Keith Gibson, Ayrshire: 762; Giraudon, Paris: 192, 368, 374, 380, 464, 569, 589, 640, 648, 701, 709, 756; Dennis Gilbert: 913; Giraudon, Paris: 238; Guggenheim Museum, New York: 895; Guildhall Library, London: 877; Sotiris Haidemenos, Athens: 139; Sonia Halliday, Weston Turville/Jane Taylor: 354; Robert Harding Picture Library Ltd, London: Cover (Roy Rainford), 10, 297, 603, 624, 628, 655, 778, 902; Hedrich-Blessing, Chicago: 897; Clive Hicks, London: 23, 32, 74, 83, 130, 138, 148, 152, 159, 177, 181, 184, 186, 194, 195, 197, 209, 211, 214, 216, 219, 221, 226, 229, 246, 251, 252, 254, 257, 267, 284, 514, 761; R. Higginson: 223, 534, 535, 592, 627, 632, 698, 742; Courtesy of Gerald D. Hines College of Architecture (photo: N. Laos): 915; Hirmer Fotoarchiv, Munich: 4, 19, 26, 36, 40, 43, 48, 64, 116, 120, 128, 146, 187, 196, 203; Michael Holford, Loughton, Essex: 170, 237, 372, 366, 566, 705; 367; Angelo Hornak, London: 164, 165, 262, 371, 498, 499,

503, 511, 509, 552, 565, 573, 773, 774, 867; Tim Imrie, London: 611; Institut de France, Paris/Bulloz: 317; Yasuhiro Ishimoto: 936; Instituo Centrale per il Catalogo e la Documentazione, Rome: 340; Italian State Tourist Office, London: 870; John F. Kennedy Library, Boston: 910; Peter Kent, London: 652; A. F. Kersting, London: 11, 16, 18, 24, 27, 33, 39, 44, 46, 47, 102, 110, 123, 129, 135, 147, 158, 162, 163, 172, 178, 179, 180, 182, 185, 190, 193, 204, 206, 210, 213, 218, 222, 225, 236, 241, 242, 244, 260, 261, 263, 264, 265, 277, 285, 286, 289, 290, 300, 320, 321, 341, 342, 353, 362, 375, 377, 384, 388, 392, 394, 397, 401, 403, 404, 406, 414, 428, 440, 461, 468, 470, 487, 486, 490, 493, 494, 495, 500, 510, 512, 513, 515, 517, 518, 519, 525, 536, 541, 544, 545, 548, 549, 550, 554, 556, 557, 567, 568, 570, 571, 601, 622, 630, 647, 659, 660, 665, 666, 667, 671, 672, 673, 674, 675, 692, 693, 741, 851, 876, 886, 889, 892, 904; G. E. Kidder Smith, New York: 610, 619, 858; Léon Krier, London: 946; Ralph Lieberman, North Adams, MA: 93, 156, 175, 207, 308, 309, 343, 356, 732, 756, 780, 781, 783, 793, 900; Louisiana Office of Tourism/Al Godoy: 916; The Mansell Collection, London/Alinari: 107, 435, 696, 865; Anderson: 122, 125, 134, 208, 315, 325, 328, 345; Marin Museum Karlskrona/Lasse Carlsson: 602; John Massey Stewart, London: 607; Claude Mercier: 943; Mitsuo Matsuoka: 937; Padre Ettore Molinaro, Brà: 450; Musée des Arts Décoratifs, Paris: 836; Musée de la Ville de Paris/SPADEM 1986: 582; Musée des Beaux-Arts, Dijon: 581; Museum of Finish Architecture, Helsinki: 702, 853, 854, 855, 862, 863, 864, 906, 907, 908, 909; Museum of Modern Art, New York/Mies van der Rohe Archive: 830; Werner Neumeister, Munich: 713; Netherlands Information Service, The Hague/Bart Hofmeester: 398; Peter Newark's American Pictures, Bath: 626, 628; New York Convention & Visitors' Bureau: 799; Novosti Press Agency, London: 141, 142, 704, 708, 894; Tomio Ohashi, Tokyo: 935; Richard Payne, Houston, TX: 914; Courtesy of Pei, Cobb, Freed and Partners: (photo by Timothy Hursley) 955; Polish Agency Interpress, Warsaw: 280, 600;

Courtesy of Porphyrios Associates: 948; Josephine Powell, Rome: 127; Prestel Verlag, Munich/Joseph H. Biller: 161; Albert Renger-Patzsch, Wamel: 491; Réunion des Musées Nationaux, Paris: 5, 420; Christian Richters, Münster: Frontispiece, 938, 952; Roger-Viollet, Paris: 849, 850; Aldo Rossi, Milan: 902; Jean Roubier, Paris: 835; Royal Commission on Historical Monuments (England), London: 561, 562, 888; Scala, Florence: 160, 355; Diede von Schawen: 923; Helga Schmidt-Glassner, Stuttgart: 166, 168, 268, 269, 273, 274, 275, 276, 278, 279, 389, 390, 395, 479, 480, 481, 484, 483, 679, 685, 686, 688, 691; Ronald Sheridan's Photo Library, Harrow on the Hill: 296; John Simpson and Partners Ltd, London: 949; John Sims, London: 200; Edwin Smith, Saffron Walden: 62, 78, 80, 92, 96, 97, 103, 137, 339, 360, 402, 427, 506, 543, 551, 553, 656, 657, 695, 779; Society of Antiquaries, London: 258; Spectrum Colour Library, London: 169; Staatliche Museen zu Berlin: 59, 112; Phil Starling: 922; Stedelijk Museum, Amsterdam: 828; Stirling Foundation, London: 921; Wim Swaan, London: 61, 171, 176, 199, 201, 202, 230, 234, 239, 243, 281, 291, 295, 306, 337, 415, 423, 430, 431, 437, 441, 443, 445, 446, 447, 455, 462, 465, 467, 471, 472, 476, 478, 486, 504, 505, 520, 521, 522, 526, 527; Thorvaldsens Museum, Copenhagen/Ole Woldbye: 699; Topham Picture Library, Edenbridge: 523, 662, 796, 887; TWA, London: 905; Unilever Historical Archives, Wirrall: 744; United Photos De Boer b.v. Haarlem: 400; Varga/Arte Phot, Paris: 508; Serena Vergano, Barcelona: 950; Victoria & Albert Museum, London: 559, 668; Vizcaya-Dade County Art Museum, Miami: 797; Paul Wakefield, London: 885; Frank Lloyd Wright Foundation, Taliesin: 791; Yan, Toulouse: 189; Zefa, London: 615; (K. Prädel): 399; Alexander Zielcke, Florence: 365

The majority of the plans and diagrams of buildings were specially drawn by Duncan Birmingham.

Index

Index

Index